Ninja Foodi

XL Pro Air Oven

Complete Cookbook

1500 Easy & Tasty Ninja Foodi XL Pro Air Fryer Oven Recipes for Beginners to Air Fry, Air Roast, Bake, Toast, Pizza, and More

Karen Palmer

CONTENTS

Introduction

Are you looking for a new smart Air Fryer oven that will help you cook all sorts of meals? Well, you are about to get lucky, as we are introducing you to the amazing Ninja Foodi Smart XL Air Fryer Oven. We all know Ninja Foodi due to its variety of kitchen appliances. From the first toast, they presented the latest Air Fryer ovens; all came with quality and durability offered by Ninja Foodi. As of today, there is a range of innovations that Ninja Foodi introduced in the tech world. The smartest Ninja Foodi Smart Air Fryer Oven is proven to be the most successful model of this range due to its smart features. In this air fryer oven cookbook, you can learn all about the Ninja Foodi smart Air Fryer Oven and will get to know various recipes that you can cook using its smart cooking functions.

Fundamentals of Ninja Foodi Smart XL Pro Air Oven

What Is Ninja Foodi Smart XL Pro Air Oven?

The smarter version of the Ninja DT201 Air Fryer Oven, also known as the Ninja Foodi Smart XL Pro Air Oven has made a huge buzz because of its amazing cooking features. The integrated thermometer is the main difference between the two if you're having trouble choosing. You can connect the thermometer to the appliance and insert it into the food to read the internal temperature with a click of a button. When the desired internal temperature is reached, the oven shut off on its own. All that's left to do is remove it and give it 15 to 30 minutes to rest. The guidebook includes a list of all the temperature ranges for every type of protein, just in case. This practical thermometer can be used to cook beef, pork, poultry, fish, or any combination thereof. Its 12-lb capacity is more than enough to hold an entire chicken or perhaps a medium-sized turkey. In comparison to conventional ovens, the Ninja Foodi Smart XL Pro Air Oven can be preheated in just 90 seconds.

Benefits of Using It

The Ninja Foodi Air Fryer oven due to its capacious build and power-saving technology has offered several benefits to all its consumers. Besides these basic reasons to buy this multipurpose cooking appliance, here are a few other advantages to accrue out of it:

Multi-Rack Cooking Option

This is perhaps my favorite feature of this appliance and it is rarely found in other appliances of this sort. Because of its XL capacity that machine has four rack levels and each level can be used to cook using a different function. For instance, for Air Frying, Air Roast and Broil you can use the top rack whereas for the whole roast mode the lowest rack level would be suitable. The keys to select the rack level are given on one side of the display screen and you can adjust the rack level by using them after setting up the cooking mode, time and temperature.

XL Capacity

The size of the Ninja Foodi XL Pro Air Fryer Oven takes it to the top of the list when compared to other toaster ovens. Its great capacity is specially designed to accommodate all food types, in varied serving sizes. So, whether you want to cook a whole chicken inside or what to Air fryer a large batch of fries for a family of 6 or 8, the appliance is powerful enough to cook all of that in just a few minutes. So, this high-power Air Fryer Oven is perfect to use for large families and to feed your guests. The XL capacity of the Ninja Foodi XL Pro Air Fryer Oven can cook the following in a single layer:

- 12" Pizza
- Six Toast Slices
- 2 lbs. of fries
- Whole chicken
- Whole Turkey Multi-Rack Cooking Option

Smart Convection Fan

The Foodi Smart XL Pro is stocked with clever features that make living easy, just like other Ninja appliances. You can prepare dishes like a professional chef if you follow the instruction guide. The convection fan regulator for multi-speed circulation is the coolest clever feature. Of course, it's not as glamorous a feature as the digital display panel, smart thermometer, or other bells and whistles. However, in every cooking mode, the function is what makes the most difference.

Advanced Control Panel

Although the control panel and digital display initially appear intimidating, the menu setup is relatively simple. For instance, it even indicates the rack position to utilize for the best results when you choose what you're cooking and how you want it cooked. The thermometer is the cherry on top. It even switches to "stay warm" mode when the internal target temperature is reached, taking all of the guessing out of roasting.

Dehydrator

Powerful but accurate, the infrared heating system has numerous parts. The Ninja DT251 enables you to dehydrate to the ideal level because it can achieve a minimum temperature of 85 degrees. You can buy additional dehydrating racks despite the fact that it only comes with one. The XL capacity can then be utilized fully by employing all four rack slots. For later use, dehydrate any surplus seasonal fruits, or make your own handmade trail mixes. Even better, you can manufacture your own beef, venison, or other dried meats.

Features of the Control Panel

The control panel of the appliance is present on the front top portion of the Air Fryer Oven. It is an all-black panel that looks amazing when the keys light up. The display is at the center of the panel and it has keys on one side of the cooking modes listed and a power button on the other side of it. Here are the operational keys that you can find on the control panel:

The Power Button: It is present on one corner of the control panel and it should be pressed to turn ON/OFF the appliance:

Time Display: Once the timer starts ticking, the time display on the screen shows the time.

Preheat: This sign flashes on the display screen when the unit is preheating. If the oven is already preheated then it won't preheat again and the sign won't appear on the screen.

Slices: This sign illuminates the panel when you select the Toast or Bagel cooking function and lets you select the number of slices that need to be toasted.

Temperature Display: This part of the display shows the cooking temperature selected. It is important to remember here that time and temperature values always return to the settings, last set and used in the previous session of cooking.

Rack Level: This sign illuminates to indicate which of the 4 rack levels are selected for the cooking. When you select a cooking mode, the machine automatically selects the rack level according to it.

Level: Once the cooking mode is selected you can use the rack level keys to change the level as per your recipe requirement.

Function +/- Buttons: These keys are provided to move from one cooking function to another and you can see the listed cooking modes on the left of the display lighting up.

Time/Slices +/- Keys: The keys used to increase or decrease the time are there to adjust the time as per the recipe requirements and these keys can also be used to select the number of slices when you are using the BAGEL

or TOAST function. By pressing the +/- keys for the time you can add or minus 1 minute under 1 hour or 5 minutes over 1 hour. To switch the 1-minute increment to 5 minutes, you can press and hold the +/- keys for 2 seconds.

Temp/Shade +/- Keys: Like the timer keys, the TEMP keys can also be used for two different sets of settings. Firstly, they are used to increase or decrease the value of temperature by 5 degrees. You can hold the keys for 2 seconds to change the increment value to10 degrees as well. Secondly, they can be used to select the "shade" or brownness of the bread, buns or bagels when the TOAST or BAGEL modes are selected. There are 7 shade levels that you can select using these keys- 1 being the lights and the 7 being the darkest level. Upon selecting the shade level, the appliance automatically selects the temperature required to bring that level of brownness, so in this way, you get consistent results.

Start/Stop Key: When the cooking function, time, and temperature are selected the START/STOP key is pressed to initiate preheating and then cooking. You can also use this key to stop the function manually.

Shade: This sign lights up on the display screen when you select the Toast or Bagel function.

Light Key: This key is pressed to light the bulb inside the appliance. It lets you see the progress of the food cooked inside the oven.

Straight from the Store

When it comes to electric appliances, it is important to inspect all the parts of the appliance before giving it a test run. The Ninja Foodi XL Pro Air Fryer Oven toaster oven comes with the following basic elements and accessories.
• The Ninja Foodi 10-in-1 Air Fryer Oven Base unit
• Air Fry Basket
• 2 Wire Racks
• Removable Crumb Tray
• Roast Tray
• Sheet Pan(s)

Inside the Ninja Foodi XL Pro Air Fryer Oven, there are four grooves on both sides which are there to insert racks for each of the four levels. These grooves are used to insert four rack trays in the oven. The uppermost grooves can be used to insert the trays when the food needs to be broiled. The center grooves are for Air frying and Roasting purposes. The lowermost level is used to place the food which needs to be baked, whole-roasted, reheated, or dehydrated. A Crumb tray is inserted at the bottom to protect the bottom of the oven from the food particle during cooking.

Step-By-Step Using It

If you are getting your hands on this Ninja Foodi Air Fryer Oven for the first time then here is what you need to do. After unboxing the appliance remove and discard all the packaging material and tapes. Check all the parts of the appliance and see if they are intact. If not then you can call customer support before taking any risks. Remove the accessories from the inside of the appliance then wash the wire rack, sheet pan, roast tray, air fry basket, and removable crumb tray using soapy water, then rinse and dry them. Put the accessories back in their places and plug in the oven to start using them. Next, you can use the appliance for any individual mode of cooking. Here is how you can operate it:

Whole Roast

Press the "+/-" buttons until the WHOLE ROAST option lights up on the control panel. The time and temperature will be displayed by default. Select the 2nd LEVEL button so that "2 LEVEL" displays on the display when cooking two layers. To choose a cook time of up to 4 hours, hit the TIME/SLICES "+/-" buttons. To choose a temperature between 250 degrees F and 450 degrees F, use the TEMP/SHADE "+/-" buttons. To start preheating, press START/PAUSE. Place the ingredients either directly on the sheet pan or the roasting pan. Place the roasting tray on the sheet pan and on the wire rack of the "1st" Level as soon as the machine beeps to indicate that it has finished preheating. Shut the oven door. Place the sheet pan on the "1st" Level and use the air fry basket on the 4th Level when cooking on two layers. The appliance will beep and "COOK END" will show up on the display when cook time is finished.

Air Roast

Press the "+/-" buttons until the AIR ROAST option lights up on the control panel. The time and temperature will be displayed by default. Select the 2nd LEVEL button so that "2 LEVEL" displays on the display when cooking two layers. To choose a cook time of up to 4 hours, Hit the TIME/SLICES "+/-" buttons. To choose a temperature between 250 degrees F and 450 degrees F, use the TEMP/SHADE "+/-" buttons. To start preheating, press START/PAUSE. Put the ingredients on the baking sheet. Place the roast tray on the sheet pan, and placed it on the wire rack on the "1st" Level as soon as the appliance beeps to indicate that it has finished preheating. Shut the oven door. Use the sheet pan as the first layer when cooking on two levels, and the air fry basket as the second layer when cooking on level three. The appliance will beep and "cook end" will show up on the display when cook time is finished.

Air Fry

Press the "+/-" buttons until the AIR FRY option lights up on the control panel, to pick the function. The time and temperature will be displayed by default. Select the 2nd LEVEL button so that "2 LEVEL" displays on the display when cooking two layers. To choose a cook time of up to 4 hours, Hit the TIME/SLICES "+/-" buttons. Select a temperature between 250 degrees F and 450 degrees F by using the TEMP/SHADE "+/-" buttons. To start preheating, press START/PAUSE. Place the contents in the roast tray with a sheet pan and the air fry basket. Put the basket on the sheet pan if the ingredients are fatty, greasy, or marinated. For dry ingredients, use an air fryer basket. Insert the basket into the rack level(s) indicated on the control panel as soon as the appliance beeps to indicate that it has warmed. If using a sheet pan as well, slide both into the oven at the same time, the pan on the wire rack below the basket in the upper rack. Shut the oven door. The appliance will beep and "COOK END" will show up on the display when cook time is finished. As soon as the device is preheated, the timer will begin to count down. Simply Hit the TIME "+/-" buttons to add more time if the ingredients are not prepared to go into the oven.

Bake

Press the "+/-" buttons until the BAKE option lights up on the control panel. The time and temperature will be displayed by default. Select the 2nd LEVEL button so that "2 LEVEL" displays on the display when cooking two layers. To choose a cook time of up to 4 hours, hit the TIME/SLICES "+/-" buttons. To choose a temperature between 180 degrees F and 450 degrees F, use the TEMP/SHADE "+/-" buttons. To start preheating, press START/PAUSE. Put the ingredients in the cake pan, air fryer basket, casserole dish, or sheet pan. Place

the sheet pan, placed on the wire rack as soon as the appliance beeps to indicate that it has reached preheating. Shut the oven door. You can switch on the light during cooking to monitor the process. The appliance will beep and "COOK END" will show up on the display when cook time is finished.

Dehydrate

Press the "+/-" buttons to pick the function when DEHYDRATE option lights up on the control panel. It will show the standard time and temperature settings. To have "2 LEVEL" appear on the display when dehydrating two layers, select the 2 LEVEL button. To choose a dehydration time of up to 24 hours, use the TIME/SLICES "+/-" buttons. A temperature between 85 degrees F and 200 degrees F can be chosen by using the TEMP/SHADE "+/-" buttons. Ingredients should be added to the air fry basket before placing it in the oven. Press START/PAUSE to start cooking and close the oven door. The appliance will beep and the phrase "COOK END" will show up on the display when the cooking time is over.

Broil

Press the "+/-" buttons until the BROIL option lights up on the control panel. The time and temperature will be displayed by default. Select a cook time of up to 30 minutes by pressing the TIME/SLICES "+/-" buttons. The TEMP/SHADE "+/-" buttons should be pressed to choose HI or LO. Put the ingredients on the baking sheet. Close the oven door after setting the sheet pan, placed it on the wire rack and click START/STOP to begin cooking. The appliance will beep and "COOK END" will appear on the display when cook time is over.

Toast

Press the "+/-" buttons until the TOAST option lights up

on the control panel. Slice count and level of darkness will automatically be set to default. To choose the number of slices of bread, use the TIME/SLICES "+/-" buttons. 9 slices can be toasted at once. To choose a level of darkness, hit the TEMP/SHADE "+/-" buttons. Place the wire rack with the bread pieces on it. To start cooking, close the oven door and select START/PAUSE. The appliance will beep and "COOK END" will appear on the display when cook time is over.

Bagel

Press the "+/-" buttons until the BAGEL option lights up on the control panel. The default slice count and amount of darkness will be shown. The number of slices can be chosen by using the TIME/SLICES "+/-" buttons. Up to nine bagel pieces can be toasted at once. Choose the level of darkness by pressing the TEMP "+/-" buttons. Put the cut-side-up side of the bagels in the center of the wire rack. To start cooking, close the oven door and select START/PAUSE. The appliance will beep and "COOK END" will show up on the display when cook time is finished.

Pizza

Press the "+/-" buttons until the Pizza option lights up on the control panel. The default slice count and amount of darkness will be shown. The time can be chosen by using the TIME/SLICES "+/-" buttons. Choose the temperature settings by pressing the TEMP "+/-" buttons. Put the pizza in the center of the wire rack. To start cooking, close the oven door and select START/PAUSE. The appliance will beep and "COOK END" will show up on the display when cook time is finished.

Reheat

Press the "+/-" buttons until the REHEAT option lights up on the control panel. To choose a reheat time of up to four hours, use the TIME/SLICES "+/-" buttons. To choose a temperature between 100 degrees F and 450 degrees F, use the TEMP/ SHADE "+/-" buttons. To keep food warm, choose below 180 degrees F. Food should be placed on a sheet pan or in a container suitable for the oven, which should then be placed on a wire rack. To start warming, close the oven door and hit START/PAUSE. The appliance will beep and "COOK END" will appear on the display when cook time is over.

Using the Foodi Smart Thermometer

Before inserting the cord into the thermometer jack, make sure it is free of any debris and that there are no knots. Take the thermometer out of the cupboard. The thermometer on the right side of the device can then be removed by unwinding the cord from the cord wrap. Into the jack, insert the thermometer. When the plug can no longer fit into the jack and you hear it click into place, push down hard.

Once the thermometer is connected and the thermometer mode is turned on by pressing the PRESET or MANUAL button, the thermometer icon will turn on in the display. Choose the desired cooking mode (such as Whole Roast) and adjust the cooking temperature as necessary. Press PRESET and use the FUNCTION "+/-" buttons to select your desired food type and the TEMP "+/-" buttons to set the internal doneness of your food. There is no need to select a cook time because the appliance will detect when your food is cooking and immediately turn off the heating element. If you choose the MANUAL option, utilize the suggested internal cook temperatures. Close the door after adding the accessory

needed for the cook function you've chosen. To start the preheating, press START/STOP.

Insert the thermometer horizontally into the thickest section of the protein piece while the unit is preheating. When the unit has heated up and beeps, open the door, set the food inside with the thermometer inserted, and then cover the thermometer cord with the door.

The target and current thermometer temperatures will be displayed on the display to show you the progress. To view the oven temperature and the amount of time since the cook began, press PRESET or MANUAL. When the goal thermometer temperature is attained, the device will automatically shut off. It will beep and say "COOK END" on the display. Put the protein on a platter and give it five minutes to rest before serving.

Tips for Using Accessories

Accessories for the Ninja Foodi Smart XL Pro Air Oven include an air fry basket, two wire racks, two sheet pans, a roast tray, and a thermometer. You also get a smart thermometer that is housed in a magnetic container. Like wired headphones, it functions. A jack can be found at the handle's bottom right corner. A crumb tray is also present beneath the heating element. Along with removing food debris, it keeps greases from sinking to the bottom of your oven. For the Ninja DT251's 10 capabilities, those accessories are adequate. For processing a sizable quantity of fruits and beef jerky, the business also sells a dehydrating kit, a 2-inch casserole plate, and a muffin pan.

Roasting Pan: Use a roasting tray on a sheet pan for cooking with

convection (such as whole roasting, air roasting, and air frying), or when cooking oily items like entire chickens, chicken wings, bacon, marinated meats, or oiled vegetables.

Basket Air Fry: Install before using the air fryer mode. It is inserted into level 2 of the cooking chamber for best results.

Cooking Tray: Reduces smoke and grease splash by fitting on top of the sheet pan and catching grease from food that has been roasted or air-fried.

Sheet Pan: Place the sheet pan(s) atop the wire rack. Only wash by hand. On some models, an additional sheet pan is not accessible.

Crumb Tray: When the oven is being used, it must stay installed at the base of the cooking chamber to catch all the crumbs and dripping. You can wash it after cooking, once it is cooled, using soap water and a soft sponge.

Cleaning and Caring for Ninja Foodi Smart XL Pro Air Oven

The Ninja Foodi DT251's accessories cannot be placed in the dishwasher, which is bad news. But that holds true for all ovens, regardless of size. Heat and powerful chemicals will eventually cause the metal's finish to deteriorate or possibly be damaged. The only method that works is hand washing such components. Cover the sheet pan with aluminum foil to capture the grease from the roast tray and make cleanup a little easier. There is now one fewer component to manage. The part that will probably be the hardest to maintain is the roast tray.

If you're having difficulties removing stubborn greases with a brush, soaking it overnight will work. The air fryer basket operates similarly.

Every-Day Cleaning

After each usage, the appliance needs to be completely cleaned. Unplug the appliance from the outlet and give it time to cool. Remove the crumb tray from the oven and empty it. Use a gentle, moist sponge to remove any food spatter from the internal walls and glass door of the appliance after each use. Use a moist towel to wipe the outside of the main unit and the control panel clean. You could use a gentle spray solution or non-abrasive liquid cleaner. Before cleaning, apply the cleaner on the sponge rather than the oven's surface.

Before placing food on top of accessories, we advise smearing them with the suggested cooking oil or covering them with baking paper or aluminum foil. Avoid covering roast tray openings with foil or parchment paper.

Thermometer Cleaning

The thermometer and its holder should not be cleaned in the dishwasher. Remove the thermometer from the device and let it cool completely before cleaning. Hand washing is possible for the thermometer tip and silicone grip. To completely clean the thermometer, submerge the silicone grip and stainless steel tip in warm, soapy water. It is not allowed to immerse the cord or jack in liquid. Never use liquid cleaning products in close proximity to the thermometer jack.

Deep Cleaning

Before deep cleaning the appliance, unplug it from the outlet and give it time to cool. Remove all of the unit's attachments, including the crumb tray, and wash each one separately. To wash the air fry basket more completely, use a non-abrasive cleaning brush. It is advised to hand wash accessories. The wire racks and air fryer basket can be cleaned in the dishwasher, however over time, wear may occur more quickly. Avoid using a dishwasher for a roast tray, sheet pan, or crumb tray.

The interior and glass door of the oven should be cleaned with a soft cloth and warm, soapy water. Abrasive cleansers, scrubbing brushes, and chemical cleaners should not be used as they will harm the oven. Sheet pans and roasting trays should be soaked in warm, soapy water overnight to remove stubborn grease before being washed with a nonabrasive sponge or brush. Dry all components completely before re-entering the oven.

Frequently Asked Questions & Notes

The oven won't turn on; why?

Ascertain that the power cord is firmly inserted into the outlet. Change the outlet where the power cord is plugged in. If necessary, reset the circuit breaker. Activate the power switch.

Is it possible to use a sheet pan rather than an air fry basket with the air fry function?

Yes, however, the results may vary in crispiness.

Do the cook times and temperatures for conventional oven recipes need to be changed?

Keep an eye on your meal while it's cooking for the greatest outcomes.

Can I reset the device to its factory defaults?

Even if you disconnect the oven, it will remember the last setting you used for each function. Hit the Light and 2 LEVEL buttons at the same time for 5 seconds to return the oven's settings to default for each function.

Why do the heating elements seem to be on and off repeatedly?

That is normal. The power levels of the heating components can be changed to precisely manage the temperature for each function in the oven.

Why does the oven door have steam coming out of it?

That is typical. High-moisture foodstuffs could create steam around the door.

Why is water flowing from under the door onto the counter?

That is typical. Foods having a high moisture content, such as frozen bread, may produce condensation that drips onto the surface and down the inside of the door.

Why is the apparatus producing smoke?

When cooking any fatty items or utilizing the Air Fry, Air Roast, or Whole Roast modes, make sure the roast tray is being used. If the issue still exists, try running a Toast cycle on shade 7 with the accessories off. This will burn off any further grease on the smoking heating

components.

Despite the fact that I used the thermometer, why is my meal overcooked or undercooked?

To obtain the most precise reading, it is important to place the thermometer longitudinally into the ingredient's thickest area. Make sure to give the meal rest for three to five minutes to finish cooking. Refer to the section on using the Foodi Thermometer for more details on recommended doneness when using the MANUAL function and doneness temperatures when using the PRESET function.

Will the thermometer grip melt if it touches hot oven elements?

Make sure the grip doesn't come into contact with any of the oven's heated elements.

How can I get the sheet pan clean?

Before cleaning the sheet pan with food that has stuck to it, soak it. When cooking, line the sheet pan with baking paper or aluminum foil to make cleanup simpler.

Why did the device trip a circuit breaker while it was in use?

The device needs to be connected via an outlet with a 15-amp circuit breaker because it consumes 1800 watts of power. The unit must also be the only appliance connected to an outlet while it is in operation. Make sure the appliance is the only one plugged into an outlet on a 15-amp breaker to prevent tripping the breaker.

What do these errors: "CALL CUSt SrVC" followed by "Er0" – "Er3" mean?

If you see this on the display screen then immediately turn off the appliance, unplug it and call customer support to help.

Precautionary Measures

Hazards occur, not because we are not doing anything wrong, but sometimes because of the lack of precautionary measures. You can reduce the risk of such hazards by keeping these measures in mind.

- While cooking, avoid using any kind of aerosol spray or flavoring.
- When putting something in or taking something out of the oven, be careful, especially when it's hot. Outlet voltages can change, which might have an impact on how well your product works. Use a thermometer to ensure that your food is prepared to the proper temperatures to avoid any potential illnesses.
- Keep food away from hot sources. Overloading the oven with food might endanger users' safety, result in property damage or personal injury, or both.
- A toaster oven cannot be used to cook large items or metal utensils since doing so increases the risk of an electrical fire or shock.
- Don't put the following items, with the exception of parchment paper, in the oven: paper, cardboard, plastic, roasting bags, etc.
- When using containers made of any material other than metal or glass, extreme attention should be taken.
- Keep the oven away from hot surfaces. The glass door and oven surfaces get warm both during and after use. Always use oven mitts and available handles to avoid burns or personal injury.

4-Week Diet Plan

Week 1

Day 1:
Breakfast: Egg Mozzarella Swirls
Lunch: Eggplant Panini
Snack: Yam Chips
Dinner: Tropical Shrimp with Spicy Mayo
Dessert: Cranberries Cauliflower Pudding

Day 2:
Breakfast: Chard Casserole
Lunch: Spinach Potato Samosa
Snack: Spicy Nuts
Dinner: Beef Cheeseburger Sliders
Dessert: Sweet Butter Fritters

Day 3:
Breakfast: Sausages and Veggie Egg Casserole
Lunch: Roasted Cauliflower
Snack: Sweet Onion Rings
Dinner: Pistachio Crusted Rack of Lamb
Dessert: Chocolate Coconut Brownies

Day 4:
Breakfast: Almond Coconut Oatmeal
Lunch: Crusty Chili Tofu
Snack: Paprika Carrot Slices
Dinner: Duck with Cranberry
Dessert: Homemade Blueberry Pancakes

Day 5:
Breakfast: Fried Cheese Hot Dogs
Lunch: Roasted Carrots
Snack: Butter Sriracha Chicken Wings
Dinner: Creamy Chicken Salad
Dessert: Strawberry Hand Tarts

Day 6:
Breakfast: Chives Cream Muffins
Lunch: Sweet Potato Bites
Snack: Eggplant Fries
Dinner: Ham Tilapia Fillets
Dessert: Fried Bananas with Ice Cream

Day 7:
Breakfast: Creamy Eggs Bake
Lunch: Crispy Zucchini
Snack: Golden Beet Chips
Dinner: Crispy Fried Chicken Skin
Dessert: Tropical Pineapple Cake

Week 2

Day 1:
Breakfast: Sausages Egg Squares
Lunch: Herbed Yellow Squash and Carrots
Snack: Oats Poppers
Dinner: Sea Scallop with Greens
Dessert: Double Lemon Cake

Day 2:
Breakfast: Green Beans Egg Bake
Lunch: Bacon-Wrapped Tots
Snack: Cajun Butter Snack
Dinner: Chinese Chicken Wings
Dessert: Sweet Cherry Pie

Day 3:
Breakfast: Butter Almond Donuts
Lunch: Burrata-Stuffed Tomatoes
Snack: Sweet Potato Fries
Dinner: Italian Sea Bas
Dessert: Tasty Apple Turnovers

Day 4:
Breakfast: Okra Egg Hash
Lunch: Garlic Mushrooms
Snack: Tomato and Basil Bruschetta
Dinner: Beef Stuffed Bell Peppers
Dessert: Healthy Banana Oatmeal Cookies

Day 5:
Breakfast: Cheese Omelet with Onion
Lunch: Sweet Casserole
Snack: Mixed Cheesy Veggie Bites
Dinner: Lamb Scallion Balls
Dessert: Strawberry Chocolate Cups

Day 6:
Breakfast: Eggs & Cheese Toast
Lunch: Smashed Baby Potatoes
Snack: Home-Fried Cheese Sticks
Dinner: Turkey Meatloaves
Dessert: Lime Merengues

Day 7:
Breakfast: Cheesy Bacon Scrambled Eggs
Lunch: Spinach Cheese Tart
Snack: Herbed Pork Skewers
Dinner: Chili Duck Bites
Dessert: Currant Cookies

Week 3

Day 1:
Breakfast: Cheesy Asparagus Omelet
Lunch: Eggplant Mozzarella Lasagna
Snack: Spicy Kale Chips
Dinner: Cheesy Fish Fingers
Dessert: Coconut Currant Pudding

Day 2:
Breakfast: Peanut Butter & Banana Toast
Lunch: Thyme Zucchini Patties
Snack: BBQ Meatballs
Dinner: Kielbasa with Pineapple
Dessert: Cream Cheesecake

Day 3:
Breakfast: Green Feta Frittatas
Lunch: Fried Green Tomato Salad
Snack: Cheese Jalapeno Poppers
Dinner: Mustard Basil Lamb
Dessert: Chocolate Chunk Hazelnut Cookies

Day 4:
Breakfast: Fryer Sausage
Lunch: Asparagus with Cheese
Snack: Air Fried Pumpkin Seeds
Dinner: Tuna and Vegie Salad
Dessert: Nutella Torte

Day 5:
Breakfast: Hard Boiled Eggs
Lunch: Fried Brussels Sprouts with Ham
Snack: Garlic and Bread-Stuffed Mushrooms
Dinner: Spicy Chicken Drumsticks
Dessert: Orange Butter Cake

Day 6:
Breakfast: Brown Bread
Lunch: Buttery Garlicky Air fried Potatoes
Snack: Ricotta Eggs Balls
Dinner: Southern-Style Fried Shrimp
Dessert: Cherry Turnovers

Day 7:
Breakfast: Walnuts Granola
Lunch: Elote Corn Salad
Snack: Pancetta-Wrapped Shrimp
Dinner: Boneless Ribeye Steaks
Dessert: Carrot Cake with Icing

Week 4

Day 1:
Breakfast: Sweet Pumpkin Oatmeal
Lunch: Zucchini with Kimchi Sauce
Snack: Cheese Apple Pie Rolls
Dinner: Cumin Turkey
Dessert: Berry Pies

Day 2:
Breakfast: Salmon Egg Scramble
Lunch: Mushroom, Zucchini and Bean Burgers
Snack: Air Fried Spare Ribs
Dinner: Fried Shrimp
Dessert: Charred Caramelized Pineapple with Mint and Lime

Day 3:
Breakfast: Healthy French Toast
Lunch: Colorful Roasted Vegetable Stromboli
Snack: Air Fried Blooming Onion
Dinner: Spiced Lamb Chops
Dessert: Apple Crumble

Day 4:
Breakfast: Cheesy Egg Pockets
Lunch: Delicious Cauliflower Steaks Gratin
Snack: Homemade Roasted Mixed Nuts
Dinner: Fish Croquettes
Dessert: Chocolate Almond Cakes

Day 5:
Breakfast: Baked Strawberries and Cream Oatmeal
Lunch: Spicy Gujarati Green Beans
Snack: Crispy Carrot Chips
Dinner: Beef Steak
Dessert: Bananas Bread Pudding

Day 6:
Breakfast: Cheese Bread Cups
Lunch: Crispy Bacon Wrapped Asparagus
Snack: Sweet Chicken Wings
Dinner: Parmesan Pork Meatballs
Dessert: Boston Cream Donut

Day 7:
Breakfast: Bacon Egg Muffins
Lunch: Asian Balsamic Fennel
Snack: Tomato Chips with Cheese
Dinner: Cornish Game Hens with Thai Cucumber Salad
Dessert: Sweet Chocolate Soufflés

Chapter 1 Breakfast Recipes

Egg Mozzarella Swirls

Prep time: 15 minutes | Cook time: 12 minutes | Servings: 6

1 tablespoon coconut flour	2 tablespoons butter, softened
½ cup mozzarella cheese, shredded	¼ teaspoon baking powder
1 teaspoon truvia	1 egg, beaten
	Cooking spray

1. In a suitable bowl, mix up almond flour, coconut flour, mozzarella cheese, Truvia, butter, baking powder, and egg. Knead the soft and non-sticky dough. 2. Then Select the Air Fry mode. Set the Ninja Foodi Smart XL Pro temperature to 355°F/180°C. Select Level "3" and set the time on your Ninja Foodi Smart XL Pro Air Fryer Oven to 12 minutes. Press Start/Pause to begin preheating. Continue to the next step when it is done preheating. 3. Meanwhile, roll up the cheese dough and cut it into 6 pieces. Make the swirl from every dough piece. 4. Grease its air fryer basket with cooking oil spray. 5. Place the cheese swirls in the air fryer in one layer, insert its air fryer basket in the level 3 and cook them for 12 minutes until they are light brown. 6. Repeat the same step with remaining uncooked dough. It is recommended to serve the cheese Danish warm.
Per Serving: Calories 199; Fat 17.9g; Sodium 525mg; Carbs 1.1g; Fiber 0.3g; Sugar 0.6g; Protein 9.9g

Chard Casserole

Prep time: 5 minutes | Cook time: 15 minutes | Servings: 4

4 eggs, whisked	1 cup tomatoes, cubed
1 teaspoon olive oil	Black pepper and salt to the taste
3 ounces Swiss chard, chopped	

1. In a suitable bowl, mix the eggs with the rest of the recipe ingredients except the oil and whisk well. 2. Grease a suitable pan that fits the fryer with the oil, pour the swish chard mix, place this pan on the rack in the level 3 and cook on "Air Fry" Mode, and set its temperature to 360°F/180°C for 15 minutes. 3. Divide between plates and serve for breakfast.
Per Serving: Calories 241; Fat 16.8 g; Sodium 225 mg; Carbs 8g; Fiber 0.4g; Sugar 1.1g; Protein 15.4g

Chives Cream Muffins

Prep time: 15 minutes | Cook time: 12 minutes | Servings: 4

4 slices of ham	1 egg, beaten
¼ teaspoon baking powder	1 teaspoon chives, chopped
4 tablespoons coconut flour	1 teaspoon olive oil
4 teaspoons heavy cream	½ teaspoon white pepper

1. Select the Air Fry mode. Set the Ninja Foodi Smart XL Pro temperature to 365°F/185°C. Select Level "3" and set the time on your Ninja Foodi Smart XL Pro Air Fryer Oven to 12 minutes. Press Start/Pause to begin preheating. Continue to the next step when it is done preheating. 2. Meanwhile, mix up baking powder, coconut flour, heavy cream, egg, chives, and white pepper. Stir the ingredients until getting a smooth mixture. 3. Finely chop the ham and add it in the muffin liquid. Brush the air fryer muffin molds with olive oil. Then pour the muffin batter in the molds. 4. Place this rack in its air fryer basket and place the molds on it. Cook the muffins for 12 minutes (365°F/185°C). Cool the muffins to the room temperature and remove them from the molds.
Per Serving: Calories 202; Fat 15.9g; Sodium 720 mg; Carbs 3.9g; Fiber 1.3g; Sugar 1.6g; Protein 12.4g

Okra Egg Hash

Prep time: 5 minutes | Cook time: 20 minutes | Servings: 4

2 cups okra	4 eggs, whisked
1 tablespoon butter, melted	A pinch of black pepper and salt

1. Grease a suitable pan that fits the air fryer with the butter. 2. In a suitable bowl, mix the okra with eggs, black pepper and salt, whisk and pour into the pan. 3. Introduce the pan in its air fryer basket. Insert its air fryer basket into the level 3 of the oven and close the door. Cook on "Air Fry" Mode, select level 3, and set its temperature to 350°F/175°C for 20 minutes. 4. Divide the mix between plates and serve.
Per Serving: Calories 149; Fat 12 g; Sodium 132 mg; Carbs 10.5g; Fiber 2.6g; Sugar 4.6g; Protein 1.5g

Salmon Egg Scramble

Prep time: 5 minutes | Cook time: 20 minutes | Servings: 4

A drizzle of olive oil	4 eggs, whisked
1 spring onion, chopped	A pinch of black pepper and salt
1 cup smoked salmon, skinless, boneless and flaked	¼ cup baby spinach
	4 tablespoons parmesan, grated

1. In a suitable bowl, mix the eggs with the rest of the recipe ingredients except the oil and whisk well. 2. Select the Air Fry mode. Set the Ninja Foodi Smart XL Pro temperature to 365°F/185°C. Select Level "3" and set the time on your Ninja Foodi Smart XL Pro Air Fryer Oven to 20 minutes. Press Start/Pause to begin preheating. Continue to the next step when it is done preheating. 3. Pour the eggs and salmon mix into a pan and transfer to the level 3 of the fryer and cook for 20 minutes. Divide between plates and serve for breakfast.
Per Serving: Calories 315; Fat 28.6 g; Sodium 1020 mg; Carbs 3.1g; Fiber 0.6g; Sugar 1.7g; Protein 11.7g

Cheesy Chicken Stuffed Peppers

Prep time: 15 minutes | Cook time: 5 minutes | Servings: 2

2 medium green peppers	1 tablespoon cream cheese
1 chili pepper, chopped	½ cup mozzarella, shredded
4 ounces chicken, shredded	¼ teaspoon chili powder

1. Remove the seeds from the bell peppers. 2. After this, Select the Air Fry mode. Set the Ninja Foodi Smart XL Pro temperature to 375°F/190°C. Select Level "3" and set the time on your Ninja Foodi Smart XL Pro Air Fryer Oven to 5 minutes. Press Start/Pause to begin preheating. Continue to the next step when it is done preheating. 3. Meanwhile, in the bowl mix up chili pepper, shredded chicken, cream cheese, and shredded mozzarella. Add chili powder and stir the prepared mixture until homogenous. 4. After this, fill the bell peppers with chicken mixture and wrap in the foil. Put the peppers in the preheated air fryer and cook for 5 minutes.
Per Serving: Calories 396; Fat 25.8 g; Sodium 565 mg; Carbs 5.6g; Fiber 0.3g; Sugar 1.7g; Protein 36.4g

Mushrooms Cream Spread

Prep time: 5 minutes | Cook time: 20 minutes | Servings: 4

1 cup white mushrooms	A pinch of black pepper and salt
¼ cup mozzarella, shredded	Cooking spray
½ cup coconut cream	

1. Put the mushrooms in your air fryer's basket, grease with cooking spray and cook on "Air Fry" Mode, select level 3, and set its temperature to 370°F/185°C for 20 minutes. 2. Transfer the cooked mushrooms to a blender, then add the remaining recipe ingredients, pulse well, divide into bowls and serve as a spread.
Per Serving: Calories 161; Fat 7.9 g; Sodium 595 mg; Carbs 10.8g; Fiber 1.7g; Sugar 0.5g; Protein 13.2g

Sausages and Veggie Egg Casserole

Prep time: 10 minutes | Cook time: 20 minutes | Servings: 4

1 tablespoon olive oil	¼ teaspoon ground paprika
3 spring onions, chopped	10 ounces Italian sausages
1 green bell pepper, sliced	1 teaspoon olive oil
¼ teaspoon salt	4 eggs
¼ teaspoon ground turmeric	

1. Select the Air Fry mode. Set the Ninja Foodi Smart XL Pro temperature to 360°F/180°C. Select Level "3" and set the time on your Ninja Foodi Smart XL Pro Air Fryer Oven to 20 minutes. Press Start/Pause to begin preheating. Continue to the next step when it is done preheating. 2. Then pour olive oil in its air fryer basket. Add bell pepper and spring onions. 3. Then sprinkle the vegetables with ground turmeric and salt. Insert its air fryer basket into the level 3 of the oven and close the door. Cook them for 5 minutes. 4. When the time is finished, shake its air fryer basket gently. 5. Chop the sausages roughly and add in its air fryer basket. Cook the ingredients for 10 minutes. 6. Then crack the eggs over the sausages and cook the casserole for 10 minutes more.
Per Serving: Calories 281; Fat 15.5 g; Sodium 262 mg; Carbs 27.5g; Fiber 2.2g; Sugar 5g; Protein 8.5g

Tuna Salad

Prep time: 5 minutes | Cook time: 15 minutes | Servings: 4

½ pound smoked tuna, flaked
1 cup arugula
2 spring onions, chopped
1 tablespoon olive oil
A pinch of black pepper and salt

1. In a suitable bowl, put all the recipe ingredients except the oil and the arugula and whisk. 2. Select the Air Fry mode. Set the Ninja Foodi Smart XL Pro temperature to 365°F/185°C. Select Level "3" and set the time on your Ninja Foodi Smart XL Pro Air Fryer Oven to 15 minutes. Press Start/Pause to begin preheating. Continue to the next step when it is done preheating. 3. Add the tuna mix to its air fryer basket, stir well, insert its air fryer basket in the level 3 and cook for 15 minutes. In a salad bowl, toss the arugula leaves with the tuna mix, toss and serve for breakfast.
Per Serving: Calories 208; Fat 10.5 g; Sodium 1755 mg; Carbs 26.9g; Fiber 4.1g; Sugar 2.5g; Protein 2.9g

Ham Quiche

Prep time: 10 minutes | Cook time: 15 minutes | Servings: 4

4 ounces ham, chopped
1 cup cheddar cheese, shredded
1 tablespoon chives, chopped
½ zucchini, grated
¼ cup heavy cream
1 tablespoon almond flour
½ teaspoon salt
½ teaspoon black pepper
½ teaspoon dried oregano
5 eggs, beaten
1 teaspoon coconut oil, softened

1. In the big bowl mix up ham, cheese, chives, zucchini, heavy cream, almond flour, salt, black pepper, oregano, and eggs. Stir the ingredients with the help of the fork until you get a homogenous mixture. 2. After this, Select the Air Fry mode. Set the Ninja Foodi Smart XL Pro temperature to 365°F/185°C. Select Level "3" and set the time on your Ninja Foodi Smart XL Pro Air Fryer Oven to 15 minutes. Press Start/Pause to begin preheating. Continue to the next step when it is done preheating. 3. Then gently grease its air fryer basket with coconut oil. Pour the ham mixture in its air fryer basket. Insert its air fryer basket into the level 3 of the oven and close the door. Cook the quiche for 15 minutes. 4. Then check if the quiche mixture is crusty, cook for extra 5 minutes if needed.
Per Serving: Calories 235; Fat 18.5 g; Sodium 64 mg; Carbs 9.6g; Fiber 4.1g; Sugar 2.4g; Protein 11.9g

Cheese Egg Cups

Prep time: 10 minutes | Cook time: 6 minutes | Servings: 2

2 eggs
2 ounces mozzarella, grated
1 ounces parmesan, grated
1 teaspoon coconut oil, melted
¼ teaspoon chili powder

1. Crack the eggs and separate egg yolks and egg whites. Then whisk the egg whites till the soft peaks. Separately whisk the egg yolks until smooth and add chili powder. 2. Then carefully add egg whites, parmesan, and mozzarella. Stir the ingredients. 3. Brush the silicone egg molds with coconut oil. Then put the cheese-egg mixture in the molds with the help of the spoon. Transfer the molds in its air fryer basket. Insert its air fryer basket into the level 3 of the oven and close the door. Cook on "Air Fry" Mode, select level 3, and set its temperature to 385°F/195°C for 6 minutes.
Per Serving: Calories 216; Fat 6.9 g; Sodium 31 mg; Carbs 38.5g; Fiber 5.6g; Sugar 6.7g; Protein 6.7g

Coconut Eggs Spread

Prep time: 5 minutes | Cook time: 8 minutes | Servings: 4

1 tablespoon olive oil
1 and ½ cup coconut cream
8 eggs, whisked
½ cup mint, chopped
Black pepper and salt to the taste

1. In a suitable bowl, mix the cream with salt, pepper, eggs and mint, whisk, pour into the air fryer. 2. Greased with the oil, spread, cook on "Air Fry" Mode, select level 3, and set its temperature to 350°F/185°C for 8 minutes, divide between plates and serve.
Per Serving: Calories 451; Fat 8.4 g; Sodium 134 mg; Carbs 59.6g; Fiber 8.2g; Sugar 4.8g; Protein 32.9g

Cheesy Mascarpone Pancake

Prep time: 10 minutes | Cook time: 8 minutes | Servings: 2

5 eggs, beaten
¼ cup almond flour
½ teaspoon baking powder
1 teaspoon apple cider vinegar
¼ cup cheddar cheese, shredded
1 teaspoon butter
1 tablespoon mascarpone
½ teaspoon sesame oil

1. Brush its air fryer basket with sesame oil. Then in the mixing bowl mix up all remaining ingredients. Stir the liquid until homogenous. Pour it in the air fryer pan and place it in the air fryer. 2. Insert its air fryer basket into the level 3 of the oven and close the door. Select Air Fry mode, cook the pancake for 8 minutes at 360°F/180°C Select Level "3". 3. Remove the cooked pancake from the air fryer pan and cut it into servings.
Per Serving: Calories 164; Fat 16.9 g; Sodium 99 mg; Carbs 3.2g; Fiber 0.8g; Sugar 0.2g; Protein 2.3g

Coconut Cauliflower Rice Pudding

Prep time: 5 minutes | Cook time: 20 minutes | Servings: 4

1 cup cauliflower rice
½ cup coconut, shredded
3 cups coconut milk
2 tablespoons stevia

1. In a suitable pan that fits the air fryer, mix all the recipe ingredients and whisk well. 2. Introduce the in your air fryer and cook on "Air Fry" Mode, select level 3, and set its temperature to 360°F/180°C for 20 minutes. 3. Divide into bowls and serve for breakfast.
Per Serving: Calories 134; Fat 11 g; Sodium 14 mg; Carbs 8.7g; Fiber 4.2g; Sugar 4.5g; Protein 2.2 g

Chicken and Cheese Lasagna

Prep time: 10 minutes | Cook time: 25 minutes | Servings: 2

1 egg, beaten
1 tablespoon heavy cream
1 teaspoon cream cheese
2 tablespoons almond flour
¼ teaspoon salt
¼ cup coconut cream
1 teaspoon dried basil
1 teaspoon keto tomato sauce
¼ cup mozzarella, shredded
1 teaspoon butter, melted
½ cup ground chicken

1. Make the lasagna batter: in the bowl mix up egg, heavy cream, cream cheese, and almond flour. Add coconut cream. Stir the liquid until smooth. 2. Then Select the Air Fry mode. Set the Ninja Foodi Smart XL Pro temperature to 355°F/180°C. Select Level "3" and set the time on your Ninja Foodi Smart XL Pro Air Fryer Oven to 25 minutes. Press Start/Pause to begin preheating. Continue to the next step when it is done preheating. 3. Brush its air fryer basket with butter. Pour ½ part of lasagna batter in its air fryer basket and flatten it in one layer. 4. Then in the separated bowl mix up tomato sauce, basil, salt, and ground chicken. Put the chicken mixture over the prepared batter in the air fryer. Add beaten egg. 5. Then top it with remaining lasagna batter and sprinkle with shredded mozzarella. Insert its air fryer basket into the level 3 of the oven and close the door. Cook the lasagna for 25 minutes.
Per Serving: Calories 281; Fat 15.5 g; Sodium 262 mg; Carbs 27.5g; Fiber 2.2g; Sugar 5g; Protein 8.5g

Chia and Hemp Seeds Pudding

Prep time: 4 minutes | Cook time: 2 minutes | Servings: 2

1 teaspoon hemp seeds
1 teaspoon chia seeds
1 tablespoon almond flour
1 teaspoon coconut flakes
1 teaspoon walnuts, chopped
½ teaspoon flax meal
¼ teaspoon vanilla extract
½ teaspoon erythritol
½ cup of coconut milk
¼ cup water, boiled

1. Put hemp seeds, chia seeds, almond flour, coconut flakes, walnuts, flax meal, vanilla extract, coconut milk, and water in the big bowl. Stir the prepared mixture until homogenous and pour it into 2 mason jars. 2. Leave the mason jars in the cold place for 4 hours. Then top the surface of the pudding with erythritol. 3. Place the mason jars in its air fryer basket. Insert its air fryer basket into the level 3 of the oven and close the door. 4. Cook the pudding for 2 minutes on "Air Fry" mode, select level 3 and set its temperature to 400°F/200°C until you get the light brown crust.
Per Serving: Calories 187; Fat 10.9 g; Sodium 2512 mg; Carbs 12g; Fiber 1.7 g; Sugar 4.9g; Protein 13.7g

Mozzarella Bell Peppers Sauté

Prep time: 5 minutes | Cook time: 15 minutes | Servings: 4

1 red bell pepper, roughly chopped
1 celery stalk, chopped
2 green onions, sliced
2 tablespoons butter, melted
½ cup mozzarella cheese, shredded
A pinch of black pepper and salt
6 eggs, whisked

1. In a suitable bowl, mix all the recipe ingredients except the butter and whisk well. 2. Select "Air Fry" mode, and level 3. Set the Ninja Foodi Smart XL Pro temperature to 360°F/180°C, then add the butter, heat it up, then add the celery and bell peppers mix, insert its air fryer basket in the level 3 and cook for 15 minutes, shaking the fryer once. 3. Divide the mix between plates and serve for breakfast.
Per Serving: Calories 170; Fat 13.1 g; Sodium 6 mg; Carbs 14.8 g; Fiber 2.5g; Sugar 9g; Protein 1.9g

Almond Coconut Oatmeal

Prep time: 5 minutes | Cook time: 15 minutes | Servings: 4

2 cups almond milk
1 cup coconut, shredded
2 teaspoons stevia
2 teaspoons vanilla extract

1. In a suitable pan that fits your air fryer, mix all the recipe ingredients, stir well, introduce the pan in the machine and cook on "Air Fry" Mode, select level 3, and set its temperature to 360°F/180°C for 15 minutes. 2. Divide into bowls and serve for breakfast.
Per Serving: Calories 117; Fat 5.8 g; Sodium 1460 mg; Carbs 9.9g; Fiber 3.3g; Sugar 3.3g; Protein 6.7g

Creamy Eggs Bake

Prep time: 10 minutes | Cook time: 20 minutes | Servings: 2

2 eggs
4 ounces double Gloucester cheese, grated'
1 teaspoon coconut flour
¼ cup heavy cream
1 tablespoon butter
1 tablespoon scallions, chopped

1. Place the eggs on the rack and insert the rack in the air fryer. Cook on Air Fry mode and Select Level "3". Cook the eggs for 17 minutes at 250°F/120°C and set the time on your Ninja Foodi Smart XL Pro Air Fryer Oven to 10 minutes. Press Start/Pause to begin preheating. Continue to the next step when it is done preheating. 2. Then cool the eggs in cold water and peel. Cut the eggs into halves. In the bowl mix up cheese, heavy cream, butter, and coconut flour. Microwave the prepared mixture for 1 minute until it is liquid. 3. Place the egg halves in the 2 ramekins. Pour the cheese mixture over the eggs and top with scallions. 4. Place the ramekins in its air fryer basket. Insert its air fryer basket into the level 3 of the oven and close the door. Cook them for 3 minutes at 400°F/200°C. Select Level "3".
Per Serving: Calories 278; Fat 13 g; Sodium 15 mg; Carbs 38.5g; Fiber 4.2g; Sugar 2.4g; Protein 4.8g

Sausages Egg Squares

Prep time: 20 minutes | Cook time: 20 minutes | Servings: 4

½ cup almond flour
¼ cup butter, melted
1 egg yolk
½ teaspoon baking powder
¼ teaspoon salt
6 ounces sausage meat
¼ teaspoon black pepper
Cooking spray

1. Make the prepared dough: in the mixing bowl mix up almond flour, butter, egg yolk, and baking powder. Add salt and knead the non-sticky dough. 2. In the separated bowl mix up black pepper and sausage meat. Roll up the prepared dough with the help of the rolling pin. Then cut the prepared dough into squares. Place the sausage meat in the center of dough squares and secure them in the shape of the puff. 3. Then Select the Air Fry mode. Set the Ninja Foodi Smart XL Pro temperature to 320°F/160°C. Select Level "3" and set the time on your Ninja Foodi Smart XL Pro Air Fryer Oven to 20 minutes. Press Start/Pause to begin preheating. Continue to the next step when it is done preheating. 4. Line its air fryer basket with baking paper. Put the sausage puffs over the baking paper and spray them with cooking spray. Insert its air fryer basket into the level 3 of the oven and close the door. Cook the meal for 20 minutes.
Per Serving: Calories 343; Fat 13.1 g; Sodium 1333 mg; Carbs 5.7g; Fiber 0.1g; Sugar 0.2g; Protein 43.6g

Parmesan Egg Scramble

Prep time: 5 minutes | Cook time: 20 minutes | Servings: 4

8 eggs, whisked
2 tablespoons oregano, chopped
Black pepper and salt to the taste
2 tablespoons parmesan, grated
¼ cup coconut cream

1. In a suitable bowl, mix the eggs with all the recipe ingredients and whisk. 2. Pour this into a suitable pan that fits your air fryer, introduce it in the preheated fryer and cook on "Air Fry" Mode, select level 3, and set its temperature to 350°F/175°C for 20 minutes, stirring often. 3. Divide the scramble between plates and serve for breakfast.
Per Serving: Calories 178; Fat 14.6 g; Sodium 67 mg; Carbs 12.4g; Fiber 4.8 g; Sugar 6.1g; Protein 2.9 g

Sausages Muffins

Prep time: 10 minutes | Cook time: 12 minutes | Servings: 4

4 teaspoons coconut flour
1 tablespoon coconut cream
1 egg, beaten
½ teaspoon baking powder
6 ounces sausage meat
1 teaspoon spring onions, chopped
½ teaspoon ground coriander
1 teaspoon sesame oil
½ teaspoon salt

1. In the mixing bowl mix up coconut flour, coconut cream, egg, baking powder, minced onion, and ground coriander. Add salt and whisk the prepared mixture until smooth. 2. After this, then add the sausage meat and stir the muffin batter. 3. Select the Air Fry mode. Set the Ninja Foodi Smart XL Pro temperature to 385°F/195°C. Select Level "3" and set the time on your Ninja Foodi Smart XL Pro Air Fryer Oven to 12 minutes. Press Start/Pause to begin preheating. Continue to the next step when it is done preheating. 4. Brush the muffin molds with sesame oil and pour the prepared batter inside. 5. Place the rack in its air fryer basket. Put the muffins on a rack. Insert its air fryer basket into the level 3 of the oven and close the door. Cook the meal for 12 minutes.
Per Serving: Calories 157; Fat 10.1 g; Sodium 423 mg; Carbs 1.6g; Fiber 0.5g; Sugar 0.4g; Protein 14.9g

Zucchini Watercress Salad

Prep time: 4 minutes | Cook time: 15 minutes | Servings: 2

1 cup watercress, torn
1 tablespoon olive oil
2 cups zucchini, roughly cubed
1 cup parmesan cheese, grated
Cooking spray

1. Grease a suitable pan that fits the air fryer with the cooking spray, then add all the recipe ingredients except the cheese, sprinkle the cheese on top and cook on "Air Fry" Mode, select level 3, and set its temperature to 390°F/200°C for 15 minutes. 2. Divide into bowls and serve for breakfast.
Per Serving: Calories 169; Fat 7.1 g; Sodium 42 mg; Carbs 28.5g; Fiber 2.1g; Sugar 13.4g; Protein 1.2g

Fried Cheese Hot Dogs

Prep time: 15 minutes | Cook time: 8 minutes | Servings: 3

6 small pork sausages
½ cup almond flour
½ cup mozzarella cheese, shredded
2 eggs, beaten
1 tablespoon mascarpone
Cooking spray

1. Pierce the hot dogs with wooden coffee sticks to get the sausages on the sticks". 2. Then in the bowl mix up almond flour, mozzarella cheese, and mascarpone. Microwave the prepared mixture for 15 seconds until you get a melted mixture. 3. Then stir the egg in the cheese mixture and whisk it until smooth. Coat every sausage stick in the cheese mixture. 4. Then Select the Air Fry mode. Set the Ninja Foodi Smart XL Pro temperature to 375°F/190°C. Select Level "3" and set the time on your Ninja Foodi Smart XL Pro Air Fryer Oven to 4 minutes. Press Start/Pause to begin preheating. Continue to the next step when it is done preheating. Grease its air fryer basket with cooking oil spray 5. Place the sausage stick in its air fryer basket. Insert its air fryer basket into the level 3 of the oven and close the door. Cook them for 4 minutes from each side until they are light brown.
Per Serving: Calories 363; Fat 17.1 g; Sodium 1065 mg; Carbs 19.8g; Fiber 3.4g; Sugar 12.9g; Protein 33.7g

Tomato Greens Salad

Prep time: 5 minutes | Cook time: 15 minutes | Servings: 4

1 teaspoon olive oil
2 cups mustard greens
A pinch of black pepper and salt

½ pound cherry tomatoes, cubed
2 tablespoons chives, chopped

1. Preheat on "Air Fry" mode, select level 3 and set its temperature to 360°F/180°C, then add all the recipe ingredients, toss, cook for 15 minutes shaking halfway, divide into bowls and serve for breakfast.
Per Serving: Calories 283; Fat 6.6g; Sodium 693mg; Carbs 8.5g; Fiber 1.4g; Sugar 3.4g; Protein 45.2g

Cabbage Pork Hash

Prep time: 15 minutes | Cook time: 20 minutes | Servings: 4

1 Chinese cabbage, shredded
¼ cup chicken broth
½ teaspoon keto tomato sauce
1 green bell pepper, chopped
1 teaspoon salt
6 ounces pork loin, chopped

1 tablespoon apple cider vinegar
1 teaspoon sesame oil
½ teaspoon chili flakes
½ teaspoon salt
¼ teaspoon black pepper
1 teaspoon ground turmeric

1. Put Chinese cabbage in the bowl. Add chicken broth, tomato sauce, bell pepper, and salt. Mix up the ingredients and transfer in its air fryer basket. 2. Select the Air Fry mode. Insert its air fryer basket into the level 3 of the oven and close the door. Cook the cabbage for 5 minutes at 365°F/185°C. 3. Meanwhile, in the mixing bowl mix up black pepper, turmeric, salt, chili flakes, sesame oil, and apple cider vinegar. 4. Add chopped pork loin and mix up the ingredients. Add the meat in its air fryer basket. Insert its air fryer basket into the level 3 of the oven and close the door. Cook the cabbage hash for 10 minutes at 385°F/195°C. Select Level "3". 5. Then shake the hash well and cook it for 5 minutes more.
Per Serving: Calories 183; Fat 0.4 g; Sodium 4347 mg; Carbs 5.6g; Fiber 0.6g; Sugar 8.4g; Protein 40.2g

Green Beans, Radish and Egg Salad

Prep time: 5 minutes | Cook time: 15 minutes | Servings: 4

1 and ¾ cups radishes, chopped
½ pound green beans, trimmed
A pinch of black pepper and salt

4 eggs, whisked
Cooking spray
1 tablespoon cilantro, chopped

1. Grease a suitable pan that fits the air fryer with the cooking spray, then add all the recipe ingredients, toss and cook on "Air Fry" Mode, select level 3, and set its temperature to 360°F/180°C for 15 minutes. 2. Divide between plates and serve for breakfast.
Per Serving: Calories 210; Fat 5.4 g; Sodium 110 mg; Carbs 18.5g; Fiber 2.4g; Sugar 13.1g; Protein 23.5g

Cauliflower Spinach Rice

Prep time: 5 minutes | Cook time: 15 minutes | Servings: 4

12 ounces' cauliflower rice
3 tablespoons stevia
2 tablespoons olive oil

2 tablespoons lime juice
1-pound fresh spinach, torn
1 red bell pepper, chopped

1. In your air fryer, mix all the recipe ingredients, toss, Cook on "Air Fry" Mode, select level 3, and set its temperature to 370°F/185°C for 15 minutes, shaking halfway, divide between plates and serve for breakfast.
Per Serving: Calories 273; Fat 24 g; Sodium 1181 mg; Carbs 12.8g; Fiber 1g; Sugar 1.4g; Protein 20g

Lemony Cinnamon Raspberries

Prep time: 5 minutes | Cook time: 12 minutes | Servings: 2

1 cup raspberries
2 tablespoons lemon juice

2 tablespoons butter
1 teaspoon cinnamon powder

1. In your air fryer, mix all the recipe ingredients, toss, cover. Cook on "Air Fry" Mode, select level 3, and set its temperature to 350°F/175°C for 12 minutes, divide into bowls and serve for breakfast.
Per Serving: Calories 297; Fat 18.4 g; Sodium 1151 mg; Carbs 11.6g; Fiber 0.6g; Sugar 10.9g; Protein 20.5g

Coconut Almond Cookies

Prep time: 10 minutes | Cook time: 8 minutes | Servings: 4

4 tablespoons coconut flour
½ teaspoon baking powder
1 teaspoon lemon juice
¼ teaspoon vanilla extract
¼ teaspoon lemon zest, grated

2 eggs, beaten
¼ cup of organic almond milk
1 teaspoon avocado oil
¼ teaspoon Himalayan pink salt

1. In the big bowl, mix up all the recipe ingredients from the list above. Knead the soft dough and cut it into 4 pieces. 2. Select the Air Fry mode. Set the Ninja Foodi Smart XL Pro temperature to 400°F/200°C. Select Level "3" and set the time on your Ninja Foodi Smart XL Pro Air Fryer Oven to 8 minutes. Press Start/Pause to begin preheating. Continue to the next step when it is done preheating. 3. Then line its air fryer basket with baking paper. Roll the prepared dough pieces in the balls and press them gently to get the shape of flat cookies. 4. Place the cookies in the air fryer. Insert its air fryer basket into the level 3 of the oven and close the door. And cook them for 8 minutes.
Per Serving: Calories 70; Fat 10.5 g; Sodium 503 mg; Carbs 21.4g; Fiber 3.1g; Sugar 1.9g; Protein 6.6g

Mozzarella Mushroom Bake

Prep time: 5 minutes | Cook time: 20 minutes | Servings: 4

2 garlic cloves, minced
1 teaspoon olive oil
2 celery stalks, chopped
½ cup white mushrooms, chopped
½ cup red bell pepper, chopped

Black pepper and salt to the taste
1 teaspoon oregano, dried
7 ounces mozzarella, shredded
1 tablespoon lemon juice

1. Select "Air Fry" mode, and level 3. Set the Ninja Foodi Smart XL Pro temperature to 350°F/175°C, then add the oil and heat it up. 2. Add garlic, celery, mushrooms, bell pepper, salt, pepper, oregano, mozzarella and the lemon juice, toss and cook for 20 minutes. 3. Divide between plates and serve for breakfast.
Per Serving: Calories 206; Fat 6.4 g; Sodium 911 mg; Carbs 28.9g; Fiber 3.6g; Sugar 20.4g; Protein 11g

Cauliflower Ham Quiche

Prep time: 10 minutes | Cook time: 15 minutes | Servings: 4

5 eggs, beaten
½ cup heavy cream
1 teaspoon ground nutmeg
¼ teaspoon ground cardamom
¼ teaspoon salt
1 teaspoon black pepper

1 teaspoon butter, softened
¼ cup spring onions, chopped
¼ cup cauliflower florets
5 ounces ham, chopped
3 ounces provolone cheese, grated

1. Pour the beaten eggs in the bowl. Add heavy cream, ground nutmeg, ground cardamom, black pepper, and salt. 2. After this, pour the liquid in the air fryer round pan. Add butter, onion, cauliflower florets, ham, and cheese. Gently stir the quiche liquid. 3. Place it in its air fryer basket. Select the Air Fry mode. Insert its air fryer basket into the level 3 of the oven and close the door. Cook the quiche for 15 minutes at 385°F/195°C. Select Level "3".
Per Serving: Calories 322; Fat 14 g; Sodium 679 mg; Carbs 1.1g; Fiber 0.2g; Sugar 0.7g; Protein 45.5g

Cream Cheese Wontons

Prep time: 15 minutes | Cook time: 2 minutes | Servings: 4

½ teaspoon garlic powder
1 ounces scallions, chopped
1 teaspoon fresh dill, chopped

4 tablespoons cream cheese
8 wonton wraps
Cooking spray

1. In the mixing bowl mix up garlic powder, scallions, fresh dill, and cream cheese. Then fill the wonton wraps with cream cheese mixture and fold them. 2. Select the Air Fry mode. Set the Ninja Foodi Smart XL Pro temperature to 355°F/180°C. Select Level "3" and set the time on your Ninja Foodi Smart XL Pro Air Fryer Oven to 2 minutes. Press Start/Pause to begin preheating. Continue to the next step when it is done preheating. 3. Place the wonton wraps in its air fryer basket. Insert its air fryer basket into the level 3 of the oven and close the door. And cook them for 2 minutes until they are light brown.
Per Serving: Calories 62; Fat 22.6 g; Sodium 242 mg; Carbs 22.9g; Fiber 1.4g; Sugar 0.5g; Protein 3.4g

Cinnamon Pudding

Prep time: 4 minutes | Cook time: 12 minutes | Servings: 2

½ teaspoon cinnamon powder
¼ teaspoon allspice, ground
4 tablespoons erythritol
4 eggs, whisked
2 tablespoons heavy cream
Cooking spray

1. In a suitable bowl, mix all the recipe ingredients except the cooking spray, whisk well and pour into a ramekin greased with cooking spray. 2. Add the basket to your air fryer, put the ramekin inside and cook on "Air Fry" Mode, select level 3, and set its temperature to 400°F/200°C for 12 minutes. Divide into bowls and serve for breakfast.
Per Serving: Calories 100; Fat 2g; Sodium 480mg; Carbs 4g; Fiber 2g; Sugar 0g; Protein 18g

Bacon Cheese Pockets

Prep time: 15 minutes | Cook time: 4 minutes | Servings: 6

6 wontons wrap
1 egg yolk, whisked
2 ounces bacon, chopped, cooked
½ cup edam cheese, shredded
1 teaspoon sesame oil
½ teaspoon black pepper

1. Put the chopped bacon in the bowl. Add edam cheese and black pepper. Stir the ingredients gently with the help of the fork. 2. After this, put the prepared mixture on the wonton wrap and fold it in the shape of the pocket. Repeat the steps with remaining filling and wonton wraps. 3. Select the Air Fry mode. Set the Ninja Foodi Smart XL Pro temperature to 400°F/200°C. Select Level "3" and set the time on your Ninja Foodi Smart XL Pro Air Fryer Oven to 2 minutes. Press Start/Pause to begin preheating. Continue to the next step when it is done preheating. 4. Brush every wonton pocket with whisked egg yolk. 5. Then brush the air fryer with sesame oil and spread the pockets inside. Cook the meal for 2 minutes from each side.
Per Serving: Calories 180; Fat 3.2g; Sodium 133mg; Carbs 32g; Fiber 1.1g; Sugar 1.8g; Protein 9g

Green Beans Egg Bake

Prep time: 5 minutes | Cook time: 20 minutes | Servings: 4

1 pound green beans, roughly chopped
Cooking spray
2 eggs, whisked
Black pepper and salt to the taste
1 tablespoon sweet paprika
4 ounces sour cream

1. Grease a suitable pan that fits your air fryer with the cooking spray and mix all the recipe ingredients inside. 2. Put the pan in its air fryer basket. Insert its air fryer basket into the level 3 of the oven and close the door. Cook on "Air Fry" Mode, and set its temperature to 360°F/180°C for 20 minutes. Divide between plates and serve.
Per Serving: Calories 229; Fat 1.9 | Sodium 567mg; Carbs 1.9g; Fiber 0.4g; Sugar 0.6g; Protein 11.8g

Egg, Bean and Mushroom Burrito

Prep time: 10 minutes | Cook time: 15 minutes | Servings: 2

2 tablespoons canned black beans, rinsed and drained
¼ cup baby portobello mushrooms, sliced
1 teaspoon olive oil
Pinch of kosher salt
1 large egg
1 slice low-fat cheddar cheese
1 eight-inch whole grain flour tortilla
Hot sauce

1. Select Level 3. 2. Select the "AIR FRY" function of Ninja Foodi Smart XL Pro Air Oven, set temperature to 360°F/180°C and time to 5 minutes. Select START/STOP to begin preheating. 3. Spray the air fryer sheet pan with nonstick cooking spray, then place the black beans and baby portobello mushrooms in the sheet pan, drizzle with the olive oil, and season with the kosher salt. 4. Place the sheet pan into the air fryer; cook for 5 minutes, then pause the fryer to crack the egg on top of the beans and mushrooms. Cook for 8 more minutes or until the egg is cooked as desired. 5. Pause the fryer again, top the egg with cheese, and cook for 1 more minute. 6. Remove the pan from the fryer, then use a spatula to place the bean mixture on the whole grain flour tortilla. Fold in the sides and roll from front to back. 7. Serve warm with the hot sauce on the side.
Per Serving: Calories 277; Fat 12g; Sodium 306mg; Carbs 26g; Fiber 6g; Sugar 2g; Protein 16g

Herbed Parmesan Balls

Prep time: 20 minutes | Cook time: 9 minutes | Servings: 3

1 teaspoon garlic powder
1 ounces parmesan, grated
½ cup cheddar cheese, shredded
1 egg, beaten
1 tablespoon cream cheese
1 teaspoon dried dill
1 teaspoon dried cilantro
1 teaspoon dried parsley
Cooking spray

1. Mix up parmesan and cheddar cheese. Add garlic powder, egg, cream cheese, dried dill, cilantro, and parsley. Stir the prepared mixture until homogenous. With the help of the scoop make the cheese balls and put them in the freezer for 15 minutes. 2. Select the Air Fry mode. Set the Ninja Foodi Smart XL Pro temperature to 400°F/200°C. Select Level "3" and set the time on your Ninja Foodi Smart XL Pro Air Fryer Oven to 9 minutes. Press Start/Pause to begin preheating. Continue to the next step when it is done preheating. 3. Then Grease its air fryer basket with cooking oil spray Put the frozen cheese balls in its air fryer basket. Insert its air fryer basket into the level 3 of the oven and close the door. Cook them for 9 minutes until they are golden.
Per Serving: Calories 122; Fat 7.5 g; Sodium 465 mg; Carbs 9g; Fiber 3.8g; Sugar 2.8g; Protein 7.4g

Zucchini Onion Cakes

Prep time: 5 minutes | Cook time: 8 minutes | Servings: 4

8 ounces zucchinis, chopped
2 spring onions, chopped
2 eggs, whisked
Black pepper and salt to the taste
¼ teaspoon sweet paprika, chopped
Cooking spray

1. In a suitable bowl, mix all the recipe ingredients except the cooking spray, stir well and shape medium fritters out of this mix. 2. Put the basket in the air fryer, then add the fritters inside, grease them with cooking spray and cook on "Air Fry" Mode, select level 3, and set its temperature to 400°F/200°C for 8 minutes. Divide the fritters between plates and serve for breakfast.
Per Serving: Calories 179; Fat 7.5 g; Sodium 242 mg; Carbs 16g; Fiber 0.6g; Sugar 6.8g; Protein 10 6g

Beef Stuffed Peppers Rings

Prep time: 10 minutes | Cook time: 11 minutes | Servings: 2

1 large green bell pepper
½ cup ground beef
1 egg, beaten
½ teaspoon salt
½ teaspoon black pepper
½ teaspoon Italian seasonings
1 teaspoon coconut oil, melted

1. Remove the seeds from the pepper and wash it. Then cut the pepper into 2 rings. 2. In the bowl mix egg, ground beef, salt, black pepper, and Italian seasonings. Select the Air Fry mode. Set the Ninja Foodi Smart XL Pro temperature to 385°F/195°C. Select Level "3" and set the time on your Ninja Foodi Smart XL Pro Air Fryer Oven to 11 minutes. Press Start/Pause to begin preheating. Continue to the next step when it is done preheating. 3. Brush its air fryer basket with coconut oil. Place the pepper rings in the air fryer and fill them with ground beef mixture. 4. Insert its air fryer basket into the level 3 of the oven and close the door. Cook the meal at 385°F/195°C for 11 minutes.
Per Serving: Calories 208; Fat 10.5 g; Sodium 1755 mg; Carbs 26.9g; Fiber 4.1g; Sugar 2.5g; Protein 2.9g

Artichokes Frittata

Prep time: 5 minutes | Cook time: 12 minutes | Servings: 4

1-pound artichoke hearts, steamed and chopped
Black pepper and salt to the taste
4 eggs, whisked
1 green onion, chopped
2 tablespoons parsley, chopped
Cooking spray

1. Grease a suitable pan that fits your air fryer with cooking spray. In a suitable bowl, mix all the other ingredients, whisk well and pour evenly into the pan. 2. Introduce the pan in the air fryer, cook on "Air Fry" Mode, select level 3, and set its temperature to 390°F/200°C for 12 minutes, divide between plates and serve for breakfast.
Per Serving: Calories 235; Fat 18.5 g; Sodium 64 mg; Carbs 9.6g; Fiber 4.1g; Sugar 2.4g; Protein 11.9g

Mozzarella Sticks

Prep time: 15 minutes | Cook time: 7 minutes | Servings: 2

4 ounces mozzarella
2 tablespoons coconut flakes
1 egg, beaten
1 teaspoon turmeric powder

1 tablespoon heavy cream
½ teaspoon black pepper
Cooking spray

1. Cut mozzarella into 2 sticks. Then in the mixing bowl mix up heavy cream, egg, and black pepper. Dip the cheese sticks in the liquid. 2. After this, coat every cheese stick with coconut flakes. Select the Air Fry mode. Set the Ninja Foodi Smart XL Pro temperature to 400°F/200°C. Select Level "3" and set the time on your Ninja Foodi Smart XL Pro Air Fryer Oven to 7 minutes. Press Start/Pause to begin preheating. Continue to the next step when it is done preheating. 3. Then grease its air fryer basket with cooking oil spray. Put mozzarella sticks in the air fryer. 4. Insert its air fryer basket into the level 3 of the oven and close the door. And cook them for 7 minutes until they are light brown.
Per Serving: Calories 281; Fat 15.5 g; Sodium 262 mg; Carbs 27.5g; Fiber 2.2g; Sugar 5g; Protein 8.5g

Endives Egg Frittata

Prep time: 5 minutes | Cook time: 15 minutes | Servings: 6

1 endive, shredded
6 eggs, whisked
A pinch of black pepper and salt

1 teaspoon sweet paprika
2 teaspoons cilantro, chopped
Cooking spray

1. In a suitable bowl, mix all the recipe ingredients except the cooking spray and stir well. 2. Grease a baking pan with the cooking spray, pour the frittata mix and spread well. 3. Put the pan in its air fryer basket. Insert its air fryer basket into the level 3 of the oven and close the door. Cook on "Air Fry" Mode, select level 3, and set its temperature to 370°F/185°C for 15 minutes. Divide between plates and serve them for breakfast.
Per Serving: Calories 117; Fat 5.8 g; Sodium 1460 mg; Carbs 9.9g; Fiber 3.3g; Sugar 3.3g; Protein 6.7g

Oregano Cod Sticks

Prep time: 15 minutes | Cook time: 6 minutes | Servings: 2

10 ounces cod fillet
¼ cup almond flour
1 tablespoon coconut flour
1 egg white

1 teaspoon dried oregano
½ teaspoon onion powder
½ teaspoon salt
1 teaspoon avocado oil

1. Chop the cod fillet and put it in the blender. Add coconut flour, egg white, dried oregano, salt, and onion powder. Blend the prepared mixture until smooth. 2. Then make the medium sticks from the fish mixture and coat them in the almond flour. 3. Brush its air fryer basket with avocado oil. Then place the cod sticks in one layer of the air fryer. Select the Air Fry mode. Cook the fish sticks for 6 minutes at 400°F/200°C. Select Level "3" and set the time on your Ninja Foodi Smart XL Pro Air Fryer Oven to 10 minutes. 4. Flip the fish sticks after 3 minutes of cooking.
Per Serving: Calories 281; Fat 15.5 g; Sodium 262 mg; Carbs 27.5g; Fiber 2.2g; Sugar 5g; Protein 8.5g

Tortilla Cheese Sandwich

Prep time: 15 minutes | Cook time: 3 minutes | Servings: 2

2 tortillas
2 cheddar cheese slices
2 deli ham slices

2 lettuce leaves
2 teaspoons mascarpone
¼ teaspoon chives, chopped

1. Cut every tortilla into halves. In the shallow bowl mix up chives and mascarpone. Spread the tortilla halves with mascarpone mixture. 2. Then place cheese and ham on 2 tortilla halves. Add leaves and top them with remaining tortilla halves. 3. Select the Air Fry mode. Set the Ninja Foodi Smart XL Pro temperature to 400°F/200°C. Select Level "3" and set the time on your Ninja Foodi Smart XL Pro Air Fryer Oven to 3 minutes. Press Start/Pause to begin preheating. Continue to the next step when it is done preheating. 4. Place the tortilla sandwiches in its air fryer basket. Insert its air fryer basket into the level 3 of the oven and close the door. Cook them for 3 minutes.
Per Serving: Calories 363; Fat 17.1 g; Sodium1065 mg; Carbs 19.8g; Fiber 3.4g; Sugar 12.9g; Protein 33.7g

Cheesy Bok Choy Mix

Prep time: 5 minutes | Cook time: 15 minutes | Servings: 4

7 ounces bok choy, torn
7ounces baby spinach, torn
2 tablespoons olive oil
2 eggs, whisked

2 tablespoons coconut cream
3 ounces mozzarella, shredded
Black pepper and salt to the taste

1. In your air fryer, mix all the recipe ingredients except the mozzarella and toss them gently. Sprinkle the mozzarella on top. Cook on "Air Fry" Mode, select level 3, and set its temperature to 360°F/180°Cfor 15 minutes, divide between plates and serve.
Per Serving: Calories 134; Fat 11 g; Sodium 14 mg; Carbs 8.7g; Fiber 4.2g; Sugar 4.5g; Protein 2.2 g

Mascarpone Almond Cheesecake Bites

Prep time: 20 minutes | Cook time: 3 minutes | Servings: 4

4 tablespoons cream cheese
4 teaspoons erythritol
¼ teaspoon vanilla extract

1 tablespoon mascarpone
4 tablespoons coconut milk
4 tablespoons almond flour

1. Mix up cream cheese with erythritol, vanilla extract, and mascarpone. 2. Make the cheesecake balls (bites) and put them on the baking paper. Refrigerate the cheesecake balls for 10-15 minutes. 3. Then Select the Air Fry mode. Set the Ninja Foodi Smart XL Pro temperature to 300°F/150°C. Select Level "3" and set the time on your Ninja Foodi Smart XL Pro Air Fryer Oven to 3 minutes. Press Start/Pause to begin preheating. Continue to the next step when it is done preheating. 4. Dip the frozen bites in the coconut milk and coat in the almond flour. Cook them in the air fryer for 3 minutes.
Per Serving: Calories 164; Fat 16.9 g; Sodium 99 mg; Carbs 3.2g; Fiber 0.8g; Sugar 0.2g; Protein 2.3g

Artichoke, Zucchini and Egg Mix

Prep time: 5 minutes | Cook time: 20 minutes | Servings: 4

½ pound artichokes, trimmed and chopped
2 zucchinis, sliced
4 spring onions, chopped

2 tomatoes, cut into quarters
4 eggs, whisked
Cooking spray
Black pepper and salt to the taste

1. Grease a suitable pan with cooking spray, and mix all the other ingredients inside. 2. Put the pan in its air fryer basket. Insert its air fryer basket into the level 3 of the oven and close the door. Cook on "Air Fry" Mode, select level 3, and set its temperature to 350°F/175°C for 20 minutes. Divide between plates and serve.
Per Serving: Calories 170; Fat 13.1 g; Sodium 6 mg; Carbs 14.8 g; Fiber 2.5g; Sugar 9g; Protein 1.9g

Mozzarella Tomato Bowls

Prep time: 5 minutes | Cook time: 15 minutes | Servings: 4

1-pound cherry tomatoes, halved
1 cup mozzarella, shredded
Cooking spray

Black pepper and salt to the taste
1 teaspoon basil, chopped

1. Grease the tomatoes with the cooking spray, season with black pepper and salt, sprinkle the mozzarella on top, place them all in your air fryer's basket. 2. Insert its air fryer basket into the level 3 of the oven and close the door. Cook on "Air Fry" Mode, select level 3, and set its temperature to 330°F/165°C for 15 minutes, divide into bowls, sprinkle the basil on top and serve.
Per Serving: Calories 178; Fat 14.6 g; Sodium 67 mg; Carbs 12.4g; Fiber 4.8 g; Sugar 6.1g; Protein 2.9 g

Berries Bowls

Prep time: 5 minutes | Cook time: 15 minutes | Servings: 4

1 and ½ cups coconut milk
½ cup blackberries

2 teaspoons stevia
½ cup coconut, shredded

1. In your air fryer's pan, mix all the recipe ingredients, stir, cover and cook on "Air Fry" Mode, select level 3, and set its temperature to 360°F/180°C for 15 minutes. Divide into bowls and serve for breakfast.
Per Serving: Calories 169; Fat 7.1 g; Sodium 42 mg; Carbs 28.5g; Fiber 2.1g; Sugar 13.4g; Protein 1.2g

Tofu Cabbage Wraps

Prep time: 15 minutes | Cook time: 9 minutes | Servings: 4

4 tortillas	1 teaspoon lemon juice
5 ounces tofu, cubed	½ cup white cabbage, shredded
1 teaspoon mustard	4 teaspoons cream cheese
1 teaspoon avocado oil	2 chipotles, chopped

1. Select the Air Fry mode. Set the Ninja Foodi Smart XL Pro temperature to 400°F/200°C. Select Level "3" and set the time on your Ninja Foodi Smart XL Pro Air Fryer Oven to 9 minutes. Press Start/Pause to begin preheating. Continue to the next step when it is done preheating. 2. Meanwhile, mix up mustard with avocado oil and lemon juice. Place the tofu cubes in the mustard mixture and coat them well. 3. Then put the tofu in its air fryer basket, insert its air fryer basket into the level 3 of the oven and close the door. And cook for 9 minutes. 4. Shake the tofu during cooking for 2-3 times to avoid burning. 4. Then place the tofu on the tortillas. Add shredded cabbage, chipotles, and cream cheese. Fold the wraps.
Per Serving: Calories 187; Fat 10.9 g; Sodium 2512 mg; Carbs 12g; Fiber 1.7 g; Sugar 4.9g; Protein 13.7g

Butter Almond Donuts

Prep time: 20 minutes | Cook time: 10 minutes | Servings: 4

1 cup almond flour	1 teaspoon vanilla extract
1 tablespoon flax meal	1 teaspoon heavy cream
2 tablespoons erythritol	1 teaspoon butter, melted
2 eggs, beaten	1 tablespoon psyllium husk
1 teaspoon baking powder	powder

1. Make the prepared dough: mix up almond flour, flax meal, eggs, baking powder, vanilla extract, heavy cream, and butter. Add psyllium husk and knead the soft but non-sticky dough. 2. Then make the donuts balls and leave them for 10 minutes in a warm place. 3. Select the Air Fry mode. Set the Ninja Foodi Smart XL Pro temperature to 355°F/180°C. Select Level "3" and set the time on your Ninja Foodi Smart XL Pro Air Fryer Oven to 10 minutes. Press Start/Pause to begin preheating. Continue to the next step when it is done preheating. Line its air fryer basket with baking paper. Put the donuts inside. 4. Insert its air fryer basket into the level 3 of the oven and close the door. And cook them for 10 minutes until they are light brown. Then coat every donut in erythritol.
Per Serving: Calories 183; Fat 0.4 g; Sodium 4347 mg; Carbs 5.6g; Fiber 0.6g; Sugar 8.4g; Protein 40.2g

Avocado Cabbage Salad

Prep time: 5 minutes | Cook time: 15 minutes | Servings: 4

2 cups red cabbage, shredded	1 small avocado, peeled, pitted
A drizzle of olive oil	and sliced
1 red bell pepper, sliced	Black pepper and salt to the taste

1. Grease your air fryer with the oil, then add all the recipe ingredients, toss, cover and Insert its air fryer basket into the level 3 of the oven and close the door. 2. Cook on "Air Fry" Mode, select level 3, and set its temperature to 400°F/200°C for 15 minutes. Divide into bowls and serve cold for breakfast.
Per Serving: Calories 297; Fat 18.4 g; Sodium 1151 mg; Carbs 11.6g; Fiber 0.6g; Sugar 10.9g; Protein 20.5g

Cheesy Pea Protein Muffins

Prep time: 5 minutes | Cook time: 15 minutes | Servings: 4

1 cup almond flour	½ cup chicken or turkey strips
1 teaspoon baking powder	3 tablespoons pea protein
3 eggs	1 cup cream cheese
1 cup mozzarella cheese, shredded	1 cup almond milk

1. Install the wire rack on Level 3. Select the "BAKE" function of Ninja Foodi Smart XL Pro Air Oven, set temperature to 390°F/200°C and time to 15 minutes. Select START/STOP to begin preheating. 2. Mix all the ingredients in a mixing bowl and stir with a wooden spoon. Fill muffin cups with mixture ¾ full and bake for 15-minutes and enjoy!
Per Serving: Calories 293; Fat 13.8g; Sodium 855mg; Carbs 28g; Fiber 8g; Sugar 11g; Protein 19g

Raspberries Bowls

Prep time: 5 minutes | Cook time: 15 minutes | Servings: 4

2 cups almond milk	¼ teaspoon nutmeg, ground
½ cups raspberries	2 teaspoons stevia
1 and ½ cups coconut, shredded	Cooking spray
½ teaspoon cinnamon powder	

1. Grease the air fryer's pan with cooking spray. mix all the recipe ingredients inside, cover and cook on "Air Fry" Mode, select level 3, and set its temperature to 360°F/180°C for 15 minutes. Divide into bowls and serve for breakfast.
Per Serving: Calories 210; Fat 5.4 g; Sodium 110 mg; Carbs 18.5g; Fiber 2.4g; Sugar 13.1g; Protein 23.5g

Strawberries Coconut Mix

Prep time: 5 minutes | Cook time: 15 minutes

2 cups coconut milk	½ cup coconut, shredded
¼ cup strawberries	2 teaspoons stevia
¼ teaspoon vanilla extract	Cooking spray

1. Grease the air fryer's pan with the cooking spray. then add all the recipe ingredients inside and toss. Cook on "Air Fry" Mode, select level 3, and set its temperature to 365°F/185°C for 15 minutes, divide into bowls and serve for breakfast.
Per Serving: Calories 157; Fat 10.1 g; Sodium 423 mg; Carbs 1.6g; Fiber 0.5g; Sugar 0.4g; Protein 14.9g

Tofu Tempeh Scramble

Prep time: 10 minutes | Cook time: 12 minutes | Servings: 3

3 eggs, beaten	1 teaspoon coconut oil, melted
3 ounces tempeh	¼ teaspoon chili flakes
2 ounces tofu	1 teaspoon apple cider vinegar
1 tablespoon mascarpone	½ teaspoon salt

1. Finely chop the tofu and tempeh and place it in the air fryer. Add chili flakes, apple cider vinegar, and coconut oil. 2. Select Air Fry mode. Shake the ingredients gently and cook them for 8 minutes at 395°F/200°C. Select Level "3" and set the time on your Ninja Foodi Smart XL Pro Air Fryer Oven to 10 minutes. Press Start/Pause to begin preheating. Continue to the next step when it is done preheating. 3. Shake the ingredients after 4 minutes of cooking. 4. After this, pour the beaten eggs over the tempeh and tofu and stir well. Cook the scramble for 2 minutes at 400°F/200°C. Select Level "3" and set the time on your Ninja Foodi Smart XL Pro Air Fryer Oven to 10 minutes. Press Start/Pause to begin preheating. Continue to the next step when it is done preheating. 5. Then scramble the prepared mixture with the help of the fork and cook for 2 minutes more.
Per Serving: Calories 273; Fat 24 g; Sodium 1181 mg; Carbs 12.8g; Fiber 1g; Sugar 1.4g; Protein 20g

Granola-Stuffed Apples

Prep time: 15 minutes | Cook time: 10 minutes | Servings: 4

4 Granny Smith or other firm apples	¾ teaspoon cinnamon
1 cup (100g) granola	2 tablespoons (28g) unsalted butter, melted
2 tablespoons (19g) light brown sugar	1 cup (240ml) water or apple juice

1. Install the wire rack on Level 3. 2. Select the "BAKE" function of Ninja Foodi Smart XL Pro Air Oven, set temperature to 350°F/175°C and time to 20 minutes. 3. Select START/STOP to begin preheating. Working one apple at a time, cut a circle around the apple stem and scoop out the core, taking care not to cut completely to the bottom. Repeat with the remaining apples. 4. In a small bowl, combine the granola, brown sugar, and cinnamon. Pour the melted butter over the ingredients and stir with a fork. Divide the granola mixture among the apples, packing it tightly into the empty cavity. 5. Place the apples in the sheet pan on the wire rack for the air fryer. Pour the water or juice around the apples. Bake for 20 minutes until the apples are soft all the way through. 6. Serve warm with a dollop of crème fraîche or yogurt, if desired.
Per Serving: Calories 200; Fat 15.6g; Sodium 165mg; Carbs 5g; Fiber 1g; Sugar 2g; Protein 10g

Spinach and Egg Salad

Prep time: 5 minutes | Cook time: 10 minutes | Servings: 4

1 tablespoon lime juice
4 eggs, hard boiled, peeled and sliced
2 cups baby spinach

Black pepper and salt to the taste
3 tablespoons heavy cream
2 tablespoons olive oil

1. In your air fryer, mix the spinach with cream, eggs, black pepper and salt, cover and cook on "Air Fry" Mode, select level 3, and set its temperature to 360°F/180°Cfor 6 minutes. 2. Transfer this to a suitable bowl, then add the lime juice and oil, toss and serve for breakfast.
Per Serving: Calories 149; Fat 12 g; Sodium 132 mg; Carbs 10.5g; Fiber 2.6g; Sugar 4.6g; Protein 1.5g

Green Beans, Onion and Egg Bowls

Prep time: 5 minutes | Cook time: 20 minutes | Servings: 2

1 cup green beans, halved
2 spring onions, chopped
4 eggs, whisked

Black pepper and salt to the taste
¼ teaspoon cumin, ground

1. Select "Air Fry" mode, and level 3. Set the Ninja Foodi Smart XL Pro temperature to 360°F/180°. then add all the recipe ingredients, toss, cover, cook for 20 minutes, divide into bowls and serve for breakfast.
Per Serving: Calories 380; Fat 7.7g; Sodium 403 mg; Carbs 7.6g; Fiber 0.1g; Sugar 5.4g; Protein 65.7g

Brown Bread

Prep time: 10 minutes | Cook time: 28 minutes | Servings: 4

8 ounces of almond flour
1 ounce of liquid stevia
1 egg

2 tablespoons butter
½ cup pumpkin seeds

1. Mix all the recipe ingredients in a suitable bowl, except the butter and egg. Keep mixing with hands. Add the butter and knead mixture. 2. Let the bread dough rest, keep it covered and warm for about 2-hours until it doubles in size. Once this happens, divide the prepared dough into small balls of about 1-ounce each and place in a baking paper. 3. Top with pumpkin seeds. Brush the balls with the egg and allow dough to rest for 40-minutes. 4. Place the prepared dough balls in a baking tray. Cook on Air Fry mode, insert its air fryer basket into the level 3 of the oven and close the door. and place in air fryer at 330°F/165°C for 28 minutes until brown and cooked.
Per Serving: Calories 220; Fat 13g; Sodium 542mg; Carbs 0.9g; Fiber 0.3g; Sugar 0.2g; Protein 5.6g

Hard Boiled Eggs

Prep time: 10 minutes | Cook time: 15 minutes | Servings: 6

6 large eggs

1. Select the Air Fry mode. Set the Ninja Foodi Smart XL Pro temperature to 365°F/185°C. Select Level "3" and set the time on your Ninja Foodi Smart XL Pro Air Fryer Oven to 15 minutes. Press Start/Pause to begin preheating. Continue to the next step when it is done preheating. 2. Insert the basket in the level 3 of the Ninja Foodi Smart XL Pro Oven. Place the eggs in the fryer basket then fry at 260°F/125°C for 15 minutes. 3. Transfer the hard boiled eggs into cold water to cool off. 4. Peel the shells and enjoy as desired.
Per Serving: Calories 258; Fat 12.4g; Sodium 79mg; Carbs 34.3g; Fiber 1g; Sugar 17g; Protein 3.2g

Fryer Sausage

Prep time: 10 minutes | Cook time: 20 minutes | Servings: 5

5 uncooked sausage links

1. Prepare the fryer basket with parchment paper then add in the sausage. 2. Insert its air fryer basket into the level 3 of the oven and close the door. Cook on "Air Fry" Mode, select level 3, and set its temperature to 360°F/180°Cfor 15 minutes then flip the sausage over and cook for an extra 5 minutes. 3. Allow the sausage to cool off for a bit then serve and enjoy as desired.
Per Serving: Calories 284; Fat 16g; Sodium 252mg; Carbs 31.6g;

Fiber 0.9g; Sugar 6.6g; Protein 3.7g

Walnuts Granola

Prep time: 4 minutes | Cook time: 8 minutes | Servings: 6

1 cup avocado, peeled, pitted and cubed
½ cup coconut flakes
2 tablespoons ghee, melted

¼ cup walnuts, chopped
¼ cup almonds, chopped
2 tablespoons stevia

1. In a suitable pan that fits your air fryer. mix all the recipe ingredients, toss, put the pan in the fryer and cook on "Bake" mode, select level 3, and set its temperature to 320°F/160°C for 8 minutes. Divide into bowls and serve right away.
Per Serving: Calories 239; Fat 48.3 g; Sodium 598 mg; Carbs 98g; Fiber 2.5g; Sugar 4.9g; Protein 7.6g

Breakfast Beet Salad

Prep time: 10 minutes | Cook time: 65 minutes | Servings: 4

¾ cup of crumbled feta cheese
2 cups mixed baby spinach
½ teaspoon thyme leaves, minced
1 teaspoon marjoram, fresh, minced
1 teaspoon parsley, fresh, minced
½ tablespoon liquid stevia
1 ½ teaspoons Dijon mustard

2 cloves of minced garlic
¼ cup red onion, minced
3 tablespoons red wine vinegar
Black pepper and salt to taste
2 tablespoons olive oil
7 large beets, stems trimmed
Pistachios for garnishing

1. Cook on Air Fry mode, select level 3. Preheat your air fryer to 390°F/200°C. Wash the beets and dry them. Place the beets on piece of aluminum foil and add to a suitable baking sheet. 2. Drizzle with oil and bake for 20-minutes in oven. 3. Season with black pepper and salt. Transfer beets to air fryer and cook for an additional 45-minutes. 4. Remove them from air fryer and place in fridge. 5. In a mixing bowl, mix onion, garlic, stevia, and mustard. Whisk these ingredients until they are well blended. Stir in the herbs and season with black pepper and salt. 6. When the beets are chilled, cut them into half-inch slices. Garnish with lettuce and pistachios.
Per Serving: Calories 353; Fat 5g; Sodium 818mg; Carbs 53.2g; Fiber 4.4g; Sugar 8g; Protein 1.3g

Delicious Shakshuka

Prep time: 10 minutes | Cook time: 35 minutes | Servings: 2

Tomato Sauce:
3 tablespoons (45ml) extra-virgin olive oil
1 small yellow onion, diced
1 jalapeño pepper, seeded and minced
1 red bell pepper, diced
2 cloves garlic, minced
Shakshuka:
4 eggs
1 tablespoon (15ml) heavy cream
1 tablespoon (1g) chopped

1 teaspoon cumin
1 teaspoon sweet paprika
Pinch cayenne pepper
1 tablespoon (16g) tomato paste
1 can (28 ounces, or 800g) whole plum tomatoes with juice
2 teaspoons granulated sugar

cilantro
Kosher salt and pepper to taste

1. Select the "AIR FRY" function of Ninja Foodi Smart XL Pro Air Oven and select Level 3. 2. Set the temperature to 300°F/150°C and time to 12 minutes. Select START/STOP to begin preheating. Sauté the onion and peppers in hot oil over medium heat, spice with salt, and sauté until softened, about 10 minutes. 3. Add the garlic and spices and sauté a few additional minutes until fragrant. Add the tomato paste and stir to combine. Add the plum tomatoes along with their juice—breaking up the tomatoes with a spoon—and the sugar. 4. Boil the mix to high heat. Lower down and manage to simmer until the tomatoes thicken, about 10 minutes. Turn off the heat. 5. Crack the eggs into a 7-inch (18 cm) round cake pan. Remove a cup of tomato sauce from the skillet and spoon it over the egg whites only, leaving the yolks exposed. Drizzle the cream over the yolks. 6. Place the pan on a wire rack on Level. Close the door to begin cooking. Cook for 12 minutes until the whites of eggs are cooked and the yolks are still runny. 7. Remove the pan from the air fryer and garnish with chopped cilantro. Season with salt and pepper. 8. Serve immediately with crusty bread to mop up the sauce.
Per Serving: Calories 429; Fat 32.4g; Sodium 325mg; Carbs 5g; Fiber 1g; Sugar 3g; Protein 28g

Cheesy Asparagus Frittata

Prep time: 15 minutes | Cook time: 15 minutes | Servings: 2-4

1 cup (134g) asparagus spears, cut into 1-inch (2.5 cm) pieces	1 tablespoon (15ml) milk
1 teaspoon vegetable oil	2 ounces (55g) goat cheese
6 eggs	1 tablespoon (3g) minced chives
	Kosher salt and pepper

1. Select the "AIR FRY" function of Ninja Foodi Smart XL Pro Air Oven and select Level. 2. Set the temperature to 400°F/200°C and time to 5 minutes. Select START/STOP to begin preheating. Toss the asparagus pieces with the vegetable oil in a small bowl. 3. Place the asparagus in a 7-inch (18 cm) round air fryer sheet pan. Place the pan on a wire rack on Level 3. 4. Close the door to begin cooking. Cook it for 5 minutes until the asparagus is softened and slightly wrinkled. Remove the pan. 5. Whisk the eggs with milk and pour the mixture over the asparagus in the sheet pan. Crumble cheese over the eggs and add the chives, if using. 6. Spice with a pinch of salt and pepper. Air fry at 320°F/160°C for 20 minutes until the eggs are cooked through. 7. Serve immediately.
Per Serving: Calories 173; Fat 13.6g; Sodium 281mg; Carbs 3g; Fiber 1g; Sugar 1g; Protein 10g

Sweet Potato and Black Bean Burritos

Prep time: 10 minutes | Cook time: 25 minutes | Servings: 6

2 sweet potatoes, cut into a small dice	lightly packed, divided
1 tablespoon (15ml) vegetable oil	6 eggs, scrambled
Kosher salt and pepper to taste	¾ cup (90g) grated Cheddar or Monterey Jack cheese, divided
6 large flour tortillas	Vegetable oil for heating
1 can (16 ounces, or 455g) refried black beans, divided	Salsa, Roasted Garlic Guacamole, and sour cream
1½ cups (45g) baby spinach,	

1. Select the "AIR FRY" function of Ninja Foodi Smart XL Pro Air Oven, set temperature to 400°F/200°C and time to 10 minutes. Select START/STOP to begin preheating. 2. Toss the sweet potatoes with the vegetable oil, season with salt and pepper, then place in air fryer basket. Select Level 3. 3. Close the door to begin cooking. Cook the potatoes for 10 minutes. Remove and set aside. 4. Take a flour tortilla and spread ¼ cup (59.5g) of the refried beans down the center, leaving a border at each end. Top with ¼ cup (8g) of the spinach leaves. 5. Sprinkle ¼ cup (27.5g) plus 2 tablespoons (14g) of sweet potato cubes on top of the spinach. Top with one-sixth of the scrambled eggs and 2 tablespoons grated cheese. 6. To wrap the burrito, fold the long side over the ingredients, then fold in the short sides and roll. Repeat with the remaining ingredients and tortillas. 7. Wrap each burrito tightly in foil and combine in a large, gallon-size freezer bag. Freeze for up to 3 months. 8. To heat, place the burrito, still wrapped in foil, in the air fryer and cook at 350°F/180°C for 20 minutes, flipping once halfway through. 9. Remove the burrito from the foil, brush the outside of the tortilla with 1 teaspoon oil, and heat for an additional 3 to 5 minutes, turning once. 10. Serve with salsa, roasted Garlic Guacamole, or sour cream as desired.
Per Serving: Calories 1052; Fat 50g; Sodium 438mg; Carbs 7g; Fiber 0g; Sugar 7g; Protein 132g

Eggs in a Basket

Prep time: 10 minutes | Cook time: 10 minutes | Servings: 1

1 thick slice country, sourdough, or Italian bread	butter, melted
	1 egg
2 tablespoons (28g) unsalted	Kosher salt and pepper to taste

1. Install the wire rack on Level 3. 2. Select the "BAKE" function of Ninja Foodi Smart XL Pro Air Oven, set temperature to 300°F/150°C and time to 8 minutes. 3. Select START/STOP to begin preheating. Brush the bottom of the air fryer sheet pan with melted butter. Using a biscuit cutter, cut a hole out of the middle of the bread and set it aside. 4. Place bread in the air fryer cake pan. Crack the egg in the bread hole, not breaking the yolk. Season with salt and pepper. 5. Place the cut-out bread hole next to the slice of bread. Place the sheet pan into the air fryer. 6. Bake at 300°F/150°C for 6 to 8 minutes until the white of egg sets and the yolk is still runny. Using a silicone spatula, remove the bread slice to a plate. 7. Serve with the cut-out bread circle on the side or place it on the egg.
Per Serving: Calories 134; Fat 9.8g; Sodium 394mg; Carbs 2g; Fiber 0g; Sugar 1g; Protein 9g

Streusel French Toast with Aromatic Cinnamon

Prep time: 10 minutes | Cook time: 15 minutes | Servings: 4

Streusel

½ cup (63g) all-purpose flour	Pinch kosher salt
¼ cup (50g) granulated sugar	4 tablespoons (55g) unsalted butter, melted
¼ cup (38g) light brown sugar	
½ teaspoon cinnamon	

French Toast

2 eggs	Pinch nutmeg
¼ cup (60ml) milk	4 slices brioche, challah, or white bread, preferably slightly stale
1 teaspoon vanilla extract	
½ teaspoon cinnamon	Maple syrup for serving

1. To make the streusel, combine the flour, sugars, cinnamon, and salt in a medium bowl. Pour the melted butter over the dry ingredients and stir with a fork to combine. Transfer the mixture to a plastic bag and place it in the freezer while you prepare the French toast. 2. To make the French toast, mix the eggs, milk, vanilla, cinnamon, and nutmeg in a medium bowl. Select the "AIR FRY" function of Ninja Foodi Smart XL Pro Air Oven, set temperature to 375°F/190°C and time to 5 minutes. Select START/STOP to begin preheating. 3. Line the air fryer basket with parchment paper to prevent sticking. Dunk each slice of bread in the egg mixture, making sure both sides are coated. Hold the bread over the bowl for a moment to allow any excess liquid to slide off. 4. Place the bread in the air fryer basket. Select Level 3. Cook for 5 minutes. 5. Open the air fryer and turn the bread over. Top each slice of bread with 2 tablespoons (40g) of streusel. 6. Cook for an additional 4 minutes until the bread is crispy and browned and the streusel is puffy and golden. 7. Serve warm with maple syrup.
Per Serving: Calories 227; Fat 9.8g; Sodium 525mg; Carbs 7g; Fiber 2g; Sugar 4g; Protein 28g

Delicious Grilled Cheese Sandwiches

Prep time: 5 minutes | Cook time: 7 minutes | Servings: 2

4 slices of brown bread	shredded
½ cup sharp cheddar cheese,	¼ cup butter, melted

1. Select Level 3. Select the "AIR FRY" function of Ninja Foodi Smart XL Pro Air Oven, set temperature to 360°F/180°C and time to 5 minutes. Select START/STOP to begin preheating. 2. Place cheese and butter into separate bowls. Melt butter and brush it onto the 4 slices of bread. Place cheese on 2 sides of bread slices. 3. Put sandwiches together and place them into the air fryer basket. Cook in air fryer for 5-minutes and serve warm
Per Serving: Calories 409; Fat 18.9g; Sodium 214mg; Carbs 10g; Fiber 1g; Sugar 9g; Protein 48g

Creamy Biscuits

Prep time: 15 minutes | Cook time: 18 minutes | Servings: 7

1 cup (125g) self-rising flour	Vegetable oil for spraying
½ cup (120ml) plus 1 tablespoon (15ml) heavy cream	2 tablespoons (28g) unsalted butter

1. Slide air fry basket into rails of Level 3. 2. Select the "AIR FRY" function of Ninja Foodi Smart XL Pro Air Oven, set temperature to 325°F/160°C and time to 18 minutes. Select START/STOP to begin preheating. 3. Place the flour in a medium bowl and whisk to remove any lumps. Make a well in the center of the flour. Slowly pour in the cream in a steady stream and continue stirring until the dough mostly comes together. 4. With your hands, gather the dough, incorporating any dry flour, and form it into a ball. 5. Place it on a floured surface and pat it into a rectangle that is ½ to ¾ inch (1.3 to 2 cm) thick. Fold in half. Turn and repeat. 6. One more time, pat the dough into a ¾-inch-thick (2 cm) rectangle. Using a 2-inch (5 cm) biscuit cutter, cut out biscuits—close together to minimize waste—taking care not to twist the cutter when pulling it up. You should be able to cut out 5 biscuits. Gather up any scraps and cut out 1 or 2 more biscuits. (These may be misshapen and slightly tougher than the first 5 biscuits, but still delicious.)7. Spray the air fryer basket with vegetable oil to prevent sticking. Place it in the air fryer basket so that they are barely touching. Cook for 15 to 18 minutes until the tops are browned and the insides fully cooked. 8. Remove the biscuits to a plate, brush the tops with melted butter, if using, and serve.
Per Serving: Calories 76; Fat 5.7g; Sodium 63mg; Carbs 1g; Fiber 0g; Sugar 1g; Protein 5g

Pecan Nuts Stuffed Cinnamon Buns

Prep time: 10 minutes | Cook time: 30 minutes | Servings: 9

¾ cup unsweetened almond milk	1 tablespoon coconut oil, melted
4 tablespoons sugar-free maple syrup	3 tablespoons water
½ cup pecan nuts, toasted	1 tablespoon ground flaxseed
3 teaspoons cinnamon powder	1½ tablespoons active yeast
1½ cups almond flour, sifted	2 ripe bananas, sliced
1 cup whole grain flour, sifted	4 dates, pitted
	¼ cup icing sugar

1. Heat the almond milk to lukewarm and add the syrup and yeast. Allow the yeast to activate for about 10-minutes. Mix flaxseed and water separately to make egg replacement. Allow flaxseed to soak for 2-minutes. 2. Add coconut oil. Pour the flaxseed mixture into yeast mixture. In another bowl, add both types of flour, and 2 teaspoons cinnamon powder. 3. Pour into the yeast-flaxseed mixture and combine until dough is formed. Knead the dough on a floured surface for about 10-minutes. Place the kneaded dough into a greased bowl and cover it with a tea towel. Leave in a warm and dark area to rise for 1 hour. Make the filling by mixing the pecans, dates and banana slices and remaining teaspoon of cinnamon powder. 4. Install the wire rack on Level 3. Select the "BAKE" function of Ninja Foodi Smart XL Pro Air Oven, set temperature to 390°F/200°C and time to 30 minutes. Select START/STOP to begin preheating. Roll the risen dough on a floured surface until it is thin. 5. Spread the pecan mixture over the dough. Roll dough and cut it into nine slices. Place inside of dish that will fit into your air fryer and cook for 30-minutes. 6. Once cook time is completed, sprinkle with icing sugar.
Per Serving: Calories 69; Fat 7.2g; Sodium 486mg; Carbs 2g; Fiber 1g; Sugar 0g; Protein 0g

Baked Strawberries and Cream Oatmeal

Prep time: 10 minutes | Cook time: 15 minutes | Servings: 4

1 cup (170g) sliced strawberries	½ teaspoon baking powder
1 egg	½ teaspoon cinnamon
¾ cup (180ml) milk	½ teaspoon ginger
¼ cup (60ml) heavy cream	Pinch salt
1 cup (80g) rolled oats	1 tablespoon (14g) unsalted butter
2 tablespoons (19g) brown sugar	

1. Place the sliced strawberries in the bottom of the cake pan for the air fryer, reserving a few for garnish. In a bowl, whisk the egg along with milk and cream and pour it over the strawberries in the pan. 2. In a small bowl, combine the rolled oats, brown sugar, baking powder, spices, and salt. Combine well the dry and wet ingredients in the cake pan and stir to combine. 3. Allow to rest for 10 minutes. Place the reserved strawberries on top of the oatmeal. 4. Install the wire rack on Level 3. Select the "BAKE" function of Ninja Foodi Smart XL Pro Air Oven, set temperature to 320°F/160°C and time to 15 minutes. Select START/STOP to begin preheating. 5. Place the sheet pan in the air fryer and bake at 320°F/160°C for 15 minutes until the oatmeal is warmed through and puffed. Spoon the oatmeal into bowls.
Per Serving: Calories 509; Fat 40.6g; Sodium 525mg; Carbs 8g; Fiber 2g; Sugar 5g; Protein 28g

Sweet Pumpkin Oatmeal

Prep time: 10 minutes | Cook time: 10 minutes | Servings: 2

1 cup rolled oats	¼ cup canned pumpkin puree
2 tablespoons raisins	2 tablespoons maple syrup
¼ teaspoon ground cinnamon	1 cup low-fat milk
Pinch of kosher salt	

1. Install the wire rack on Level 3. 2. Select the "BAKE" function of Ninja Foodi Smart XL Pro Air Oven, set temperature to 300°F/150°C and time to 10 minutes. Select START/STOP to begin preheating. 3. In a medium bowl, combine the rolled oats, raisins, ground cinnamon, and kosher salt, then stir in the pumpkin puree, maple syrup, and low-fat milk. 4. Spray the air fryer sheet pan with nonstick cooking spray, then pour the oatmeal mixture into the pan. Place the sheet pan into the air fryer and cook for 10 minutes. 5. Remove the oatmeal from the fryer and allow to cool in the pan on a wire rack for 5 minutes before serving.
Per Serving: Calories 301; Fat 4g; Sodium 140mg; Carbs 57g; Fiber 6g; Sugar 26g; Protein 10g

Blueberry Oat Squares Bites

Prep time: 10 minutes | Cook time: 14 minutes | Servings: 6

1 cup all-purpose flour	¼ cup light brown sugar, packed
1 cup quick-cook oats	¼ cup unsweetened applesauce
¼ teaspoon baking powder	¼ cup canola oil
Pinch of kosher salt	¼ cup low-fat milk
¼ teaspoon ground cinnamon	1 cup fresh blueberries
1 large egg, beaten	1 teaspoon confectioners' sugar

1. Install the wire rack on Level 3. 2. Select the "BAKE" function of Ninja Foodi Smart XL Pro Air Oven, set temperature to 390°F/200°C and time to 14 minutes. Select START/STOP to begin preheating. 3. In a large bowl, whisk together the all-purpose flour, quick-cook oats, baking powder, kosher salt, and ground cinnamon. Set aside. 4. In a separate large bowl, combine the egg, light brown sugar, unsweetened applesauce, canola oil, and low-fat milk. 5. Add the egg mixture to the flour mixture, stirring until just combined, then gently fold in the blueberries. 6. Spray the air fryer sheet pan with nonstick cooking spray, then pour the batter into the pan. 7. Place the sheet pan into the air fryer. Cook for 12–14 minutes or until golden brown and a toothpick comes out clean when inserted through the middle. 8. Remove the pan from the fryer and allow to cool on a wire rack for 10 minutes. 9. Dust the confectioners' sugar on top before cutting and serving.
Per Serving: Calories 236; Fat 11g; Sodium 61mg; Carbs 32g; Fiber 2g; Sugar 12g; Protein 4g

Green Feta Frittatas

Prep time: 5 minutes | Cook time: 11 minutes | Servings: 2

1 cup kale, chopped	2 tablespoons water
1 teaspoon olive oil	Pinch of kosher salt
4 large eggs, beaten	3 tablespoons crumbled feta

1. Select Level 3. 2. Select the "AIR FRY" function of Ninja Foodi Smart XL Pro Air Oven, set temperature to 360°F/180°C and time to 3 minutes. Select START/STOP to begin preheating. 3. Spray the air fryer sheet pan with nonstick cooking spray, then place the kale in the pan, drizzle with the olive oil, and Place the pan into the air fryer, cook for 3 minutes. 4. While the kale cooks, whisk together the eggs, water, and kosher salt in a large bowl. 5. Pause the fryer to pour the eggs into the pan and sprinkle the feta on top. Reduce the heat to 300°F/150°C and cook for 8 more minutes. 6. Remove the frittata from the fryer and allow to cool in the pan on a wire rack for 5 minutes before cutting and serving.
Per Serving: Calories 216; Fat 15g; Sodium 354mg; Carbs 5g; Fiber 1g; Sugar 2g; Protein 16g

Sweet Avocado & Blueberry Muffins

Prep time: 5 minutes | Cook time: 15 minutes | Servings: 12

2 eggs	2 ripe avocados, peeled, pitted, mashed
1 cup blueberries	
2 cups almond flour	2 tablespoons liquid Stevia
1 teaspoon baking soda	1 cup plain Greek yogurt
⅛ teaspoon salt	1 teaspoon vanilla extract
For Streusel Topping:	
2 tablespoons Truvia sweetener	4 tablespoons almond flour
4 tablespoons butter, softened	

1. Make the streusel topping by mixing Truvia, flour, and butter until you form a crumbly mixture. Place this mixture in the freezer for a while. 2. Meanwhile, make the muffins by sifting together flour, baking powder, baking soda and salt and set aside. Add avocados and liquid Stevia to a bowl and mix well. Adding in one egg at a time, continue to beat. Add the vanilla extract and yogurt and beat again. Add in flour mixture a bit at a time and mix well. Add the blueberries into the mixture and gently fold them in. 3. Pour the batter into greased muffin cups, then add mixture until they are half-full. Sprinkle the streusel topping mixture on top of muffin mixture and place muffin cups in the air fryer basket. 4. Install the wire rack on Level 3. Select the "BAKE" function of Ninja Foodi Smart XL Pro Air Oven, set temperature to 355°F/180°C and time to 10 minutes. Select START/STOP to begin preheating. Place the air fryer basket in and cook for 10-minutes. 5. Remove the muffin cups from the air fryer and allow them to cool. Cool completely then serve.
Per Serving: Calories 139; Fat 3.2g; Sodium 45mg; Carbs 26g; Fiber 4g; Sugar 8g; Protein 3g

Fried Apples with Steel-Cut Oats

Prep time: 10 minutes | Cook time: 40 minutes | Servings: 2

1 cup dry steel-cut oats
4 cups water
Pinch of kosher salt
1 large Gala apple, cored and cut

into 10 slices
⅛ teaspoon ground cinnamon
1 tablespoon granulated sugar

1. In a medium saucepan, combine the steel-cut oats, water, and kosher salt. Bring the mixture to a boil, reduce the heat to a simmer, and cook uncovered for 30 minutes or until the oats are tender. Set aside. 2. Slide basket into rails of Level 3. Select the "AIR FRY" function of Ninja Foodi Smart XL Pro Air Oven, set temperature to 390°F/200°C and time to 10 minutes. Select START/STOP to begin preheating. 3. Spray the fryer basket with nonstick cooking spray, then place the apple slices in the basket and Place it into the air fryer, cook for 10 minutes. 4. While the apples cook, combine the ground cinnamon and granulated sugar in a small bowl and set aside. 5. Remove the apple slices from the fryer and place on a serving plate. Sprinkle 1 teaspoon of the cinnamon sugar mix on the apples. 6. Allow the apples to cool for 5 minutes, then serve on top of the cooked oats.
Per Serving: Calories 183; Fat 3g; Sodium 36mg; Carbs 36g; Fiber 5g; Sugar 8g; Protein 5g

Homemade Apple Fritters

Prep time: 10 minutes | Cook time: 10 minutes | Servings: 5

Fritters
2 firm apples, such as Granny Smith, peeled, cored, and diced
Juice from 1 lemon
½ teaspoon cinnamon
1 cup (125g) all-purpose flour
1½ teaspoons baking powder
½ teaspoon kosher salt
Glaze
1¼ cups (125g) powdered sugar, sifted

2 tablespoons (26g) granulated sugar
2 eggs
¼ cup (60ml) milk
2 tablespoons (28g) unsalted butter, melted
Vegetable oil for spraying

½ teaspoon vanilla extract
¼ cup (60ml) water

1. Select the "AIR FRY" function of Ninja Foodi Smart XL Pro Air Oven, set temperature to 360°F/180°C and time to 8 minutes. Select START/STOP to begin preheating. 2. To make the fritters, toss the diced apples with lemon juice and cinnamon in a small bowl, set aside. In a bowl, mix the flour with baking powder, and salt. 3. In a bowl, whisk the sugar and eggs until the mixture is pale yellow. mix in the milk with melted butter. 4. Mix the wet and dry ingredients in the large bowl and stir to combine. Fold in the diced apples. 5. Brush the air fryer basket with oil or line it with parchment paper to prevent sticking. Working in 3 batches and using a spring-loaded cookie scoop, ice cream scoop, or ¼-cup measure, scoop 5 balls of dough directly onto the air fryer basket. 6. Spray the fritters with oil. Place the sheet pan into the air fryer on Level 3. Cook for 7 to 8 minutes until the outside is browned and the inside is fully cooked. 7. Whisk together the powdered sugar, vanilla, and water in a small bowl. Drizzle the glaze over the fritters or dip the tops of the fritters directly in the glaze, letting any excess drip off.
Per Serving: Calories 248; Fat 21.1g; Sodium 429mg; Carbs 2g; Fiber 0g; Sugar 1g; Protein 12g

Sweet Raspberry Yogurt Cake

Prep time: 10 minutes | Cook time: 8 minutes | Servings: 4

½ cup whole wheat pastry flour
⅛ teaspoon kosher salt
¼ teaspoon baking powder
½ cup whole milk vanilla yogurt

2 tablespoons canola oil
2 tablespoons maple syrup
¾ cup fresh raspberries
1 teaspoon confectioners' sugar

1. Select Level 3. 2. Select the "AIR FRY" function of Ninja Foodi Smart XL Pro Air Oven, set temperature to 390°F/200°C and time to 8 minutes. Select START/STOP to begin preheating. 3. In a large bowl, combine the whole wheat pastry flour, kosher salt, and baking powder, then stir in the whole milk vanilla yogurt, canola oil, and maple syrup and gently fold in the raspberries. 4. Spray the air fryer sheet pan with nonstick cooking spray, then pour the cake batter into the pan and Place the sheet pan into the air fryer; cook for 8 minutes. 5. Remove the cake from the fryer and allow to cool in the pan on a wire rack for 10 minutes, then sift the confectioners' sugar on top before cutting and serving.
Per Serving: Calories 222; Fat 8g; Sodium 82mg; Carbs 25g; Fiber 3g; Sugar 12g; Protein 3g

Caramelized Banana with Yogurt

Prep time: 5 minutes | Cook time: 5 minutes | Servings: 1

1 banana, cut into ¾ -inch slices
6 oz. nonfat plain Greek yogurt

3 tablespoons Toasted Granola with Almonds

1. Select the "AIR FRY" function of Ninja Foodi Smart XL Pro Air Oven, set temperature to 390°F/200°C and time to 5 minutes. Select START/STOP to begin preheating. 2. Spray the air fryer basket with nonstick cooking spray, then place the banana slices in the basket and slide basket into rails of Level 3; cook for 5 minutes. 3. Allow to cool in the fryer for 5 minutes, then remove the banana slices from the fryer. 4. Spread the plain Greek yogurt on a serving plate, then place the banana slices on the yogurt and top with the toasted granola before serving.
Per Serving: Calories 249; Fat 1g; Sodium 96mg; Carbs 40g; Fiber 4g; Sugar 23g; Protein 18g

Healthy French Toast

Prep time: 8 minutes | Cook time: 8 minutes | Servings: 2

2 slices whole grain bread
1 large egg
½ cup low-fat milk
⅛ teaspoon ground cinnamon

½ teaspoon vanilla extract
2 teaspoons maple syrup
1 teaspoon confectioners' sugar

1. Install the wire rack on Level 3. 2. Select the "BAKE" function of Ninja Foodi Smart XL Pro Air Oven, set temperature to 360°F/180°C and time to 8 minutes. Select START/STOP to begin preheating. 3. Spray the air fryer sheet pan with nonstick cooking spray, then cut the whole grain bread into small pieces or strips and place in the pan. Set aside. 4. In a medium bowl, whisk together the egg, low-fat milk, ground cinnamon, vanilla extract, and 2 teaspoons of maple syrup. 5. Pour the egg mixture over the bread, then press it down with a spatula to make sure all the bread is coated. Place the soaked toast on sheet pan and cook for 8 minutes. 6. Remove the French toast from the fryer and allow to cool in the pan on a wire rack for 5 minutes, then dust with the confectioners' sugar and drizzle 2 tablespoons of maple syrup on top before serving.
Per Serving: Calories 221; Fat 4g; Sodium 239mg; Carbs 37g; Fiber 2g; Sugar 21g; Protein 9g

Toasted Granola with Nuts

Prep time: 5 minutes | Cook time: 8-10 minutes | Servings: 5

⅔ cup rolled oats
⅓ cup shredded sweetened coconut
⅓ cup sliced almonds

1 teaspoon canola oil
2 teaspoons honey
¼ teaspoon kosher salt

1. Select Level 3. 2. Select the "AIR FRY" function of Ninja Foodi Smart XL Pro Air Oven, set temperature to 390°F/200°C and time to 5 minutes. Select START/STOP to begin preheating. 3. In a medium bowl, combine the rolled oats, shredded sweetened coconut, sliced almonds, canola oil, honey, and kosher salt. 4. Place a small piece of parchment paper on the bottom of the air fryer sheet pan, then pour the mixture into the pan and distribute it evenly. 5. Place the sheet pan into the air fryer, cook for 5 minutes, pause the fryer to gently stir the granola, and cook for 3 more minutes. 6. Remove the granola from the fryer and allow to cool in the pan on a wire rack for 5 minutes, then transfer the granola to a serving plate to cool completely before serving.
Per Serving: Calories 163; Fat 9g; Sodium 94mg; Carbs 18g; Fiber 3g; Sugar 7g; Protein 4g

Salmon & Carrot Breakfast

Prep time: 5 minutes | Cook time: 15 minutes | Servings: 2

1 lb. salmon, chopped
2 cups feta, crumbled
4 bread slices

3 tablespoons pickled red onion
2 cucumbers, sliced
1 carrot, shredded

1. Select Level 3. Select the "AIR FRY" function of Ninja Foodi Smart XL Pro Air Oven, set temperature to 300°F/150°C and time to 15 minutes. Select START/STOP to begin preheating. 2. Add salmon and feta to a bowl. Add carrot, red onion and cucumber and mix well. 3. In a sheet pan, make a layer of bread and then pour the salmon mix over it. Air fry it for 15-minutes.
Per Serving: Calories 56; Fat 2.2g; Sodium 177mg; Carbs 5g; Fiber 1g; Sugar 1g; Protein 5g

Cheese Omelet with Onion

Prep time: 15 minutes | Cook time: 13 minutes | Servings: 2

3 eggs
1 large yellow onion, diced
2 tablespoons cheddar cheese, shredded
½ teaspoon soy sauce
Salt and pepper to taste
Olive oil cooking spray

1. Select Level 3. Select the "AIR FRY" function of Ninja Foodi Smart XL Pro Air Oven, set temperature to 390°F/200°C and time to 7 minutes. Select START/STOP to begin preheating. 2. In a bowl whisk together eggs, soy sauce, pepper, and salt. Spray with olive oil cooking spray a small pan that will fit inside of your air fryer. Add onions to the pan and spread them around. Air fry onions for 7-minutes. 3. Pour the beaten egg mixture over the cooked onions and sprinkle the top with shredded cheese. Place back into the air fryer and cook for 6-minutes more. 4. Remove from the air fryer and serve omelet with toasted multi-grain bread.
Per Serving: Calories 427; Fat 18.3g; Sodium 603mg; Carbs 44g; Fiber 6g; Sugar 3g; Protein 23g

Red Onion Omelet Cups with Bell Pepper

Prep time: 5 minutes | Cook time: 10 minutes | Servings: 2

4 large eggs
½ bell pepper, finely chopped
1 tablespoon red onion, finely chopped
¼ teaspoon kosher salt
¼ teaspoon freshly ground black pepper
2 tablespoons shredded cheddar cheese

1. Select the "AIR FRY" function of Ninja Foodi Smart XL Pro Air Oven, set temperature to 390°F/200°C and time to 8 minutes. Select START/STOP to begin preheating. 2. In a large bowl, whisk together the eggs, then stir in the bell pepper, red onion, kosher salt, and black pepper. 3. Spray two 3-inch ramekins with nonstick cooking spray, then pour half the egg mixture into each ramekin and place the ramekins in the fryer basket. Slide basket into rails of Level 3, cook for 8 minutes. 4. Pause the fryer, sprinkle 1 tablespoon of shredded cheddar cheese on top of each cup, and cook for 2 more minutes. 5. Remove the ramekins from the fryer and allow to cool on a wire rack for 5 minutes, then turn the omelet cups out on plates and sprinkle some black pepper on top before serving.
Per Serving: Calories 176; Fat 12g; Sodium 333mg; Carbs 2g; Fiber 0g; Sugar 1g; Protein 14g

Mini Cheeseburger Sliders

Prep time: 5 minutes | Cook time: 10 minutes | Servings: 6

1 lb. ground beef
6 slices of cheddar cheese
6 dinner rolls
Salt and black pepper to taste

1. Select Level 3. Select the "AIR FRY" function of Ninja Foodi Smart XL Pro Air Oven, set temperature to 390°F/200°C and time to 11 minutes. Select START/STOP to begin preheating. 2. Form 6 beef patties each about 2.5 ounces and season with salt and black pepper. Add the burger patties to the air fryer basket and cook them for 10-minutes. 3. Remove the burger patties from the air fryer; place the cheese on top of burgers and return to air fryer and cook for another minute. 4. Remove and put burgers on dinner rolls and serve warm.
Per Serving: Calories 4; Fat 0.1g; Sodium 0mg; Carbs 1g; Fiber 1g; Sugar 0g; Protein 0g

Creamy Tomato & Egg Scramble

Prep time: 5 minutes | Cook time: 10 minutes | Servings: 2

2 eggs
1 tomato, chopped
Dash of salt
1 teaspoon butter
¼ cup cream

1. In a bowl, whisk the eggs, salt, and cream until fluffy. Select Level 3. Select the "AIR FRY" function of Ninja Foodi Smart XL Pro Air Oven, set temperature to 300°F/150°C and time to 10 minutes. Select START/STOP to begin preheating. 2. Add butter to baking pan and place into air fryer. Once the butter is melted, add the egg mixture to baking pan and tomato then cook for 10-minutes. 3. Whisk the eggs until fluffy then serve warm.
Per Serving: Calories 104; Fat 2.5g; Sodium 29mg; Carbs 18g; Fiber 4g; Sugar 2g; Protein 3g

Classic Fries

Prep time: 10 minutes | Cook time: 20 minutes | Servings: 2

1 lb. small red potatoes, diced
2 teaspoons olive oil
¼ cup yellow onion, finely chopped
¼ teaspoon kosher salt
¼ teaspoon freshly ground black pepper

1. Select the "AIR FRY" function of Ninja Foodi Smart XL Pro Air Oven, set temperature to 360°F/180°C and time to 20 minutes. Select START/STOP to begin preheating. 2. In a medium bowl, toss the red potatoes and olive oil, then add the onion, kosher salt, and black pepper, tossing again to coat. 3. Spray the fryer basket with nonstick cooking spray, then place the mixture in the basket and place the basket into the air fryer on Level 3; cook for 20 minutes or until golden brown, pausing the fryer every 5 minutes to shake the basket. 4. Remove the fries from the fryer, place on a plate lined with a paper towel, and allow to cool for 5 minutes before serving.
Per Serving: Calories 102; Fat 2g; Sodium 161mg; Carbs 19g; Fiber 2g; Sugar 2g; Protein 2g

BLT Sandwich

Prep time: 5 minutes | Cook time: 15 minutes | Servings: 3

6 ounces bacon, thick-cut
2 tablespoons brown sugar
2 teaspoons chipotle chile powder
1 teaspoon cayenne pepper
1 tablespoon Dijon mustard
1 heads lettuce, torn into leaves
2 medium tomatoes, sliced
6 (½-inch) slices white bread

1. Slide air fry basket into rails of Level 3. 2. Select the "AIR FRY" function of Ninja Foodi Smart XL Pro Air Oven, set temperature to 400°F/200°C and time to 10 minutes. Select START/STOP to begin preheating. 3. Toss the bacon with the sugar, chipotle chile powder, cayenne pepper, and mustard. Place the bacon in the Air Fryer basket. 4. Then, cook the bacon for 10 minutes, tossing the basket halfway through the cooking time. Assemble your sandwiches with the bacon, lettuce, and tomato. 5. Bon appétit!
Per Serving: Calories 401; Fat 23.3g; Sodium 411mg; Carbs 32.3g; Fiber 6.4g; Sugar 9.5g; Protein 14.2g

Avocado Egg-in-a-Hole

Prep time: 5 minutes | Cook time: 10 minutes | Servings: 1

1 slice whole grain bread
1 large egg
⅛ teaspoon kosher salt
¼ cup avocado, diced
¼ cup tomato, diced
Pinch of freshly ground black pepper

1. Install the wire rack on Level 3. Select the "BAKE" function of Ninja Foodi Smart XL Pro Air Oven, set temperature to 360°F/180°C and time to 7 minutes. Select START/STOP to begin preheating. 2. Spray the air fryer sheet pan with nonstick cooking spray, then use a ring mold or a sharp knife to cut a 3-inch hole in the center of the whole grain bread. Place the bread slice and the circle in the pan. 3. Crack the egg into the hole, then season with the kosher salt. Place the pan into the air fryer; cook for 5–7 minutes or until the egg is cooked as desired. 4. Remove the pan from the fryer and allow to cool on a wire rack for 5 minutes before transferring the toast to a plate, then sprinkle the avocado, tomato, and black pepper on top before serving.
Per Serving: Calories 220; Fat 12g; Sodium 406mg; Carbs 18g; Fiber 5g; Sugar 4g; Protein 10g

Italian Sausage Sandwich

Prep time: 5 minutes | Cook time: 20 minutes | Servings: 3

1 pound sweet Italian sausage
6 white bread slices
2 teaspoons mustard

1. Select the "AIR FRY" function of Ninja Foodi Smart XL Pro Air Oven, set temperature to 370°F/185°C and time to 15 minutes. Select START/STOP to begin preheating. 2. Place the sausage in a lightly greased Air fryer basket. Slide basket into rails of Level 3. 3. Air fry the sausage for 15 minutes, tossing the basket halfway through the cooking time. 4. Assemble the sandwiches with the bread, mustard, and sausage, and serve immediately.
Per Serving: Calories 407; Fat 14.5g; Sodium 336mg; Carbs 31.8g; Fiber 6.6g; Sugar 7.6g; Protein 28.8g

Cheesy Egg Pockets

Prep time: 10 minutes | Cook time: 35 minutes | Servings: 4

1 large egg, beaten
Pinch of kosher salt
½ sheet puff pastry
1 slice cheddar cheese, divided into 4 pieces

1. Install the wire rack on Level 3. Select the "BAKE" function of Ninja Foodi Smart XL Pro Air Oven, set temperature to 330°F/165°C and time to 5 minutes. Select START/STOP to begin preheating. 2. Pour the egg into the air fryer sheet pan, season with the kosher salt, and cook for 3 minutes. Pause the fryer, gently scramble the egg, and cook for 2 more minutes. Remove the egg from the fryer, keeping the fryer on, and set the egg aside to slightly cool. 3. Roll the puff pastry out flat and divide into 4 pieces. 4. Place a piece of cheddar cheese and ¼ of the egg on one side of a piece of pastry, fold the pastry over the egg and cheese, and use a fork to press the edges closed. Repeat this process with the remaining pieces. 5. Place 2 pockets in the fryer and cook for 15 minutes or until golden brown. Repeat this process with the other 2 pockets. 6. Remove the pockets from the fryer and allow to cool on a wire rack for 5 minutes before serving.
Per Serving: Calories 218; Fat 15g; Sodium 143mg; Carbs 14g; Fiber 0g; Sugar 0g; Protein 6g

Smoky Potatoes with Chipotle Ketchup

Prep time: 15 minutes | Cook time: 25 minutes | Servings: 4

2 cups (220g) diced (½ inch [1.3 cm]) waxy red potatoes
2 teaspoons vegetable oil, divided
Kosher salt to taste
½ cup (80g) chopped yellow onion
1 cup (150g) chopped red bell pepper
1¾ cups (420g) ketchup
2 chipotle peppers in adobo
1 tablespoon (15ml) adobo sauce
½ teaspoon smoked paprika

1. In a bowl, toss the potatoes with 1 teaspoon of oil and season with a pinch of salt. Slide basket into rails of Level 3. 2. Select the "AIR FRY" function of Ninja Foodi Smart XL Pro Air Oven, set temperature to 400°F/200°C and time to 10 minutes. Select START/STOP to begin preheating. Place them in the air fryer basket and cook for 10 minutes. 3. In a bowl toss the onion and pepper with the remaining teaspoon of oil and season with salt. 4. After 10 minutes, add the onion and pepper to the air fryer basket and toss to combine. Cook for further 10 -12 minutes until the peppers are softened and charred at the edges and the potatoes are crispy outside and cooked through. 5. While the vegetables are cooking, prepare the chipotle ketchup. Combine the ketchup, 2 chipotle peppers, and 1 tablespoon (15ml) of the adobo sauce in a blender and puree until smooth. 6. Pour the chipotle ketchup into a serving bowl. Toss cooked vegetables with the smoked paprika. 7. Serve immediately with chipotle ketchup on the side.
Per Serving: Calories 314; Fat 25g; Sodium 138mg; Carbs 2g; Fiber 0g; Sugar 1g; Protein 17g

Spicy Sweet Potato Hash

Prep time: 10 minutes | Cook time: 20 minutes | Servings: 4

2 large sweet potatoes
½ small red onion, cut into large chunks
1 green bell pepper, cut into large chunks
1 jalapeño pepper, seeded and sliced
½ teaspoon kosher salt
¼ teaspoon freshly ground black pepper (plus extra for serving)
1 teaspoon olive oil
1 large egg, poached

1. Select Level 3. Select the "AIR FRY" function of Ninja Foodi Smart XL Pro Air Oven, set temperature to 390°F/200°C and time to 16 minutes. Select START/STOP to begin preheating. 2. Cook the sweet potatoes on high in the microwave until softened but not completely cooked (3–4 minutes), then set aside to cool for 10 minutes. 3. Remove the skins from the sweet potatoes, then cut the sweet potatoes into large chunks. 4. In a large bowl, combine the sweet potatoes, red onion, green bell pepper, jalapeño pepper, kosher salt, black pepper, and olive oil, tossing gently. 5. Spray the fryer basket with nonstick cooking spray, then pour the mixture into the basket. Slide basket into rails of Level 3 and cook for 8 minutes. 6. Pause the fryer to shake the basket, then cook for 8 more minutes or until golden brown.7. Remove the hash from the fryer, place on a plate lined with a paper towel, and allow to cool for 5 minutes, then add the poached egg, sprinkle black pepper on top, and serve.
Per Serving: Calories 121; Fat 3g; Sodium 174mg; Carbs 22g; Fiber 4g; Sugar 7g; Protein 4g

Cheesy Bacon & Egg Quesadilla

Prep time: 5 minutes | Cook time: 5 minutes | Servings: 1

1 large egg
⅛ teaspoon kosher salt
1 eight-inch whole wheat tortilla
¼ cup shredded cheddar cheese
1 slice cooked bacon, chopped

1. Select Level 3. Select the "AIR FRY" function of Ninja Foodi Smart XL Pro Air Oven, set temperature to 360°F/180°C and time to 5 minutes. Select START/STOP to begin preheating. 2. Pour the egg into the air fryer sheet pan and season with the kosher salt. Cook for 3 minutes, then pause the fryer, gently scramble the egg, and cook for 2 more minutes. 3. Remove the egg from the fryer, keeping the fryer on, and set the egg aside to slightly cool. 4. Spray the fryer basket with nonstick cooking spray, then layer the cooked egg, shredded cheddar cheese, and bacon on the tortilla. Fold in half, place in the basket, slide basket into rails of Level 3 and cook for 5 minutes. 5. Remove the quesadilla from the fryer and allow to cool on a wire rack for 2–3 minutes before serving.
Per Serving: Calories 335; Fat 19g; Sodium 480mg; Carbs 25g; Fiber 2g; Sugar 1g; Protein 19g

Cherry Tomatoes and Sausage Frittata

Prep time: 5 minutes | Cook time: 15 minutes | Servings: 3

6 eggs
8 cherry tomatoes, halved
2 tablespoons parmesan cheese, shredded
1 Italian sausage, diced
Salt and pepper to taste

1. Install the wire rack on Level 3. Select the "BAKE" function of Ninja Foodi Smart XL Pro Air Oven, set temperature to 355°F/180°C and time to 5 minutes. Select START/STOP to begin preheating. 2. Add the tomatoes and sausage to baking dish. Place the baking dish into air fryer and cook for 5-minutes. 3. Meanwhile, add eggs, salt, pepper, cheese, and oil into mixing bowl and whisk well. Remove the baking dish from air fryer and pour the egg mixture on top, spreading evenly. 4. Placing the dish back into the air fryer and bake for an additional 5-minutes. 5. Remove from air fryer and slice into wedges and serve.
Per Serving: Calories 162; Fat 9.4g; Sodium 68mg; Carbs 21g; Fiber 4g; Sugar 16g; Protein 1g

Sweet Apple Compote

Prep time: 5 minutes | Cook time: 15 minutes | Servings: 4

2 medium apples, peeled and diced
⅛ teaspoon ground cinnamon
2 teaspoons honey
Juice of ½ lemon
2 tablespoon raisins
⅔ cup water

1. Install the wire rack on Level 3. Select the "BAKE" function of Ninja Foodi Smart XL Pro Air Oven, set temperature to 360°F/180°C and time to 15 minutes. Select START/STOP to begin preheating. 2. Spray the air fryer sheet pan with nonstick cooking spray, then combine the apples, ground cinnamon, honey, lemon juice, raisins, and water in the pan. Cook for 12–15 minutes or until the apples are tender. 3. Remove the compote from the fryer and allow to cool in the pan on a wire rack for 5 minutes before serving.
Per Serving: Calories 65; Fat 0g; Sodium 3mg; Carbs 17g; Fiber 1g; Sugar 14g; Protein 0g

Banana Cookies

Prep time: 5 minutes | Cook time: 20 minutes | Servings: 6

3 ripe bananas
1 teaspoon vanilla extract
⅓ cup olive oil
1 cup dates, pitted and chopped
2 cups rolled oats

1. Select Level 3. Select the "AIR FRY" function of Ninja Foodi Smart XL Pro Air Oven, set temperature to 350°F/175°C and time to 20 minutes. Select START/STOP to begin preheating. 2. In a bowl, mash bananas and add the rest of the ingredients and mix well. Allow ingredients to rest in the fridge for 10-minutes. 3. Cut some parchment paper to fit inside of your air fryer basket. Drop a teaspoonful of mixture on parchment paper, making sure not to overlap the cookies. 4. Cook the cookies for 20-minutes and serve with some almond milk.
Per Serving: Calories 288; Fat 23.3g; Sodium 308mg; Carbs 6g; Fiber 1g; Sugar 5g; Protein 14g

Tasty Spinach Balls

Prep time: 10 minutes | Cook time: 10 minutes | Servings: 4

1 carrot, peeled and grated
2 slices of bread, toasted and make into breadcrumbs
1 tablespoon corn flour
1 tablespoon nutritional yeast
½ teaspoon garlic, minced
1 egg, beaten
½ teaspoon garlic powder
½ onion, chopped
1 package fresh spinach, blanched and chopped

1. Select Level 3. Select the "AIR FRY" function of Ninja Foodi Smart XL Pro Air Oven, set temperature to 390°F/200°C and time to 10 minutes. Select START/STOP to begin preheating. 2. Blend ingredients in a bowl, except the breadcrumbs. Make small balls with the mixture and roll them over the bread crumbs. 3. Place the spinach balls in sheet pan and cook for 10-minutes. Serve warm.
Per Serving: Calories 138; Fat 10.6g; Sodium 102mg; Carbs 1g; Fiber 0g; Sugar 1g; Protein 9g

Cherry, Almond and Oat Bars

Prep time: 10 minutes | Cook time: 17 minutes | Servings: 8

2 cups old-fashioned oats
½ cup quinoa, cooked
½ cup chia seeds
½ cup prunes, pureed
¼ teaspoon salt
2 teaspoons liquid Stevia
¾ cup almond butter
½ cup dried cherries, chopped
½ cup almonds, sliced

1.Select Level 3. Select the "AIR FRY" function of Ninja Foodi Smart XL Pro Air Oven, set temperature to 375°F/190°C and time to 15 minutes. Select START/STOP to begin preheating. 2. In a large mixing bowl, add quinoa, chia seeds, oats, cherries, and almonds. In a saucepan over medium heat melt almond butter, liquid Stevia and coconut oil for 2-minutes and stir to combine. 3. Add salt and prunes and mix well. Pour into baking dish that will fit in air fryer and cook for 15-minutes. 4. Allow to cool for an hour once cook time is completed, then slice the bars and serve.
Per Serving: Calories 151; Fat 7.5g; Sodium 621mg; Carbs 20g; Fiber 5g; Sugar 2g; Protein 5g

Cheesy Bacon Scrambled Eggs

Prep time: 5 minutes | Cook time: 10 minutes | Servings: 4

¼ teaspoon onion powder
4 eggs, beaten
3-ounces bacon, cooked, chopped
½ cup cheddar cheese, grated
3 tablespoons Greek yogurt
¼ teaspoon garlic powder
Salt and pepper to taste

1. Select Level 3. Select the "AIR FRY" function of Ninja Foodi Smart XL Pro Air Oven, set temperature to 330°F/165°C and time to 5 minutes. Select START/STOP to begin preheating. 2. Whisk eggs in a bowl, add salt and pepper to taste along with yogurt, garlic powder, onion powder, cheese, and bacon, stir. 3. Add the egg mixture into an oven-proof baking dish. Place into air fryer and cook for 10-minutes. 4. Scramble eggs and serve warm.
Per Serving: Calories 25; Fat 0.1g; Sodium 546mg; Carbs 3g; Fiber 1g; Sugar 0g; Protein 3g

Pecan Rolled Granola

Prep time: 5 minutes | Cook time: 5 minutes | Servings: 6

1½ cups rolled oats
½ cup pecans, roughly chopped
Dash of salt
½ cup raisins
½ cup sunflower seeds
2 tablespoons butter, melted
1 teaspoon liquid Stevia

1. Install the wire rack on Level 3. Select the "BAKE" function of Ninja Foodi Smart XL Pro Air Oven, set temperature to 350°F/175°C and time to 5 minutes. Select START/STOP to begin preheating. 2. In a mixing bowl, combine oats, seeds, pecans and a dash of salt and stir well. In a small bowl mix butter with Stevia then add to the oat mixture. 3. Spray the sheet pan with cooking spray and add in the oat mixture. Place in the air fryer and bake for 5 minutes, Stir halfway through. 4. Remove from air fryer and pour into bowl to cool. Add the sunflower seeds and raisins and stir. 5. Eat immediately or store in an airtight container.
Per Serving: Calories 34; Fat 2.3g; Sodium 122mg; Carbs 1g; Fiber 0g; Sugar 0g; Protein 2g

Pumpkin Pie Toast

Prep time: 5 minutes | Cook time: 20 minutes | Servings: 4

2 large, beaten eggs
4 slices of cinnamon swirl bread
¼ cup milk
¼ cup pumpkin purée
¼ teaspoon pumpkin spices
¼ cup butter

1. Install the wire rack on Level 3. Select the "BAKE" function of Ninja Foodi Smart XL Pro Air Oven, set temperature to 340°F/170°C and time to 10 minutes. Select START/STOP to begin preheating. 2. In a large mixing bowl, mix milk, eggs, pumpkin purée and pie spice. Whisk until mixture is smooth. 3. In the egg mixture dip the bread on both sides. Place 2 slices of bread onto the air fryer sheet pan and cook for 10-minutes. Serve pumpkin pie toast with butter.
Per Serving: Calories 80; Fat 6g; Sodium 444mg; Carbs 6g; Fiber 1g; Sugar 4g; Protein 1g

Egg Casserole with Ham

Prep time: 5 minutes | Cook time: 12 minutes | Servings: 2

1 cup day-old whole grain bread, cubed
3 large eggs, beaten
2 tablespoon water
⅛ teaspoon kosher salt
1 oz. prosciutto, roughly chopped
1 oz. slice pepper jack cheese, roughly chopped
1 tablespoon fresh chives, chopped

1. Install the wire rack on Level 3. 2. Select the "BAKE" function of Ninja Foodi Smart XL Pro Air Oven, set temperature to 360°F/180°C and time to 12 minutes. Select START/STOP to begin preheating. 3. Spray the air fryer sheet pan with nonstick cooking spray, then place the bread cubes in the pan. 4. In a medium bowl, whisk together the eggs and water, then stir in the kosher salt, prosciutto, pepper jack cheese, and chives. 5. Pour the egg mixture over the bread cubes and cook for 10–12 minutes or until the eggs have set and the top is golden brown. 6. Remove the casserole from the fryer and allow to cool in the pan on a wire rack for 5 minutes before cutting and serving.
Per Serving: Calories 248; Fat 6g; Sodium 557mg; Carbs 11g; Fiber 3g; Sugar 2g; Protein 19g

Cheesy Bacon, Ham and Eggs

Prep time: 5 minutes | Cook time: 10 minutes | Servings: 4

4 eggs
⅓ cup ham, cooked and chopped into small pieces
⅓ cup bacon, cooked, chopped into small pieces
⅓ cup cheddar cheese, shredded

1. In a medium-sized mixing bowl, whisk the eggs, add the ham, bacon, and cheese and stir until well combined. Add to sheet pan that is sprayed with cooking spray. 2. Select Level 3. Select the "AIR FRY" function of Ninja Foodi Smart XL Pro Air Oven, set temperature to 300°F/150°C and time to 10 minutes. Select START/STOP to begin preheating. 3. Place pan into air fryer and cook for 10 minutes then remove when cooking time is completed and serve warm.
Per Serving: Calories 217; Fat 21.8g; Sodium 207mg; Carbs 7g; Fiber 4g; Sugar 3g; Protein 2g

Crispy Avocado Fries

Prep time: 5 minutes | Cook time: 8 minutes | Servings: 2

2 eggs, beaten
2 large avocados, peeled, pitted, cut into 8 slices each
¼ teaspoon pepper
½ teaspoon cayenne pepper
Salt to taste
Juice of ½ a lemon
½ cup of whole wheat flour
1 cup whole wheat breadcrumbs
Greek yogurt to serve

1. Add flour, salt, pepper and cayenne pepper to bowl and mix. Add bread crumbs into another bowl. Beat eggs in a third bowl. 2. First, dredge the avocado slices in the flour mixture. Next, dip them into the egg mixture and finally dredge them in the breadcrumbs. 3. Place avocado fries into the air fryer basket. Install the wire rack on Level 2. Select the "AIR FRY" function of Ninja Foodi Smart XL Pro Air Oven, set temperature to 390°F/200°C and time to 6 minutes. Select START/STOP to begin preheating. Place the air fryer basket into the air fryer and cook for 6-minutes. 4. When cook time is completed, transfer the avocado fries onto a serving platter. Sprinkle with lemon juice and serve with Greek yogurt.
Per Serving: Calories 33; Fat 3.5g; Sodium 1mg; Carbs 1g; Fiber 0g; Sugar 0g; Protein 0g

Cheesy Asparagus Omelet

Prep time: 5 minutes | Cook time: 8 minutes | Servings: 2

3 eggs
5 steamed asparagus tips
2 tablespoons of warm milk
1 tablespoon parmesan cheese,

grated
Salt and pepper to taste
Non-stick cooking spray

1. Select Level 3. Select the "AIR FRY" function of Ninja Foodi Smart XL Pro Air Oven, set temperature to 320°F/160°C and time to 8 minutes. Select START/STOP to begin preheating. 2. Mix in a large bowl, eggs, cheese, milk, salt and pepper then blend them. Spray a sheet pan with non-stick cooking spray. 3. Pour the egg mixture into the pan and add the asparagus, then place pan into the air fryer. Cook it for 8-minutes. 4. Serve warm.
Per Serving: Calories 74; Fat 1.9g; Sodium 685mg; Carbs 9g; Fiber 7g; Sugar 2g; Protein 9g

Baked Eggs with Spinach

Prep time: 5 minutes | Cook time: 8 minutes | Servings: 4

1 lb. of spinach, chopped
7 ounces sliced ham
4 eggs

1 tablespoon olive oil
4 tablespoons milk
Salt and pepper to taste

1. Install the wire rack on Level 3. Select the "BAKE" function of Ninja Foodi Smart XL Pro Air Oven, set temperature to 300°F/150°C and time to 8 minutes. Select START/STOP to begin preheating. 2. Butter the inside of 4 ramekins. In each ramekin, place spinach on bottom, one egg, 1 tablespoon of milk, salt, and pepper. 3. Place ramekins in air fryer basket and cook for 8-minutes.
Per Serving: Calories 23; Fat 1.3g; Sodium 40mg; Carbs 2g; Fiber 1g; Sugar 1g; Protein 1g

Baked Spinach Quiche

Prep time: 5 minutes | Cook time: 15 minutes | Servings: 2

2 eggs
1 large yellow onion, diced
1¾ cups whole wheat flour
1½ cups spinach, chopped
¾ cup cottage cheese

Salt and black pepper to taste
2 tablespoons olive oil
¾ cup butter
¼ cup milk

1. Install the wire rack on Level 3. Select the "BAKE" function of Ninja Foodi Smart XL Pro Air Oven, set temperature to 355°F/180°C and time to 15 minutes. Select START/STOP to begin preheating. 2. Add the flour, butter, salt, and milk to the bowl and knead dough until smooth and refrigerate for 15-minutes. 3. Place a frying pan over medium heat and add the oil to it. When the oil is heated, add the onions into the pan and sauté them. 4. Add spinach to pan and cook until it wilts. Drain excess moisture from spinach. 5. Whisk the eggs together and add cheese to bowl and mix. Take the dough out of the fridge and divide into 8 equal parts. Roll the dough into a round that will fit into the bottom of quiche mold. Place the rolled dough into molds. 6. Place the spinach filling over dough. Place molds into air fryer basket and place basket inside of air fryer and cook for 15-minutes. Remove quiche from molds and serve warm or cold.
Per Serving: Calories 88; Fat 7.1g; Sodium 143mg; Carbs 4g; Fiber 3g; Sugar 1g; Protein 4g

Cheese Bread Cups

Prep time: 5 minutes | Cook time: 15 minutes | Servings: 2

2 eggs
2 tablespoons cheddar cheese, grated
Salt and pepper to taste

1 ham slice, cut into 2 pieces
1 bread slices, flatten with rolling pin

1. Select Level 3. Select the "AIR FRY" function of Ninja Foodi Smart XL Pro Air Oven, set temperature to 300°F/150°C and time to 15 minutes. Select START/STOP to begin preheating. 2. Spray the inside of 2 ramekins with cooking spray. Place 2 flat pieces of bread into each ramekin. Add the ham slice pieces into each ramekin. 3. Crack an egg in each ramekin then sprinkle with cheese. Season with salt and pepper. Place the ramekins into air fryer and cook for 15-minutes. 4. Serve warm.
Per Serving: Calories 354; Fat 7.9g; Sodium 704mg; Carbs 6g; Fiber 3.6g; Sugar 6g; Protein 18g

Breaded Cod Nuggets

Prep time: 5 minutes | Cook time: 10 minutes | Servings: 4

1 lb. of cod
For Breading:
2 eggs, beaten
2 tablespoons olive oil
1 cup almond flour
¾ cup breadcrumbs

1 teaspoon dried parsley
Pinch of sea salt
½ teaspoon black pepper

1. Install the wire rack on Level 3. Select the "BAKE" function of Ninja Foodi Smart XL Pro Air Oven, set temperature to 390°F/200°C and time to 10 minutes. Select START/STOP to begin preheating. 2. Cut the cod into strips about 1-inch by 2-inches in length. Blend breadcrumbs, olive oil, salt, parsley and pepper in a food processor. 3. In three separate bowls, add breadcrumbs, eggs, and flour. Place each piece of fish into flour, then the eggs and lastly the breadcrumbs. 4. Add pieces of cod to air fryer basket and cook for 10-minutes. Serve warm.
Per Serving: Calories 42; Fat 2.8g; Sodium 126mg; Carbs 4g; Fiber 1g; Sugar 1g; Protein 1g

Bacon Egg Muffins

Prep time: 5 minutes | Cook time: 6 minutes | Servings: 2

2 whole wheat English muffins
4 slices of bacon

Pepper to taste
2 eggs

1. Crack an egg each into ramekins. Season with pepper. 2. Select Level 3. Select the "AIR FRY" function of Ninja Foodi Smart XL Pro Air Oven, set temperature to 390°F/200°C and time to 6 minutes. Select START/STOP to begin preheating. 3. Place the ramekins with the bacon and muffins alongside in the wire rack and cook for 6 minutes. 4. Remove the muffins from the air fryer after a few minutes and split them. 5. When the bacon and eggs are done cooking, add two pieces of bacon and one egg to each egg muffin and serve immediately.
Per Serving: Calories 716; Fat 62.6g; Sodium 302mg; Carbs 18g; Fiber 8g; Sugar 2g; Protein 34g

Vegetable Patties

Prep time: 5 minutes | Cook time: 15 minutes | Servings: 2

1 cup almond flour
½ cup milk
1 tablespoon parmesan cheese, grated
3 eggs
1 potato, grated
1 beet, peeled and grated

1 carrot, grated
1 zucchini, grated
1 tablespoon olive oil
¼ teaspoon nutmeg
1 teaspoon onion powder
1 teaspoon garlic powder
½ teaspoon black pepper

1. Select Level 3. Select the "AIR FRY" function of Ninja Foodi Smart XL Pro Air Oven, set temperature to 390°F/200°C and time to 15 minutes. Select START/STOP to begin preheating. 2. Mix the zucchini, potato, beet, carrot, eggs, milk, almond flour and parmesan in a bowl. Place olive oil into oven-safe dish. Form patties with vegetable mix and flatten to form patties. 3. Place patties into dish and cook in air fryer for 15-minutes. Serve with sliced tomatoes, sour cream, and toast.
Per Serving: Calories 134; Fat 2.8g; Sodium 64mg; Carbs 26g; Fiber 4g; Sugar 8g; Protein 3g

Egg White Cups with Spinach and Tomato

Prep time: 5 minutes | Cook time: 10 minutes | Servings: 1

2 egg whites, beaten
2 tablespoons tomato, chopped
2 tablespoons spinach, chopped

Pinch of kosher salt
Red pepper flakes

1. Slide basket into rails of Level 3. 2. Select the "AIR FRY" function of Ninja Foodi Smart XL Pro Air Oven, set temperature to 300°F/150°C and time to 5 minutes. Select START/STOP to begin preheating. 3. Spray a 3-inch ramekin with nonstick cooking spray, then combine the egg whites, tomato, spinach, kosher salt, and red pepper flakes (if using) in the ramekin. 4. Place the ramekin in the air fryer basket and cook for 10 minutes or until the eggs have set. 5. Remove the ramekin from the fryer and allow to cool on a wire rack for 5 minutes before serving.
Per Serving: Calories 40; Fat 0g; Sodium 184mg; Carbs 1g; Fiber 1g; Sugar 1g; Protein 7g

Peanut Butter & Banana Toast

Prep time: 5 minutes | Cook time: 6 minutes | Servings: 1

2 slices of whole wheat bread
1 teaspoon of sugar-free maple syrup

1 sliced banana
2 tablespoons of peanut butter

1. Install the wire rack on Level 3. Select the "BAKE" function of Ninja Foodi Smart XL Pro Air Oven, set temperature to 330°F/165°C and time to 6 minutes. Select START/STOP to begin preheating. 2. Evenly coat both sides of the slices of bread with peanut butter. Add the sliced banana and drizzle with some sugar-free maple syrup. 3. Place toast directly on wire rack and cook for 6 minutes. Serve warm.
Per Serving: Calories 101; Fat 5.4g; Sodium 106mg; Carbs 8g; Fiber 3g; Sugar 3g; Protein 7g

Cheese & Egg Sandwich

Prep time: 5 minutes | Cook time: 6 minutes | Servings: 1

1-2 eggs
1-2 slices of cheddar or Swiss cheese

A bit of butter
1 roll sliced in half, Kaiser bun, English muffin, etc.

1. Butter your sliced roll on both sides. Place the eggs in an oven-safe dish and whisk. Add seasoning if you wish, such as dill, chives, oregano, and salt. 2. Place the egg dish, roll and cheese into the air fryer. Make sure the buttered sides of the roll are facing upwards. 3. Select Level 3. Select the "AIR FRY" function of Ninja Foodi Smart XL Pro Air Oven, set temperature to 390°F/200°C and time to 6 minutes. Select START/STOP to begin preheating. Cook them for 6 minutes. 4. Place the egg and cheese between the pieces of roll and serve warm. You might like to try adding slices of avocado and tomatoes to this breakfast sandwich!
Per Serving: Calories 292; Fat 24.3g; Sodium 660mg; Carbs 5g; Fiber 0g; Sugar 3g; Protein 14g

Zucchini & Cream Muffins

Prep time: 5 minutes | Cook time: 15 minutes | Servings: 5

1 tablespoon cream cheese
Half a cup zucchini, shredded
1 tablespoon plain yogurt
1 egg
1 cup of milk
2 tablespoons of warmed coconut

oil
Pinch of sea salt
2 teaspoons baking powder
1 teaspoon cinnamon
1 tablespoon liquid Stevia
4 cups whole wheat flour

1. Select Level 3. Select the "AIR FRY" function of Ninja Foodi Smart XL Pro Air Oven, set temperature to 350°F/175°C and time to 12 minutes. Select START/STOP to begin preheating. Mix all your dry ingredients in a mixing bowl. Stir to combine. 2. In another mixing bowl combine all of the wet ingredients (coconut oil, milk, yogurt, liquid Stevia, and egg. Whisk these until evenly combined. 3. In a large bowl, combine both the wet and dry ingredients and use a hand mixer to whisk them. Stir in the shredded zucchini and fold in the cream cheese. 4. Place five muffin cups into your air fryer. Fill each cup ¾ full of mixture. Cook muffins for 12-minutes. Serve warm or cold.
Per Serving: Calories 193; Fat 8.9g; Sodium 93mg; Carbs 2g; Fiber 1g; Sugar 0g; Protein 25g

Oriental Tofu & Mushroom Omelet

Prep time: 5 minutes | Cook time: 24 minutes | Servings: 1

½ cup fresh Shimeji mushrooms, sliced
2 eggs, whisked
Salt and pepper to taste
1 clove of garlic, minced

A handful of sliced tofu
2 tablespoons onion, finely chopped
Cooking spray

1. Select Level 3. Select the "AIR FRY" function of Ninja Foodi Smart XL Pro Air Oven, set temperature to 355°F/180°C and time to 4 minutes. Select START/STOP to begin preheating. 2. Spray sheet pan with cooking spray. Add onions and garlic. Air fry them for 4-minutes. 3. Place the tofu and mushrooms over the onions and add salt and pepper to taste. 4. Whisk the eggs and pour them over tofu and mushrooms. Air fry again for 20-minutes. 5. Serve warm.
Per Serving: Calories 153; Fat 2.8g; Sodium 28mg; Carbs 26g; Fiber 1g; Sugar 1g; Protein 6g

Eggs & Cheese Toast

Prep time: 5 minutes | Cook time: 15 minutes | Servings: 2

⅛ teaspoon of black pepper
¼ teaspoon salt
½ teaspoon Italian seasoning
¼ teaspoon balsamic vinegar
¼ teaspoon sugar-free maple syrup
1 cup sausages, chopped into small pieces

2 eggs
2 slices of whole wheat toast
3 tablespoons cheddar cheese, shredded
6-slices tomatoes
Cooking spray
A little mayonnaise to serve

1. Select Level 3. Select the "AIR FRY" function of Ninja Foodi Smart XL Pro Air Oven, set temperature to 320°/160°C and time to 10 minutes. Select START/STOP to begin preheating. 2. Spray baking dish with cooking spray. Place the bread slices at the bottom of the dish. Sprinkle the sausages over bread. Lay the tomatoes over it. Sprinkle top with cheese. 3. Beat the eggs and then pour over top of bread slices. Drizzle vinegar and maple syrup over eggs. Season with Italian seasoning, salt, and pepper, then sprinkle some more cheese on top. 4. Place the baking dish in the air fryer basket and cooked for 10-minutes. Remove from air fryer and add spot of mayonnaise and serve.
Per Serving: Calories 147; Fat 7.3g; Sodium 56mg; Carbs 20g; Fiber 5g; Sugar 11g; Protein 4g

Cheese Bacon & Egg Sandwiches

Prep time: 3 minutes | Cook time: 8 minutes | Servings: 2

2 large eggs
¼ teaspoon kosher salt, divided
¼ teaspoon freshly ground black pepper, divided (plus extra for serving)

2 slices Canadian bacon
2 slices American cheese
2 whole grain English muffins, sliced in half

1. Slide basket into rails of Level 3. 2. Select the "AIR FRY" function of Ninja Foodi Smart XL Pro Air Oven, set temperature to 360°F/180°C and time to 5 minutes. Select START/STOP to begin preheating. 3. Spray two 3-inch ramekins with nonstick cooking spray, then crack one egg into each ramekin and add half the kosher salt and half the black pepper to each egg. 4. Place the ramekins in the fryer basket and cook for 5 minutes. Pause the fryer and top each partially cooked egg with a slice of Canadian bacon and a slice of American cheese. 5. Cook for 3 more minutes or until the cheese has melted and the egg yolk has just cooked through. 6. Remove the ramekins from the fryer and allow to cool on a wire rack for 2–3 minutes, then flip the eggs, bacon, and cheese out onto English muffins and sprinkle some black pepper on top before serving.
Per Serving: Calories 305; Fat 5g; Sodium 618mg; Carbs 26g; Fiber 3g; Sugar 3g; Protein 22g

Delicious Huevos Rancheros

Prep time: 20 minutes | Cook time: 25 minutes | Servings: 4

4 large eggs
¼ teaspoon kosher salt
¼ cup masa harina (corn flour)
1 teaspoon olive oil

¼ cup warm water
½ cup salsa
¼ cup crumbled queso fresco or feta cheese

1. Select Level 3. Select the "AIR FRY" function of Ninja Foodi Smart XL Pro Air Oven, set temperature to 330°F/165°C and time to 5 minutes. Select START/STOP to begin preheating. with the 2. Crack the eggs into the air fryer sheet pan, season with the kosher salt, and cook for 3 minutes. Pause the fryer, gently scramble the eggs, and cook for 2 more minutes. Remove the eggs from the fryer, keeping the fryer on, and set the eggs aside to slightly cool. 3. Preheat the air fryer to 390°F/200°C. 4. In a medium bowl, combine the masa harina, olive oil, and ¼ teaspoon of kosher salt by hand, then slowly pour in the water, stirring until a soft dough forms. 5. Divide the dough into 4 equal balls, then place each ball between 2 pieces of parchment paper and use a pie plate or a rolling pin to flatten the dough. 6. Spray the air fryer sheet pan with nonstick cooking spray, then place one flattened tortilla in the pan and cook for 5 minutes. Repeat this process with the remaining tortillas. 7. Remove the tortillas from the fryer and place on a serving plate, then top each tortilla with the scrambled eggs, salsa, and cheese before serving.
Per Serving: Calories 142; Fat 8g; Sodium 333mg; Carbs 8g; Fiber 1g; Sugar 2g; Protein 8g

Chapter 2 Vegetable and Sides Recipes

Roasted Cauliflower

Prep time: 10 minutes | Cook time: 20 minutes | Servings: 2

1 head cauliflower
½ lemon, juiced
½ tablespoon olive oil
1 teaspoon curry powder
Black pepper and salt to taste

1. Wash the cauliflower and remove its leaves and core. Cut it into florets of comparable size. 2. Cook on Air Roast mode, select level 3. Grease your roast tray with oil and preheat it for 2-minutes at 390°F/200°C. Mix fresh lemon juice and curry powder, then add the cauliflower florets and stir. Use black pepper and salt as seasoning and stir again. Cook for 20-minutes and serve warm.
Per Serving: Calories 229; Fat 1.9 | Sodium 567mg; Carbs 1.9g; Fiber 0.4g; Sugar 0.6g; Protein 11.8g

Eggplant Panini

Prep time: 10 minutes | Cook time: 25 minutes | Servings: 2

1 medium eggplant, cut into ½ inch slices
½ cup mayonnaise
2 tablespoons milk
Black pepper to taste
½ teaspoon garlic powder
½ teaspoon onion powder
1 tablespoon dried parsley
½ teaspoon Italian seasoning
½ cup breadcrumbs
Salt to taste
Fresh basil, chopped for garnishing
¾ cup tomato sauce
2 tablespoons parmesan, grated cheese
2 cups grated mozzarella cheese
2 tablespoons olive oil
4 slices artisan Italian bread
Cooking spray

1. Cover both sides of eggplant with salt. Place them between sheets of paper towels. Set aside for 30-minutes to get rid of excess moisture. 2. In a mixing bowl, mix Italian seasoning, breadcrumbs, parsley, onion powder, garlic powder and season with black pepper and salt. In another small bowl, whisk mayonnaise and milk until smooth.3. Cook on Air Fry mode and select Level "3". Preheat your air fryer to 400°F/200°C and set the time to 15 minutes. Remove the excess salt from eggplant slices. Cover both sides of eggplant with mayonnaise mixture. 4. Press the eggplant slices into the breadcrumb mixture. Use cooking spray on both sides of eggplant slices. Air fry slices in batches for 15-minutes, turning over when halfway done. Each bread slice must be greased with olive oil. 5. On a cutting board, place two slices of bread with oiled sides down. 6. Layer mozzarella cheese and grated parmesan cheese. Place eggplant on cheese. 7. Cover with tomato sauce and add remaining mozzarella and parmesan cheeses. 8. Garnish with chopped fresh basil. Put the second slice of bread oiled side up on top. 9. Take preheated panini press and place sandwiches on it. Close the lid and cook for 10-minutes. 10. Slice panini into halves and serve.
Per Serving: Calories 185; Fat 11g; Sodium 355mg; Carbs 21g; Fiber 5.8g; Sugar 3g; Protein 4.7g

Cheesy Cauliflower Tots

Prep time: 10 minutes | Cook time: 15 minutes | Servings: 6

3 cups cauliflower florets
1 tablespoon coconut flour
1 teaspoon fine salt
1 large egg, beaten
1 (8-ounce) package cream
cheese, softened
½ cup finely chopped onions
1 teaspoon smoked paprika
Chopped fresh parsley, for garnish
Ranch dressing (here), for serving

1. Spray its air fryer basket with avocado oil. Select the Air Fry mode. Set the Ninja Foodi Smart XL Pro temperature to 400°F/200°C. Select Level "3" and set the time on your Ninja Foodi Smart XL Pro Air Fryer Oven to 10 minutes. Press Start/Pause to begin preheating. Continue to the next step when it is done preheating. 2. Place the cauliflower in a food processor and pulse until it resembles grains of rice. 3. Place the riced cauliflower in a medium-sized bowl, sprinkle the coconut flour and salt on top, and toss well to coat. Add the egg, cream cheese, onions, and paprika and mix well to mix. 4. Form the cauliflower–cream cheese mixture into 24 tater tot shapes. Place them in its air fryer basket, leaving space between them, insert its air fryer basket in level 3 and cook for 15 minutes, until golden. 5. Remove the tots from the air fryer and place them on a serving plate. Garnish with chopped parsley, if desired, and serve with ranch dressing on the side for dipping, if desired.
Per Serving: Calories 190; Fat 18g; Sodium 150mg; Carbs 0.6g; Fiber 0.4g; Sugar 0.4g; Protein 7.2g

Spinach Potato Samosa

Prep time: 10 minutes | Cook time: 15 minutes | Servings: 2

1½ cups of almond flour
½ teaspoon baking soda
1 teaspoon garam masala
1 teaspoon coriander, chopped
¼ cup green peas
½ teaspoon sesame seeds
¼ cup potatoes, boiled, small chunks
2 tablespoons olive oil
¾ cup boiled and blended spinach puree
Salt and chili powder to taste

1. In a suitable bowl, mix baking soda, salt, and flour to make the prepared dough. Add 1 tablespoon of oil. 2. Add the spinach puree and mix until the prepared dough is smooth. Place in fridge for twenty-minutes. 3. In the pan add one tablespoon of oil, then add potatoes, peas and cook for 5-minutes. 4. Add the sesame seeds, garam masala, coriander, and stir. Knead the prepared dough and make the small ball using a rolling pin. 5. Form balls, make into cone shapes, which are then filled with stuffing that is not yet fully cooked. Make sure flour sheets are well sealed. 6. Preheat on "Air Fry" Mode, and set its temperature to 390°F/200°C. Place samosa in air fryer basket. Insert its air fryer basket into the level 3 of the oven and close the door. and cook for 15 minutes.
Per Serving: Calories 122; Fat 1.8g; Sodium 794mg; Carbs 17g; Fiber 8.9g; Sugar 1.6g; Protein 1.9g

Roasted Carrots

Prep time: 10 minutes | Cook time: 12 minutes | Servings: 2

1 tablespoon honey
Black pepper and salt to taste
3 cups of baby carrots
1 tablespoon olive oil

In a mixing bowl, mix carrots, honey, and olive oil. Season with black pepper and salt. Cook on Air Roast mode, select level 3 and begin preheating. Cook in air fryer at 390°F/200°C for 12-minutes.
Per Serving: Calories 163; Fat 11.5g; Sodium 918mg; Carbs 8.3g; Fiber 4.2g; Sugar 0.2g; Protein 7.4g

Crispy Baby Corn

Prep time: 10 minutes | Cook time: 10 minutes | Servings: 4

1 cup almond flour
1 teaspoon garlic powder
¼ teaspoon chili powder
4 baby corns, boiled
Salt to taste
½ teaspoon carom seeds
Pinch of baking soda

1. In a suitable bowl, then add flour, chili powder, garlic powder, baking soda, carom seed, and salt. Mix well. 2. Pour a little water into the prepared batter to make a nice batter. Dip boiled baby corn into the prepared batter to coat. 3. Cook on Air Fry mode and select Level "3". Preheat your air fryer to 350°F/175°C and set the time to 10 minutes. Line its air fryer basket with foil and place the baby corns on foil. Insert its air fryer basket into the level 3 of the oven and close the door. Cook baby corns for 10-minutes.
Per Serving: Calories 284; Fat 7.9g; Sodium 704mg; Carbs 38.1g; Fiber 1.9g; Sugar 1.9g; Protein 14.8g

Fried Brussels Sprouts

Prep time: 5 minutes | Cook time: 8 minutes | Servings: 4

2 cups brussels sprouts, trimmed and halved
3 tablespoons ghee or coconut oil, melted
1 teaspoon fine salt or smoked salt
Dash of lime or lemon juice
Thinly sliced parmesan cheese, for serving (optional; omit for dairy-free)
Lemon slices, for serving

1. Spray its air fryer basket with avocado oil. Select the Air Fry mode. Set the Ninja Foodi Smart XL Pro temperature to 400°F/200°C. Select Level "3" and set the time on your Ninja Foodi Smart XL Pro Air Fryer Oven to 8 minutes. Press Start/Pause to begin preheating. Continue to the next step when it is done preheating. 2. In a suitable bowl, toss the brussels sprouts, ghee, and salt. Add the lime or lemon juice. 3. Place the brussels sprouts in its air fryer basket. Insert its air fryer basket into the level 3 of the oven and close the door. and cook for 8 minutes, until crispy, shaking the basket after 5 minutes. Serve with thinly sliced parmesan and lemon slices, if desired.
Per Serving: Calories 282; Fat 15g; Sodium 526mg; Carbs 20g; Fiber 0.6g; Sugar 3.3g; Protein 16g

Bacon-Wrapped Tots

Prep time: 10 minutes | Cook time: 13 minutes | Servings: 6

1 recipe keto tots (here)
12 thin-cut slices bacon, cut in half crosswise
½ cup shredded cheddar cheese (about 2 ounces)
¼ cup sliced green onions, for garnish
½ cup full-fat sour cream, for serving

1. Spray its air fryer basket with avocado oil. Select the Air Fry mode. Set the Ninja Foodi Smart XL Pro temperature to 400°F/200°C. Select Level "3" and set the time on your Ninja Foodi Smart XL Pro Air Fryer Oven to 10 minutes. Press Start/Pause to begin preheating. Continue to the next step when it is done preheating. 2. Wrap a piece of bacon around each tot and secure it with a toothpick. Place the wrapped tots in its air fryer basket, leaving space between them. 3. Insert its air fryer basket into the level 3 of the oven and close the door. Cook for 13 minutes, until the bacon is crisp to your liking. Remove the tots from the air fryer, place them on a serving plate, and sprinkle the cheese over the hot tots. Garnish with the green onions and serve with the sour cream.
Per Serving: Calories 267; Fat 12g; Sodium 165mg; Carbs 39g; Fiber 1.4g; Sugar 22g; Protein 3.3g

Tasty Cheese Sticks

Prep time: 10 minutes | Cook time: 5 minutes | Servings: 4

1 (16-ounce) package mozzarella cheese
½ teaspoon salt
1 teaspoon garlic powder
1 teaspoon onion powder
1 teaspoon cayenne pepper
1 cup breadcrumbs
1 cup almond flour
2 eggs, beaten

1. Cut the mozzarella cheese into 3 (½ inch) sticks. Add beaten eggs in small bowl. In a suitable bowl, add flour. In another small bowl, mix breadcrumbs, cayenne pepper, onion powder, garlic powder, and salt. 2. Dip cheese sticks into beaten egg, then dip into flour, then return to egg, and coat with breadcrumbs. 3. Place coated cheese in the fridge for 20-minutes. 4. Select the Air Fry mode, Preheat your air fryer to 400°F/200°C. Spray air fryer basket with cooking spray. 5. Place the coated cheese sticks into air fryer and insert its air fryer basket into the level 3 of the oven and close the door. Cook for 5-minutes. Serve hot!
Per Serving: Calories 275; Fat 1.4g; Sodium 582mg; Carbs 31.5g; Fiber 1.1g; Sugar 0.1g; Protein 2.8g

Crusty Chili Tofu

Prep time: 10 minutes | Cook time: 12 minutes | Servings: 4

¼ cup cornmeal
15-ounces extra firm tofu, drained, cubed
Black pepper and salt to taste
1 teaspoon chili flakes
¾ cup cornstarch
Oil

1. Line its air fryer basket with aluminum foil and brush with oil. 2. Select the Air Fry mode, preheat your air fryer to 370°F/185°C. Mix all the recipe ingredients in a suitable bowl. Place in air fryer, insert its air fryer basket into the level 3 of the oven and close the door. And cook for 12-minutes.
Per Serving: Calories 206; Fat 3.4g; Sodium 174mg; Carbs 35g; Fiber 9.4g; Sugar 5.9g; Protein 10.6g

Potato Au Gratin

Prep time: 10 minutes | Cook time: 15 minutes | Servings: 4

¼ cup milk
3 tablespoons cheddar cheese, grated
3 potatoes, peeled and sliced
¼ teaspoon nutmeg
¼ teaspoon pepper
¼ teaspoon salt
¼ cup coconut cream

1. Select the Air Fry mode, preheat air fryer to 400°F/200°C. 2. Add the cream and milk into a suitable bowl and season with salt, pepper, and nutmeg. Coat potato slices in milk and cream mixture. 3. Spread the potato slices in an oven-safe dish and pour remaining cream on top of potato slices. 4. Sprinkle the top with grated cheese. 5. Place into air fryer basket, insert its air fryer basket into the level 3 of the oven and close the door. And cook for 15-minutes.
Per Serving: Calories 297; Fat 1g; Sodium 291mg; Carbs 35g; Fiber 1g; Sugar 9g; Protein 2g

Crispy Cauliflower Florets

Prep time: 10 minutes | Cook time: 20 minutes | Servings: 2

1 egg, beaten
2 tablespoons parmesan cheese, grated
2 cups cauliflower florets, boiled
¼ cup almond flour
1 tablespoon olive oil
Salt to taste
½ tablespoon mixed herbs
½ teaspoon chili powder
½ teaspoon garlic powder
½ cup breadcrumbs

1. In a suitable bowl, mix garlic powder, breadcrumbs, chili powder, mixed herbs, salt, and cheese. 2. Add olive oil to the breadcrumb mixture and mix well. 3. Place flour in a suitable bowl and place the egg in another bowl. 4. Dip the cauliflower florets into the beaten egg, then in flour, and coat with breadcrumbs. 5. Cook on Air Fry mode and Select Level "3", preheat your air fryer to 350°F/175°C and set the time to 10 minutes. Place the coated cauliflower florets inside air fryer basket. Insert its air fryer basket into the level 3 of the oven and close the door. And cook for 20-minutes.
Per Serving: Calories 270; Fat 14.6g; Sodium 394mg; Carbs 31.3g; Fiber 7.5g; Sugar 9.7g; Protein 6.4g

Delicious Fried Corn

Prep time: 10 minutes | Cook time: 10 minutes | Servings: 8

4 ears of corn
Black pepper and salt to taste
3 teaspoons vegetable oil

1. Remove the husks from corn, wash and pat them dry. Cut if needed to fit into air fryer basket. 2. Drizzle with vegetable oil and season with black pepper and salt. Insert its air fryer basket into the level 3 of the oven and close the door. Cook on "Air Fry" Mode, select level 3, and set its temperature to 400°F/200°C for 10-minutes.
Per Serving: Calories 208; Fat 5g; Sodium 1205mg; Carbs 34.1g; Fiber 7.8g; Sugar 2.5g; Protein 5.9g

Spicy Chipotle Nuts

Prep time: 10 minutes | Cook time: 4 minutes | Servings: 8

2 cups mixed nuts
1 teaspoon chipotle chili powder
1 teaspoon salt
1 teaspoon pepper
1 tablespoon butter, melted
1 teaspoon ground cumin

In a suitable bowl, put the mixed nuts, then add all the recipe ingredients and toss to coat. Cook on Air Fry mode, preheat your air fryer to 350°F/175°C for 4 minutes. Add mixed nuts into air fryer basket, insert its air fryer basket into the level 3 of the oven and close the door. And cook for 4-minutes.
Per Serving: Calories 350; Fat 2.6g; Sodium 358mg; Carbs 64.6g; Fiber 14.4g; Sugar 3.3g; Protein 19.9g

Cauliflower Steaks

Prep time: 10 minutes | Cook time: 15 minutes | Servings: 4

¼ cup avocado oil
¼ cup lemon juice
2 cloves garlic, minced
1 teaspoon grated fresh ginger
1 tablespoon turmeric powder
1 teaspoon fine salt
1 medium head cauliflower
Full-fat sour cream (or kite hill brand almond milk yogurt for dairy-free), for serving
Extra-virgin olive oil, for serving
Chopped fresh cilantro leaves, for garnish

1. Select the Air Fry mode. Set the Ninja Foodi Smart XL Pro temperature to 400°F/200°C. Select Level "3" and set the time on your Ninja Foodi Smart XL Pro Air Fryer Oven to 15 minutes. Press Start/Pause to begin preheating. Continue to the next step when it is done preheating. 2. In a suitable shallow dish, mix the avocado oil, lemon juice, garlic, ginger, turmeric, and salt. Slice the cauliflower into ½-inch steaks and place them in the marinade. Cover and refrigerate for almost 20 minutes or overnight. 3. Remove the cauliflower steaks from the marinade and place them in its air fryer basket. Insert its air fryer basket into the level 3 of the oven and close the door. Cook for 15 minutes, until soft and slightly charred on the edges. 4. Serve with sour cream and a drizzle of olive oil, and sprinkle with chopped cilantro leaves.
Per Serving: Calories 100; Fat 2g; Sodium 480mg; Carbs 4g; Fiber 2g; Sugar 0g; Protein 8g

Roasted Tawa Veggies

Prep time: 10 minutes | Cook time: 25 minutes | Servings: 4

¼ cup okra
2 teaspoons garam masala
1 teaspoon red chili powder
1 teaspoon amchur powder
¼ cup taro root

¼ cup potato
¼ cup eggplant
Salt to taste
Olive oil for brushing

1. Cut potato and taro root into fries and soak in salt water for 10 minutes. Cut okra and eggplant into four pieces. Rinse potatoes and taro root and pat dry. 2. Add the spices to potatoes, taro roots, okra, and eggplant. 3. Cooke on Air Roast mode and select level 3. Brush pan with oil and preheat to 390°F/200°C and cook for 10 minutes. Lower the heat to 355°F /180°C and cook for an additional 15-minutes.
Per Serving: Calories 288; Fat 6.9g; Sodium 761mg; Carbs 46g; Fiber 4g; Sugar 12g; Protein 9.6g

Mediterranean Veggie Fry

Prep time: 10 minutes | Cook time: 20 minutes | Servings: 4

1 large zucchini, sliced
1 green pepper, sliced
1 large parsnip, peeled and cubed
Black pepper and salt to taste
2 tablespoons honey
2 cloves garlic, crushed

1 teaspoon mixed herbs
1 teaspoon mustard
6 tablespoons olive oil, divided
4 cherry tomatoes
1 medium carrot, peeled and cubed

1. Add the zucchini, green pepper, parsnip, cherry tomatoes, carrot to bottom of air fryer. Cover ingredients with 3 tablespoons of oil and adjust the time to 15-minutes. Cook on "Air Fry" Mode, select level 3, and set its temperature to 360°F. 2. Prepare your marinade by combining remaining ingredients in air fryer safe baking dish. Mix marinade and vegetables in baking dish and stir well. 3. Sprinkle with black pepper and salt. Cook it at 390°F/200°C for 5-minutes.
Per Serving: Calories 260; Fat 16g; Sodium 585mg; Carbs 3.1g; Fiber 1.3g; Sugar 0.2g; Protein 5.5g

Sweet Potato Bites

Prep time: 10 minutes | Cook time: 15 minutes | Servings: 2

2 sweet potatoes, diced
½ cup parsley, chopped
2 tablespoons honey

2 tablespoons olive oil
2 teaspoons cinnamon
1 teaspoon red chili flakes

1. Select the Air Fry mode, preheat your air fryer to 350°F/175°C. Add all the recipe ingredients in a suitable mixing bowl and toss well. 2. Place the sweet potato mixture into air fryer basket. Insert its air fryer basket into the level 3 of the oven and close the door. 3. Cook in preheated air fryer for 15-minutes.
Per Serving: Calories 266; Fat 6.3g; Sodium 193mg; Carbs 39.1g; Fiber 7.2g; Sugar 5.2g; Protein 14.8g

Cauliflower with Ranch Dressing Dip

Prep time: 5 minutes | Cook time: 12 minutes Servings: 4

4 cups cauliflower florets
2 tablespoons dried parsley
1 tablespoon plus 1 teaspoon onion powder
2 teaspoons garlic powder
1½ teaspoons dried dill weed

1 teaspoon dried chives
1 teaspoon fine salt or smoked salt
1 teaspoon black pepper
Ranch dressing (here), for serving

1. Select the Air Fry mode. Set the Ninja Foodi Smart XL Pro temperature to 400°F/200°C. Select Level "3" and set the time on your Ninja Foodi Smart XL Pro Air Fryer Oven to 12 minutes. Press Start/Pause to begin preheating. Continue to the next step when it is done preheating. 2. Place the cauliflower in a suitable bowl and spray it with avocado oil. 3. Place the parsley, onion powder, garlic powder, dill weed, chives, salt, and pepper in a suitable bowl and stir to mix well. Sprinkle the ranch seasoning over the cauliflower. 4. Place the cauliflower in its air fryer basket. Insert its air fryer basket into the level 3 of the oven and close the door. and cook for 12 minutes, until soft and crisp on the edges. Serve with ranch dressing for dipping.
Per Serving: Calories 180; Fat 3.2g; Sodium 133mg; Carbs 32g; Fiber 1.1g; Sugar 1.8g; Protein 9g

Baked Parsley Potatoes

Prep time: 10 minutes | Cook time: 40 minutes | Servings: 3

3 baking potatoes, washed
Parsley for garnishing
1 tablespoon olive oil

Salt to taste
2 garlic cloves, crushed

1. Prepare the potatoes: make holes using a fork in them. Season potatoes with salt and cover with garlic puree and olive oil. 2. Layer the potatoes in its air fryer basket and Insert its air fryer basket into the level 3 of the oven and close the door. Cook on "Air Fry" Mode, select level 3, and set its temperature to 390°F/200°C and cook for 40-minutes.
Per Serving: Calories 248; Fat 30g; Sodium 660mg; Carbs 5g; Fiber 0g; Sugar 0g; Protein 4g

Parmesan Potato balls

Prep time: 10 minutes | Cook time: 4 minutes | Servings: 4

4 potatoes, diced and boiled
2 tablespoons flour
1 egg yolk
1 tablespoon olive oil

3 tablespoons breadcrumbs
Nutmeg to taste
Black pepper and salt to taste
3 tablespoons parmesan cheese

1. Mash potatoes and add all the recipe ingredients except breadcrumbs and oil to the bowl. 2. Mix ingredients and make into medium size balls. Mix breadcrumbs and olive oil separately. Coat balls with breadcrumbs. 3. Preheat on "Air Fry" Mode, and set its temperature to 390°F/200°C and cook for 4 minutes.
Per Serving: Calories 257; Fat 10.4g; Sodium 431mg; Carbs 20g; Fiber 0g; Sugar 1.6g; Protein 2g

Herbed Yellow Squash and Carrots

Prep time: 10 minutes | Cook time: 30 minutes | Servings: 4

2 cups yellow squash, sliced
½ teaspoon salt
½ teaspoon pepper
1 tablespoon thyme leaves

1 tablespoon oregano, chopped
2 tablespoons olive oil
1 cup carrots, sliced

1. In a suitable bowl, add, yellow squash and carrots, then add oregano, oil, and thyme. Season with pepper and salt. Toss well. Place vegetables in air fryer basket and Insert its air fryer basket into the level 3 of the oven and close the door. Cook on Air Fry mode for 400°F/200°C for 30-minutes.
Per Serving: Calories 399; Fat 16g; Sodium 537mg; Carbs 28g; Fiber 3g; Sugar 10g; Protein 5g

Parmesan Beef Tart

Prep time: 10 minutes | Cook time: 25 minutes Servings: 4

½ cup grated parmesan cheese (about 1½ ounces)
1 cup heavy cream, very warm
⅛ teaspoon fine salt
⅛ teaspoon ground white pepper
1 large egg
1 large egg yolk

For serving/garnish:
2 cups arugula
1 cup heirloom cherry tomatoes, halved
4 slices Italian cured beef (omit for vegetarian)
Black pepper

1. Select the Air Fry mode. Set the Ninja Foodi Smart XL Pro temperature to 350°F/175°C. Select Level "3" and set the time on your Ninja Foodi Smart XL Pro Air Fryer Oven to 25 minutes. Press Start/Pause to begin preheating. Continue to the next step when it is done preheating. Grease four 4-ounce ramekins well. 2. Place the parmesan in a medium-sized bowl and pour in the warm cream. Stir well to mix and add the black pepper and salt. 3. In a separate medium-sized bowl, beat the egg and yolk until well mixed. Gradually stir in the warm parmesan mixture. 4. Pour the egg-and-cheese mixture into the prepared ramekins, cover the ramekins with foil, and place them in a casserole dish that will fit in your air fryer. 5. Pour boiling water into the casserole dish until the water reaches halfway up the sides of the ramekins. Place the casserole dish in the air fryer and bake until the flan is just set (the prepared mixture will jiggle slightly when moved), about 25 minutes. Check after 20 minutes. 6. Let the flan rest for 15 minutes. Serve with arugula, halved cherry tomatoes, and slices of Italian cured beef, if desired. Garnish with black pepper, if desired.
Per Serving: Calories 206; Fat 3.4g; Sodium 174mg; Carbs 35g; Fiber 9.4g; Sugar 5.9g; Protein 10.6g

Chapter 2 Vegetable and Sides Recipes | 35

Healthy Yellow Beans

Prep time: 10 minutes | Cook time: 10 minutes | Servings: 2

1-pound Yellow beans washed, and ends trimmed
1 lime, juiced

¼ teaspoon olive oil
Black pepper and salt to taste

1. Place the yellow beans in air fryer basket and pour the lime juice over beans. Season beans with black pepper and salt. Drizzle the beans with olive oil. 2. Insert its air fryer basket into the level 3 of the oven and close the door. Select the Air Fry mode, cook beans at 400°F/200°C for 10-minutes.
Per Serving: Calories 196; Fat 7.1g; Sodium 492mg; Carbs 21.6g; Fiber 2.9g; Sugar 0.8g; Protein 13.4g

Kale Chips

Prep time: 10 minutes | Cook time: 3 minutes | Servings: 2

1 head of kale
1 teaspoon soy sauce

1 tablespoon olive oil

Tear up kale into 1 ½-inch pieces. Wash clean and dry thoroughly. Toss with olive oil and soy sauce. Select the Air Fry mode, fry in air fryer at 390°F/200°C for 3-minutes.
Per Serving: Calories 275; Fat 1.4g; Sodium 582mg; Carbs 31.5g; Fiber 1.1g; Sugar 0.1g; Protein 9.8g

Crispy Zucchini

Prep time: 10 minutes | Cook time: 20 minutes | Servings: 6

4 egg whites
6 medium zucchinis, thinly sliced
4 tablespoons parmesan cheese, grated

½ teaspoon garlic powder
1 cup breadcrumbs
Black pepper and salt to taste

1. Select the Air Fry mode, preheat your air fryer to400°F/200°C. 2. Whisk salt, pepper and egg whites in small bowl. In another bowl, mix garlic powder, breadcrumbs, and parmesan cheese. 3. Dip zucchini slices into egg whites then coat them with breadcrumbs. 4. Place coated zucchini in air fryer basket and Insert its air fryer basket into the level 3 of the oven and close the door. cook for 20-minutes.
Per Serving: Calories 275; Fat 1.4g; Sodium 582mg; Carbs 31.5g; Fiber 1.1g; Sugar 0.1g; Protein 2.8g

Crispy Potato Tots

Prep time: 10 minutes | Cook time: 8 minutes | Servings: 2

1 large potato, diced
Black pepper and salt to taste

1 teaspoon onion, minced
1 tablespoon olive oil

1. Cover potatoes with water in saucepan and boil over medium-high heat. Drain the potatoes and place in a suitable bowl and mash potatoes. 2. Add olive oil, onion, pepper and salt to mashed potatoes and mix well. 3. Make small tots from potato mixture and place into air fryer basket. Insert its air fryer basket into the level 3 of the oven and close the door. Cook on "Air Fry" Mode, select level 3, and set its temperature to 380°F/195°C for 8-minutes. Shake basket. Insert its air fryer basket into the level 3 of the oven and close the door. Cook for another 5-minutes. Serve hot!
Per Serving: Calories 220; Fat 1.7g; Sodium 178mg; Carbs 1.7g; Fiber 0.2g; Sugar 0.2g; Protein 2.9g

Baked Potatoes

Prep time: 10 minutes | Cook time: 20 minutes | Servings: 4

4 potatoes
Black pepper and salt to taste

Olive oil as needed

1. Peel potatoes then cut them in half. Select the Air Fry mode, preheat your air fryer to 355°F/180°C Brush potatoes gently with oil, season with black pepper and salt. then cook in preheated air fryer for 10 minutes. Brush again with oil and insert its air fryer basket into the level 3 of the oven and close the door. cook for another 10 minutes.
Per Serving: Calories 268; Fat 10.4g; Sodium 411mg; Carbs 0.4g; Fiber 0.1g; Sugar 0.1g; Protein 4.6

Fried Asparagus

Prep time: 10 minutes | Cook time: 10 minutes | Servings: 4

10 asparagus spears,
Woody ends chopped off
Black pepper and salt to taste

1 garlic clove, minced
4 tablespoons olive oil

1. Select the Air Fry mode, preheat air fryer to400°F/200°C. for 5-minutes. Mix the garlic and oil in a suitable bowl. 2. Coat the asparagus with oil mixture and place it into air fryer basket. Season asparagus with black pepper and salt. 3. Insert its air fryer basket into the level 3 of the oven and close the door. cook for 10 minutes.
Per Serving: Calories 346; Fat 16.1g; Sodium 882mg; Carbs 1.3g; Fiber 0.5g; Sugar 0.5g; Protein 4.2g

Crispy Sweet Potato Wedges

Prep time: 10 minutes | Cook time: 20 minutes | Servings: 2

2 large sweet potatoes, cut into wedges
Black pepper and salt to taste
1 tablespoon red pepper flakes

1 teaspoon cumin
1 teaspoon mustard powder
1 teaspoon chili powder
1 tablespoon olive oil

1. Select the Air Fry mode, preheat air fryer to 350°F/175°C. Place all the recipe ingredients in a mixing bowl and stir well. 2. Add sweet potato wedges into air fryer basket. Insert its air fryer basket into the level 3 of the oven and close the door. And cook for 20-minutes. Make sure to shake the basket every 5-minutes.
Per Serving: Calories 223; Fat 11.7g; Sodium 721mg; Carbs 13.6g; Fiber 0.7g; Sugar 8g; Protein 5.7g

Fried Tomatoes

Prep time: 10 minutes | Cook time: 20 minutes | Servings: 2

2 tomatoes
Black pepper and salt to taste

Herbs of choice
Cooking spray

1. Cut the tomatoes in half. Spray the bottoms of them lightly with cooking spray. Turn all halves cut side up. Spray lightly with cooking spray. 2. Sprinkle with black pepper and your choice of dried herbs, such as oregano, parsley, basil, sage, thyme, etc. 3. Place the tomato halves on the top tray of air fryer with cut-side up. Insert its air fryer basket into the level 3 of the oven and close the door. Cook on Air Fry mode, turn air fryer to 320°F/160°C for 20 minutes.
Per Serving: Calories 256; Fat 16.4g; Sodium 1321mg; Carbs 19.2g; Fiber 2.2g; Sugar 4.2g; Protein 5.2g

Tomatoes Parmesan Provençal

Prep time: 10 minutes | Cook time: 15 minutes | Servings: 4

4 small ripe tomatoes connected on the vine
¼ teaspoon fine salt
¼ teaspoon black pepper
½ cup powdered parmesan cheese (about 1½ ounces)
For Garnish:
Fresh parsley leaves
Black pepper

2 tablespoons chopped fresh parsley
¼ cup minced onions
2 cloves garlic, minced
½ teaspoon chopped fresh thyme leaves

Sprig of fresh basil

1. Spray its air fryer basket with avocado oil. Select the Air Fry mode. Set the Ninja Foodi Smart XL Pro temperature to 350°F/175°C. Select Level "3" and set the time on your Ninja Foodi Smart XL Pro Air Fryer Oven to 15 minutes. Press Start/Pause to begin preheating. Continue to the next step when it is done preheating. 2. Slice the tops off the tomatoes without removing them from the vine. Do not discard the tops. Use a suitable spoon to scoop the seeds out of the tomatoes. Sprinkle the insides of the tomatoes with the black pepper and salt. 3. In a medium-sized bowl, mix the cheese, parsley, onions, garlic, and thyme. Stir to mix well. Divide the prepared mixture evenly among the tomatoes. 4. Spray avocado oil on the tomatoes and place them in its air fryer basket. Place the tomato tops in its air fryer basket next to, not on top of, the filled tomatoes. Insert its air fryer basket into the level 3 of the oven and close the door. Cook for 15 minutes, until the filling is golden and the tomatoes are soft yet still holding their shape. 5. Garnish with fresh parsley, black pepper, and a sprig of basil. Serve warm, with the tomato tops on the vine.
Per Serving: Calories 73; Fat 22g; Sodium 517mg; Carbs 3.3g; Fiber 0.2g; Sugar 1.4g; Protein 1.1g

Tasty Broccoli Florets

Prep time: 5 minutes | Cook time: 8 minutes | Servings: 4

4 cups broccoli florets
3 tablespoons melted ghee or butter-flavored coconut oil
1½ teaspoons fine salt or smoked

salt
Mayonnaise, for serving (optional; omit for egg-free)

1. Spray its air fryer basket with avocado oil. Select the Air Fry mode. Set the Ninja Foodi Smart XL Pro temperature to 400°F/200°C. Select Level "3" and set the time on your Ninja Foodi Smart XL Pro Air Fryer Oven to 10 minutes. Press Start/Pause to begin preheating. Continue to the next step when it is done preheating. 2. Place the broccoli in a suitable bowl. Drizzle it with the ghee, toss to coat, and sprinkle it with the salt. Transfer the broccoli to its air fryer basket. Insert its air fryer basket into the level 3 of the oven and close the door. and cook for 8 minutes, until soft and crisp on the edges.
Per Serving: Calories 47; Fat 1g; Sodium 518mg; Carbs 7g; Fiber 1.5g; Sugar 3.4g; Protein 2g

Air fried Spiral Sliced Zucchini

Prep time: 5 minutes | Cook time: 8 minutes | Servings: 2

1 (12-inch) zucchini
Special equipment:
Spiral slicer

1. Spray its air fryer basket with avocado oil. Select the Air Fry mode. Set the Ninja Foodi Smart XL Pro temperature to 400°F/200°C. Select Level "3" and set the time on your Ninja Foodi Smart XL Pro Air Fryer Oven to 8 minutes. Press Start/Pause to begin preheating. Continue to the next step when it is done preheating. 2. Cut the ends off the zucchini to create nice even edges. If you desire completely white noodles, peel the zucchini. Using a spiral slicer, cut the zucchini into long, thin noodles. 3. Spread out the zucchini noodles in its air fryer basket in a single layer, insert its air fryer basket into the level 3 of the oven and close the door. and cook for 8 minutes, until soft. Serve.
Per Serving: Calories 209; Fat 7.5g; Sodium 321mg; Carbs 34.1g; Fiber 4g; Sugar 3.8g; Protein 4.3g

Air-Fried Carrots

Prep time: 10 minutes | Cook time: 12 minutes | Servings: 4

2 cups carrots, peeled and chopped
¼ cup coriander

1 tablespoon olive oil
1 teaspoon cumin

1. Coat the carrots with cumin and oil. 2. Insert its air fryer basket into the level 3 of the oven and close the door. Cook on "Air Fry" Mode, select level 3, and set its temperature to 390°F/200°C for 12-minutes. Sprinkle with coriander over the carrots. Serve and enjoy!
Per Serving: Calories 105; Fat 25g; Sodium 532mg; Carbs 2.3g; Fiber 0.4g; Sugar 2g; Protein 8.3g

Cauliflower Rice

Prep time: 5 minutes | Cook time: 8 minutes | Servings: 4

2 cups cauliflower florets
⅓ cup sliced green onions, plus more for garnish
3 tablespoons wheat-free tamari or coconut aminos
1 clove garlic, smashed

1 teaspoon grated fresh ginger
1 teaspoon fish sauce or fine salt (see note)
1 teaspoon lime juice
⅛ teaspoon black pepper

1. Select the Air Fry mode. Set the Ninja Foodi Smart XL Pro temperature to 375°F/190°C. Select Level "3" and set the time on your Ninja Foodi Smart XL Pro Air Fryer Oven to 8 minutes. Press Start/Pause to begin preheating. Continue to the next step when it is done preheating. 2. Add the cauliflower to a food processor and pulse until it resembles grains of rice. 3. Place all the recipe ingredients, including the riced cauliflower, in a suitable bowl and stir well to mix. 4. Transfer the cauliflower mixture to a 6-inch pie pan or a casserole dish that will fit in your air fryer. Insert the air fryer dish into the level 3 of the oven and close the door. Cook for 8 minutes, until soft, shaking halfway through. Garnish with sliced green onions before serving.
Per Serving: Calories 185; Fat 11g; Sodium 355mg; Carbs 21g; Fiber 5.8g; Sugar 3g; Protein 4.7g

Garlic Mushrooms

Prep time: 5 minutes | Cook time: 10 minutes | Servings: 4

3 tablespoons unsalted butter
1 (8-ounce) package button mushrooms, sliced

2 cloves garlic, minced
3 sprigs fresh thyme leaves
½ teaspoon fine salt

1. Spray its air fryer basket with avocado oil. Select the Air Fry mode. Set the Ninja Foodi Smart XL Pro temperature to 400°F/200°C. Select Level "3" and set the time on your Ninja Foodi Smart XL Pro Air Fryer Oven to 10 minutes. Press Start/Pause to begin preheating. Continue to the next step when it is done preheating. 2. Place all the recipe ingredients in a medium-sized bowl. Use a spoon or your hands to coat the mushroom slices. 3. Place the mushrooms in its air fryer basket in one layer; work in batches if necessary. Insert its air fryer basket into the level 3 of the oven and close the door. Cook for 10 minutes, until slightly crispy and brown. Garnish with thyme sprigs before serving.
Per Serving: Calories 122; Fat 1.8g; Sodium 794mg; Carbs 17g; Fiber 8.9g; Sugar 1.6g; Protein 14.9g

Sweet Casserole

Prep time: 15 minutes | Cook time: 55 minutes Servings: 6

2 cups cauliflower florets
1 cup chicken broth or water
1 cup canned pumpkin puree
⅓ cup unsalted butter, melted (or coconut oil for dairy-free), plus more for the pan
¼ cup swerve confectioners'-style
Topping:
1 cup chopped pecans
½ cup blanched almond flour or pecan meal
½ cup swerve confectioners

sweetener or equivalent amount of liquid or powdered sweetener
¼ cup unsweetened, unflavored almond milk or heavy cream
2 large eggs, beaten
1 teaspoon fine salt
1 teaspoon vanilla extract

⅓ cup unsalted butter, melted
Chopped fresh parsley leaves, for garnish

1. Select the Air Fry mode. Set the Ninja Foodi Smart XL Pro temperature to 350°F/175°C. Select Level "3" and set the time on your Ninja Foodi Smart XL Pro Air Fryer Oven to 10 minutes. Press Start/Pause to begin preheating. Continue to the next step when it is done preheating. 2. Put the cauliflower florets in an air fryer-compatible 6-inch pie pan or casserole dish. To the pie pan, add the broth. Cook the cauliflower in the air fryer for 20 minutes, or until extremely soft. 3. Transfer the cauliflower to a food processor after it has been drained. You'll need the pie pan in the following step, so set it aside. Cauliflower should be thoroughly smoothened. Blend the pumpkin, eggs, almond milk, butter, sugar, salt, and vanilla until creamy. 4. Butter-grease the pie pan you used to cook the cauliflower. Fill the pan with the prepared mixture of cauliflower and pumpkin. Place aside. 5. Create the topping by thoroughly combining all the topping recipe components in a good bowl. Over the cauliflower-pumpkin mixture, crumble the topping. Cook in the air fryer for 30 to 35 minutes, or until thoroughly heated and the top is golden. If preferred, garnish the food with fresh parsley before serving.
Per Serving: Calories 163; Fat 11.5g; Sodium 918mg; Carbs 8.3g; Fiber 4.2g; Sugar 0.2g; Protein 7.4g

Roasted rainbow Carrots

Prep time: 5 minutes | Cook time: 12 minutes | Servings: 2

10 to 12 heirloom or rainbow carrots (about 1 pound), scrubbed but not peeled
1 teaspoon olive oil
salt and freshly ground black

pepper
1 tablespoon butter
1 teaspoon fresh orange zest
1 teaspoon chopped fresh thyme

1. Select Level 3. Select the "AIR FRY" function of Ninja Foodi Smart XL Pro Air Oven, set temperature to 400°F/200°C and time to 12 minutes. Select START/STOP to begin preheating. 2. Scrub the carrots and halve them lengthwise. Toss them in the olive oil, season with salt and freshly ground black pepper and transfer to the air fryer. 3. Air-fry for 12 minutes, shaking the basket every once in a while to rotate the carrots as they cook. 4. As soon as the carrots have finished cooking, add the butter, orange zest and thyme and toss all the ingredients together in the air fryer basket to melt the butter and coat evenly. 5. Serve warm.
Per Serving: Calories 170; Fat 8g; Sodium 345mg; Carbs 24g; Fiber 7g; Sugar 11g; Protein 2g

Burrata-Stuffed Tomatoes

Prep time: 5 minutes | Cook time: 5 minutes | Servings: 4

4 medium tomatoes
½ teaspoon fine salt
4 (2-ounce) burrata balls

Fresh basil leaves, for garnish
Extra-virgin olive oil, for drizzling

1. Select the Air Fry mode. Set the Ninja Foodi Smart XL Pro temperature to 300°F/150°C. Select Level "3" and set the time on your Ninja Foodi Smart XL Pro Air Fryer Oven to 10 minutes. Press Start/Pause to begin preheating. Continue to the next step when it is done preheating. 2. Core the tomatoes and scoop out the seeds and membranes using a melon baller or spoon. Sprinkle the insides of all the tomatoes with the salt. 3. Stuff each tomato with a ball of burrata. Insert its air fryer basket into the level 3 of the oven and close the door. cook for 5 minutes, until the cheese has softened. 4. Garnish with basil leaves and drizzle with olive oil. Serve warm.
Per Serving: Calories 102; Fat 7.6g; Sodium 545mg; Carbs 1.5g; Fiber 0.4g; Sugar 0.7g; Protein 7.1g

Spinach Cheese Tart

Prep time: 10 minutes | Cook time: 40 minutes | Servings: 6

Crust:
1 cup blanched almond flour
1 cup grated parmesan cheese
Filling:
4 ounces cream cheese (½ cup), softened
1 (8-ounce) package frozen chopped spinach, thawed and drained
½ cup artichoke hearts, drained

1 large egg

and chopped
⅓ cup shredded parmesan cheese, plus more for topping
1 large egg
1 clove garlic, minced
¼ teaspoon fine salt

1. Select the Air Fry mode. Set the Ninja Foodi Smart XL Pro temperature to 350°F/175°C. Select Level "3" and set the time on your Ninja Foodi Smart XL Pro Air Fryer Oven to 10 minutes. Press Start/Pause to begin preheating. Continue to the next step when it is done preheating.2. Make the crust: place the almond flour and cheese in a suitable bowl and mix until well mixed. Add the egg and mix until the prepared dough is well mixed and stiff.3. Press the prepared dough into a 6-inch pie pan. Bake for 8 to 10 minutes, until it starts to brown lightly.4. Meanwhile, make the filling: place the cream cheese in a suitable bowl and stir to break it up. Add the spinach, artichoke hearts, cheese, egg, garlic, and salt. Stir well to mix.5. Pour the spinach mixture into the prebaked crust and sprinkle with additional parmesan. Place in its air fryer basket. Insert its air fryer basket into the level 3 of the oven and close the door. Cook for 25 to 30 minutes, until cooked through.
Per Serving: Calories 103; Fat 8.4g; Sodium 117mg; Carbs 3.5g; Fiber 0.9g; Sugar 1.5g; Protein 5.1g

Cheesy Summer Vegetables Drizzle with Balsamic

Prep time: 5 minutes | Cook time: 17 minutes | Servings: 2

1 cup balsamic vinegar
1 zucchini, sliced
1 yellow squash, sliced
2 tablespoons olive oil
1 clove garlic, minced
½ teaspoon Italian seasoning

salt and freshly ground black pepper
½ cup cherry tomatoes, halved
2 ounces crumbled goat cheese
2 tablespoons chopped fresh basil, plus more leaves for garnish

1. Place the balsamic vinegar in a small saucepot on the stovetop. Boil the vinegar to a boil, lower the heat and manage to simmer uncovered for 20 minutes, until the mixture reduces and thickens. Set aside to cool. 2. Select Level 3. Select the "AIR FRY" function of Ninja Foodi Smart XL Pro Air Oven, set temperature to 390°F/200°C and time to 17 minutes. Select START/STOP to begin preheating. 3. Combine the zucchini and yellow squash in a large bowl. Add the olive oil, minced garlic, Italian seasoning, salt and pepper and toss to coat. 4. Air-fry the vegetables for 10 minutes, shaking the basket several times during the cooking process. Add the cherry tomatoes and continue to air-fry for another 5 minutes. Sprinkle the goat cheese over the vegetables and air-fry for 2 more minutes. 5. Drizzle with the balsamic reduction and season with freshly ground black pepper. Garnish with the fresh basil leaves.
Per Serving: Calories 360; Fat 19g; Sodium 114mg; Carbs 37g; Fiber 3g; Sugar 23g; Protein 8g

Crunchy Mac 'N' Cheese

Prep time: 10 minutes | Cook time: 15 minutes Servings: 4

2 cups frozen chopped cauliflower, thawed
2 ounces cream cheese (¼ cup), softened
¼ cup shredded gruyere or Swiss
¼ teaspoon fine salt
Topping:
¼ cup pork dust
¼ cup unsalted butter, melted
For Garnish:
Chopped fresh thyme or chives

cheese
¼ cup shredded sharp cheddar cheese
2 tablespoons finely diced onions
3 tablespoons beef broth

4 slices bacon, finely diced

1. Select the Air Fry mode. Set the Ninja Foodi Smart XL Pro temperature to 375°F/190°C. Select Level "3" and set the time on your Ninja Foodi Smart XL Pro Air Fryer Oven to 15 minutes. Press Start/Pause to begin preheating. Continue to the next step when it is done preheating. 2. Place the cauliflower on a paper towel and pat dry. Cut any large pieces of cauliflower into ½-inch pieces. 3. In a medium-sized bowl, stir the cream cheese, gruyere, cheddar, and onions. Slowly stir in the broth and mix well. Add the salt and stir to mix. Add the cauliflower and stir gently to mix the cauliflower into the cheese sauce. 4. Grease four 4-ounce ramekins with butter. Divide the cauliflower mixture among the ramekins, filling each three-quarters full. 5. Make the topping: in a suitable bowl, stir the pork dust, butter, and bacon until well mixed. Divide the topping among the ramekins. 6. Place the ramekins in the air fryer (if you're using a suitable air fryer, work in batches if necessary) and cook for 15 minutes, until the topping is browned and the bacon is crispy. 7. Garnish with fresh thyme or chives, if desired.8. Store leftovers in the ramekins covered with foil. Reheat in a preheated 375°F/190°C air fryer for 6 minutes, until the cauliflower is heated through and the top is crispy.
Per Serving: Calories 284; Fat 7.9g; Sodium 704mg; Carbs 38.1g; Fiber 1.9g; Sugar 1.9g; Protein 4.8g

Roasted Paprika Asparagus

Prep time: 5 minutes | Cook time: 10 minutes | Servings: 3

¾-pound fresh asparagus, trimmed
Coarse sea salt and ground black

pepper, to taste
1 teaspoon paprika
2 tablespoons olive oil

1. Install the wire rack on Level 3. Select the "AIR ROAST" function of Ninja Foodi Smart XL Pro Air Oven, set temperature to 400°F/200°C and time to 6 minutes. Select START/STOP to begin preheating. 2. Toss the asparagus with salt, black pepper, paprika, and olive oil. Transfer the asparagus spears to the air fryer basket. Place the basket in the air fryer. 3.Cook the asparagus for about 6 minutes, tossing them halfway through the cooking time. 4. Bon appétit!
Per Serving: Calories 110; Fat 6.3g; Sodium 304mg; Carbs 9.2g; Fiber 2.9g; Sugar 2.9g; Protein 2.9g

Air Fried Bok Choy

Prep time: 10 minutes | Cook time: 10 minutes | Servings: 4

2 tablespoons olive oil
2 tablespoons reduced-sodium soy sauce
2 teaspoons sesame oil
2 teaspoons chili-garlic sauce

2 cloves garlic, minced
1 head (about 1 pound) bok choy, sliced lengthwise into quarters
2 teaspoons black sesame seeds

1. Select the Air Fry mode. Set the Ninja Foodi Smart XL Pro temperature to 400°F/200°C. Select Level "3" and set the time on your Ninja Foodi Smart XL Pro Air Fryer Oven to 10 minutes. Press Start/Pause to begin preheating. Continue to the next step when it is done preheating. 2. In a suitable bowl, mix the olive oil, soy sauce, sesame oil, chili-garlic sauce, and garlic. Add the bok choy and toss, massaging the leaves with your hands if necessary, until thoroughly coated. 3. Spread the bok choy in the basket of the air fryer. Insert its air fryer basket into the level 3 of the oven and close the door. Tossing halfway through the cooking time to shake the basket, air fry for 7 to 10 minutes until the bok choy is soft and the tips of the leaves begin to crisp. Remove from the basket and let cool for a few minutes before coarsely chopping. Serve sprinkled with the sesame seeds.
Per Serving: Calories 174; Fat 13g; Sodium 552mg; Carbs 25g; Fiber 1.2g; Sugar 1.2g; Protein 7.7g

Buckwheat Bean Patties

Prep time: 5 minutes | Cook time: 15 minutes | Servings: 4

1 cup buckwheat, soaked
overnight and rinsed
1 cup canned kidney beans,
drained and well rinsed
¼ cup walnuts, chopped
1 tablespoon olive oil

1 small onion, chopped
1 teaspoon smoked paprika
Sea salt and ground black pepper,
to taste
½ cup bread crumbs

1. Select the "AIR FRY" function of Ninja Foodi Smart XL Pro Air Oven, set temperature to 380°F/200°C and time to 15 minutes. Select START/STOP to begin preheating. Mix all ingredients until everything is well combined. Form the mixture into four patties and arrange them in a lightly greased air fryer basket. 2. Slide basket into rails of Level 3. Cook the burgers for about 15 minutes until cooked through. Turn them over halfway through the cooking time. 3. Bon appétit!
Per Serving: Calories 198; Fat 8.7g; Sodium 236mg; Carbs 24.2g; Fiber 5.3g; Sugar 2.2g; Protein 8g

Garlic Breadsticks

Prep time: 10 minutes | Cook time: 12 minutes Servings: 6

Dough:
1¾ cups shredded mozzarella
cheese (about 7 ounces)
2 tablespoons unsalted butter
Garlic butter:
3 tablespoons unsalted butter,
softened
Topping:
½ cup shredded parmesan cheese
(about 2 ounces)
For serving:
½ cup marinara sauce

1 large egg, beaten
¾ cup blanched almond flour
⅛ teaspoon fine salt

2 cloves garlic, minced

1 teaspoon dried basil leaves
1 teaspoon dried oregano leaves

1. Select the Air Fry mode. Set the Ninja Foodi Smart XL Pro temperature to 400°F/195°C. Select Level "3" and set the time on your Ninja Foodi Smart XL Pro Air Fryer Oven to 10 minutes. Press Start/Pause to begin preheating. Continue to the next step when it is done preheating. Place a piece of parchment paper in a 6-inch square casserole dish and spray it with avocado oil. 2. Make the prepared dough: place the mozzarella cheese and butter in a microwave-safe bowl and microwave for 1 to 2 minutes, until the cheese is entirely melted. Stir well. Add the egg and, using a hand mixer on low speed, mix well. Add the almond flour and salt and mix well with the hand mixer. 3. Lay a piece of parchment paper on the countertop and place the prepared dough on it. Knead it for about 3 minutes; the prepared dough should be thick yet pliable. (note: if the prepared dough is too sticky, 4. Chill it in the refrigerator for an hour or overnight.) Place the prepared dough in the prepared casserole dish and use your hands to spread it out to fill the bottom of the casserole dish. 5. Make the garlic butter: in a suitable dish, stir the butter and garlic until well mixed. 6. Spread the garlic butter on top of the prepared dough. Top with the parmesan, basil, and oregano. Place in its air fryer basket. Insert its air fryer basket into the level 3 of the oven and close the door. Cook for 10 minutes, until golden and cooked through. 7. Cut into 1-inch-wide breadsticks and serve with marinara sauce, if desired.
Per Serving: Calories 270; Fat 14.6g; Sodium 394mg; Carbs 31.3g; Fiber 7.5g; Sugar 9.7g; Protein 6.4g

Crunchy Kohlrabi Fries

Prep time: 10 minutes | Cook time: 30 minutes | Servings: 4

2 pounds kohlrabi, peeled and cut
into ¼–½-inch fries

2 tablespoons olive oil
Black pepper and salt

1. Select the Air Fry mode. Set the Ninja Foodi Smart XL Pro temperature to 400°F/200°C. Select Level "3" and set the time on your Ninja Foodi Smart XL Pro Air Fryer Oven to 30 minutes. Press Start/Pause to begin preheating. Continue to the next step when it is done preheating. 2. In a suitable bowl, mix the kohlrabi and olive oil. Season to taste with black pepper and salt. Toss gently until thoroughly coated. 3. Spread the kohlrabi in a single layer in its air fryer basket. Insert its air fryer basket into the level 3 of the oven and close the door. Tossing halfway through the cooking time to shake the basket, air fry for 20 to 30 minutes until the fries are browned and crunchy.
Per Serving: Calories 280; Fat 2g; Sodium 821mg; Carbs 34.6g; Fiber 0g; Sugar 0g; Protein 10g

Parmesan Bruschetta

Prep time: 10 minutes | Cook time: 8 minutes | Servings: 6

1 small tomato, diced
2 tablespoons chopped fresh basil
leaves
1 teaspoon dried oregano leaves
¼ teaspoon fine salt
3 tablespoons unsalted butter,

softened
1 clove garlic, minced
1 recipe hot dog buns, cut into
twelve ½-inch-thick slices
¼ cup plus 2 tablespoons
shredded parmesan cheese

1. Spray its air fryer basket with avocado oil. Select the Air Fry mode. Set the Ninja Foodi Smart XL Pro temperature to 360°F/180°C Select Level "3" and set the time on your Ninja Foodi Smart XL Pro Air Fryer Oven to 4 minutes. Press Start/Pause to begin preheating. Continue to the next step when it is done preheating. 2. In a suitable bowl, stir the tomato, basil, oregano, and salt until well mixed. Set aside. 3. In another small bowl, mix the butter and garlic. Spread the garlic butter on one side of each hot dog bun slice. 4. Place the slices in its air fryer basket buttered side down, spaced about ⅛ inch apart. Insert its air fryer basket into the level 3 of the oven and close the door. Cook for 4 minutes. Remove the slices from the air fryer, flip them so that the buttered side is up, and top each slice with 1½ tablespoons of parmesan and a dollop of the tomato mixture. 5. Increase the air fryer temperature to 390°F/200°C and return the slices to its air fryer basket. Cook for another 4 minutes, until the bread is crispy and the cheese is melted. 6. Serve immediately
Per Serving: Calories 231; Fat 9g; Sodium 271mg; Carbs 32.8g; Fiber 6.4g; Sugar 7g; Protein 6.3g

Curried Cauliflower

Prep time: 10 minutes | Cook time: 20 minutes | Servings: 4

¼ cup olive oil
2 teaspoons curry powder
½ teaspoon salt
¼ teaspoon black pepper
1 head cauliflower, cut into bite-

size florets
½ red onion, sliced
2 tablespoons freshly chopped
parsley, for garnish

1. Select the Air Fry mode. Set the Ninja Foodi Smart XL Pro temperature to 400°F/200°C. Select Level "3" and set the time on your Ninja Foodi Smart XL Pro Air Fryer Oven to 20 minutes. Press Start/Pause to begin preheating. Continue to the next step when it is done preheating. 2. In a suitable bowl, mix curry powder, the olive oil, salt, and pepper. Add the cauliflower and onion. Toss gently until the vegetables are completely coated with the oil mixture. Transfer the vegetables to the basket of the air fryer. 3. Insert its air fryer basket into the level 3 of the oven and close the door. Tossing halfway through the cooking time to shake the basket, air fry for 20 minutes until the cauliflower is soft and beginning to brown. Top with the parsley, if desired, before serving.
Per Serving: Calories 351; Fat 11g; Sodium 150mg; Carbs 3.3g; Fiber 0.2g; Sugar 1g; Protein 3.2g

Roasted Broccoli with Sesame

Prep time: 10 minutes | Cook time: 10 minutes | Servings: 4

6 cups broccoli florets, cut into
bite-size pieces
1 tablespoon olive oil
¼ teaspoon salt
2 tablespoons sesame seeds
2 tablespoons rice vinegar

2 tablespoons reduced-sodium
soy sauce
2 tablespoons sesame oil
½ teaspoon swerve sugar
replacement
¼ teaspoon red pepper flakes

1. Select the Air Fry mode. Set the Ninja Foodi Smart XL Pro temperature to 400°F/200°C. Select Level "3" and set the time on your Ninja Foodi Smart XL Pro Air Fryer Oven to 10 minutes. Press Start/Pause to begin preheating. Continue to the next step when it is done preheating. 2. In a suitable bowl, toss the broccoli with the olive oil and salt until thoroughly coated. 3. Transfer the broccoli to its air fryer basket. Insert its air fryer basket into the level 3 of the oven and close the door. Tossing halfway through the cooking time to shake the basket, air fry for 10 minutes until the stems are soft and the edges are beginning to crisp. 4. Meanwhile, in the same large bowl, whisk the sesame seeds, vinegar, soy sauce, sesame oil, swerve, and red pepper flakes (if using). 5. Transfer the broccoli to the bowl and toss until thoroughly coated with the seasonings. Serve warm or at room temperature.
Per Serving: Calories 200; Fat 32g; Sodium 721mg; Carbs 2.6g; Fiber 0g; Sugar 0g; Protein 7.4g

Eggplant Mozzarella Lasagna

Prep time: 10 minutes | Cook time: 40 minutes | Servings: 4

1 small eggplant (about ¾ pound), sliced into rounds
2 teaspoons salt
1 tablespoon olive oil
1 cup shredded mozzarella, divided
1 cup ricotta cheese
1 large egg
¼ cup grated parmesan cheese
½ teaspoon dried oregano
1½ cups no-sugar-added marinara
1 tablespoon chopped fresh parsley

1. Coat a 6-cup casserole dish that fits in your air fryer with olive oil; set aside. 2. Spread the eggplant slices in a single layer on a suitable baking sheet and sprinkle with the salt. Let sit for 10 minutes. You can wipe off excess water and salt with a paper towel. Parmesan Zucchini-Tart. 3. Select the Air Fry mode. Set the Ninja Foodi Smart XL Pro temperature to 350°F/175°C. Select Level "3" and set the time on your Ninja Foodi Smart XL Pro Air Fryer Oven to 6 minutes. Press Start/Pause to begin preheating. Continue to the next step when it is done preheating. 4. Brush the eggplant with the olive oil and spread in a single layer in its air fryer basket. Insert its air fryer basket into the level 3 of the oven and close the door. Tossing halfway through the cooking time to turn the eggplant, air fry for 6 minutes until softened. Transfer the eggplant back to the baking sheet and let cool. 5. In a suitable bowl, mix ½ cup of the mozzarella with the ricotta, egg, parmesan, and oregano. To assemble the lasagna, spread a spoonful of marinara in the bottom of the casserole dish, followed by a layer of eggplant, a layer of the cheese mixture, and a layer of marinara. Repeat the layers until all of the ingredients are used, ending with the remaining ½ cup of mozzarella. Scatter the parsley on top. Cover the baking dish with foil. 6. Increase the air fryer to 370°F/185°C. Insert its air fryer basket into the level 3 of the oven and close the door. air fry for 30 minutes. Uncover the dish and continue baking for 10 minutes longer until the cheese begins to brown.
Per Serving: Calories 208; Fat 5g; Sodium 1205mg; Carbs 34.1g; Fiber 7.8g; Sugar 2.5g; Protein 5.9g

Vegetable Lasagna

Prep time: 10 minutes | Cook time: 45 minutes | Servings: 6

1 zucchini, sliced
1 yellow squash, sliced
8 ounces mushrooms, sliced
1 red bell pepper, cut into strips
1 tablespoon olive oil
2 cups ricotta cheese
2 cups grated mozzarella cheese,
Béchamel Sauce:
3 tablespoons butter
3 tablespoons flour
2½ cups milk
½ cup grated Parmesan cheese
divided
1 egg
1 teaspoon salt
freshly ground black pepper
¼ cup shredded carrots
½ cup chopped fresh spinach
8 lasagna noodles, cooked

½ teaspoon salt
Freshly ground black pepper
Pinch of ground nutmeg

1. Select Level 3. Select the "AIR FRY" function of Ninja Foodi Smart XL Pro Air Oven, set temperature to 400°F/200°C and time to 10 minutes. Select START/STOP to begin preheating. 2. Toss the zucchini, yellow squash, mushrooms and red pepper in a large bowl with the olive oil and season with salt and pepper. Air-fry for 10 minutes, shaking the basket once or twice while the vegetables cook. 3. While the vegetables are cooking, make the béchamel sauce and cheese filling. Add flour in melted butter and whisk, cooking for a couple of minutes. Add in milk and whisk until smooth. 4. Boil the mix and manage simmer until the sauce thickens. Stir in cheese and spice with the salt, pepper and nutmeg. Set the sauce aside. 5. Combine the ricotta cheese, 1¼ cups of the mozzarella cheese, egg, salt and pepper in a large bowl and stir until combined. Fold in the carrots and spinach. 6. When the vegetables have finished cooking, build the lasagna. Use a baking dish that is 6 inches in diameter and 4 inches high. Spread bechamel sauce on the bottom baking dish. 7. Top with two lasagna noodles, cut to fit the dish and overlapping each other a little. Spoon a third of the ricotta cheese mixture and then a third of the roasted veggies on top of the noodles. 8. Pour ½ cup of béchamel sauce on top and then repeat these layers two more times: noodles – cheese mixture – vegetables – béchamel sauce. Sprinkle the mozzarella cheese over the top. 9. Cover with foil, loosely so the aluminum doesn't touch the cheese. 10. Air-fry for 45 minutes, removing the foil for the last 2 minutes, to slightly brown the cheese on top.
Per Serving: Calories 162; Fat 5.3g; Sodium 1006mg; Carbs 3g; Fiber 2g; Sugar 0g; Protein 25g

Parmesan Zucchini Tart

Prep time: 10 minutes | Cook time: 60 minutes | Servings: 6

½ cup grated parmesan cheese, divided
1½ cups almond flour
1 tablespoon coconut flour
½ teaspoon garlic powder
¾ teaspoon salt, divided
¼ cup unsalted butter, melted
1 zucchini, thinly sliced
1 cup ricotta cheese
3 eggs
2 tablespoons heavy cream
2 cloves garlic, minced
½ teaspoon dried tarragon

1. Select the Air Fry mode. Set the Ninja Foodi Smart XL Pro temperature to 330°F/165°C. Select Level "3" and set the time on your Ninja Foodi Smart XL Pro Air Fryer Oven to 15 minutes. Press Start/Pause to begin preheating. Continue to the next step when it is done preheating. Coat a round 6-cup pan with olive oil and set aside. 2. In a suitable bowl, whisk ¼ cup of the parmesan with the almond flour, coconut flour, garlic powder, and ¼ teaspoon of the salt. Stir in the melted butter until the prepared dough resembles coarse crumbs. Press the prepared dough tightly into the bottom and up the sides of the prepared pan. Insert its air fryer basket into the level 3 of the oven and close the door. Air fry for 12 to 15 minutes until the crust begins to brown. Let cool to room temperature. 3. Meanwhile, place the zucchini in a colander and sprinkle with the remaining ½ teaspoon salt. Toss gently to distribute the salt and let sit for 30 minutes. 4. In a suitable bowl, whisk the ricotta, eggs, heavy cream, garlic, and tarragon. Gently stir in the zucchini slices. Pour the cheese mixture into the cooled crust and sprinkle with the remaining ¼ cup parmesan. 5. Increase the air fryer to 350°F/175°C. Select Level "3" and set the time on your Ninja Foodi Smart XL Pro Air Fryer Oven to 10 minutes. Press Start/Pause to begin preheating. Continue to the next step when it is done preheating. Place the pan in its air fryer basket, insert its air fryer basket into the level 3 of the oven and close the door. And air fry for 45 to 50 minutes, until set and a tester inserted into the center of the tart comes out clean. Serve warm or at room temperature.
Per Serving: Calories 250; Fat 2.6g; Sodium 358mg; Carbs 64.6g; Fiber 14.4g; Sugar 3.3g; Protein 9.9g

Crispy Bacon Wrapped Asparagus

Prep time: 10 minutes | Cook time: 10 minutes | Servings: 4

8 slices reduced-sodium bacon, cut in half
16 thick (about 1 pound)
asparagus spears, trimmed of woody ends

1. Select the Air Fry mode. Set the Ninja Foodi Smart XL Pro temperature to 350°F/175°C. Select Level "3" and set the time on your Ninja Foodi Smart XL Pro Air Fryer Oven to 10 minutes. Press Start/Pause to begin preheating. Continue to the next step when it is done preheating. 2. Wrap half a slice of bacon in the center of each stalk of asparagus. 3. Working in batches, if necessary, spread seam-side down in a single layer in its air fryer basket. Insert its air fryer basket into the level 3 of the oven and close the door. Cook for 10 minutes until the bacon is crisp and the stalks are soft.
Per Serving: Calories 220; Fat 13g; Sodium 542mg; Carbs 0.9g; Fiber 0.3g; Sugar 0.2g; Protein 5.6g

Buttery Mushrooms with Tomatoes

Prep time: 5 minutes | Cook time: 10 minutes | Servings: 4

1 pound cremini mushrooms, sliced
1 large tomato, sliced
2 tablespoons butter, melted
1 teaspoon rosemary, minced
1 teaspoon parsley, minced
1 teaspoon garlic, minced
Coarse sea salt and ground black pepper, to taste

1. Select Level 3. Select the "AIR FRY" function of Ninja Foodi Smart XL Pro Air Oven, set temperature to 400°F/200°C and time to 7 minutes. Select START/STOP to begin preheating. 2. Toss the mushrooms and tomatoes with the remaining ingredients. Toss until they are well coated on all sides. 3. Arrange the mushrooms in the Air Fryer basket. Place the basket into the air fryer, and cook your mushrooms for about 7 minutes, shaking the basket halfway through the cooking time. 4. Bon appétit!
Per Serving: Calories 84; Fat 6.3g; Sodium 132mg; Carbs 6.1g; Fiber 4.1g; Sugar 2g; Protein 2.8g

Butter Cauliflower with Garlic Blue Cheese Dip

Prep time: 10 minutes | Cook time: 10 minutes | Servings: 4

1 large head cauliflower, chopped into florets
1 tablespoon olive oil
Garlic Blue Cheese Dip
½ cup mayonnaise
¼ cup sour cream
2 tablespoons heavy cream
1 tablespoon fresh lemon juice

Black pepper and salt
¼ cup unsalted butter, melted
¼ cup hot sauce

1 clove garlic, minced
¼ cup crumbled blue cheese
Black pepper and salt

1. Select the Air Fry mode. Set the Ninja Foodi Smart XL Pro temperature to 400°F/200°C. Select Level "3" and set the time on your Ninja Foodi Smart XL Pro Air Fryer Oven to 10 minutes. Press Start/Pause to begin preheating. Continue to the next step when it is done preheating. 2. In a suitable bowl, mix the cauliflower and olive oil. Season to taste with black pepper and salt. Toss until the vegetables are thoroughly coated. 3. Working in batches, place half of the cauliflower in its air fryer basket. Insert its air fryer basket into the level 3 of the oven and close the door. Tossing halfway through the cooking time to shake the basket, air fry for 8 to 10 minutes until the cauliflower is evenly browned. Transfer to a suitable bowl and repeat with the remaining cauliflower. 4. In a suitable bowl, whisk the melted butter and hot sauce. 5. To make the dip: in a suitable bowl, mix the mayonnaise, sour cream, heavy cream, lemon juice, garlic, and blue cheese. Season to taste with black pepper and salt. 6. Just before serving, pour the butter mixture over the cauliflower and toss gently until thoroughly coated. Serve with the dip on the side.
Per Serving: Calories 248; Fat 30g; Sodium 660mg; Carbs 5g; Fiber 0g; Sugar 0g; Protein 4g

Cauliflower Gnocchi

Prep time: 10 minutes | Cook time: 30 minutes | Servings: 4

5 cups cauliflower florets
⅔ cup almond flour
½ teaspoon salt

¼ cup unsalted butter, melted
¼ cup grated parmesan cheese

1. In a food processor fitted with a metal blade, pulse the cauliflower until finely chopped. Transfer the cauliflower to a suitable microwave-safe bowl and cover it with a paper towel. Microwave for 5 minutes. Spread the cauliflower on a towel to cool. 2. When cool enough to handle, draw up the sides of the towel and squeeze tightly over a sink to remove the excess moisture. Return the cauliflower to the food processor and whirl until creamy. Sprinkle in the flour and salt and pulse until a sticky dough comes together. 3. Transfer the prepared dough to a workspace lightly floured with almond flour. Shape the prepared dough into a ball and divide into 4 equal sections. Roll each section into a rope 1 inch thick. Slice the prepared dough into squares with a sharp knife. 4. Select the Air Fry mode. Set the Ninja Foodi Smart XL Pro temperature to 400°F/200°C. Select Level "3" and set the time on your Ninja Foodi Smart XL Pro Air Fryer Oven to 30 minutes. Press Start/Pause to begin preheating. Continue to the next step when it is done preheating. 5. Place the gnocchi in a single layer in the basket of the air fryer and spray liberally with olive oil. Insert its air fryer basket into the level 3 of the oven and close the door. Tossing halfway through the cooking time to turn the gnocchi, air fry for 25 to 30 minutes until air fry for 25 to 30 minutes until the edges are golden and crispy. Transfer to a suitable bowl and toss with the melted butter and parmesan cheese.
Per Serving: Calories 257; Fat 10.4g; Sodium 431mg; Carbs 20g; Fiber 0g; Sugar 1.6g; Protein 2g

Buttery Sweet Potatoes

Prep time: 15 minutes | Cook time: 25 minutes | Servings: 2

2 sweet potatoes, peeled and halved
1 tablespoon butter, melted

1 teaspoon dried dill weed
Sea salt and red pepper flakes, crushed

1. Install the wire rack on Level 3. Select the "AIR ROAST" function of Ninja Foodi Smart XL Pro Air Oven, set temperature to 380°F/195°C and time to 15 minutes. Select START/STOP to begin preheating. 2. Toss the sweet potatoes with the remaining ingredients. Cook the sweet potatoes for 15 minutes, shaking them halfway through the cooking time. 3. Taste and adjust the seasonings. Bon appétit!
Per Serving: Calories 163; Fat 5.8g; Sodium 323mg; Carbs 26.2g; Fiber 3.6g; Sugar 5.4g; Protein 2g

Cauliflower with Gremolata

Prep time: 10 minutes | Cook time: 20 minutes | Servings: 4

2 tablespoons olive oil
1 tablespoon Italian seasoning
1 large head cauliflower, outer leaves removed and sliced
Gremolata
1 bunch Italian parsley (about 1 cup packed)
2 cloves garlic
Zest of 1 small lemon, plus 1–2

lengthwise through the core into thick "steaks"
Black pepper and salt
¼ cup parmesan cheese

teaspoons lemon juice
½ cup olive oil
Black pepper and salt to taste

1. Select the Air Fry mode. Set the Ninja Foodi Smart XL Pro temperature to 400°F/200°C. Select Level "3" and set the time on your Ninja Foodi Smart XL Pro Air Fryer Oven to 20 minutes. Press Start/Pause to begin preheating. Continue to the next step when it is done preheating. 2. In a suitable bowl, mix the olive oil and Italian seasoning. Brush both sides of each cauliflower "steak" liberally with the oil. Season to taste with black pepper and salt. 3. Spread the cauliflower in a single layer in its air fryer basket. Insert its air fryer basket into the level 3 of the oven and close the door. Tossing halfway through the cooking time to turn the "steaks," air fry for 15 to 20 minutes until the cauliflower is soft and the edges begin to brown. Sprinkle with the parmesan and air fry for 5 minutes longer. 4. To make the gremolata: in a food processor fitted with a metal blade, mix the parsley, garlic, and lemon zest and juice. With the motor running, then add the olive oil in a steady stream until the prepared mixture forms a bright green sauce. Season to taste with black pepper and salt. Serve the cauliflower steaks with the gremolata spooned over the top.
Per Serving: Calories 205; Fat 15g; Sodium 482mg; Carbs 17g; Fiber 3g; Sugar 2g; Protein 5g

Broccoli- Fritters

Prep time: 10 minutes | Cook time: 25 minutes | Servings: 4

1 cup broccoli florets
1 cup shredded mozzarella cheese
¾ cup almond flour
½ cup flaxseed meal, divided
2 teaspoons baking powder

1 teaspoon garlic powder
Black pepper and salt
2 eggs, lightly beaten
½ cup ranch dressing

1. Select the Air Fry mode. Set the Ninja Foodi Smart XL Pro temperature to 400°F/200°C. Select Level "3" and set the time on your Ninja Foodi Smart XL Pro Air Fryer Oven to 25 minutes. Press Start/Pause to begin preheating. Continue to the next step when it is done preheating. 2. In a food processor fitted with a metal blade, pulse the broccoli until very finely chopped. 3. Transfer the broccoli to a suitable bowl and add the mozzarella, almond flour, ¼ cup of the flaxseed meal, baking powder, and garlic powder. Stir until thoroughly mixed. Season to taste with black pepper and salt. Add the eggs and stir again to form a sticky dough. Shape the prepared dough into 1¼-inch fritters. 4. Place the remaining ¼ cup flaxseed meal in a shallow bowl and roll the fritters in the meal to form an even coating. 5. Spread the fritters in a single layer in the basket of the air fryer and spray liberally with olive oil. Insert its air fryer basket into the level 3 of the oven and close the door. Tossing halfway through the cooking time to shake the basket, air fry for 20 to 25 minutes until the fritters are golden and crispy. Serve with the ranch dressing for dipping.
Per Serving: Calories 208; Fat 24g; Sodium 715mg; Carbs 0.8g; Fiber 0.1g; Sugar 0.1g; Protein 1.9g

Roasted Fennel

Prep time: 5 minutes | Cook time: 15 minutes | Servings: 4

1-pound fennel bulbs, trimmed and sliced
2 tablespoons olive oil
1 teaspoon fresh garlic, minced

1 teaspoon dried parsley flakes
Kosher salt and ground black pepper, to taste

1. Select the "AIR FRY" function of Ninja Foodi Smart XL Pro Air Oven, set temperature to 370°F/185°C and time to 15 minutes. Select START/STOP to begin preheating. Toss all ingredients in a mixing bowl. 2. Place the basket in the air fryer on Level 3; Cook the fennel for about 15 minutes or until cooked through, check your fennel halfway through the cooking time. 3. Bon appétit!
Per Serving: Calories 97; Fat 6.9g; Sodium 211mg; Carbs 8.4g; Fiber 3.5g; Sugar 4.4g; Protein 1.4g

Crispy Sesame Tofu

Prep time: 10 minutes | Cook time: 20 minutes | Servings: 4

1 (16-ounce) block extra-firm tofu	1 tablespoon olive oil
2 tablespoons reduced-sodium soy sauce	1 tablespoon chili-garlic sauce
1 tablespoon toasted sesame oil	1½ teaspoons black sesame seeds
	1 scallion, thinly sliced

1. Press the tofu for at least 15 minutes by wrapping it in paper towels and setting a heavy pan on top so that the moisture drains. 2. Slice the tofu into bite-size cubes and transfer to a suitable bowl. Drizzle with the soy sauce, sesame oil, olive oil, and chili-garlic sauce. Cover and refrigerate for 1 hour or up to overnight. 3. Select the Air Fry mode. Set the Ninja Foodi Smart XL Pro temperature to 400°F/200°C. Select Level "3" and set the time on your Ninja Foodi Smart XL Pro Air Fryer Oven to 20 minutes. Press Start/Pause to begin preheating. Continue to the next step when it is done preheating. 4. Spread the tofu in a single layer in its air fryer basket. Pausing to shake the pan halfway through the cooking time, air fry for 15 to 20 minutes until crisp. Serve with any juices that accumulate in the bottom of the air fryer, sprinkled with the sesame seeds and sliced scallion.
Per Serving: Calories 275; Fat 1.4g; Sodium 582mg; Carbs 31.5g; Fiber 1.1g; Sugar 0.1g; Protein 9.8g

Mushroom Stuffed with Spinach

Prep time: 10 minutes | Cook time: 14 minutes | Servings: 4

2 tablespoons olive oil	½ cup chopped marinated artichoke hearts
4 large portobello mushrooms, stems removed and gills scraped out	1 cup frozen spinach, thawed and squeezed dry
½ teaspoon salt	½ cup grated parmesan cheese
¼ teaspoon pepper	2 tablespoons chopped fresh parsley
4 ounces goat cheese, crumbled	

1. Rub the olive oil over the portobello mushrooms until thoroughly coated. Sprinkle both sides with the black pepper and salt. Place top-side down on a clean work surface. 2. In a suitable bowl, mix the goat cheese, artichoke hearts, and spinach. Mash with the back of a fork until thoroughly mixed. Divide the cheese mixture among the mushrooms and sprinkle with the parmesan cheese. 3. Select the Air Fry mode. Set the Ninja Foodi Smart XL Pro temperature to 400°F/200°C. Select Level "3" and set the time on your Ninja Foodi Smart XL Pro Air Fryer Oven to 14 minutes. Press Start/Pause to begin preheating. Continue to the next step when it is done preheating. 4. Insert its air fryer basket into the level 3 of the oven and close the door. Air fry for 14 minutes until the mushrooms are soft and the cheese has begun to brown. Top with the parsley just before serving.
Per Serving: Calories 220; Fat 1.7g; Sodium 178mg; Carbs 1.7g; Fiber 0.2g; Sugar 0.2g; Protein 2.9g

Healthy Potato Latkes

Prep time: 15 minutes | Cook time: 60 minutes | Servings: 6

1 russet potato	Freshly ground black pepper
¼ onion	Canola or vegetable oil, in a spray bottle
2 eggs, lightly beaten	Chopped chives, for garnish
⅓ cup flour	Apple sauce
½ teaspoon baking powder	Sour cream
1 teaspoon salt	

1. Shred the potato and onion with a coarse box grater or a food processor with the shredding blade. squeeze the excess water of shredded vegetables. 2. Transfer the onion and potato to a large bowl and add the eggs, flour, baking powder, salt and black pepper. Mix well and prepare patties, about ¼-cup of mixture each. Brush or spray both sides of the latkes with oil. 3. Select the "AIR FRY" function of Ninja Foodi Smart XL Pro Air Oven, set temperature to 400°F/200°C and time to 13 minutes. Select START/STOP to begin preheating. 4. Air-fry the latkes in batches. Transfer one layer of the latkes to the air fryer basket and Place the basket in the air fryer. Slide basket into rails of Level 3, air-fry for 12 to 13 minutes, flipping them over halfway through the cooking time. 5. Transfer the finished latkes to a platter and cover with aluminum foil, or place them in a warm oven to keep warm. 6. Garnish the latkes with chopped chives and serve with sour cream and applesauce.
Per Serving: Calories 60; Fat 1g; Sodium 123mg; Carbs 12g; Fiber 1g; Sugar 0g; Protein 2g

Fried Zucchini Mix

Prep time: 10 minutes | Cook time: 7 minutes | Servings: 4

2 medium zucchini, thinly sliced	Zest and juice of ½ lemon
5 tablespoons olive oil, divided	1 clove garlic, minced
¼ cup chopped fresh parsley	¼ cup crumbled feta cheese
2 tablespoons chopped fresh mint	Black pepper

1. Select the Air Fry mode. Set the Ninja Foodi Smart XL Pro temperature to 400°F/200°C. Select Level "3" and set the time on your Ninja Foodi Smart XL Pro Air Fryer Oven to 7 minutes. Press Start/Pause to begin preheating. Continue to the next step when it is done preheating. 2. In a suitable bowl, toss the zucchini slices with 1 tablespoon of the olive oil. 3. Spread the zucchini in an even layer in its air fryer basket. Insert its air fryer basket into the level 3 of the oven and close the door. Tossing halfway through the cooking time to shake the basket, air fry for 5 to 7 minutes until soft and lightly browned per side. 4. Meanwhile, in a suitable bowl, mix the remaining 4 tablespoons olive oil, parsley, mint, lemon zest, lemon juice, and garlic. 5. Spread the zucchini on a plate and drizzle with the dressing. Sprinkle the feta and black pepper on top. Serve warm or at room temperature.
Per Serving: Calories 346; Fat 16.1g; Sodium 882mg; Carbs 1.3g; Fiber 0.5g; Sugar 0.5g; Protein 4.2g

Roasted Brussels Sprouts with Gorgonzola

Prep time: 10 minutes | Cook time: 25 minutes | Servings: 4

½ cup pecans	Black pepper and salt
1½ pounds fresh brussels sprouts, trimmed and quartered	¼ cup crumbled gorgonzola cheese
2 tablespoons olive oil	

1. Spread the pecans in a single layer of the air fryer and set the heat to 350°F/175°C. Cook on Air Fry mode. Select Level "3" and set the time on your Ninja Foodi Smart XL Pro Air Fryer Oven to 5 minutes. Press Start/Pause to begin preheating. Continue to the next step when it is done preheating. Air fry for 3 to 5 minutes until the pecans are lightly browned and fragrant. Transfer the pecans to a plate and continue preheating the air fryer, increasing the heat to 400°F/200°C. Select Level "3" and set the time on your Ninja Foodi Smart XL Pro Air Fryer Oven to 20 minutes. Press Start/Pause to begin preheating. Continue to the next step when it is done preheating. 2. In a suitable bowl, toss the brussels sprouts with the olive oil and season with black pepper and salt to taste. 3. Spread the brussels sprouts in a single layer in its air fryer basket. Insert its air fryer basket into the level 3 of the oven and close the door. Pausing halfway through the baking time to shake the basket, air fry for 20 to 25 minutes until the sprouts are soft and starting to brown on the edges. 4. Transfer the sprouts to a serving bowl and top with the toasted pecans and gorgonzola. Serve warm or at room temperature.
Per Serving: Calories 268; Fat 10.4g; Sodium 411mg; Carbs 0.4g; Fiber 0.1g; Sugar 0.1g; Protein 10.6g

Delicious Cauliflower Steaks Gratin

Prep time: 5 minutes | Cook time: 13 minutes | Servings: 2

1 head cauliflower	leaves
1 tablespoon olive oil	3 tablespoons grated Parmigiano-Reggiano cheese
Salt and freshly ground black pepper	2 tablespoons panko breadcrumbs
½ teaspoon chopped fresh thyme	

1. Select Level 3. Select the "AIR FRY" function of Ninja Foodi Smart XL Pro Air Oven, set temperature to 370°F/185°C and time to 10 minutes. Select START/STOP to begin preheating. 2. Cut two steaks out of the center of the cauliflower. To do this, cut the cauliflower in half and then cut one slice about 1-inch thick off each. 3. Brush the cauliflower with olive oil and spice with salt, freshly ground black pepper and fresh thyme. 4. Place the cauliflower steaks into the air fryer basket and air-fry for 6 minutes. Turn the steaks over and air-fry for another 4 minutes. 5. Combine the Parmesan cheese and panko breadcrumbs and sprinkle the mixture over the tops of both steaks and air-fry for another 3 minutes until the cheese has melted and the breadcrumbs have browned. 6. Serve this with some sautéed bitter greens and air-fried blistered tomatoes.
Per Serving: Calories 1646; Fat 146g; Sodium 498mg; Carbs 10g; Fiber 2g; Sugar 2g; Protein 77g

Cheesy Green Bean and Mushroom Casserole

Prep time: 10 minutes | Cook time: 22 minutes | Servings: 4

1 pound fresh green beans, ends trimmed, strings removed, and chopped into 2-inch pieces
1 (8-ounce) package sliced brown mushrooms
½ onion, sliced
1 clove garlic, minced
1 tablespoon olive oil
½ teaspoon salt
¼ teaspoon black pepper
4 ounces cream cheese
½ cup chicken stock
¼ teaspoon ground nutmeg
½ cup grated cheddar cheese

1. Select the Air Fry mode. Set the Ninja Foodi Smart XL Pro temperature to 400°F/200°C. Select Level "3" and set the time on your Ninja Foodi Smart XL Pro Air Fryer Oven to 10 minutes. Press Start/Pause to begin preheating. Continue to the next step when it is done preheating. Coat a 6-cup casserole dish with olive oil and set aside. 2. In a suitable bowl, mix the green beans, mushrooms, onion, garlic, olive oil, salt, and pepper. Toss well until the vegetables are thoroughly coated with the oil and seasonings. 3. Transfer the prepared mixture to its air fryer basket. Insert its air fryer basket into the level 3 of the oven and close the door. Tossing halfway through the cooking time to shake the basket, air fry for 10 minutes until soft. 4. While the vegetables are cooking, in a 2-cup glass measuring cup, warm the cream cheese and chicken stock in the microwave on high for 1 to 2 minutes until the cream cheese is melted. Add the nutmeg and whisk until smooth. 5. Transfer the vegetables to the prepared casserole dish and pour the cream cheese mixture over the top. Top with the cheddar cheese. Air fry for 10 minutes until the cheese is melted and beginning to brown.
Per Serving: Calories 353; Fat 5g; Sodium 818mg; Carbs 53.2g; Fiber 4.4g; Sugar 8g; Protein 7.3g

Thyme Zucchini Patties

Prep time: 10 minutes | Cook time: 10 minutes | Servings: 4

2 zucchinis, grated (about 1 pound)
1 teaspoon salt
¼ cup almond flour
¼ cup grated parmesan cheese
1 large egg
¼ teaspoon dried thyme
¼ teaspoon ground turmeric
¼ teaspoon black pepper
1 tablespoon olive oil
½ lemon, sliced into wedges

1. Place the zucchini in a suitable colander and sprinkle with the salt. Let sit for 5 to 10 minutes. Squeeze as all the liquid from the zucchini and place in a suitable mixing bowl. Add the almond flour, parmesan, egg, thyme, turmeric, and black pepper. Stir gently until thoroughly mixed. 2. Select the Air Fry mode. Set the Ninja Foodi Smart XL Pro temperature to 400°F/200°C. Select Level "3" and set the time on your Ninja Foodi Smart XL Pro Air Fryer Oven to 10 minutes. Press Start/Pause to begin preheating. Continue to the next step when it is done preheating. Cut a piece of parchment paper slightly smaller than the bottom of the air fryer. 3. Shape the prepared mixture into 8 patties and spread on the parchment paper. Brush lightly with the olive oil. Insert its air fryer basket into the level 3 of the oven and close the door. Tossing halfway through the cooking time to turn the patties, air fry for 10 minutes until golden. Serve warm with the lemon wedges.
Per Serving: Calories 223; Fat 11.7g; Sodium 721mg; Carbs 13.6g; Fiber 0.7g; Sugar 8g; Protein 5.7g

Colorful Winter Vegetable Patties

Prep time: 5 minutes | Cook time: 15 minutes | Servings: 3

1 carrot, shredded
1 parsnip, shredded
1 onion, chopped
1 garlic clove, minced
½ cup all-purpose flour
1 teaspoon cayenne pepper
Sea salt and ground black pepper, to taste
2 eggs, whisked

1. Select Level 3. Select the "AIR FRY" function of Ninja Foodi Smart XL Pro Air Oven, set temperature to 380°F/195°C and time to 15 minutes. Select START/STOP to begin preheating. 2. Mix all of the ingredients until everything is well combined. Form the mixture into three patties. 3. Place the basket with patties into the air fryer; cook the burgers for about 15 minutes or until cooked through. 4. Bon appétit!
Per Serving: Calories 184; Fat 3.3g; Sodium 366mg; Carbs 8g; Fiber 4.3g; Sugar 5.6g; Protein 8g

Fried Green Tomato Salad

Prep time: 10 minutes | Cook time: 10 minutes | Servings: 4

4 green tomatoes
½ teaspoon salt
1 large egg, lightly beaten
Buttermilk Dressing
1 cup mayonnaise
½ cup sour cream
2 teaspoons fresh lemon juice
2 tablespoons finely chopped fresh parsley
½ cup peanut flour
1 tablespoon creole seasoning
1 (5-ounce) bag arugula

1 teaspoon dried dill
1 teaspoon dried chives
½ teaspoon salt
½ teaspoon garlic powder
½ teaspoon onion powder

1. Slice the tomatoes into ½-inch slices and sprinkle with the salt. Let sit for 5 to 10 minutes. 2. Place the egg in a suitable shallow bowl. In another small shallow bowl, mix the peanut flour and creole seasoning. Dip tomato slice into the egg wash, then dip into the flour mixture, turning to coat evenly. 3. Select the Air Fry mode. Set the Ninja Foodi Smart XL Pro temperature to 400°F/200°C. Select Level "3" and set the time on your Ninja Foodi Smart XL Pro Air Fryer Oven to 10 minutes. Press Start/Pause to begin preheating. Continue to the next step when it is done preheating. 4. Working in batches if necessary, spread the tomato slices in a single layer in its air fryer basket and spray both sides lightly with olive oil. Insert its air fryer basket into the level 3 of the oven and close the door. Air fry until browned and crisp, 8 to 10 minutes. 5. To make the buttermilk dressing: in a suitable bowl, whisk the mayonnaise, sour cream, lemon juice, parsley, dill, chives, salt, garlic powder, and onion powder. 6. Serve the tomato slices on top of a bed of the arugula with the dressing on the side.
Per Serving: Calories 316; Fat 12.2g; Sodium 587mg; Carbs 12.2g; Fiber 1g; Sugar 1.8g; Protein 5.8g

Pork Rind Crusted Okra

Prep time: 10 minutes | Cook time: 10 minutes | Servings: 4

1 egg
½ cup milk
½ cup crushed pork rinds
¼ cup grated parmesan cheese
¼ cup almond flour
1 teaspoon garlic powder
¼ teaspoon black pepper
½ pound fresh okra, stems removed and chopped into 1-inch slices

1. In a shallow bowl, whisk the egg and milk. 2. In a second shallow bowl, mix the pork rinds, parmesan, almond flour, garlic powder, and black pepper. 3. Dip the okra into the egg mixture followed by the pork rind mixture. Press lightly to ensure an even coating. 4. Select the Air Fry mode. Set the Ninja Foodi Smart XL Pro temperature to 400°F/200°C. Select Level "3" and set the time on your Ninja Foodi Smart XL Pro Air Fryer Oven to 10 minutes. Press Start/Pause to begin preheating. Continue to the next step when it is done preheating. 5. Working in batches if necessary, spread the okra in a single layer in its air fryer basket and spray lightly with olive oil. Insert its air fryer basket into the level 3 of the oven and close the door. Tossing halfway through the cooking time to turn the okra, air fry for 10 minutes until soft and golden. Serve warm.
Per Serving: Calories 336; Fat 27.1g; Sodium 66mg; Carbs 1.1g; Fiber 0.4g; Sugar 0.2g; Protein 1.7g

Herby Italian Peppers

Prep time: 10 minutes | Cook time: 15 minutes | Servings: 3

3 Italian peppers, seeded and halved
1 tablespoon olive oil
Kosher salt and ground black pepper, to taste
1 teaspoon cayenne pepper
1 tablespoon fresh parsley, chopped
1 tablespoon fresh basil, chopped
1 tablespoon fresh chives, chopped

1. Select the "AIR FRY" function of Ninja Foodi Smart XL Pro Air Oven, set temperature to 400°F/200°C and time to 5 minutes. Select START/STOP to begin preheating. Toss the peppers with the olive oil, salt, black pepper, and cayenne pepper; place the peppers in the air fryer basket. 2. Place the basket in the air fryer on Level 3. Cook the peppers for about 13 minutes, shaking the basket halfway through the cooking time. 3. Taste, adjust the seasonings, and serve with the fresh herbs. Bon appétit!
Per Serving: Calories 77; Fat 4.6g; Sodium 359mg; Carbs 7.2g; Fiber 2.4g; Sugar 5g; Protein 1.4g

Asparagus with Cheese

Prep time: 5 minutes | Cook time: 10 minutes | Servings: 4

1-pound asparagus, trimmed	Sea salt and cayenne pepper, to
1 tablespoon sesame oil	taste
½ teaspoon onion powder	½ cup Pecorino cheese, preferably
½ teaspoon granulated garlic	freshly grated

1. Select the "AIR FRY" function of Ninja Foodi Smart XL Pro Air Oven, set temperature to 400°F/200°C and time to 6 minutes. Select START/STOP to begin preheating. 2. Toss the asparagus with the sesame oil, onion powder, granulated garlic, salt, and cayenne pepper. Arrange the asparagus spears in the air fryer basket. 3. Place the basket in the air fryer on Level 3. Cook the asparagus for about 6 minutes, tossing them halfway through the cooking time. 4. Top the asparagus with the cheese. Bon appétit!
Per Serving: Calories 120; Fat 8.5g; Sodium 244mg; Carbs 5.9g; Fiber 2.8g; Sugar 2.6g; Protein 6.9g

Cheesy Eggplant

Prep time: 15 minutes | Cook time: 50 minutes | Servings: 4 to 6

1 medium eggplant, cut into slices	freshly ground black pepper
kosher salt	2 tablespoons milk
½ cup breadcrumbs	½ cup mayonnaise
2 teaspoons dried parsley	1 cup tomato sauce
½ teaspoon Italian seasoning	1 (14-ounce) can diced tomatoes
½ teaspoon garlic powder	1 teaspoon Italian seasoning
½ teaspoon onion powder	2 cups grated mozzarella cheese
½ teaspoon salt	½ cup grated Parmesan cheese

1. Lay the eggplant slices on a baking sheet and sprinkle kosher salt generously over the top. Let the eggplant sit for 15 minutes while you prepare the rest of the ingredients. 2. Combine the breadcrumbs with parsley, Italian seasoning, garlic and onion powder, salt and black pepper in a dish. Whisk the milk with mayonnaise in a bowl until smooth. 3. Select Level 3. Select the "AIR FRY" function of Ninja Foodi Smart XL Pro Air Oven, set temperature to 400°F/200°C and time to 15 minutes. Select START/STOP to begin preheating. 4. Brush off salt from the eggplant slices and then coat both sides of each slice with the mayonnaise mixture. Dip the eggplant into the breadcrumbs. Place the eggplant on a Ninja sheet pan and grease both sides with olive oil. Air-fry the eggplant slices for 15 minutes, turning halfway through the cooking time. 5.While the eggplant is cooking, prepare the components of the eggplant Parmesan. Mix the tomato sauce, diced tomatoes and Italian seasoning in a bowl. Combine the mozzarella and Parmesan cheeses in a second bowl. 6. When all of the eggplant cooked build the dish with all the ingredient components. Cover the bottom of a 1½-quart round baking dish (6-inches in diameter) with a few tablespoons of the tomato sauce mixture. 7. Top with one third of the eggplant, tomato sauce and cheese. Repeat two more times, finishing with cheese on top. Cover with foil and Air-fry at 350°F/175°C for 30 minutes. 8. Remove the foil and air-fry for an additional 5 minutes to brown the cheese on top. Let the eggplant Parmesan rest for a few minutes to set up and cool to an edible temperature before serving.
Per Serving: Calories 184; Fat 7.4g; Sodium 103mg; Carbs 7g; Fiber 1g; Sugar 1g; Protein 22g

Mexican Sweet Potatoes

Prep time: 15 minutes | Cook time: 35 minutes | Servings: 4

1 pound sweet potatoes, scrubbed,	pepper, to taste
prick with a fork	½ teaspoon cayenne pepper
1 tablespoon olive oil	4 tablespoons salsa
Coarse sea salt and ground black	

1. Slide basket into rails of Level 3. Select the "AIR FRY" function of Ninja Foodi Smart XL Pro Air Oven, set temperature to 380°F/195°C and time to 35 minutes. Select START/STOP to begin preheating. 2. Sprinkle the sweet potatoes with olive oil, salt, black pepper, and cayenne pepper. Place the basket in the air fryer, cook the sweet potatoes for 35 minutes, checking them halfway through the cooking time. 3.Split the tops open with a knife. Top each potato with salsa and serve. 4. Bon appétit!
Per Serving: Calories 128; Fat 3.5g; Sodium 146mg; Carbs 22.1g; Fiber 3g; Sugar 2.1g; Protein 3g

Jerk Rubbed Grilled Corn

Prep time: 5 minutes | Cook time: 6 minutes | Servings: 4

1 teaspoon ground allspice	⅛ teaspoon ground cayenne
1 teaspoon dried thyme	pepper
½ teaspoon ground ginger	1 teaspoon salt
½ teaspoon ground cinnamon	2 tablespoons butter, melted
¼ teaspoon ground nutmeg	4 ears of corn, husked

1. Select the "AIR FRY" function of Ninja Foodi Smart XL Pro Air Oven, set temperature to 380°F/195°C and time to 6 minutes. Select START/STOP to begin preheating. 2. Combine all the spices in a bowl. Grease the corn evenly with the melted butter and then sprinkle the spices generously on all sides of each ear of corn. 3. Transfer the ears of corn to the air fryer basket. It's ok if they are crisscrossed on top of each other. Slide basket into rails of Level 3. Air-fry for 6 minutes, rotating the ears as they cook. 4. Brush more butter on at the end and sprinkle with any remaining spice mixture.
Per Serving: Calories 110; Fat 6g; Sodium 85mg; Carbs 15g; Fiber 2g; Sugar 2g; Protein 2g

Cheesy Mushrooms

Prep time: 5 minutes | Cook time: 10 minutes | Servings: 4

1-pound chestnut mushrooms,	Sea salt and ground black pepper,
quartered	to taste
1 tablespoon olive oil	4 tablespoons Pecorino Romano
1 garlic clove, pressed	cheese, shredded

1. Select the "AIR FRY" function of Ninja Foodi Smart XL Pro Air Oven, set temperature to 400°F/200°C and time to 7 minutes. Select START/STOP to begin preheating. 2. Toss the mushrooms with the oil, garlic, salt, and black pepper. Toss until they are well coated on all sides. 3. Arrange the mushrooms in the Air Fryer basket. Slide basket into rails of Level 3. 4. Cook your mushrooms for about 7 minutes, shaking the basket halfway through the cooking time. 5. Afterwards, toss the mushrooms with the cheese and serve immediately!
Per Serving: Calories 83; Fat 5.1g; Sodium 136mg; Carbs 6.4g; Fiber 1.7g; Sugar 3.4g; Protein 4g

Fried Brussels Sprouts with Ham

Prep time: 5 minutes | Cook time: 15 minutes | Servings: 4

1 pound Brussels sprouts,	Sea salt and freshly ground black
trimmed	pepper, to season
1 tablespoon peanut oil	2 (ounces) ham, diced

1. Select the "AIR FRY" function of Ninja Foodi Smart XL Pro Air Oven, set temperature to 380°F/195°C and time to 13 minutes. Select START/STOP to begin preheating. 2. Toss the Brussels sprouts with the remaining ingredients; then, arrange the Brussels sprouts in the Air Fryer basket. 3. Slide basket into rails of Level 3; cook the Brussels sprouts for 13 minutes, shaking the basket halfway through the cooking time. 4. Serve warm and enjoy!
Per Serving: Calories 93; Fat 4.3g; Sodium 311mg; Carbs 10.2g; Fiber 4.3g; Sugar 2.4g; Protein 6.2g

Asian Balsamic Fennel

Prep time: 5 minutes | Cook time: 15 minutes | Servings: 4

1-pound fennel bulbs, trimmed	crushed
and sliced	1 tablespoon balsamic vinegar
2 tablespoons sesame oil	1 tablespoon soy sauce
Sea salt and ground black pepper,	1 tablespoon sesame seeds, lightly
to taste	toasted
1 teaspoon red pepper flakes,	

1. Select Level 3. Select the "AIR FRY" function of Ninja Foodi Smart XL Pro Air Oven, set temperature to 370°F/185°C and time to 15 minutes. Select START/STOP to begin preheating. Toss the fennel with the sesame oil, salt, black pepper, and red pepper flakes. 2. Place the fennel in air fryer basket and cook the fennel for about 15 minutes or until cooked through; check your fennel halfway through the cooking time. 3.Toss the warm fennel with vinegar, soy sauce, and sesame seeds. Bon appétit!
Per Serving: Calories 114; Fat 8.3g; Sodium 144mg; Carbs 9.1g; Fiber 3.8g; Sugar 5.2g; Protein 2g

Spicy Gujarati Green Beans

Prep time: 5 minutes | Cook time: 10 minutes | Servings: 3

¾ pound fresh green beans, trimmed
1 garlic clove, minced
2 tablespoons olive oil
1 tablespoon soy sauce
1 teaspoon black mustard seeds
1 dried red chile pepper, crushed
Sea salt and ground black pepper, to taste

1. Select the "AIR FRY" function of Ninja Foodi Smart XL Pro Air Oven, set temperature to 380°F/195°C and time to 8 minutes. Select START/STOP to begin preheating. 2. Toss the green beans with the remaining ingredients; then arrange them in the Air Fryer basket. 3. Slide basket into rails of Level 3, cook the green beans for 8 minutes, tossing the basket halfway through the cooking time. 4. Enjoy!
Per Serving: Calories 136; Fat 9.8g; Sodium 239mg; Carbs 2.7g; Fiber 3.3g; Sugar 4.9g; Protein 2.7g

Crispy-Bottom Rice with Currants and Pistachios

Prep time: 10 minutes | Cook time: 25 minutes | Servings: 2

1 tablespoon olive oil
¼ teaspoon ground turmeric
2 cups cooked white basmati, jasmine, or other long-grain rice
¼ cup dried currants
¼ cup roughly chopped pistachios
Kosher salt and freshly ground black pepper
1 tablespoon thinly sliced fresh cilantro

1. Select Level 3. Select the "AIR FRY" function of Ninja Foodi Smart XL Pro Air Oven, set temperature to 300°F/150°C and time to 25 minutes. Select START/STOP to begin preheating. Combine the olive oil and turmeric in the bottom of a 7-inch round cake pan. 2. In a bowl, combine the rice, currants, and pistachios, season with salt and pepper, then spoon the rice over the oil, making sure to not stir the oil up into the rice. Very gently press the rice into an even layer. 3. Place the pan in the air fryer and cook until the rice is warmed through and the bottom is toasted and crispy, 20 to 25 minutes. 4. Break up the crust on the bottom of the rice, sprinkle with the cilantro, and serve warm.
Per Serving: Calories 567; Fat 16.3g; Sodium 478mg; Carbs 19g; Fiber 14g; Sugar 6g; Protein 18g

Colorful Roasted Vegetable Stromboli

Prep time: 9 minutes | Cook time: 20 minutes | Servings: 2

½ onion, thinly sliced
½ red pepper, julienned
½ yellow pepper, julienned
olive oil
1 small zucchini, thinly sliced
1 cup thinly sliced mushrooms
1½ cups chopped broccoli
1 teaspoon Italian seasoning
salt and freshly ground black
pepper
1 (14-ounce) tube refrigerated pizza dough
2 cups grated mozzarella cheese
¼ cup grated Parmesan cheese
½ cup sliced black olives, optional
Dried oregano
Pizza or marinara sauce

1. Select Level 3. Select the "AIR FRY" function of Ninja Foodi Smart XL Pro Air Oven, set temperature to 400°F/200°C and time to 7 minutes. Select START/STOP to begin preheating. 2. Toss the onions and peppers with a little olive oil and air-fry the vegetables for 7 minutes, shaking the basket once or twice while the vegetables cook. 3. Add the zucchini, mushrooms, broccoli and Italian seasoning to the basket. Add a little more olive oil and season with salt and freshly ground black pepper. 4. Air-fry for an additional 7 minutes, shaking the basket halfway through. Let the vegetables cool slightly while you roll out the pizza dough. 5. Press the pizza dough into a 13-inch by 11-inch rectangle, with the long side closest to you. Spread the mozzarella and Parmesan cheeses on the dough leaving an empty 1-inch border from the edge farthest away from you. 6. Spoon the roasted vegetables over the cheese, sprinkle the olives (if using) over everything and top with the remaining cheese. 7. Start rolling the stromboli toward the empty border. Tuck the dough ends and pinch to shut. Place the seam down and shape it to a U-shape to fit into the air fryer basket. 8. Cut small slits with a sharp knife evenly in the top of the dough, lightly brush the stromboli with a little oil and sprinkle with some dried oregano. 9. Grease the air fryer sheet pan with oil and transfer the U-shaped stromboli to the air fryer. Air-fry for 15 minutes, flipping the stromboli over after the first 10 minutes. 10. To remove, carefully flip over. Cut it into 2-inch slices and serve with pizza or marinara sauce.
Per Serving: Calories 387; Fat 26.3g; Sodium 602mg; Carbs 12g; Fiber 8g; Sugar 1g; Protein 26g

Cheesy Beans

Prep time: 5 minutes | Cook time: 9 minutes | Servings: 2

½ pound green beans
1 tablespoon sesame oil
Sea salt and ground black pepper,
to taste
2 ounces cheddar cheese, grated

1. Install the wire rack on Level 3. Select the "BAKE" function of Ninja Foodi Smart XL Pro Air Oven, set temperature to 380°F/195°C and time to 7 minutes. Select START/STOP to begin preheating. 2. Toss the green beans with the sesame oil; then, arrange them in the air fryer basket. 3. Place the basket in the air fryer, cook the green beans for 7 minutes, tossing the basket halfway through the cooking time. 4. Toss the warm green beans with the salt, black pepper, and cheese; stir to combine well. Enjoy!
Per Serving: Calories 154; Fat 9.6g; Sodium 444mg; Carbs 13g; Fiber 3.4g; Sugar 6.9g; Protein 6.4g

Buttery Garlicky Air Fried Potatoes

Prep time: 10 minutes | Cook time: 18 minutes | Servings: 3

¾ pound potatoes, quartered
1 tablespoon butter, melted
1 teaspoon garlic, pressed
1 teaspoon dried oregano
Sea salt and ground black pepper, to taste

1. Select the "AIR FRY" function of Ninja Foodi Smart XL Pro Air Oven, set temperature to 400°F/200°C and time to 18 minutes. Select START/STOP to begin preheating. Toss the potatoes with the remaining ingredients until well coated on all sides. 2. Arrange the potatoes in the Air Fryer basket. 3. Slide basket into rails of Level 3; cook the potatoes for about 18 minutes, shaking the basket halfway through the cooking time. 4. Serve warm and enjoy!
Per Serving: Calories 123; Fat 4g; Sodium 213mg; Carbs 20.1g; Fiber 2.5g; Sugar 0.9g; Protein 2.3g

Mushroom Patties

Prep time: 5 minutes | Cook time: 15 minutes | Servings: 3

¾-pound brown mushrooms, chopped
1 large eggs, whisked
½ cup breadcrumbs
½ cup parmesan cheese, grated
1 small onion, minced
1 garlic clove, minced
Sea salt and ground black pepper, to taste
1 tablespoon olive oil

1. Slide basket into rails of Level 3. Select the "AIR FRY" function of Ninja Foodi Smart XL Pro Air Oven, set temperature to 380°F/195°C and time to 15 minutes. Select START/STOP to begin preheating. 2. Mix all ingredients until everything is well combined. Form the mixture into three patties. 3. Place the basket in the air fryer, cook the burgers for about 15 minutes or until cooked through. Bon appétit!
Per Serving: Calories 184; Fat 11.1g; Sodium 332mg; Carbs 14g; Fiber 1.5g; Sugar 4g; Protein 9.4g

Curried Cauliflower with Yogurt

Prep time: 5 minutes | Cook time: 12 minutes | Servings: 2

4 cups cauliflower florets (about half a large head)
1 tablespoon olive oil
Cool Yogurt Drizzle
¼ cup plain yogurt
2 tablespoons sour cream
1 teaspoon lemon juice
pinch cayenne pepper
salt
1 teaspoon curry powder
½ cup toasted, chopped cashews

salt
1 teaspoon honey
1 tablespoon chopped cilantro,

1. Select the "AIR FRY" function of Ninja Foodi Smart XL Pro Air Oven, set temperature to 400°F/200°C and time to 12 minutes. Select START/STOP to begin preheating. 2. Toss the cauliflower florets with the olive oil, salt and curry powder, coating evenly. 3. Transfer the cauliflower to the air fryer basket and slide basket into rails of Level 3, air-fry for 12 minutes, shaking the basket twice during the cooking process. 4. While the cauliflower is cooking, make the cool yogurt drizzle by combining all ingredients in a bowl. 5. Serve it warm with the cool yogurt either underneath or drizzled over the top. Scatter the cashews and cilantro leaves around.
Per Serving: Calories 270; Fat 21g; Sodium 478mg; Carbs 18g; Fiber 5g; Sugar 5g; Protein 9g

Spicy Chinese Asparagus

Prep time: 5 minutes | Cook time: 10 minutes | Servings: 4

1-pound asparagus
4 teaspoons Chinese chili oil
½ teaspoon garlic powder

1 tablespoon soy sauce
½ teaspoon red pepper flakes, crushed

1. Select the "AIR FRY" function of Ninja Foodi Smart XL Pro Air Oven, set temperature to 400°F/200°C and time to 6 minutes. Select START/STOP to begin preheating. 2. Toss the asparagus with the remaining ingredients. Arrange the asparagus spears in the Air Fryer basket. 3. Slide basket into rails of Level 3, cook the asparagus for about 6 minutes, tossing them halfway through the cooking time. Bon appétit!
Per Serving: Calories 75; Fat 6g; Sodium 111mg; Carbs 5.6g; Fiber 2.5g; Sugar 2.9g; Protein 2.8g

Fried Tomatoes with Sriracha Mayo

Prep time: 10 minutes | Cook time: 24 minutes | Servings: 4

3 green tomatoes
salt and freshly ground black pepper
⅓ cup all-purpose flour
2 eggs
½ cup buttermilk
Sriracha Mayo
½ cup mayonnaise
1 to 2 tablespoons sriracha hot

1 cup panko breadcrumbs
1 cup cornmeal
olive oil, in a spray bottle
fresh thyme sprigs or chopped fresh chives

sauce
1 tablespoon milk

1. Cut the tomatoes in slices. Pat dry tomatoes slice and season generously with salt and pepper. 2. Place the flour in the first shallow dish, whisk the eggs and buttermilk together in the other dish, and combine the panko breadcrumbs and cornmeal in the third one. 3. Select Level 3. Select the "AIR FRY" function of Ninja Foodi Smart XL Pro Air Oven, set temperature to 400°F/200°C and time to 8 minutes. Select START/STOP to begin preheating. 4. Dredge the spiced slices in flour Then dip into the egg and finally press in the breadcrumbs. 5. Spray the air-fryer basket with oil. Transfer prepared tomato slices in and spray with olive oil. Air-fry for 8 minutes. Flip them and grease with oil, and air-fry for further 4 minutes until golden brown. 6. For sriracha mayo: Mix the mayonnaise, sriracha hot sauce and milk in a bowl. Stir well until smooth. 7. Serve the fried tomatoes hot with the sriracha mayo on the side.
Per Serving: Calories 340; Fat 5g; Sodium 321mg; Carbs 62g; Fiber 5g; Sugar 9g; Protein 12g

Delicious Falafel

Prep time: 5 minutes | Cook time: 10 minutes | Servings: 4

1 cup dried chickpeas
½ onion, chopped
1 clove garlic
¼ cup fresh parsley leaves
1 teaspoon salt
¼ teaspoon crushed red pepper
Tomato Salad
2 tomatoes, seeds removed and diced
½ cucumber, finely diced
¼ red onion, finely diced and rinsed with water
1 teaspoon red wine vinegar

flakes
1 teaspoon ground cumin
½ teaspoon ground coriander
1 to 2 tablespoons flour
olive oil

1 tablespoon olive oil
salt and freshly ground black pepper
2 tablespoons chopped fresh parsley

1. Soak chickpeas overnight on the counter. Then drain the them and place them in a food processor, along with the onion, garlic, parsley, spices and 1 tablespoon of flour. Pulse until coarse paste consistency appears in a processor. Knead and mix them together. 2. Scoop portions of the mix and shape into balls. Place the balls on a plate and refrigerate for at least 30 minutes. You should have between 12 and 14 balls. 3. Select Level 3. Select the "AIR FRY" function of Ninja Foodi Smart XL Pro Air Oven, set temperature to 380°F/195°C and time to 10 minutes. Select START/STOP to begin preheating. 4. Spray the falafel balls with oil and place them in the air fryer. Air-fry for 10 minutes, rolling them over and spraying them with oil again halfway through the cooking time so that they cook and brown evenly. 5. Serve with pita bread, hummus, cucumbers, hot peppers, tomatoes or any other fillings you might like.
Per Serving: Calories 203; Fat 10.9g; Sodium 402mg; Carbs 2g; Fiber 0g; Sugar 1g; Protein 23g

Smashed Baby Potatoes

Prep time: 5 minutes | Cook time: 18 minutes | Servings: 3 to 4

1½ pounds baby red or baby Yukon gold potatoes
¼ cup butter, melted
1 teaspoon olive oil
½ teaspoon paprika

1 teaspoon dried parsley
salt and freshly ground black pepper
2 scallions, finely chopped

1. Boil salted water. Boil potatoes for 18 minutes or until the potatoes are fork-tender. 2. Drain and place them to a cutting board to cool slightly. Spray or brush the bottom of a drinking glass with a little oil. Smash or flatten the potatoes by slowly pressing the glass down on each potato. 3. Try not to completely flatten the potato or smash it so hard that it breaks apart. Combine the melted butter, olive oil, paprika, and parsley together. 4. Select Level 3. Select the "AIR FRY" function of Ninja Foodi Smart XL Pro Air Oven, set temperature to 400°F/200°C and time to 18 minutes. Select START/STOP to begin preheating. 5. Spray the air fryer basket with oil and transfer one layer of the smashed potatoes into the basket. Grease with butter mixture and spice generously with salt and freshly ground black pepper. 6. Air-fry for 10 minutes. Carefully flip the potatoes over and air-fry for an additional 8 minutes until crispy and lightly browned. 7. Keep the potatoes warm. Sprinkle minced scallions over the potatoes and serve warm.
Per Serving: Calories 240; Fat 14g; Sodium 704mg; Carbs 28g; Fiber 2g; Sugar 2g; Protein 4g

Egg-Stuffed Peppers

Prep time: 5 minutes | Cook time: 15 minutes | Servings: 3

3 bell peppers, seeded and halved
1 tablespoon olive oil
3 eggs

3 tablespoons green onion, chopped
Sea salt and ground black pepper

1. Select Level 3. Select the "AIR FRY" function of Ninja Foodi Smart XL Pro Air Oven, set temperature to 390°F/200°C and time to 10 minutes. Select START/STOP to begin preheating. 2.Toss the peppers with the oil; place them in the Air Fryer basket. 3. Crack an egg into each bell pepper half. Sprinkle your peppers with the salt and black pepper. 4. Place the basket in the air fryer, cook the peppers for about 10 minutes. Top the peppers with green onions. Continue to cook for 4 minutes more. 5. Bon appétit!
Per Serving: Calories 143; Fat 9.1g; Sodium 203mg; Carbs 7.8g; Fiber 2.6g; Sugar 5.4g; Protein 6.4g

Cheese Broccoli Stuffed Potatoes

Prep time: 12 minutes | Cook time: 30 minutes | Servings: 2

2 large russet potatoes, scrubbed
1 tablespoon olive oil
salt and freshly ground black pepper
2 tablespoons butter
¼ cup sour cream
3 tablespoons half-and-half (or

milk)
1¼ cups grated Cheddar cheese, divided
¾ teaspoon salt
freshly ground black pepper
1 cup frozen baby broccoli florets, thawed and drained

1. Install the wire rack on Level 3. Select the "AIR ROAST" function of Ninja Foodi Smart XL Pro Air Oven, set temperature to 400°F/200°C and time to 30 minutes. Select START/STOP to begin preheating. 2. Rub the potatoes all over with olive oil and season generously with salt and freshly ground black pepper. Place the spiced potatoes into the air fryer sheet pan and air-fry for 30 minutes, turning the potatoes over halfway through the cooking process. 3. Let them rest for 5 minutes. Cut a large oval out of the top of both potatoes. Leaving half an inch of potato flesh around the edge of the potato, scoop the inside of the potato out and into a large bowl to prepare the potato filling. 4. Mash the scooped potato filling with a fork and add the butter, sour cream, half-and-half, 1 cup of the grated Cheddar cheese, salt and pepper to taste. Mix well and then fold in the broccoli florets. 5. Stuff the hollowed out potato shells with the potato and broccoli mixture. Mound the filling high in the potatoes – you will have more filling than room in the potato shells. 6. Transfer the stuffed potatoes back to the air fryer basket and air-fry at 360°F/180°C for 10 minutes. 7. Spread the Cheddar cheese on top of each stuffed potato, lower the heat to 330°F/165°C and air-fry for an additional minute or two to melt cheese.
Per Serving: Calories 295; Fat 21.2g; Sodium 94mg; Carbs 3g; Fiber 1g; Sugar 1g; Protein 23g

Potato and Cauliflower Stuffed Turnovers

Prep time: 10 minutes | Cook time: 35 minutes | Servings: 4

Dough:

2 cups all-purpose flour	¼ teaspoon dried thyme
½ teaspoon baking powder	¼ cup canola oil
1 teaspoon salt	½ to ⅔ cup water
Freshly ground black pepper	

Turnover Filling:

1 tablespoon canola or vegetable oil	2 cups cauliflower florets
1 onion, finely chopped	½ cup frozen peas
1 clove garlic, minced	2 tablespoons chopped fresh cilantro
1 tablespoon grated fresh ginger	Salt and freshly ground black pepper
½ teaspoon cumin seeds	
½ teaspoon fennel seeds	2 tablespoons butter, melted
1 teaspoon curry powder	mango chutney, for serving
2 russet potatoes, diced	

1. Start by making the dough. Mix the flour along with baking powder, salt, pepper and dried thyme in a mixing bowl or the bowl of a stand mixer. 2. Drizzle in the canola oil and pinch it together with your fingers to turn the flour into a crumby mixture. Stir in the water. Knead it for 5 minutes until it is smooth. Let the dough rest while you make the turnover filling. 3. Pre-heat a large skillet on the stovetop over medium-high heat. Add the oil and sauté the onion until it starts to become tender – about 4 minutes. 4. Add the garlic, ginger and cook for another minute. Add the dried spices and toss everything to coat. Add the potatoes and cauliflower to the skillet and pour in 1½ cups of water. 5. Simmer everything together for 20 to 25 minutes, or until the potatoes are soft and most of the water has evaporated. Stir well, crushing the potatoes and cauliflower a little as you do so. Stir in the peas and cilantro, season to taste with salt and freshly ground black pepper and set aside to cool. 6. Divide the dough into 4 balls. Roll the dough balls out into ¼-inch thick circles. Divide the cooled potato filling between the dough circles, placing an empty border around the edge of the dough. 7. Wet the dough edges with water and fold one edge of the circle over to meet the other edge of the circle, creating a half moon. Pinch the edges together with your fingers and then press the edge with the tines of a fork to decorate and seal. 8. Select Level 3. Select the "AIR FRY" function of Ninja Foodi Smart XL Pro Air Oven, set temperature to 380°F/195°C and time to 15 minutes. Select START/STOP to begin preheating. 9. Spray or brush the air fryer basket with oil. Brush the turnovers with the melted butter and place 2 turnovers into the air fryer basket. Air-fry for 15 minutes. 10. Flip the turnovers over and air-fry for another 5 minutes. Repeat with the remaining 2 turnovers. 11. Serving warm with mango chutney.
Per Serving: Calories 144; Fat 6.6g; Sodium 171mg; Carbs 2g; Fiber 0g; Sugar 1g; Protein 19g

Hasselback Potatoes with Sour Cream and Pesto

Prep time: 15 minutes | Cook time: 40 minutes | Servings: 2

2 russet potatoes	leaf parsley leaves
5 tablespoons olive oil	1 tablespoon chopped walnuts
Kosher salt and freshly ground black pepper	1 tablespoon grated parmesan cheese
¼ cup roughly chopped fresh chives	1 teaspoon fresh lemon juice
2 tablespoons packed fresh flat-	1 small garlic clove, peeled
	¼ cup sour cream

1. Place the potatoes on a hard surface and lay a chopstick or thin-handled wooden spoon to the side of each potato. Thinly slice the potatoes crosswise, letting the chopstick or spoon handle stop the blade of your knife, and stop ½ inch short of each end of the potato. Rub the potatoes with 1 tablespoon of the olive oil and season with salt and pepper. 2. Select Level 3. Select the "AIR FRY" function of Ninja Foodi Smart XL Pro Air Oven, set temperature to 375°F/190°C and time to 40 minutes. Select START/STOP to begin preheating. 3. Place the potatoes, cut-side up, in the air fryer and cook until golden brown and crisp on the outside and tender inside, about 40 minutes, drizzling the insides with olive oil and spice with salt and pepper halfway through. 4. Meanwhile, in a small blender or food processor, combine the remaining 3 tablespoons olive oil, the walnuts, parmesan, chives, parsley, lemon juice, and garlic and puree until smooth. Season the chive pesto with salt and pepper. 5. Transfer the potatoes to plates. Drizzle the potatoes with the pesto, letting it drip down into the grooves, then dollop each with sour cream and serve hot.
Per Serving: Calories 143; Fat 7.5g; Sodium 5mg; Carbs 19g; Fiber 3g; Sugar 3g; Protein 3g

Sweet Butternut Squash

Prep time: 5 minutes | Cook time: 15 minutes | Servings: 2 to 3

1 butternut squash, peeled	2 tablespoons honey
olive oil, in a spray bottle	Pinch ground cinnamon
Salt and freshly ground black pepper	Pinch ground nutmeg
	Chopped fresh sage
2 tablespoons butter, softened	

1. Select Level 3. Select the "AIR FRY" function of Ninja Foodi Smart XL Pro Air Oven, set temperature to 370°F/185°C and time to 5 minutes. Select START/STOP to begin preheating. 2. Cut the neck of the butternut squash into disks about ½-inch thick. Brush or spray the disks with oil and season with salt and freshly ground black pepper. 3. Transfer the butternut disks to the air fryer in one layer (or just ever so slightly overlapping). Air-fry for 5 minutes. 4. While the butternut squash is cooking, combine the butter, honey, cinnamon and nutmeg in a small bowl. Brush this mixture on the butternut squash, flip the disks over and brush the other side as well. Continue to air-fry for another 5 minutes. 5. Flip the disks once more, brush with more of the honey butter and air-fry for another 5 minutes. The butternut should be browning nicely around the edges. 6. Remove the butternut squash from the air-fryer and repeat with additional batches if necessary. Transfer to a serving platter, sprinkle with the fresh sage and serve.
Per Serving: Calories 310; Fat 8g; Sodium 578mg; Carbs 63g; Fiber 9g; Sugar 20g; Protein 5g

Cheesy Spinach Calzone

Prep time: 10 minutes | Cook time: 20 minutes | Servings: 2

⅔ cup frozen chopped spinach, thawed

1 cup grated mozzarella cheese	1 store-bought or homemade
1 cup ricotta cheese	pizza dough
½ teaspoon Italian seasoning	2 tablespoons olive oil
½ teaspoon salt	Pizza or marinara sauce
Freshly ground black pepper	

1. Drain and squeeze all the water out of the thawed spinach and set it aside. Mix the mozzarella cheese, ricotta cheese, Italian seasoning, salt and freshly ground black pepper together in a bowl. Stir in the chopped spinach. 2. Divide the dough, stretch or roll one half of the dough into a 10-inch circle. Spread the cheese and spinach mixture on half of the dough, leaving about one inch of dough empty around the edge. 3. Fold the half of the dough over the cheese mixture, almost to the edge of the bottom in a half moon. Fold the edge up over the top edge and crimp the dough around the edges in order to make the crust and seal the calzone. Brush the dough with olive oil. 4. Select Level 3. Select the "AIR FRY" function of Ninja Foodi Smart XL Pro Air Oven, set temperature to 360°F/180°C and time to 10 minutes. Select START/STOP to begin preheating. 5. Grease the air fryer basket with olive oil. Air-fry the calzones one at a time for 10 minutes, flipping the calzone over halfway through. 6. Serve with warm pizza or marinara sauce if desired.
Per Serving: Calories 463; Fat 15.5g; Sodium 553mg; Carbs 366g; Fiber 3g; Sugar 3g; Protein 41g

Sour and Spicy Brussels Sprouts

Prep time: 10 minutes | Cook time: 25 minutes | Servings: 2

¼ cup Thai sweet chili sauce	2 small shallots, cut into ¼-inch-thick slices
2 tablespoons black vinegar or balsamic vinegar	Kosher salt and freshly ground black pepper
½ teaspoon hot sauce, such as Tabasco	2 teaspoons lightly packed fresh cilantro leaves
8 ounces Brussels sprouts, trimmed (large sprouts halved)	

1. Select Level 3. Select the "AIR FRY" function of Ninja Foodi Smart XL Pro Air Oven, set temperature to 375°F/190°C and time to 20 minutes. Select START/STOP to begin preheating. 2. In a bowl, whisk the chili sauce, vinegar, and hot sauce. Add the Brussels sprouts and shallots, season with salt and pepper, and toss to combine. 3. Scrape the Brussels sprouts and sauce into a 7-inch round cake pan, metal cake pan, or foil pan. 4. Place in the Ninja air fryer and cook, stirring every 5 minutes, until the sauce reduced to a sticky glaze, about 20 minutes. 5. Transfer the Brussels sprouts to plates. Sprinkle with the cilantro and serve warm.
Per Serving: Calories 153; Fat 39g; Sodium 108mg; Carbs 25g; Fiber 6g; Sugar 2g; Protein 37g

Fried Eggplant with Harissa Yogurt

Prep time: 10 minutes | Cook time: 20 minutes | Servings: 2

1 eggplant, cut crosswise into
½-inch-thick slices
2 tablespoons vegetable oil
Kosher salt
Ground black pepper

½ cup plain yogurt
2 tablespoons harissa paste
1 garlic clove, grated
2 teaspoons honey

1. Select Level 3. Select the "AIR FRY" function of Ninja Foodi Smart XL Pro Air Oven, set temperature to 400°F/200°C and time to 15 minutes. Select START/STOP to begin preheating. 2. In a bowl, toss the eggplant and oil, spice with salt and pepper. Transfer to air fryer and cook, shaking every 5 minutes, until the eggplant caramelized and soft, about 15 minutes. 3. Meanwhile, in a bowl, whisk the yogurt, harissa, and garlic, spread onto a serving plate. 4. Place the warm eggplant over the yogurt and spread the honey just before serving.
Per Serving: Calories 18; Fat 0.3g; Sodium 7mg; Carbs 1g; Fiber 0g; Sugar 0g; Protein 2g

Whole Roasted Cauliflower

Prep time: 15 minutes | Cook time: 30 minutes | Servings: 2 to 4

3 tablespoons olive oil
2 tablespoons red wine vinegar
2 tablespoons Worcestershire sauce
2 tablespoons grated parmesan cheese
1 tablespoon Dijon mustard
4 garlic cloves, minced
4 oil-packed anchovy fillets,

drained and finely minced
Kosher salt and freshly ground black pepper
1 small head cauliflower (about 1 pound), green leaves trimmed and stem trimmed flush with the bottom of the head
1 tablespoon roughly chopped fresh flat-leaf parsley

1. Install the wire rack on Level 3. Select the "AIR ROAST" function of Ninja Foodi Smart XL Pro Air Oven, set temperature to 340°F/170°C and time to 25 minutes. Select START/STOP to begin preheating. 2. In a liquid measuring cup, whisk together the olive oil, vinegar, Worcestershire, parmesan, mustard, garlic, anchovies, and salt and pepper to taste. 3. Place the cauliflower head upside down on a cutting board and use a paring knife to make an "x" through the full length of the core. 4. Transfer the cauliflower head to a large bowl and pour half the dressing over it. Turn the cauliflower head to coat it in the dressing, then let it rest, stem-side up, in the dressing for 10 minutes and up to 30 minutes to allow the dressing to seep into all its nooks and crannies. 5. Transfer the cauliflower head, stem-side down, to the roast tray on sheet pan in the air fryer and cook for 25 minutes. 6. Drizzle the remaining dressing over the cauliflower and cook at 400°F/200°C until the top of the cauliflower is golden brown and the core is tender, about 5 minutes more. 7. Remove the pan from the air fryer and transfer the cauliflower to a large plate. Sprinkle with the parsley, if you like, and serve hot.
Per Serving: Calories 18; Fat 7.9g; Sodium 704mg; Carbs 6g; Fiber 3.6g; Sugar 6g; Protein 18g

Sweet And Savory Roast Carrots

Prep time: 1 minutes | Cook time: 25 minutes | Servings: 2

1½ tablespoons agave syrup or honey
1 tablespoon soy sauce
1 tablespoon vegetable oil
¼ teaspoon crushed red chile flakes
¼ teaspoon ground coriander

¼ teaspoon freshly ground black pepper
1 pound carrots, peeled and cut on an angle into ½-inch-thick slices
1 tablespoon finely chopped fresh flat-leaf parsley

1. Select Level 3. Select the "AIR FRY" function of Ninja Foodi Smart XL Pro Air Oven, set temperature to 375°F/190°C and time to 20 minutes. Select START/STOP to begin preheating. 2. In a bowl, combine the agave syrup, soy sauce, oil, chile flakes, coriander, black pepper, and carrots and toss to coat evenly. Transfer the carrots and dressing to a 7-inch round cake pan. 3. Place in the air fryer and cook stirring every 5 minutes, until the dressing is reduced to a glaze and the carrots are lightly caramelized and tender, about 20 minutes. 4. Sprinkle with the parsley before serving.
Per Serving: Calories 232; Fat 8.5g; Sodium 465mg; Carbs 38g; Fiber 1g; Sugar 15g; Protein 2g

Zucchini with Kimchi Sauce

Prep time: 10 minutes | Cook time: 20 minutes | Servings: 2

2 medium zucchini, ends trimmed (about 6 ounces each)
2 tablespoons olive oil
½ cup kimchi, finely chopped
¼ cup finely chopped fresh cilantro
¼ cup chopped parsley

2 tablespoons rice vinegar
2 teaspoons Asian chili-garlic sauce
1 teaspoon grated fresh ginger
Kosher salt and freshly ground black pepper

1. Select Level 3. Select the "AIR FRY" function of Ninja Foodi Smart XL Pro Air Oven, set temperature to 400°F/200°C and time to 15 minutes. Select START/STOP to begin preheating. 2. Brush the zucchini with half of the olive oil, place in the air fryer, and cook, turning halfway through, until lightly charred on the outside and tender, about 15 minutes. 3. In a bowl, mix the oil, with kimchi, cilantro, parsley, vinegar, chili-garlic sauce, and ginger. 4. Once the zucchini is finished cooking, transfer it to a colander and let it cool for 5 minutes. Using your fingers, pinch and break the zucchini into bite-size pieces, letting them fall back into the colander. 5. Season the zucchini with salt and pepper, toss to combine, then let sit a further 5 minutes to allow some of its liquid to drain. 6. Pile the zucchini atop the kimchi sauce on a plate and sprinkle with more parsley to serve.
Per Serving: Calories 718; Fat 23g; Sodium 964mg; Carbs 8g; Fiber 5g; Sugar 2g; Protein 37g

Elote Corn Salad

Prep time: 5 minutes | Cook time: 10 minutes | Servings: 2

2 ears of corn, shucked
1 tablespoon unsalted butter, at room temperature
1 teaspoon chili powder
¼ teaspoon garlic powder
Kosher salt and freshly ground black pepper
1 cup lightly packed fresh cilantro

leaves
1 tablespoon sour cream
1 tablespoon mayonnaise
1 teaspoon adobo sauce
2 tablespoons crumbled queso fresco
Lime wedges, for serving

1. Select Level 3. Select the "AIR FRY" function of Ninja Foodi Smart XL Pro Air Oven, set temperature to 400°F/200°C and time to 10 minutes. Select START/STOP to begin preheating. 2. Brush the corn all over with the butter, then sprinkle with the chili powder and garlic powder, and season with salt and pepper. 3. Place the corn in the air fryer and cook, turning halfway through, until charred and tender, about 10 minutes. 4. Transfer the it on cutting board, cut the kernels off and move to a bowl. Add the cilantro and toss to combine well. 5. In a bowl, stir the sour cream, mayonnaise, and adobo sauce. Spoon the adobo dressing over the top of corn. 6. Spice with the queso fresco and serve with lime wedges on the side.
Per Serving: Calories 218; Fat 2.4g; Sodium 641mg; Carbs 14g; Fiber 6g; Sugar 2g; Protein 19g

Charred Okra with Peanut Sauce

Prep time: 10 minutes | Cook time: 25 minutes | Servings: 2

¾ pound okra pods
2 tablespoons vegetable oil
Kosher salt and freshly ground black pepper
1 large shallot, minced
1 garlic clove, minced
½ Scotch bonnet chile, minced

(seeded if you want a milder sauce)
1 tablespoon tomato paste
1 cup vegetable stock or water
2 tablespoons natural peanut butter
Juice of ½ lime

1. Select Level 3. Select the "AIR FRY" function of Ninja Foodi Smart XL Pro Air Oven, set temperature to 400°F/200°C and time to 16 minutes. Select START/STOP to begin preheating. 2. In a bowl, toss the okra with 1 tablespoon of the oil and season with salt and pepper. Transfer the okra to the air fryer and cook, shaking the basket halfway through, until the okra is tender and lightly charred at the edges, about 16 minutes. 3. In a skillet, cook the shallot, garlic, and chile and cook, stirring, until soft, about 2 minutes. 4. Add tomato paste and cook for 30 seconds, then stir in the vegetable stock and peanut butter. Lower the heat to manage to simmer and cook until the sauce is reduced slightly and thickened, 3 to 4 minutes. 5. Remove from the heat, stir in the lime juice, and season with salt and pepper. 6. Place the peanut sauce on a plate, then pile the okra on top and serve hot.
Per Serving: Calories 18; Fat 1g; Sodium 106mg; Carbs 2g; Fiber 0g; Sugar 2g; Protein 0g

Stuffed Zucchini Boats

Prep time: 5 minutes | Cook time: 20 minutes | Servings: 2

Olive oil
½ cup onion, finely chopped
1 clove garlic, finely minced
½ teaspoon dried oregano
¼ teaspoon dried thyme
¾ cup couscous
1½ cups chicken stock, divided
1 tomato, seeds removed and finely chopped
½ cup coarsely chopped Kalamata olives

½ cup grated Romano cheese
¼ cup pine nuts, toasted
1 tablespoon chopped fresh parsley
1 teaspoon salt
Freshly ground black pepper
1 egg, beaten
1 cup grated mozzarella cheese, divided
2 thick zucchini

1. Pre-heat a sauté pan on the stovetop and add the oil and sauté the onion until it just starts to soften–about 4 minutes. Stir in the garlic, dried oregano and thyme. 2. Add the couscous and sauté for just a minute. Add 1¼ cups of the chicken stock and simmer over low heat for 3 to 5 minutes, until liquid has been absorbed and the couscous is soft. Remove the pan from heat and set it aside to cool slightly. 3. Fluff the couscous and add the tomato, Kalamata olives, Romano cheese, pine nuts, parsley, salt and pepper. Mix well. Add the remaining chicken stock, the egg and ½ cup of the mozzarella cheese. Stir to ensure everything is combined. 4. Cut each zucchini in half lengthwise. Then, trim each half of the zucchini into four 5-inch lengths. 5. Use a spoon to scoop out the center of the zucchini, leaving some flesh around the sides. Grease zucchini with olive oil and spice the cut side with salt and pepper. 6. Select Level 3. Select the "BAKE" function of Ninja Foodi Smart XL Pro Air Oven, set temperature to 380°F/195°C and time to 19 minutes. Select START/STOP to begin preheating. 7. Divide the couscous filling between the four zucchini boats. Press the filling and fill the inside of the zucchini. The filling should be mounded into the boats and rounded on top. 8. Transfer the zucchini boats to the air fryer basket and drizzle the stuffed zucchini boats with olive oil. Air-fry for 19 minutes. 9. Then, spread the mozzarella cheese on zucchini, pressing it down onto the filling lightly to prevent it from blowing around in the air fryer. Air-fry for one more minute to melt the cheese. 10. Transfer the finished zucchini boats to a serving platter and garnish with the chopped parsley.
Per Serving: Calories 494; Fat 36g; Sodium 690mg; Carbs 17g; Fiber 11g; Sugar 2g; Protein 28g

Mushroom, Zucchini and Bean Burgers

Prep time: 10 minutes | Cook time: 50 minutes | Servings: 4

1 cup diced zucchini, (about ½ medium zucchini)
1 tablespoon olive oil
Salt and freshly ground black pepper
1 cup chopped brown mushrooms (about 3 ounces)
1 small clove garlic
1 (15-ounce) can black beans, drained and rinsed
Mayonnaise, tomato, avocado and lettuce, for serving

1 teaspoon lemon zest
1 tablespoon chopped fresh cilantro
½ cup plain breadcrumbs
1 egg, beaten
½ teaspoon salt
Freshly ground black pepper
Whole-wheat pita bread, burger buns or brioche buns

1. Select Level 3. Select the "AIR FRY" function of Ninja Foodi Smart XL Pro Air Oven, set temperature to 400°F/200°C and time to 6 minutes. Select START/STOP to begin preheating. 2. Toss the zucchini with the olive oil, season with salt and freshly ground black pepper and air-fry for 6 minutes, shaking the basket once or twice while it cooks. 3. Transfer the zucchini to a food processor with the mushrooms, garlic and black beans and process until still a little chunky but broken down and pasty. 4. Transfer the mixture to a bowl. Add the lemon zest, cilantro, breadcrumbs and egg and mix well. Spice with salt and ground black pepper. Shape the mixture into four burger patties and refrigerate for at least 15 minutes. 5. Transfer two of the veggie burgers to the air fryer basket and air-fry for 12 minutes, flipping the burgers gently halfway through the cooking time. 6. Keep the burgers warm by loosely tenting them with foil while you cook the remaining two burgers. Return the first batch of burgers back into the air fryer with the second batch for the last two minutes of cooking to re-heat. 7. Serve on toasted whole-wheat pita bread, burger buns or brioche buns with some mayonnaise, tomato, avocado and lettuce.
Per Serving: Calories 314; Fat 27.2g; Sodium 182mg; Carbs 0g; Fiber 0g; Sugar 0g; Protein 17g

Cheese Soufflés with Asparagus and Mushroom

Prep time: 7 minutes | Cook time: 14 minutes | Servings: 3

Butter
Grated Parmesan cheese
3 button mushrooms, thinly sliced
8 spears asparagus, sliced ½-inch long
1 teaspoon olive oil
1 tablespoon butter
4½ teaspoons flour
Pinch paprika

Pinch ground nutmeg
Salt and freshly ground black pepper
½ cup milk
½ cup grated Gruyère cheese or other Swiss cheese (about 2 ounces)
2 eggs, separated

1. Butter three 6-ounce ramekins and dust with grated Parmesan cheese. 2. Select Level 3. Select the "AIR FRY" function of Ninja Foodi Smart XL Pro Air Oven, set temperature to 400°F/200°C and time to 7 minutes. Select START/STOP to begin preheating. 3. Toss the mushrooms and asparagus in a bowl with the olive oil. Transfer the vegetables to the air fryer and air-fry for 7 minutes, shaking the basket once or twice to redistribute the ingredients while they cook. 4. While the vegetables are cooking, make the soufflé base. Add the melted butter in flour, stir and cook for a minute or two. 5. Add the paprika, nutmeg, salt and pepper. Whisk the milk in and manage to a simmer to thicken. Stir in the cheese, to melt. 6. Let the mix cool for few minutes and then whisk the egg yolks in, one at a time. Stir in the cooked mushrooms and asparagus. Let this soufflé base cool. 7. In a bowl, whisk the egg whites till soft peak stage. Fold the whipped egg whites into the soufflé base, adding a little at a time. 8. Transfer the batter carefully to the buttered ramekins, leaving about ½-inch at the top. Place the ramekins in the air fryer and air-fry for 14 minutes. 9. The soufflés should have risen nicely and be brown on top. Serve immediately.
Per Serving: Calories 543; Fat 38.1g; Sodium 134mg; Carbs 27g; Fiber 1g; Sugar 0g; Protein 23g

Maitake Mushrooms with Sesame

Prep time: 10 minutes | Cook time: 15 minutes | Servings: 2

1 tablespoon soy sauce
3 teaspoons vegetable oil
2 teaspoons toasted sesame oil
1 garlic clove, minced
7 ounces maitake mushrooms

½ teaspoon flaky sea salt
½ teaspoon sesame seeds
½ teaspoon finely chopped fresh thyme leaves

1. Select Level 3. Select the "AIR FRY" function of Ninja Foodi Smart XL Pro Air Oven, set temperature to 300°F/150°C and time to 10 minutes. Select START/STOP to begin preheating. 2. In a bowl, mix soy sauce with 1 teaspoon of the vegetable oil, the sesame oil, and garlic. Place the maitake mushrooms in more or less a single layer in the air fryer, then drizzle with the soy sauce mixture. 3. Cook for 10 minutes. Sprinkle with the sea salt, sesame seeds, and thyme, then drizzle with the remaining 2 teaspoons vegetable oil. 4. Cook until the mushrooms are crisp at the edges and tender inside, about 5 minutes more. 5. Remove the mushrooms from the air fryer, transfer to plates, and serve hot.
Per Serving: Calories 605; Fat 31g; Sodium 833mg; Carbs 51g; Fiber 6g; Sugar 5g; Protein 74g

Sweet-Roasted Tomatoes

Prep time: 5 minutes | Cook time: 20 minutes | Servings: 2

10 ounces cherry tomatoes, halved
Kosher salt
2 tablespoons maple syrup
1 tablespoon vegetable oil

2 sprigs fresh thyme, stems removed
1 garlic clove, minced
Freshly ground black pepper

1. Select Level 3. Select the "AIR FRY" function of Ninja Foodi Smart XL Pro Air Oven, set temperature to 325°F/160°C and time to 20 minutes. Select START/STOP to begin preheating. 2. Place the tomatoes in a colander and sprinkle liberally with salt. Let stand for 10 minutes to drain. 3. Transfer the tomatoes cut-side up to a 7-inch round cake pan then drizzle with the maple syrup, followed by the oil. 4. Sprinkle with the thyme leaves and garlic and season with pepper. Place it in the air fryer and cook until the tomatoes are soft, collapsed, and lightly caramelized on top, about 20 minutes. 5. Serve with the tomatoes to a plate and drizzle with the juices from the pan to serve.
Per Serving: Calories 240; Fat 4.3g; Sodium 278mg; Carbs 47g; Fiber 7g; Sugar 3g; Protein 6g

Charred Sweet Potatoes

Prep time: 5 minutes | Cook time: 20 minutes | Servings: 2

4 small sweet potatoes, scrubbed clean (3 ounces each)
2 tablespoons olive oil
Kosher salt and freshly ground black pepper

2 tablespoons honey
½ teaspoon smoked paprika
Smoked or regular sea salt, for serving

1. Select Level 3. Select the "AIR FRY" function of Ninja Foodi Smart XL Pro Air Oven, set temperature to 375°F/190°C and time to 20 minutes. Select START/STOP to begin preheating. 2. In a bowl, toss together the sweet potatoes and olive oil, spice with salt and pepper, and toss again to coat evenly. 3. Transfer the sweet potatoes to the air fryer and cook, flipping halfway through, until tender on the inside and the skins are crisp and slightly blistered, about 20 minutes. 4. In a bowl, mix the honey and smoked paprika. When the potatoes are done, split them down the middle like a baked potato and lightly press the ends toward the middle to expose the flesh. 5. Transfer to plates, drizzle with the paprika honey, and sprinkle with the smoked salt before serving.
Per Serving: Calories 365; Fat 12.4g; Sodium 717mg; Carbs 29g; Fiber 3g; Sugar 10g; Protein 19g

Brussels Sprouts with Cheese

Prep time: 5 minutes | Cook time: 13 minutes | Servings: 4

1 pound Brussels sprouts, trimmed
1 tablespoon olive oil
Sea salt and ground black pepper,

to taste
4 ounces Provolone cheese, crumbled

1. Select the "AIR FRY" function of Ninja Foodi Smart XL Pro Air Oven, set temperature to 380°F/195°C and time to 10 minutes. Select START/STOP to begin preheating. 2. Toss the Brussels sprouts with the olive oil and spices until they are well coated on all sides; then, arrange the Brussels sprouts in the Air Fryer basket. 3. Slide basket into rails of Level 3, cook the Brussels sprouts for 10 minutes, shaking the basket halfway through the cooking time. 4. Toss the Brussels sprouts with the cheese and serve warm. Enjoy!
Per Serving: Calories 183; Fat 11.8g; Sodium 144mg; Carbs 11.8g; Fiber 4.5g; Sugar 3.2g; Protein 11.4g

Mole Cauliflower

Prep time: 5 minutes | Cook time: 35 minutes | Servings: 2

8 ounces medium cauliflower florets
1 tablespoon vegetable oil
Kosher salt and freshly ground black pepper
1½ cups vegetable broth
2 tablespoons New Mexico chile powder (or regular chili powder)
2 tablespoons salted roasted

peanuts
1 tablespoon sesame seeds
1 tablespoon finely chopped golden raisins
1 teaspoon kosher salt
1 teaspoon dark brown sugar
½ teaspoon dried oregano
¼ teaspoon cayenne pepper
⅛ teaspoon ground cinnamon

1. In a bowl, toss the cauliflower with the oil and season with salt and black pepper. Select Level 3. Select the "AIR FRY" function of Ninja Foodi Smart XL Pro Air Oven, set temperature to 375°F/190°C and time to 10 minutes. Select START/STOP to begin preheating. 2. Place the cauliflower into the air fryer sheet pan and cook until the cauliflower is lightly browned, about 10 minutes, stirring halfway through. 3. Meanwhile, in a small blender, combine the broth, chile powder, peanuts, sesame seeds, raisins, salt, brown sugar, oregano, cayenne, and cinnamon and puree until smooth. 4. Pour into a small saucepan or skillet and bring to a simmer over medium heat, then cook until reduced 3 to 5 minutes. 5. Pour the hot mole sauce over the cauliflower in the pan, stir to coat, then cook until the sauce is thickened and lightly charred on the cauliflower, about 5 minutes more. 6. Sprinkle with more sesame seeds and serve warm.
Per Serving: Calories 205; Fat 5.8g; Sodium 1481mg; Carbs 1g; Fiber 0g; Sugar 0g; Protein 35g

Chinese Chili-Roasted Broccoli

Prep time: 5 minutes | Cook time: 15 minutes | Servings: 2

12 ounces broccoli florets
2 tablespoons Asian hot chili oil
1 teaspoon ground Sichuan peppercorns
2 garlic cloves, chopped

One ginger, peeled and finely chopped
Kosher salt and freshly ground black pepper

1. Select Level 3. Select the "AIR FRY" function of Ninja Foodi Smart XL Pro Air Oven, set temperature to 375°F/190°C and time to 10 minutes. Select START/STOP to begin preheating. 2. In a bowl, toss together the broccoli, chili oil, Sichuan peppercorns, garlic, ginger, and salt and black pepper to taste. 3. Transfer to the air fryer basket and cook, shaking the basket halfway through, until lightly charred and tender, about 10 minutes. 4. Serve warm.
Per Serving: Calories 722; Fat 39g; Sodium 140mg; Carbs 7g; Fiber 2g; Sugar 4g; Protein 18g

Spicy Tangy Tahini Kale

Prep time: 5 minutes | Cook time: 15 minutes | Servings: 2 to 4

¼ cup tahini
¼ cup fresh lemon juice
2 tablespoons olive oil
1 teaspoon sesame seeds
½ teaspoon garlic powder

¼ teaspoon cayenne pepper
4 cups packed torn kale leaves
Kosher salt and freshly ground black pepper

1. Select Level 3. Select the "AIR FRY" function of Ninja Foodi Smart XL Pro Air Oven, set temperature to 350°F/175°C and time to 15 minutes. Select START/STOP to begin preheating. 2. In a bowl, whisk the tahini, lemon juice, olive oil, sesame seeds, garlic powder, and cayenne until smooth. Add the kale leaves, season with salt and black pepper, and toss in the dressing until completely coated. 3. Transfer the kale leaves to a 7-inch round cake or pizza pan , metal cake pan, or foil pan. 4. Place in the air fryer and cook stirring every 5 minutes, until the kale wilted and the top is lightly browned, about 15 minutes. 5. Serve warm.
Per Serving: Calories 300; Fat 24g; Sodium 117mg; Carbs 3g; Fiber 3g; Sugar 2g; Protein 18g

Chapter 3 Poultry Mains Recipes

Cornish Game Hens with Thai Cucumber Salad

Prep time: 10 minutes | Cook time: 23 minutes | Servings: 2

2 (1¼-pound) Cornish game hens, giblets discarded
6 tablespoons chopped fresh cilantro
2 tablespoons packed light brown sugar
1 tablespoon fish sauce
2 garlic cloves, minced
2 teaspoons grated lime zest
1 Thai chile, stemmed, seeded, and minced
1 tablespoon lime juice
2 teaspoons vegetable oil
1 teaspoon ground coriander
Black pepper and salt
1 English cucumber, halved lengthwise and sliced thin
1 small shallot, sliced thin
2 tablespoons chopped dry-roasted peanuts

1. lightly spray air-fryer basket with vegetable oil spray. To handle 1 hen at a time, cut along both sides of the hen's backbone with kitchen shears to remove it. Flatten hens and lay breast side up on counter. Using sharp chef's knife, cut through center of breast to make 2 halves. 2. Using your fingers, gently loosen skin covering breast and thighs. Pat hens dry with paper towels. Using metal skewer, poke 10 to 15 holes in fat deposits on top of breasts and thighs. Tuck wingtips underneath hens. 3. Mix ¼ cup cilantro, 4 teaspoons sugar, 2 teaspoons fish sauce, garlic, lime zest, 1 teaspoon oil, coriander, ½ teaspoon pepper, and ⅛ teaspoon salt in bowl. Rub cilantro mixture evenly under skin of hens and set aside to marinate for 10 minutes. 4. Spread hens breast side up in prepared basket. Insert its air fryer basket into the level 3 of the oven and close the door. Cook on Air Fry mode, set its temperature to 400°F/200°C and set the time to23 minutes, rotating hens halfway through (do not flip). Transfer hens to a cutting board, bandage loosely with aluminum foil, and leave for 5 minutes. 5. Meanwhile, whisk lime juice, Thai chile, remaining 2 teaspoons sugar, remaining 1 teaspoon fish sauce, and remaining 1 teaspoon oil in medium serving bowl. Add cucumber, shallot, and remaining 2 tablespoons cilantro and toss to coat. Season with black pepper and salt to taste and sprinkle with peanuts. Serve hens with cucumber salad and lime wedges.
Per Serving: Calories 210; Fat 17.8g; Sodium 619mg; Carbs 21g; Fiber 1.4g; Sugar 1.8g; Protein 3.4g

Buttery Turkey with Mushroom

Prep time: 5 minutes | Cook time: 25 minutes | Servings: 4

6 cups leftover turkey meat, skinless, boneless and shredded
A pinch of black pepper and salt
1 tablespoon parsley, chopped
1 cup chicken stock
3 tablespoons butter, melted
1 pound mushrooms, sliced
2 spring onions, chopped

1. Heat up a suitable pan that fits the air fryer with the butter over medium-high heat, then add the mushrooms and sauté for about 5 minutes. 2. Add the rest of the recipe ingredients, toss, put the pan in the machine. 3. Insert its air fryer basket into the level 3 of the oven and close the door. Cook on "Air Fry" Mode, select level 3, and set its temperature to 370°F/185°C for 20 minutes. Divide everything between plates and serve.
Per Serving: Calories 324; Fat 17.8 g; Sodium 363 mg; Carbs 8.9g; Fiber 0.5g; Sugar 1.9g; Protein 36.6g

Spicy Chicken Drumsticks

Prep time: 10 minutes | Cook time: 22 minutes | Servings: 2

2 teaspoons paprika
1 teaspoon packed brown sugar
1 teaspoon garlic powder
½ teaspoon dry mustard
½ teaspoon salt
Pinch pepper
4 (5-ounce) chicken drumsticks, trimmed
1 teaspoon vegetable oil
1 scallion, sliced

1. Mix paprika, sugar, garlic powder, mustard, salt, and pepper in bowl. Pat drumsticks dry with paper towels. Using metal skewer, poke 10 to 15 holes in skin of each drumstick. Rub liberally with oil and sprinkle evenly with spice mixture. 2. Spread drumsticks in air-fryer basket, spaced evenly apart, alternating ends. Insert its air fryer basket into the level 3 of the oven and close the door. set its temperature to 400°F/200°C. Cook for 25 minutes on "Air Fry" mode, flipping and rotating chicken halfway through, until chicken is crisp. 3. Transfer the prepared chicken to serving platter and let rest for 5 minutes. Sprinkle with scallion. Serve.
Per Serving: Calories 267; Fat 15.2 g; Sodium 479 mg; Carbs 13.9g; Fiber 0.1g; Sugar 12.9g; Protein 20.6g

Ricotta Adobo Chicken

Prep time: 15 minutes | Cook time: 18 minutes | Servings: 3

3 chicken thighs, boneless
2 teaspoons adobo sauce
1 teaspoon ricotta cheese
1 teaspoon dried thyme
Cooking spray to

1. In the mixing bowl mix up adobo sauce and ricotta cheese, then add dried thyme and churn the mixture. 2. Then brush the chicken thighs with adobo sauce mixture and leave for 10 minutes to marinate. 3. Select the Air Fry mode. Set the Ninja Foodi Smart XL Pro temperature to 385°F/195°C. Select Level "3" and set the time on your Ninja Foodi Smart XL Pro Air Fryer Oven to 18 minutes. Press Start/Pause to begin preheating. Continue to the next step when it is done preheating. 4. Spray its air fryer basket with cooking spray and put the chicken thighs inside. 5. Insert its air fryer basket into the level 3 of the oven and close the door. Cook them for 18 minutes.
Per Serving: Calories 398; Fat 27 g; Sodium 416mg; Carbs 34.9g; Fiber 6.5g; Sugar 6.9g; Protein 11.6g

Teriyaki Chicken

Prep time: 10 minutes | Cook time: 27 minutes | Servings: 2

¼ cup chicken broth
1½ tablespoons soy sauce
½ teaspoon grated fresh ginger
⅛ teaspoon red pepper flakes
4 (5-ounce) bone-in chicken thighs, trimmed
1 tablespoon sugar
1 tablespoon mirin
½ teaspoon cornstarch
6 ounces snow peas, strings removed
1 garlic clove, minced
⅛ teaspoon grated lemon zest plus ½ teaspoon juice
¼ teaspoon salt
Pinch pepper

1. Whisk broth, soy sauce, ginger, and pepper flakes in large bowl. Pat chicken dry with paper towels. Using metal skewer, poke skin side of chicken 10 to 15 times. Add to bowl with broth mixture and toss to coat; set aside to marinate for 10 minutes. 2. Remove chicken from marinade and pat dry with paper towels. Measure out 2 tablespoons remaining marinade and mix with sugar, mirin, and cornstarch in bowl; discard remainder. Microwave, stirring occasionally, until thickened and bubbling, about 1 minute, set aside. 3. Spread chicken skin side up in air-fryer basket, spaced evenly apart. Cook on Air Fry mode, insert its air fryer basket into the level 3 of the oven and close the door. and set its temperature to 400°F/200°C and set the time to 20 minutes. Cook until chicken is golden, crisp, and registers 195 degrees °F/90°C, 20 to 25 minutes, rotating chicken halfway through (do not flip). Brush chicken skin with thickened marinade mixture. Return basket to air fryer oven and cook until chicken is well browned, about 5 minutes. Transfer the prepared chicken to serving platter, cover with aluminum foil, and let rest for 5 minutes. Measure out ½ teaspoon fat from air-fryer drawer; discard remainder. 4. While chicken rests, toss reserved fat, snow peas, garlic, lemon zest, salt, and pepper in bowl and transfer to now-empty basket. Insert its air fryer basket into the level 3 of the oven and close the door. cook until snow peas are crisp-soft, 2 to 3 minutes. Transfer to serving bowl and toss with lemon juice. Serve with chicken.
Per Serving: Calories 396; Fat 23.2g; Sodium 622mg; Carbs 0.7g; Fiber 0g; Sugar 0g; Protein 5.6g

Chili Duck Bites

Prep time: 15 minutes | Cook time: 15 minutes | Servings: 4

8 ounces duck breast, skinless, boneless
1 teaspoon erythritol
½ teaspoon salt
1 teaspoon chili pepper
1 tablespoon butter, softened
½ teaspoon minced garlic
½ teaspoon dried dill

1. Cut the duck breast into small pieces (bites). Then sprinkle them with salt, chili pepper, erythritol, dried dill, and minced garlic. Leave the duck pieces for 10-15 minutes to marinate. 2. Meanwhile, Select the Air Fry mode. Set the Ninja Foodi Smart XL Pro temperature to 365°F/185°C. Select Level "3" and set the time on your Ninja Foodi Smart XL Pro Air Fryer Oven to 10 minutes. Press Start/Pause to begin preheating. Continue to the next step when it is done preheating. Sprinkle the duck bites with butter and put in the air fryer. 3. Insert its air fryer basket into the level 3 of the oven and close the door. Cook the duck bites for 10 minutes. Then shake well and cook for 5 minutes more at 400°F/200°C.
Per Serving: Calories 416; Fat 8.3 g; Sodium 208 mg; Carbs 22.9g; Fiber 0.5g; Sugar 19g; Protein 60.6g

Tandoori Chicken

Prep time: 10 minutes | Cook time: 20 minutes | Servings: 2

3 garlic cloves, minced
1 tablespoon grated fresh ginger
1½ teaspoons garam masala
1 teaspoon ground cumin
1 teaspoon chili powder
1 teaspoon vegetable oil

Black pepper and salt
½ cup plain whole-milk yogurt
4 teaspoons lime juice
4 (5-ounce) bone-in chicken thighs, trimmed

1. Mix garlic, ginger, garam masala, cumin, chili powder, oil, ¼ teaspoon salt, and ¼ teaspoon pepper in large bowl and microwave, about 30 seconds. Set aside to cool slightly, then stir in ¼ cup yogurt and 1 tablespoon lime juice. 2. Pat chicken dry with paper towels. Using metal skewer, poke skin side of chicken 10 to 15 times. Add to bowl with yogurt-spice mixture and toss to coat; set aside to marinate for 10 minutes. Meanwhile, mix remaining ¼ cup yogurt and remaining 1 teaspoon lime juice in clean bowl; season with black pepper and salt to taste and set aside. 3. Remove the marinated chicken from marinade and let the excess drip off, and spread skin side up in air-fryer basket, spaced evenly apart. Cook on Air Fry mode. Insert its air fryer basket into the level 3 of the oven and close the door. Set its temperature to 400°F/200°C and set the time to 20 minutes. Cook until chicken is well browned and crisp, 20 to 30 minutes, rotating chicken halfway through. 4. Transfer the prepared chicken to serving platter, tent loosely with aluminum foil, and let rest for 5 minutes. Serve with reserved yogurt-lime sauce.
Per Serving: Calories 382; Fat 32.5 g; Sodium 1363 mg; Carbs 3.2g; Fiber 0.2g; Sugar 1.9g; Protein 19.1g

Chicken Lettuce Wraps

Prep time: 10 minutes | Cook time: 12 minutes | Servings: 4

1 pound boneless, skinless chicken thighs, trimmed
1 teaspoon vegetable oil
2 tablespoons lime juice
1 shallot, minced
1 tablespoon fish sauce, plus extra for serving
2 teaspoons packed brown sugar
1 garlic clove, minced
⅛ teaspoon red pepper flakes

1 mango, peeled, and diced
⅓ cup chopped fresh mint
⅓ cup chopped fresh cilantro
⅓ cup chopped fresh Thai basil
1 head bibb lettuce (8 ounces), leaves separated
¼ cup dry-roasted peanuts, chopped
2 Thai chiles, stemmed and sliced thin

1. Pat the boneless chicken dry with paper towels and rub liberally with oil. Place chicken in air-fryer basket. Insert its air fryer basket into the level 3 of the oven and close the door. set its temperature to 400°F/200°C. Cook until chicken registers 175 degrees °F/80°C, for 12 to 16 minutes on "Air Fry" Mode. Flip once cooked half way through 2. Meanwhile, whisk lime juice, shallot, fish sauce, sugar, garlic, and pepper flakes in large bowl; set aside.3. Transfer the cooked chicken to a cutting board, cool slightly, and use two forks to cut it into bite-sized pieces. Add shredded chicken, mango, mint, cilantro, and basil to bowl with dressing and toss to coat. Serve chicken in lettuce leaves, passing peanuts, Thai chiles, and extra fish sauce separately.
Per Serving: Calories 398; Fat 37.8 g; Sodium 1463 mg; Carbs 2.5g; Fiber 0.2g; Sugar 0.5g; Protein 13.6g

Bacon Partridges

Prep time: 15 minutes | Cook time: 20 minutes | Servings: 6

18 ounces partridges, trimmed
3 ounces bacon, sliced
1 teaspoon minced ginger
1 tablespoon avocado oil

½ teaspoon garlic powder
1 teaspoon salt
½ teaspoon smoked paprika

1. Rub the partridges with minced ginger and sprinkle with garlic powder, salt, and smoked paprika. Then wrap the poultry in the sliced bacon and sprinkle with avocado oil. 2. Select the Air Fry mode. Set the Ninja Foodi Smart XL Pro temperature to 375°F/190°C. Select Level "3" and set the time on your Ninja Foodi Smart XL Pro Air Fryer Oven to 20 minutes. Press Start/Pause to begin preheating. Continue to the next step when it is done preheating. 3. Place the wrapped partridges in its air fryer basket. Insert its air fryer basket into the level 3 of the oven and close the door. Cook them for 20 minutes. 4. Flip them on another side after 10 minutes of cooking.
Per Serving: Calories 351; Fat 11g; Sodium 150mg; Carbs 3.3g; Fiber 0.2g; Sugar 1g; Protein 33.2g

Jerk Chicken

Prep time: 10 minutes | Cook time: 27 minutes | Servings: 2

1 tablespoon packed brown sugar
1 teaspoon ground allspice
1 teaspoon pepper
1 teaspoon garlic powder
¾ teaspoon dry mustard
¾ teaspoon dried thyme
½ teaspoon salt

¼ teaspoon cayenne pepper
2 (10-ounce) chicken leg quarters, trimmed
1 teaspoon vegetable oil
1 scallion, green part only, sliced thin
Lime wedges

1. Mix sugar, allspice, pepper, garlic powder, mustard, thyme, salt, and cayenne in bowl. Pat chicken dry with paper towels. Using metal skewer, poke 10 to 15 holes in skin of each chicken leg. Rub liberally with oil and sprinkle evenly with spice mixture. 2. Spread chicken skin side up in air-fryer basket, spaced evenly apart. Cook on Air Fry mode. Insert its air fryer basket into the level 3 of the oven and close the door. set its temperature to 400°F/200°C and set the time to 27 minutes. Cook until chicken is well browned and crisp and registers 195°F /90°C, 27 to 30 minutes, rotating chicken halfway through. 3. Transfer the prepared chicken to plate, tent loosely with aluminum foil, and let rest for 5 minutes. Sprinkle with scallion. Serve with lime wedges.
Per Serving: Calories 368; Fat 32.8 g; Sodium 507 mg; Carbs 0.6g; Fiber 0.1g; Sugar 1.1g; Protein 18.5g

Spicy Chicken Drumsticks with Cheese

Prep time: 10 minutes | Cook time: 22 minutes | Servings: 2

1½ teaspoons paprika
½ teaspoon cayenne pepper
¼ teaspoon salt
¼ teaspoon pepper
4 (5-ounce) chicken drumsticks, trimmed
1 teaspoon vegetable oil

3 tablespoons hot sauce
2 tablespoons unsalted butter
2 teaspoons molasses
¼ teaspoon cornstarch
2 tablespoons crumbled blue cheese

1. Mix paprika, cayenne, salt, and pepper in bowl. Pat drumsticks dry with paper towels. Using metal skewer, poke 10 to 15 holes in skin of each drumstick. Rub liberally with oil and sprinkle evenly with spice mixture. 2. Spread drumsticks in air-fryer basket, spaced evenly apart, alternating ends. Insert its air fryer basket into the level 3 of the oven and close the door. set its temperature to 400°F/200°C. Cook on Air Fry mode for 22 to 25 minutes, flipping chicken halfway through. Transfer the prepared chicken to large plate, tent loosely with aluminum foil, and let rest for 5 minutes. 3. Meanwhile, microwave hot sauce, butter, molasses, and cornstarch in large bowl, stirring occasionally, until hot, about 1 minute. Add chicken and toss to coat. Transfer to serving platter and sprinkle with blue cheese. Serve.
Per Serving: Calories 257; Fat 17 g; Sodium 674 mg; Carbs 13.9g; Fiber 4.2; Sugar 5.9g; Protein 13.6g

Turkey Cheese Burgers

Prep time: 10 minutes | Cook time: 12 minutes | Servings: 2

½ slice sandwich bread, torn into ½-inch pieces
2 tablespoons plain yogurt
Black pepper and salt
8 ounces ground turkey
1 ounce Monterey jack cheese,

shredded (¼ cup)
2 hamburger buns, toasted if desired
½ tomato, sliced thin
1 cup baby arugula

1. Mash bread, yogurt, ¼ teaspoon salt, and ¼ teaspoon pepper to paste in medium bowl using fork. Break up ground turkey into small pieces over bread mixture in bowl, then add Monterey jack, and lightly knead with hands until mixture forms cohesive mass. 2. Divide turkey mixture into 2 lightly packed balls, then gently flatten each into 1-inch-thick patty. Press center of each patty with your fingertips to create ¼-inch-deep depression. Season with black pepper and salt. 3. Spread patties in air-fryer basket, spaced evenly apart. Cook on Air Fry mode. Insert its air fryer basket into the level 3 of the oven and close the door. Set its temperature to 350°F/175°C and set the time to 12 minutes. Cook until burgers are browned and register 160°F/70°C, 12 to 16 minutes, flipping and rotating burgers halfway through. 4. Transfer burgers to large plate, tent loosely with aluminum foil, and let rest for 5 minutes. 5. Serve.
Per Serving: Calories 341; Fat 24.6 g; Sodium 401 mg; Carbs 12g; Fiber 0.1g; Sugar 11.9g; Protein 18.6g

Turkey Meatloaves

Prep time: 10 minutes | Cook time: 25 minutes | Servings: 2

1 shallot, minced	1 tablespoon whole milk
1 tablespoon vegetable oil	1 tablespoon Worcestershire sauce
1 garlic clove, minced	¼ teaspoon salt
½ teaspoon minced fresh thyme	¼ teaspoon pepper
or ⅛ teaspoon dried	1-pound ground turkey
Pinch cayenne pepper	¼ cup ketchup
1 slice white sandwich bread, torn	1 tablespoon cider vinegar
into ½-inch pieces	1 tablespoon packed brown sugar
1 large egg, lightly beaten	½ teaspoon hot sauce

1. Fold 1 long sheet of aluminum foil into a 4-inch wide sling to use with the air fryer basket. Lay a layer of foil across the basket widthwise, pressing it into the bottom and up the sides. If necessary, fold any extra foil so that the edges are flush with the top of the basket. Spray foil and the basket with vegetable oil spray sparingly. 2. Microwave shallot, oil, garlic, thyme, and cayenne in large bowl until fragrant, about 1 minute. Add bread, egg, milk, Worcestershire, salt, and pepper and mash mixture to paste using fork. Break up ground turkey into small pieces over bread mixture and knead with hands until well mixed. Shape turkey mixture into two 5 by 3-inch loaves. Spread loaves on sling in prepared basket, spaced evenly apart. 3. Mix ketchup, vinegar, sugar, and hot sauce in small bowl, then brush loaves with half of ketchup mixture. Cook on Air Fry mode. Insert its air fryer basket into the level 3 of the oven and close the door. set its temperature to 350°F /175°C. Cook until meatloaves register 160°F/80°C, 25 to 30 minutes, brushing with remaining ketchup mixture and rotating meatloaves using sling halfway through. 4. Using foil sling, carefully remove meatloaves from basket. Serve.
Per Serving: Calories 634; Fat 19.6 g; Sodium 1263 mg; Carbs 13.1g; Fiber 1.5g; Sugar 8.6g; Protein 96g

Chicken Fritters

Prep time: 20 minutes | Cook time: 16 minutes | Servings: 8

1-pound chicken breast, skinless,	1 teaspoon dried dill
boneless	½ teaspoon salt
3 ounces coconut flakes	1 egg yolk
1 tablespoon ricotta cheese	1 teaspoon avocado oil
1 teaspoon mascarpone	

1. Cut the chicken breast into the tiny pieces and put them in the bowl. 2. Add coconut flakes, ricotta cheese, mascarpone, dried dill, salt, and egg yolk. 3. Then make the chicken fritters with the help of the fingertips. 4. Select the Air Fry mode. Set the Ninja Foodi Smart XL Pro temperature to 360°F/180°C Select Level "3" and set the time on your Ninja Foodi Smart XL Pro Air Fryer Oven to 16 minutes. Press Start/Pause to begin preheating. Continue to the next step when it is done preheating. Line its air fryer basket with baking paper and put the chicken cakes in the air fryer. 5. Sprinkle the chicken fritters with avocado oil and cook for 8 minutes. Then flip the chicken fritters on another side and cook them for 8 minutes more.
Per Serving: Calories 506; Fat 48.3 g; Sodium 608 mg; Carbs 158.9g; Fiber 6.5g; Sugar 83.9g; Protein 12.6g

Crispy Buttermilk Fried Chicken

Prep time: 10 minutes | Cook time: 15 minutes | Servings: 4

1-pound chicken breast halves	1 cup all-purpose flour
Sea salt	½ teaspoon onion powder
Ground black pepper, to taste	1 teaspoon garlic powder
1 cup buttermilk	1 teaspoon smoked paprika

1. Select Level 3. Select the "AIR FRY" function of Ninja Foodi Smart XL Pro Air Fryer Oven, set temperature to 380°F/195°C and time to 12 minutes. Select START/STOP to begin preheating. 2. Toss together the chicken pieces, salt, and black pepper in a large bowl to coat. Stir in the buttermilk until the chicken is coated on all sides. Place the chicken in your refrigerator for about 6 hours. 3. In a shallow bowl, thoroughly combine the flour, onion powder, garlic powder, and smoked paprika. 4. Dredge the chicken in the spiced flour; shake off any excess and transfer them to a lightly oiled Air Fryer basket. 5. Cook the chicken breasts for 12 minutes, turning them over halfway through the cooking time. Enjoy!
Per Serving: Calories 266; Fat 3.9g; Sodium 478mg; Carbs 26.7g; Fiber 0.8g; Sugar 3g; Protein 28.2g

Fried Chicken with Thyme

Prep time: 20 minutes | Cook time: 75 minutes | Servings: 4

16 ounces whole chicken	1 teaspoon salt
1 tablespoon dried thyme	1 tablespoon avocado oil
1 teaspoon ground cumin	

1. Cut the chicken into halves and sprinkle it with dried thyme, cumin, and salt. Then brush the chicken halves with avocado oil. 2. Select the Air Fry mode. Set the Ninja Foodi Smart XL Pro temperature to 365°F/185°C. Select Level "3" and set the time on your Ninja Foodi Smart XL Pro Air Fryer Oven to 60 minutes. Press Start/Pause to begin preheating. Continue to the next step when it is done preheating. 3. Put the chicken halves in its air fryer basket. Insert its air fryer basket into the level 3 of the oven and close the door. Cook them for 60 minutes. 4. Then flip the chicken halves on another side and cook them for 15 minutes more.
Per Serving: Calories 148; Fat 0.3 g; Sodium 3 mg; Carbs 38.9g; Fiber 0.5g; Sugar 33.9g; Protein 0.6g

Mascarpone Chicken Fillets

Prep time: 15 minutes | Cook time: 12 minutes | Servings: 4

1 tablespoon fresh basil, chopped	1 tablespoon nut oil
4 ounces mozzarella, sliced	1 teaspoon chili flakes
12 ounces chicken fillet	1 teaspoon mascarpone

1. Brush the air fryer pan with nut oil. Then cut the chicken fillet on 4 Servings and beat them gently with a kitchen hammer. 2. After this, sprinkle the chicken fillets with chili flakes and put in the air fryer pan in one layer. Top the fillets with fresh basil and sprinkle with mascarpone. 3. After this, top the chicken fillets with sliced mozzarella. 4. Select the Air Fry mode. Set the Ninja Foodi Smart XL Pro temperature to 375°F/190°C. Select Level "3" and set the time on your Ninja Foodi Smart XL Pro Air Fryer Oven to 12 minutes. 5. Put the pan with caprese chicken fillets in its air fryer basket. Insert its air fryer basket into the level 3 of the oven and close the door. Cook them for 12 minutes.
Per Serving: Calories 386; Fat 10.3 g; Sodium 238 mg; Carbs 72.9g; Fiber 4.5g; Sugar 59g; Protein 2.6g

Turkey and Spinach

Prep time: 5 minutes | Cook time: 15 minutes | Servings: 4

1-pound turkey meat, ground and	2 tablespoons coconut aminos
browned	4 cups spinach leaves
1 tablespoon garlic, minced	A pinch of black pepper and salt
1 tablespoon ginger, grated	

1. In a suitable pan that fits your air fryer, mix all the recipe ingredients and toss. 2. Put the pan in its air fryer basket. Insert its air fryer basket into the level 3 of the oven and close the door. Cook on "Air Fry" Mode, select level 3, and set its temperature to 380°F/195°C for 15 minutes divide everything into bowls and serve.
Per Serving: Calories 116; Fat 2.3 g; Sodium 15 mg; Carbs 18.9g; Fiber 4.5g; Sugar 2.2g; Protein 6g

Chinese Chicken Wings

Prep time: 15 minutes | Cook time: 20 minutes | Servings: 6

6 chicken wings	1 teaspoon minced garlic
1 tablespoon coconut aminos	2 tablespoons apple cider vinegar
1 teaspoon ground ginger	1 tablespoon olive oil
1 teaspoon salt	1 chili pepper, chopped

1. Put the chicken wings in the bowl and sprinkle with coconut aminos and ground ginger. Add salt, minced garlic, apple cider vinegar, olive oil, and chopped chili. Mix up the chicken wings and leave them for 15 minutes to marinate. 2. Meanwhile, Select the Air Fry mode. Set the Ninja Foodi Smart XL Pro temperature to 380°F/195°C. Select Level "3" and set the time on your Ninja Foodi Smart XL Pro Air Fryer Oven to 20 minutes. Press Start/Pause to begin preheating. Continue to the next step when it is done preheating. 3. Place the marinated chicken wings in the air fryer. Insert its air fryer basket into the level 3 of the oven and close the door. and cook them for 20 minutes. Flip the chicken wings from time to time to avoid the burning.
Per Serving: Calories 257; Fat 10.4g; Sodium 431mg; Carbs 20g; Fiber 0g; Sugar 1.6g; Protein 21g

Tasty Thyme Chicken Breast

Prep time: 10 minutes | Cook time: 17 minutes | Servings: 3

1-pound chicken breast, skinless, boneless	1 teaspoon salt
1 teaspoon garlic powder	½ teaspoon black pepper
1 teaspoon dried thyme	½ teaspoon cayenne pepper
	2 teaspoons sunflower oil

1. Sprinkle the chicken breast with garlic powder, dried thyme, salt, black pepper, and cayenne pepper. 2. Then gently brush the chicken with sunflower oil and put it in the air fryer. Cook on Air Fry mode. Insert its air fryer basket into the level 3 of the oven and close the door. Set the time on your Ninja Foodi Smart XL Pro Air Fryer Oven to 17 minutes. Slice the cooked chicken into Servings.
Per Serving: Calories 213; Fat 4.1 g; Sodium 303 mg; Carbs 37.9g; Fiber 1.5g; Sugar 1.9g; Protein 6.6g

Turkey and Asparagus

Prep time: 5 minutes | Cook time: 25 minutes | Servings: 4

1-pound turkey breast soft loins, cut into strips	1 tablespoon lemon juice
1-pound asparagus, trimmed and cut into medium pieces	1 teaspoon coconut aminos
	2 tablespoons olive oil
A pinch of black pepper and salt	2 garlic cloves, minced
	¼ cup chicken stock

1. Heat up a suitable pan that fits the air fryer with the oil over medium-high heat, then add the meat and brown for 2 minutes per side. 2. Add the rest of the recipe ingredients, toss, put the pan in the machine. Insert its air fryer basket into the level 3 of the oven and close the door. Cook on "Air Fry" Mode, select level 3, and set its temperature to 380°F/195°C for 20 minutes. 3. Divide everything between plates and serve
Per Serving: Calories 249; Fat 5.7 g; Sodium 574 mg; Carbs 23.9g; Fiber 0.9g; Sugar 1.9g; Protein 3.6g

Ground Turkey with Green Beans

Prep time: 5 minutes | Cook time: 25 minutes | Servings: 4

1-pound turkey meat, ground	1 pound green beans, trimmed and halved
A pinch of black pepper and salt	
2 tablespoons olive oil	2 teaspoons garlic powder
2 teaspoons parsley flakes	

1. Heat up a suitable pan that fits the air fryer with the oil over medium-high heat, then add the meat and brown it for 5 minutes. 2. Add the remaining recipe ingredients, toss, put the pan in the machine. Insert its air fryer basket into the level 3 of the oven and close the door. and cook on "Air Fry" Mode, select level 3, and set its temperature to 370°F/185°C for 20 minutes. 3. Divide between plates and serve.
Per Serving: Calories 416; Fat 8.3 g; Sodium 208 mg; Carbs 22.9g; Fiber 0.5g; Sugar 19g; Protein 60.6g

Sliced Duck and Lettuce Salad

Prep time: 5 minutes | Cook time: 20 minutes | Servings: 4

2 duck breasts, boneless and skin on	12 cherry tomatoes, halved
	1 tablespoon balsamic vinegar
1 teaspoon coconut oil, melted	3 cups lettuce leaves, torn
A pinch of black pepper and salt	12 mint leaves, torn
2 shallots, sliced	
For the Dressing:	
1 tablespoon lemon juice	2 and ½ tablespoons olive oil
½ tablespoon balsamic vinegar	½ teaspoon mustard

1. Heat up a suitable pan that fits your air fryer with the coconut oil over medium heat, then add the duck breasts skin side down and cook for 3 minutes. 2. Add salt, pepper, shallots, tomatoes and 1 tablespoon balsamic vinegar, toss, put the pan in the fryer and cook on "Air Fry" Mode, select level 3, and set its temperature to 370°F/185°C for 17 minutes. 3. Cool this mix down, thinly slice the duck breast and put it along with the tomatoes and shallots in a suitable bowl. 4. Add mint and salad leaves and toss. 5. In a separate bowl, mix ½ tablespoon vinegar with lemon juice, oil and mustard and whisk well. Pour this over the duck salad, toss and serve.
Per Serving: Calories 379; Fat 19g; Sodium 184mg; Carbs 12.3g; Fiber 0.6g; Sugar 2g; Protein 37.7g

Lemongrass Chicken Breast

Prep time: 25 minutes | Cook time: 20 minutes | Servings: 5

15 ounces chicken breast, skinless, boneless	2 teaspoons apple cider vinegar
	1 teaspoon lemon juice
1 teaspoon lemongrass	1 tablespoon sunflower oil
1 teaspoon black pepper	1 teaspoon dried basil
1 teaspoon salt	½ teaspoon ground coriander
1 teaspoon chili powder	2 tablespoons water
1 teaspoon smoked paprika	1 tablespoon heavy cream

1. Make the marinade: in the bowl mix up lemongrass, black pepper, salt, chili powder, smoked paprika, apple cider vinegar, lemon juice, sunflower oil, dried basil, ground coriander, water, and heavy cream. 2. Then chop the chicken breast roughly and put it in the marinade. Stir it well and leave for 20 minutes in the fridge. 3. Then Select the Air Fry mode. Set the Ninja Foodi Smart XL Pro temperature to 375°F/190°C. Select Level "3" and set the time on your Ninja Foodi Smart XL Pro Air Fryer Oven to 20 minutes. Press Start/Pause to begin preheating. Continue to the next step when it is done preheating. 4. Put the marinated chicken breast pieces in the air fryer. Insert its air fryer basket into the level 3 of the oven and close the door. and cook them for 20 minutes. Shake the chicken pieces after 10 minutes of cooking to avoid burning. 5.The cooked chicken breast pieces should have a light brown color.
Per Serving: Calories 351; Fat 20.3 g; Sodium 298 mg; Carbs 40.9g; Fiber 0.5g; Sugar 35.5g; Protein3.6g

Ground Turkey with Cabbage

Prep time: 5 minutes | Cook time: 25 minutes | Servings: 4

1-pound turkey meat, ground	shredded
A pinch of black pepper and salt	1 tablespoon sweet paprika, chopped
2 tablespoons butter, melted	
1-ounce chicken stock	1 tablespoon parsley, chopped
1 small red cabbage head,	

1. Heat up a suitable pan that fits the air fryer with the butter, then add the meat and brown for 5 minutes. 2. Add all the other ingredients, toss, put the pan in its air fryer basket. Insert its air fryer basket into the level 3 of the oven and close the door. Cook on "Air Fry" Mode, select level 3, and set its temperature to 380°F/195°C for 20 minutes. Divide everything between plates and serve.
Per Serving: Calories 426; Fat 36.3 g; Sodium 248 mg; Carbs 22.1g; Fiber 2g; Sugar 10.9g; Protein 6.6g

Cheesy Turkey Cubes

Prep time: 5 minutes | Cook time: 20 minutes | Servings: 4

1 big turkey breast, skinless, boneless and cubed	¼ cup cheddar cheese, grated
	¼ teaspoon garlic powder
Black pepper and salt to the taste	1 tablespoon olive oil

1. Rub the turkey cubes with the oil, season with salt, pepper and garlic powder and dredge in cheddar cheese. 2. Put the turkey bits in your air fryer's basket. Insert its air fryer basket into the level 3 of the oven and close the door. And cook on "Air Fry" Mode, select level 3, and set its temperature to 380°F/195°C for 20 minutes. Divide between plates and serve with a side salad.
Per Serving: Calories 477; Fat 13.3 g; Sodium 128 mg; Carbs 89.5g; Fiber 6.5g; Sugar 59.2g; Protein 5.4g

Herbed Duck Legs

Prep time: 5 minutes | Cook time: 30 minutes | Servings: 4

4 duck legs	4 teaspoons thyme, dried
A pinch of black pepper and salt	2 tablespoons olive oil
3 teaspoons fennel seeds, crushed	

In a suitable bowl, mix the duck legs with all the other ingredients and toss well. Put the duck legs in your air fryer's basket. Insert its air fryer basket into the level 3 of the oven and close the door. and cook on "Air Fry" Mode, select level 3, and set its temperature to 380°F/195°C for 15 minutes per side. Divide between plates and serve
Per Serving: Calories 266; Fat 6.3g; Sodium 193mg; Carbs 39.1g; Fiber 7.2g; Sugar 5.2g; Protein 14.8g

Spicy Chicken Bites

Prep time: 15 minutes | Cook time: 10 minutes | Servings: 5

15 ounces chicken fillet
1 tablespoon peanut oil
1 teaspoon chili sauce
1 teaspoon lemon zest, grated
½ teaspoon onion powder
1 egg, beaten
½ teaspoon salt

1. Cut the chicken fillet on 5 pieces and sprinkle with chili sauce, lemon zest, onion powder, and salt. 2. Then dip every chicken piece in the beaten egg. 3. Select the Air Fry mode. Set the Ninja Foodi Smart XL Pro temperature to 400°F/200°C. Select Level "3" and set the time on your Ninja Foodi Smart XL Pro Air Fryer Oven to 10 minutes. Press Start/Pause to begin preheating. Continue to the next step when it is done preheating. 4. Sprinkle its air fryer basket with peanut oil. Put the prepared chicken bites in the air fryer in one layer. Insert its air fryer basket into the level 3 of the oven and close the door. and cook them for 5 minutes from each side.
Per Serving: Calories 276; Fat 2.1 g; Sodium 18 mg; Carbs 65.9g; Fiber 4.5g; Sugar 59g; Protein 26g

Turkey with Broccoli

Prep time: 5 minutes | Cook time: 25 minutes | Servings: 4

1-pound turkey meat, ground
2 garlic cloves, minced
1 teaspoon ginger, grated
2 teaspoons coconut aminos
3 tablespoons olive oil
2 broccoli heads, florets separated and then halved
A pinch of black pepper and salt
1 teaspoon chili paste

1. Heat up a suitable pan that fits the air fryer with the oil over medium heat, then add the meat and brown for 5 minutes. 2. Add the rest of the recipe ingredients, toss, put the pan in the fryer. 3. Insert its air fryer basket into the level 3 of the oven and close the door. and cook on "Air Fry" Mode, select level 3, and set its temperature to 380°F/195°C for 20 minutes. Divide everything between plates and serve.
Per Serving: Calories 416; Fat 8.3 g; Sodium 208 mg; Carbs 22.9g; Fiber 0.5g; Sugar 19g; Protein 60.6g

Turkey with Chili Kale

Prep time: 5 minutes | Cook time: 25 minutes | Servings: 4

1-pound turkey meat, ground
A pinch of black pepper and salt
2 tablespoons olive oil
1 teaspoon coconut aminos
2 spring onions, minced
4 cups kale, chopped
1 tablespoon garlic, chopped
1 red chili pepper, chopped
½ cup chicken stock

1. Heat up a suitable pan that fits your air fryer with the oil over medium heat, then add the meat, salt, pepper, spring onions and the garlic, stir and sauté for 5 minutes. 2. Add the rest of the recipe ingredients, toss, put the pan in the fryer and cook on "Air Fry" Mode, select level 3, and set its temperature to 380°F/195°C for 20 minutes. Divide between plates and serve
Per Serving: Calories 244; Fat 15g; Sodium 232mg; Carbs 12.3g; Fiber 0.4g; Sugar 2g; Protein 13g

Balsamic Ginger Duck

Prep time: 10 minutes | Cook time: 30 minutes | Servings: 4

12 ounces duck legs
1 tablespoon balsamic vinegar
1 teaspoon Splenda
½ teaspoon minced ginger
½ teaspoon harissa
1 tablespoon avocado oil

1. Rub the duck legs with minced ginger, harissa, Splenda, and avocado oil. Then sprinkle the duck legs with ½ tablespoon of balsamic vinegar. 2. Select the Air Fry mode. Set the Ninja Foodi Smart XL Pro temperature to385°F/195°C. Select Level "3" and set the time on your Ninja Foodi Smart XL Pro Air Fryer Oven to 30 minutes. Press Start/Pause to begin preheating. Continue to the next step when it is done preheating. 3. Place the duck legs in the air fryer. Insert its air fryer basket into the level 3 of the oven and close the door. and cook them for 30 minutes. Sprinkle the cooked duck legs with the balsamic vinegar and place it in the serving plates.
Per Serving: Calories 209; Fat 7.5g; Sodium 321mg; Carbs 34.1g; Fiber 4g; Sugar 3.8g; Protein 4.3g

Cumin Turkey

Prep time: 5 minutes | Cook time: 25 minutes | Servings: 4

1-pound turkey meat, cubed and browned
A pinch of black pepper and salt
1 green bell pepper, chopped
3 garlic cloves, chopped
1 and ½ teaspoons cumin, ground
12 ounces veggies stock
1 cup tomatoes, chopped

1. In a suitable pan that fits your air fryer, mix the turkey with the rest of the recipe ingredients, toss, put the pan in the machine and cook on "Air Fry" Mode, select level 3, and set its temperature to 380°F/195°C for 25 minutes. 2. Divide into bowls and serve.
Per Serving: Calories 305; Fat 25g; Sodium 532mg; Carbs 2.3g; Fiber 0.4g; Sugar 2g; Protein 18.3g

Chicken Celery Mix

Prep time: 15 minutes | Cook time: 9 minutes | Servings: 4

1 teaspoon fennel seeds
½ teaspoon ground celery
½ teaspoon salt
1 tablespoon olive oil
12 ounces chicken fillet

1. Cut the chicken fillets on 4 chicken chops. In the shallow bowl mix up fennel seeds and olive oil. Rub the chicken chops with salt and ground celery. 2. Select the Air Fry mode. Set the Ninja Foodi Smart XL Pro temperature to 365°F/185°C. Select Level "3" and set the time on your Ninja Foodi Smart XL Pro Air Fryer Oven to 9 minutes. Press Start/Pause to begin preheating. Continue to the next step when it is done preheating. 3. Brush the chicken chops with the fennel oil and place it in its air fryer basket. Cook them for 9 minutes.
Per Serving: Calories 255; Fat 4.2g; Sodium 963mg; Carbs 21.5g; Fiber 0.8g; Sugar 5.7g; Protein 8.1g

Turkey and Spinach Bowls

Prep time: 5 minutes | Cook time: 25 minutes | Servings: 4

1-pound turkey meat, ground
Black pepper and salt to the taste
2 tablespoons olive oil
10 ounces keto tomato sauce
1 tablespoon oregano, chopped
2 cups spinach

1. Heat up a suitable pan that fits your air fryer with the oil over medium heat, then add the turkey, oregano, black pepper and salt, stir and brown for 5 minutes. Add the tomato sauce, toss, put the pan in the machine and cook on "Air Fry" Mode, select level 3, and set its temperature to 370°F/185°C for 15 minutes. Add spinach, toss, cook for 5 minutes more, divide everything into bowls and serve.
Per Serving: Calories 267; Fat 12g; Sodium 165mg; Carbs 39g; Fiber 1.4g; Sugar 22g; Protein 3.3g

Chicken Patties

Prep time: 10 minutes | Cook time: 10 minutes | Servings: 6

1-pound ground chicken
⅓ cup shredded cheddar cheese (omit for dairy-free)
2 tablespoons diced onions, or ¼
Coating:
1 cup pork dust (see here)
For Serving:
Cornichons
Mayonnaise
teaspoon onion powder
2 tablespoons mayonnaise
1 teaspoon dill pickle juice
1 teaspoon fine sea salt

Prepared yellow mustard

1. Spray the air fryer basket with avocado oil. Select Level 3. Select the "AIR FRY" function of Ninja Foodi Smart XL Pro Air Oven, set temperature to 375°F/190°C and time to 10 minutes. Select START/STOP to begin preheating. 2. Place the ingredients for the patties in a medium-sized bowl and use your hands to combine well. Form the mixture into six 3½-inch patties. 3. Place the pork dust in a shallow bowl. Dredge each patty in the pork dust and use your hands to press the pork dust into a crust around the patty. 4. Working in batches if necessary, place the patties in the air fryer basket, leaving space between them, and cook for 5 minutes. 5. Flip the patties with a spatula and cook for another 5 minutes, or until the coating is golden brown and the chicken is no longer pink inside. 6. Serve the patties with cornichons, mayo, and mustard, if desired. 7. Store leftovers in an airtight container in the refrigerator for up to 3 days.
Per Serving: Calories 354; Fat 7.9g; Sodium 704mg; Carbs 6g; Fiber 3.6g; Sugar 6g; Protein 18g

Turkey Pie

Prep time: 15 minutes | Cook time: 30 minutes | Servings: 6

10 ounces ground turkey
3 tablespoons coconut oil, softened
½ teaspoon baking powder
1 egg, beaten
1 cup coconut flour
1 teaspoon xanthan gum
¼ teaspoon salt
1 teaspoon chili flakes
2 spring onions, chopped
1 teaspoon smoked paprika
1 teaspoon dried parsley
1 teaspoon sesame oil

1. Make the pie dough: in the mixing bowl mix up coconut oil, baking powder, egg, coconut flour, and xanthan gum. Add salt and knead the non-sticky soft dough. 2. Line the air fryer baking pan with parchment. Cut the prepared dough into halves and roll up with the help of the rolling pin. 3. Put the first put of dough in the baking pan and flatten it gently with the help of the fingertips. 4. Then in the mixing bowl, mix up ground turkey, chili flakes, diced onion, smoked paprika, and dried parsley. 5. Put the ground turkey mixture over the flattened dough. Cover the ground turkey with remaining dough. Secure the edges of the pie and brush it with the sesame oil. 6. Select the Air Fry mode. Set the Ninja Foodi Smart XL Pro temperature to 380°F/195°C. Select Level "3" and set the time on your Ninja Foodi Smart XL Pro Air Fryer Oven to 30 minutes. Press Start/Pause to begin preheating. Continue to the next step when it is done preheating. 7. Put the pie in its air fryer basket. Insert its air fryer basket into the level 3 of the oven and close the door. Cook it for 30 minutes. Cool the cooked pie to the room temperature and then remove it from the baking pan. Cut the pie into the Servings.
Per Serving: Calories 183; Fat 15g; Sodium 402mg; Carbs 2.5g; Fiber 0.4g; Sugar 1.1g; Protein 10g

Duck with Mushroom and Cauliflower

Prep time: 5 minutes | Cook time: 20 minutes | Servings: 4

2 ounces mushrooms, sliced
2 tablespoons olive oil
2 cups cauliflower florets, riced
½ cup walnuts, toasted and chopped
2 cups chicken stock
A pinch of black pepper and salt
½ cup parsley, chopped
2 pounds duck breasts, boneless and skin scored

1. Heat up a suitable pan that fits the air fryer with the oil over medium-high heat, then add the duck breasts skin side down and brown for 4 minutes. 2. Add the mushrooms, cauliflower, black pepper and salt, insert its air fryer basket in the level 3 and cook for 1 minute more. 3. Add the stock, introduce the pan in its air fryer basket. Insert its air fryer basket into the level 3 of the oven and close the door. Cook on "Air Fry" Mode, select level 3, and set its temperature to 380°F/195°C for 15 minutes. Divide the mix between plates, sprinkle the parsley and walnuts on top and serve.
Per Serving: Calories 273; Fat 22g; Sodium 517mg; Carbs 3.3g; Fiber 0.2g; Sugar 1.4g; Protein 16.1g

Hot Jalapeno Cheese Chicken Breasts

Prep time: 5 minutes | Cook time: 20 minutes | Servings: 2

2 oz. full-fat cream cheese, softened
4 slices sugar-free bacon, cooked and crumbled
¼ cup pickled jalapenos, sliced
½ cup sharp cheddar cheese, shredded and divided
2 x 6-oz. boneless skinless chicken breasts

1. In a bowl, mix cream cheese, bacon, jalapeno slices, and half of the cheddar cheese until well-combined. 2. Cut parallel slits in the chicken breasts of about ¾ the length – make sure not to cut all the way down. You should be able to make between six and eight slices, depending on the size of the chicken breast. 3.Insert evenly sized dollops of the cheese mixture into the slits of the chicken breasts. Top the chicken with sprinkles of the rest of the cheddar cheese. Place the chicken in air fryer sheet pan. 4. Install the wire rack on Level 3. Select the "AIR ROAST" function of Ninja Foodi Smart XL Pro Air Oven, set temperature to 350°F/175°C and time to 20 minutes. Select START/STOP to begin preheating. cook the chicken breasts for twenty minutes. 5.Test with a meat thermometer. The chicken should be at 165°F/75°C when fully cooked. Serve hot and enjoy!
Per Serving: Calories 216; Fat 10.4g; Sodium 311mg; Carbs 14g; Fiber 1g; Sugar 2g; Protein 18g

Creamy Duck Strips

Prep time: 15 minutes | Cook time: 17 minutes | Servings: 5

12 ounces duck breast, skinless, boneless
½ cup coconut flour
⅓ cup heavy cream
1 teaspoon salt
1 teaspoon white pepper

1. Cut the duck breast on the small strips (fingers) and sprinkle with salt and white pepper. Then dip the duck fingers in the heavy cream and coat in the coconut flour. 2. Select the Air Fry mode. Set the Ninja Foodi Smart XL Pro temperature to 375°F/190°C. Select Level "3" and set the time on your Ninja Foodi Smart XL Pro Air Fryer Oven to 10 minutes. Press Start/Pause to begin preheating. Continue to the next step when it is done preheating. 3. Put the duck fingers in its air fryer basket in one layer. Insert its air fryer basket into the level 3 of the oven and close the door. and cook them for 10 minutes. Then flip the duck fingers on another side and cook them for 7 minutes more.
Per Serving: Calories 190; Fat 18g; Sodium 150mg; Carbs 0.6g; Fiber 0.4g; Sugar 0.4g; Protein 7.2g

Air Fried Duck Legs

Prep time: 10 minutes | Cook time: 16 minutes | Servings: 2

2 duck legs
1 teaspoon olive oil
½ teaspoon ground cumin
1 teaspoon salt
1 tablespoon scallions, chopped

1. In the shallow bowl mix up ground cumin and salt. Then rub the duck legs with the spice mixture. After this, mix up the scallions and olive oil. 2. Sprinkle the duck legs with the scallions' mix. 2. Select the Air Fry mode. Set the Ninja Foodi Smart XL Pro temperature to385°F/195°C. Select Level "3" and set the time on your Ninja Foodi Smart XL Pro Air Fryer Oven to 16 minutes. Press Start/Pause to begin preheating. Continue to the next step when it is done preheating. 3. Put the duck legs in the air fryer. Insert its air fryer basket into the level 3 of the oven and close the door. and cook them for 8 minutes. Then flip the duck legs on another side and cook for 8 minutes.
Per Serving: Calories 282; Fat 15g; Sodium 526mg; Carbs 20g; Fiber 0.6g; Sugar 3.3g; Protein 16g

Chili Chicken Skin

Prep time: 10 minutes | Cook time: 30 minutes | Servings: 4

½ teaspoon chili paste
8 ounces chicken skin
1 teaspoon sesame oil
½ teaspoon chili powder
½ teaspoon salt

1.In the shallow bowl mix up chili paste, sesame oil, chili powder, and salt. Then brush the chicken skin with chili mixture well and leave for 10 minutes to marinate. 2. Meanwhile, Select the Air Fry mode. Set the Ninja Foodi Smart XL Pro temperature to 365°F/185°C. Select Level "3" and set the time on your Ninja Foodi Smart XL Pro Air Fryer Oven to 20 minutes. Press Start/Pause to begin preheating. Continue to the next step when it is done preheating. 3. Put the marinated chicken skin in its air fryer basket. Insert its air fryer basket into the level 3 of the oven and close the door. Cook it for 20 minutes. When the time is finished, flip the chicken skin on another side and cook it for 10 minutes more until the chicken skin is crunchy.
Per Serving: Calories 275; Fat 1.4g; Sodium 582mg; Carbs 31.5g; Fiber 1.1g; Sugar 0.1g; Protein 29.8g

Spicy Duck Legs

Prep time: 5 minutes | Cook time: 25 minutes | Servings: 4

4 duck legs
2 garlic cloves, minced
1 teaspoon five spice
A pinch of black pepper and salt
2 tablespoons olive oil
1 teaspoon hot chili powder

1. In a suitable bowl, mix the duck legs with all the other ingredients and rub them well. 2. Put the duck legs in your air fryer's basket. Insert its air fryer basket into the level 3 of the oven and close the door. And cook on "Air Fry" Mode, select level 3, and set its temperature to 380°F/195°C for 25 minutes, flipping them halfway. Divide between plates and serve.
Per Serving: Calories 199; Fat 11.1g; Sodium 297mg; Carbs 14.9g; Fiber 1g; Sugar 2.5g; Protein 9.9g

Thyme Duck

Prep time: 15 minutes | Cook time: 17 minutes | Servings: 4

1-pound duck breast, skinless, boneless
2 ounces preserved lime, sliced
1 teaspoon apple cider vinegar
1 tablespoon olive oil
½ teaspoon salt
½ teaspoon dried thyme

1.Cut the duck breast on 4 pieces and sprinkle with salt, dried thyme, apple cider vinegar, and oil. Mix up the duck pieces well and put on the foil. 2. Then pot the reserved lime over the duck and wrap the foil. Select the Air Fry mode. Set the Ninja Foodi Smart XL Pro temperature to 375°F/190°C and put the wrapped duck breast in its air fryer basket. Insert its air fryer basket into the level 3 of the oven and close the door. Cook it for 17 minutes.
Per Serving: Calories 260; Fat 16g; Sodium 585mg; Carbs 3.1g; Fiber 1.3g; Sugar 0.2g; Protein 25.5g

Chicken Rolls

Prep time: 15 minutes | Cook time: 10 minutes | Servings: 4

4 wonton wraps
8 ounces chicken fillet
1 garlic clove, diced
1 teaspoon keto tomato sauce
1 teaspoon butter, melted
¼ teaspoon chili flakes
½ teaspoon ground turmeric

1. Slice the chicken on the small strips and sprinkle with chili flakes, ground turmeric, and butter. 2. Select the Air Fry mode. Set the Ninja Foodi Smart XL Pro temperature to 365°F/185°C. Select Level "3" and set the time on your Ninja Foodi Smart XL Pro Air Fryer Oven to 10 minutes. Press Start/Pause to begin preheating. Continue to the next step when it is done preheating. 3. Put the sliced chicken in the air fryer. Insert its air fryer basket into the level 3 of the oven and close the door. and cook it for 10 minutes. 4. Then transfer the chicken in the bowl. Add tomato sauce and diced garlic. 5. Mix up the chicken and place it on the wonton wraps. Roll them.
Per Serving: Calories 348; Fat 30g; Sodium 660mg; Carbs 5g; Fiber 0g; Sugar 0g; Protein 14g

Cinnamon Balsamic Duck

Prep time: 5 minutes | Cook time: 20 minutes | Servings: 2

2 duck breasts, boneless and skin scored
A pinch of black pepper and salt
¼ teaspoon cinnamon powder
4 tablespoons stevia
3 tablespoons balsamic vinegar

1. In a suitable bowl, mix the duck breasts with the rest of the recipe ingredients and rub well. 2. Put the duck breasts in your air fryer's basket. Insert its air fryer basket into the level 3 of the oven and close the door. and cook on "Air Fry" Mode, select level 3, and set its temperature to 380°F/195°C for 10 minutes per side. 3. Divide everything between plates and serve.
Per Serving: Calories 297; Fat 1g; Sodium 291mg; Carbs 35g; Fiber 1g; Sugar 9g; Protein 29g

Chicken Wings with Vinegar Sauce

Prep time: 10 minutes | Cook time: 12 minutes | Servings: 4

4 chicken wings
1 teaspoon erythritol
1 teaspoon water
1 teaspoon apple cider vinegar
1 teaspoon salt
¼ teaspoon ground paprika
½ teaspoon dried oregano
Cooking spray

1. Sprinkle the chicken wings with salt and dried oregano. 2. Then Select the Air Fry mode. Set the Ninja Foodi Smart XL Pro temperature to 400°F/200°C. Select Level "3" and set the time on your Ninja Foodi Smart XL Pro Air Fryer Oven to 8 minutes. Press Start/Pause to begin preheating. Continue to the next step when it is done preheating. 3. Place the chicken wings in its air fryer basket. Insert its air fryer basket into the level 3 of the oven and close the door. Cook them for 8 minutes. Flip the chicken wings on another side after 4 minutes of cooking. 4. Meanwhile, mix up erythritol, water, apple cider vinegar, and ground paprika in the saucepan and bring the liquid to boil. Stir the liquid well and cook it until erythritol is dissolved. 5. After this, liberally brush the chicken wings with sweet erythritol liquid and cook them in the air fryer at 400°F/200°C for 4 minutes more.
Per Serving: Calories 274; Fat 9.5 g; Sodium 3542 mg; Carbs 6.3g; Fiber 0.9g; Sugar 4.6g; Protein 40.5g

Duck Blackberry Mix

Prep time: 5 minutes | Cook time: 25 minutes | Servings: 4

4 duck breasts, boneless and skin scored
A pinch of black pepper and salt
2 tablespoons olive oil
1 and ½ cups chicken stock
2 spring onions, chopped
4 garlic cloves, minced
1 and ½ cups blackberries, pureed
2 tablespoons butter, melted

1.Heat up a suitable pan that fits the air fryer with the oil and the butter over medium-high heat, then add the duck breasts skin side down and sear for 5 minutes. 2. Add the remaining recipe ingredients, toss, put the pan in the air fryer. Insert its air fryer basket into the level 3 of the oven and close the door. And cook on "Air Fry" Mode, select level 3, and set its temperature to 370°F/185°C for 20 minutes. 3. Divide the duck and sauce between plates and serve.
Per Serving: Calories 237; Fat 19g; Sodium 518mg; Carbs 7g; Fiber 1.5g; Sugar 3.4g; Protein 12g

Almond Crusted Duck

Prep time: 5 minutes | Cook time: 30 minutes | Servings: 4

4 duck legs
Juice of ½ lemon
Zest of ½ lemon, grated
1 tablespoon cardamom, crushed
¼ teaspoon allspice
2 tablespoons almonds, toasted and chopped
2 tablespoons olive oil

1. In a suitable bowl, mix the duck legs with the remaining recipe ingredients except the almonds and toss. 2. Put the duck legs in your air fryer's basket. Insert its air fryer basket into the level 3 of the oven and close the door. And cook on "Air Fry" Mode, select level 3, and set its temperature to 380°F/195°C for 15 minutes per side. 3. Divide the duck legs between plates, sprinkle the almonds on top and serve with a side salad.
Per Serving: Calories 399; Fat 16g; Sodium 537mg; Carbs 28g; Fiber 3g; Sugar 10g; Protein 35g

Cinnamon Duck with Olives

Prep time: 5 minutes | Cook time: 25 minutes | Servings: 2

2 duck legs
1 teaspoon cinnamon powder
1 tablespoon olive oil
1 garlic clove, minced
A pinch of black pepper and salt
2 ounces black olives, pitted and sliced
Juice of ½ lime
1 tablespoon parsley, chopped

1. In a suitable bowl, mix the duck legs with cinnamon, oil, garlic, black pepper and salt, and rub well. 2. Heat up a suitable pan that fits the air fryer over medium-high heat, then add duck legs and brown for 2-3 minutes per side. 3. Add the remaining recipe ingredients to the pan, put the pan in its air fryer basket. Insert its air fryer basket into the level 3 of the oven and close the door. Cook on "Air Fry" Mode, select level 3, and set its temperature to 400°F/200°C for 10 minutes per side. Divide between plates and serve.
Per Serving: Calories 336; Fat 6g; Sodium 181mg; Carbs 1.3g; Fiber 0.2g; Sugar 0.4g; Protein 69.2g

Duck with Peppers Sauce

Prep time: 5 minutes | Cook time: 25 minutes | Servings: 4

4 duck breast fillets, skin-on
1 tablespoon balsamic vinegar
4 tablespoons olive oil
1 red bell pepper, peeled and chopped
¼ cup basil, chopped
1 tablespoon pine nuts
1 teaspoon tarragon
1 garlic clove, minced
1 tablespoon lemon juice

1. Heat up a suitable pan that fist your air fryer with half of the oil over medium heat, then add the duck fillets skin side up and cook for 2-3 minutes. Add the vinegar, toss and cook for 2 minutes more. 2. In a blender, mix the rest of the oil with the remaining recipe ingredients and pulse well. 3. Pour this over the duck, put the pan in the fryer and cook on "Air Fry" Mode, select level 3, and set its temperature to 370°F/185°C for 16 minutes. Divide everything between plates and serve.
Per Serving: Calories 220; Fat 1.7g; Sodium 178mg; Carbs 1.7g; Fiber 0.2g; Sugar 0.2g; Protein 32.9g

Peppercorn Duck

Prep time: 5 minutes | Cook time: 30 minutes | Servings: 4

4 duck legs, skin on	10 peppercorns, crushed
Juice of ½ lemon	1 tablespoon balsamic vinegar
1 teaspoon cinnamon powder	1 tablespoon olive oil
1 teaspoon vanilla extract	A pinch of black pepper and salt

1. Heat up a suitable pan with the oil over medium-high heat, then add the duck legs and sear them for 3 minutes per side. 2. Transfer to a suitable pan that fits the air fryer, then add the remaining recipe ingredients, toss, put the pan in its air fryer basket. Insert its air fryer basket into the level 3 of the oven and close the door. Cook on "Air Fry" Mode, select level 3, and set its temperature to 380°F/195°C for 22 minutes. 3. Divide duck legs and cooking juices between plates and serve.
Per Serving: Calories 308; Fat 24g; Sodium 715mg; Carbs 0.8g; Fiber 0.1g; Sugar 0.1g; Protein 21.9g

Duck Meatballs

Prep time: 20 minutes | Cook time: 10 minutes | Servings: 6

1-pound ground duck	1 teaspoon dried cilantro
½ teaspoon ground cloves	2 tablespoons almond flour
½ teaspoon ground nutmeg	Cooking spray
½ teaspoon salt	

1. In the mixing bowl mix up ground duck, ground cloves, ground nutmeg, salt, dried cilantro, and almond flour. With the help of the fingertips make the duck meatballs and sprinkle them with cooking spray. 2. Select the Air Fry mode. Set the Ninja Foodi Smart XL Pro temperature to385°F/195°C. Select Level "3" and set the time on your Ninja Foodi Smart XL Pro Air Fryer Oven to 10 minutes. Press Start/Pause to begin preheating. Continue to the next step when it is done preheating. 3. Put the duck meatballs in its air fryer basket in one layer and cook them for 5 minutes. Then flip the meatballs on another side and cook them for 5 minutes more.
Per Serving: Calories 275; Fat 1.4g; Sodium 582mg; Carbs 31.5g; Fiber 1.1g; Sugar 0.1g; Protein 29.8g

Duck Breasts with Mushrooms

Prep time: 5 minutes | Cook time: 25 minutes | Servings: 6

6 duck breasts, boneless, skin on and scored	¼ pound oyster mushrooms, sliced
1 tablespoon balsamic vinegar	½ bunch coriander, chopped
1 tablespoon coconut aminos	2 tablespoons olive oil
A pinch of black pepper and salt	3 garlic cloves, minced
2 courgettes, sliced	

1. Heat up a suitable pan that fits your air fryer with the oil over medium heat, then add the duck breasts skin side down and sear for 5 minutes. 2. Add the rest of the recipe ingredients, cook for 2 minutes more, transfer the pan to the air fryer and cook on "Air Fry" Mode, select level 3, and set its temperature to 380°F/195°C for 20 minutes. 3. Divide everything between plates and serve.
Per Serving: Calories 275; Fat 1.4g; Sodium 582mg; Carbs 31.5g; Fiber 1.1g; Sugar 0.1g; Protein 29.8g

Crispy Coconut Chicken Fillet

Prep time: 15 minutes | Cook time: 9 minutes | Servings: 5

15 ounces chicken fillet	½ cup coconut flour
5 eggs, beaten	1 teaspoon dried oregano
1 teaspoon salt	Cooking spray

1.Cut the chicken fillet on 5 chops and beat them gently with the help of the kitchen hammer. After this, sprinkle the chicken chops with dried oregano and salt. Dip every chicken chop in the beaten eggs and coat in the coconut flour. 2. Select the Air Fry mode. Set the Ninja Foodi Smart XL Pro temperature to 360°F/180°C Select Level "3" and set the time on your Ninja Foodi Smart XL Pro Air Fryer Oven to 9 minutes. Press Start/Pause to begin preheating. Continue to the next step when it is done preheating. 3. Place the chicken in the air fryer in one layer and cook for 5 minutes. Then flip them on another side and cook for 4 minutes more until the schnitzels are light brown.
Per Serving: Calories 380; Fat 29g; Sodium 821mg; Carbs 34.6g; Fiber 0g; Sugar 0g; Protein 30g

Duck and Eggplant Mix

Prep time: 5 minutes | Cook time: 25 minutes | Servings: 4

1-pound duck breasts, skinless, boneless and cubed	2 tablespoons olive oil
2 eggplants, cubed	1 tablespoon sweet paprika
A pinch of black pepper and salt	½ cup keto tomato sauce

1. Heat up a suitable pan that fits your air fryer with the oil over medium heat, then add the duck pieces and brown for 5 minutes. 2. Add the rest of the recipe ingredients, toss, introduce the pan in the fryer and cook on "Air Fry" Mode, select level 3, and set its temperature to 370°F/185°C for 20 minutes. 3. Divide between plates and serve.
Per Serving: Calories 374; Fat 13g; Sodium 552mg; Carbs 25g; Fiber 1.2g; Sugar 1.2g; Protein 37.7g

Za'atar Chicken Drumsticks

Prep time: 10 minutes | Cook time: 18 minutes | Servings: 4

1-pound chicken drumsticks, bone-in	½ teaspoon lemon zest, grated
1 tablespoon Za'atar	1 teaspoon chives, chopped
1 teaspoon garlic powder	1 tablespoon avocado oil

1. In the mixing bowl mix up Za'atar, garlic powder, lemon zest, chives, and avocado oil. Then rub the chicken drumsticks with the Za'atar mixture. 2. Select the Air Fry mode. Set the Ninja Foodi Smart XL Pro temperature to 375°F/190°C. Select Level "3" and set the time on your Ninja Foodi Smart XL Pro Air Fryer Oven to 18 minutes. Press Start/Pause to begin preheating. Continue to the next step when it is done preheating. 3. Put the chicken drumsticks in its air fryer basket. Insert its air fryer basket into the level 3 of the oven and close the door. Cook for 15 minutes. Then flip the drumsticks on another side and cook them for 3 minutes more.
Per Serving: Calories 268; Fat 10.4g; Sodium 411mg; Carbs 0.4g; Fiber 0.1g; Sugar 0.1g; Protein 40.6g

Creamy Curry Duck

Prep time: 5 minutes | Cook time: 25 minutes | Servings: 4

15 ounces duck breasts, skinless, boneless and cubed	Black pepper and salt to the taste
1 tablespoon olive oil	5 ounces heavy cream
2 shallots, chopped	1 teaspoon curry powder
	½ bunch coriander, chopped

1. Heat up a suitable pan that fits your air fryer with the oil over medium heat, then add the duck, toss and brown for 5 minutes. 2. Add the rest of the recipe ingredients, toss, introduce the pan in its air fryer basket. Insert its air fryer basket into the level 3 of the oven and close the door. Cook on "Air Fry" Mode, select level 3, and set its temperature to 370°F/185°C for 20 minutes. 3. Divide the mix into bowls and serve.
Per Serving: Calories 220; Fat 13g; Sodium 542mg; Carbs 0.9g; Fiber 0.3g; Sugar 0.2g; Protein 25.6g

Tasty Yogurt Chicken Thighs

Prep time: 25 minutes | Cook time: 20 minutes | Servings: 4

4 chicken thighs, skinless, boneless	1 teaspoon dried cilantro
2 tablespoons plain yogurt	½ teaspoon ground cloves
1 teaspoon cayenne pepper	1 tablespoon apple cider vinegar
	1 teaspoon olive oil

1.Make the marinade: in the mixing bowl mix up plain yogurt, cayenne pepper, dried cilantro, ground cloves, and apple cider vinegar. Then put the chicken thighs in the marinade and mix up well. Marinate the chicken for 20 minutes in the fridge. 2. Then Select the Air Fry mode. Set the Ninja Foodi Smart XL Pro temperature to 380°F/195°C. Select Level "3" and set the time on your Ninja Foodi Smart XL Pro Air Fryer Oven to 20 minutes. Press Start/Pause to begin preheating. Continue to the next step when it is done preheating. 3. Sprinkle the chicken thighs with olive oil and place in the air fryer. Cook them for 20 minutes.
Per Serving: Calories 353; Fat 5g; Sodium 818mg; Carbs 53.2g; Fiber 4.4g; Sugar 8g; Protein 7.3g

Cheesy Duck Asparagus Mix

Prep time: 5 minutes | Cook time: 25 minutes | Servings: 4

2 duck breast fillets, boneless
½ cup keto tomato sauce
A drizzle of olive oil
Black pepper and salt to the taste

1 cup red bell pepper, chopped
½ pound asparagus, trimmed and halved
½ cup cheddar cheese, grated

1. Heat up a suitable pan that fits your air fryer with the oil over medium heat, then add the duck fillets and brown for 5 minutes. 2. Add the rest of the recipe ingredients except the cheese, toss, put the pan in its air fryer basket. Insert its air fryer basket into the level 3 of the oven and close the door. Cook on "Air Fry" Mode, select level 3, and set its temperature to 370°F/185°C for 20 minutes. 3. Sprinkle the cheese on top, divide the mix between plates and serve.
Per Serving: Calories 346; Fat 16.1g; Sodium 882mg; Carbs 1.3g; Fiber 0.5g; Sugar 0.5g; Protein 48.2g

Air Fried Partridge

Prep time: 15 minutes | Cook time: 14 minutes | Servings: 4

10 ounces partridges
1 teaspoon dried rosemary

1 tablespoon butter, melted
1 teaspoon salt

1. Cut the partridges into the halves and sprinkle with dried rosemary and salt. Then brush them with melted butter. 2. Select the Air Fry mode. Set the Ninja Foodi Smart XL Pro temperature to385°F/195°C. Select Level "3" and set the time on your Ninja Foodi Smart XL Pro Air Fryer Oven to 14 minutes. Press Start/Pause to begin preheating. Continue to the next step when it is done preheating. 3. Put the partridge halves in its air fryer basket. Insert its air fryer basket into the level 3 of the oven and close the door. Cook them for 8 minutes. Then flip the poultry on another side and cook for 6 minutes more.
Per Serving: Calories 223; Fat 11.7g; Sodium 721mg; Carbs 13.6g; Fiber 0.7g; Sugar 8g; Protein 15.7g

Duck with Cranberry

Prep time: 5 minutes | Cook time: 25 minutes | Servings: 4

4 duck breasts, boneless, skin-on and scored
A pinch of black pepper and salt

1 tablespoon olive oil
¼ cup balsamic vinegar
½ cup dried cranberries

1. Heat up a suitable pan that fits your air fryer with the oil over medium-high heat, then add the duck breasts skin side down and cook for 5 minutes. 2. Add the rest of the recipe ingredients, toss, put the pan in the fryer and cook on "Air Fry" Mode, select level 3, and set its temperature to 380°F/195°C for 20 minutes. Divide between plates and serve.
Per Serving: Calories 400; Fat 32g; Sodium 721mg; Carbs 2.6g; Fiber 0g; Sugar 0g; Protein 27.4g

Duck with Strawberry Sauce

Prep time: 15 minutes | Cook time: 15 minutes | Servings: 4

1-pound duck breast, skinless, boneless
1 tablespoon erythritol
2 tablespoons water
1 ounces strawberry

½ teaspoon salt
½ teaspoon ground paprika
¼ teaspoon ground cinnamon
1 teaspoon chili powder
1 teaspoon sesame oil

1. Rub the duck breast with salt and chili powder. Then brush it with sesame oil. 2. Select the Air Fry mode. Set the Ninja Foodi Smart XL Pro temperature to 380°F/195°C. Select Level "3" and set the time on your Ninja Foodi Smart XL Pro Air Fryer Oven to 12 minutes. Press Start/Pause to begin preheating. Continue to the next step when it is done preheating. 3. Put the duck breast in its air fryer basket. Insert its air fryer basket into the level 3 of the oven and close the door. Cook it for 12 minutes. 4. Meanwhile, make the sweet sauce: in the small bowl mix up erythritol, water, ground paprika, and ground cinnamon. Mash the strawberry and add it in the erythritol mixture. Stir it well and microwave it for 10 seconds. 5. Then stir the sauce and microwave it for 10 seconds more. Repeat the same steps 2 times more. 6. Then rush the duck breast with ½ part of sweet sauce and cook for 3 minutes more. 7. Slice the cooked duck breast and sprinkle it with remaining sauce.
Per Serving: Calories 305; Fat 15g; Sodium 482mg; Carbs 17g; Fiber 3g; Sugar 2g; Protein 35g

Cheese Stuffed Chicken Fillets

Prep time: 15 minutes | Cook time: 11 minutes | Servings: 2

8 ounces' chicken fillet
3 ounces blue cheese
½ teaspoon salt

½ teaspoon thyme
1 teaspoon sesame oil

1. Cut the fillet into halves and beat them gently with the help of the kitchen hammer. After this, make the horizontal cut in every fillet. Sprinkle the chicken with salt and thyme. 2. Then fill it with blue cheese and secure the cut with the help of the toothpick. Sprinkle the stuffed chicken fillets with sesame oil. 3. Select the Air Fry mode. Set the Ninja Foodi Smart XL Pro temperature to 385°F/195°C. Select Level "3" and set the time on your Ninja Foodi Smart XL Pro Air Fryer Oven to 11 minutes. Press Start/Pause to begin preheating. Continue to the next step when it is done preheating. 4. Put the chicken fillets in its air fryer basket. Insert its air fryer basket into the level 3 of the oven and close the door. Cook them for 7 minutes. 5. Then carefully flip the chicken fillets on another side and cook for 4 minutes more.
Per Serving: Calories 316; Fat 12.2g; Sodium 587mg; Carbs 12.2g; Fiber 1g; Sugar 1.8g; Protein 25.8g

Cheesy Fried Chicken

Prep time: 10 minutes | Cook time: 20 minutes | Servings: 4

1 egg, whisked
½ cup parmesan cheese, preferably freshly grated
½ cup tortilla chips, crushed
½ teaspoon onion powder

½ teaspoon garlic powder
1 teaspoon red chili powder
1 ½ pounds chicken breasts, boneless skinless cut into strips

1. Install the wire rack on Level 3. Select the "AIR ROAST" function of Ninja Foodi Smart XL Pro Air Oven, set temperature to 380°F/195°C and time to 12 minutes. Select START/STOP to begin preheating. 2. Whisk the egg in a shallow bowl. In a separate bowl, whisk the parmesan cheese, tortilla chips, onion powder, garlic powder, and red chili powder. 3. Dip the chicken into the egg mixture. Then, roll the chicken pieces over the cheese mixture. 4. Cook the chicken for 12 minutes, turning them over halfway through the cooking time. Bon appétit!
Per Serving: Calories 427; Fat 23.1g; Sodium 633mg; Carbs 11.1g; Fiber 0.9g; Sugar 0.6g; Protein 41.4g

Chicken Strips with Mushrooms and Peppers

Prep time: 10 minutes | Cook time: 22 minutes | Servings: 5

1-pound chicken breast, skinless, boneless
1 teaspoon minced ginger
½ teaspoon minced garlic
1 tablespoon coconut aminos
1 teaspoon lemon juice
5 ounces cremini mushrooms,

sliced
¼ cup bell pepper, sliced
5 ounces cauliflower, chopped
1 teaspoon ground paprika
½ teaspoon cayenne pepper
1 tablespoon avocado oil
1 teaspoon salt

1. Select the Air Fry mode. Set the Ninja Foodi Smart XL Pro temperature to 375°F/190°C. Select Level "3" and set the time on your Ninja Foodi Smart XL Pro Air Fryer Oven to 8 minutes. Press Start/Pause to begin preheating. Continue to the next step when it is done preheating. 2. In the mixing bowl mix up sliced mushrooms, cauliflower, and bell pepper. Sprinkle the ingredients with salt, ½ tablespoon avocado oil, cayenne pepper, and ground paprika. 3. Mix up the vegetables and place them in its air fryer basket. Cook the ingredients for 5 minutes. 4. Then shake them well and cook for 3 minutes more. 5. Transfer the cooked vegetables into the bowl. Then Select the Air Fry mode. Set the Ninja Foodi Smart XL Pro temperature to 380°F/195°C. Select Level "3" and set the time on your Ninja Foodi Smart XL Pro Air Fryer Oven to 10 minutes. Press Start/Pause to begin preheating. Continue to the next step when it is done preheating. 6. Slice the chicken breast into the strips. Sprinkle the sliced chicken breast with minced ginger, minced garlic, and sprinkle with coconut aminos and lemon juice. 7. Place the chicken breast in its air fryer basket. Insert its air fryer basket into the level 3 of the oven and close the door. Cook it for 13 minutes. 8. Then add cooked vegetables and mix up the meal. Cook it for 1 minute more.
Per Serving: Calories 437; Fat 28g; Sodium 1221mg; Carbs 22.3g; Fiber 0.9g; Sugar 8g; Protein 30.3g

Creamy Duck with Tomatoes

Prep time: 5 minutes | Cook time: 25 minutes | Servings: 4

2 spring onions, chopped
2 tablespoons butter, melted
4 garlic cloves, minced
1 and ½ teaspoons coriander, ground
Black pepper and salt to the taste
15 ounces tomatoes, crushed
¼ cup lemon juice
1 and ½ pounds duck breast, skinless, boneless and cubed
½ cup cilantro, chopped
½ cup chicken stock
½ cup heavy cream

1. Heat up a suitable pan that fits your air fryer with the butter over medium heat, then add the duck pieces and cook for 5 minutes. 2. Add the rest of the recipe ingredients except the cilantro, toss, introduce the pan in the fryer and cook on "Air Fry" Mode, select level 3, and set its temperature to 370°F/185°C for 20 minutes. Divide between plates and sprinkle with coriander. Serve.
Per Serving: Calories 352; Fat 9.1g; Sodium 1294mg; Carbs 3.9g; Fiber 1g; Sugar 1g; Protein 61g

Parsley Duck Fillets

Prep time: 10 minutes | Cook time: 25 minutes | Servings: 4

4 duck breast fillets, boneless, skin-on and scored
2 tablespoons olive oil
2 tablespoons parsley, chopped
Black pepper and salt to the taste
1 cup chicken stock
1 teaspoon balsamic vinegar

1. Heat up a suitable pan that fits your air fryer with the oil over medium heat, then add the duck breasts skin side down and sear for 5 minutes. 2. Add the rest of the recipe ingredients, toss, put the pan in the fryer and cook on "Air Fry" Mode, select level 3, and set its temperature to 380°F/195°C for 20 minutes. Divide everything between plates and serve
Per Serving: Calories 336; Fat 27.1g; Sodium 66mg; Carbs 1.1g; Fiber 0.4g; Sugar 0.2g; Protein 19.7g

Spicy Marinated Chicken

Prep time: 10 minutes | Cook time: 15 minutes | Servings: 2

¾-pound chicken breasts, boneless, skinless
1 teaspoon garlic, minced
½ cup red wine
¼ cup hot sauce
1 tablespoon Dijon mustard
Sea salt and cayenne pepper, to taste

1. Select Level 3. Select the "AIR FRY" function of Ninja Foodi Smart XL Pro Air Oven, set temperature to 380°F/195°C and time to 12 minutes. Select START/STOP to begin preheating. 2. Place the chicken, garlic, red wine, hot sauce, and mustard in a ceramic bowl. Cover and let it marinate for about 3 hours in your refrigerator. 3. Place the chicken in the Air Fryer basket. Cook the chicken breasts for 12 minutes, turning them over halfway through the cooking time. 4. Spice it with the salt and cayenne pepper to taste. Bon appétit!
Per Serving: Calories 313; Fat 16g; Sodium 542mg; Carbs 3.7g; Fiber 0.9g; Sugar 2g; Protein 36.5g

Chicken Liver Spread

Prep time: 10 minutes | Cook time: 8 minutes | Servings: 6

1-pound chicken liver
2 tablespoons ghee
1 teaspoon salt
1 teaspoon smoked paprika
¼ cup hot water

1. Select the Air Fry mode. Set the Ninja Foodi Smart XL Pro temperature to 400°F/200°C. Select Level "3" and set the time on your Ninja Foodi Smart XL Pro Air Fryer Oven to 8 minutes. Press Start/Pause to begin preheating. Continue to the next step when it is done preheating. 2. Wash and trim the chicken liver and spread it in its air fryer basket. Cook the ingredients for 5 minutes. 3. Then flip them on another side and cook for 3 minutes more. 4. When the chicken liver is cooked, transfer it in the blender. Add ghee, salt, and smoked paprika. Add hot water and blend the prepared mixture until smooth. 5. Then transfer the cooked chicken pâté in the bowl and store it in the fridge for up to 3 days.
Per Serving: Calories 374; Fat 25g; Sodium 275mg; Carbs 7.3g; Fiber 0g; Sugar 6g; Protein 12.3g

Easy Turkey Schnitzel

Prep time: 10 minutes | Cook time: 25 minutes | Servings: 3

1½ pounds turkey thighs, skinless, boneless
1 egg, beaten
½ cup all-purpose flour
½ cup seasoned breadcrumbs
½ teaspoon red pepper flakes, crushed
Sea salt
Ground black pepper, to taste
1 tablespoon olive oil

1. Select Level 3. Select the "AIR FRY" function of Ninja Foodi Smart XL Pro Air Oven, set temperature to 380°F/195°C and time to 22 minutes. Select START/STOP to begin preheating. 2. Flatten the turkey thighs with a mallet. Whisk the egg in a bowl. Place the flour in another bowl. 3. Then, place the breadcrumbs, red pepper, salt, and black pepper in another bowl. Dip in the flour, then, in the egg, and roll them in the breadcrumb mixture. 4. Place the breaded turkey thighs in the Air Fryer basket. Mist your schnitzel with the olive oil and transfer them to the basket. 5. Cook the schnitzel for 22 minutes, turning them over halfway through the cooking time. Bon appétit!
Per Serving: Calories 579; Fat 27.4g; Sodium 456mg; Carbs 30.3g; Fiber 1.6g; Sugar 2g; Protein 51g

Sesame Crusted Duck

Prep time: 10 minutes | Cook time: 20 minutes | Servings: 4

2 pounds duck breast, skinless, boneless and cubed
½ cup spring onions, chopped
Black pepper and salt to the taste
1 tablespoon olive oil
2 garlic cloves, minced
¼ teaspoon red pepper flakes, crushed
1 tablespoon sesame seeds, toasted

1. Heat up a suitable pan that fits your air fryer with the oil over medium heat, then add the meat, toss and brown for 5 minutes. 2. Add the rest of the recipe ingredients except the sesame seeds, toss, introduce in the fryer and cook on "Air Fry" Mode, select level 3, and set its temperature to 380°F/195°C for 15 minutes. 3. Add sesame seeds, toss, divide between plates and serve.
Per Serving: Calories 316; Fat 17g; Sodium 271mg; Carbs 4.3g; Fiber 0.9g; Sugar 2.1g; Protein 35g

Air Fried Chicken Satay

Prep time: 10 minutes | Cook time: 14 minutes | Servings: 4

4 chicken wings
1 teaspoon olive oil
1 teaspoon tomato sauce
1 teaspoon dried cilantro
½ teaspoon salt

1. String the chicken wings on the wooden skewers. Then in the shallow bowl mix up olive oil, tomato sauce, dried cilantro, and salt. Spread the chicken skewers with the tomato mixture. 2. Select the Air Fry mode. Set the Ninja Foodi Smart XL Pro temperature to 390°F/200°C. Select Level "3" and set the time on your Ninja Foodi Smart XL Pro Air Fryer Oven to 14 minutes. Press Start/Pause to begin preheating. Continue to the next step when it is done preheating. 3. Spread the chicken satay in its air fryer basket. Insert this air fryer basket into the level 3 of the oven and close the door. Cook the meal for 10 minutes. 4. Then flip the chicken satay on another side and cook it for 4 minutes more.
Per Serving: Calories 264; Fat 17g; Sodium 129mg; Carbs 0.9g; Fiber 0.3g; Sugar 0g; Protein 27g

Thyme Paprika Duck

Prep time: 5 minutes | Cook time: 25 minutes | Servings: 4

1-pound duck breasts, skinless, boneless and cubed
Black pepper and salt to the taste
1 tablespoon olive oil
½ teaspoon sweet paprika
¼ cup chicken stock
1 teaspoon thyme, chopped

1. Heat up a suitable pan that fits your air fryer with the oil over medium heat, then add the duck pieces, and brown them for 5 minutes. 2. Add the rest of the recipe ingredients, toss, put the pan in the machine and cook on "Air Fry" Mode, select level 3, and set its temperature to 380°F/195°C for 20 minutes. Divide between plates and serve
Per Serving: Calories 283; Fat 6.6g; Sodium 693mg; Carbs 8.5g; Fiber 1.4g; Sugar 3.4g; Protein 45.2g

Buttery Chicken Wings

Prep time: 5 minutes | Cook time: 15 minutes | Servings: 2

¾-pound chicken wings, boneless
1 tablespoon butter, room
temperature

½ teaspoon garlic powder
½ teaspoon shallot powder
½ teaspoon mustard powder

1. Select Level 3. Select the "AIR FRY" function of Ninja Foodi Smart XL Pro Air Oven, set temperature to 380°F/195°C and time to 18 minutes. Select START/STOP to begin preheating. 2. Toss the chicken wings with the remaining ingredients. Cook the chicken wings for 18 minutes, turning them over halfway through the cooking time.
Per Serving: Calories 265; Fat 11.7g; Sodium 322mg; Carbs 0.5g; Fiber 0.9g; Sugar 0.5g; Protein 37.5g

Herbed Turkey Drumsticks

Prep time: 10 minutes | Cook time: 45 minutes | Servings: 5

2 pounds turkey drumsticks,
bone-in
2 tablespoons olive oil
Kosher salt

Ground black pepper, to taste
1 teaspoon dried thyme
1 teaspoon dried rosemary
1 teaspoon garlic, minced

1. Select Level 3. Select the "AIR FRY" function of Ninja Foodi Smart XL Pro Air Oven, set temperature to 400°F/200°C and time to 40 minutes. Select START/STOP to begin preheating. 2. Toss the turkey drumsticks with the remaining ingredients. 3. Cook the turkey drumsticks for 40 minutes, turning them over halfway through the cooking time. Bon appétit!
Per Serving: Calories 341; Fat 21.7g; Sodium 324mg; Carbs 0.5g; Fiber 0.1g; Sugar 0.1g; Protein 35.5g

Peppery Chicken Fillets

Prep time: 10 minutes | Cook time: 20 minutes | Servings: 4

1-pound chicken fillets
2 tablespoons butter
2 bell peppers, seeded and sliced
1 teaspoon garlic, minced

Sea salt
Ground black pepper, to taste
1 teaspoon red pepper flakes

1. Install the wire rack on Level 3. Select the "AIR ROAST" function of Ninja Foodi Smart XL Pro Air Oven, set temperature to 380°F/195°C and time to 15 minutes. Select START/STOP to begin preheating. 2. Toss the chicken fillets with the butter and place them in the Air Fryer basket. Top the chicken with bell peppers, garlic, salt, black pepper, and red pepper flakes. 3. Cook the chicken and peppers for 15 minutes, tossing the basket halfway through the cooking time. 4. Serve warm and enjoy!
Per Serving: Calories 305; Fat 22.8g; Sodium 642mg; Carbs 2.3g; Fiber 0.4g; Sugar 1.1g; Protein 21.6g

Orange Duck

Prep time: 15 minutes | Cook time: 45 minutes | Servings: 4

1-pound duck legs
¼ cup orange sauce

Sea salt and red pepper flakes,
crushed

1. Install the wire rack on Level 3. Select the "AIR ROAST" function of Ninja Foodi Smart XL Pro Air Oven, set temperature to 400°F/200°C and time to 40 minutes. Select START/STOP to begin preheating. 2. Toss the duck legs with the remaining ingredients. 3. Cook the duck legs for 40 minutes, turning them over halfway through the cooking time. Bon appétit!
Per Serving: Calories 471; Fat 44.1g; Sodium 311mg; Carbs 2.9g; Fiber 0.3g; Sugar 2.1g; Protein 13.1g

Herbed Chicken Wings

Prep time: 10 minutes | Cook time: 11 minutes | Servings: 4

1 tablespoon emperor herbs
chicken spices

8 chicken wings
Cooking spray

1. Cook on Air Fry mode and Select Level "3". Liberally sprinkle the chicken wings with emperor herbs chicken spices and place in the preheated to 400°F/200°C air fryer. Cook the chicken wings for 6 minutes from each side.
Per Serving: Calories 351; Fat 31g; Sodium 1329mg; Carbs 1.5g; Fiber 0.8g; Sugar 0.4g; Protein 24g

Chicken Cheese Dinner Rolls

Prep time: 5 minutes | Cook time: 15 minutes | Servings: 4

1-pound chicken, ground
½ cup tortilla chips, crushed
2 ounces cheddar cheese, grated
1 teaspoon dried parsley flakes
1 teaspoon cayenne pepper

½ teaspoon paprika
Kosher salt
Ground black pepper
4 dinner rolls

1. Install the wire rack on Level 3. Select the "AIR ROAST" function of Ninja Foodi Smart XL Pro Air Oven, set temperature to 380°F/195°C and time to 17 minutes. Select START/STOP to begin preheating. 2. Mix the chicken, tortilla chips, cheese, and spices until everything is well combined. Now, roll the mixture into four patties. 3. Cook the burgers for about 17 minutes or until cooked through; turn over halfway through the cooking time. 4. Serve your burgers in dinner rolls. Bon appétit!
Per Serving: Calories 575; Fat 25.3g; Sodium 369mg; Carbs 37g; Fiber 3.2g; Sugar 4.6g; Protein 49.7g

Cheesy Ham Stuffed Chicken

Prep time: 5 minutes | Cook time: 22 minutes | Servings: 4

1-pound chicken breasts, skinless,
boneless and cut into 4 slices
4 ounces goat cheese, crumbled
4 ounces ham, chopped
1 egg

¼ cup all-purpose flour
¼ cup parmesan cheese, grated
½ teaspoon onion powder
½ teaspoon garlic powder

1. Pound the chicken breasts with a mallet. 2. Stuff each piece of chicken with cheese and ham. Roll them up and secure with toothpicks. 3. In a shallow bowl, mix the remaining ingredients until well combined. Dip the chicken rolls into the egg/flour mixture. 4. Place the stuffed chicken in the Air Fryer basket. Install the wire rack on Level 3. Select the "AIR ROAST" function of Ninja Foodi Smart XL Pro Air Oven, set temperature to 400°F/200°C and time to 22 minutes. Select START/STOP to begin preheating. 5. Cook the stuffed chicken breasts for about 22 minutes, turning them over halfway through the cooking time. 6. Bon appétit!
Per Serving: Calories 486; Fat 32.3g; Sodium 589mg; Carbs 7.9g; Fiber 0.2g; Sugar 0.8g; Protein 39.3g

Country Chicken Tenders

Prep time: 5 minutes | Cook time: 15 minutes | Servings: 4

¾ lb. of chicken tenders
For Breading:
2 tablespoons olive oil
1 teaspoon black pepper
½ teaspoon salt

½ cup seasoned breadcrumbs
½ cup all-purpose flour
2 eggs, beaten

1. Select Level 3. Select the "AIR FRY" function of Ninja Foodi Smart XL Pro Air Oven, set temperature to 330°F/165°C and time to 10 minutes. Select START/STOP to begin preheating. 2. In three separate bowls, set aside breadcrumbs, eggs, and flour. Season the breadcrumbs with salt and pepper. Add olive oil to the breadcrumbs and mix well. 3. Place chicken tenders into flour, then dip into eggs and finally dip into breadcrumbs. Press to ensure that the breadcrumbs are evenly coating the chicken. 4. Shake off excess breading and place in the air fryer basket. Cook the chicken tenders for 10-minutes in the air fryer. 5. Serve warm.
Per Serving: Calories 271; Fat 9.3g; Sodium 15mg; Carbs 43g; Fiber 6g; Sugar 2g; Protein 5g

Italian Chicken Drumsticks

Prep time: 10 minutes | Cook time: 25 minutes | Servings: 4

4 chicken drumsticks, bone-in
1 tablespoon butter
½ teaspoon cayenne pepper

1 teaspoon Italian herb mix
Sea salt
Ground black pepper, to taste

1. Select Level 3. Select the "AIR FRY" function of Ninja Foodi Smart XL Pro Air Oven, set temperature to 370°F/185°C and time to 20 minutes. Select START/STOP to begin preheating. Pat the chicken drumsticks dry with paper towels. Toss the chicken with the all ingredients. 2. Cook the chicken drumsticks for 20 minutes, turning them over halfway through the cooking time. Bon appétit!
Per Serving: Calories 235; Fat 14.8g; Sodium 422mg; Carbs 0.3g; Fiber 0.3g; Sugar 0.1g; Protein 23.3g

Lemon Turkey with Parsley

Prep time: 10 minutes | Cook time: 40 minutes | Servings: 5

2 pounds turkey wings	1 teaspoon poultry seasoning mix
2 tablespoons olive oil	2 tablespoons fresh parsley,
½ teaspoon garlic powder	roughly chopped
½ teaspoon onion powder	1 lemon, cut into slices

1. Select Level 3. Select the "AIR FRY" function of Ninja Foodi Smart XL Pro Air Oven, set temperature to 400°F/200°C and time to 40 minutes. Select START/STOP to begin preheating. 2. Toss the turkey wings with olive oil, garlic powder, onion powder, and poultry seasoning mix. 3. Cook the turkey wings for 40 minutes, turning them over halfway through the cooking time. 4. Let it rest for 10 minutes before carving and serving. Garnish the turkey wings with the parsley and lemon slices. 5. Bon appétit!
Per Serving: Calories 411; Fat 27.8g; Sodium 411mg; Carbs 1.3g; Fiber 0.2g; Sugar 0.3g; Protein 36.5g

Chicken Cutlets with Steamed Broccoli

Prep time: 5 minutes | Cook time: 15 minutes | Servings: 4

1-pound chicken cutlets	Sea salt
1-pound broccoli florets	Ground black pepper, to taste
1 tablespoon olive oil	

1. Select Level 3. Select the "AIR FRY" function of Ninja Foodi Smart XL Pro Air Oven, set temperature to 380°F/195°C and time to 6 minutes. Select START/STOP to begin preheating. 2. Pat the chicken dry with kitchen towels. Place the chicken cutlets in a lightly greased Air Fryer basket. 3. Cook the chicken cutlets for 6 minutes, turning them over halfway through the cooking time. 4. Turn the heat to 400 °F/200°C and add in the remaining ingredients. Continue to cook for 6 minutes more. 5. Bon appétit!
Per Serving: Calories 313; Fat 20.8g; Sodium 444mg; Carbs 7.5g; Fiber 2g; Sugar 1.9g; Protein 24.5g

Creamy Chicken Salad

Prep time: 5 minutes | Cook time: 20 minutes | Servings: 4

1-pound chicken breasts, skinless	1 tablespoon lemon juice
and boneless	Sea salt and ground black pepper
¼ cup mayonnaise	½ cup celery, chopped
¼ cup sour cream	

1. Select Level 3. Select the "AIR FRY" function of Ninja Foodi Smart XL Pro Air Oven, set temperature to 380°F/195°C and time to 5 minutes. Select START/STOP to begin preheating. 2. Pat dry the chicken and place the chicken in a lightly oiled air fryer basket. Cook the chicken breasts for 12 minutes, turning them over halfway through the cooking time. 3. Shred the chicken breasts using two forks; transfer it to a salad bowl and add in the remaining ingredients. 4. Toss to combine and serve well chilled. Bon appétit!
Per Serving: Calories 315; Fat 23g; Sodium 478mg; Carbs 2.8g; Fiber 0.4g; Sugar 0.9g; Protein 24.5g

Spicy Chicken

Prep time: 10 minutes | Cook time: 15 minutes | Servings: 4

1-pound chicken breasts,	1 teaspoon garlic, minced
boneless, skinless	1 teaspoon black peppercorns,
½ cup rice wine	whole
1 tablespoon stone-ground	1 teaspoon chili powder
mustard	¼ teaspoon sea salt

1. Install the wire rack on Level 3. Select the "AIR ROAST" function of Ninja Foodi Smart XL Pro Air Oven, set temperature to 380°F/195°C and time to 12 minutes. Select START/STOP to begin preheating. 2. Place the chicken, wine, mustard, garlic, and whole peppercorns in a ceramic bowl. Cover and let it marinate for about 3 hours in your refrigerator. 3. Discard the marinade and place the chicken breasts in the Air Fryer basket. 4. Cook the chicken breasts for 12 minutes, turning them over halfway through the cooking time. 5. Season the chicken with the chili powder and salt. Serve immediately and enjoy!
Per Serving: Calories 206; Fat 11g; Sodium 421mg; Carbs 1g; Fiber 0.2g; Sugar 0.4g; Protein 24.2g

Tangy Ranch Chicken Wings

Prep time: 10 minutes | Cook time: 25 minutes | Servings: 3

1-pound chicken wings, boneless	Kosher salt
2 tablespoons olive oil	Ground black pepper
1 teaspoon Ranch seasoning mix	

1. Select Level 3. Select the "AIR FRY" function of Ninja Foodi Smart XL Pro Air Oven, set temperature to 380°F/195°C and time to 22 minutes. Select START/STOP to begin preheating. 2. Pat the chicken dry with kitchen towels. Toss the chicken with the remaining ingredients. 3. Cook the chicken wings for 22 minutes, turning them over halfway through the cooking time. Bon appétit!
Per Serving: Calories 273; Fat14.3g; Sodium 357mg; Carbs 0.5g; Fiber 0.5g; Sugar 0.4g; Protein 33.2g

Roasted Turkey with Scallions

Prep time: 10 minutes | Cook time: 40 minutes | Servings: 4

1½ pounds turkey legs	Sea salt
1 tablespoon butter, melted	Ground black pepper
1 teaspoon hot paprika	2 tablespoons scallions, chopped
1 teaspoon garlic, pressed	

1. Install the wire rack on Level 3. Select the "AIR ROAST" function of Ninja Foodi Smart XL Pro Air Oven, set temperature to 400°F/200°C and time to 40 minutes. Select START/STOP to begin preheating. Toss the turkey legs with the remaining ingredients, except for the scallions. 2. Cook the turkey legs for 40 minutes, turning them over halfway through the cooking time. 3. Garnish the roasted turkey legs with the fresh scallions and enjoy!
Per Serving: Calories 279; Fat 14.4g; Sodium 678mg; Carbs 1.8g; Fiber 0.5g; Sugar 0.7g; Protein 33.6g

Turkey and Avocado Sliders

Prep time: 10 minutes | Cook time: 25 minutes | Servings: 4

1-pound turkey, ground	½ cup breadcrumbs
1 tablespoon olive oil	Kosher salt
1 avocado, peeled, pitted and	Ground black pepper
chopped	8 small rolls
2 garlic cloves, minced	

1. Select Level 3. Select the "AIR FRY" function of Ninja Foodi Smart XL Pro Air Oven, set temperature to 380°F/195°C and time to 20 minutes. Select START/STOP to begin preheating. 2. Mix the turkey, olive oil, avocado, garlic, breadcrumbs, salt, and black pepper until everything is well combined. Form the mixture into eight small patties. 3. Cook the patties for about 20 minutes or until cooked through; turn over halfway through the cooking time. 4. Serve your patties in the prepared rolls and enjoy!
Per Serving: Calories 519; Fat 22.4g; Sodium 711mg; Carbs 48g; Fiber 5g; Sugar 6.7g; Protein 31.6g

Chicken Fajita Rolls

Prep time: 10 minutes | Cook time: 25 minutes | Servings: 2

2 x 6-oz. boneless skinless	¼ medium white onion, sliced
chicken breasts	1 tablespoon coconut oil, melted
1 green bell pepper, sliced	1 teaspoons taco seasoning mix

1. Cut chicken in half and place each one between two sheets of cooking parchment. Using a mallet, pound the chicken to flatten to a quarter-inch thick. 2. Place the chicken on a flat surface, with the short end facing you. Place four slices of pepper and three slices of onion at the end of each piece of chicken. 3. Roll up the chicken tightly, making sure not to let any veggies fall out. Secure with some toothpicks or with butcher's string. 4. Coat the chicken with coconut oil and then with taco seasoning. Place into your air fryer. 5. Install the wire rack on Level 3. Select the "AIR ROAST" function of Ninja Foodi Smart XL Pro Air Oven, set temperature to 390°F/200°C and time to 25 minutes. Select START/STOP to begin preheating. 6. Cook the chicken for twenty-five minutes. Serve the rolls immediately with your favorite dips and sides.
Per Serving: Calories 276; Fat 16g; Sodium 70mg; Carbs 1g; Fiber 0g; Sugar 0g; Protein 30g

Tasty Chicken Salad Sandwich

Prep time: 10 minutes | Cook time: 20 minutes | Servings: 4

1-pound chicken breasts, boneless and skinless
1 stalks celery, chopped
1 carrot, chopped
1 small onion, chopped
1 cup mayonnaise
Sea salt
Ground black pepper, to taste
4 sandwich buns

1. Select Level 3. Select the "AIR FRY" function of Ninja Foodi Smart XL Pro Air Oven, set temperature to 380°F/195°C and time to 12 minutes. Select START/STOP to begin preheating. 2. Pat dry the chicken and place the chicken in a lightly oiled basket. Cook the chicken breasts for 12 minutes, turning them over halfway through the cooking time. 3. Shred the chicken breasts using two forks; transfer it to a salad bowl and add in the celery, carrot, onion, mayo, salt, and pepper. 4. Toss to combine and serve in sandwich buns. Enjoy!
Per Serving: Calories 522; Fat 31.4g; Sodium 478mg; Carbs 27.1g; Fiber 2.5g; Sugar 5.2g; Protein 31.6g

Thai Hot Drumettes

Prep time: 5 minutes | Cook time: 25 minutes | Servings: 3

1-pound chicken drumettes, bone-in
Sea salt and freshly ground black pepper, to taste
¼ cup Thai hot sauces
2 tablespoons sesame oil
1 teaspoon tamari sauce

1. Install the wire rack on Level 3. Select the "AIR ROAST" function of Ninja Foodi Smart XL Pro Air Oven, set temperature to 390°F/200°C and time to 22 minutes. Select START/STOP to begin preheating. Toss the chicken drumettes with the remaining ingredients. 2. Cook the chicken drumettes for 22 minutes, turning them over halfway through the cooking time. Bon appétit!
Per Serving: Calories 260; Fat 13.3g; Sodium 432mg; Carbs 0.5g; Fiber 0.5g; Sugar 0.4g; Protein 31.2g

Italian Garlicky Chicken Thighs

Prep time: 10 minutes | Cook time: 20 minutes | Servings: 4

4 skin-on bone-in chicken thighs
2 tablespoons unsalted butter, melted
3 teaspoons Italian herbs
½ teaspoon garlic powder
¼ teaspoon onion powder

1. Install the wire rack on Level 3. Select the "AIR ROAST" function of Ninja Foodi Smart XL Pro Air Oven, set temperature to 380°F/195°C and time to 20 minutes. Select START/STOP to begin preheating. 2. Using a brush, coat the chicken thighs with the melted butter. Combine the herbs with the garlic powder and onion powder, then massage into the chicken thighs. Place the thighs in the fryer. 3. Cook for 20 minutes, turning the chicken halfway through to cook on the other side. 4. When the thighs have achieved a golden color, test the temperature with a meat thermometer. 5. Once they have reached 165°F/75°C, remove from the fryer and serve.
Per Serving: Calories 350; Fat 16.7g; Sodium 428mg; Carbs 22g; Fiber 1g; Sugar 3g; Protein 28g

Classic Teriyaki Chicken Wings

Prep time: 10 minutes | Cook time: 35 minutes | Servings: 4

¼ teaspoon ground ginger
2 teaspoons minced garlic
½ cup sugar-free teriyaki sauce
2 lbs. chicken wings
2 teaspoons baking powder

1. Install the wire rack on Level 3. Select the "AIR ROAST" function of Ninja Foodi Smart XL Pro Air Oven, set temperature to 400°F/200°C and time to 25 minutes. Select START/STOP to begin preheating. 2. In a bowl, mix the ginger with garlic, and teriyaki sauce. Place the chicken wings in a separate, larger bowl and pour the mixture over them. Toss to coat until the chicken is well covered. Refrigerate for at least an hour. 3. Remove the marinated wings from the fridge and add the baking powder, tossing again to coat. Then place the chicken in the basket of your air fryer. 4. Cook for 25 minutes, giving the basket a shake intermittently throughout the cooking time. 5 .When the wings are 165°F/75°C and golden in color, remove from the fryer and serve immediately.
Per Serving: Calories 433; Fat 37g; Sodium 192mg; Carbs 14g; Fiber 1g; Sugar 4g; Protein 11g

Garlicky Nutty Meatballs

Prep time: 5 minutes | Cook time: 15 minutes | Servings: 2

½ lb. boneless chicken thighs
1 teaspoon minced garlic
1¼ cup roasted pecans
½ cup mushrooms
1 teaspoon extra virgin olive oil

1. Select Level 3. Select the "AIR FRY" function of Ninja Foodi Smart XL Pro Air Oven, set temperature to 375°F/190°C and time to 5 minutes. Select START/STOP to begin preheating. 2. Cube the chicken thighs. Place them in the food processor along with the garlic, pecans, and other seasonings as desired. Pulse until a smooth consistency is achieved. 3. Chop the mushrooms finely. Add to the chicken mixture and combine. Shape the mix into balls and brush them with olive oil. 4. Put the balls into the fryer and cook for eighteen minutes. Serve hot.
Per Serving: Calories 505; Fat 38.1g; Sodium 264mg; Carbs 6g; Fiber 2g; Sugar 3g; Protein 34g

Chimichurri Chicken Drumsticks

Prep time: 10 minutes | Cook time: 20 minutes | Servings: 4

8 chicken drumsticks
½ cup chimichurri sauce
¼ cup lemon juice

1. Coat the chicken drumsticks with chimichurri sauce and refrigerate in an airtight container for no less than an hour, ideally overnight. 2. Remove the chicken from refrigerator and allow return to room temperature for roughly twenty minutes. 3. Select Level 3. Select the "AIR FRY" function of Ninja Foodi Smart XL Pro Air Oven, set temperature to 400°F/200°C and time to 18 minutes. Select START/STOP to begin preheating. 4. Cook the drumsticks for 18 minutes in the preheated air fryer. Drizzle with lemon juice to taste and enjoy.
Per Serving: Calories 281; Fat 17.2g; Sodium 407mg; Carbs 4g; Fiber 2g; Sugar 1g; Protein 28g

Easy Chili Chicken

Prep time: 5 minutes | Cook time: 15 minutes | Servings: 1

1 lb. skinless, boneless chicken breast
1 teaspoon chili flakes
1 teaspoon garlic powder
½ cup flour
1 tablespoon olive oil cooking spray

1. Install the wire rack on Level 3. Select the "AIR ROAST" function of Ninja Foodi Smart XL Pro Air Oven, set temperature to 365°F/185°C and time to 10 minutes. Select START/STOP to begin preheating. Spray with olive oil. 2. Cut the chicken into 1-inches cubes and place in a bowl. Toss with the chili flakes, garlic powder, and additional seasonings to taste and make sure to coat entirely. 3. Add the coconut flour and toss once more. Cook the chicken in the fryer for 10 minutes. 4. Turn over and cook for a further 5 minutes before serving.
Per Serving: Calories 281; Fat 17.2g; Sodium 407mg; Carbs 4g; Fiber 2g; Sugar 1g; Protein 28g

Buttery Lemon Pepper Chicken

Prep time: 5 minutes | Cook time: 25 minutes | Servings: 4

½ teaspoon garlic powder
2 teaspoons baking powder
8 chicken legs
4 tablespoons salted butter,
melted
1 tablespoon lemon pepper seasoning

1. In a bowl mix the garlic powder and baking powder, then use this mixture to coat the chicken legs. Lay the chicken in the basket of your fryer. 2. Install the wire rack on Level 3. Select the "AIR ROAST" function of Ninja Foodi Smart XL Pro Air Oven, set temperature to 375°F/190°C and time to 5 minutes. Select START/STOP to begin preheating. 3. Cook the chicken legs for twenty-five minutes. Halfway through, turn them over and allow to cook on the other side. 4. When the chicken has turned golden brown, test with a thermometer to ensure it has reached an ideal temperature of 165°F/75°C. 5. Remove from the fryer. Mix together the melted butter and lemon pepper seasoning and toss with the chicken legs until the chicken is coated all over. 6. Serve hot.
Per Serving: Calories 145; Fat 7.2g; Sodium 66mg; Carbs 7g; Fiber 2g; Sugar 2g; Protein 15g

Crispy Fried Chicken Skin

Prep time: 5 minutes | Cook time: 5 minutes | Servings: 2

1 lb. chicken skin
1 teaspoon butter

½ teaspoon chili flakes
1 teaspoon dill

1. Install the wire rack on Level 3. Select the "AIR ROAST" function of Ninja Foodi Smart XL Pro Air Oven, set temperature to 360°F/180°C and time to 6 minutes. Select START/STOP to begin preheating. 2. Cut the chicken skin into slices. 3. Heat the butter until melted and pour it over the chicken skin. Toss with chili flakes, dill, and any additional seasonings to taste, making sure to coat well. 4. Cook the skins in the fryer for 3 minutes. Turn and cook for another 3 minutes. 5. Serve immediately or save them for later – they can be eaten hot or at room temperature.
Per Serving: Calories 685; Fat 35g; Sodium 239mg; Carbs 4g; Fiber 2g; Sugar 1g; Protein 26g

Southern Hot Fried Chicken

Prep time: 10 minutes | Cook time: 20 minutes | Servings: 2

2 x 6-oz. boneless skinless chicken breasts
2 tablespoons hot sauce

½ teaspoon onion powder
1 tablespoon chili powder
2 oz. pork rinds, finely ground

1. Install the wire rack on Level 3. Select the "AIR ROAST" function of Ninja Foodi Smart XL Pro Air Oven, set temperature to 350°F/175°C and time to 13 minutes. Select START/STOP to begin preheating. 2. Cut the chicken in half lengthwise and rub in the hot sauce. Combine the onion powder with the chili powder, then rub into the chicken. Leave to marinate for at least a half hour. 3. Use the ground pork rinds to coat the chicken breasts in the ground pork rinds, covering them thoroughly. Place the chicken in your fryer. 4. Cook the chicken for 13 minutes. Flip it and cook for another 13 minutes or until golden. 5. Test the chicken with a meat thermometer. When fully cooked, it should reach 165°F/75°C. Serve hot.
Per Serving: Calories 170; Fat 7.9g; Sodium 204mg; Carbs 3g; Fiber 0g; Sugar 2g; Protein 19g

Delicious Chicken Goulash

Prep time: 5 minutes | Cook time: 15 minutes | Servings: 2

2 chopped bell peppers
2 diced tomatoes
1 lb. ground chicken

½ cup chicken broth
Salt and pepper

1. Select Level 3. Select the "AIR FRY" function of Ninja Foodi Smart XL Pro Air Oven, set temperature to 365°F/185°C and time to 5 minutes. Select START/STOP to begin preheating. 2. Cook the bell pepper for five minutes. 3. Add in the diced tomatoes and ground chicken. Combine well, then allow to cook for a further six minutes. 4. Pour in broth, and spice to taste with salt and pepper. Cook for another six minutes before serving.
Per Serving: Calories 169; Fat 1.5g; Sodium 629mg; Carbs 36g; Fiber 6g; Sugar 14g; Protein 8g

Roasted Pecan Chicken Thighs

Prep time: 10 minutes | Cook time: 27 minutes | Servings: 1

1 lb. chicken thighs
Salt and pepper
2 cups roasted pecans

1 cup water
1 cup flour

1. Install the wire rack on Level 3. Select the "AIR ROAST" function of Ninja Foodi Smart XL Pro Air Oven, set temperature to 400°F/200°C and time to 27 minutes. Select START/STOP to begin preheating. 2. Spice the chicken with salt and pepper, then set aside. 3. Pulse the roasted pecans in a food processor until a flour-like consistency is achieved. 4. Fill a dish with the water, another with the flour, and a third with the pecans. 5. Coat the thighs with the flour. Mix the remaining flour with the processed pecans. 6. Dredge the thighs in the water and then press into the -pecan mix, ensuring the chicken is completely covered. 7. Cook the chicken in the fryer for twenty-two minutes, with an extra five minutes added if you would like the chicken a darker-brown color. Check the temperature has reached 165°F/75°C before serving.
Per Serving: Calories 426; Fat 22.6g; Sodium 357mg; Carbs 36g; Fiber 2g; Sugar 19g; Protein 20g

Greek Meatballs

Prep time: 5 minutes | Cook time: 12 minutes | Servings: 1

½ oz. finely ground pork rinds
1 lb. ground chicken
1 teaspoon Greek seasoning

⅓ cup feta, crumbled
⅓ cup frozen spinach, drained and thawed

1. In a bowl, place all ingredients and combine using your hands. Take equal-sized portions of this mixture and roll each into a 2-inch ball. Place the balls in your fryer. 2. Select Level 3. Select the "AIR FRY" function of Ninja Foodi Smart XL Pro Air Oven, set temperature to 350°F/175°C and time to 12 minutes. Select START/STOP to begin preheating. Cook the meatballs for twelve minutes, in several batches if necessary. 3. Once they are golden, ensure they have reached an ideal temperature of 165°F/75°C and remove from the fryer. 4. Keep each batch warm while you move on to the next one. Serve with Tzatziki if desired.
Per Serving: Calories 629; Fat 61g; Sodium 64mg; Carbs 3g; Fiber 1g; Sugar 1g; Protein 18g

Cheesy Buffalo Chicken Tenders

Prep time: 5 minutes | Cook time: 15 minutes | Servings: 4

1 egg
1 cup mozzarella cheese, shredded

¼ cup buffalo sauce
1 cup cooked chicken, shredded
¼ cup feta cheese

1. Combine all ingredients. Line the basket of your fryer with a suitably sized piece of parchment paper. Lay the mixture into the fryer and press it into a circle about half an inch thick. Crumble the feta cheese over it. 2. Install the wire rack on Level 3. Select the "AIR ROAST" function of Ninja Foodi Smart XL Pro Air Oven, set temperature to 400°F/200°C and time to 8 minutes. Select START/STOP to begin preheating. 3. Cook for eight minutes. Turn the fryer off and allow the chicken to rest inside before removing with care. 4. Cut the mixture into slices and serve hot.
Per Serving: Calories 227; Fat 11.2g; Sodium 412mg; Carbs 1g; Fiber 0g; Sugar 1g; Protein 31g

Spicy Garlicky Chicken Tenders

Prep time: 10 minutes | Cook time: 20 minutes | Servings: 1

¼ cup hot sauce
1 lb. boneless skinless chicken tenders

1 teaspoon garlic powder
1½ oz. pork rinds, finely ground
1 tsp chili powder

1. Toss the hot sauce and chicken tenders together in a bowl, ensuring the chicken is completely coated. 2. In another bowl, combine the garlic powder, ground pork rinds, and chili powder. Use this mixture to coat the tenders, covering them well. Place the chicken into your fryer, taking care not to layer pieces on top of one another. 3. Select Level 3. Select the "AIR FRY" function of Ninja Foodi Smart XL Pro Air Oven, set temperature to 375°F/190°C and time to 20 minutes. Select START/STOP to begin preheating. 4. Cook the chicken for twenty minutes until cooked all the way through and golden. Serve warm with your favorite dips and sides.
Per Serving: Calories 342; Fat 11.8g; Sodium 683mg; Carbs 24g; Fiber 4g; Sugar 1g; Protein 38g

Cheesy Chicken with Pepperoni Pizza

Prep time: 5 minutes | Cook time: 15 minutes | Servings: 6

2 cups cooked chicken, cubed
20 slices pepperoni
1 cup sugar-free pizza sauce

1 cup mozzarella cheese, shredded
¼ cup parmesan cheese, grated

1. Select Level 3. Select the "AIR FRY" function of Ninja Foodi Smart XL Pro Air Oven, set temperature to 375°F/190°C and time to 15 minutes. Select START/STOP to begin preheating. 2. Place the chicken into the base of a four-cup baking dish and add the pepperoni and pizza sauce on top. Mix well so as to completely coat the meat with the sauce. 3. Add the parmesan and mozzarella on top of the chicken, then place the baking dish into your fryer. Cook for 15 minutes. 4. When everything is bubbling and melted, remove from the fryer. Serve hot.
Per Serving: Calories 191; Fat 13g; Sodium 574mg; Carbs 5g; Fiber 1g; Sugar 3g; Protein 13g

Delicious Chicken Pizza Crusts

Prep time: 10 minutes | Cook time: 25 minutes | Servings: 1

½ cup mozzarella, shredded
¼ cup parmesan cheese, grated
1 lb. ground chicken

1. Select Level 3. Select the "PIZZA" function of Ninja Foodi Smart XL Pro Air Oven, set temperature to 375°F/190°C and time to 25 minutes. Select START/STOP to begin preheating. 2. In a bowl, mix up all ingredients and then spread the mixture out, dividing it into four parts of equal size. 3. Cut a parchment paper into four circles, roughly six inches in diameter, and put the chicken mix onto the center of each piece, flattening the mixture to fill out the circle. 4. Cook for 25 minutes. Halfway through, turn the crust over to cook on the other side. Keep each batch warm while you move onto the next one. 5. Once all the crusts are cooked, top with cheese and the toppings of your choice. If desired, cook the topped crusts for an additional five minutes. 6. Serve hot, or freeze and save for later!
Per Serving: Calories 291; Fat 15.4g; Sodium 96mg; Carbs 3g; Fiber 1g; Sugar 2g; Protein 33g

Sweet Strawberry Turkey

Prep time: 10 minutes | Cook time: 40 minutes | Servings: 2

2 lb. turkey breast
1 tablespoon olive oil
Salt and pepper
1 cup fresh strawberries

1. Select Level 3. Select the "AIR FRY" function of Ninja Foodi Smart XL Pro Air Oven, set temperature to 375°F/190°C and time to 30 minutes. Select START/STOP to begin preheating. 2. Massage the turkey breast with olive oil, before seasoning with a generous amount of salt and pepper. 3. Cook the turkey in the fryer for fifteen minutes. Flip the turkey and cook for a further fifteen minutes. 4. During these last fifteen minutes, blend the strawberries in a food processor until a smooth consistency has been achieved. 5. Heap the strawberries over the turkey, then cook for a final seven minutes and enjoy.
Per Serving: Calories 253; Fat 13.4g; Sodium 663mg; Carbs 7g; Fiber 3g; Sugar 2g; Protein 26g

Delicious Chimichurri Turkey

Prep time: 15 minutes | Cook time: 55 minutes | Servings: 1

1 lb. turkey breast
½ cup chimichurri sauce
½ cup butter
¼ cup parmesan cheese, grated
¼ teaspoon garlic powder

1 Massage the chimichurri sauce into the turkey breast, then refrigerate in an airtight container for at least a half hour. 2. In the meantime, prepare the herbed butter. Mix together the butter, parmesan, and garlic powder, using a hand mixer if desired. 3. Install the wire rack on Level 3. Select the "AIR ROAST" function of Ninja Foodi Smart XL Pro Air Oven, set temperature to 350°F/175°C and time to 40 minutes. Select START/STOP to begin preheating. 4. Place the turkey in the fryer and allow to cook for twenty minutes. Flip and cook on the other side for a further twenty minutes. 5. Take care when removing the turkey from the fryer. Place it on a serving dish and enjoy with the herbed butter.
Per Serving: Calories 217; Fat 7.9g; Sodium 998mg; Carbs 17g; Fiber 4g; Sugar 8g; Protein 19g

Roasted Chicken with Butter and Garlic

Prep time: 10 minutes | Cook time: 60 minutes | Servings: 1

½ cup butter
1 teaspoon pepper
3 tablespoons garlic, minced
1 whole chicken

1. Install the wire rack on Level 3. Select the "AIR ROAST" function of Ninja Foodi Smart XL Pro Air Oven, set temperature to 350°F/175°C and time to 60 minutes. Select START/STOP to begin preheating. 2. Soft butter at room temperature, then mix well in a small bowl with the pepper and garlic. 3. Massage the butter into the chicken. Any remaining butter can go inside the chicken. 4. Cook the chicken in the fryer for half an hour. Flip, then cook on the other side for another thirty minutes. 5. Test the temperature of the chicken by sticking a meat thermometer into the thigh to make sure it has reached 165°F/75°C. Let sit for ten minutes before you carve it and serve.
Per Serving: Calories 381; Fat 36g; Sodium 2mg; Carbs 16g; Fiber 1g; Sugar 13g; Protein 0g

Chicken & Spiced Tomatoes

Prep time: 5 minutes | Cook time: 35 minutes | Servings: 1

1 lb. boneless chicken breast
Salt and pepper
1 cup butter
1 cup tomatoes, diced
1½ teaspoons paprika
1 teaspoon pumpkin pie spices

1. Select Level 3. Select the "AIR FRY" function of Ninja Foodi Smart XL Pro Air Oven, set temperature to 375°F/190°C and time to 15 minutes. Select START/STOP to begin preheating. 2. Cut the chicken into relatively thick slices and put them in the fryer. Sprinkle with salt and pepper to taste. Cook for fifteen minutes. 3. Melt the butter before adding the tomatoes, paprika, and pumpkin pie spices. Leave simmering while the chicken finishes cooking. 4. Pour the tomato mixture over the cooked chicken in serving plate. Serve hot.
Per Serving: Calories 106; Fat 6.9g; Sodium 1mg; Carbs 12g; Fiber 2g; Sugar 10g; Protein 0g

Coconut Chicken

Prep time: 5 minutes | Cook time: 35 minutes | Servings: 4

1½ cups coconut milk
2 tablespoons garam masala
1½ lbs. chicken thighs
¾ tablespoon coconut oil, melted

1. Combine the coconut oil and garam masala together in a bowl. Pour the mixture over the chicken thighs and leave to marinate for a half hour. 2. Select Level 3. Select the "AIR FRY" function of Ninja Foodi Smart XL Pro Air Oven, set temperature to 375°F/190°C and time to 15 minutes. Select START/STOP to begin preheating. 3. Cook the chicken into the fryer for fifteen minutes. 4. Add in the coconut milk, giving it a good stir, then cook for an additional ten minutes. 5. Remove the chicken and place on a serving dish. Make sure to pour all of the coconut "gravy" over it and serve immediately.
Per Serving: Calories 118; Fat 7.2g; Sodium 232mg; Carbs 14g; Fiber 1g; Sugar 11g; Protein 2g

Roasted Chicken with Onion

Prep time: 10 minutes | Cook time: 80 minutes | Servings: 6

6 lb. whole chicken
1 teaspoon olive oil
1 tablespoon minced garlic
1 white onion, peeled and halved
3 tablespoons butter

1. Install the wire rack on Level 3. Select the "AIR ROAST" function of Ninja Foodi Smart XL Pro Air Oven, set temperature to 360°F/180°C and time to 75 minutes. Select START/STOP to begin preheating. 2. Grease the chicken with oil and the minced garlic. 3. Place the peeled and halved onion, as well as the butter, inside of the chicken. 4. Cook the chicken in the fryer for seventy-five minutes. 5. Take care when removing the chicken from the fryer, then carve and serve.
Per Serving: Calories 87; Fat 5.6g; Sodium 42mg; Carbs 9g; Fiber 0g; Sugar 6g; Protein 0g

Chicken Meatballs with Penne Pasta

Prep time: 5 minutes | Cook time: 15 minutes | Servings: 4

1 cup chicken meat, ground
1 sweet red pepper, minced
¼ cup green onions, chopped
1 green garlic, minced
4 tablespoons friendly bread crumbs
½ teaspoon cumin powder
1 tablespoon fresh coriander, minced
½ teaspoon sea salt
¼ teaspoon mixed peppercorns, ground
1 package penne pasta, cooked

1. Select Level 3. Select the "AIR FRY" function of Ninja Foodi Smart XL Pro Air Oven, set temperature to 350°F/175°C and time to 15 minutes. Select START/STOP to begin preheating. 2. Put the chicken, red pepper, green onions, and garlic into a mixing bowl and stir together to combine. 3. Throw in the seasoned bread crumbs and all of the seasonings. Combine again. 4. Use your hands to mold equal amounts of the mixture into small balls, each one roughly the size of a golf ball. 5. Put them in the fryer and cook for 15 minutes. Shake once or twice throughout the cooking time for even results. 6. Serve with cooked penne pasta.
Per Serving: Calories 429; Fat 32g; Sodium 325mg; Carbs 5g; Fiber 1g; Sugar 3g; Protein 5g

Crispy Popcorn Chicken

Prep time: 10 minutes | Cook time: 15 minutes | Servings: 4

½ cup mayonnaise
1 teaspoon prepared yellow mustard
½ cup finely shredded cheddar cheese (about 2 ounces)
½ cup pork dust (see here)
¼ teaspoon garlic powder
¼ teaspoon onion powder

¼ teaspoon smoked paprika
1 pound boneless, skinless chicken breasts, cut into ½-inch pieces
Chopped fresh parsley, for garnish
Ranch Dressing (here), for serving

1. Spray the air fryer basket with avocado oil. Select Level 3. Select the "AIR FRY" function of Ninja Foodi Smart XL Pro Air Oven, set temperature to 400°F/200°C and time to 15 minutes. Select START/STOP to begin preheating. 2. In a large bowl, mix together the mayonnaise and mustard. In a separate medium-sized bowl, mix together the cheese, pork dust, garlic powder, onion powder, and paprika until well combined. 3. Add the chicken pieces to the mayonnaise mixture and stir well to coat. One at a time, roll the coated chicken pieces in the pork dust mixture and spray them with avocado oil, then place them in the air fryer basket, leaving space between them. 4. Cook the chicken for 12 to 15 minutes, until the internal temperature reaches 165°F/75°C and the coating is golden brown. 5. Garnish with fresh parsley, if desired, and serve with ranch dressing, if desired. Store leftovers in an airtight container in the fridge for up to 4 days.
Per Serving: Calories 354; Fat 7.9g; Sodium 704mg; Carbs 6g; Fiber 3.6g; Sugar 6g; Protein 18g

Sweet Saucy Chicken Sausages

Prep time: 5 minutes | Cook time: 15 minutes | Servings: 4

4 chicken sausages
2 tablespoons honey
¼ cup mayonnaise

2 tablespoons Dijon mustard
1 tablespoon balsamic vinegar
½ teaspoon dried rosemary

1. Select Level 3. Select the "AIR FRY" function of Ninja Foodi Smart XL Pro Air Oven, set temperature to 350°F/175°C and time to 13 minutes. Select START/STOP to begin preheating. 2. Place the sausages on the sheet pan of your fryer and cook for about 13 minutes, flipping halfway. 3. Make the sauce by whisking the rest of the ingredients. 4. Pour the sauce over the warm sausages before serving.
Per Serving: Calories 350; Fat 22.5g; Sodium 166mg; Carbs 38g; Fiber 1g; Sugar 25g; Protein 1g

Cabbage Potato Cakes & Cajun Chicken Wings

Prep time: 10 minutes | Cook time: 30 minutes | Servings: 4

4 large-sized chicken wings
1 teaspoon Cajun seasoning
1 teaspoon maple syrup
¾ teaspoon sea salt flakes
¼ teaspoon red pepper flakes, crushed
1 teaspoon onion powder
1 teaspoon porcini powder
½ teaspoon celery seeds
1 small-seized head of cabbage, shredded
1 cup mashed potatoes

1 small-sized brown onion, coarsely grated
1 teaspoon garlic puree
1 medium whole egg, well whisked
½ teaspoon table salt
½ teaspoon ground black pepper
1½ tablespoons flour
¾ teaspoon baking powder
1 heaped tablespoon cilantro
1 tablespoon sesame oil

1. Select Level 3. Select the "AIR FRY" function of Ninja Foodi Smart XL Pro Air Oven, set temperature to 390°F/200°C and time to 30 minutes. Select START/STOP to begin preheating. 2. Pat the chicken wings dry. Place them in the fryer and cook for 25 - 30 minutes, ensuring they are cooked through. 3. Make the rub by combining the Cajun seasoning, maple syrup, sea salt flakes, red pepper, onion powder, porcini powder, and celery seeds. 4. Mix together the shredded cabbage, potato, onion, garlic puree, egg, table salt, black pepper, flour, baking powder and cilantro. 5. Separate the cabbage mixture into 4 portions and use your hands to mold each one into a cabbage-potato cake. 6. Douse each cake with the sesame oil. 7. Bake the cabbage-potato cakes in the fryer for 10 minutes, turning them once through the cooking time. You will need to do this in multiple batches. 8. Serve the cakes and the chicken wings together.
Per Serving: Calories 138; Fat 10.6g; Sodium 102mg; Carbs 1g; Fiber 0g; Sugar 1g; Protein 9g

Maple-Glazed Chicken

Prep time: 5 minutes | Cook time: 15 minutes | Servings: 4

2½ tablespoons maple syrup
1 tablespoon tamari soy sauce
1 tablespoon oyster sauce
1 teaspoon fresh lemon juice
1 teaspoon minced fresh ginger

1 teaspoon garlic puree
Seasoned salt
Ground pepper
2 boneless, skinless chicken breasts

1. Select Level 3. Select the "AIR FRY" function of Ninja Foodi Smart XL Pro Air Oven, set temperature to 365°F/185°C and time to 15 minutes. Select START/STOP to begin preheating. 2. In a bowl, mix the maple syrup, tamari sauce, oyster sauce, lemon juice, fresh ginger and garlic puree. This is your marinade. 3. Sprinkle the chicken with salt and pepper. Coat the chicken breasts with the marinade. Place some foil over the bowl and refrigerate for 3 hours, or overnight if possible. 4. Remove the chicken from the marinade. Place it in the Air Fryer and fry for 15 minutes flipping each one once or twice throughout. 5. Add the remaining marinade to a pan over medium heat. Allow the marinade to simmer for 3-5 minutes until it has reduced by half. 6. Pour over the cooked chicken and serve.
Per Serving: Calories 200; Fat 15.6g; Sodium 165mg; Carbs 5g; Fiber 1g; Sugar 2g; Protein 10g

Delicious Chicken Cordon Bleu

Prep time: 5 minutes | Cook time: 15 minutes | Servings: 4

8 (4 ounces each) thin-sliced chicken breast cutlets
¾ teaspoon kosher salt
Freshly ground black pepper
4 slices (1 ounce each) reduced-sodium deli ham, halved lengthwise
4 slices (1 ounce each) low-sodium Swiss cheese, halved

lengthwise
1 large egg
2 large egg whites
¾ cup bread crumbs, regular or gluten-free
2 tablespoons grated Parmesan cheese
Olive oil spray

1. Season the chicken cutlets with ¾ teaspoon salt and pepper to taste. Working with one at a time, place a cutlet on a work surface and put a half-slice of ham and cheese on top. Roll the chicken up, then set aside, seam side down. 2. In a bowl, beat together the whole egg and egg whites. In a shallow bowl, mix the bread crumbs and Parmesan. 3. Dip the chicken into the egg mixture, then into the bread crumbs, gently pressing to adhere. Spray both sides with oil. 4. Select Level 3. Select the "AIR FRY" function of Ninja Foodi Smart XL Pro Air Oven, set temperature to 400°F/200°C and time to 12 minutes. Select START/STOP to begin preheating. 5. Working in batches, place chicken rolls seam side down in the air fryer basket. Cook for 12 minutes, flipping halfway, until golden and cooked through. 6. Serve immediately.
Per Serving: Calories 497; Fat 15.5g; Sodium 983mg; Carbs 16g; Fiber 1g; Sugar 2g; Protein 69g

Herbed Cornish Hen

Prep time: 15 minutes | Cook time: 30 minutes | Servings: 2

1 cornish hen (about 2 pounds)
½ teaspoon ground cumin
½ teaspoon dried oregano
½ teaspoon garlic powder

½ teaspoon kosher salt
⅛ teaspoon freshly ground black pepper
1 teaspoon unsalted butter, melted

1. Discard the giblets from the hen or reserve for another use. Using kitchen shears, cut off the neck and along both sides of the backbone to remove. Trim any excess fat, then cut the hen in half along the breastbone. Trim off the wing tips. 2. In a bowl, combine the cumin with oregano, garlic powder, salt, and pepper. 3. Place the hen skin side up on a work surface. Brush the skin with the melted butter, then season with the spices. 4. Install the wire rack on Level 3. Select the "AIR ROAST" function of Ninja Foodi Smart XL Pro Air Oven, set temperature to 380°F/195°C and time to 30 minutes. Select START/STOP to begin preheating. 5. Transfer the hen to the air fryer basket, skin side down. Cook for about 30 minutes, flipping halfway, until golden and the internal temperature reaches 165°F/75°C. Cover with foil for 5 minutes before serving. 6. To make this even lighter, remove the skin and you'll save around 250 calories and 25 grams of total fat per serving.
Per Serving: Calories 499; Fat 35.5g; Sodium 400mg; Carbs 1g; Fiber 0g; Sugar 0g; Protein 41g

Pickle-Brined Chicken Tenders

Prep time: 5 minutes | Cook time: 22 minutes | Servings: 4

12 chicken tenders
1¼ cups dill pickle juice
1 large egg
1 large egg white
½ teaspoon kosher salt
Freshly ground black pepper
½ cup seasoned bread crumbs
½ cup seasoned panko bread crumbs
Olive oil spray

1. Add the chicken with the pickle juice in a bowl. Cover it and let it marinate for 8 hours in the refrigerator. 2. Drain and pat dry the chicken. 3. In a bowl, beat the whole egg, egg white, salt, and pepper to taste. In a shallow bowl, combine both bread crumbs. 4. Dredge the chicken in the egg, then into the bread crumbs. Generously spray both sides of the chicken with oil. 5. Select Level 3. Select the "AIR FRY" function of Ninja Foodi Smart XL Pro Air Oven, set temperature to 400°F/200°C and time to 12 minutes. Select START/STOP to begin preheating. 6. Place the chicken in the air fryer basket. Cook for 10 to 12 minutes, flipping halfway, until cooked through, crispy, and golden. Serve immediately.
Per Serving: Calories 257; Fat 5.5g; Sodium 742mg; Carbs 14g; Fiber 1g; Sugar 1g; Protein 35g

Spiced Chicken with Avocado Salsa

Prep time: 10 minutes | Cook time: 15 minutes | Servings: 4

Chicken
Kosher salt
4 (6-ounce) boneless, skinless chicken breasts
¾ teaspoon garlic powder
½ teaspoon onion powder
½ teaspoon ground cumin
Avocado Salsa
½ cup finely diced red onion
3 tablespoons fresh lime juice
10 ounces avocado (2 medium Hass), diced
½ teaspoon ancho chile powder
½ teaspoon sweet paprika
½ teaspoon dried oregano
⅛ teaspoon crushed red pepper flakes
Olive oil spray

1 tablespoon chopped fresh cilantro
Kosher salt

1. For the chicken: Fill a large bowl with lukewarm water and add ¼ cup salt. Stir to dissolve. Let the water cool to room temperature. Add the chicken to the water and refrigerate for at least 1 hour to brine. Remove the chicken from the water and pat dry with paper towels. 2. In a small bowl, combine ¾ teaspoon salt, the garlic powder, onion powder, cumin, ancho powder, paprika, oregano, and pepper flakes. Spritz the chicken all over with oil, then rub with the spice mix. 3. Install the wire rack on Level 3. Select the "AIR ROAST" function of Ninja Foodi Smart XL Pro Air Oven, set temperature to 380°F/195°C and time to 10 minutes. Select START/STOP to begin preheating. 4. Place the chicken in the air fryer basket. Cook for about 10 minutes, flipping halfway, until browned and cooked through. 5. Meanwhile, for the avocado salsa: In a medium bowl, combine the onion and lime juice. Fold in avocado and cilantro and season with ¼ teaspoon salt. 6. Serve the chicken topped with the salsa.
Per Serving: Calories 324; Fat 15g; Sodium 490mg; Carbs 10g; Fiber 5.5g; Sugar 2g; Protein 38g

Delicious Turkey Quinoa Skewers

Prep time: 5 minutes | Cook time: 10 minutes | Servings: 8

1 cup red quinoa, cooked
1½ cups water
14 oz. ground turkey
2 small eggs, beaten
1 teaspoon ground ginger
2½ tablespoons vegetable oil
1 cup chopped fresh parsley
2 tablespoons seasoned friendly bread crumbs
¾ teaspoon salt
1 heaped teaspoon fresh rosemary, finely chopped
½ teaspoon ground allspice

1. In a bowl, mix ingredients together using your hands, kneading the mixture well. 2. Mold equal amounts of the mixture into small balls. 3. Select Level 3. Select the "AIR FRY" function of Ninja Foodi Smart XL Pro Air Oven, set temperature to 380°F/195°C and time to 10 minutes. Select START/STOP to begin preheating. 4. Place the balls in the fryer basket and fry for 8-10 minutes. 5. Skewer them and serve with the dipping sauce of your choice.
Per Serving: Calories 76; Fat 5.7 g; Sodium 63mg; Carbs 2g; Fiber 0g; Sugar 2g; Protein 3g

Traditional Provençal Chicken

Prep time: 5 minutes | Cook time: 25 minutes | Servings: 4

4 medium-sized skin-on chicken drumsticks
1½ teaspoons herbs de Provence
Salt and pepper to taste
1 tablespoon rice vinegar
2 tablespoons olive oil
2 garlic cloves, crushed
12 oz. crushed canned tomatoes
1 small-size leek, thinly sliced
2 slices smoked bacon, chopped

1. Select Level 3. Select the "AIR FRY" function of Ninja Foodi Smart XL Pro Air Oven, set temperature to 360°F/180°C and time to 25 minutes. Select START/STOP to begin preheating. 2. Season the chicken drumsticks with herbs de Provence, salt and pepper. Pour over a light drizzling of the rice vinegar and olive oil. Cook in the sheet pan for 8-10 minutes. 3. Pause the fryer. Add in the rest of ingredients, give them a stir, and resume cooking for 15 more minutes, checking them occasionally to ensure they don't overcook. 4. Serve with rice and lemon wedges.
Per Serving: Calories 288; Fat 23.3g; Sodium 308mg; Carbs 6g; Fiber 1g; Sugar 5g; Protein 2g

Cheesy Caprese Chicken

Prep time: 5 minutes | Cook time: 20 minutes | Servings: 4

Tomatoes
1-pint heirloom cherry tomatoes, halved
4 large garlic cloves, slightly smashed
Chicken
2 (8-ounce) boneless, skinless chicken breasts
½ teaspoon kosher salt
Freshly ground black pepper
1 tablespoon prepared pesto
1 large egg, beaten
½ cup seasoned bread crumbs, whole wheat or gluten-free
1 teaspoon olive oil
¼ teaspoon kosher salt
¼ teaspoon freshly ground black pepper

2 tablespoons freshly grated Parmesan cheese
Olive oil spray
4 ounces fresh mozzarella cheese, thinly sliced
2 tablespoons balsamic glaze
Chopped fresh basil, for garnish

1. Select Level 3. Select the "AIR FRY" function of Ninja Foodi Smart XL Pro Air Oven, set temperature to 400°F/200°C and time to 5 minutes. Select START/STOP to begin preheating. 2. For the tomatoes: In a medium bowl, combine the tomatoes, garlic, oil, salt, and pepper, tossing to coat. Place the air fryer basket and cook for 4 to 5 minutes, shaking the basket a few times, until the tomatoes are soft. 3. Meanwhile, for the chicken: Halve each chicken breast horizontally to make a total of 4 cutlets. Place the chicken between parchment paper. With meat mallet pound to a ¼-inch thickness. Spice with the salt and pepper to taste and evenly coat with the pesto. 4. Place the egg in a shallow bowl. Combine the bread crumbs with Parmesan in a separate shallow bowl. Dip the chicken into the egg, then coat in the bread crumb mixture, gently pressing to adhere. Spray both sides with oil. 5. Preheat the air fryer to 400°F/200°C again. 6. Place them in the air fryer basket. Cook for 7 minutes, flipping halfway, until golden and cooked through. 7. Top each cutlet with 1 ounce of the mozzarella and one-quarter of the tomatoes. Return the cutlets to the air fryer basket, in batches, and cook for about 2 minutes to melt the cheese. 8. Remove from the air fryer, drizzle with the balsamic glaze, and top with the basil. Serve immediately.
Per Serving: Calories 364; Fat 15.5g; Sodium 868mg; Carbs 20g; Fiber 3g; Sugar 10g; Protein 36g

Pepperoni and Cheese Stuffed Chicken

Prep time: 5 minutes | Cook time: 15 minutes | Servings: 4

4 small boneless, skinless chicken breasts
¼ cup pizza sauce
½ cup Colby cheese, shredded
16 slices pepperoni
Salt and pepper, to taste
1½ tablespoons olive oil
1½ tablespoons dried oregano

1. Install the wire rack on Level 3. Select the "AIR ROAST" function of Ninja Foodi Smart XL Pro Air Oven, set temperature to 370°F/175°C and time to 15 minutes. Select START/STOP to begin preheating. 2. Flatten the chicken breasts with a rolling pin. 3. Top the chicken with equal amounts of each ingredient and roll the fillets around the stuffing. Secure with a small skewer or two toothpicks. 4. Roast in the fryer on the sheet pan for 13 - 15 minutes.
Per Serving: Calories 105; Fat 5g; Sodium 233mg; Carbs 7g; Fiber 2g; Sugar 4g; Protein 8g

Tasty Turkey Cutlets with Arugula Salad

Prep time: 5 minutes | Cook time: 10 minutes | Servings: 4

4 turkey breast cutlets (18 ounces total)
Kosher salt and freshly ground black pepper
1 large egg, beaten
½ cup seasoned bread crumbs, regular or gluten-free
2 tablespoons grated Parmesan
cheese
Olive oil spray
6 cups (4 ounces) baby arugula
1 tablespoon olive oil
1 tablespoon lemon juice
1 lemon cut into wedges for serving
Shaved Parmesan

1. One at a time, place a cutlet between two sheets of parchment paper or plastic wrap. Pound meat to a ¼-inch thickness. Season the cutlets with ½ teaspoon salt (total) and pepper to taste. 2. Place the egg in a shallow medium bowl. In a separate bowl, combine the bread crumbs and Parmesan. 3. Dip the turkey cutlets in the egg, then in the bread crumb mixture, gently pressing to adhere. Shake off the excess bread crumbs and place on a work surface. Spray both sides with oil. 4. Select Level 3. Select the "AIR FRY" function of Ninja Foodi Smart XL Pro Air Oven, set temperature to 400°F/200°C and time to 8 minutes. Select START/STOP to begin preheating. 5. Working in batches, place the turkey cutlets in the air fryer basket. Cook for 8 minutes, flipping halfway, until golden brown and the center is cooked. 6. Place the arugula in a bowl and toss with the oil, lemon juice, ¼ teaspoon salt, and pepper to taste. 7. To serve, place a cutlet on each plate and top with 1½ cups arugula salad. Serve with lemon wedges, and top with some shaved Parmesan, if desired.
Per Serving: Calories 244; Fat 6.5g; Sodium 534mg; Carbs 9g; Fiber 1g; Sugar 2g; Protein 36g

Chicken Tenders with Marinara Sauce

Prep time: 10 minutes | Cook time: 8 minutes | Servings: 6

2 large eggs
1 cup pork dust
2 teaspoons Italian seasoning
1 pound boneless, skinless chicken tenders
½ cup marinara sauce, for serving

1. Spray the air fryer basket with avocado oil. Select Level 3. Select the "AIR FRY" function of Ninja Foodi Smart XL Pro Air Oven, set temperature to 390°F/200°C and time to 8 minutes. Select START/STOP to begin preheating. 2. In a medium-sized bowl, lightly beat the eggs. In another medium-sized bowl, combine the pork dust and Italian seasoning. 3. One at a time, dip the chicken tenders in the eggs, shake off the excess egg, then dredge the tenders in the pork dust mixture. 4. Using your hands, press the coating into each tender, coating it well. Place the tenders in the air fryer basket, leaving space between them. 5. Cook the tenders for 8 minutes, or until the internal temperature reaches 165°F/75°C and they are golden brown, flipping halfway through. Transfer the chicken tenders to a platter and serve with the marinara sauce. 6. Store leftovers in an airtight container in the refrigerator for up to 4 days.
Per Serving: Calories 354; Fat 7.9g; Sodium 704mg; Carbs 6g; Fiber 3.6g; Sugar 6g; Protein 18g

Seasoned Chicken Tenders

Prep time: 5 minutes | Cook time: 10 minutes | Servings: 4

Seasoning
1 teaspoon kosher salt
½ teaspoon garlic powder
½ teaspoon onion powder
½ teaspoon chili powder
Chicken
8 chicken breast tenders (1-pound total)
¼ teaspoon sweet paprika
¼ teaspoon freshly ground black pepper

2 tablespoons mayonnaise

1. For the seasoning: In a bowl, combine the salt, garlic powder, onion powder, chili powder, paprika, and pepper. 2. For the chicken: Add the chicken in a bowl and add the mayonnaise. Mix well to coat all over, then sprinkle with the seasoning mix. 3. Select Level 3. Select the "AIR FRY" function of Ninja Foodi Smart XL Pro Air Oven, set temperature to 375°F/190°C and time to 7 minutes. Select START/STOP to begin preheating. 4. Place a single layer of the chicken in the air fryer basket. Cook for 6 to 7 minutes, flipping halfway, until cooked through in the center. 5. Serve immediately.
Per Serving: Calories 183; Fat 8.5g; Sodium 457mg; Carbs 0g; Fiber 0g; Sugar 0g; Protein 24g

Asian-Style Turkey Meatballs with Hoisin Sauce

Prep time: 5 minutes | Cook time: 20 minutes | Servings: 4

Meatballs
1⅓ pounds 93% lean ground turkey
¼ cup panko bread crumbs, regular or gluten-free
3 chopped scallions, plus more for garnish
¼ cup chopped fresh cilantro
1 large egg
1 tablespoon grated fresh ginger
1 garlic clove, minced
1 tablespoon reduced-sodium soy sauce or tamari
2 teaspoons toasted sesame oil
¾ teaspoon kosher salt
Olive oil spray
Hoisin Sauce
2 tablespoons hoisin sauce
2 tablespoons fresh orange juice
1 tablespoon reduced-sodium soy sauce or tamari

1. For the meatballs: In a bowl, combine the turkey, panko, scallions, cilantro, egg, ginger, garlic, sesame oil, soy sauce, and salt. Gently mix with until combined. Roll into 12 meatballs (¼ cup each) and spritz with oil. 2. Select Level 3. Select the "AIR FRY" function of Ninja Foodi Smart XL Pro Air Oven, set temperature to 380°F/195°C and time to 9 minutes. Select START/STOP to begin preheating. 3. Place meatballs in the air fryer basket. Cook for about 9 minutes, flipping halfway, until cooked through in the center and browned. 4. Meanwhile, for the hoisin sauce: In a small saucepan, combine the hoisin sauce, orange juice, and soy sauce and boil over medium-low heat. 5. Lower the heat and manage to simmer until reduced slightly, 2 to 3 minutes.
Per Serving: Calories 313; Fat 16.5g; Sodium 755mg; Carbs 10g; Fiber 1g; Sugar 4g; Protein 31g

Delicious Chicken Piccata

Prep time: 5 minutes | Cook time: 10 minutes | Servings: 4

Chicken
2 (8-ounce) boneless, skinless chicken breasts
¼ teaspoon kosher salt
Freshly ground black pepper
Sauce
1 tablespoon whipped butter
½ cup reduced-sodium chicken broth
¼ cup dry white wine
For Serving
1 lemon, sliced
2 large egg whites
⅔ cup seasoned bread crumbs
Olive oil spray

Juice of 1 lemon, lemon halves reserved
Freshly ground black pepper
1 tablespoon capers, drained

Chopped fresh parsley leaves

1. Cut the chicken horizontally for 4 cutlets. Pound it to a ¼-inch thickness. Spice with the salt and pepper to taste. 2. In a bowl, beat the egg whites with little water. Place the bread crumbs on a deep plate. Dip chicken in the egg, then in the bread crumbs. Generously spray both sides of the chicken with olive oil. 3. Select Level 3. Select the "AIR FRY" function of Ninja Foodi Smart XL Pro Air Oven, set temperature to 370°F/175°C and time to 6 minutes. Select START/STOP to begin preheating. 4. Working in batches, place the chicken cutlets in the air fryer. Cook for about 6 minutes, flipping halfway, until cooked through, crisp, and golden. 5. For the sauce: In a skillet, melt the butter and add the chicken broth along with wine, lemon juice, and pepper to taste. Boil until the liquid is reduced by half. Discard the lemon halves and stir in the capers.
Per Serving: Calories 232; Fat 6g; Sodium 691mg; Carbs 13g; Fiber 2g; Sugar 2g; Protein 29g

Refreshing Romaine Slaw

Prep time: 5 minutes | Cook time: 15 minutes | Servings: 4

5 cups shredded romaine lettuce
¼ cup slivered red onion
1½ tablespoons olive oil
1½ tablespoons apple cider
vinegar
4 teaspoons fresh lime juice
¼ teaspoon kosher salt
Freshly ground black pepper

1. In a bowl, mix the lettuce, onion, oil, vinegar, lime juice, salt, and pepper to taste. 2. Toss well and serve right away.
Per Serving: Calories 60; Fat 5g; Sodium 76mg; Carbs 3g; Fiber 1.5g; Sugar 1g; Protein 1g

Cornflake-Crusted Chicken with Romaine Slaw

Prep time: 10 minutes | Cook time: 35 minutes | Servings: 4

Chicken

8 bone-in chicken drumsticks (30 ounces total), skin removed	½ teaspoon sweet paprika
½ teaspoon kosher salt	¼ teaspoon garlic powder
2 large eggs	¼ teaspoon chili powder
	Olive oil spray

Crumb Coating

1⅔ cups (3½ ounces) cornflakes	1 teaspoon dried thyme
Olive oil spray	½ teaspoon garlic powder
1 teaspoon kosher salt	½ teaspoon onion powder
1 tablespoon dried parsley	¼ teaspoon chili powder
1½ teaspoons sweet paprika	Romaine Slaw for serving
1 teaspoon dried marjoram	

1. For the chicken: Season the chicken with the salt. Whisk the eggs with 1 teaspoon water, the paprika, garlic powder, and chili powder. Set aside. 2. For the crumb coating: Place the cornflakes in a zip-top bag and crush them. Place to a shallow bowl. Spritz the cornflakes with a little oil, then add the salt, parsley, paprika, marjoram, thyme, garlic powder, onion powder, and chili powder. Mix well to combine. 3. Dip drumstick in the egg mix, then in the crumbs. 4. Select Level 3. Select the "AIR FRY" function of Ninja Foodi Smart XL Pro Air Oven, set temperature to 350°F/175°C and time to 28 minutes. Select START/STOP to begin preheating. 5. Place the chicken in the air fryer basket. Cook for about 28 minutes, flipping halfway, until the chicken is cooked through and golden. Serve with the slaw.
Per Serving: Calories 346; Fat 11g; Sodium 693mg; Carbs 15g; Fiber 1g; Sugar 2g; Protein 45g

Spiced Yogurt-Marinated Chicken Thighs with Vegetables

Prep time: 10 minutes | Cook time: 22 minutes | Servings: 4

¼ cup whole-milk yogurt (not Greek)	8 (4-ounce) boneless, skinless chicken thighs, trimmed
3 garlic cloves, minced	7 ounces shishito peppers
2 tablespoons fresh lemon juice	2 medium vine tomatoes, quartered
1 teaspoon grated fresh ginger	Olive oil spray
1 teaspoon garam masala	1 tablespoon chopped fresh cilantro, for garnish
¼ teaspoon ground turmeric	1 lemon, cut into wedges
¼ teaspoon cayenne pepper	
1¼ teaspoons kosher salt	

1. In a bowl, stir the yogurt, garlic, lemon juice, ginger, garam masala, turmeric, cayenne, and 1 teaspoon of the salt. Place the chicken and marinade in a zip-top bag. Marinate the chicken in the refrigerator for at least 2 hours, or overnight. 2. Slide basket into rails of Level 3. Select the "AIR FRY" function of Ninja Foodi Smart XL Pro Air Oven, set temperature to 400°F/200°C and time to 14 minutes. Select START/STOP to begin preheating. 3. Remove the chicken from the marinade. Place chicken in the air fryer basket. Cook for about 14 minutes, flipping halfway, until slightly browned and cooked through. Set the cooked chicken aside and tent with foil. 4. Spritz the shishito peppers and tomatoes all over with oil. Place in the air fryer basket and cook for 8 minutes, shaking halfway, until soft and slightly charred. Sprinkle with the remaining ¼ teaspoon salt. 5. Transfer the chicken and vegetables to plates. Garnish with cilantro and serve with the lemon wedges on the side.
Per Serving: Calories 321; Fat 10g; Sodium 563mg; Carbs 11g; Fiber 2g; Sugar 5g; Protein 46g

Chicken Chimichangas with Sour Sauce

Prep time: 5 minutes | Cook time: 10 minutes | Servings: 4

Pico De Gallo

½ cup tomato, diced	1 teaspoon fresh lime juice
3 tablespoons onion	¼ teaspoon kosher salt
1 tablespoon chopped cilantro	Freshly ground black pepper

Chimichangas

12 ounces shredded chicken breast	1 (4-ounce) can green chiles, drained
Juice of ½ orange	4 (7- to 8-inch) low-carb whole wheat tortillas
Juice of ½ lime	½ cup (2 ounces) shredded pepper Jack cheese
1 garlic clove, minced	
1 teaspoon ground cumin	
Olive oil spray	

For Serving

3 cups lettuce, shredded	4 ounces avocado, diced
4 tablespoons sour cream	

1. In a bowl, Add the tomato, onion along with cilantro, lime juice, salt, pepper, mix well to combine. 2. For the chimichangas: In a bowl, combine the chicken, orange juice, lime juice, garlic, cumin, and drained chiles. Mix well to incorporate. 3. Place the chicken mixture (almost ¾ cup) on tortillas. Sprinkle with cheese. Lift and wrap it around the filling. 4. Select Level 3. Select the "AIR FRY" function of Ninja Foodi Smart XL Pro Air Oven, set temperature to 400°F/200°C and time to 8 minutes. Select START/STOP to begin preheating. 5. Lightly grease the chimichangas with oil. Place in the air fryer basket. Cook for 7 to 8 minutes, flipping halfway, until golden and crisp. 6. To serve: Place ¾ cup lettuce top with chimichanga along with pico de gallo, sour cream, and avocado. Garnish with cilantro. 7. Serve immediately.
Per Serving: Calories 391; Fat 18.5g; Sodium 716mg; Carbs 30g; Fiber 16.5g; Sugar 5g; Protein 40g

Healthy Turkey Meatloaves

Prep time: 5 minutes | Cook time: 20 minutes | Servings: 4

Meatloaves

1 pound 93% lean ground turkey	¼ cup chopped scallions
⅓ cup bread crumbs, regular or gluten-free	2 tablespoons chopped fresh cilantro
⅓ cup canned black beans, rinsed and drained	1 large egg, beaten
⅓ cup frozen corn	1 tablespoon tomato paste
¼ cup jarred chunky mild salsa	1 teaspoon kosher salt
¼ cup minced onion	½ teaspoon ground cumin

Glaze

2 tablespoons ketchup	2 tablespoons jarred mild salsa

1. For the meatloaves: In a medium bowl, combine the turkey, bread crumbs, beans, corn, salsa, onion, scallions, cilantro, egg, tomato paste, salt, and cumin and mix well. Divide the mixture into 4 equal portions and shape into 1-inch-thick round patties. 2. For the glaze: In a small bowl, stir together the ketchup and salsa. 3. Select Level 3. Select the "AIR FRY" function of Ninja Foodi Smart XL Pro Air Oven, set temperature to 350°F/175°C and time to 18 minutes. Select START/STOP to begin preheating. 4. Working in batches, place the meatloaves in the air fryer basket. Cook for about 18 minutes, flipping halfway, until the center is cooked through. 5. Brush the meatloaves with the glaze and return to the air fryer and cook for about 2 minutes to heat through. 6. Serve immediately.
Per Serving: Calories 279; Fat 11.5g; Sodium 695mg; Carbs 18g; Fiber 3g; Sugar 4g; Protein 26g

Traditional Tarragon Chicken

Prep time: 5 minutes | Cook time: 35 minutes | Servings: 4

2 cups roasted vegetable broth	½ cup of spring onions, chopped
2 chicken breasts, cut into halves	1 Serrano pepper, deveined and chopped
¾ teaspoon fine sea salt	1 bell pepper, deveined and chopped
¼ teaspoon mixed peppercorns, freshly cracked	1 tablespoon tamari sauce
1 teaspoon cumin powder	½ chopped fresh tarragon
1½ teaspoons sesame oil	
1½ tablespoons Worcester sauce	

1. Select Level 3. Select the "AIR FRY" function of Ninja Foodi Smart XL Pro Air Oven, set temperature to 380°F/195°C and time to 18 minutes. Select START/STOP to begin preheating. 2. Cook the vegetable broth and chicken breasts in a large saucepan for 10 minutes. Lower the heat and simmer for another 10 minutes. 3. Let the chicken cool briefly. Then tear the chicken into shreds with a stand mixer or two forks. 4. Coat the shredded chicken with the salt, cracked peppercorns, cumin, sesame oil and the Worcester sauce. 5. Transfer to the Air Fryer and air fry for 18 minutes, or longer as needed. 6. In the meantime, cook the remaining ingredients over medium heat in a skillet, until the vegetables are tender and fragrant. 7. Take the skillet off the heat. Stir in the shredded chicken, incorporating all the ingredients well. Serve immediately.
Per Serving: Calories 173; Fat 13.6g; Sodium 281mg; Carbs 3g; Fiber 1g; Sugar 1g; Protein 10g

Chapter 4 Beef, Pork, and Lamb Recipes

Parmesan Pork Meatballs

Prep time: 15 minutes | Cook time: 10 minutes | Servings: 4

12 ounces ground pork
2 ounces parmesan, grated
1 teaspoon Italian seasonings
1 teaspoon black pepper
1 teaspoon chili flakes
1 teaspoon fresh parsley, chopped
1 teaspoon avocado oil
1 teaspoon salt

1. Mix up ground pork, parmesan, Italian seasoning, black pepper, chili flakes, parsley, and salt. Make 4 balls from the mixture. 2. Select the Air Fry mode. Set the Ninja Foodi Smart XL Pro temperature to 365°F/185°C. Select Level "3" and set the time on your Ninja Foodi Smart XL Pro Air Fryer Oven to 10 minutes. Press Start/Pause to begin preheating. Continue to the next step when it is done preheating. 3. Then brush its air fryer basket with avocado oil. Put the pork balls inside. 4. Insert its air fryer basket into the level 3 of the oven and close the door. Cook them at 365°F/185°C for 10 minutes.
Per Serving: Calories 373; Fat 8.5 g; Sodium 4928 mg; Carbs 0.8g; Fiber 0.3g; Sugar 7.6g; Protein 74.5g

Boneless Ribeye Steaks

Prep time: 35 minutes | Cook time: 12 minutes | Servings: 2–4

2 (8-ounces) boneless ribeye steaks
4 teaspoons Worcestershire sauce
½ teaspoon garlic powder
Pepper, to taste
4 teaspoons olive oil
Salt, to taste

1. Season steaks on both sides with Worcestershire sauce. Use the back of a spoon to spread. 2. Rub both sides of steaks with garlic powder and coarsely black pepper to taste. 3. Drizzle both sides of steaks with olive oil, again using the back of a spoon to spread evenly over surfaces. 4. Allow steaks to marinate for 30 minutes. 5. place both steaks in air fryer basket. Insert its air fryer basket into the level 3 of the oven and close the door. Cook on "Air Fry" Mode, select level 3, and set its temperature to 390°F/200°C for 5 minutes per side. Serve.
Per Serving: Calories 597; Fat 17.1 g; Sodium 723 mg; Carbs 66.5g; Fiber 9.3g; Sugar 45g; Protein 48.6g

Air Fried Calf's Liver

Prep time: 15 minutes | Cook time: 4–5 minutes | Servings: 4

1 pound sliced calf's liver
Black pepper and salt
2 eggs
2 tablespoons milk
½ cup whole wheat flour
1½ cups panko breadcrumbs
½ cup plain breadcrumbs
½ teaspoon salt
¼ teaspoon pepper
Oil for misting or cooking spray

1. Cut liver slices crosswise into strips about ½-inch wide. Sprinkle with black pepper and salt to taste. 2. Beat egg and milk in a shallow dish. 3. Place wheat flour in a second shallow dish. 4. In a third shallow dish, mix panko, plain breadcrumbs, ½ teaspoon salt, and ¼ teaspoon pepper. 5. Preheat on "Air Fry" Mode, and set its temperature to 390°F/200°C. Select Level "3" and set the time on your Ninja Foodi Smart XL Pro Air Fryer Oven to 10 minutes. Press Start/Pause to begin preheating. Continue to the next step when it is done preheating. 6. Dip liver strips in flour, egg wash, and then breadcrumbs, pressing in coating slightly to make crumbs stick. 7. Cooking half the liver at a time, place strips in air fryer basket in a single layer, close but not touching. 8. Cook on "Air Fry" Mode, select level 3, and set its temperature to 390°F/200°C for 4 to 5 minutes until done to your preference. 9. Repeat step 7 to cook remaining liver.
Per Serving: Calories 379; Fat 20.9 g; Sodium 1598 mg; Carbs 10g; Fiber 2.2g; Sugar 2.1g; Protein 37g

Pork Stuffed Calzones

Prep time: 30 minutes | Cook time: 7–8 minutes | Servings: 8

Filling
¼ pound ground pork sausage
½ teaspoon chile powder
¼ teaspoon ground cumin
⅛ teaspoon garlic powder
⅛ teaspoon onion powder
⅛ teaspoon oregano
½ cup ricotta cheese
1-ounce sharp cheddar cheese,
shredded
2 ounces pepper jack cheese, shredded
1 4-ounce can chopped green chiles, drained
Oil for misting or cooking spray
Salsa, sour cream, or guacamole

Crust
2 cups white wheat flour
1 package (¼ ounce) rapid rise yeast
1 teaspoon salt
½ teaspoon chile powder
½ teaspoon ground cumin
1 cup warm water (125°F/50°C)
2 teaspoons olive oil

1. Crumble sausage into air fryer baking pan and stir in the filling seasonings: chile powder, cumin, garlic powder, onion powder, and oregano. Cook on "Air Fry" Mode, select level 3, and set its temperature to 390°F/200°C for 2 minutes. Stir, breaking apart, insert its air fryer basket in the level 3 and cook for 3 to 4 minutes, until well done. 2. To make dough, mix flour, yeast, salt, chile powder, and cumin. Stir in warm water and oil until soft dough forms. Turn out onto lightly floured board and knead for 3 or 4 minutes. Let dough rest for 10 minutes. 3. Place the three cheeses in a medium bowl. Add cooked sausage and chiles and stir until well mixed. cut dough into 8 pieces. 4. Working with 4 pieces of the prepared dough, press each into a circle about 5 inches in diameter. Top each dough circle with 2 heaping tablespoons of filling. Fold over into a half-moon shape and press edges together. Seal edges firmly to prevent leakage. Spray both sides with oil spray. 5. Place 4 calzones in air fryer basket. Insert its air fryer basket into the level 3 of the oven and close the door. Cook on "Air Fry" Mode, select level 3, and set its temperature to 360°F/180°C for 5 minutes. Mist with oil or spray and cook for 2 to 3 minutes, until crust is done and nicely browned. 6. While the first batch is cooking, press out the remaining dough, fill, and shape into calzones. 7. Spray both sides with oil or cooking spray and cook for 5 minutes. If needed, mist with oil and continue cooking for 2 to 3 minutes longer. This second batch will cook a little faster than the first because your air fryer is already hot.8. Serve plain or with salsa, sour cream, or guacamole.
Per Serving: Calories 183; Fat 0.4 g; Sodium 4347 mg; Carbs 5.6g; Fiber 0.6g; Sugar 8.4g; Protein 40.2g

Lamb Stuffed Pita Pockets

Prep time: 15 minutes | Cook time: 5–7 minutes | Servings: 4

Dressing
1 cup plain yogurt
1 tablespoon lemon juice
1 teaspoon dried dill weed, crushed
1 teaspoon ground oregano
½ teaspoon salt
Meatballs
½ pound ground lamb
1 tablespoon diced onion
1 teaspoon dried parsley
1 teaspoon dried dill weed, crushed
¼ teaspoon oregano
¼ teaspoon coriander
¼ teaspoon ground cumin
¼ teaspoon salt
4 pita halves
Suggested Toppings
Red onion, slivered
Seedless cucumber, thinly sliced
Crumbled feta cheese
Sliced black olives
Chopped fresh peppers

1. Mix all the dressing ingredients and refrigerate while preparing lamb. 2. Mix all meatball ingredients in a suitable bowl and stir to distribute seasonings. 3. Shape meat mixture into 12 small meatballs, rounded or slightly flattened if you prefer. 4. Cook on "Air Fry" Mode, select level 3, and set its temperature to 390°F/200°C°C for 5 to 7 minutes, until well done. Remove and drain on paper towels. 5. To serve, pile meatballs in pita pockets and drizzle with dressing. Put the suggested toppings in pita pockets, if desired.
Per Serving: Calories 445; Fat 28.2 g; Sodium 322 mg; Carbs 6.2g; Fiber 2.2g; Sugar 1.4g; Protein 43.7g

Spiced Lamb Chops

Prep time: 30 minutes | Cook time: 20 minutes | Servings: 2–3

2 teaspoons oil
½ teaspoon ground rosemary
½ teaspoon lemon juice
1-pound lamb chops,
approximately 1-inch thick
Black pepper and salt
Cooking spray

1. Mix the oil, rosemary, and lemon juice and rub into all sides of the lamb chops. Season to taste with black pepper and salt. 2. Spray air fryer basket with nonstick spray and place lamb chops in it. 3. Cook on "Air Fry" Mode, select level 3, and set its temperature to 360°F/180°C for 20 minutes. For rare chops, stop cooking after about 12 minutes and check for doneness.
Per Serving: Calories 362; Fat 22.6 g; Sodium 242 mg; Carbs 2.9g; Fiber 1.4g; Sugar 0.5g; Protein 37.4g

Italian Sausage with Peppers

Prep time: 10 minutes | Cook time: 21–25 minutes | Servings: 6

1 6-ounce can tomato paste	1 tablespoon extra-virgin olive oil
⅔ cup water	½ large onion, cut in 1-inch
1 8-ounce can tomato sauce	chunks
1 teaspoon dried parsley flakes	4 ounces fresh mushrooms, sliced
½ teaspoon garlic powder	1 large green bell pepper, diced
⅛ teaspoon oregano	8 ounces spaghetti, cooked
½ pound mild Italian bulk sausage	Parmesan cheese for serving

1. In a suitable saucepan or skillet, stir the tomato paste, water, tomato sauce, parsley, garlic, and oregano. Heat on stovetop over very low heat while preparing meat and vegetables. 2. Break sausage into small chunks, about ½-inch pieces. Place in air fryer baking pan. 3. Cook on "Air Fry" Mode, select level 3, and set its temperature to 390°F/200°C°C for 5 minutes. Stir. Cook 5 to 7 minutes longer until sausage is well done. Remove from pan, drain on paper towels, and add to the sauce mixture. 4. If any sausage grease remains in baking pan, pour it off or use paper towels to soak it up. 5. Place olive oil, onions, and mushrooms in pan and stir. Cook for 5 minutes or just until soft. Using a slotted spoon, transfer onions and mushrooms from baking pan into the sauce and sausage mixture. 6. Place bell pepper chunks in air fryer baking pan and cook for 6 to 8 minutes until soft. When done, stir into sauce with sausage and other vegetables. 7. Serve over cooked spaghetti with plenty of parmesan cheese.
Per Serving: Calories 210; Fat 5.4 g; Sodium 110 mg; Carbs 18.5g; Fiber 2.4g; Sugar 13.1g; Protein 23.5g

Air Fried Wax Bean

Prep time: 10 minutes | Cook time: 10 minutes | Servings: 4

1-pound fresh wax beans, trimmed	1 teaspoon garlic powder
2 teaspoons olive oil	½ teaspoon cumin powder
½ teaspoon onion powder	Black pepper and salt, to taste

1. Toss the wax beans with the remaining recipe ingredients. 2. Cook on Air Fry mode, select level 3. Air Fry the wax beans at 390°F/200°C for about 6 minutes, tossing the basket halfway through the cooking time. 3. Enjoy!
Per Serving: Calories 76; Fat 4.2 g; Sodium 135 mg; Carbs 2.4g; Fiber 0.5g; Sugar 0.3g; Protein 6.2g

Meatball Subs with Marinara

Prep time: 15 minutes | Cook time: 9–11 minutes | Servings: 4–8

Marinara Sauce

1 (15-ounce) can diced tomatoes	½ teaspoon oregano
1 teaspoon garlic powder	⅛ teaspoon salt
1 teaspoon dried basil	1 tablespoon robust olive oil

Meatballs

¼ pound ground turkey	1 teaspoon garlic powder
¾ pound very lean ground beef	¼ teaspoon smoked paprika
1 tablespoon milk	¼ teaspoon crushed red pepper
½ cup corn bread pieces	1½ teaspoons dried parsley
1 egg	¼ teaspoon oregano
¼ teaspoon salt	2 teaspoons Worcestershire sauce
½ teaspoon dried onion	

Sandwiches

4 large whole-grain sub or hoagie rolls, split	Jalapeño or banana peppers
Toppings, sliced or chopped:	Red or green bell pepper
Mushrooms	Red onions
	Grated cheese

1. Place all marinara ingredients in saucepan and bring to a boil. Lower heat and simmer 10 minutes, uncovered. 2. Mix all meatball recipe ingredients in large bowl and stir. Mixture should be well blended but don't overwork it. Excessive mixing will toughen the meatballs. 3. Divide meat into 16 equal portions and shape into balls. 4. Cook on Air Fry mode and select level 3. Cook the balls at 360°F/180°Cuntil meat is done and juices run clear, about 9 to 11 minutes. 5. While meatballs are cooking, taste marinara. If you prefer stronger flavors, then add more seasoning and simmer another 5 minutes. 6. When meatballs finish cooking, drain them on paper towels. 7. To assemble subs, place 4 meatballs on each sub roll, spoon sauce over meat, and add preferred toppings. Serve with additional marinara for dipping.
Per Serving: Calories 487; Fat 15 g; Sodium 4856 mg; Carbs 0g; Fiber 0g; Sugar 0g; Protein 85.4g

Beef Steak

Prep time: 10 minutes | Cook time: 15 minutes | Servings: 4

2 eggs	½ teaspoon pepper
½ cup buttermilk	1-pound beef cube steaks
1½ cups flour	Black pepper and salt
¾ teaspoon salt	Oil for misting or cooking spray

1. Beat eggs and buttermilk in a shallow dish. 2. In another shallow dish, stir the flour, ½ teaspoon salt, and ¼ teaspoon pepper. 3. Season cube steaks with remaining black pepper and salt to taste. Dip in flour, buttermilk egg wash, and then flour again. 4. Spray both sides of steaks with oil or cooking spray. 5. Cooking in 2 batches, place steaks in air fryer basket in single layer. Cook on "Air Fry" Mode, select level 3, and set its temperature to 360°F/180°Cfor 10 minutes. Spray tops of steaks with oil and cook 5 minutes until meat is well done. 6. Repeat to cook remaining steaks.
Per Serving: Calories 512; Fat 7.1 g; Sodium 42 mg; Carbs 28.5g; Fiber 2.1g; Sugar 13.4g; Protein 1.2g

Meat Pies

Prep time: 20 minutes | Cook time: meat 10–12 minutes | Servings: 8 pies

Filling

½ pound lean ground beef	½ teaspoon garlic powder
¼ cup finely chopped onion	½ teaspoon red pepper flakes
¼ cup finely chopped green bell pepper	1 tablespoon low sodium Worcestershire sauce
⅛ teaspoon salt	

Crust

2 cups self-rising flour	1 egg
¼ cup butter, finely diced	1 tablespoon water or milk
1 cup milk	Oil for misting or cooking spray
Egg wash	

1. Mix all filling ingredients well and shape into 4 small patties. 2. Cook on Air Fry mode and Select Level "3". Cook patties in air fryer basket at 390°F/200°C for 10 to 12 minutes until well done. 3. Place patties in large bowl and use fork and knife to crumble meat into very small pieces. Set aside. 4. To make the crust, use a pastry blender or fork to cut the butter into the flour until well mixed. Add milk and stir until dough stiffens. 5. Divide dough into 8 equal portions. 6. On a floured surface, roll each portion of dough into a circle. The circle should be thin and about 5 inches in diameter, but don't worry about getting a perfect shape. Uneven circles result in a rustic look that many people prefer. 7. Spoon 2 tablespoons of meat filling onto each dough circle. 8. Brush egg wash all the way around the edge of dough circle, about ½-inch deep. (see tip.) 9. Fold each circle in half and press dough with tines of a dinner fork to seal the edges all the way around. 10. Brush tops of sealed meat pies with egg wash. 11. Cook filled pies in a single layer in air fryer basket at 360°F/180°C for 4 minutes. Spray tops with oil or cooking spray, turn pies over, and spray bottoms with oil or cooking spray. Cook for an additional 2 minutes. 12. Repeat previous step to cook remaining pies.
Per Serving: Calories 273; Fat 24 g; Sodium 1181 mg; Carbs 12.8g; Fiber 1g; Sugar 1.4g; Protein 20g

Pepperoni Pizza Pockets

Prep time: 10 minutes | Cook time: 8–10 minutes | Servings: 4

4 bread slices, 1-inch thick
Olive oil for misting
24 slices pepperoni (about 2 ounces)
1 ounce roasted red peppers, drained and patted dry
1-ounce pepper jack cheese cut into 4 slices
Pizza sauce

1. Spray both sides of bread slices with olive oil. 2. Stand slices upright and cut a deep slit in the top to create a pocket—almost to the bottom crust but not all the way through. 3. Stuff each bread pocket with 6 slices of pepperoni, a suitable strip of roasted red pepper, and a slice of cheese. 4. Place bread pockets in air fryer basket, standing up. Cook on "Air Fry" Mode, select level 3, and set its temperature to 360°F/180°Cfor 8 to 10 minutes, until filling is heated through and bread is lightly browned. Serve while hot as is or with pizza sauce for dipping.
Per Serving: Calories 596; Fat 10.8 g; Sodium 7429 mg; Carbs 14.9g; Fiber 1.9g; Sugar 21.9g; Protein 112.2g

Pizza Tortilla Rolls

Prep time: 15 minutes | Cook time: 7–8 minutes | Servings: 4

1 teaspoon butter
½ medium onion, slivered
½ red or green bell pepper, julienned
4 ounces fresh white mushrooms, chopped
8 flour tortillas (6- or 7-inch size)
½ cup pizza sauce
8 thin slices deli ham
24 pepperoni slices (about 1½ ounces)
1 cup shredded mozzarella cheese (about 4 ounces)
Oil for misting or cooking spray

1. Place butter, onions, bell pepper, and mushrooms in air fryer baking pan. Cook on "Air Fry" Mode, select level 3, and set its temperature to 390°F/200°C or 3 minutes. Mix and cook 3 to 4 minutes longer until just crisp and soft. Remove pan and set aside. 2. Spread roughly 2 teaspoons of pizza sauce on each tortilla half before assembling the rolls. Add three slices of pepperoni and a piece of ham on top. On top of the cheese, distribute the sautéed vegetables among the tortillas. 3. Tortillas should be rolled, then oiled and, if necessary, fastened with toothpicks. 4. Place 4 rolls in air fryer basket. Insert its air fryer basket into the level 3 of the oven and close the door. Cook for 4 minutes. Turn and cook 3 to 4 minutes, until heated through and lightly browned. 5. Repeat step 4 to cook remaining pizza rolls.
Per Serving: Calories 559; Fat 23.8 g; Sodium 430 mg; Carbs 18.3g; Fiber 0.3g; Sugar 17.6g; Protein 65.8g

Tasty Pork & Beef Egg Rolls

Prep time: 30 minutes | Cook time: 7–8 minutes | Servings: 8 egg rolls

¼ pound very lean ground beef
¼ pound lean ground pork
1 tablespoon soy sauce
1 teaspoon olive oil
½ cup grated carrots
2 green onions, chopped
2 cups grated napa cabbage
¼ cup chopped water chestnuts
¼ teaspoon salt
¼ teaspoon garlic powder
¼ teaspoon black pepper
1 egg
1 tablespoon water
8 egg roll wraps
Oil for misting or cooking spray

1. In a suitable skillet, brown beef and pork with soy sauce. Remove cooked meat from skillet, drain, and set aside. 2. Pour off any excess grease from skillet. Add olive oil, carrots, and onions. Sauté until barely soft, about 1 minute. 3. Stir in cabbage, cover, insert its air fryer basket in the level 3 and cook for 1 minute or just until cabbage slightly wilts. Remove from heat. 4. In a suitable bowl, mix the cooked meats and vegetables, water chestnuts, salt, garlic powder, and pepper. Stir well. If needed, then add more salt to taste. 5. Beat egg and water in a suitable bowl. 6. Fill egg roll wrappers, using about ¼ cup of filling for each wrap. Roll up and brush all over with egg wash to seal. Spray very lightly with olive oil or cooking spray. 7. Place 4 egg rolls in air fryer basket. Insert its air fryer basket into the level 3 of the oven and close the door. Cook on "Air Fry" Mode, select level 3, and set its temperature to 390°F/200°C for 4 minutes. Turnover and cook 3 to 4 more minutes, until golden and crispy. 8. Repeat to cook remaining egg rolls.
Tip: if needed, drain filling in colander before placing in wrappers. Wet filling can prevent the wraps from crisping.
Per Serving: Calories 467; Fat 18.1 g; Sodium 438 mg; Carbs 6.6g; Fiber 0.5g; Sugar 5.5g; Protein 66.1g

Kielbasa with Pineapple

Prep time: 15 minutes | Cook time: 10 minutes | Servings: 2–4

Kielbasa chunks with pineapple & peppers
¾ pound kielbasa sausage
1 cup bell pepper chunks (any color)
1 8-ounce can pineapple chunks in juice, drained
1 tablespoon barbeque seasoning
1 tablespoon soy sauce
Cooking spray

1. Cut sausage into ½-inch slices. 2. In a medium bowl, toss all the recipe ingredients together. 3. Grease the Ninja Foody Smart Xl Pro's air fryer basket with nonstick cooking spray. 4. Pour sausage mixture into the basket. 5. Cook on "Air Fry" Mode, select level 3, and set its temperature to 390°F/200°C°C for approximately 5 minutes. Shake basket. Insert its air fryer basket into the level 3 of the oven and close the door. Cook an additional 5 minutes.
Per Serving: Calories 319; Fat 14.7 g; Sodium 92 mg; Carbs 30.3g; Fiber 4g; Sugar 12.3g; Protein 24g

Saucy Pork Chops

Prep time: 5 minutes | Cook time: 16–20 minutes | Servings: 2

2 bone-in, center cut pork chops, 1-inch thick (10 ounces each)
2 teaspoons Worcestershire sauce
Black pepper and salt
Cooking spray

1. Rub the Worcestershire sauce into both sides of pork chops. 2. Season with black pepper and salt to taste. 3. Grease the Ninja Foodi Smart XL Pro's air fryer basket with cooking spray and place the chops in basket side by side. 4. Cook on "Air Fry" Mode, select level 3, and set its temperature to 360°F/180°C for 16 to 20 minutes until well done. Let rest for 5 minutes before serving.
Per Serving: Calories 540; Fat 26.8 g; Sodium 309 mg; Carbs 2.6g; Fiber 0.4g; Sugar 1.2g; Protein 69.9g

Air Fryer Steak Tips

Prep time: 10 minutes | Cook time: 8 minutes | Servings 4

⅓ cup soy sauce
1 cup water
¼ cup freshly squeezed lemon juice
3 tablespoons brown sugar
1 teaspoon garlic powder
1 teaspoon ground ginger
1 teaspoon dried parsley
2 pounds steak tips, cut into 1-inch cubes

1. In a suitable mixing bowl, make the marinade. Mix the soy sauce, water, lemon juice, brown sugar, garlic powder, ginger, and parsley. 2. Place the meat in the marinade, then cover and refrigerate for at least 1 hour. 3. Select the Air Fry mode. Set the Ninja Foodi Smart XL Pro temperature to 400°F/200°C. Select Level "3" and set the time on your Ninja Foodi Smart XL Pro Air Fryer Oven to 4 minutes. Press Start/Pause to begin preheating. Continue to the next step when it is done preheating. Spray its air fryer basket with olive oil. 4. When the steak is done, place it in the greased air fryer basket. 5. Set the timer and cook for 4 minutes. 6. Using tongs, flip the meat. 7. Reset the timer and cook for 4 minutes more.
Per Serving: Calories 322; Fat 14 g; Sodium 679 mg; Carbs 1.1g; Fiber 0.2g; Sugar 0.7g; Protein 45.5g

Sausage Calzone

Prep time: 30 minutes | Cook time: 7–8 minutes | Servings: 8 calzones

Crust
2 cups white wheat flour
1 package (¼ ounce) instant yeast
1 teaspoon salt
Filling
¼ pound Italian sausage
½ cup ricotta cheese
4 ounces mozzarella cheese, shredded
½ teaspoon dried basil
1 cup warm water (125°F/52°C)
2 teaspoons olive oil

¼ cup grated parmesan cheese
Oil for misting or cooking spray
Marinara sauce for serving

1. Crumble Italian sausage into air fryer baking pan and cook on "Air Fry" Mode, select level 3, and set its temperature to 390°F/200°C for 5 minutes. Stir, breaking apart, insert its air fryer basket in the level 3 and cook for 3 to 4 minutes, until well done. 2. To make dough, mix flour, yeast, salt, and basil. Add warm water and oil and stir until a soft dough forms. Turn out onto lightly floured board and knead for 3 or 4 minutes. Let dough rest for 10 minutes. 3. to make filling, mix the three cheeses in a medium bowl and mix well. Stir in the cooked sausage. cut dough into 8 pieces. 4. Working with 4 pieces of the prepared dough, press each into a circle about 5 inches in diameter. Top each dough circle with 2 heaping tablespoons of filling. Fold over to create a half-moon shape and press edges firmly together. Be sure that edges are firmly sealed to prevent leakage. Spray both sides with oil spray. 5. Place 4 calzones in air fryer basket. Insert its air fryer basket into the level 3 of the oven and close the door. Cook on "Air Fry" Mode, select level 3, and set its temperature to 360°F/180°Cfor 5 minutes. Mist with oil and cook for 2 to 3 minutes, until crust is done and nicely browned. 6. While the first batch is cooking, press out the remaining dough, fill, and shape into calzones. 7. Spray both sides with oil and cook for 5 minutes. If needed, mist with oil and continue cooking for 2 to 3 minutes longer. This second batch will cook a little faster than the first because your air fryer is already hot. Serve.
Per Serving: Calories 384; Fat 20.5g; Sodium 449 mg; Carbs 5.1g; Fiber 2.1g; Sugar 0.7g; Protein 45g

Sweet and Sour Meat Loaves

Prep time: 15 minutes | Cook time: 17–19 minutes | Servings: 4

Sauce
¼ cup white vinegar
¼ cup brown sugar
2 tablespoons Worcestershire
sauce
½ cup ketchup

Meat loaves
1 pound very lean ground beef
⅔ cup dry bread (approx. 1 slice torn into small pieces)
1 egg
⅓ cup minced onion
1 teaspoon salt
2 tablespoons ketchup

1. In a suitable saucepan, mix all sauce ingredients and bring to a boil. Remove from heat and stir to ensure that brown sugar dissolves completely. 2. In a suitable bowl, mix the beef, bread, egg, onion, salt, and ketchup. Mix well. 3. Divide the prepared meat mixture into 4 portions and shape each into a thick, round patty. Patties will be about 3 to 3½ inches in diameter, and all four should fit easily into its air fryer basket at once. 4. Cook on "Air Fry" Mode, select level 3, and set its temperature to 360°F/180°C for 16 to 18 minutes, until meat is well done. Baste tops of mini loaves with a suitable amount of sauce, insert its air fryer basket in the level 3 and cook 1 minute. 5. Serve hot with additional sauce on the side.
Per Serving: Calories 457; Fat 10.1 g; Sodium 423 mg; Carbs 1.6g; Fiber 0.5g; Sugar 0.4g; Protein 14.9g

Pork Loin with Orange Marmalade

Prep time: 10 minutes | Cook time: 45–50 minutes | Servings: 8

1 tablespoon lime juice
1 tablespoon orange marmalade
1 teaspoon coarse brown mustard
1 teaspoon curry powder
1 teaspoon dried lemongrass
2-pound boneless pork loin roast
Black pepper and salt
Cooking spray

1. Mix the lime juice, marmalade, mustard, curry powder, and lemongrass. 2. Rub mixture all over the surface of the pork loin. Season to taste with black pepper and salt. 3. Spray air fryer basket with nonstick spray and place pork roast diagonally in basket. 4. Cook on "Air Fry" Mode, select level 3, and set its temperature to 360°F/180°C for approximately 45 to 50 minutes. 5. Wrap roast in foil and let rest for 10 minutes before slicing.
Per Serving: Calories 297; Fat 18.4 g; Sodium 1151 mg; Carbs 11.6g; Fiber 0.6g; Sugar 10.9g; Protein 20.5g

Beef Steaks

Prep time: 5 minutes | Cook time: 8–12 minutes | Servings: 4

4 small beef cube steaks
Black pepper and salt
½ cup flour
Oil for misting or cooking spray

1. Cut cube steaks into 1-inch-wide strips. 2. Sprinkle with black pepper and salt to taste. 3. Roll in flour to coat all sides. 4. Spray air fryer basket with cooking spray or oil. 5. Place steak strips in air fryer basket in single layer, very close but not touching. Spray top of steak strips with oil or cooking spray. 6. Cook on "Air Fry" Mode, select level 3, and set its temperature to 390°F/200°C for 4 minutes, turn strips over, and spray with oil or cooking spray. 7. Cook 4 more minutes and test with fork for doneness. Steak fingers should be crispy outside with no red juices inside. If needed, cook an additional 2 to 4 minutes until well done. (don't eat beef cube steak rare.) 8. Repeat steps 5 through 7 to cook remaining strips.
Per Serving: Calories 370; Fat 10.5 g; Sodium 503 mg; Carbs 21.4g; Fiber 3.1g; Sugar 1.9g; Protein 46.6g

Beef Stuffed Bell Peppers

Prep time: 20 minutes | Cook time: 22 minutes | Servings: 4

¼ pound lean ground pork
¾ pound lean ground beef
¼ cup onion, minced
1 15-ounce can red gold crushed tomatoes
1 teaspoon Worcestershire sauce
1 teaspoon barbeque seasoning
1 teaspoon honey
½ teaspoon dried basil
½ cup cooked brown rice
½ teaspoon garlic powder
½ teaspoon oregano
½ teaspoon salt
2 small bell peppers

1. Place pork, beef, and onion in air fryer baking pan and cook on "Air Fry" Mode, select level 3, and set its temperature to 360°F/180°Cfor

5 minutes. 2. Stir to break apart chunks and cook 3 more minutes. Continue cooking and stirring in 2-minute intervals until meat is well done. Remove from pan and drain. 3. In a suitable saucepan, mix the tomatoes, Worcestershire, barbeque seasoning, honey, and basil. Stir well to mix in honey and seasonings. 4. In a suitable bowl, mix the cooked meat mixture, rice, garlic powder, oregano, and salt. Add ¼ cup of the seasoned crushed tomatoes. Stir until well mixed. 5. Cut peppers in half and remove their stems and seeds. 6. Stuff each pepper half with one fourth of the meat mixture. 7. Place the peppers in air fryer basket. Insert its air fryer basket into the level 3 of the oven and close the door. Cook for 12 minutes, until peppers are crisp soft. 8. Heat remaining tomato sauce. Serve peppers with warm sauce spooned over top.
Per Serving: Calories 206; Fat 6.4 g; Sodium 911 mg; Carbs 28.9g; Fiber 3.6g; Sugar 20.4g; Protein 11g

Pork Cutlets

Prep time: 20 minutes | Cook time: 7–9 minutes | Servings: 4

Aloha salsa
1 cup fresh pineapple, chopped in small pieces
¼ cup red onion, finely chopped
¼ cup green or red bell pepper, chopped
½ teaspoon ground cinnamon
1 teaspoon low-sodium soy sauce
⅛ teaspoon crushed red pepper
⅛ teaspoon black pepper
2 eggs
2 tablespoons milk
¼ cup flour
¼ cup panko breadcrumbs
4 teaspoons sesame seeds
1 pound boneless, thin pork cutlets (⅜- to ½-inch thick)
Lemon pepper and salt
¼ cup cornstarch
Oil for misting or cooking spray

1. In a suitable bowl, stir all the recipe ingredients for salsa. Cover and refrigerate while cooking pork. 2. Preheat on "Air Fry" Mode, and set its temperature to 390°F/200°C. Select Level "3" and set the time on your Ninja Foodi Smart XL Pro Air Fryer Oven to 9 minutes. Press Start/Pause to begin preheating. Continue to the next step when it is done preheating. 3. Beat eggs and milk in shallow dish. 4. Now in another shallow dish, mix the flour, panko, and sesame seeds. 5. Sprinkle pork cutlets with lemon pepper and salt to taste. Most lemon pepper seasoning contains salt, so go easy adding extra. 6. Dip pork cutlets in cornstarch, egg mixture, and then panko coating. Spray both sides with oil or cooking spray. 7. Cook cutlets for 3 minutes. Turn cutlets over, spraying both sides, and continue cooking for 4 to 6 minutes until well done. 8. Serve fried cutlets with salsa on the side.
Per Serving: Calories 363; Fat 17.1 g; Sodium1065 mg; Carbs 19.8g; Fiber 3.4g; Sugar 12.9g; Protein 33.7g

Breaded Pork Cutlets

Prep time: 10 minutes | Cook time: 7 minutes | Servings: 4

8 thin boneless pork loin cutlets
¾ teaspoon adobo seasoning salt
1 large egg, beaten
1 teaspoon sazon seasoning
½ cup 2 tablespoons bread crumbs
Olive oil spray
5 ounces avocado (from 1 medium Hass), sliced
1 large tomato, sliced
2 limes, cut into wedges, for serving

1. Working one at a time, place a pork cutlet between two sheets of plastic wrap. Use a heavy skillet or meat mallet to pound the pork to a ¼-inch thickness, being careful not to tear the meat. 2. Season the cutlets on both sides with the adobo seasoning. 3. In a shallow bowl, beat the egg with 1 teaspoon water and the sazon. Place the bread crumbs in a second shallow bowl. Dip the cutlets into the egg mixture and let the excess drip off, then dip them in the bread crumbs. Place the cutlets on a work surface and press lightly with the flat side of a heavy knife to help the bread crumbs adhere. Liberally spray both sides with oil. 4. Select the Air Fry mode. Set the Ninja Foodi Smart XL Pro temperature to 400°F/200°C. Select Level "3" and set the time on your Ninja Foodi Smart XL Pro Air Fryer Oven to 7 minutes. Press Start/Pause to begin preheating. Continue to the next step when it is done preheating. 5. Working in batches, place the cutlets in its air fryer basket. Cook for 7 minutes, flip when cooked halfway through, until golden and the center is no longer pink. 6. Divide the cutlets among 4 plates and serve with the avocado, tomato, and lime wedges. Serve immediately.
Per Serving: Calories 467; Fat 20.6 g; Sodium 424 mg; Carbs 19.4g; Fiber 1.1g; Sugar 17.6g; Protein 50.4g

Pork Loin Schnitzel

Prep time: 15 minutes | Cook time: 14–16 minutes | Servings: 4

4 thin boneless pork loin chops	¼ teaspoon marjoram
2 tablespoons lemon juice	1 cup plain breadcrumbs
½ cup flour	2 eggs, beaten
1 teaspoon salt	Oil for misting or cooking spray

1. Rub the lemon juice into all sides of pork chops. 2. Mix the flour, salt, and marjoram. 3. Place flour mixture on a sheet of wax paper. 4. Place breadcrumbs on another sheet of wax paper. 5. Roll pork chops in flour, dip in beaten eggs, then roll in breadcrumbs. Mist all sides with oil or cooking spray. 6. Spray Ninja Foodi Smart XL Pro air fryer basket with cooking spray and place pork chops in basket. 7. Cook on "Air Fry" Mode, select level 3, and set its temperature to 390°F/200°C for 7 minutes. Turn, mist again, insert its air fryer basket in the level 3 and cook for another 7 or 8 minutes, until well done. Serve with lemon wedges.
Per Serving: Calories 467; Fat 19.8 g; Sodium 958 mg; Carbs 2.6g; Fiber 0.1g; Sugar 2.2g; Protein 65.7g

Beef Stir-Fry

Prep time: 10 minutes | Cook time: 10 minutes | Servings: 4 to 6

For the Marinade

¼ cup hoisin sauce	1 tablespoon soy sauce
2 teaspoons minced garlic	1 teaspoon ground ginger
1 teaspoon sesame oil	¼ cup water

For the Stir-Fry

1-pound beef top sirloin steak, sliced	1 red bell pepper, julienned
½ cup diced red onion	1 yellow bell pepper, julienned
1 green bell pepper, cut into 1-inch strips	1 pound of broccoli florets
	1 teaspoon stir-fry oil

1. In a suitable mixing bowl, make the marinade. Mix the hoisin sauce, garlic, sesame oil, soy sauce, ginger, and water. 2. Add the steak, then cover and let marinate in the refrigerator for about 30 minutes. 3. In a suitable bowl, mix the vegetables and the stir-fry oil and toss until the vegetables are thoroughly coated with oil. 4. Place the vegetables in its air fryer basket. 5. Select the Air Fry mode. Set the Ninja Foodi Smart XL Pro temperature to 250°F/120°C. Select Level "3" and set the time on your Ninja Foodi Smart XL Pro Air Fryer Oven to 2 minutes. Press Start/Pause to begin preheating. Continue to the next step when it is done preheating. Set the timer and steam for 2 minutes. Check and make sure that the vegetables are soft. If not, then add another 2 to 3 minutes. 6. Once the vegetables are done, transfer them to a suitable bowl and place the meat into the air fryer. 7. Select the Air Fry mode. Set the Ninja Foodi Smart XL Pro temperature to 360°F/180°C. Select Level "3" and set the time on your Ninja Foodi Smart XL Pro Air Fryer Oven to 4 minutes. Press Start/Pause to begin preheating. Continue to the next step when it is done preheating. Set the timer and fry for 4 minutes. 8. Pour the vegetables back into its air fryer basket and shake.9. Release its air fryer basket. Pour the meat and vegetables into a suitable bowl and serve.
Per Serving: Calories 556; Fat 37.8 g; Sodium 1792 mg; Carbs 16.5g; Fiber 0.5g; Sugar 0g; Protein 29.8g

Air Fried Chili Steaks

Prep time: 10 minutes | Cook time: 14 minutes | Servings: 4

1½ pounds flank steak	Salt
Black pepper	
⅓ cup olive oil	4 teaspoons minced garlic
⅓ cup freshly squeezed lime juice	1 teaspoon ground cumin
½ cup chopped fresh cilantro	1 teaspoon chili powder

1. Spray its air fryer basket with olive oil. 2. Place the flank steak in a suitable mixing bowl. Season with black pepper and salt. 3. Add the olive oil, lime juice, cilantro, garlic, cumin, and chili powder and toss to coat the steak. 4. For the best flavor, let the steak marinate in the refrigerator for about 1 hour. 5. Place the steak in its air fryer basket. 6. Select the Air Fry mode. Set the Ninja Foodi Smart XL Pro temperature to 400°F/200°C. Select Level "3" and set the time on your Ninja Foodi Smart XL Pro Air Fryer Oven to 10 minutes. Press Start/Pause to begin preheating. Continue to the next step when it is done preheating. Set the timer and grill for 7 minutes. 7. Using tongs, flip the steak. 8. Reset the timer and grill for 7 minutes more. 9. Cook the steak to your desired level of doneness. For medium-rare texture, cook to an internal temperature of 135°F/55°C, or for medium, 145°F/60°C. Select Level "3" and set the time on your Ninja Foodi Smart XL Pro Air Fryer Oven to 10 minutes. Press Start/Pause to begin preheating. Continue to the next step when it is done preheating. Be careful not to overcook the steak, or it will dry out. 10. Serve.
Per Serving: Calories 556; Fat 37.8 g; Sodium 1792 mg; Carbs 16.5g; Fiber 0.5g; Sugar 0g; Protein 29.8g

Venison Meal

Prep time: 10 minutes | Cook time: 10–12 minutes | Servings: 4

2 eggs	¼ teaspoon pepper
¼ cup milk	1-pound venison backstrap, sliced
1 cup whole wheat flour	Black pepper and salt
½ teaspoon salt	Oil for misting or cooking spray

1. Beat eggs and milk in a shallow dish. 2. In another shallow dish, mix the flour, salt, and pepper. Stir to mix well. 3. Sprinkle venison steaks with additional black pepper and salt to taste. Dip in flour, egg wash, then in flour again, pressing in coating. 4. Spray steaks with oil or cooking spray on both sides. 5. Cooking in 2 batches, place steaks in its air fryer basket in a single layer. Cook on "Air Fry" Mode, select level 3, and set its temperature to 360°F/180°C for 8 minutes. Spray with oil, turn over, and spray other side. Cook for 2 minutes longer, until coating is crispy brown and meat is done to your liking. 6. Repeat to cook remaining venison.
Per Serving: Calories 546; Fat 40 g; Sodium 231 mg; Carbs 3.1g; Fiber 0.2g; Sugar 0.9g; Protein 40.4g

Moroccan Lemon Lamb Cutlets

Prep time: 5 minutes | Cook time: 30 minutes | Servings: 4

8 lamb cutlets	1 tablespoon cumin, ground
A pinch of black pepper and salt	1 tablespoon coriander seeds
4 tablespoons olive oil	Zest of 2 lemons, grated
½ cup mint leaves	3 tablespoons lemon juice
6 garlic cloves	

1. In a blender, mix all the recipe ingredients except the lamb and pulse well. 2. Rub the lamb cutlets with this mix, place them in your air fryer's basket. Insert its air fryer basket into the level 3 of the oven and close the door. 3. Cook on "Air Fry" Mode, select level 3, and set its temperature to 380°F/195°C for 15 minutes per side. Serve with a side salad.
Per Serving: Calories 291; Fat 14.8 g; Sodium 1363 mg; Carbs 5.2g; Fiber 0.5g; Sugar 4.9g; Protein 33.6g

Grilled Rib Eye Steaks with Herb Butter

Prep time: 10 minutes | Cook time: 8 minutes | Servings: 4

For the Herb Butter

1 cup unsalted butter	1 teaspoon minced shallot
1 garlic clove, roasted and peeled	1 teaspoon minced fresh parsley
1 tablespoon salt	1 teaspoon minced fresh sage
1 teaspoon black pepper	1 teaspoon minced fresh rosemary

For the Steak

4 (10- to 12-ounce) rib eye steaks	Black pepper
Salt	

To make the herb butter 1. In a suitable bowl, mix the butter, roasted garlic, salt, pepper, shallot, parsley, sage, and rosemary until the herbs are fully and evenly incorporated into the butter. 2. Cover the butter and refrigerate for about 1 hour.
To make the steak 1. Select the Air Fry mode. Set the Ninja Foodi Smart XL Pro temperature to 400°F/200°C. Select Level "3" and set the time on your Ninja Foodi Smart XL Pro Air Fryer Oven to 4 minutes. Press Start/Pause to begin preheating. Continue to the next step when it is done preheating. 2. Season the steaks with black pepper and salt. 3. Place the steaks into its air fryer basket. Grill for 4 minutes. 4. Using tongs, flip the steaks. 5. Reset the timer and grill for 4 minutes more. Cook the steaks to your desired level of doneness. For medium-rare doneness, cook to an internal temperature of 135°F/55°C, or for medium, 145°F/65°C. 6. Place a dab of the butter on each steak. (keep any remaining herb butter in the refrigerator for up to two days.)
Per Serving: Calories 667; Fat 18.4 g; Sodium 1526 mg; Carbs 22.5g; Fiber 3.2g; Sugar 2.9g; Protein 101.2g

Beef Sloppy Joes

Prep time: 10 minutes | Cook time: 21 minutes | Servings: 4

Oil for misting or cooking spray	1½ teaspoons brown sugar
1 pound very lean ground beef	1¼ teaspoons low-sodium
1 teaspoon onion powder	Worcestershire sauce
⅓ cup ketchup	½ teaspoon salt
¼ cup water	½ teaspoon vinegar
½ teaspoon celery seed	⅛ teaspoon dry mustard
1 tablespoon lemon juice	Hamburger or slider buns

1. Spray air fryer basket with olive oil. 2. Break raw ground beef into small chunks and pile into basket. 3. Cook on "Air Fry" Mode, select level 3, and set its temperature to 390°F/200°C for 5 minutes. Stir to break apart and cook 3 minutes. Stir and cook 2 to 4 minutes longer until meat is well done. 4. Remove meat from air fryer, drain, and use a knife and fork to crumble into small pieces. 5. Give your air fryer basket a quick rinse to remove any bits of meat. 6. Place all the remaining recipe ingredients except the buns in a 6 x 6-inch baking pan and mix together. 7. Add meat and stir well. 8. Cook on "Air Fry" Mode, select level 3, and set its temperature to 330°F/165°C for 5 minutes. Stir and cook for 2 minutes. 9. Scoop onto buns.
Per Serving: Calories 328; Fat 28.7 g; Sodium 95 mg; Carbs 7.4g; Fiber 2.8g; Sugar 0.7g; Protein 13g

Beef Hamburgers

Prep time: 10 minutes | Cook time: 8 minutes | Servings: 4

2 slices crustless bread	4 hamburger buns
¼ cup milk	6 slices foolproof air fryer bacon,
1½ pounds lean ground beef	for topping
1 teaspoon salt	Lettuce, sliced tomato, and pickle,
½ teaspoon black pepper	for topping
1 teaspoon minced garlic	

1. Cut the bread into 1-inch pieces. 2. Put the bread pieces in a suitable mixing bowl and pour the milk over them. Let sit for about 5 minutes. 3. In a medium bowl, then add the ground beef, the bread and milk mixture, salt, pepper, and minced garlic. 4. Using your hands, mix, making sure that the bread and milk mixture is broken down. 5. Divide the meat into fourths and form into patties. You should have 4 (6-ounce) patties. 6. Place the patties into its air fryer basket. 7. Select the Air Fry mode. Set the Ninja Foodi Smart XL Pro temperature to 400°F/200°C. Select Level "3" and set the time on your Ninja Foodi Smart XL Pro Air Fryer Oven to 4 minutes. Press Start/Pause to begin preheating. Continue to the next step when it is done preheating. Set the timer and grill for 4 minutes. 8. Using a spatula, flip and cook for 4 minutes more. 9. Assemble your patties by placing it in a hamburger bun and topping each burger with 1 or 2 slices of cooked bacon. Serve with a choice of toppings.
Per Serving: Calories 346; Fat 16.8 g; Sodium 1585 mg; Carbs 5.7g; Fiber 1g; Sugar 2.9g; Protein 42.2g

Air Fryer Beef and Pork Meatloaf

Prep time: 10 minutes | Cook time: 15 minutes | Servings: 4

2 tablespoons unsalted butter	1 tablespoon Worcestershire sauce
½ cup diced onion	1 tablespoon soy sauce
½ cup diced green bell pepper	1 teaspoon salt
1-pound lean ground beef	½ teaspoon black pepper
1-pound ground pork	1 cup bread crumbs, divided
2 large eggs	⅓ cup ketchup, divided

1. Grease 3 mini loaf pans with cooking spray. 2. Heat the butter in a medium sauté pan or skillet over medium-low heat. Add the onions and green peppers and sauté until both are soft. Let the onions and green peppers cool to room temperature. 3. Meanwhile, in a suitable bowl, mix the beef and pork. 4. Add the eggs and mix well, then mix in the Worcestershire sauce, soy sauce, salt, and pepper. 5. Add ½ cup of bread crumbs and mix well. Add more bread crumbs as needed. You only want to add enough bread crumbs to make the prepared mixture stick together; if you add too much, your meatloaf will be dry. 6. Mix in the green peppers and onions. 7. Evenly divide the meatloaf mixture among the 3 mini loaf pans. Gently pat the meat into the pan, so each pan is evenly filled. 8. Divide the ketchup among the loaf pans and spread it in an even layer over each loaf. 9. Select the Air Fry mode. Set the Ninja Foodi Smart XL Pro temperature to 330°F/165°C. Select Level "3" and set the time on your Ninja Foodi Smart XL Pro

Air Fryer Oven to 15 minutes. Press Start/Pause to begin preheating. Continue to the next step when it is done preheating. Set the timer and cook for 15 minutes. 10. Check if the internal temperature of each meatloaf has reached 160°F/70°C. Add more time if needed. 11. Using silicone oven mitts, remove the mini pans from the air fryer and let rest for about 5 minutes before serving.
Per Serving: Calories 669; Fat 43.4 g; Sodium 156 mg; Carbs 36.2g; Fiber 14.9g; Sugar 4.3g; Protein 38.4g

Italian Meatballs

Prep time: 10 minutes | Cook time: 10 minutes | Servings: 4 to 6

2 tablespoons olive oil, divided	2 teaspoons minced garlic
1 onion, diced	2 teaspoons salt
1-pound ground beef	1 teaspoon black pepper
1-pound ground pork	½ teaspoon red pepper flakes
⅓ cup plain bread crumbs	1 teaspoon Italian seasoning
2 large eggs	2 tablespoons grated parmesan
¼ cup minced fresh parsley	cheese

1. Spray its air fryer basket with olive oil. 2. In a suitable skillet, heat 1 tablespoon of olive oil over medium-low heat. Add the onions and sauté until soft. Let cool slightly. 3. In a suitable bowl, mix the cooked onions, ground beef, ground pork, bread crumbs, eggs, black pepper, parsley, garlic, salt, red pepper flakes, Italian seasoning, and grated parmesan cheese. 4. Form the prepared mixture into meatballs about 1.5 inches in diameter. 5. Place the meatballs in the greased air fryer basket in a single layer. (you may have to cook the meatballs in more than one batch.) 6. Select the Air Fry mode. Set the Ninja Foodi Smart XL Pro temperature to 400°F/200°C. Select Level "3" and set the time on your Ninja Foodi Smart XL Pro Air Fryer Oven to 5 minutes. Press Start/Pause to begin preheating. Continue to the next step when it is done preheating. Set the timer and fry for 5 minutes. 7. Using tongs, flip the meatballs. 8. Reset the timer and fry for 5 minutes more.
Per Serving: Calories 407; Fat 11.5 g; Sodium 412 mg; Carbs 31.9g; Fiber 1.3g; Sugar 25.9g; Protein 42.2g

Herbed Lamb Chops

Prep time: 10 minutes | Cook time: 7 minutes | Servings: 4 to 6

2 teaspoons dried rosemary	¼ cup olive oil
2 teaspoons dried thyme	¼ cup freshly squeezed lemon
2 teaspoons dried oregano	juice
2 teaspoons salt	2 pounds lamb chops
2 teaspoons ground coriander	

1. In a suitable resealable plastic bag, mix the rosemary, thyme, oregano, salt, coriander, olive oil, and lemon juice. Seal the bag and shake to mix. 2. Seal the lamb chops into the bag, and refrigerate for at least 1 hour. 3. Add the lamb chops into the air fryer. 4. Select the Air Fry mode. Set the Ninja Foodi Smart XL Pro temperature to 390°F/200°C. Select Level "3" and set the time on your Ninja Foodi Smart XL Pro Air Fryer Oven to 3 minutes. Press Start/Pause to begin preheating. 5. Continue to the next step when it is done preheating. Set the timer and cook for 3 minutes. Using tongs, flip the lamb chops. 6. Reset the timer and cook for 4 minutes more for medium-rare. Add 1 to 2 minutes for well-done.
Per Serving: Calories 286; Fat 9.8 g; Sodium 270 mg; Carbs 11.9g; Fiber 0.9g; Sugar 1.2g; Protein 36.2g

Spicy Buttered Beef Rib Eye Steaks

Prep time: 15 minutes | Cook time: 17 minutes | Servings: 4

1-pound beef rib eye steak, bone-in (4 steaks)	½ teaspoon ground paprika
	½ teaspoon ground ginger
1 tablespoon butter	½ teaspoon chipotle powder
1 teaspoon garlic, diced	1 teaspoon salt
½ teaspoon lime zest, grated	½ teaspoon chili flakes

1. Rub the meat steaks with garlic, lime zest, ground paprika, ground ginger, chipotle powder, salt, and chili flakes, then melt the butter and brush the meat with it. 2. Put the steaks in its air fryer basket. Cook on Air Fry mode. Insert its air fryer basket into the level 3 of the oven and close the door. 3. Cook them for 17 minutes at 400°F/200°C. Flip the meat on another side after 10 minutes of cooking.
Per Serving: Calories 475; Fat 24.8 g; Sodium 508 mg; Carbs 4.1g; Fiber 0.9g; Sugar 1.9g; Protein 58g

Spicy Cube Steaks

Prep time: 10 minutes | Cook time: 8 minutes | Servings: 4 to 6

1½ cups all-purpose flour
1 teaspoon black pepper
1 teaspoon salt
½ teaspoon smoked paprika
½ teaspoon onion powder
½ teaspoon garlic powder

½ teaspoon baking soda
½ teaspoon baking powder
1½ cup buttermilk
2 tablespoons hot sauce
2 large eggs
4 cube steaks

1. Spray its air fryer basket with olive oil. 2. In a suitable mixing bowl, mix the flour, pepper, salt, paprika, onion powder, garlic powder, baking soda, and baking powder. 3. In a separate small mixing bowl, mix the buttermilk, hot sauce, and eggs. 4. Dip the cube steaks in the flour mixture, shake off the excess, then dip them in the buttermilk mixture, shaking off the excess, then dip them back in the flour mixture. 5. As you complete the cycle, place the steaks in the greased air fryer basket in a single layer. Be careful not to overcrowd the basket. Spray the coated steaks liberally with olive oil. 6. Select the Air Fry mode. Set the Ninja Foodi Smart XL Pro temperature to 400°F/200°C. Select Level "3" and set the time on your Ninja Foodi Smart XL Pro Air Fryer Oven to 4 minutes. 7. Start/Pause to begin preheating. Continue to the next step when it is done preheating. Set the timer and fry for 4 minutes. 8. Using tongs, flip the steaks. Spray liberally with olive oil. 9. Reset the timer and fry for 4 minutes more.
Per Serving: Calories 263; Fat 9.1 g; Sodium 110 mg; Carbs 8.3g; Fiber 2.6g; Sugar 3.6g; Protein 37.5g

Cheesy Garlic Pork Chops

Prep time: 10 minutes | Cook time: 17 minutes | Servings: 4

3 cups bread crumbs
½ cup grated parmesan cheese
2 tablespoons vegetable oil
2 teaspoons salt
2 teaspoons sweet paprika

½ teaspoon onion powder
¼ teaspoon garlic powder
6 (½-inch-thick) bone-in pork chops

1.Spray its air fryer basket with olive oil. 2. In a suitable resealable bag, mix the bread crumbs, parmesan cheese, oil, salt, paprika, onion powder, and garlic powder. Seal the bag and shake it a few times in order for the spices to blend together. 3. Place the pork chops, one by one, in the bag and shake to coat. 4. Place the pork chops in the greased air fryer basket in a single layer. Be careful not to overcrowd the basket. (you may have to cook the pork chops in more than one batch.) Spray the chops liberally with olive oil to avoid powdery, uncooked breading. 5. Select the Air Fry mode. Set the Ninja Foodi Smart XL Pro temperature to 360°F/180°C Select Level "3" and set the time on your Ninja Foodi Smart XL Pro Air Fryer Oven to 10 minutes. Press Start/Pause to begin preheating. Continue to the next step when it is done preheating. Set the timer and cook for 10 minutes. 6. Using tongs, flip the chops. Spray them liberally with olive oil. 7. Reset the timer and cook for 7 minutes more. 8. Check that the pork has reached an internal temperature of 145°F/63°C. Add Cooking time if needed.
Per Serving: Calories 291; Fat 15.2 g; Sodium 544 mg; Carbs 13g; Fiber 0.9g; Sugar 10.9g; Protein 26.5g

Beef Crunch Wraps

Prep time: 5 minutes | Cook time: 2 minutes | Servings: 6

6 wheat tostadas
2 cups sour cream
2 cups Mexican blend cheese
2 cups shredded lettuce
12 ounces low-sodium nacho cheese

3 Roma tomatoes
6 12-inch wheat tortillas
1⅓ cups water
2 packets low-sodium taco seasoning
2 pounds of lean ground beef

1. Select Level 3. Select the "AIR FRY" function of Ninja Foodi Smart XL Pro Air Oven, set temperature to 400°F/200°C and time to 2 minutes. Select START/STOP to begin preheating. 2. Make beef according to taco seasoning packets. Place ⅔ cup prepared beef, 4 tablespoons cheese, 1 tostada, ⅓ cup sour cream, ⅓ cup lettuce, ⅙ of tomatoes and ⅓ cup cheese on each tortilla. 3. Fold up the tortillas edges and repeat with the remaining ingredients. Lay the folded sides of tortillas down into the air fryer and spray with olive oil. Cook 2 minutes till browned.
Per Serving: Calories 311; Fat 6g; Sodium 112mg; Carbs 15g; Fiber 6g; Sugar 12g; Protein 2g

Air Fried Rack of Lamb

Prep time: 10 minutes | Cook time: 10 minutes | Servings: 4

¼ cup freshly squeezed lemon juice
1 teaspoon oregano
2 teaspoons minced fresh rosemary
1 teaspoon minced fresh thyme

2 tablespoons minced garlic
Salt
Black pepper
2 to 4 tablespoons olive oil
1 lamb rib rack (7 to 8 ribs)

1. In a suitable mixing bowl, mix the lemon juice, oregano, rosemary, thyme, garlic, salt, pepper, and olive oil and mix well. 2. Rub the prepared mixture over the lamb, covering all of the meat. 3. Place the rack of lamb in the air fryer. 4. Select the Air Fry mode. Set the Ninja Foodi Smart XL Pro temperature to 360°F/180°°C. Select Level "3" and set the time on your Ninja Foodi Smart XL Pro Air Fryer Oven to 10 minutes. Press Start/Pause to begin preheating. Continue to the next step when it is done preheating. Set the timer and cook for 10 minutes. 5. After 10 minutes, measure the internal temperature of the rack of lamb. Medium-rare is 135°F/55°C, medium is 145°F/60°C, and well-done is 170°F/75°C.
Per Serving: Calories 236; Fat 13.2 g; Sodium 502 mg; Carbs 6.3g; Fiber 0.9g; Sugar 4.4g; Protein 23.2g

Beef Cheeseburger Sliders

Prep time: 10 minutes | Cook time: 8 minutes | Servings: 4

Sliders
1 pound 90% lean ground beef
¼ cup (1 ounce) shredded reduced-fat cheddar cheese
1 tablespoon yellow mustard
Special Sauce
2 tablespoons light mayonnaise
2 teaspoons ketchup
½ teaspoon yellow mustard
½ teaspoon dill pickle juice
For Serving
4 large outer leaves iceberg lettuce, each halved lengthwise
8 (¼-inch-thick) slices tomato

¾ teaspoon kosher salt
¼ teaspoon onion powder
⅛ teaspoon black pepper

⅛ teaspoon onion powder
⅛ teaspoon garlic powder
⅛ teaspoon sweet paprika

(from 2 small)
2 slices red onion, rings separated
8 dill pickle chips

1. For the sliders, combine the meat, cheddar, mustard, salt, onion powder, and pepper in a suitable bowl. Form the meat into 8 patties that are each approximately 12 inch thick. To make a dimple, press your finger into the center of each patty (this will help maintain their flat shape when they cook). 2. To make the sauce, combine the ketchup, mayonnaise, mustard, pickle juice, onion powder, garlic powder, and paprika in a bowl and whisk to combine well. 3. Select the Air Fry mode. Set the Ninja Foodi Smart XL Pro temperature to 400°F/200°C. Select Level "3" and set the time on your Ninja Foodi Smart XL Pro Air Fryer Oven to 8 minutes. Press Start/Pause to begin preheating. Continue to the next step when it is done preheating. 4. Spread a single layer of sliders in the air fryer basket while working in batches. Cook for 8 minutes for medium-rare, flip when cooked halfway through. (The temperature and time are the same for an air fryer that resembles a toaster oven. 5. A slice of tomato, a slider, an onion, special sauce, and pickles should be placed on each plate after the two lettuce halves have been placed. Serve right away.
Per Serving: Calories 433; Fat 8.7 g; Sodium 364 mg; Carbs 4.9g; Fiber 1.1g; Sugar 1.9g; Protein 33.2g

Mustard Basil Lamb

Prep time: 10 minutes | Cook time: 30 minutes | Servings: 4

8 lamb cutlets
A pinch of black pepper and salt
A drizzle of olive oil
2 garlic cloves, minced
¼ cup mustard

1 tablespoon chives, chopped
1 tablespoon basil, chopped
1 tablespoon oregano, chopped
1 tablespoon mint chopped

1. In a suitable bowl, mix the lamb with the rest of the recipe ingredients and rub well. 2. Put the cutlets in your air fryer's basket. Insert its air fryer basket into the level 3 of the oven and close the door. Cook on "Air Fry" Mode, select level 3, and set its temperature to 380°F/195°C for 15 minutes per side. 3. Divide between plates and serve with a side salad.
Per Serving: Calories 248; Fat 11.8 g; Sodium 421 mg; Carbs 2.2g; Fiber 0.4g; Sugar 1.5g; Protein 33.3g

Beef with Horseradish Cream

Prep time: 10 minutes | Cook time: 35 minutes | Servings: 8

Beef

1 (2-pound) trimmed top round roast, tied
1 teaspoon kosher salt
1 teaspoon olive oil

1 tablespoon Dijon mustard
1 teaspoon prepared horseradish
1 garlic clove, minced

Horseradish-chive cream

⅔ cup sour cream
2¼ tablespoons prepared horseradish
2¼ tablespoons Dijon mustard

1 tablespoon minced chives
¼ teaspoon kosher salt
Black pepper

1. For the beef: remove the roast from the refrigerator and let it reach room temperature, about 1 hour. Pat dry with paper towels. Season with the salt. 2. In a suitable bowl, mix the oil, mustard, horseradish, and garlic. Rub the outside of the roast with the mixture. 3. Select the Air Fry mode. Set the Ninja Foodi Smart XL Pro temperature to 325°F/165°C. Select Level "3" and set the time on your Ninja Foodi Smart XL Pro Air Fryer Oven to 10 minutes. Press Start/Pause to begin preheating. Continue to the next step when it is done preheating. 4. Place the roast in its air fryer basket. Cook for 30 to 35 minutes, flip when cooked halfway through, until browned and a thermometer inserted in the center reads 125°F/50°C to 130°F/55°C for medium rare. (for a toaster oven–style air fryer, cook on "Air Fry" Mode, select level 3, and set its temperature to 300°F/150°C for 25 to 30 minutes.) 5. Meanwhile, for the horseradish-chive cream: in a medium bowl, mix the sour cream, horseradish, mustard, chives, salt, and pepper to taste and mix until smooth. Refrigerate until ready to use. 6. Transfer the roast to a cutting board, tent with foil, and let rest for 10 to 15 minutes before carving. Thinly slice and serve with the horseradish cream on the side. 7. Skinny scoop if you don't have time to let the roast come to room temperature before you cook it, then add about 5 minutes to the cooking time. Larger roasts will require more time in the air fryer.

Per Serving: Calories 499; Fat 23.8 g; Sodium 197 mg; Carbs 0.9g; Fiber 0.3g; Sugar 0.1g; Protein 65.6g

Garlic Leg of Lamb

Prep time: 15 minutes | Cook time: 21 minutes | Servings: 2

9 ounces leg of lamb, boneless
1 teaspoon minced garlic
2 tablespoons butter, softened

½ teaspoon dried dill
½ teaspoon salt

1. In the shallow bowl mix up minced garlic, butter, dried dill, and salt. 2. Then rub the leg of lamb with butter mixture and place it in the preheated air fryer. 3. Cook on "Air Fry" Mode, select level 3, cook it at 380°F/195°C for 21 minutes.

Per Serving: Calories 360; Fat 30.8 g; Sodium 584 mg; Carbs 1.3g; Fiber 0.5g; Sugar 0.2g; Protein 18.6g

Lamb Scallion Balls

Prep time: 5 minutes | Cook time: 30 minutes | Servings: 4

1 and ½ pounds lamb, ground
1 scallion, chopped
A pinch of black pepper and salt
½ cup pine nuts, toasted and chopped

1 tablespoon thyme, chopped
2 garlic cloves, minced
1 tablespoon olive oil
1 egg, whisked

1. In a suitable bowl, mix the lamb with the rest of the recipe ingredients except the oil, stir well and shape medium meatballs out of this mix. 2. Grease the meatballs with the oil, put them in your air fryer's basket. Insert its air fryer basket into the level 3 of the oven and close the door. Cook on "Air Fry" Mode, select level 3, and set its temperature to 380°F/195°C for 15 minutes per side. 3. Divide between plates and serve with a side salad.

Per Serving: Calories 292; Fat 9.4 g; Sodium 349 mg; Carbs 2.5g; Fiber 0.4g; Sugar 1.6g; Protein 46.6g

Pork Soft loin

Prep time: 10 minutes | Cook time: 30 minutes | Servings: 4 to 6

¼ cup olive oil
¼ cup soy sauce
¼ cup freshly squeezed lemon

juice
1 garlic clove, minced
1 tablespoon Dijon mustard

1 teaspoon salt
½ teaspoon black pepper

2 pounds pork soft loin

1. The marinade should be made in a good mixing bowl. Olive oil, soy sauce, lemon juice, garlic powder, Dijon mustard, salt, and pepper should all be combined. 2. Pour the leftover marinade over the tender loin after placing it in a convenient basin. For about an hour, cover and marinate in the refrigerator. 3. Put the air fryer basket with the tender piece of marinated pork inside. 4. Select the Air Roast mode. Set the Ninja Foodi Smart XL Pro temperature to 400°F/200°C. Select Level "3" and set the time on your Ninja Foodi Smart XL Pro Air Fryer Oven to 10 minutes. Press Start/Pause to begin preheating. Continue to the next step when it is done preheating. Set a timer for 10 minutes and roast. 5. Flip the pork over with tongs and baste it with half of the marinade that was saved. 6. Set the timer for 10 more minutes of roasting. 7. Flip the pig over with tongs and bats with the remaining marinade. 8. For a total cooking time of 30 minutes, reset the timer and roast for an additional 10 minutes.

Per Serving: Calories 562; Fat 31.2 g; Sodium 198 mg; Carbs 1.9g; Fiber 1.1g; Sugar 0.9g; Protein 66g

Baby Back Ribs with Barbecue Sauce

Prep time: 10 minutes | Cook time: 23 to 25 minutes | Servings: 4

1 rack baby back ribs
1 tablespoon garlic powder
1 teaspoon black pepper

2 tablespoons salt
1 cup barbecue sauce (any type)

1. Dry the ribs with a paper towel. 2. Season the ribs liberally with the garlic powder, pepper, and salt. 3. Place the seasoned ribs into the air fryer. 4. Select the Air Fry mode. Set the Ninja Foodi Smart XL Pro temperature to 400°F/200°C. Select Level "3" and set the time on your Ninja Foodi Smart XL Pro Air Fryer Oven to 10 minutes. Press Start/Pause to begin preheating. Continue to the next step when it is done preheating. Set the timer and grill for 10 minutes. 5. Using tongs, flip the ribs. 6. Reset the timer and grill for another 10 minutes. 7. Once the ribs are cooked, use a pastry brush to brush on the barbecue sauce, then set the timer and grill for a final 3 to 5 minutes.

Per Serving: Calories 386; Fat 9.8 g; Sodium 50mg; Carbs 6.2g; Fiber 1.7g; Sugar 3.1g; Protein 19.2g

Pork Lettuce Wraps

Prep time: 10 minutes | Cook time: 10 minutes | Servings: 4

Pork

1-pound pork soft loin, cut into 12 (½-inch-thick) slices
¼ teaspoon kosher salt
⅛ teaspoon black pepper
3 scallions, chopped

3 garlic cloves, crushed
¼ cup reduced-sodium soy sauce
1 tablespoon gochujang
1 tablespoon light brown sugar
1 tablespoon grated fresh ginger

Gochujang Sauce

2 tablespoons gochujang
2 tablespoons mirin

1 teaspoon toasted sesame oil

For Serving

2¼ cups cooked brown rice
12 baby romaine or green leaf lettuce leaves

½ tablespoon sesame seeds
2 scallions, sliced

1. For the pork: place the pork slices in a suitable bowl and season with the black pepper and salt. In a suitable bowl, mix the scallions, garlic, soy sauce, gochujang, brown sugar, and ginger and mix well. Pour over the pork and toss to coat. 2. Cover with plastic wrap and marinate in the refrigerator overnight. 3. Select the Air Fry mode. Set the Ninja Foodi Smart XL Pro temperature to 400°F/200°C. Select Level "3" and set the time on your Ninja Foodi Smart XL Pro Air Fryer Oven to 10 minutes. Press Start/Pause to begin preheating. Continue to the next step when it is done preheating. 4. Working in batches, spread a single layer of pork (discarding the excess marinade) in the air fryer. 5. Cook for about 10 minutes, flip halfway through cooking until browned and no longer pink in the center. 6. For the gochujang sauce: in a suitable bowl, mix the gochujang, mirin, and sesame oil and mix until smooth. 7. To serve: place 3 tablespoons brown rice on each lettuce leaf. Top with a slice of pork, 1 teaspoon of the gochujang sauce, and some of the sesame seeds and scallions. 8. Wrap the leaves over the rice and pork into little burrito-like bundles and eat right away.

Per Serving: Calories 391; Fat 12.3 g; Sodium 2031 mg; Carbs 23.9g; Fiber 3.7g; Sugar 13.9g; Protein 46.2g

Pizza-Stuffed Peppers

Prep time: 10 minutes | Cook time: 10 minutes | Servings: 4

1 (8-ounce) link sweet Italian pork sausage	1 cup marinara sauce
4 medium bell peppers	1½ cups (6 ounces) shredded mozzarella cheese
Olive oil spray	12 slices turkey pepperoni, halved

1. Select the Air Fry mode. Set the Ninja Foodi Smart XL Pro temperature to 370°F/185°C. Select Level "3" and set the time on your Ninja Foodi Smart XL Pro Air Fryer Oven to 10 minutes. Press Start/Pause to begin preheating. Continue to the next step when it is done preheating. 2. Place the sausage in its air fryer basket. Insert its air fryer basket into the level 3 of the oven and close the door. Cook for 10 minutes, flip when cooked halfway through, until cooked. (for a toaster oven–style air fryer, Cook on "Air Fry" Mode, select level 3, and set its temperature to 350°F/175°C; the timing remains the same.) Set aside to cool, then chop into small pieces. 3. Halve the peppers lengthwise and remove the seeds. Spray both sides with oil. 4. Reduce the air fryer temperature to 350°F/175°C. Select Level "3" and set the time on your Ninja Foodi Smart XL Pro Air Fryer Oven to 10 minutes. Press Start/Pause to begin preheating. Continue to the next step when it is done preheating. 5. Place the peppers in its air fryer basket. Insert its air fryer basket into the level 3 of the oven and close the door. Cook for 6 to 8 minutes, flip when cooked halfway through, until slightly softened. Transfer to a plate. 6. Fill each pepper half with 2 tablespoons marinara and top with 3 tablespoons mozzarella, a few pieces of sausage, and 3 pepperoni halves. 7. Working in batches, return the stuffed peppers in a single layer to the air fryer. Cook for 7 minutes, until the cheese is melted and the sauce is hot. Serve immediately.
Per Serving: Calories 237; Fat 12.8 g; Sodium 162 mg; Carbs 3.9g; Fiber 0.9g; Sugar 1.9g; Protein 31.7g

Apple-Stuffed Pork Chops

Prep time: 10 minutes | Cook time: 5 minutes | Servings: 4

Pork

4 (6½ ounces each) bone-in, center-cut loin pork chops, trimmed	¼ teaspoon ground cinnamon
	¼ teaspoon ground nutmeg
1 teaspoon kosher salt	¼ teaspoon sweet paprika
½ teaspoon dried sage	⅛ teaspoon black pepper
½ teaspoon garlic powder	2 teaspoons Dijon mustard
	2 teaspoons pure maple syrup

Apple Stuffing

½ tablespoon unsalted butter	½ teaspoon kosher salt
1 large sweet apple (honey crisp or gala), peeled and thinly sliced	½ teaspoon dried sage
	½ teaspoon garlic powder
½ medium onion, chopped	¼ teaspoon ground cinnamon
¼ cup chopped celery	¼ teaspoon ground nutmeg

1. For the pork: working with one chop at a time, place the pork between two sheets of plastic wrap. Use a heavy skillet or meat mallet to pound the pork to a ¾-inch thickness, being careful not to tear the meat. Cut a pocket in each chop horizontally, making sure not to cut all the way through. 2. In a suitable bowl, mix the salt, sage, garlic powder, cinnamon, nutmeg, paprika, and pepper. Season the inside and outside of each pork chop with the spice mix. 3. In a suitable bowl, mix the mustard and maple syrup. 4. For the apple stuffing: in a suitable skillet, melt the butter over medium heat. Add the apple, onion, celery, salt, sage, garlic powder, cinnamon, and nutmeg. Cover and cook, stirring occasionally, until the apple and vegetables are softened, about 15 minutes. Dividing evenly, stuff the apple mixture (about ¼ cup each) into the pork chops. 5. Select the Air Fry mode. Set the Ninja Foodi Smart XL Pro temperature to 400°F/200°C. Select Level "3" and set the time on your Ninja Foodi Smart XL Pro Air Fryer Oven to 10 minutes. Press Start/Pause to begin preheating. Continue to the next step when it is done preheating. 6. Working in batches, place the stuffed pork chops in its air fryer basket. Cook for 3 minutes. Flip the chops and brush the tops with the mustard-maple mixture. 7. Continue cooking for 3 to 4 minutes, until just cooked through. (for a toaster oven–style air fryer, cook on "Air Fry" Mode, select level 3, and set its temperature to 375°F/190°C for 3 minutes, then for 2 to 3 minutes.) Carefully remove the chops with tongs to a platter. Serve.
Per Serving: Calories 244; Fat 13.3 g; Sodium 144 mg; Carbs 3g; Fiber 0.9g; Sugar 0.7g; Protein 32.2g

Glazed Lamb Chops

Prep time: 10 minutes | Cook time: 12 minutes | Servings: 4

8 (3½-ounce) bone-in lamb loin chops, trimmed	3 tablespoons honey
3 garlic cloves, crushed	½ tablespoon light brown sugar
¼ cup soy sauce or tamari	¼ teaspoon crushed red pepper flakes
¼ teaspoon Chinese five-spice powder	Scallions, sliced into long, thin strips

1. Place the lamb chops in a suitable bowl and season with the garlic, soy sauce, five-spice, and honey, tossing to coat well. Cover with plastic wrap and marinate in the refrigerator for 2 hours, or as long as overnight. 2. Select the Air Fry mode. Set the Ninja Foodi Smart XL Pro temperature to 400°F/200°C. Select Level "3" and set the time on your Ninja Foodi Smart XL Pro Air Fryer Oven to 5 minutes. Press Start/Pause to begin preheating. Continue to the next step when it is done preheating. 3. Working in batches, spread a single layer of chops (reserve the marinade) in its air fryer basket. Insert its air fryer basket into the level 3 of the oven and close the door. Cook for 5 minutes. 4. Flip the chops, brush the tops with the marinade, and sprinkle with the brown sugar and pepper flakes. Continue cooking until the top is browned and caramelized, 4 to 5 minutes for medium to medium-rare doneness; for well done, cook an additional 1 to 2 minutes. 5. Top with the scallions and serve.
Per Serving: Calories 324; Fat 17.8 g; Sodium 363 mg; Carbs 8.9g; Fiber 0.5g; Sugar 1.9g; Protein 36.6g

Sirloin Steak with Guacamole

Prep time: 10 minutes | Cook time: 10 minutes | Servings: 4

Guacamole

1 small Hass avocado (4 ounces)	Steak
¼ cup diced tomato	10 ounces top sirloin steak (½ to ¾ inch thick)
2 tablespoons diced red onion	
2 teaspoons chopped fresh cilantro	1 large garlic clove, minced
2 teaspoons fresh lime juice	½ teaspoon kosher salt
½ teaspoon kosher salt	1 teaspoon ground cumin
black pepper	black pepper
	¼ lime

For Serving

3 cups chopped romaine lettuce	bought or homemade (see the chimichanga recipe, this page)
¼ cup (1 ounce) shredded Monterey jack cheese	1 jalapeño, sliced thin
½ cup Pico de Gallo, store-	Lime wedges

1. For the guacamole: in a suitable bowl, mash the avocado, then add the red onion, cilantro, tomato, lime juice, salt, and pepper to taste. Mix and set aside. 2. For the steak: season the steak with the garlic, salt, cumin, and pepper to taste. 3. Select the Air Fry mode. Set the Ninja Foodi Smart XL Pro temperature to 400°F/200°C. Select Level "3" and set the time on your Ninja Foodi Smart XL Pro Air Fryer Oven to 10 minutes. Press Start/Pause to begin preheating. Continue to the next step when it is done preheating. 4. Place the steak in its air fryer basket. Cook, flip when cooked halfway through, until cooked to your desired doneness, 7 to 10 minutes for medium, depending on the thickness of your steak. (for a toaster oven–style air fryer, the temperature and timing remain the same.) Let the steak rest for 5 minutes. 5. Add the lime juice over the steak and thinly slice. Serve with guacamole.
Per Serving: Calories 457; Fat 28.8 g; Sodium 712 mg; Carbs 7.8g; Fiber 2.9g; Sugar 3.9g; Protein 42g

Ribs with Chimichurri Mix

Prep time:10 minutes | Cook time: 35 minutes | Servings: 4

1-pound pork baby back ribs, boneless	2 tablespoons chimichurri sauce
	½ teaspoon salt

1. Sprinkle the ribs with salt and brush with chimichurri sauce. 2. Then Select the Air Fry mode. Set the Ninja Foodi Smart XL Pro temperature to 365°F/185°C. Select Level "3" and set the time on your Ninja Foodi Smart XL Pro Air Fryer Oven to 35 minutes. Press Start/Pause to begin preheating. 3. Continue to the next step when it is done preheating. Put the pork ribs in its air fryer basket. Insert its air fryer basket into the level 3 of the oven and close the door. Cook for 35 minutes.
Per Serving: Calories 325; Fat 27 g; Sodium 58 mg; Carbs 2.2g; Fiber 0.2g; Sugar 0.2g; Protein 18.3g

Roasted Rosemary Lamb Cutlets

Prep time: 5 minutes | Cook time: 30 minutes | Servings: 4

8 lamb cutlets
2 tablespoons olive oil
A pinch of black pepper and salt
2 tablespoons rosemary, chopped
2 garlic cloves, minced
A pinch of cayenne pepper

1. In a suitable bowl, mix the lamb with the rest of the recipe ingredients and rub well. 2. Put the lamb in the fryer's basket. Insert its air fryer basket into the level 3 of the oven and close the door. Cook on "Air Fry" Mode, select level 3, and set its temperature to 380°F/195°C for 30 minutes, flipping them halfway. 3. Divide the cutlets between plates and serve.
Per Serving: Calories 319; Fat 21.2 g; Sodium 63 mg; Carbs 14g; Fiber 3.5g; Sugar 8.9g; Protein 19.6g

Sesame Flank Steak

Prep time: 10 minutes | Cook time: 12 minutes | Servings: 4

6 tablespoons reduced-sodium soy sauce or tamari
2 tablespoons toasted sesame oil
2 tablespoons sugar
1 tablespoon grated fresh ginger
1 shallot, minced
1 garlic clove, minced
¼ teaspoon crushed red pepper flakes
1½ pounds flank steak
1 scallion, thinly sliced
Toasted sesame seeds, for topping

1. In a suitable bowl, mix the soy sauce, sesame oil, sugar, ginger, shallot, garlic, and pepper flakes and mix until the sugar dissolves. Add the steak and massage the marinade into the meat. Cover with plastic wrap and let marinate overnight in the refrigerator. 2. Select the Air Fry mode. Set the Ninja Foodi Smart XL Pro temperature to 400°F/200°C. Select Level "3" and set the time on your Ninja Foodi Smart XL Pro Air Fryer Oven to 12 minutes. Press Start/Pause to begin preheating. Continue to the next step when it is done preheating. 3. Remove the steak from the marinade (discard the marinade). Working in two batches if needed, place the steak in its air fryer basket. Cook, flip when cooked halfway through, until charred on the outside and cooked to your desired doneness, about 12 minutes for medium rare. 4. Let rest for 5 minutes before very thinly slicing across the grain. Transfer to a platter. Serve topped with the scallion and sesame seeds. 5. Skinny scoop if the steak is too large for your air fryer, cut it into two pieces.
Per Serving: Calories 301; Fat 11.2g; Sodium 413 mg; Carbs 4.7g; Fiber 0.3g; Sugar 3.5g; Protein 42.9g

Peppermint Lamb with Celery Ribs

Prep time: 15 minutes | Cook time: 12 minutes | Servings:4

1-pound lamb chops
2 ounces celery ribs, chopped
½ teaspoon lemon zest, grated
½ teaspoon garlic, minced
½ teaspoon peppermint
1 tablespoon ghee
½ teaspoon black pepper
1 teaspoon olive oil

1. Put the celery ribs in the blender. Add lemon zest, garlic, peppermint, ghee, black pepper, and olive oil. Pulse the prepared mixture for 1-2 minutes. 2. Cook on Air Fry mode, Select Level "3", set its temperature on your Ninja Foodi Smart XL Pro Air Fryer Oven to 400°F/200°C. for 12 minutes. Press Start/Pause to begin preheating. Continue to the next step when it is done preheating. 3. Then carefully rub the lamb chops with blended mixture and put the meat in the air fryer, cook the lamb chops for 6 minutes from each side, Serve.
Per Serving: Calories 629; Fat 40.5 g; Sodium 584 mg; Carbs 16.9g; Fiber 4.1g; Sugar 9.3g; Protein 50.3g

Spicy Lamb Chops

Prep time: 5 minutes | Cook time: 20 minutes | Servings: 4

4 lamb chops
4 garlic cloves, minced
½ teaspoon chili powder
¼ teaspoon smoked paprika
2 tablespoons olive oil
A pinch of black pepper and salt

1. In a suitable bowl, mix the lamb with the rest of the recipe ingredients and toss well. 2. Transfer the chops to your air fryer's basket. Insert its air fryer basket into the level 3 of the oven and close the door. 3. Cook on "Air Fry" Mode, select level 3, and set its temperature to 390°F/200°C for 10 minutes per side. Serve with a side salad, if desired.
Per Serving: Calories 413; Fat 30.8 g; Sodium 1279 mg; Carbs 2.4g; Fiber 0.5g; Sugar 1.3g; Protein 31.6g

Spicy Pork Riblets

Prep time: 30 minutes | Cook time: 40 minutes | Servings: 4

1-pound pork riblets
2 tablespoons erythritol
½ teaspoon ground paprika
½ teaspoon chili powder
1 teaspoon yellow mustard
2 tablespoons apple cider vinegar
1 teaspoon keto tomato sauce
¼ cup of water
1 teaspoon salt

1. In the mixing bowl mix up erythritol, ground paprika, chili powder, yellow mustard, apple cider vinegar, tomato sauce, and water. Add salt. Whisk the prepared mixture until homogenous. 2. Then put the pork riblets in the homogenous mixture and mix up well. Leave the meat for 20 minutes in this sauce. 3. After this, Select the Air Fry mode. Set the Ninja Foodi Smart XL Pro temperature to 355°F/180°C. Select Level "3" and set the time on your Ninja Foodi Smart XL Pro Air Fryer Oven to 40 minutes. Press Start/Pause to begin preheating. 4. Continue to the next step when it is done preheating. Put the pork riblets in its air fryer basket. Insert its air fryer basket into the level 3 of the oven and close the door. 5. Cook them for 40 minutes. Flip the pork ribs on another side after 20 minutes of cooking.
Per Serving: Calories 404; Fat 20.3 g; Sodium 8 mg; Carbs 3.4g; Fiber 1g; Sugar 1.2g; Protein 53.4g

Marjoram Lamb Chops

Prep time: 5 minutes | Cook time: 25 minutes | Servings: 4

4 lamb chops
2 tablespoons olive oil
Black pepper and salt to the taste
1 tablespoon marjoram, chopped
3 garlic cloves, minced
1 teaspoon thyme, dried
½ cup keto tomato sauce

1. Heat up a suitable pan that fits the air fryer with the oil over medium-high heat, then add the lamb chops and brown for 5 minutes. 2. Add the rest of the recipe ingredients, toss, put the pan in the fryer and cook on "Air Fry" Mode, select level 3, and set its temperature to 390°F/200°C for 20 minutes more. 3. Divide into bowls and serve right away.
Per Serving: Calories 416; Fat 8.3 g; Sodium 208 mg; Carbs 22.9g; Fiber 0.5g; Sugar 19g; Protein 60.6g

Cayenne Beef Oxtails

Prep time: 15 minutes | Cook time: 65 minutes | Servings: 6

2-pound beef oxtail
1 teaspoon salt
1 teaspoon cayenne pepper
1 tablespoon sesame oil
⅓ teaspoon ground coriander
2 tablespoons apple cider vinegar
½ teaspoon dried thyme
1 tablespoon ghee

1. Chop the oxtail roughly and sprinkle with salt, cayenne pepper, sesame oil, ground coriander, and apple cider vinegar. Add dried thyme and shake the oxtail well. 2. Then put the meat in the air fryer baking pan and add ghee. Select the Air Fry mode. Set the Ninja Foodi Smart XL Pro temperature to 360°F/180°C Select Level "3" and set the time on your Ninja Foodi Smart XL Pro Air Fryer Oven to 65 minutes. Press Start/Pause to begin preheating. 3. Continue to the next step when it is done preheating. Put the pan with the oxtail in its air fryer basket. Insert its air fryer basket into the level 3 of the oven and close the door. Cook it for 65 minutes.
Per Serving: Calories 382; Fat 32.5 g; Sodium 1363 mg; Carbs 3.2g; Fiber 0.2g; Sugar 1.9g; Protein 19.1g

Lamb Chops with Lemon Yogurt Sauce

Prep time: 5 minutes | Cook time: 30 minutes | Servings: 4

4 lamb chops
A pinch of black pepper and salt
1 cup Greek yogurt
2 tablespoons coconut oil, melted
1 teaspoon lemon zest, grated
½ teaspoon turmeric powder

1. In a suitable bowl, mix the lamb chops with the rest of the recipe ingredients and toss well. 2. Put the chops in your air fryer's basket. Insert its air fryer basket into the level 3 of the oven and close the door. Cook on "Air Fry" Mode, select level 3, and set its temperature to 380°F/195°C for 15 minutes per side. 3. Divide between plates and serve.
Per Serving: Calories 368; Fat 32.8 g; Sodium 507 mg; Carbs 0.6g; Fiber 0.1g; Sugar 1.1g; Protein 18.5g

Lamb with Coconut Cilantro Sauce

Prep time: 5 minutes | Cook time: 30 minutes | Servings: 4

1-pound lamb, cubed
1 cup coconut cream
3 tablespoons sweet paprika

2 tablespoons olive oil
2 tablespoons cilantro, chopped
Black pepper and salt to the taste

1. Heat up a suitable pan that fits your air fryer with the oil over medium-high heat, then add the meat and brown for 5 minutes. 2. Add the rest of the recipe ingredients, toss, put the pan in its air fryer basket. Insert its air fryer basket into the level 3 of the oven and close the door. 3. Cook on "Air Fry" Mode, select level 3, and set its temperature to 380°F/195°C for 25 minutes. Divide everything into bowls and serve.
Per Serving: Calories 324; Fat 17.8 g; Sodium 363 mg; Carbs 8.9g; Fiber 0.5g; Sugar 1.9g; Protein 36.6g

Air Fried Pork Belly

Prep time: 15 minutes | Cook time: 55 minutes | Servings: 6

1-pound pork belly
1 teaspoon Splenda
1 teaspoon salt

1 teaspoon white pepper
1 teaspoon butter, softened
½ teaspoon onion powder

1. Sprinkle the pork belly with salt, white pepper, and onion powder. 2. Then Select the Air Fry mode. Set the Ninja Foodi Smart XL Pro temperature to385°F/195°C. Select Level "3" and set the time on your Ninja Foodi Smart XL Pro Air Fryer Oven to 45 minutes. Press Start/ Pause to begin preheating. Continue to the next step when it is done preheating. 3. Put the pork belly in its air fryer basket. Insert its air fryer basket into the level 3 of the oven and close the door. Cook it for 45 minutes. 4. Then turn the pork belly on another side and spread it with butter. 5. After this, top the pork belly with Splenda and cook it at 400°F/200°C for 10 minutes.
Per Serving: Calories 398; Fat 37.8 g; Sodium 1463 mg; Carbs 2.5g; Fiber 0.2g; Sugar 0.5g; Protein 13.6g

Crusted Lamb Chops

Prep time: 15 minutes | Cook time: 8 minutes | Servings: 4

1-pound lamb chops
1 egg, beaten
½ teaspoon salt

½ cup coconut flour
cooking spray

1. Chop the lamb chops into small pieces (popcorn) and sprinkle with salt. Then add a beaten egg and stir the meat well. 2. After this, then add coconut flour and shake the lamb popcorn until all meat pieces are coated. 3. Select the Air Fry mode. Set the Ninja Foodi Smart XL Pro temperature to 380°F/195°C. Select Level "3" and set the time on your Ninja Foodi Smart XL Pro Air Fryer Oven to 8 minutes. Press Start/ Pause to begin preheating. Continue to the next step when it is done preheating. 4. Put the lamb popcorn in the air fryer and spray it with cooking spray. Cook the lamb popcorn for 4 minutes. 5. Then shake the meat well and cook it for 4 minutes more.
Per Serving: Calories 267; Fat 15.2 g; Sodium 479 mg; Carbs 13.9g; Fiber 0.1g; Sugar 12.9g; Protein 20.6g

Lamb Meatloaf

Prep time: 5 minutes | Cook time: 35 minutes | Servings: 4

2 pounds lamb, ground
A pinch of black pepper and salt
½ teaspoon hot paprika
A drizzle of olive oil
2 tablespoons parsley, chopped
2 tablespoons cilantro, chopped
1 teaspoon cumin, ground

¼ teaspoon cinnamon powder
1 teaspoon coriander, ground
1 egg
2 tablespoons keto tomato sauce
4 scallions, chopped
1 teaspoon lemon juice

1. In a suitable bowl, mix the lamb with the rest of the recipe ingredients except the oil and stir really well. 2. Grease a loaf pan that fits the air fryer with the oil, then add the lamb mix and shape the meatloaf. 3. Put the pan in its air fryer basket. Insert its air fryer basket into the level 3 of the oven and close the door. Cook on "Air Fry" Mode, select level 3, and set its temperature to 380°F/195°C for 35 minutes. Slice and serve.
Per Serving: Calories 324; Fat 17.8 g; Sodium 363 mg; Carbs 8.9g; Fiber 0.5g; Sugar 1.9g; Protein 36.6g

Beef Carne Asada

Prep time: 15 minutes | Cook time: 14 minutes | Servings: 4

¼ lime
2 tablespoons orange juice
1 teaspoon dried cilantro
1 chili pepper, chopped
1 tablespoon sesame oil

1 tablespoon apple cider vinegar
½ teaspoon chili paste
½ teaspoon ground cumin
½ teaspoon salt
1-pound beef skirt steak

1. Chop the lime roughly and put it in the blender. Add orange juice, dried cilantro, chili pepper, sesame oil, apple cider vinegar, chili paste, ground cumin, and salt. Blend the prepared mixture until smooth. Cut the skirt steak on 4 Servings. 2. Then brush every steak with blended lime mixture and leave for 10 minutes to marinate. 3. Meanwhile, Select the Air Fry mode. Set the Ninja Foodi Smart XL Pro temperature to 400°F/200°C. Select Level "3" and set the time on your Ninja Foodi Smart XL Pro Air Fryer Oven to 14 minutes. Press Start/Pause to begin preheating. Continue to the next step when it is done preheating. 4. Put the steaks in the air fryer in one layer and cook them for 7 minutes. Flip the meat on another side and cook it for 7 minutes more.
Per Serving: Calories 341; Fat 24.6 g; Sodium 401 mg; Carbs 12g; Fiber 0.1g; Sugar 11.9g; Protein 18.6g

Beef and Cheese Egg Rolls

Prep time: 15 minutes | Cook time: 10 minutes | Servings: 3

6 egg roll wrappers
6 chopped dill pickle chips
1 tablespoon yellow mustard
3 tablespoons cream cheese
3 tablespoons shredded cheddar cheese

½ cup chopped onion
½ cup chopped bell pepper
¼ teaspoon onion powder
¼ teaspoon garlic powder
8 ounces of raw lean ground beef

1. Select Level 3. Select the "AIR FRY" function of Ninja Foodi Smart XL Pro Air Oven, set temperature to 390°F/200°C and time to 9 minutes. Select START/STOP to begin preheating. 2. In a skillet, add seasonings, beef, onion, and bell pepper. Stir and crumble beef till fully cooked and vegetables are soft. 3. Take skillet off the heat and add cream cheese, mustard, and cheddar cheese, stirring till melted. 4. Pour the beef mixture into a bowl and fold in pickles. Lay out egg wrappers and place ⅙ of beef mixture into each one. Moisten egg roll wrapper edges with water. Fold sides to the middle and seal them with water. Repeat with all other egg rolls. 5. Place rolls into the air fryer, one batch at a time. Cook for 7-9 minutes.
Per Serving: Calories 112; Fat 2g; Sodium 12mg; Carbs 8g; Fiber 1g; Sugar 6g; Protein 0g

Beef and Cabbage Egg Rolls with Brandy Mustard Sauce

Prep time: 5 minutes | Cook time: 20 minutes | Servings: 5

Olive oil
½ cup orange marmalade
5 slices of Swiss cheese
Brandy Mustard Sauce:
1/16th teaspoon pepper
2 tablespoons whole grain mustard
1 teaspoon dry mustard powder
1 cup heavy cream
½ cup chicken stock

4 cups corned beef and cabbage
1 egg
10 egg roll wrappers

¼ cup brandy
¾ cup dry white wine
¼ teaspoon curry powder
½ tablespoon cilantro
1 minced shallot
2 tablespoons ghee

1. For mustard sauce, Cook shallots in ghee until softened. Add brandy along with wine, boil on low heat. Cook until liquids reduce. Add stock and seasonings. Manage to Simmer 5 minutes. Low the heat and whisk in heavy cream. Cook on low till sauce thicken. Place it in the fridge. 2. Select the "AIR FRY" function of Ninja Foodi Smart XL Pro Air Oven, set temperature to 390°F/200°C and time to 10 minutes. Select START/STOP to begin preheating. 3. Whisk the egg and set to the side. Lay out an egg wrapper and brush the edges with egg wash. Place corned beef mix and cabbage into the center along with marmalade and Swiss cheese. 4. Fold the bottom corner over filling. Fold gently and make sure the filling is completely sealed. 5. Place rolls into the air fryer basket. Slide basket into rails of Level 3. Grease rolls with olive oil. Cook 10 minutes, shaking halfway through cooking. 6. Serve with Brandy Mustard sauce and devour!
Per Serving: Calories 134; Fat 9.8g; Sodium 394mg; Carbs 2g; Fiber 0g; Sugar 1g; Protein 9g

Lamb Meatballs

Prep time: 15 minutes | Cook time: 7 minutes | Servings: 4

½ teaspoon lime zest, grated
1 tablespoon lime juice
10 ounces ground lamb
1 teaspoon black pepper

1 garlic clove, minced
½ teaspoon minced ginger
1 teaspoon avocado oil

1. In the mixing bowl mix up lime zest, lime juice, ground lamb, minced garlic, and ginger. With the help of the scooper make the meatballs and put them in the freezer for 5-10 minutes. 2. Meanwhile, Select the Air Fry mode. Set the Ninja Foodi Smart XL Pro temperature to 380°F/195°C. Select Level "3" and set the time on your Ninja Foodi Smart XL Pro Air Fryer Oven to 7 minutes. Press Start/Pause to begin preheating. Continue to the next step when it is done preheating. 3. Brush its air fryer basket with avocado oil from inside and put the meatballs. Cook them for 7 minutes.
Per Serving: Calories 398; Fat 27 g; Sodium 416mg; Carbs 34.9g; Fiber 6.5g; Sugar 6.9g; Protein 11.6g

Beef Hamburgers with Mayonnaise

Prep time: 10 minutes | Cook time: 10 minutes | Servings: 4

For the Burgers
¼ cup chopped green scallions
½ teaspoon salt
1 tablespoon soy sauce
1 tablespoon sesame oil
1-pound lean ground beef
For the Mayonnaise
¼ cup mayonnaise
¼ cup chopped green scallions
1 tablespoon gochujang

2 teaspoons sugar
2 tablespoons gochujang
2 teaspoons minced ginger
2 teaspoons minced garlic

1 tablespoon coconut oil
2 teaspoons sesame seeds
4 hamburger buns, to serve

1. Using a suitable mixing bowl, then add in onions, sugar, oil, ginger, garlic, soy sauce, gochujang, salt and ground beef then incorporate together. 2. Allow the beef to marinate for an hour then mold into four different patties. 3. Place the patties into the fryer basket then insert the basket in the level 3 of the Ninja Foodi Smart XL Pro Oven. Air fry on Air Fry mode for 10 minutes at 360°F/180°C Select Level "3". 4. In the meantime, mix the scallions, sesame seeds, oil, gochujang and mayonnaise together. 5. Serve the burger along with the mayonnaise mixture and enjoy as desired.
Per Serving: Calories 192; Fat 9.3g; Sodium 133mg; Carbs 27.1g; Fiber 1.4g; Sugar 19g; Protein 3.2g

Sirloin Steak with Sausage gravy

Prep time: 10 minutes | Cook time: 15 minutes | Servings: 2

1 teaspoon pepper
2 cups almond milk
2 tablespoons almond flour
6 ounces ground sausage meat
1 teaspoon pepper
1 teaspoon salt
1 teaspoon garlic powder

1 teaspoon onion powder
1 cup panko breadcrumbs
1 cup almond flour
3 beaten eggs
6 ounces sirloin steak, pounded
till thin

1. Slide basket into rails of Level 3. Select the "AIR FRY" function of Ninja Foodi Smart XL Pro Air Oven, set temperature to 370°F/175°C and time to 12 minutes. Select START/STOP to begin preheating. 2. Season panko breadcrumbs with spices. Dredge steak in flour, then egg, and then seasoned panko mixture. Place into air fryer basket. Cook 12 minutes. 3. To make sausage gravy, cook sausage and drain off fat, but reserve 2 tablespoons. Add flour to sausage and mix until incorporated. 4. Gradually mix in milk over medium to high heat till it becomes thick. Season mixture with pepper and cook 3 minutes longer. 5. Serve steak topped with gravy and enjoy!
Per Serving: Calories 30; Fat 13g; Sodium 12mg; Carbs 49g; Fiber 4g; Sugar 6g; Protein 3g

Easy Roast Beef

Prep time: 10 minutes | Cook time: 45 minutes | Servings: 6 to 8

Roast beef
1 tablespoon olive oil

Seasonings of choice

1. Install the wire rack on Level 3. Select the "AIR ROAST" function of Ninja Foodi Smart XL Pro Air Oven, set temperature to 390°F/200°C and time to 30 minutes. Select START/STOP to begin preheating. 2. Place roast in a bowl and toss with olive oil and desired seasonings. Put seasoned roast into the air fryer and cook for 30 minutes. 3. Flip roast when the timer sounds and cook another 15 minutes.
Per Serving: Calories 429; Fat 32.4g; Sodium 325mg; Carbs 5g; Fiber 1g; Sugar 3g; Protein 28g

Crispy Mongolian-style Beef

Prep time: 10 minutes | Cook time: 12 minutes | Servings: 6 to 10

Olive oil
½ cup almond flour
Sauce:
½ cup chopped green onion
1 teaspoon red chili flakes
1 teaspoon almond flour
½ cup brown sugar
1 teaspoon hoisin sauce
½ cup water

2 pounds beef tenderloin or beef
chuck, sliced into strips

½ cup rice vinegar
½ cup low-sodium soy sauce
1 tablespoon chopped garlic
1 tablespoon finely chopped
ginger
2 tablespoons olive oil

1. Install the wire rack on Level 3. Select the "AIR ROAST" function of Ninja Foodi Smart XL Pro Air Oven, set temperature to 300°F/150°C and time to 10 minutes. Select START/STOP to begin preheating. 2. Toss beef strips in almond flour, ensuring they are coated well. Add to air fryer and cook 10 minutes. 3. Meanwhile, add all sauce ingredients to the pan and bring to a boil. Mix well. Add beef strips to the sauce and cook 2 minutes. 4. Serve over cauliflower rice!
Per Serving: Calories 173; Fat 13.6g; Sodium 281mg; Carbs 3g; Fiber 1g; Sugar 1g; Protein 10g

Fried Beef Taco Egg Rolls

Prep time: 15 minutes | Cook time: 12 minutes | Servings: 4

1 teaspoon cilantro
2 chopped garlic cloves
1 tablespoon olive oil
1 cup shredded Mexican cheese
½ packet taco seasoning

½ can cilantro lime rotel
½ chopped onion
16 egg roll wrappers
1-pound lean ground beef

1. Select Level 3. Select the "AIR FRY" function of Ninja Foodi Smart XL Pro Air Oven, set temperature to 400°F/200°C and time to 12 minutes. Select START/STOP to begin preheating. 2. Add onions and garlic to a skillet, cooking till fragrant. Then add taco seasoning, pepper, salt, and beef, cooking till beef is broken up into tiny pieces and cooked thoroughly. Add Rotel and stir well. 3. Lay out egg wrappers and brush with water to soften a bit. Load wrappers with beef filling and add cheese to each. Fold diagonally to close and use water to secure edges. 4. Brush filled egg wrappers with olive oil and add to the air fryer. Cook 8 minutes, flip, and cook another 4 minutes. 5. Sprinkled with cilantro, serve.
Per Serving: Calories 1052; Fat 50g; Sodium 438mg; Carbs 7g; Fiber 0g; Sugar 7g; Protein 132g

Sweet Honey Mesquite Pork Chops

Prep time: 5 minutes | Cook time: 10 minutes | Servings: 2

2 tablespoons mesquite seasoning
¼ cup honey
1 tablespoon olive oil

1 tablespoon water
freshly ground black pepper
2 bone-in center pork chops

1. In a shallow glass dish, whisk the mesquite seasoning, honey, olive oil, water and black pepper together. Pierce the chops all over and on both sides with a fork or meat tenderizer. Add the pork chops to the marinade and massage the marinade into the chops. Cover and marinate for 30 minutes. 2. Select Level 3. Select the "AIR FRY" function of Ninja Foodi Smart XL Pro Air Oven, set temperature to 400°F/200°C and time to 6 minutes. Select START/STOP to begin preheating. 3. Transfer the pork chops to the air fryer basket and pour half of the marinade over the chops, reserving the remaining marinade. Air-fry the pork chops for 6 minutes. 4. Flip and pour the marinade on top. Air-fry for an additional 3 minutes at 330°F/165°C. Then, increase the air fryer temperature to 400°F/200°C and air-fry the pork chops for an additional minute. 5. Let them rest for 5 minutes before serving. If you'd like a sauce for these chops, pour the cooked marinade from the bottom of the air fryer over the top.
Per Serving: Calories 69; Fat 7.2g; Sodium 486mg; Carbs 2g; Fiber 1g; Sugar 0g; Protein 0g

Lamb with Rhubarb

Prep time: 5 minutes | Cook time: 30 minutes | Servings: 4

1 and ½ pound lamb ribs	1 tablespoon fennel seeds, ground
A pinch of black pepper and salt	1 tablespoon coriander seeds, ground
1 tablespoon black peppercorns, ground	4 rhubarb stalks, chopped
1 tablespoon white peppercorns, ground	¼ cup balsamic vinegar
	2 tablespoons olive oil

1. Heat up a suitable pan that fits your air fryer with the oil over medium heat, then add the lamb and brown for 2 minutes. 2. Add the rest of the recipe ingredients, toss, bring to a simmer for 2 minutes and take off the heat. 3. Put the pan in the fryer and cook on "Air Fry" Mode, select level 3, and set its temperature to 380°F/195°C or 25 minutes. 4. Divide everything into bowls and serve.
Per Serving: Calories 257; Fat 17 g; Sodium 674 mg; Carbs 13.9g; Fiber 4.2; Sugar 5.9g; Protein 13.6g

Delicious Corned Beef Egg Rolls

Prep time: 5 minutes | Cook time: 8 minutes | Servings: 2 to 3

Swiss cheese	Sliced deli corned beef
Can of sauerkraut	Egg roll wrappers

1. Slide basket into rails of Level 3. Select the "AIR FRY" function of Ninja Foodi Smart XL Pro Air Oven, set temperature to 400°F/200°C and time to 8 minutes. Select START/STOP to begin preheating. 2. Cut corned beef and Swiss cheese into thin slices. Drain sauerkraut and dry well. Take egg roll wrapper and moisten edges with water. 3. Stack center with corned beef and cheese till you reach desired thickness. Top off with sauerkraut. Fold the corner over the edge of filling. Bring up sides and glue with water. 4. Add to air fryer basket and spritz with olive oil. Cook 4 minutes, then flip and cook another 4 minutes.
Per Serving: Calories 227; Fat 9.8g; Sodium 525mg; Carbs 7g; Fiber 2g; Sugar 4g; Protein 28g

Spicy Herbed Roast Beef

Prep time: 15 minutes | Cook time: 30 minutes | Servings: 5 to 6

½ teaspoon fresh rosemary	1 teaspoon salt
1 teaspoon dried thyme	4-pound top round roast beef
¼ teaspoon pepper	2 teaspoons olive oil

1. Install the wire rack on Level 3. Select the "AIR ROAST" function of Ninja Foodi Smart XL Pro Air Oven, set temperature to 360°F/180°C and time to 20 minutes. Select START/STOP to begin preheating. 2. Rub olive oil all over beef. Mix rosemary, thyme, pepper, and salt together and proceed to rub all sides of beef with spice mixture. 3. Place seasoned beef into air fryer and cook 20 minutes. Allow it to rest for at least 10 minutes before slicing to serve.
Per Serving: Calories 248; Fat 21.1g; Sodium 429mg; Carbs 2g; Fiber 0g; Sugar 1g; Protein 12g

Regular Beef Empanadas

Prep time: 15 minutes | Cook time: 10 minutes | Servings: 4

1 teaspoon water	1 cup picadillo
1 egg white	8 Goya empanada discs (thawed)

1. Select Level 3. Select the "AIR FRY" function of Ninja Foodi Smart XL Pro Air Oven, set temperature to 325°F/160°C and time to 8 minutes. Select START/STOP to begin preheating. 2. Spray basket with olive oil. Place 2 tablespoons of picadillo into the center of each disc. Fold disc in half and use a fork to seal edges. Repeat with all ingredients. 3. Whisk egg white with water and brush tops of empanadas with egg wash. Add 2-3 empanadas to the air fryer, cooking 8 minutes until golden. 4. Repeat till you cook all the filled empanadas.
Per Serving: Calories 200; Fat 15.6g; Sodium 165mg; Carbs 5g; Fiber 1g; Sugar 2g; Protein 10g

Simple Beef Patties

Prep time: 10 minutes | Cook time: 10 minutes | Servings: 4

1-pound lean ground beef	1 teaspoon dried parsley

½ teaspoon dried oregano	½ teaspoon garlic powder
½ teaspoon pepper	Few drops of liquid smoke
½ teaspoon salt	1 teaspoon Worcestershire sauce
½ teaspoon onion powder	

1. Select Level 3. Select the "AIR FRY" function of Ninja Foodi Smart XL Pro Air Oven, set temperature to 350°F/175°C and time to 10 minutes. Select START/STOP to begin preheating. 2. Mix all seasonings together till combined. Place beef in a bowl and add seasonings. Mix well, but do not overmix. 3. Make 4 patties from the mixture and, using your thumb, make an indent in the center of each patty. 4. Add patties to air fryer basket and cook 10 minutes. No need to turn!
Per Serving: Calories 76; Fat 5.7g; Sodium 63mg; Carbs 1g; Fiber 0g; Sugar 1g; Protein 5g

Roasted Beef Stuffed Peppers

Prep time: 5 minutes | Cook time: 25 minutes | Servings: 4

4 ounces shredded cheddar cheese	8 ounces lean ground beef
½ teaspoon pepper	1 teaspoon olive oil
½ teaspoon salt	1 minced garlic clove
1 teaspoon Worcestershire sauce	½ chopped onion
½ cup tomato sauce	2 green peppers

1. Select Level 3. Select the "AIR FRY" function of Ninja Foodi Smart XL Pro Air Oven, set temperature to 390°F/200°C and time to 20 minutes. Select START/STOP to begin preheating. 2. Spray with olive oil. Cut stems off bell peppers and remove seeds. Cook in boiling salted water for 3 minutes. Sauté garlic and onion together in a skillet until golden in color. 3. Take skillet off the heat. Mix pepper, salt, Worcestershire sauce, ¼ cup of tomato sauce, half of cheese and beef together. 4. Divide meat mixture into pepper halves. Top filled peppers with remaining cheese and tomato sauce. Place filled peppers in air fryer and bake 15-20 minutes.
Per Serving: Calories 509; Fat 40.6g; Sodium 525mg; Carbs 8g; Fiber 2g; Sugar 5g; Protein 28g

Tasty Steak and Broccoli

Prep time: 10 minutes | Cook time: 15 minutes | Servings: 4

1 minced garlic clove	⅓ cup sherry
1 sliced ginger root	2 teaspoons sesame oil
1 tablespoon olive oil	⅓ cup oyster sauce
1 teaspoon almond flour	1 pounds of broccoli
1 teaspoon sweetener of choice	¾ pound round steak
1 teaspoon low-sodium soy sauce	

1. Select Level 3. Select the "AIR FRY" function of Ninja Foodi Smart XL Pro Air Oven, set temperature to 400°F/200°C and time to 12 minutes. Select START/STOP to begin preheating. 2. Remove stems from broccoli and slice into florets. Slice steak into thin strips. Combine sweetener, soy sauce, sherry, almond flour, sesame oil, and oyster sauce together, stirring till sweetener dissolves. 3. Put strips of steak into the mixture and allow to marinate for 45 minutes to 2 hours. 4. Add broccoli and marinated steak to air fryer. Place garlic, ginger, and olive oil on top. Cook 12 minutes. Serve with cauliflower rice!
Per Serving: Calories 288; Fat 23.3g; Sodium 308mg; Carbs 6g; Fiber 1g; Sugar 5g; Protein 14g

Herbed Beef Roast with Onion

Prep time: 15 minutes | Cook time: 45 minutes | Servings: 4

1½ pounds beef eye round roast	1 onion, sliced
1 tablespoon olive oil	1 rosemary sprig
Sea salt	1 thyme sprig
Ground black pepper, to taste	

1. Select Level 3. Select the "AIR FRY" function of Ninja Foodi Smart XL Pro Air Oven, set temperature to 390°F/200°C and time to 45 minutes. Select START/STOP to begin preheating. 2. Toss the beef with the olive oil, salt, and black pepper; place the beef in the Air Fryer basket. 3. Cook the beef eye round roast for 45 minutes, turning it over halfway through the cooking time. 4. Top the beef with the onion, rosemary, and thyme. Continue to cook an additional 10 minutes. Enjoy!
Per Serving: Calories 268; Fat 13.6g; Sodium 348mg; Carbs 1.2g; Fiber 0.2g; Sugar 0.6g; Protein 35.2g

Hoisin Glazed Pork Chops

Prep time: 5 minutes | Cook time: 12 minutes | Servings: 2 to 3

3 tablespoons hoisin sauce
¼ cup honey
1 tablespoon soy sauce
3 tablespoons rice vinegar
2 tablespoons brown sugar
1½ teaspoons grated fresh ginger

2 teaspoons Sriracha sauce
2 to 3 bone-in center cut pork chops, 1-inch thick (about 1¼ pounds)
chopped scallions, for garnish

1. Combine the hoisin sauce, honey, soy sauce, rice vinegar, brown sugar, ginger, and Sriracha sauce in a small saucepan. Whisk the ingredients and boil over medium-high heat on the stovetop. Lower the heat and manage to simmer the sauce until it has reduced in volume and thickened slightly – about 10 minutes. 2. Select Level 3. Select the "AIR FRY" function of Ninja Foodi Smart XL Pro Air Oven, set temperature to 400°F/200°C and time to 5 minutes. Select START/STOP to begin preheating. 3. Place the pork chops into the air fryer basket and pour half the hoisin BBQ sauce over the top. Air-fry for 6 minutes. 4. Then, flip the chops over, pour the remaining hoisin BBQ sauce on top and air-fry for 5 to 6 more minutes, depending on the thickness of the pork chops. The internal temperature of the pork chops should be 155°F/70°C when tested with an instant-read thermometer. 5. You can spoon a little of the sauce from the bottom drawer of the air fryer over the top if desired. Sprinkle with chopped scallions and serve.
Per Serving: Calories 293; Fat 13.8g; Sodium 855mg; Carbs 28g; Fiber 8g; Sugar 11g; Protein 19g

Cheesy Bacon and Pear Stuffed Pork Chops

Prep time: 5 minutes | Cook time: 6 to 18 minutes | Servings: 3

4 slices bacon, chopped
1 tablespoon butter
½ cup finely diced onion
⅓ cup chicken stock
1½ cups seasoned stuffing cubes
1 egg, beaten
½ teaspoon dried thyme
½ teaspoon salt

⅛ teaspoon black pepper
1 pear, finely diced
⅓ cup crumbled blue cheese
3 boneless center-cut pork chops (2-inch thick)
Olive oil
Salt and freshly ground black pepper

1. Select Level 3. Select the "AIR FRY" function of Ninja Foodi Smart XL Pro Air Oven, set temperature to 400°F/200°C and time to 6 minutes. Select START/STOP to begin preheating. 2. Place the bacon into the air fryer basket and air-fry for 6 minutes, stirring halfway through the cooking time. Pour out the grease from the bottom of the air fryer. 3. To make the stuffing, melt the butter in a medium saucepan over medium heat on the stovetop. Cook the onion for a few minutes, until it starts to soften. Add the chicken stock and simmer for 1 minute. Add the stuffing cubes. Stir until the stock has been absorbed. Add the bacon, egg, dried thyme, salt and freshly ground black pepper, and stir until combined. Fold in the diced pear and crumbled blue cheese. 4. Place the chops on a cutting board. Using the palm of your hand to hold the chop flat and steady, slice into the side of the pork chop to make a pocket in the center of the chop. Leave about an inch of chop uncut and make sure you don't cut all the way through the pork chop. Brush chops with olive oil and season with salt and freshly ground black pepper. Stuff each pork chop with a third of the stuffing, packing the stuffing tightly inside the pocket. 5. Preheat the air fryer to 360°F/180°C. Spray or brush the sides of the air fryer basket with oil. Place the chops in the air fryer basket with the open stuffed edge of the pork chop facing the outside edges of the basket. 6. Air-fry the pork chops for 18 minutes, turning the pork chops over halfway through the cooking time. Let rest and then transfer to a serving platter.
Per Serving: Calories 151; Fat 7.5g; Sodium 621mg; Carbs 20g; Fiber 5g; Sugar 2g; Protein 5g

Herbed Tenderloin with Fried Apples

Prep time: 5 minutes | Cook time: 23 minutes | Servings: 2 to 3

1 pork tenderloin (about 1-pound)
2 tablespoons coarse brown mustard
Salt and freshly ground black pepper
1½ teaspoons finely chopped

fresh rosemary, plus sprigs for garnish
2 apples, cored and cut into 8 wedges
1 tablespoon butter, melted
1 teaspoon brown sugar

1. Select Level 3. Select the "AIR FRY" function of Ninja Foodi Smart XL Pro Air Oven, set temperature to 370°F/185°C and time to 10 minutes. Select START/STOP to begin preheating. 2. Cut the pork tenderloin in half so that you have two pieces that fit into the air fryer basket. Brush the mustard onto both halves of the pork tenderloin and then season with salt, pepper and the rosemary. 3. Place the pork tenderloin halves into the air fryer basket and cook for 10 minutes. Turn the pork over and air-fry for an additional 5 to 8 minutes. 4. If your pork tenderloin is especially thick, you may need to add a minute or two, but it's better to check the pork and add time, than to overcook it. Let the pork rest for 5 minutes. 5. In the meantime, toss the apple wedges with the butter and brown sugar and air-fry at 400°F/200°C for 8 minutes, shaking the basket once or twice during the cooking process so the apples cook and brown evenly. 6. Slice the pork on the bias. Serve with the fried apples scattered over the top and a few sprigs of rosemary as garnish.
Per Serving: Calories 25; Fat 0.1g; Sodium 546mg; Carbs 3g; Fiber 1g; Sugar 0g; Protein 3g

Pistachio Crusted Rack of Lamb

Prep time: 5 minutes | Cook time: 19 minutes | Servings: 2

½ cup finely chopped pistachios
3 tablespoons panko breadcrumbs
1 teaspoon chopped fresh rosemary
2 teaspoons chopped fresh oregano

Salt and freshly ground black pepper
1 tablespoon olive oil
1 rack of lamb, bones trimmed of fat
1 tablespoon Dijon mustard

1. Select Level 3. Select the "AIR FRY" function of Ninja Foodi Smart XL Pro Air Oven, set temperature to 380°F/195°C and time to 12 minutes. Select START/STOP to begin preheating. 2. Combine the pistachios, breadcrumbs, rosemary, oregano, salt and pepper in a small bowl. Grease in the oil and stir to combine. 3. Season the rack of lamb with salt and pepper on all sides and transfer it to the air fryer basket with the fat side facing up. Air-fry the lamb for 12 minutes. 4. Remove the lamb and brush the fat side of the lamb rack with the Dijon mustard. Coat the rack with pistachio mixture, pressing the breadcrumbs onto the lamb with your hands and rolling the bottom of the rack in any of the crumbs that fall off. 5. Return the rack of lamb to the air fryer and air-fry for another 3 to 7 minutes. Add or subtract a couple of minutes for lamb that is more or less well cooked. 6. Let the lamb rest for at least 5 minutes. Then, slice into chops and serve.
Per Serving: Calories 56; Fat 2.2g; Sodium 177mg; Carbs 5g; Fiber 1g; Sugar 1g; Protein 5g

Hot Paprika Pork Loin Roast

Prep time: 5 minutes | Cook time: 20 minutes | Servings: 4

1½ pounds top loin roasts, sliced into four pieces
2 tablespoons olive oil
1 teaspoon hot paprika

Sea salt and ground black pepper
1 tablespoon Dijon mustard
1 teaspoon garlic, pressed

1. Select Level 3. Select the "AIR FRY" function of Ninja Foodi Smart XL Pro Air Oven, set temperature to 400°F/200°C and time to 15 minutes. Select START/STOP to begin preheating. 2. Place all ingredients in a lightly greased Air Fryer basket. Cook the pork for 15 minutes, turning it over halfway through the cooking time.
Per Serving: Calories 352; Fat 1.9g; Sodium 414mg; Carbs 1.9g; Fiber 0.6g; Sugar 0.6g; Protein 36.4g

Hot and Spicy Rib Roast

Prep time: 10 minutes | Cook time: 55 minutes | Servings: 4

1½ pounds pork center cut rib roast
2 teaspoons butter, melted
1 teaspoon red chili powder
1 teaspoon paprika

1 teaspoon garlic powder
½ teaspoon onion powder
Sea salt and ground black pepper, to taste
2 tablespoons tamari sauce

1. Install the wire rack on Level 3. Select the "AIR ROAST" function of Ninja Foodi Smart XL Pro Air Oven, set temperature to 360°F/180°C and time to 55 minutes. Select START/STOP to begin preheating. 2. Toss all ingredients in a lightly greased Air Fryer basket. Cook the pork for 55 minutes, turning it over halfway through the cooking time. 3. Serve warm and enjoy!
Per Serving: Calories 383; Fat 17.9g; Sodium 269mg; Carbs 3.2g; Fiber 1.1g; Sugar 1g; Protein 49.9g

Lamb Koftas with Cucumber-Yogurt Dip

Prep time: 5 minutes | Cook time: 8 minutes | Servings: 3 to 4

For the Lamb:

1-pound ground lamb	1 egg, beaten
1 teaspoon ground cumin	½ teaspoon salt
1 teaspoon ground coriander	Freshly ground black pepper
2 tablespoons chopped fresh mint	

For the Cucumber-Yogurt Dip:

½ English cucumber, grated (1 cup)	1 cup plain yogurt
Salt	1 tablespoon olive oil
½ clove garlic, finely minced	1 tablespoon chopped fresh dill
	Freshly ground black pepper

1. For the lamb: Combine ingredients and mix well. Divide the mixture into 10 portions. Make ball from portions and then by cupping the meatball in your hand, shape it into an oval. 2. Select Level 3. Select the "AIR FRY" function of Ninja Foodi Smart XL Pro Air Oven, set temperature to 400°F/200°C and time to 8 minutes. Select START/STOP to begin preheating. 3. Air-fry the koftas for 8 minutes. 4. For the cucumber-yogurt dip: Place the grated cucumber in a strainer and sprinkle with salt. Let this drain while the koftas are cooking. 5. Meanwhile, combine the garlic, yogurt, oil and fresh dill in a bowl. Just before serving, stir the cucumber into the yogurt sauce and season to taste with freshly ground black pepper. 6. Serve warm with the cucumber-yogurt dip.

Per Serving: Calories 217; Fat 21.8g; Sodium 207mg; Carbs 7g; Fiber 4g; Sugar 3g; Protein 2g

Cheese Lamb Hamburgers

Prep time: 5 minutes | Cook time: 15 minutes | Servings: 3 to 4

2 teaspoons olive oil	½ cup black olives, finely chopped
⅓ onion, finely chopped	⅓ cup crumbled feta cheese
1 clove garlic, minced	½ teaspoon salt
1-pound ground lamb	Freshly ground black pepper
2 tablespoons fresh parsley, finely chopped	4 thick pita breads
1½ teaspoons fresh oregano, finely chopped	Toppings and condiments

1. Pre-heat a skillet on the stovetop. Cook the onion in olive oil until tender, but not browned. Add in the garlic and cook. Place the cooked onion and garlic to a bowl and add the lamb, parsley along with oregano, olives, cheese, salt and pepper. Mix the ingredients. 2. Divide the mix into 4 portions and form the hamburgers. 3. Select Level 3. Select the "AIR FRY" function of Ninja Foodi Smart XL Pro Air Oven, set temperature to 370°F/175°C and time to 5 minutes. Select START/STOP to begin preheating. 4. Air-fry the burgers for 5 minutes. Flip the burgers over and air-fry for another 8 minutes. Cook the breads in the air fryer for 2 minutes. 5. Place the burgers into the toasted breads, and serve with a tzatziki sauce or some mayonnaise.

Per Serving: Calories 74; Fat 1.9g; Sodium 685mg; Carbs 9g; Fiber 7g; Sugar 2g; Protein 9g

Herbed Porterhouse Steak

Prep time: 5 minutes | Cook time: 15 minutes | Servings: 4

1½ pounds Porterhouse steak	1 teaspoon dried parsley
1 tablespoon olive oil	1 teaspoon dried oregano
Kosher salt	½ teaspoon dried basil
Ground black pepper	2 tablespoons butter
½ teaspoon cayenne pepper	2 garlic cloves, minced

1. Select Level 3. Select the "ROAST" function of Ninja Foodi Smart XL Pro Air Oven, set temperature to 400°F/200°C and time to 12 minutes. Select START/STOP to begin preheating. 2. Toss the steak with the remaining ingredients; place the steak in the Air Fryer basket. Cook the steak for 12 minutes, turning it over halfway through the cooking time. 3. Bon appétit!

Per Serving: Calories 326; Fat 19.6g; Sodium 458mg; Carbs 1.9g; Fiber 0.4g; Sugar 0.6g; Protein 35.6g

Delicious Beef Burgers

Prep time: 5 minutes | Cook time: 20 minutes | Servings: 3

¾-pound ground beef	1 small onion, chopped
2 cloves garlic, minced	Kosher salt

Ground black pepper	3 hamburger buns

1. Select Level 3. Select the "AIR FRY" function of Ninja Foodi Smart XL Pro Air Oven, set temperature to 380°F/195°C and time to 15 minutes. Select START/STOP to begin preheating. 2. Mix the beef, garlic, onion, salt, and black pepper until everything is well combined. Form the mixture into three patties. 3. Cook the burgers for about 15 minutes or until cooked through; serve your burgers on the prepared buns and enjoy!

Per Serving: Calories 392; Fat 16.6g; Sodium 222mg; Carbs 32.3g; Fiber 1.8g; Sugar 5.3g; Protein 28.8g

The London Broil

Prep time: 10 minutes | Cook time: 30 minutes | Servings: 3

1 pound London broil	1 tablespoon paprika
¼ cup soy sauce	Sea salt and ground black pepper, to taste
¼ cup fresh lemon juice	
2 garlic cloves, minced	

1. Select Level 3. Select the "AIR FRY" function of Ninja Foodi Smart XL Pro Air Oven, set temperature to 400°F/200°C and time to 28 minutes. Select START/STOP to begin preheating. 2. Toss the beef with the remaining ingredients and let it marinate for an hour. Place the beef in a lightly oiled Air Fryer basket and discard the marinade. 3. Cook the beef for 28 minutes, turning it over halfway through the cooking time. Bon appétit!

Per Serving: Calories 220; Fat 9.6g; Sodium 369mg; Carbs 6.3g; Fiber 1g; Sugar 3.6g; Protein 24.2g

Herbed Buttery Strip Steak

Prep time: 10 minutes | Cook time: 20 minutes | Servings: 4

1½ pounds New York strip steak	1 teaspoon paprika
2 tablespoons butter, melted	1 teaspoon dried thyme
Sea salt	1 teaspoon dried rosemary
Ground black pepper, to taste	

1. Install the wire rack on Level 3. Select the "AIR ROAST" function of Ninja Foodi Smart XL Pro Air Oven, set temperature to 400°F/200°C and time to 15 minutes. Select START/STOP to begin preheating. 2. Toss the beef with the remaining ingredients; place the beef in the Air Fryer basket. 3. Cook the beef for 15 minutes, turning it over halfway through the cooking time. Enjoy!

Per Serving: Calories 218; Fat 12.6g; Sodium 456mg; Carbs 1.4g; Fiber 0.4g; Sugar 0.6g; Protein 23.6g

Cheese-Stuffed Meatballs

Prep time: 10 minutes | Cook time: 16 minutes | Servings: 4

1-pound ground beef	½ teaspoon ground black pepper
¼ cup diced onions	1 cup mushrooms (about 8 ounces), finely chopped
1 large egg	½ cup tomato sauce
1½ teaspoons smoked paprika	1 dozen (½-inch) cubes cheddar cheese
½ teaspoon fine sea salt	
½ teaspoon garlic powder	

For Serving:

Prepared yellow mustard	ketchup
Sugar-free or reduced-sugar	

1. Spray the air fryer basket with avocado oil. Select Level 3. Select the "AIR FRY" function of Ninja Foodi Smart XL Pro Air Oven, set temperature to 375°F/190°C and time to 8 minutes. Select START/STOP to begin preheating. 2. In a large bowl, mix together the ground beef, onions, egg, paprika, salt, garlic powder, and pepper until well combined. Add the mushrooms and slowly stir in the tomato sauce. The meat mixture should be very moist but still hold its shape when rolled into meatballs. 3. Divide the meat mixture into 12 equal portions. Place 1 cube of cheese in the center of each portion and form the meat around the cheese into a 2-inch meatball. Arrange the meatballs in a single layer in the air fryer basket, leaving space between them. 4. Cook the meatballs for 8 minutes, flip them over, and lower the temperature to 325°F/160°C. Cook for another 6 to 8 minutes, until cooked through. 5. Serve with mustard and ketchup, if desired. Store leftovers in an airtight container in the refrigerator for up to 4 days or in the freezer for up to 2 months.

Per Serving: Calories 354; Fat 7.9g; Sodium 704mg; Carbs 6g; Fiber 3.6g; Sugar 6g; Protein 18g

Healthy Keto Turtles

Prep time: 15 minutes | Cook time: 15 minutes | Servings: 4

1-pound ground beef
1 teaspoon fine sea salt
½ teaspoon ground black pepper
4 hot dogs
For Serving:
Prepared yellow mustard

8 whole peppercorns
2 large dill pickles
2 slices bacon

Cornichons

1. Create the turtle shells: Form the ground beef into 4 equal-sized patties. Season the outsides of the patties with the salt and pepper. 2. Make the turtle heads: Slice 1½ inches off one end of each hot dog. Use your thumb to make an indent in the side of each ground beef patty and press in a hot dog end for the head. Use the tip of a sharp knife to score 2 spots in each hot dog end for the eyes. Place a whole peppercorn in each slot. 3. Make the turtle legs: Cut the rest of the hot dogs in half lengthwise, then cut each half in half crosswise (you should have sixteen 1½-inch pieces). Place one piece of hot dog flat side down under each front corner of the patties. (You will have 8 hot dog pieces left over.)4. Decorate the shells: Cut the dill pickles into ⅛-inch-thick slices that are about 3 inches long. Place the pickle slices parallel to each other on top of the ground beef patties, spaced about half an inch apart. 5. Slice the bacon into ¼-inch-wide and 5- to 6-inch-long strips. Place the strips on the patties, on top of and perpendicular to the pickle slices, spaced about half an inch apart. Tuck the ends of the bacon strips underneath the turtle so they don't curl up. 6. Spray the air fryer basket with avocado oil. Select Level 3. Select the "AIR FRY" function of Ninja Foodi Smart XL Pro Air Oven, set temperature to 390°F/200°C and time to 15 minutes. Select START/STOP to begin preheating. 7. Place the turtles in the air fryer basket, leaving space between them. Cook for 10 to 15 minutes, until the beef is cooked to your liking. 8. Remove from the air fryer and serve with mustard and cornichons. Store leftovers in an airtight container in the refrigerator for up to 4 days or in the freezer for up to 2 months.
Per Serving: Calories 354; Fat 7.9g; Sodium 704mg; Carbs 6g; Fiber 3.6g; Sugar 6g; Protein 18g

Fragrant Ribeye Steak

Prep time: 5 minutes | Cook time: 20 minutes | Servings: 4

1-pound ribeye steak, bone-in
2 tablespoons butter, room temperature
2 garlic cloves, minced

Sea salt and ground black pepper, to taste
2 rosemary sprigs, leaves picked, chopped

1. Install the wire rack on Level 3. Select the "AIR ROAST" function of Ninja Foodi Smart XL Pro Air Oven, set temperature to 400°F/200°C and time to 15 minutes. Select START/STOP to begin preheating. 2. Toss the ribeye steak with the butter, garlic, salt, black pepper, and rosemary; place the steak in the Air Fryer basket. 3. Cook the ribeye steak for 15 minutes, turning it over halfway through the cooking time. Bon appétit!
Per Serving: Calories 263; Fat 17.6g; Sodium 259mg; Carbs 3.7g; Fiber 0.2g; Sugar 0.6g; Protein 22.7g

Beef Brisket

Prep time: 10 minutes | Cook time: 1 hour 10 minutes | Servings: 4

1½ pounds beef brisket
2 tablespoons olive oil
3 garlic cloves, pressed
Sea salt
Ground black pepper

1 teaspoon red pepper flakes, crushed
2 tablespoons tomato ketchup
2 tablespoons Dijon mustard

1. Install the wire rack on Level 3. Select the "AIR ROAST" function of Ninja Foodi Smart XL Pro Air Oven, set temperature to 360°F/180°C and time to 70 minutes. Select START/STOP to begin preheating. 2. Toss the beef brisket with the olive oil, garlic, salt, black pepper, and red pepper; now, place the beef brisket in the Air Fryer basket. 3. Cook the beef brisket at 390 °F/200°C for 15 minutes, turn the beef over and reduce the temperature to 360 °F/180°C. Continue to cook the beef brisket for approximately 55 minutes or until cooked through. 4. Shred the beef with two forks; add in the ketchup and mustard and stir to combine well. Bon appétit!
Per Serving: Calories 414; Fat 32.4g; Sodium 147mg; Carbs 25g; Fiber 0.8g; Sugar 1.6g; Protein 3.4g

Delicious Italian Herb Filet Mignon

Prep time: 5 minutes | Cook time: 20 minutes | Servings: 4

1½ pounds filet mignon
2 tablespoons olive oil
2 cloves garlic, pressed
1 tablespoon Italian herb mix

1 teaspoon cayenne pepper
Kosher salt and freshly ground black pepper, to taste

1. Install the wire rack on Level 3. Select the "AIR ROAST" function of Ninja Foodi Smart XL Pro Air Oven, set temperature to 400°F/200°C and time to 14 minutes. Select START/STOP to begin preheating. 2. Toss the beef with the remaining ingredients; place the beef in the Air Fryer basket. Cook the beef for 14 minutes, turning it over halfway through the cooking time. Enjoy!
Per Serving: Calories 218; Fat 12.6g; Sodium 289mg; Carbs 1.4g; Fiber 0.4g; Sugar 0.6g; Protein 23.6g

Mustardy Steak Sliders

Prep time: 10 minutes | Cook time: 20 minutes | Servings: 4

1½ pounds skirt steak
1 teaspoon steak dry rub
½ teaspoon cayenne pepper
Sea salt and ground black pepper,

to taste
2 tablespoons olive oil
2 tablespoons Dijon mustard
8 Hawaiian buns

1. Select Level 3. Select the "AIR FRY" function of Ninja Foodi Smart XL Pro Air Oven, set temperature to 400°F/200°C and time to 15 minutes. Select START/STOP to begin preheating. 2. Toss the beef with the spices and olive oil; place the beef in the Air Fryer basket. Cook the beef for 15 minutes, turning it over halfway through the cooking time. 3. Cut the beef into slices and serve them with mustard and Hawaiian buns. Bon appétit!
Per Serving: Calories 541; Fat 20.7g; Sodium 436mg; Carbs 44g; Fiber 2.3g; Sugar 6.1g; Protein 44g

Bacon Salad with Crispy Croutons

Prep time: 5 minutes | Cook time: 20 minutes | Servings: 5

1-pound bacon, cut into thick slices
1 head lettuce, torn into leaves
1 tablespoon fresh chive, chopped
1 tablespoon fresh tarragon, chopped
1 tablespoon fresh parsley, chopped

2 tablespoons freshly squeezed lemon juice
2 garlic cloves, minced
Coarse sea salt and ground black pepper, to taste
1 teaspoon red pepper flakes, crushed
2 cups bread cubes

1. Select Level 3. Select the "AIR FRY" function of Ninja Foodi Smart XL Pro Air Oven, set temperature to 400°F/200°C and time to 10 minutes. Select START/STOP to begin preheating. 2. Place the bacon in the Air Fryer basket. Then, cook the bacon for 10 minutes, tossing the basket halfway through the cooking time; reserve. Air fry the bread cubes at 390°F/200°C for 6 minutes or until the bread is toasted. 3. Toss the remaining ingredients in a salad bowl; top your salad with the bacon and croutons. Bon appétit!
Per Serving: Calories 419; Fat 36.3g; Sodium 455mg; Carbs 13.4g; Fiber 1g; Sugar 2.5g; Protein 13.4g

Herbed Roast Beef

Prep time: 10 minutes | Cook time: 55 minutes | Servings: 4

1½ pounds bottom round roast
2 tablespoons olive oil
2 garlic cloves, minced
1 teaspoon rosemary

1 teaspoon parsley
1 teaspoon oregano
Sea salt and freshly ground black pepper

1. Install the wire rack on Level 3. Select the "AIR ROAST" function of Ninja Foodi Smart XL Pro Air Oven, set temperature to 390°F/200°C and time to 50 minutes. Select START/STOP to begin preheating. 2. Toss the beef with the spices, garlic, and olive oil; place the beef in the Air Fryer basket. Cook the roast beef for 50 minutes, turning it over halfway through the cooking time. 3. Cut the beef into slices and serve them with dinner rolls. Bon appétit!
Per Serving: Calories 301; Fat 16.7g; Sodium 411mg; Carbs 0.4g; Fiber 0.1g; Sugar 0.1g; Protein 35.4g
Per Serving: Calories 401; Fat 32.1g; Sodium 236mg; Carbs 2.4g; Fiber 0.4g; Sugar 0.6g; Protein 25.4g

Spicy Top Round Roast

Prep time: 10 minutes | Cook time: 55 minutes | Servings: 5

2 pounds top round roast
2 tablespoons extra-virgin olive oil
2 cloves garlic, pressed
1 tablespoon fresh rosemary, chopped

1 tablespoon fresh parsley, chopped
1 teaspoon red chili powder
Kosher salt and freshly ground black pepper, to taste

1. Install the wire rack on Level 3. Select the "AIR ROAST" function of Ninja Foodi Smart XL Pro Air Oven, set temperature to 390°F/200°C and time to 55 minutes. Select START/STOP to begin preheating. 2. Toss the beef with the remaining ingredients; place the beef in the Air Fryer basket. Cook the beef for 55 minutes, turning it over halfway through the cooking time. Enjoy!
Per Serving: Calories 270; Fat 10.9g; Sodium 236mg; Carbs 0.5g; Fiber 0.2g; Sugar 0.1g; Protein 42.2g

Tenderloin Steaks with Crispy Mushrooms

Prep time: 5 minutes | Cook time: 20 minutes | Servings: 4

1½ pounds tenderloin steaks
2 tablespoons butter, melted
1 teaspoon garlic powder
½ teaspoon mustard powder
1 teaspoon cayenne pepper

Sea salt
Ground black pepper
½ pound cremini mushrooms, sliced

1. Install the wire rack on Level 3. Select the "AIR ROAST" function of Ninja Foodi Smart XL Pro Air Oven, set temperature to 400°F/200°C and time to 10 minutes. Select START/STOP to begin preheating. 2. Toss the beef with 1 tablespoon of the butter and spices; place the beef in the Air Fryer basket. Cook the beef for 10 minutes, turning it over halfway through the cooking time. 3. Add in the mushrooms along with the remaining 1 tablespoon of the butter. Continue to cook an additional 5 minutes. Serve warm. Bon appétit!
Per Serving: Calories 310; Fat 17g; Sodium 369mg; Carbs 3.7g; Fiber 1.7g; Sugar 1.6g; Protein 41.2g

Delicious Picnic Ham

Prep time: 10 minutes | Cook time: 60 minutes | Servings: 4

1½ pounds picnic ham
2 tablespoons olive oil
2 garlic cloves, minced

2 tablespoons rice vinegar
1 tablespoon tamari sauce

1. Install the wire rack on Level 3. Select the "AIR ROAST" function of Ninja Foodi Smart XL Pro Air Oven, set temperature to 400°F/200°C and time to 60 minutes. Select START/STOP to begin preheating. 2. Cook the ham in your air fryer basket for 13 minutes. Toss the ham with the remaining ingredients; wrap the ham in a piece of aluminum foil and lower it into the Air Fryer basket. Reduce the temperature to 375 °F/190°C and cook the ham for about 30 minutes. 3. Remove the foil, turn the temperature to 400 °F/200°C, and continue to cook an additional 15 minutes or until cooked through.
Per Serving: Calories 344; Fat 21.8g; Sodium 633mg; Carbs 7.5g; Fiber 2.4g; Sugar 0.5g; Protein 28.4g

Italian-Style Pork Burgers

Prep time: 5 minutes | Cook time: 20 minutes | Servings: 4

1-pound ground pork
Sea salt
Ground black pepper
1 tablespoon Italian herb mix
1 small onion, chopped
1 teaspoon garlic, minced

¼ cup parmesan cheese, grated
¼ cup seasoned breadcrumbs
1 egg
4 hamburger buns
4 teaspoons Dijon mustard
4 tablespoons mayonnaise

1. Select Level 3. Select the "AIR FRY" function of Ninja Foodi Smart XL Pro Air Oven, set temperature to 380°F/195°C and time to 15 minutes. Select START/STOP to begin preheating. 2. In a mixing bowl, thoroughly combine the pork, spices, onion, garlic, parmesan, breadcrumbs, and egg. Form the mixture into four patties. Cook the burgers for about 15 minutes or until cooked through. 3. Serve your burgers with hamburger buns, mustard, and mayonnaise. Enjoy!
Per Serving: Calories 593; Fat 38.9g; Sodium 235mg; Carbs 30.2g; Fiber 2.7g; Sugar 5g; Protein 27.6g

Marinated London Broil

Prep time: 10 minutes | Cook time: 30 minutes | Servings: 4

1 pound London broil
Kosher salt
Ground black pepper
2 tablespoons olive oil
1 small lemon, freshly squeezed

3 cloves garlic, minced
1 tablespoon fresh parsley, chopped
1 tablespoon fresh coriander, chopped

1. Install the wire rack on Level 3. Select the "AIR ROAST" function of Ninja Foodi Smart XL Pro Air Oven, set temperature to 400°F/200°C and time to 28 minutes. Select START/STOP to begin preheating. 2. Toss the beef with the remaining ingredients and let it marinate for an hour. Place the beef in a lightly oiled Air Fryer basket and discard the marinade. 3. Cook the beef for 28 minutes, turning it over halfway through the cooking time. Bon appétit!
Per Serving: Calories 227; Fat 13.6g; Sodium 417mg; Carbs 2.7g; Fiber 0.3g; Sugar 0.9g; Protein 23.8g

Pork Schnitzel with Delicious Dill Sauce

Prep time: 10 minutes | Cook time: 24 minutes | Servings: 4 to 6

6 boneless, center cut pork chops (about 1½ pounds)
½ cup flour
1½ teaspoons salt
freshly ground black pepper
2 eggs
½ cup milk
Dill Sauce:
1 cup chicken stock
1½ tablespoons cornstarch
⅓ cup sour cream

1½ cups toasted fine breadcrumbs
1 teaspoon paprika
3 tablespoons butter, melted
2 tablespoons vegetable or olive oil
lemon wedges

1½ tablespoons chopped fresh dill
salt and pepper

1. Pound each chop until they are ½-inch thick. 2. Mix the flour, salt, and black pepper in a shallow dish. Whisk the eggs and milk together in a second shallow dish. Finally, combine the breadcrumbs and paprika in a third shallow dish. 3. Dip each flattened pork chop in the flour. Dip each chop into the egg mixture. Finally, dip them into the breadcrumbs and press the breadcrumbs onto the meat firmly. Place each finished chop on a baking sheet until they are all coated. 4. Select Level 3. Select the "AIR FRY" function of Ninja Foodi Smart XL Pro Air Oven, set temperature to 400°F/200°C and time to 4 minutes. Select START/STOP to begin preheating. 5. Combine the melted butter and the oil in a small bowl and lightly brush both sides of the coated pork chops. Do not brush the chops too heavily or the breading will not be as crispy. 6. Air-fry one schnitzel at a time for 4 minutes, turning it over halfway through the cooking time. Hold the cooked schnitzels warm on a baking pan in a 170°F/75°C oven while you finish air-frying the rest. 7. While the schnitzels are cooking, whisk the chicken stock and cornstarch together in a small saucepan over medium-high heat on the stovetop. Boil and manage simmer for 2 minutes. Add the dill and spice with salt and pepper. 8. Transfer the pork schnitzel to a platter and serve with dill sauce and lemon wedges. For a traditional meal, serve this alongside some egg noodles, spätzle or German potato salad.
Per Serving: Calories 414; Fat 21g; Sodium 369mg; Carbs 24g; Fiber 1g; Sugar 3g; Protein 30g

Delicious Herbed Meatloaf

Prep time: 10 minutes | Cook time: 30 minutes | Servings: 4

1½ pounds ground chuck
1 egg, beaten
2 tablespoons olive oil
4 tablespoons crackers, crushed
½ cup shallots, minced
2 garlic cloves, minced

1 tablespoon fresh rosemary, chopped
1 tablespoon fresh thyme, chopped
Sea salt and ground black pepper, to taste

1. Select Level 3. Select the "BAKE" function of Ninja Foodi Smart XL Pro Air Oven, set temperature to 390°F/200°C and time to 25 minutes. Select START/STOP to begin preheating. 2. Thoroughly combine all ingredients until everything is well combined. Scrape the beef mixture into a lightly oiled baking pan and transfer it to the Air Fryer basket. 3. Cook your meatloaf for 25 minutes. Bon appétit!
Per Serving: Calories 373; Fat 23.1g; Sodium 258mg; Carbs 5g; Fiber 0.6g; Sugar 1.4g; Protein 36.8g

Homemade Skirt Steak

Prep time: 5 minutes | Cook time: 15 minutes | Servings: 4

1½ pounds skirt steak
Kosher salt and freshly cracked
black pepper, to taste
1 teaspoon cayenne pepper

¼ teaspoon cumin powder
2 tablespoons olive oil
2 garlic cloves, minced

1. Install the wire rack on Level 3. Select the "AIR ROAST" function of Ninja Foodi Smart XL Pro Air Oven, set temperature to 400°F/200°C and time to 12 minutes. Select START/STOP to begin preheating. 2. Toss the steak with the other ingredients; place the steak in the Air Fryer basket. 3. Cook the steak at 400 °F/200°C for 12 minutes, turning it over halfway through the cooking time. Bon appétit!
Per Serving: Calories 305; Fat 17.5g; Sodium 369mg; Carbs 1.8g; Fiber 0.3g; Sugar 0.6g; Protein 35.2g

French Chateaubriand

Prep time: 5 minutes | Cook time: 15 minutes | Servings: 4

1-pound beef filet mignon
Sea salt
Ground black pepper
1 teaspoon cayenne pepper

3 tablespoons olive oil
1 tablespoon Dijon mustard
4 tablespoons dry French wine

1. Select Level 3. Select the "AIR FRY" function of Ninja Foodi Smart XL Pro Air Oven, set temperature to 400°F/200°C and time to 14 minutes. Select START/STOP to begin preheating. 2. Toss the filet mignon with the rest of the ingredients; place the filet mignon in the Air Fryer basket. 3. Cook the filet mignon for 14 minutes, turning it over halfway through the cooking time. Enjoy!
Per Serving: Calories 249; Fat 15.5g; Sodium 423mg; Carbs 1.8g; Fiber 0.4g; Sugar 0.8g; Protein 26.6g

Tasty Montreal Ribeye Steak

Prep time: 5 minutes | Cook time: 20 minutes | Servings: 4

1½ pounds ribeye steak, bone-in
2 tablespoons butter
1 Montreal seasoning mix

Sea salt and ground black pepper,
to taste

1. Install the wire rack on Level 3. Select the "AIR ROAST" function of Ninja Foodi Smart XL Pro Air Oven, set temperature to 400°F/200°C and time to 15 minutes. Select START/STOP to begin preheating. 2. Toss the ribeye steak with the remaining ingredients; place the ribeye steak in a lightly oiled Air Fryer basket. 3. Cook the ribeye steak for 15 minutes, turning it over halfway through the cooking time. Bon appétit!
Per Serving: Calories 357; Fat 23.5g; Sodium 247mg; Carbs 33.5g; Fiber 0.4g; Sugar 0.2g; Protein 33.5g

Delicious Italian Rump Roast

Prep time: 10 minutes | Cook time: 55 minutes | Servings: 4

1½ pounds rump roast
2 tablespoons olive oil
Sea salt
Ground black pepper, to taste

1 teaspoon Italian seasoning mix
1 onion, sliced
2 cloves garlic, peeled
¼ cup red wine

1. Install the wire rack on Level 3. Select the "AIR ROAST" function of Ninja Foodi Smart XL Pro Air Oven, set temperature to 390°F/200°C and time to 55 minutes. Select START/STOP to begin preheating. 2. Toss the rump roast with the rest of the ingredients; place the rump roast in a lightly oiled Air Fryer basket. 3. Cook the rump roast for 55 minutes, turning it over halfway through the cooking time. Bon appétit!
Per Serving: Calories 297; Fat 16.9g; Sodium 358mg; Carbs 0.7g; Fiber 0.1g; Sugar 0.2g; Protein 35.2g

Smoked Paprika Pork Loin Chops

Prep time: 5 minutes | Cook time: 20 minutes | Servings: 4

1-pound pork loin chops
1 tablespoon olive oil
Sea salt and ground black pepper,

to taste
1 tablespoon smoked paprika

1. Select Level 3. Select the "AIR FRY" function of Ninja Foodi Smart XL Pro Air Oven, set temperature to 400°F/200°C and time to 15 minutes. Select START/STOP to begin preheating. 2. Place all ingredients in a lightly greased Air Fryer basket. Cook the pork loin chops for 15 minutes, turning them over halfway through the cooking time.
Per Serving: Calories 332; Fat 1.9g; Sodium 378mg; Carbs 1.9g; Fiber 0.8g; Sugar 0.7g; Protein 23.4g

Herbed Spicy Pork Roast

Prep time: 10 minutes | Cook time: 55 minutes | Servings: 4

1½ pounds center-cut pork roast
1 tablespoon olive oil
Sea salt
Ground black pepper

1 teaspoon garlic powder
1 teaspoon hot paprika
½ teaspoon dried parsley flakes
½ teaspoon dried rosemary

1. Select Level 3. Select the "AIR FRY" function of Ninja Foodi Smart XL Pro Air Oven, set temperature to 360°F/180°C and time to 55 minutes. Select START/STOP to begin preheating. 2. Toss all ingredients in a lightly greased Air Fryer basket. Cook the pork for 55 minutes, turning it over halfway through the cooking time. 3. Serve warm and enjoy!
Per Serving: Calories 330; Fat 14.3g; Sodium 347mg; Carbs 1g; Fiber 0.3g; Sugar 0g; Protein 37.4g

Simple Pork Spareribs

Prep time: 10 minutes | Cook time: 40 minutes | Servings: 4

2 pounds pork spareribs
1 teaspoon coarse sea salt
⅓ teaspoon freshly ground black
pepper

1 tablespoon brown sugar
1 teaspoon cayenne pepper
1 teaspoon garlic powder
1 teaspoon mustard powder

1. Select Level 3. Select the "AIR FRY" function of Ninja Foodi Smart XL Pro Air Oven, set temperature to 350°F/175°C and time to 35 minutes. Select START/STOP to begin preheating. 2. Toss all ingredients in a lightly greased Air Fryer basket. Cook the pork ribs for 35 minutes, turning them over halfway through the cooking time.
Per Serving: Calories 301; Fat 8.5g; Sodium 147mg; Carbs 2.8g; Fiber 0.2g; Sugar 2g; Protein 50.1g

Delicious Sweet Pork Belly

Prep time: 5 minutes | Cook time: 20 minutes | Servings: 6

1½ pounds pork belly, cut into
pieces
¼ cup tomato sauce
1 tablespoon tamari sauce

2 tablespoons dark brown sugar
1 teaspoon garlic, minced
Sea salt and ground black pepper,
to season

1. Install the wire rack on Level 3. Select the "AIR ROAST" function of Ninja Foodi Smart XL Pro Air Oven, set temperature to 400°F/200°C and time to 17 minutes. Select START/STOP to begin preheating. 2. Toss all ingredients in your Air Fryer basket. Cook the pork belly for about 17 minutes, shaking the basket halfway through the cooking time.
Per Serving: Calories 603; Fat 60.1g; Sodium 578mg; Carbs 3.3g; Fiber 0.8g; Sugar 1.7g; Protein 11.1g

Spicy Beef Burgers

Prep time: 10 minutes | Cook time: 20 minutes | Servings: 3

¾-pound ground beef
2 tablespoons onion, minced
1 teaspoon garlic, minced
1 teaspoon cayenne pepper

Sea salt
Ground black pepper
1 teaspoon red chili powder
3 hamburger buns

1. Select Level 3. Select the "AIR FRY" function of Ninja Foodi Smart XL Pro Air Oven, set temperature to 380°F/195°C and time to 15 minutes. Select START/STOP to begin preheating. 2. Mix the beef, onion, garlic, cayenne pepper, salt, black pepper, and red chili powder until everything is well combined. Form the mixture into three patties. 3. Cook the burgers for about 15 minutes or until cooked through. Serve your burgers on the prepared buns and enjoy!
Per Serving: Calories 270; Fat 10.9g; Sodium 369mg; Carbs 0.5g; Fiber 0.2g; Sugar 0.1g; Protein 42.2g

Cheesy Pork Loin Filets with Mushrooms

Prep time: 5 minutes | Cook time: 20 minutes | Servings: 4

1½ pounds pork loin filets
Sea salt and ground black pepper, to taste
2 tablespoons olive oil
1 pound mushrooms, sliced
2 ounces blue cheese

1. Select Level 3. Select the "AIR FRY" function of Ninja Foodi Smart XL Pro Air Oven, set temperature to 400°F/200°C and time to 10 minutes. Select START/STOP to begin preheating. 2. Place the pork, salt, black pepper, and olive oil in a lightly greased Air Fryer basket. Cook the pork loin filets for 10 minutes, turning them over halfway through the cooking time. 3. Top the pork loin filets with the mushrooms. Continue cooking for 5 minutes. Top the warm pork with blue cheese. 4. Bon appétit!
Per Serving: Calories 408; Fat 18.3g; Sodium 236mg; Carbs 5g; Fiber 1.3g; Sugar 2.8g; Protein 53.4g

Pork Sausage with Crunchy Brussels Sprouts

Prep time: 5 minutes | Cook time: 20 minutes | Servings: 4

1-pound sausage links, uncooked
1 pound Brussels sprouts, halved
1 teaspoon dried thyme
1 teaspoon dried rosemary
1 teaspoon dried parsley flakes
1 teaspoon garlic powder

1. Select Level 3. Select the "AIR FRY" function of Ninja Foodi Smart XL Pro Air Oven, set temperature to 380°F/195°C and time to 15 minutes. Select START/STOP to begin preheating. 2. Place the sausage and Brussels sprouts in a lightly greased Air Fryer basket. Air fry the sausage and Brussels sprouts for 15 minutes tossing the basket halfway through the cooking time. 3. Bon appétit!
Per Serving: Calories 444; Fat 35.8g; Sodium 225mg; Carbs 11.5g; Fiber 4.4g; Sugar 2.5g; Protein 20.1g

Garlicky Rosemary Pork Butt

Prep time: 10 minutes | Cook time: 60 minutes | Servings: 4

1½ pounds pork butt
1 teaspoon butter, melted
2 garlic cloves, pressed
2 tablespoons fresh rosemary, chopped
Coarse sea salt and freshly ground black pepper, to taste

1. Select Level 3. Select the "AIR FRY" function of Ninja Foodi Smart XL Pro Air Oven, set temperature to 360°F/180°C and time to 55 minutes. Select START/STOP to begin preheating. 2. Toss all ingredients in a lightly greased Air Fryer basket. Cook the pork for 55 minutes, turning it over halfway through the cooking time. 3. Serve warm and enjoy!
Per Serving: Calories 338; Fat 22g; Sodium 522mg; Carbs 0.7g; Fiber 0.2g; Sugar 0.2g; Protein 29.7g

Pork Ribs with Zucchini

Prep time: 10 minutes | Cook time: 40 minutes | Servings: 4

1½ pounds pork loin ribs
2 cloves garlic, minced
1 tablespoon olive oil
4 tablespoons whiskey
1 teaspoon onion powder
Sea salt and ground black pepper, to taste
½-pound zucchini, sliced

1. Select Level 3. Select the "AIR FRY" function of Ninja Foodi Smart XL Pro Air Oven, set temperature to 350°F/175°C and time to 25 minutes. Select START/STOP to begin preheating. 2. Toss the pork ribs with the garlic, olive oil, whiskey and spices; place the ingredients in a lightly greased Air Fryer basket. Cook the pork ribs for 25 minutes, turning them over halfway through the cooking time. 3. Top the pork ribs with the sliced zucchini and continue cooking an additional 12 minutes. Serve immediately.
Per Serving: Calories 303; Fat 13.5g; Sodium 471mg; Carbs 7.2g; Fiber 0.9g; Sugar 4.1g; Protein 37.1g

Spicy St. Louis-Style Ribs

Prep time: 10 minutes | Cook time: 40 minutes | Servings: 4

1½ pounds St. Louis-style ribs
1 teaspoon hot sauce
1 tablespoon canola oil
Kosher salt and ground black pepper, to taste
2 garlic cloves, minced

1. Select Level 3. Select the "AIR FRY" function of Ninja Foodi Smart XL Pro Air Oven, set temperature to 350°F/175°C and time to 35 minutes. Select START/STOP to begin preheating. 2. Toss all ingredients in a lightly greased Air Fryer basket. Cook the pork ribs for 35 minutes, turning them over halfway through the cooking time.
Per Serving: Calories 360; Fat 23.6g; Sodium 478mg; Carbs 33.4g; Fiber 0.2g; Sugar 0.6g; Protein 33.4g

Spiced Ground Pork Dinner Rolls

Prep time: 5 minutes | Cook time: 20 minutes | Servings: 4

1-pound ground pork
Sea salt and freshly ground black pepper, to taste
1 teaspoon red pepper flakes, crushed
½ cup scallions, chopped
2 garlic cloves, minced
1 tablespoon olive oil
1 tablespoon soy sauce
8 dinner rolls, split

1. Select Level 3. Select the "AIR FRY" function of Ninja Foodi Smart XL Pro Air Oven, set temperature to 380°F/195°C and time to 15 minutes. Select START/STOP to begin preheating. 2. In a mixing bowl, thoroughly combine the pork, spices, scallions, garlic, olive oil, and soy sauce. Form the mixture into four patties. Cook the patties for about 15 minutes or until cooked through. 3. Serve the patties in dinner rolls and enjoy!
Per Serving: Calories 499; Fat 31.6g; Sodium 478mg; Carbs 28.2g; Fiber 2.6g; Sugar 2g; Protein 24.5g

Pork Tacos

Prep time: 10 minutes | Cook time: 60 minutes | Servings: 4

2 ancho chiles, seeded and minced
2 garlic cloves, chopped
1 tablespoon olive oil
Kosher salt
Ground black pepper, to season
1 teaspoon dried Mexican oregano
1 ½ pounds pork butt
4 corn tortillas, warmed

1. Select Level 3. Select the "AIR FRY" function of Ninja Foodi Smart XL Pro Air Oven, set temperature to 360°F/180°C and time to 55 minutes. Select START/STOP to begin preheating. 2. Toss all ingredients, except for the tortillas, in a lightly greased Air Fryer basket. Air fry the pork butt for 55 minutes, turning it over halfway through the cooking time. 3. Using two forks, shred the pork and serve in tortillas with toppings of choice. Serve immediately!
Per Serving: Calories 538; Fat 34.2g; Sodium 455mg; Carbs 11.3g; Fiber 1.6g; Sugar 0.2g; Protein 44.1g

Pork Loin Chops with Onions

Prep time: 5 minutes | Cook time: 20 minutes | Servings: 4

1½ pounds pork loin chops, boneless
2 tablespoons olive oil
½ teaspoon cayenne pepper
1 teaspoon garlic powder
Sea salt
Ground black pepper
1 onion, cut into wedges

1. Select Level 3. Select the "AIR FRY" function of Ninja Foodi Smart XL Pro Air Oven, set temperature to 400°F/200°C and time to 15 minutes. Select START/STOP to begin preheating. 2. Place all ingredients in a lightly greased Air Fryer basket. Cook the pork loin chops for 15 minutes, turning them over halfway through the cooking time.
Per Serving: Calories 358; Fat 18.6g; Sodium 633mg; Carbs 8g; Fiber 1g; Sugar 4.7g; Protein 37.3g

Chapter 5 Fish and Seafood Recipes

Fried Shrimp

Prep time: 10 minutes | Cook time: 15 minutes | Servings: 4

1 ½ pounds shrimp, cleaned and deveined
½ cup all-purpose flour
½ teaspoon shallot powder
½ teaspoon garlic powder
1 teaspoon red pepper flakes,

crushed
Black pepper and salt, to taste
2 large eggs
1 cup crackers, crushed
½ cup parmesan cheese, grated

1. In a suitable shallow bowl, mix the flour and spices. Beat the eggs in the second bowl, and mix the crackers and cheese in the third bowl. 2. Dip the shrimp in the flour mixture, then in the whisked eggs; finally, roll the shrimp over the cracker/cheese mixture until they are well coated on all sides. 3. Spread the shrimp in a well-greased air fryer cooking basket. 4. Cook the shrimp on Air Fry mode on level 3 at 400°F/200°C for about 15 minutes. 5. Bon appétit!
Per Serving: Calories 399; Fat 13 g; Sodium 626 mg; Carbs 52.9g; Fiber 8.8g; Sugar 3.9g; Protein 19.6g

Swordfish Steaks

Prep time: 10 minutes | Cook time: 10 minutes | Servings: 4

1-pound swordfish steaks
2 tablespoons olive oil
2 tablespoons fresh mint leaves, chopped

3 tablespoons fresh lemon juice
1 teaspoon garlic powder
½ teaspoon shallot powder
Black pepper and salt, to taste

1. Toss the swordfish steaks with the remaining recipe ingredients and place them in a lightly oiled air fryer cooking basket. 2. Cook the swordfish steaks on Air Fry mode on level 3 at 400°F/200°C for about 10 minutes, turning them over halfway through the cooking time. 3. Bon appétit!
Per Serving: Calories 213; Fat 4.1 g; Sodium 303 mg; Carbs 37.9g; Fiber 1.5g; Sugar 1.9g; Protein 26.6g

Fish Croquettes Muffins

Prep time: 10 minutes | Cook time: 15 minutes | Servings: 4

1-pound mackerel fillet, boneless and chopped
1 tablespoon olive oil
½ onion, chopped
2 garlic cloves, crushed
1 teaspoon hot paprika

1 tablespoon fresh cilantro, chopped
2 tablespoons fresh parsley, chopped
Black pepper and salt, to taste
4 English muffins, toasted

1. Mix all the recipe ingredients, except for the English muffins, in a suitable bowl. Shape the prepared mixture into four patties and place them in a lightly oiled air fryer cooking basket. 2. Cook the fish patties on Air Fry mode on level 3 at 400°F/200°C for about 14 minutes, turning them over halfway through the cooking time. 3. Serve on English muffins and enjoy!
Per Serving: Calories 303; Fat 3.1 g; Sodium 343 mg; Carbs 24.9g; Fiber 1.5g; Sugar 0.9g; Protein 22.6g

Air Fried Calamari

Prep time: 10 minutes | Cook time: 5 minutes | Servings: 4

1 pound calamari, sliced into rings
2 garlic cloves, minced
1 teaspoon red pepper flakes
2 tablespoons dry white wine
2 tablespoons olive oil

2 tablespoons fresh lemon juice
1 teaspoon basil, chopped
1 teaspoon dill, chopped
1 teaspoon parsley, chopped
Salt and black pepper, to taste

1. Toss all the recipe ingredients in a lightly greased air fryer cooking basket. 2. Cook your calamari on Air Fry mode on level 3 at 400°F/200°C for 5 minutes, tossing the basket halfway through the cooking time. 3. Bon appétit!
Per Serving: Calories 249; Fat 5.7 g; Sodium 574 mg; Carbs 23.9g; Fiber 0.9g; Sugar 1.9g; Protein 3.6g

Pollock Fishcakes

Prep time: 10 minutes | Cook time: 15 minutes | Servings: 4

1 pound pollock, chopped
1 teaspoon chili sauce

Black pepper and salt, to taste
4 tablespoons all-purpose

1 teaspoon smoked paprika
2 tablespoons olive oil

4 ciabatta buns

1.Mix all the recipe ingredients, except for the ciabatta buns, in a suitable bowl. Shape the prepared mixture into four patties and place them in a lightly oiled air fryer cooking basket. 2. Cook the fish patties on Air Fry mode on level 3 at 400°F/200°C for about 14 minutes, turning them over halfway through the cooking time. 3. Serve on hamburger buns and enjoy!
Per Serving: Calories 416; Fat 8.3 g; Sodium 208 mg; Carbs 22.9g; Fiber 0.5g; Sugar 19g; Protein 60.6g

Italian Squid with Cheese

Prep time: 10 minutes | Cook time: 10 minutes | Servings: 4

1 ½ pounds small squid tubes
2 tablespoons butter, melted
1 chili pepper, chopped
2 garlic cloves, minced
1 teaspoon red pepper flakes
Black pepper and salt, to taste

¼ cup dry white wine
2 tablespoons fresh lemon juice
1 teaspoon Mediterranean herb mix
2 tablespoons Parmigiano-Reggiano cheese, grated

1. Toss all the recipe ingredients, except for the Parmigiano-Reggiano cheese, in a lightly greased air fryer cooking basket. 2. Cook your squid on Air Fry mode on level 3 at 400°F/200°C for 5 minutes, tossing the basket halfway through the cooking time. 3. Top the warm squid with the cheese. Bon appétit!
Per Serving: Calories 249; Fat 5.7 g; Sodium 574 mg; Carbs 23.9g; Fiber 0.9g; Sugar 1.9g; Protein 3.6g

Air Fried Buttered Sea Bass

Prep time: 10 minutes | Cook time: 15 minutes | Servings: 3

2 tablespoons butter, room temperature
1-pound sea bass such
¼ cup dry white wine
¼ cup all-purpose flour

Black pepper and salt, to taste
1 teaspoon mustard seeds
1 teaspoon fennel seeds
2 cloves garlic, minced

1. Toss the fish with the remaining recipe ingredients; place them in a lightly oiled air fryer cooking basket. 2. Cook the fish on Air Fry mode on level 3 at 400°F/200°C for about 10 minutes, turning them over halfway through the cooking time. 3. Bon appétit!
Per Serving: Calories 297; Fat 1g; Sodium 291mg; Carbs 35g; Fiber 1g; Sugar 9g; Protein 29g

Herbed Salmon Fillets

Prep time: 10 minutes | Cook time: 15 minutes | Servings: 4

1 ½ pounds salmon fillets
2 sprigs fresh rosemary
1 tablespoon fresh basil
1 tablespoon fresh thyme
1 tablespoon fresh dill

1 small lemon, juiced
2 tablespoons olive oil
Black pepper and salt, to taste
1 teaspoon stone-ground mustard
2 cloves garlic, chopped

1. Toss the salmon with the remaining recipe ingredients; place them in a lightly oiled air fryer cooking basket. 2. Cook the salmon fillets on Air Fry mode on level 3 at 380°F/195°C for about 12 minutes, turning them over halfway through the cooking time. 3. Serve immediately and enjoy!
Per Serving: Calories 348; Fat 30g; Sodium 660mg; Carbs 5g; Fiber 0g; Sugar 0g; Protein 14g

Chili Calamari

Prep time: 10 minutes | Cook time: 10 minutes | Servings: 4

½ cup milk
1 cup all-purpose flour
2 tablespoons olive oil
1 teaspoon turmeric powder

Salt flakes and black, to taste
1 teaspoon paprika
1 red chili, minced
1 pound calamari, cut into rings

1. In a mixing bowl, thoroughly mix the milk, flour, olive oil, turmeric powder, salt, black pepper, paprika, and red chili. Mix to mix well. 2. Now, dip your calamari into the flour mixture to coat. 3. Cook your calamari on Air Fry mode on level 3 at 400°F/200°C for 5 minutes, turning them over halfway through the cooking time. 4. Bon appétit!
Per Serving: Calories 257; Fat 10.4g; Sodium 431mg; Carbs 20g; Fiber 0g; Sugar 1.6g; Protein 21g

Shrimp Hoagie Rolls

Prep time: 10 minutes | Cook time: 10 minutes | Servings: 4

1-pound shrimp, peeled and chilled
1 teaspoon olive oil
1 stalks celery, sliced
1 English cucumber, sliced
1 shallot, sliced
1 tablespoon fresh dill, roughly chopped
1 tablespoon fresh parsley,

roughly chopped
1 tablespoon fresh lime juice
1 tablespoon apple cider vinegar
½ cup mayonnaise
1 teaspoon creole seasoning mix
1 ½ teaspoons Dijon mustard
Salt and lemon pepper, to taste
4 hoagie rolls

1. Toss the shrimp and olive oil in the air fryer cooking basket. 2. Cook the shrimp on Air Fry mode on level 3 at 400°F/200°C for 6 minutes, tossing the basket halfway through the cooking time. 3. Place the shrimp in a mixing bowl along with the remaining recipe ingredients; toss to mix and serve on the prepared hoagie rolls. 4. Bon appétit!
Per Serving: Calories 399; Fat 16g; Sodium 537mg; Carbs 28g; Fiber 3g; Sugar 10g; Protein 35g

Italian Sea Bass

Prep time: 10 minutes | Cook time: 15 minutes | Servings: 4

1-pound sea bass
2 garlic cloves, minced
2 tablespoons olive oil
1 tablespoon Italian seasoning

mix
Black pepper and salt, to taste
¼ cup dry white wine

1. Toss the fish with the remaining recipe ingredients; place them in a lightly oiled air fryer cooking basket. 2. Cook the fish on Air Fry mode on level 3 at 400°F/200°C for about 15 minutes, turning them over halfway through the cooking time. 3. Bon appétit!
Per Serving: Calories 305; Fat 15g; Sodium 482mg; Carbs 17g; Fiber 3g; Sugar 2g; Protein 35g

Mustard Calamari

Prep time: 10 minutes | Cook time: 5 minutes | Servings: 4

2 cups flour
Black pepper and salt, to taste
1 teaspoon garlic, minced
1 tablespoon mustard

2 tablespoons olive oil
1 pound calamari, sliced into rings

1. In a mixing bowl, thoroughly mix the flour, salt, black pepper, garlic, mustard, and, and olive oil. Mix to mix well. 2. Now, dip your calamari into the flour mixture to coat. 3. Cook your calamari on Air Fry mode on level 3 at 400°F/200°C for 5 minutes, turning them over halfway through the cooking time. 4. Bon appétit!
Per Serving: Calories 336; Fat 6g; Sodium 181mg; Carbs 1.3g; Fiber 0.2g; Sugar 0.4g; Protein 69.2g

Cod Meatballs

Prep time: 15 minutes | Cook time: 8 minutes | Servings: 3

12 ounces cod fillet, grinded
1 teaspoon ground coriander
½ teaspoon ground cumin
½ teaspoon salt
1 teaspoon dried dill
½ teaspoon lemon zest, grated

½ teaspoon ground paprika
1 egg, beaten
1 teaspoon chives, chopped
½ teaspoon lemon juice
Cooking spray

1. In the bowl mix up grinded cod fillet, ground coriander, cumin, salt, dried dill, lemon zest, ground paprika, egg, chives, and lemon juice. Stir the prepared mixture with the help of the spoon until homogenous. 2. Select the Air Fry mode. Set the Ninja Foodi Smart XL Pro temperature to 400°F/200°C. Select Level "3" and set the time on your Ninja Foodi Smart XL Pro Air Fryer Oven to 8 minutes. Press Start/Pause to begin preheating. Continue to the next step when it is done preheating. 3. Grease its air fryer basket with cooking oil spray Make the medium size meatballs from the fish mixture and put them in the air fryer in one layer. 4. Insert its air fryer basket into the level 3 of the oven and close the door. Cook the cod cakes for 4 minutes. 5. Then flip them on another side and cook for 4 minutes more.
Per Serving: Calories 216; Fat 6.9 g; Sodium 31 mg; Carbs 38.5g; Fiber 5.6g; Sugar 6.7g; Protein 6.7g

Cheesy Fish Fingers

Prep time: 10 minutes | Cook time: 15 minutes | Servings: 4

½ cup all-purpose flour
Salt and black pepper
1 teaspoon cayenne pepper
½ teaspoon onion powder
1 tablespoon Italian parsley, chopped

1 teaspoon garlic powder
1 egg, whisked
½ cup pecorino Romano cheese, grated
1-pound monkfish, sliced into strips

1. In a shallow bowl, mix well the flour, spices, egg, and cheese. Dip the fish strips in the prepared batter until they are well coated on all sides. 2. Spread the prepared fish strips in the air fryer cooking basket. 3. Cook the fish strips on Air Fry mode on level 3 at 400°F/200°C for about 10 minutes, shaking the basket halfway through the cooking time. 4. Bon appétit!
Per Serving: Calories 308; Fat 24g; Sodium 715mg; Carbs 0.8g; Fiber 0.1g; Sugar 0.1g; Protein 21.9g

Fish Croquettes

Prep time: 10 minutes | Cook time: 15 minutes | Servings: 4

1-pound catfish, skinless, boneless and chopped
2 tablespoons olive oil
2 cloves garlic, minced

1 small onion, minced
¼ cup all-purpose flour
Black pepper and salt, to taste
½ cup breadcrumbs

1. Mix all the recipe ingredients in a suitable bowl. Shape the prepared mixture into bite-sized balls and place them in a lightly oiled air fryer cooking basket. 2. Cook the fish croquettes on Air Fry mode on level 3 at 400°F/200°C for about 14 minutes, shaking the basket halfway through the cooking time. 3. Bon appétit!
Per Serving: Calories 275; Fat 1.4g; Sodium 582mg; Carbs 31.5g; Fiber 1.1g; Sugar 0.1g; Protein 29.8g

Air Fried Mackerel

Prep time: 20 minutes | Cook time: 15 minutes | Servings: 2

8 ounces mackerel, trimmed
1 tablespoon Italian seasonings
1 teaspoon keto tomato sauce

2 tablespoons ghee, melted
½ teaspoon salt

1. Rub the mackerel with Italian seasonings, and tomato sauce. After this, rub the fish with salt and leave for 15 minutes in the fridge to marinate. 2. Meanwhile, Select the Air Fry mode. Set the Ninja Foodi Smart XL Pro temperature to 390°F/200°C. Select Level "3" and set the time on your Ninja Foodi Smart XL Pro Air Fryer Oven to 15 minutes. Press Start/Pause to begin preheating. Continue to the next step when it is done preheating. 3. When the time of marinating is finished, brush the fish with ghee and wrap in the baking paper. 4. Place the wrapped fish in its air fryer basket. Insert its air fryer basket into the level 3 of the oven and close the door. Cook it for 15 minutes.
Per Serving: Calories 551; Fat 31g; Sodium 1329mg; Carbs 1.5g; Fiber 0.8g; Sugar 0.4g; Protein 64g

Crab Meatballs

Prep time: 10 minutes | Cook time: 9 minutes | Servings: 2

10 ounces crab meat
1 garlic clove, minced
1 tablespoon green onions, chopped
1 teaspoon ground nutmeg

½ teaspoon salt
½ teaspoon ground turmeric
2 tablespoons coconut flour
1 teaspoon coconut oil, melted

1. Put the crab meat in the bowl and churn it with the help of the fork. Then add minced garlic, green onion, ground nutmeg, salt, ground turmeric, and coconut flour. Stir the prepared mixture until homogenous and make 4 crab meatballs. 2. Select the Air Fry mode. Set the Ninja Foodi Smart XL Pro temperature to 375°F/190°C. Select Level "3" and set the time on your Ninja Foodi Smart XL Pro Air Fryer Oven to 9 minutes. Press Start/Pause to begin preheating. Continue to the next step when it is done preheating. 3. Put the meatballs in the air fryer and sprinkle them with coconut oil. Cook them for 5 minutes. Then flip them on another side and cook for 4 minutes more.
Per Serving: Calories 180; Fat 3.2g; Sodium 133mg; Carbs 32g; Fiber 1.1g; Sugar 1.8g; Protein 9g

Mackerel Fish Pita Wraps

Prep time: 10 minutes | Cook time: 15 minutes | Servings: 4

1-pound mackerel fish fillets	½ teaspoon chili powder
2 tablespoons olive oil	Black pepper and salt, to taste
1 tablespoon Mediterranean seasoning mix	2 ounces feta cheese, crumbled
	4 (6-½ inch) tortillas

1. Toss the fish fillets with the olive oil; place them in a lightly oiled air fryer cooking basket. 2. Cook the fish fillets on Air Fry mode on level 3 at 400°F/200°C for about 14 minutes, turning them over halfway through the cooking time. 3. Assemble your pitas with the chopped fish and remaining ingredients and serve warm. Bon appétit!
Per Serving: Calories 380; Fat 29g; Sodium 821mg; Carbs 34.6g; Fiber 0g; Sugar 0g; Protein 30g

Butter Shrimp

Prep time: 10 minutes | Cook time: 10 minutes | Servings: 4

1-pound jumbo shrimp	chopped
2 tablespoons butter	2 tablespoons fresh chives, chopped
Salt and lemon pepper, to taste	
2 tablespoons fresh cilantro,	2 garlic cloves, crushed

1. Toss all the recipe ingredients in a lightly greased air fryer cooking basket. 2. Cook the shrimp on Air Fry mode on level 3 at 400°F/200°C for 8 minutes, tossing the basket halfway through the cooking time. 3. Bon appétit!
Per Serving: Calories 374; Fat 13g; Sodium 552mg; Carbs 25g; Fiber 1.2g; Sugar 1.2g; Protein 37.7g

Rosemary Butter Scallops

Prep time: 10 minutes | Cook time: 10 minutes | Servings: 4

1 ½ pounds sea scallops	2 rosemary sprigs, leaves picked and chopped
4 tablespoons butter, melted	
1 tablespoon garlic, minced	4 tablespoons dry white wine
Salt and black pepper, to season	

1. Toss all the recipe ingredients in a lightly greased air fryer cooking basket. 2. Cook the scallops on Air Fry mode on level 3 at 400°F/200°C for 7 minutes, tossing the basket halfway through the cooking time. 3. Bon appétit!
Per Serving: Calories 351; Fat 16g; Sodium 777mg; Carbs 26g; Fiber 4g; Sugar 5g; Protein 28g

Southern-Style Fried Shrimp

Prep time: 10 minutes | Cook time: 15 minutes | Servings: 4

1 cup all-purpose flour	1 cup seasoned breadcrumbs
1 teaspoon old bay seasoning	1 ½ pounds shrimp, peeled and deveined
Salt and lemon pepper, to taste	
½ cup buttermilk	

1. In a shallow bowl, mix the flour, spices, and buttermilk. Place the seasoned breadcrumbs in the second bowl. 2. Dip the shrimp in the prepared flour mixture, then in the breadcrumbs until they are well coated on all sides. 3. Spread the shrimp in a well-greased air fryer cooking basket. 4. Cook the shrimp at on Air Fry mode on level 3 at 400°F/200°C for about 10 minutes, shaking the basket halfway through the cooking time. 5. Bon appétit!
Per Serving: Calories 275; Fat 1.4g; Sodium 582mg; Carbs 31.5g; Fiber 1.1g; Sugar 0.1g; Protein 29.8g

Tasty Sausage-Stuffed Squid

Prep time: 10 minutes | Cook time: 10 minutes | Servings: 4

2 tablespoons olive oil	1 small Italian pepper, chopped
1 small onion, chopped	Black pepper and salt, to taste
2 cloves garlic, minced	4 ounces beef sausage, crumbled
1 tablespoon fresh parsley, chopped	1-pound squid tubes, cleaned

1. In a mixing bowl, thoroughly mix the olive oil, onion, garlic, parsley, Italian pepper, salt, black pepper, and sausage. 2. Stuff the squid tubes with the sausage filling and secure them with toothpicks. Place them in a lightly oiled air fryer cooking basket. 3. Cook the stuffed squid tubes on Air Fry mode on level 3 at 400°F/200°C for 5 minutes, turning them over halfway through the cooking time. 4. Bon appétit!
Per Serving: Calories 268; Fat 10.4g; Sodium 411mg; Carbs 0.4g; Fiber 0.1g; Sugar 0.1g; Protein 40.6g

Haddock Fishcakes

Prep time: 10 minutes | Cook time: 15 minutes | Servings: 4

1-pound haddock, boneless and	½ cup parmesan cheese, grated
¼ cup all-purpose flour	½ cup breadcrumbs
2 eggs	4 brioche buns

1. Mix all the recipe ingredients, except for the brioche buns, in a suitable bowl. Shape the prepared mixture into four patties and place them in a lightly oiled air fryer cooking basket. 2. Cook the fish patties on Air Fry mode on level 3 at 400°F/200°C for about 14 minutes, turning them over halfway through the cooking time. 3. Serve on hamburger buns and enjoy!
Per Serving: Calories 353; Fat 5g; Sodium 818mg; Carbs 53.2g; Fiber 4.4g; Sugar 8g; Protein 17.3g

Shrimp Salad

Prep time: 10 minutes | Cook time: 10 minutes | Servings: 4

1 ½ pounds shrimp, peeled and deveined	2 tablespoons chives, chopped
1 tablespoon olive oil	1 bell pepper, seeded and chopped
Black pepper and salt, to taste	1 celery stalk, trimmed and chopped
1 teaspoon fresh dill, chopped	½ cup mayonnaise
1 teaspoon fresh basil, chopped	1 teaspoon stone-ground mustard
1 tablespoon fresh parsley, chopped	1 tablespoon fresh lime juice

1. Toss the shrimp and olive oil in the air fryer cooking basket. 2. Cook the shrimp on Air Fry mode on level 3 at 400°F/200°C for 6 minutes, tossing the basket halfway through the cooking time. 3. Place the shrimp in a salad bowl; add in the remaining recipe ingredients and gently stir to mix. Serve well-chilled. 4. Bon appétit!
Per Serving: Calories 346; Fat 16.1g; Sodium 882mg; Carbs 1.3g; Fiber 0.5g; Sugar 0.5g; Protein 48.2g

Mediterranean Calamari

Prep time: 10 minutes | Cook time: 10 minutes | Servings: 4

1 pound calamari, sliced into rings	1 teaspoon garlic powder
Black pepper and salt, to taste	2 tablespoons lemon juice
1 teaspoon cayenne pepper	2 tablespoons olive oil

1. Toss all the recipe ingredients in a lightly greased air fryer cooking basket. 2. Cook your calamari on Air Fry mode on level 3 at 400°F/200°C for 5 minutes, tossing the basket halfway through the cooking time. 3. Bon appétit!
Per Serving: Calories 502; Fat 25g; Sodium 230mg; Carbs 1.5g; Fiber 0.2g; Sugar 0.4g; Protein 64.1g

Ginger Cod Fillets

Prep time: 15 minutes | Cook time: 11 minutes | Servings: 4

1-pound cod fillet	½ teaspoon salt
1 teaspoon minced ginger	½ teaspoon ground paprika
½ teaspoon ground ginger	½ teaspoon dried thyme
1 tablespoon avocado oil	

1. Rub the cod fillet with minced ginger and sprinkle with avocado oil. Leave the fish for 10 minutes to marinate. 2. Meanwhile, mix up ground ginger, salt, ground paprika, and thyme in the shallow bowl. Rub the marinated cod with the spice mixture. Select the Air Fry mode. Set the Ninja Foodi Smart XL Pro temperature to 390°F/200°C. Select Level "3" and set the time on your Ninja Foodi Smart XL Pro Air Fryer Oven to 11 minutes. Press Start/Pause to begin preheating. Continue to the next step when it is done preheating. 3. Put the cod in its air fryer basket. Insert its air fryer basket into the level 3 of the oven and close the door. Cook it for 6 minutes. 4. After this, flip the fish on another side and cook for 5 minutes more.
Per Serving: Calories 437; Fat 28g; Sodium 1221mg; Carbs 22.3g; Fiber 0.9g; Sugar 8g; Protein 30.3g

Sea Scallop with Greens

Prep time: 10 minutes | Cook time: 10 minutes | Servings: 4

1½ pounds sea scallops
Black pepper and salt, to taste
2 tablespoons olive oil
1 tablespoon balsamic vinegar
2 garlic cloves, minced

2 teaspoons fresh tarragon, minced
1 teaspoon Dijon mustard
1 cup mixed baby greens
1 small tomato, diced

1. Toss the scallops, salt, and black pepper in a lightly greased air fryer cooking basket. 2. Cook the scallops on Air Fry mode on level 3 at 400°F/200°C for 7 minutes, tossing the basket halfway through the cooking time. 3. Toss the scallops with the remaining recipe ingredients and serve at room temperature or well-chilled. 4. Bon appétit!
Per Serving: Calories 223; Fat 11.7g; Sodium 721mg; Carbs 13.6g; Fiber 0.7g; Sugar 8g; Protein 15.7g

Fish Burgers

Prep time: 10 minutes | Cook time: 15 minutes | Servings: 4

1-pound halibut, chopped
2 garlic cloves, crushed
4 tablespoons scallions, chopped
Black pepper and salt, to taste

1 teaspoon smoked paprika
A pinch of grated nutmeg
1 tablespoon olive oil
4 hamburger buns

1. Mix all the recipe ingredients, except for the hamburger buns, in a suitable bowl. Shape the prepared mixture into four patties and place them in a lightly oiled air fryer cooking basket. 2. Cook the fish patties on Air Fry mode on level 3 at 400°F/200°C for about 14 minutes, turning them over halfway through the cooking time. 3. Serve on hamburger buns and enjoy!
Per Serving: Calories 456; Fat 16.4g; Sodium 1321mg; Carbs 19.2g; Fiber 2.2g; Sugar 4.2g; Protein 55.2g

Coconut Shrimp

Prep time: 10 minutes | Cook time: 10 minutes | Servings: 4

½ cup whole wheat flour
1 cup coconut, shredded
¼ cup buttermilk
2 tablespoons olive oil
2 garlic cloves, crushed

1 tablespoon fresh lemon juice
Salt and red pepper flakes, to taste
1 ½ pounds shrimp, peeled and deveined

1. Mix the flour, coconut, buttermilk, olive oil, garlic, lemon juice, salt, and red pepper in a mixing bowl. 2. Dip the shrimp in the prepared batter and place them in a well-greased air fryer cooking basket. 3. Cook the shrimp on Air Fry mode on level 3 at 400°F/200°C for 9 minutes, tossing the basket halfway through the cooking time. 4. Bon appétit!
Per Serving: Calories 546; Fat 33.1g; Sodium 1201mg; Carbs 30g; Fiber 2.4g; Sugar 9.7g; Protein 32g

Tuna and Vegie Salad

Prep time: 10 minutes | Cook time: 15 minutes | Servings: 4

1-pound fresh tuna steak
Black pepper and salt, to taste
2 tablespoons fresh lemon juice
1 small onion, thinly sliced

1 carrot, julienned
2 cups baby spinach
2 tablespoons parsley, roughly chopped

1. Toss the fish with the black pepper and salt; place your tuna in a lightly oiled air fryer cooking basket. 2. Cook your tuna on Air Fry mode on level 3 at 400°F/200°C for about 10 minutes, turning it over halfway through the cooking time. 3. Chop your tuna with two forks and add in the remaining recipe ingredients; stir to mix and serve well-chilled. Bon appétit!
Per Serving: Calories 379; Fat 19g; Sodium 184mg; Carbs 12.3g; Fiber 0.6g; Sugar 2g; Protein 37.7g

Tangy Butter Lemon Scallops

Prep time: 10 minutes | Cook time: 10 minutes | Servings: 4

1-pound sea scallops
2 tablespoons butter, room temperature
2 tablespoons lemon juice

2 garlic cloves, crushed
Salt and fresh black pepper to taste
¼ cup dry white wine

1. Toss all the recipe ingredients in a lightly greased air fryer cooking basket. 2. Cook the scallops on Air Fry mode on level 3 at 400°F/200°C for 7 minutes, tossing the basket halfway through the cooking time. Bon appétit!
Per Serving: Calories 351; Fat 11g; Sodium 150mg; Carbs 3.3g; Fiber 0.2g; Sugar 1g; Protein 33.2g

Lobster with Butter

Prep time: 10 minutes | Cook time: 10 minutes | Servings: 4

1-pound lobster tails
4 tablespoons butter, room temperature
2 garlic cloves, minced

Salt and freshly cracked black pepper, to taste
4 tablespoons springs onions
1 tablespoon fresh lime juice

1. Butterfly the lobster by cutting through the shell and place them in a lightly oiled air fryer basket. 2. In a mixing bowl, thoroughly mix the remaining recipe ingredients. 3. Now, spread ½ of the butter mixture over the top of the lobster meat. Cook on Air Fry mode and Select Level "3". Air fry the lobster tails at 380°F/195°C for 4 minutes. 4. After that, spread another ½ of the butter mixture on top; continue to cook for a further 4 minutes. Bon appétit!
Per Serving: Calories 400; Fat 32g; Sodium 721mg; Carbs 2.6g; Fiber 0g; Sugar 0g; Protein 27.4g

Butter Calamari

Prep time: 10 minutes | Cook time: 5 minutes | Servings: 4

1 pound calamari, sliced into rings
2 tablespoons butter
2 tablespoons parsley, chopped

2 garlic cloves, minced
1 teaspoon cayenne pepper
Black pepper and salt, to taste

1. Toss all the recipe ingredients in a lightly greased air fryer cooking basket. 2. Cook your calamari on Air Fry mode on level 3 at 400°F/200°C for 5 minutes, tossing the basket halfway through the cooking time. Bon appétit!
Per Serving: Calories 316; Fat 12.2g; Sodium 587mg; Carbs 12.2g; Fiber 1g; Sugar 1.8g; Protein 25.8g

Parmesan Trout

Prep time: 5 minutes | Cook time: 15 minutes | Servings: 4

2 tablespoons olive oil
2 garlic cloves, minced
½ cup chicken stock
Black pepper and salt to the taste

4 trout fillets, boneless
¾ cup parmesan, grated
¼ cup tarragon, chopped

1. In a suitable pan that fits your air fryer, mix all the recipe ingredients except the fish and the parmesan and whisk. Add the fish and grease it well with this mix. 2. Sprinkle the parmesan on top, put the pan in its air fryer basket. Insert its air fryer basket into the level 3 of the oven and close the door. Cook on "Air Fry" Mode, select level 3, and set its temperature to 380°F/195°C for 15 minutes. 3. Divide everything between plates and serve.
Per Serving: Calories 336; Fat 27.1g; Sodium 66mg; Carbs 1.1g; Fiber 0.4g; Sugar 0.2g; Protein 19.7g

Crab with Tomato Sauce

Prep time: 5 minutes | Cook time: 20 minutes | Servings: 4

2 tablespoons olive oil
1 cup green bell pepper, chopped
4 garlic cloves, chopped
8 tomatoes, chopped
½ teaspoon garlic powder
1 teaspoon thyme, dried

1 teaspoon sweet paprika
¼ cup chicken stock
1 and ½ pound crab meat
A pinch of black pepper and salt
1 tablespoon chives, chopped

1. Heat up a suitable pan that fist the air fryer with the oil over medium heat, then add bell pepper and the garlic and sauté for 2 minutes. 2. Add the rest of the recipe ingredients except the crab meat, stir, bring to a boil and simmer for 6 minutes more. 3. Add the crab meat, put the pan in the fryer and cook on "Air Fry" Mode, select level 3, and set its temperature to 380°F/195°C for 15 minutes. Divide into bowls and serve.
Per Serving: Calories 410; Fat 17.8g; Sodium 619mg; Carbs 21g; Fiber 1.4g; Sugar 1.8g; Protein 38.4g

Sea Bass with Broccoli

Prep time: 5 minutes | Cook time: 20 minutes | Servings: 4

4 black sea bass fillets, boneless	crushed
1-pound broccoli florets	1 teaspoon lemon zest, grated
4 tablespoons butter, melted	A pinch of black pepper and salt
½ teaspoon red pepper flakes,	

1. In a suitable pan that fits your air fryer, mix the broccoli with the other ingredients except the fish and half of the butter, toss, put the pan in the fryer and cook on "Air Fry" Mode, select level 3, and set its temperature to 380°F/195°C for 8 minutes. 2. Add the fish greased with the rest of the butter, cook on "Air Fry" Mode, select level 3, and set its temperature to 380°F/195°C for 12 minutes more, divide between plates and serve.
Per Serving: Calories 396; Fat 23.2g; Sodium 622mg; Carbs 0.7g; Fiber 0g; Sugar 0g; Protein 45.6g

Ham Tilapia Fillets

Prep time: 15 minutes | Cook time: 10 minutes | Servings: 4

16 ounces tilapia fillet	½ teaspoon salt
4 ham slices	1 teaspoon dried rosemary
1 teaspoon sunflower oil	

1. Cut the tilapia on 4 servings. Sprinkle every fish serving with salt, dried rosemary, and sunflower oil. 2. Then carefully wrap the fish fillets in the ham slices and secure with toothpicks. 3. Select the Air Fry mode. Set the Ninja Foodi Smart XL Pro temperature to 400°F/200°C. Select Level "3" and set the time on your Ninja Foodi Smart XL Pro Air Fryer Oven to 10 minutes. Press Start/Pause to begin preheating. Continue to the next step when it is done preheating. 4. Put the wrapped tilapia in its air fryer basket in one layer and cook them for 10 minutes. 5. Gently flip the fish on another side after 5 minutes of cooking.
Per Serving: Calories 352; Fat 9.1g; Sodium 1294mg; Carbs 3.9g; Fiber 1g; Sugar 1g; Protein 61g

Paprika Snapper

Prep time: 5 minutes | Cook time: 14 minutes | Servings: 4

4 snapper fillets, boneless and skin scored	A pinch of black pepper and salt
2 tablespoons sweet paprika	6 spring onions, chopped
3 tablespoons olive oil	Juice of ½ lemon

1. In a suitable bowl, mix the paprika with the rest of the recipe ingredients except the fish and whisk well. 2. Rub the fish with this mix, place the fillets in your air fryer's basket. Insert its air fryer basket into the level 3 of the oven and close the door. Cook on "Air Fry" Mode, select level 3, and set its temperature to 390°F/200°C for 7 minutes per side. 3. Divide between plates and serve with a side salad.
Per Serving: Calories 391; Fat 24g; Sodium 142mg; Carbs 38.5g; Fiber 3.5g; Sugar 21g; Protein 16.6g

Spicy Parsley Trout

Prep time: 10 minutes | Cook time: 13 minutes | Servings: 4

10 ounces trout fillet	1 teaspoon dried parsley
1 teaspoon chili flakes	1 ounces cheddar cheese, shredded
½ teaspoon chili powder	
½ teaspoon salt	1 tablespoon avocado oil

1. Chop the trout and put in the air fryer baking pan. Then sprinkle the fish with chili flakes, chili powder, salt, and dried parsley. Sprinkle the trout with avocado oil and stir gently. 2. Select the Air Fry mode. Set the Ninja Foodi Smart XL Pro temperature to 390°F/200°C. Select Level "3" and set the time on your Ninja Foodi Smart XL Pro Air Fryer Oven to 10 minutes. Press Start/Pause to begin preheating. Continue to the next step when it is done preheating. 3. Cover the baking pan with foil and put it in the air fryer. Cook the fish for 10 minutes. 4. After this, remove the foil and top the trout with cheddar cheese. Cook the meal for 3 minutes at 400°F/200°C. Select Level "3". Serve.
Per Serving: Calories 268; Fat 10.4g; Sodium 411mg; Carbs 0.4g; Fiber 0.1g; Sugar 0.1g; Protein 10.6g

Char Fillets with Fennel

Prep time: 5 minutes | Cook time: 18 minutes | Servings: 4

4 char fillets, boneless	1 teaspoon caraway seeds
3 tablespoons olive oil	2 tablespoons balsamic vinegar
1 fennel bulb, sliced with a mandolin	1 tablespoon lemon juice
	1 tablespoon lemon peel, grated
A pinch of black pepper and salt	½ cup dill, chopped
5 garlic cloves, minced	

1. In a suitable pan that fits your air fryer, mix the fish with all the other ingredients, toss, introduce in its air fryer basket. 2. Insert its air fryer basket into the level 3 of the oven and close the door. Cook on "Air Fry" Mode, select level 3, and set its temperature to 390°F/200°C for 18 minutes. 3. Divide the fish between plates and serve with a side salad.
Per Serving: Calories 220; Fat 13g; Sodium 542mg; Carbs 0.9g; Fiber 0.3g; Sugar 0.2g; Protein 5.6g

Cod with Green Beans

Prep time: 15 minutes | Cook time: 15 minutes | Servings: 4

12 ounces' cod fillet	1 tablespoon avocado oil
½ cup green beans, trimmed and halved	1 teaspoon salt
	1 teaspoon ground coriander

1. Cut the cod fillet on 4 servings: and sprinkle every serving with salt and ground coriander. 2. After this, place the fish on 4 foil squares. Top them with green beans and avocado oil and wrap them into parcels. Select the Air Fry mode. Set the Ninja Foodi Smart XL Pro temperature to 400°F/200°C. Select Level "3" and set the time on your Ninja Foodi Smart XL Pro Air Fryer Oven to 15 minutes. Press Start/Pause to begin preheating. Continue to the next step when it is done preheating. 3. Place the cod parcels in its air fryer basket. Insert its air fryer basket into the level 3 of the oven and close the door. Cook them for 15 minutes. Serve.
Per Serving: Calories 353; Fat 5g; Sodium 818mg; Carbs 53.2g; Fiber 4.4g; Sugar 8g; Protein 7.3g

Spicy Red Snapper

Prep time: 5 minutes | Cook time: 15 minutes | Servings: 4

4 red snapper fillets, boneless	2 tablespoons lime juice
A pinch of black pepper and salt	1 tablespoon hot chili paste
2 garlic cloves, minced	2 tablespoons olive oil
2 tablespoons coconut aminos	

1.In a suitable bowl, mix all the recipe ingredients except the fish and whisk well. 2. Rub the fish with this mix, place it in your air fryer's basket. Insert its air fryer basket into the level 3 of the oven and close the door. Cook on "Air Fry" Mode, select level 3, and set its temperature to 380°F/195°C for 15 minutes. Serve with a side salad.
Per Serving: Calories 346; Fat 16.1g; Sodium 882mg; Carbs 1.3g; Fiber 0.5g; Sugar 0.5g; Protein 4.2g

Paprika Calamari with Ghee Mix

Prep time: 20 minutes | Cook time: 4 minutes | Servings: 2

8 ounces calamari, peeled, trimmed	½ teaspoon smoked paprika
	½ teaspoon white pepper
1 teaspoon ghee, melted	1 tablespoon apple cider vinegar
1 teaspoon fresh basil, chopped	

1. In the shallow bowl mix up melted ghee, basil, smoked paprika, white pepper, and apple cider vinegar. After this, sprinkle the calamari with ghee mixture and leave for 15 minutes to marinate. 2. After this, roughly slice the calamari. Select the Air Fry mode. Set the Ninja Foodi Smart XL Pro temperature to 400°F/200°C. Select Level "3" and set the time on your Ninja Foodi Smart XL Pro Air Fryer Oven to 4 minutes. Press Start/Pause to begin preheating. Continue to the next step when it is done preheating. 3. Put the sliced calamari in its air fryer basket. Insert its air fryer basket into the level 3 of the oven and close the door. Cook for 2 minutes. Shake the seafood well and cook for 2 minutes more.
Per Serving: Calories 351; Fat 11g; Sodium 150mg; Carbs 3.3g; Fiber 0.2g; Sugar 1g; Protein 3.2g

Air Fried Sea Bream Fillet

Prep time: 15 minutes | Cook time: 8 minutes | Servings: 4

1 tablespoon tomato sauce
1 tablespoon avocado oil
1 teaspoon black pepper
½ teaspoon salt
12 ounces sea bream fillet

1. Cut the sea bream fillet on 4 servings. After this, in the mixing bowl mix up tomato sauce, avocado oil, salt, and black pepper. Rub the fish fillets with tomato mixture from both sides. 2. Select the Air Fry mode. Set the Ninja Foodi Smart XL Pro temperature to 390°F/200°C. Select Level "3" and set the time on your Ninja Foodi Smart XL Pro Air Fryer Oven to 8 minutes. Press Start/Pause to begin preheating. Continue to the next step when it is done preheating. 3. Line its air fryer basket with foil. Put the sea bream fillets on the foil and cook them for 8 minutes.
Per Serving: Calories 223; Fat 11.7g; Sodium 721mg; Carbs 13.6g; Fiber 0.7g; Sugar 8g; Protein 5.7g

Halibut Capers Mix

Prep time: 5 minutes | Cook time: 18 minutes | Servings: 4

4 halibut fillets, boneless
A pinch of black pepper and salt
1 shallot, chopped
2 garlic cloves, minced
1 cup parsley, chopped
1 tablespoon chives, chopped
1 tablespoon lemon zest, grated
1 tablespoon capers, drained and chopped
1 tablespoon lemon juice
1 tablespoon olive oil
1 tablespoon butter, melted

1. Heat up a suitable pan that fits your air fryer with the oil and the butter over medium-high heat, then add the shallot and the garlic and sauté for 2 minutes. 2. Add the rest of the recipe ingredients except the fish, toss and sauté for 3 minutes more. 3. Add the fish, sear for 1 minute per side, toss it gently with the herbed mix, place the pan in its air fryer basket. Insert its air fryer basket into the level 3 of the oven and close the door. Cook on "Air Fry" Mode, select level 3, and set its temperature to 380°F/195°C for 12 minutes. Divide everything between plates and serve.
Per Serving: Calories 379; Fat 19g; Sodium 184mg; Carbs 12.3g; Fiber 0.6g; Sugar 2g; Protein 7.7g

Sea Bass with Rosemary Vinaigrette

Prep time: 5 minutes | Cook time: 12 minutes | Servings: 4

4 black sea bass fillets, boneless and skin scored
2 tablespoons olive oil
A pinch of black pepper and salt
3 tablespoons black olives, pitted
and chopped
3 garlic cloves, minced
1 tablespoon rosemary, chopped
Juice of 1 lime

1. In a suitable bowl, mix the oil with the olives and the rest of the recipe ingredients except the fish and whisk well. 2. Place the fish in a suitable pan that fits the air fryer, spread the rosemary vinaigrette all over, put the pan in the machine and cook on "Air Fry" Mode, select level 3, and set its temperature to 380°F/195°C for 12 minutes, flipping the fish halfway. 3. Divide between plates and serve.
Per Serving: Calories 152; Fat 9.1g; Sodium 1294mg; Carbs 3.9g; Fiber 1g; Sugar 1g; Protein 1g

Trout with Zucchinis

Prep time: 5 minutes | Cook time: 15 minutes | Servings: 4

3 zucchinis, cut in medium chunks
4 trout fillets, boneless
2 tablespoons olive oil
¼ cup keto tomato sauce
Black pepper and salt to the taste
1 garlic clove, minced
1 tablespoon lemon juice
½ cup cilantro, chopped

1. In a suitable pan that fits your air fryer, mix the fish with the other ingredients, toss, introduce in the fryer and cook on "Air Fry" Mode, select level 3, and set its temperature to 380°F/195°C for 15 minutes. 2. Divide everything between plates and serve right away.
Per Serving: Calories 264; Fat 17g; Sodium 129mg; Carbs 0.9g; Fiber 0.3g; Sugar 0g; Protein 7g

Cajun Branzino

Prep time: 10 minutes | Cook time: 8 minutes | Servings: 4

1-pound branzino, trimmed, washed
1 teaspoon Cajun seasoning
1 tablespoon sesame oil
1 tablespoon lemon juice
1 teaspoon salt

1. Rub the branzino with salt and Cajun seasoning carefully. Then sprinkle the fish with the lemon juice and sesame oil. 2. Select the Air Fry mode. Set the Ninja Foodi Smart XL Pro temperature to 380°F/195°C. Select Level "3" and set the time on your Ninja Foodi Smart XL Pro Air Fryer Oven to 8 minutes. Press Start/Pause to begin preheating. Continue to the next step when it is done preheating. 3. Place the fish in its air fryer basket. Insert its air fryer basket into the level 3 of the oven and close the door. Cook it for 8 minutes. Serve.
Per Serving: Calories 137; Fat 28g; Sodium 1221mg; Carbs 22.3g; Fiber 0.9g; Sugar 8g; Protein 10.3g

Cheesy Crab Flounder

Prep time: 10 minutes | Cook time: 12 minutes | Servings: 3

9 ounces flounder fillets
4 ounces crab meat, chopped
1 tablespoon mascarpone
½ teaspoon ground nutmeg
2 spring onions, diced
½ teaspoon dried thyme
2 ounces parmesan, grated
1 egg, beaten

1. Line the air fryer baking pan with baking paper. After this, cut the flounder fillet on3 Servings: and transfer them in the baking pan in one layer. 2. Sprinkle the fish fillets with ground nutmeg and dried thyme. Then top them with chopped crab meat, spring onions, and parmesan. 3. In the mixing bowl, mix up mascarpone and egg. Pour the liquid over the cheese. 4. Select the Air Fry mode. Set the Ninja Foodi Smart XL Pro temperature to385°F/195°C. Select Level "3" and set the time on your Ninja Foodi Smart XL Pro Air Fryer Oven to 12 minutes. Press Start/Pause to begin preheating. Continue to the next step when it is done preheating. 5. Place the baking pan with fish in its air fryer basket. Insert its air fryer basket into the level 3 of the oven and close the door. Cook the meal for 12 minutes.
Per Serving: Calories 316; Fat 12.2g; Sodium 587mg; Carbs 12.2g; Fiber 1g; Sugar 1.8g; Protein 5.8g

Delicious Caribbean Ginger Sea Bass

Prep time: 15 minutes | Cook time: 10 minutes | Servings: 2

¼ habanero, chopped
1 teaspoon Caribbean spices
8 ounces sea bass, trimmed
½ teaspoon erythritol
1 teaspoon smoked paprika
¼ teaspoon minced ginger
1 tablespoon avocado oil

1. In the mixing bowl, mix up Caribbean spices, erythritol, and smoked paprika. Then rub the sea bass with the spice mixture well. 2. In the shallow bowl, whisk minced ginger and avocado oil. Brush the fish with the ginger mixture. 3. Select the Air Fry mode. Set the Ninja Foodi Smart XL Pro temperature to 400°F/200°C. Select Level "3" and set the time on your Ninja Foodi Smart XL Pro Air Fryer Oven to 10 minutes. Press Start/Pause to begin preheating. Continue to the next step when it is done preheating. 4. Put the sea bass in its air fryer basket. Insert its air fryer basket into the level 3 of the oven and close the door. Cook it for 10 minutes. Serve.
Per Serving: Calories 210; Fat 17.8g; Sodium 619mg; Carbs 21g; Fiber 1.4g; Sugar 1.8g; Protein 3.4g

Trout with Shallots

Prep time: 5 minutes | Cook time: 12 minutes | Servings: 4

4 trout fillets, boneless
Juice of 1 lime
½ cup butter, melted
½ cup olive oil
3 garlic cloves, minced
6 shallots, chopped
A pinch of black pepper and salt

1. In a suitable pan that fits the air fryer, mix the fish with the shallots and the rest of the recipe ingredients, toss gently, put the pan in the machine and cook on "Air Fry" Mode, select level 3, and set its temperature to 390°F/200°C for 12 minutes, flipping the fish halfway. 2. Divide between plates and serve with a side salad.
Per Serving: Calories 396; Fat 23.2g; Sodium 622mg; Carbs 0.7g; Fiber 0g; Sugar 0g; Protein 5.6g

Air Fried Chorizo Squid

Prep time: 15 minutes | Cook time: 10 minutes | Servings: 2

8 ounces squid tube, trimmed, washed
4 ounces chorizo, chopped
1 teaspoon olive oil
1 teaspoon chili flakes
1 tablespoon keto mayonnaise

1. Select the Air Fry mode. Set the Ninja Foodi Smart XL Pro temperature to 400°F/200°C and put the chopped chorizo in its air fryer basket. Sprinkle it with chili flakes and olive oil and cook for 6 minutes. 2. Then shake chorizo well. Slice the squid tube into the rings and add in the air fryer. Cook the meal for 4 minutes at 400°F/200°C. Select Level "3" and set the time on your Ninja Foodi Smart XL Pro Air Fryer Oven to 10 minutes. Press Start/Pause to begin preheating. Continue to the next step when it is done preheating. 3. Shake the cooked meal well and transfer it in the plates. Sprinkle the meal with keto mayonnaise.
Per Serving: Calories 310; Fat 17g; Sodium 271mg; Carbs 4.3g; Fiber 0.9g; Sugar 2.1g; Protein 5g

Calamari with Tangy Tomato Sauce

Prep time: 5 minutes | Cook time: 8 minutes | Servings: 4

3 lbs. calamari
⅓ cup olive oil
1 tablespoon fresh oregano
1 teaspoon lemon juice
1 tablespoon garlic, minced
Sauce:
1 lb. fresh whole tomatoes
3 cloves garlic, minced
1 stalk of celery, chopped
1 tablespoon olive oil
¼ teaspoon chopped fresh lemon peel
¼ teaspoon crushed red pepper
¼ cup vinegar

½ green bell pepper
Salt and pepper to taste
½ cup onion, chopped

1. Select Level 3. Select the "AIR FRY" function of Ninja Foodi Smart XL Pro Air Oven, set temperature to 390°F/200°C and time to 6 minutes. Select START/STOP to begin preheating. 2. To make the sauce, mix all the sauce ingredients and add to blender. Blend until mixture is smooth. Clean the calamari and slice it into ½-inch rings. 3. Season calamari with vinegar, red pepper, lemon peel, garlic, lemon juice, and oregano. Add oil to air fryer sheet pan. Add calamari with its juice. Air fry for about 6-minutes. Stir once and air fry for another 2-minutes. Serve with hot with sauce.
Per Serving: Calories 298; Fat 11g; Sodium 336mg; Carbs 10.2g; Fiber g; Sugar 6g; Protein 18g

Air Fried Tilapia Fillets

Prep time: 5 minutes | Cook time: 15 minutes | Servings: 3

2 egg yolks
4 wheat buns
1 lb. tilapia fillets, sliced
1 tablespoon nectar
1 tablespoon hot sauce
3 teaspoons of sweet pickle relish
2 tablespoons mayonnaise
1 tablespoon fish sauce

1. Select Level 3. Select the "AIR FRY" function of Ninja Foodi Smart XL Pro Air Oven, set temperature to 300°F/150°C and time to 15 minutes. Select START/STOP to begin preheating. 2. Mix the fish sauce and egg yolks in a bowl. Add mayonnaise, sweet pickle relish, hot sauce, and nectar. 3. Pour mixture into round baking tray. Place tray inside air fryer with tilapia fillets inside. Cook for 15 minutes.
Per Serving: Calories 354; Fat 7.9g; Sodium 704mg; Carbs 6g; Fiber 3.6g; Sugar 6g; Protein 18g

Swordfish with Tomatoes

Prep time: 5 minutes | Cook time: 10 minutes | Servings: 2

2 1-inch thick swordfish steaks
A pinch of black pepper and salt
30 ounces tomatoes, chopped
2 tablespoons capers, drained
1 tablespoon red vinegar
2 tablespoons oregano, chopped

1. In a suitable pan that fits the air fryer, mix all the recipe ingredients, toss, put the pan in the fryer and cook on "Air Fry" Mode, select level 3, and set its temperature to 390°F/200°C for 10 minutes, flipping the fish halfway. 2. Divide the mix between plates and serve.
Per Serving: Calories 200; Fat 32g; Sodium 721mg; Carbs 2.6g; Fiber 0g; Sugar 0g; Protein 7.4g

Clam and Veggie balls

Prep time: 5 minutes | Cook time: 30 minutes | Servings: 4

2 cups clam meat
2 tablespoons olive oil
¾ cup water
1 cup chickpea flour
¼ teaspoon black pepper
½ cup shredded zucchini
1 cup shredded carrot

1.Select Level 3. Select the "AIR FRY" function of Ninja Foodi Smart XL Pro Air Oven, set temperature to 390°F/200°C and time to 30 minutes. Select START/STOP to begin preheating. 2. Mix clam meat, olive oil, shredded carrot and zucchini along with black pepper in a bowl. Form small balls using your hands. Mix chickpea flour and water to form batter. 3. Coat balls with batter. Place in air fryer and cook for 30-minutes.
Per Serving: Calories 354; Fat 7.9g; Sodium 704mg; Carbs 6g; Fiber 3.6g; Sugar 6g; Protein 18g

Tuna Stuffed Potatoes

Prep time: 5 minutes | Cook time: 30 minutes | Servings: 2

4 medium potatoes
1 teaspoon olive oil
½ tablespoon capers
Salt and pepper to taste
1 green onion, sliced
1 tablespoon Greek yogurt
½ teaspoon chili powder
½ can of tuna in oil, drained
2 boiled eggs, sliced

1. Install the wire rack on Level 3. Select the "AIR ROAST" function of Ninja Foodi Smart XL Pro Air Oven, set temperature to 355°F/180°C and time to 30 minutes. Select START/STOP to begin preheating. Soak the potatoes in water for 30-minutes. Pat dry with kitchen towel. 2. Brush the potatoes with olive oil. Place potatoes in air fryer and air fry for 30-minutes. 3. Put tuna in a bowl with yogurt and chili powder, mix well. Add half of the green onion plus salt and pepper. 4. Slit potatoes length-wise. Stuff tuna mixture in the middle of potatoes and place on a serving plate. Sprinkle with chili powder and remaining green onions over potatoes. 5. Serve with capers and a salad of your choice and topped with boiled egg slices.
Per Serving: Calories 354; Fat 7.9g; Sodium 704mg; Carbs 6g; Fiber 3.6g; Sugar 6g; Protein 18g

Teriyaki Halibut Steak

Prep time: 5 minutes | Cook time: 12 minutes | Servings: 3

1 lb. halibut steak
⅔ cup soy sauce
¼ teaspoon ginger, ground
1 garlic clove, minced
¼ cup orange juice
¼ teaspoon crushed red pepper flakes
2 tablespoon lime juice
1 teaspoon liquid stevia
½ cup mirin

1. Prepare teriyaki glaze by combining all ingredients except halibut steak in a saucepan. Bring mixture to a boil, then reduce heat by half. Set aside and allow to cool. Pour half of the glaze into a re-sealable bag with halibut and place in the fridge for 30-minutes. 2. Select Level 3. Select the "AIR FRY" function of Ninja Foodi Smart XL Pro Air Oven, set temperature to 390°F/200°C and time to 12 minutes. 3. Select START/STOP to begin preheating. Place marinated halibut in air fryer and cook for 12-minutes. 4. When finished, brush some of the remaining glazes over halibut steak.
Per Serving: Calories 354; Fat 7.9g; Sodium 704mg; Carbs 6g; Fiber 3.6g; Sugar 6g; Protein 18g

Crispy Nacho-Crusted Shrimp

Prep time: 5 minutes | Cook time: 8 minutes | Servings: 8

18 jumbo shrimps, peeled and deveined
1 egg, beaten
8-9-ounce nacho-flavored chips, crushed
Salt and pepper to taste

1. Prepare two shallow dishes, one with egg and one with crushed chips. Spice with salt and pepper. Dip shrimp in the egg and then coat in nacho crumbs. 2. Select Level 3. Select the "AIR FRY" function of Ninja Foodi Smart XL Pro Air Oven, set temperature to 350°F/175°C and time to 8 minutes. Select START/STOP to begin preheating. 3. Arrange the shrimp in the air fryer and cook for 8-minutes.
Per Serving: Calories 354; Fat 7.9g; Sodium 704mg; Carbs 6g; Fiber 3.6g; Sugar 6g; Protein 18g

Sweet and Spicy Tossed Calamari

Prep time: 5 minutes | Cook time: 13 minutes | Servings: 2

½ lb. calamari tubes, about ¼ inch wide, rinsed and patted dry
1 cup club soda
½ cup honey

Red pepper flakes to taste
1 cup almond flour
Salt and black pepper to taste
2 tablespoons sriracha

1. Select Level 3. Select the "AIR FRY" function of Ninja Foodi Smart XL Pro Air Oven, set temperature to 380°F/195°C and time to 11 minutes. Select START/STOP to begin preheating. 2. Cover calamari rings with club soda in a bowl. Set aside for 10-minutes. In another bowl, mix flour, salt, and black pepper. In a third bowl, combine honey, sriracha, and red pepper flakes. Drain the calamari, pat dry, and cover with flour mixture. 3. Grease your air fryer basket with cooking spray. Add calamari in one layer, leaving little space in between. Cook for 11-minutes. Shake basket a couple of times during the process. 4. Remove the calamari from the air fryer and cover with half of the honey sauce and place inside the air fryer again. Cook for an additional 2-minutes. 5. When ready to serve, cover with remaining sauce.
Per Serving: Calories 354; Fat 7.9g; Sodium 704mg; Carbs 6g; Fiber 3.6g; Sugar 6g; Protein 18g

Delicious Salmon & Eggs

Prep time: 5 minutes | Cook time: 10 minutes | Servings: 2

2 eggs
1 lb. salmon, seasoned and cooked
1 cup celery, chopped

1 onion, chopped
1 tablespoon olive oil
Salt and pepper to taste

1. Select Level 3. Select the "AIR FRY" function of Ninja Foodi Smart XL Pro Air Oven, set the temperature to 300°F/150°C and time to 10 minutes. Select START/STOP to begin preheating. 2. Whisk the eggs in a bowl. Add celery, onion, salt, and pepper. Add the oil to a round baking tray and pour in the egg mixture, then place in the air fryer. 3. Let it cook for 10-minutes. When done, serve with cooked salmon.
Per Serving: Calories 354; Fat 7.9g; Sodium 704mg; Carbs 6g; Fiber 3.6g; Sugar 6g; Protein 18g

Kataifi Shrimp with Lemon Garlic Sauce

Prep time: 5 minutes | Cook time: 22 minutes | Servings: 5

20 large green shrimps, peeled and deveined
7 tablespoons unsalted butter
12-ounces of kataifi pastry

Wedges of lemon or lime
Salt and pepper to taste
5 cloves of garlic, crushed
2 lemons, zested and juiced

1. In a pan, heat butter. Add the garlic and lemon zest, and sauté for about 2-minutes. Season with salt, pepper and lemon juice. Cover the shrimp with half of garlic butter sauce and set aside the remaining half of sauce. 2. Select Level 3. Select the "AIR FRY" function of Ninja Foodi Smart XL Pro Air Oven, set temperature to 360°F/180°C and time to 20 minutes. Select START/STOP to begin preheating. 3. Remove the pastry from the bag and tease out strands. On the countertop lay 6-inch strands. Roll shrimp and butter into pastry. Shrimp tail should be exposed. Repeat process for all shrimp. 4. Place the shrimp into air fryer for 10-minutes. Flip shrimp over and place back into air fryer for another 10-minutes. 5. Serve with a salad and lime or lemon wedges. Dip the shrimp into the remaining garlic butter sauce.
Per Serving: Calories 354; Fat 7.9g; Sodium 704mg; Carbs 6g; Fiber 3.6g; Sugar 6g; Protein 18g

Bread Crusted Fish

Prep time: 5 minutes | Cook time: 12 minutes | Servings: 4

4 fish fillets
1 egg

5-ounces breadcrumbs
4 tablespoons olive oil

1. Select Level 3. Select the "AIR FRY" function of Ninja Foodi Smart XL Pro Air Oven, set temperature to 350°F/175°C and time to 12 minutes. Select START/STOP to begin preheating. 2. In a bowl, mix oil and breadcrumbs. Whisk egg. Gently dip the fish into egg and then into crumb mixture. 3. Put into air fryer and cook for 12-minutes.
Per Serving: Calories 354; Fat 7.9g; Sodium 704mg; Carbs 6g; Fiber 3.6g; Sugar 6g; Protein 18g

Delicious Fish Taco

Prep time: 5 minutes | Cook time: 8 minutes | Servings: 2

1½ cups almond flour
1 can of beer
1 teaspoon baking powder
1 teaspoon sea salt
½ cup salsa
8-ounces fresh halibut, sliced into
Avocado Cream:
1 large avocado
¾ cup buttermilk

small strips
Corn tortillas
Cilantro, chopped
Cholula sauce to taste
2 tablespoons olive oil
2 chili peppers, sliced

½ lime juiced

1. Make your batter by mixing baking powder, 1 cup of flour, beer, and salt. Stir well. Cover the halibut with remaining ½ cup of flour and dip it into the batter to coat well. 2. Select Level 3. Select the "AIR FRY" function of Ninja Foodi Smart XL Pro Air oven, set temperature to 390°F/200°C and time to 8 minutes. Select START/STOP to begin preheating. 3. Grease air fry basket with olive oil. Cook the fish for 8-minutes. Mix the avocado cream ingredients in a blender until smooth. Place the corn tortillas on a plate and cover with salsa. Set aside. 4. Put the fish on top of tortillas and cover with avocado cream. 5. Add Cholula sauce, sprinkle with cilantro and top with chili slices and serve.
Per Serving: Calories 354; Fat 7.9g; Sodium 704mg; Carbs 6g; Fiber 3.6g; Sugar 6g; Protein 18g

Grilled Barramundi with Tangy Butter Sauce

Prep time: 5 minutes | Cook time: 40 minutes | Servings: 2

1 lb. small potatoes
7-ounces barramundi fillets
1 teaspoon olive oil
¼ bunch of fresh thyme, chopped
Green beans, cooked, optional
Lemon Butter Sauce:
1 scallion, chopped
½ cup thickened cream

½ cup white wine
1 bay leaf
10 black peppercorns
1 clove garlic, chopped
8-ounces unsalted butter
1 lemon, juiced
Salt and pepper to taste

1. Select Level 3. Select the "AIR FRY" function of Ninja Foodi Smart XL Pro Air Oven, set temperature to 390°F/200°C and time to 20 minutes. Select START/STOP to begin preheating. 2. In a bowl, add potatoes, salt, thyme and olive oil. Mix ingredients well. Put potatoes into air fryer basket and cook for 20-minutes. Layer the fish fillets in a basket on top of potatoes. Cook for another 20-minutes. 3. In a skillet, heat scallion and garlic over medium-high heat and add the peppercorns and bay leaf. Pour the wine in and reduce heat to low. 4. Add the thickened cream and stir to blend. Add the butter and whisk over low heat. When butter has melted, add salt, pepper, and lemon juice. Strain the sauce to remove peppercorns and bay leaf. 5. Place the fish and potatoes on a serving plate and add sauce and serve with green beans.
Per Serving: Calories 354; Fat 7.9g; Sodium 704mg; Carbs 6g; Fiber 3.6g; Sugar 6g; Protein 18g

Creamy Tilapia Bowls

Prep time: 15 minutes | Cook time: 10 minutes | Servings: 4

7 oz. tilapia fillet or flathead fish
1 teaspoon arrowroot powder
1 teaspoon ground paprika
½ teaspoon salt
½ teaspoon ground black pepper
¼ teaspoon ground cumin
½ teaspoon garlic powder

1 teaspoon lemon juice
4 oz. purple cabbage, shredded
1 jalapeno, sliced
1 tablespoon heavy cream
½ teaspoon minced garlic
Cooking spray

1. Sprinkle the tilapia fillet with arrowroot powder, ground paprika, salt, ground black pepper, ground cumin, and garlic powder. 2. Select Level 3. Select the "AIR FRY" function of Ninja Foodi Smart XL Pro Air Oven, set temperature to 385°F/195°C and time to 10 minutes. Select START/STOP to begin preheating. 3. Spray the tilapia fillet with cooking spray and place it in the air fryer. Cook the fish for 10 minutes. Meanwhile, in the bowl mix up shredded cabbage, jalapeno pepper, and lemon juice. 4. When the tilapia fillet is cooked, chop it roughly. Put the shredded cabbage mixture in the serving bowls. Top them with chopped tilapia. 5. After this, in the shallow bowl mix up minced garlic and heavy cream. Sprinkle the meal with a heavy cream mixture.
Per Serving: Calories 354; Fat 7.9g; Sodium 704mg; Carbs 6g; Fiber 3.6g; Sugar 6g; Protein 18g

Nut-Crusted Catfish

Prep time: 5 minutes | Cook time: 12 minutes | Servings: 4

½ cup pecan meal	¼ teaspoon ground black pepper
1 teaspoon fine sea salt	4 (4-ounce) catfish fillets
For Garnish:	
Fresh oregano	Pecan halves

1. Spray the air fryer basket with avocado oil. Select Level 3. Select the "AIR FRY" function of Ninja Foodi Smart XL Pro Air Oven, set temperature to 375°F/190°C and time to 12 minutes. Select START/STOP to begin preheating. 2. In a bowl, mix the pecan meal, salt, and pepper. One at a time, dredge the catfish fillets in the mixture, coating them well. Use your hands to press the pecan meal into the fillets. 3. Spray the fish with avocado oil and place them in the air fryer basket. Cook the coated catfish for 12 minutes, or until it flakes easily and the center is no longer translucent, flipping halfway through. 4. Garnish with oregano sprigs and pecan halves, if desired.
Per Serving: Calories 354; Fat 7.9g; Sodium 704mg; Carbs 6g; Fiber 3.6g; Sugar 6g; Protein 18g

Tangy Cranberry Cod

Prep time: 5 minutes | Cook time: 20 minutes | Servings: 2

3 filets cod	3 tablespoons cranberry jam
1 tablespoon olive oil	

1. Select Level 3. Select the "AIR FRY" function of Ninja Foodi Smart XL Pro Air Oven, set temperature to 390°F/200°C and time to 20 minutes. Select START/STOP to begin preheating. 2. Brush the cod filets with olive oil. Spoon a tablespoon of cranberry jam on each filet. Cook for 20-minutes.
Per Serving: Calories 354; Fat 7.9g; Sodium 704mg; Carbs 6g; Fiber 3.6g; Sugar 6g; Protein 18g

Codfish and Oysters Teriyaki with Veggies

Prep time: 5 minutes | Cook time: 10 minutes | Servings: 2

1 tablespoon olive oil	1 clove garlic, chopped
6 pieces mini king oyster mushrooms, thinly sliced	Salt to taste
2 slices (1-inch) codfish	1 green onion, minced
1 Napa cabbage leaf, sliced	Veggies, steamed of your choice
Teriyaki Sauce:	
1 teaspoon liquid stevia	2 tablespoons soy sauce
2 tablespoons mirin	

1. Make teriyaki sauce by mixing well all the ingredients then set aside. Grease the air fryer basket with oil. Place the mushrooms, garlic, Napa cabbage leaf, and salt inside. Layer the fish on top. 2. Select Level 3. Select the "AIR FRY" function of Ninja Foodi Smart XL Pro Air Oven, set temperature to 360°F/180°C and time to 5 minutes. Select START/STOP to begin preheating. 3. Place the basket in air fryer and cook for 5-minutes. Stir. Pour the teriyaki sauce over ingredients in the basket. Cook for an additional 5-minutes. 4. Serve with your choice of steamed veggies.
Per Serving: Calories 354; Fat 7.9g; Sodium 704mg; Carbs 6g; Fiber 3.6g; Sugar 6g; Protein 18g

Crispy Salmon with Dill Sauce

Prep time: 5 minutes | Cook time: 23 minutes | Servings: 4

1½ lbs. of salmon	Pinch of sea salt
4 teaspoons olive oil	
Dill Sauce:	
½ cup non-fat Greek yogurt	2 tablespoons dill, finely chopped
½ cup light sour cream	Pinch of sea salt

1. Select Level 3. Select the "AIR FRY" function of Ninja Foodi Smart XL Pro Air Oven, set temperature to 270°F/135°C and time to 23 minutes. Select START/STOP to begin preheating. 2. Cut salmon into four 6-ounce portions and drizzle 1 teaspoon of olive oil over each piece. Season with sea salt. Place salmon into basket and cook for 23-minutes. 3. Make dill sauce. In a mixing bowl, mix sour cream, yogurt, chopped dill and sea salt. Top cooked salmon with sauce and garnish with additional dill and serve.
Per Serving: Calories 354; Fat 7.9g; Sodium 704mg; Carbs 6g; Fiber 3.6g; Sugar 6g; Protein 18g

Crispy Crab Patties with Sweet 'n' Sour Sauce

Prep time: 10 minutes | Cook time: 12 minutes | Servings: 8

Patties:	
1 pound canned lump crabmeat, drained	1 tablespoon chopped fresh chives
1 (8-ounce) package cream cheese, softened	1 large egg
	1 teaspoon grated fresh ginger
Coating:	1 clove garlic, minced
1½ cups pork dust	
Dipping Sauce:	
½ cup chicken broth	¼ teaspoon grated fresh ginger
⅓ cup coconut aminos or wheat-free tamari	1 clove garlic, smashed to a paste
⅓ cup Swerve sweetener	Sliced green onions, for garnish
¼ cup tomato sauce	Fried Cauliflower Rice, for serving
1 tablespoon coconut vinegar	

1. Select Level 3. Select the "AIR FRY" function of Ninja Foodi Smart XL Pro Air Oven, set temperature to 400°F/200°C and time to 12 minutes. Select START/STOP to begin preheating. 2. In a medium-sized bowl, gently mix all the ingredients for the patties, without breaking up the crabmeat. 3. Form the crab mixture into 8 patties that are 2½ inches in diameter and ¾ inch thick. Place the pork dust in a shallow dish. Place each patty in the pork dust. 4. Use your hands to press the pork dust into the patties to form a crust. Place the patties in the air fryer, leaving space between them. Cook for 12 minutes, or until the crust is golden and crispy. 5. While the patties cook, make the dipping sauce: In a large saucepan, whisk together all the sauce ingredients. Simmer, then turn the heat down to medium until the sauce thickened, about 5 minutes. 6. Place the patties on a serving platter, drizzle with the dipping sauce, and garnish with sliced green onions, if desired. 7. Serve the dipping sauce on the side. Serve with fried cauliflower rice, if desired.
Per Serving: Calories 354; Fat 7.9g; Sodium 704mg; Carbs 6g; Fiber 3.6g; Sugar 6g; Protein 18g

Minty Trout and Crunchy Pine Nuts

Prep time: 5 minutes | Cook time: 16 minutes | Servings: 4

4 rainbow trout	½ cup mint, chopped
1 cup olive oil + 3 tablespoons	Zest of 1 lemon
Juice of 1 lemon	⅓ pine nuts
A pinch of salt and black pepper	1 avocado, peeled, pitted and roughly chopped
1 cup parsley, chopped	
3 garlic cloves, minced	

1. Select Level 3. Select the "AIR FRY" function of Ninja Foodi Smart XL Pro Air Oven, set temperature to 390°F/200°C and time to 5 minutes. Select START/STOP to begin preheating. 2. Pat dry the trout, season with salt and pepper and rub with 3 tablespoons oil. Put the fish in your air fryer's basket and cook for 8 minutes on each side. 3. Divide the fish between plates and drizzle half of the lemon juice all over. 4. In a blender, combine the oil with the remaining lemon juice, parsley, garlic, mint, lemon zest, pine nuts and the avocado and pulse well. Spread this over the trout and serve.
Per Serving: Calories 354; Fat 7.9g; Sodium 704mg; Carbs 6g; Fiber 3.6g; Sugar 6g; Protein 18g

Healthy Scallops

Prep time: 5 minutes | Cook time: 4 minutes | Servings: 2

12 medium sea scallops	¾ teaspoon ground black pepper
1 teaspoon fine sea salt	Fresh thyme leaves, for garnish

1. Spray the air fryer basket with avocado oil. Select Level 3. Select the "AIR FRY" function of Ninja Foodi Smart XL Pro Air Oven, set temperature to 390°F/200°C and time to 4 minutes. Select START/STOP to begin preheating. 2. Rinse the scallops and pat completely dry. Spray avocado oil on the scallops and season them with the salt and pepper. Place them in the air fryer basket, spacing them apart. 3. Cook for 2 minutes, then flip the scallops and cook for another 2 minutes, or until cooked through and no longer translucent. 4. Garnish with ground black pepper and thyme leaves, if desired.
Per Serving: Calories 354; Fat 7.9g; Sodium 704mg; Carbs 6g; Fiber 3.6g; Sugar 6g; Protein 18g

Tuna Croquettes

Prep time: 10 minutes | Cook time: 8 minutes | Servings: 2

2 (5-ounce) cans tuna, drained
1 (8-ounce) package cream cheese, softened
½ cup finely shredded cheddar cheese
2 tablespoons diced onions
For Serving:
Cherry tomatoes
Mayonnaise

2 teaspoons prepared yellow mustard
1 large egg
1½ cups pork dust
Fresh dill, for garnish

Prepared yellow mustard

1. Select Level 3. Select the "AIR FRY" function of Ninja Foodi Smart XL Pro Air Oven, set temperature to 400°F/200°C and time to 5 minutes. Select START/STOP to begin preheating. 2. Make the patties: In a large bowl, stir together the tuna, cream cheese, cheddar cheese, onions, mustard, and egg until well combined. 3. Place the pork dust in a shallow bowl. Form the tuna mixture into twelve 1½-inch balls. 4. Roll the balls in the pork dust and use your hands to press it into a thick crust around each ball. Flatten the balls into ½-inch-thick patties. 5. Working in batches to avoid overcrowding, place the patties in the air fryer basket, leaving space between them. Cook for 8 minutes, or until golden and crispy, flipping halfway through. 6. Garnish the croquettes with fresh dill, if desired, and serve with cherry tomatoes and dollops of mayo and mustard on the side.
Per Serving: Calories 354; Fat 7.9g; Sodium 704mg; Carbs 6g; Fiber 3.6g; Sugar 6g; Protein 18g

Garlic Butter Shrimp

Prep time: 5 minutes | Cook time: 8 minutes | Servings: 4

¼ cup unsalted butter
2 tablespoons fish stock or chicken broth
1 tablespoon lemon juice
2 cloves garlic, minced
2 tablespoons chopped fresh basil

leaves
1 tablespoon parsley
1 teaspoon red pepper flakes
1-pound shrimp,
Fresh basil sprigs, for garnish

1. Select Level 3. Select the "AIR FRY" function of Ninja Foodi Smart XL Pro Air Oven, set temperature to 350°F/175°C and time to 5 minutes. Select START/STOP to begin preheating. 2. Place the butter, fish stock, lemon juice, garlic, basil, parsley, and red pepper flakes in a 6 by 3-inch pan, stir to combine, and place in the air fryer. Cook until fragrant and the garlic has softened. 3. Add the shrimp and stir to coat the shrimp in the sauce. Cook until the shrimp are pink, stirring after 3 minutes. 4. Garnish with fresh basil sprigs and chopped parsley before serving.
Per Serving: Calories 354; Fat 7.9g; Sodium 704mg; Carbs 6g; Fiber 3.6g; Sugar 6g; Protein 18g

Tropical Shrimp with Spicy Mayo

Prep time: 10 minutes | Cook time: 6 minutes | Servings: 4

1-pound large shrimp (about 2 dozen), peeled and deveined, tails on
Fine sea salt and ground black pepper
Spicy Mayo:
½ cup mayonnaise
2 tablespoons beef or chicken broth
For Serving:
Microgreens

2 large eggs
1 tablespoon water
½ cup unsweetened coconut flakes
½ cup pork dust

½ teaspoon hot sauce
½ teaspoon cayenne pepper

Thinly sliced radishes

1. Spray the air fryer basket with avocado oil. Select Level 3. Select the "AIR FRY" function of Ninja Foodi Smart XL Pro Air Oven, set temperature to 400°F/200°C and time to 6 minutes. Select START/STOP to begin preheating. 2. Season the shrimp well on all sides with salt and pepper. 3. Crack the eggs into a shallow baking dish, add the water and a pinch of salt and pepper, and whisk to combine. In baking dish, stir the coconut flakes and pork dust until well combined. 4. Dip one shrimp in the eggs and let any excess egg drip off, then dredge both sides of the shrimp in the coconut mixture. Spray the shrimp with avocado oil and place it in the air fryer basket. Repeat with the remaining shrimp, leaving space between them in the air fryer basket. 5. Cook the shrimp in the air fryer for 6 minutes, or until cooked through and no longer translucent, flipping halfway through. 6. While the shrimp cook, make the spicy mayo: In a medium-sized bowl, stir

together all the spicy mayo ingredients until well combined. 7. Serve the shrimp on a bed of microgreens and thinly sliced radishes, if desired. Serve the spicy mayo on the side for dipping.
Per Serving: Calories 354; Fat 7.9g; Sodium 704mg; Carbs 6g; Fiber 3.6g; Sugar 6g; Protein 18g

Crispy Cheesy Cod Fillets

Prep time: 10 minutes | Cook time: 10 minutes | Servings: 4

1 large egg
½ cup powdered Parmesan cheese
1 teaspoon smoked paprika
¼ teaspoon celery salt
¼ teaspoon ground black pepper

4 (4-ounce) cod fillets
Chopped fresh oregano or parsley, for garnish
Lemon slices, for serving

1. Spray the air fryer basket with avocado oil. Select Level 3. Select the "AIR FRY" function of Ninja Foodi Smart XL Pro Air Oven, set temperature to 400°F/200°C and time to 10 minutes. Select START/STOP to begin preheating. 2. Crack the egg in a shallow bowl and beat it lightly with a fork. Combine the Parmesan cheese, paprika, celery salt, and pepper in a separate shallow bowl. 3. Dip the fillets in egg, then dredge them in the Parmesan mixture. Using your hands, press the Parmesan onto the fillets to form a nice crust. As you finish, place the fish in the air fryer basket. 4. Cook the fish for 10 minutes, or until it is cooked through and flakes easily with a fork. Garnish with parsley and serve with lemon slices, if desired.
Per Serving: Calories 354; Fat 7.9g; Sodium 704mg; Carbs 6g; Fiber 3.6g; Sugar 6g; Protein 18g

Cumin Paprika Shrimp

Prep time: 10 minutes | Cook time: 10 minutes | Servings: 4

1 teaspoon chili flakes
1 teaspoon ground cumin
½ teaspoon salt
½ teaspoon dried oregano
10 oz. shrimps, peeled

1 green bell pepper
2 spring onions, chopped
1 teaspoon apple cider vinegar
1 tablespoon olive oil
1 teaspoon smoked paprika

1. In the mixing bowl mix up chili flakes, ground cumin, salt, dried oregano, and shrimps. Shake the mixture well. 2. Select Level 3. Select the "AIR FRY" function of Ninja Foodi Smart XL Pro Air Oven, set temperature to 400°F/200°C and time to 5 minutes. Select START/STOP to begin preheating. 3. Put the spring onions in the air fryer and cook it for 3 minutes. Meanwhile, slice the bell pepper. Add it in the air fryer and cook the vegetables for 2 minutes more. 4. Then add shrimps and sprinkle the mixture with smoked paprika, olive oil, and apple cider vinegar. Shake it gently and cook for 5 minutes more. 5. Transfer the cooked fajita in the serving plates.
Per Serving: Calories 354; Fat 7.9g; Sodium 704mg; Carbs 6g; Fiber 3.6g; Sugar 6g; Protein 18g

Shrimp with Lettuce

Prep time: 10 minutes | Cook time: 9 minutes | Servings: 2

2 large eggs
1 teaspoon prepared yellow mustard
1-pound small shrimp, peeled,
For Serving:
8 large Boston lettuce leaves
¼ cup pico de gallo
¼ cup shredded purple cabbage

deveined, and tails removed
½ cup finely shredded Gouda or Parmesan cheese
½ cup pork dust

1 lemon, sliced
Guacamole

1. Select Level 3. Select the "AIR FRY" function of Ninja Foodi Smart XL Pro Air Oven, set temperature to 400°F/200°C and time to 9 minutes. Select START/STOP to begin preheating. 2. Crack the eggs into a large bowl, add the mustard, and whisk until well combined. Add in the shrimp and toss to coat. 3. In a medium-sized bowl, mix together the cheese and pork dust until well combined. 4. One at a time, roll the coated shrimp in the pork dust mixture and use your hands to press it onto each shrimp. Spray the coated shrimp with avocado oil and place them in the air fryer basket, leaving space between them. 5. Cook the shrimp for 9 minutes, or until cooked through and no longer translucent, flipping after 4 minutes. 6. Place a lettuce on a serving plate, place several shrimp on top, and top with 1½ teaspoons each of pico de gallo and purple cabbage. Squeeze some lemon juice on top and serve with guacamole, if desired.
Per Serving: Calories 354; Fat 7.9g; Sodium 704mg; Carbs 6g; Fiber 3.6g; Sugar 6g; Protein 18g

Tasty Salmon and Cauliflower Rice

Prep time: 5 minutes | Cook time: 25 minutes | Servings: 4

4 salmon fillets, boneless	½ cup chicken stock
Salt and black pepper to the taste	1 teaspoon turmeric powder
1 cup cauliflower, riced	1 tablespoon butter, melted

1. Select Level 3. Select the "AIR FRY" function of Ninja Foodi Smart XL Pro Air Oven, set temperature to 360°F/180°C and time to 25 minutes. Select START/STOP to begin preheating. 2. In a pan that fits your air fryer, mix the cauliflower rice with the other ingredients except the salmon and toss. 3. Arrange the salmon fillets over the cauliflower rice, put the pan in the fryer and cook for 25 minutes, flipping the fish after 15 minutes. 4. Divide everything between plates and serve.
Per Serving: Calories 354; Fat 7.9g; Sodium 704mg; Carbs 6g; Fiber 3.6g; Sugar 6g; Protein 18g

Parmesan-Crusted Shrimp over Pesto Zoodles

Prep time: 10 minutes | Cook time: 14 minutes | Servings: 4

2 large eggs	½ cup powdered Parmesan cheese
3 cloves garlic, minced	(about 1½ ounces)
2 teaspoons dried basil, divided	1-pound jumbo shrimp, peeled,
½ teaspoon fine sea salt	deveined, butterflied, tails
½ teaspoon ground black pepper	removed
Pesto:	
1 packed cup fresh basil	3 cloves garlic, peeled
¼ cup extra-virgin olive oil or	1 tablespoon lemon juice
avocado oil	½ teaspoon fine sea salt
¼ cup grated Parmesan cheese	¼ teaspoon ground black pepper
¼ cup roasted, salted walnuts	2 recipes Perfect Zoodles warm,
(omit for nut-free)	for serving

1. Spray the air fryer basket with avocado oil. Select Level 3. Select the "AIR FRY" function of Ninja Foodi Smart XL Pro Air Oven, set temperature to 400°F/200°C and time to 7 minutes. Select START/STOP to begin preheating. 2. In a large bowl, whisk together the eggs, garlic, 1 teaspoon of the dried basil, the salt, and the pepper. In a bowl, mix the remaining teaspoon of dried basil and the Parmesan cheese. 3. Place the shrimp in the bowl with the egg mixture and use your hands to coat the shrimp. Roll one shrimp in the Parmesan mixture and press the coating onto the shrimp with your hands. Place the coated shrimp in the air fryer basket. Repeat with the remaining shrimp, leaving space between them in the air fryer basket. 4. Cook the shrimp in the air fryer for 7 minutes, or until cooked through and no longer translucent, flipping after 4 minutes. 5. While the shrimp cook, make the pesto: Place all the ingredients for the pesto in a food processor and pulse until smooth, with a few rough pieces of basil. 6. Just before serving, toss the warm zoodles with the pesto and place the shrimp on top.
Per Serving: Calories 354; Fat 7.9g; Sodium 704mg; Carbs 6g; Fiber 3.6g; Sugar 6g; Protein 18g

Marinated Salmon with Sweet Sauce

Prep time: 5 minutes | Cook time: 6 minutes | Servings: 2

2 (4-ounce) salmon fillets (about 1¼ inches thick)

Marinade:	
¼ cup wheat-free tamari or	a few drops liquid stevia
coconut aminos	2 teaspoons grated fresh ginger
2 tablespoons lime or lemon juice	2 cloves garlic, minced
2 tablespoons sesame oil	½ teaspoon ground black pepper
2 tablespoons Swerve	Sliced green onions, for garnish
confectioners'-style sweetener, or	
Sauce:	
¼ cup beef broth	powdered sweetener
¼ cup wheat-free tamari	1 tablespoon tomato sauce
3 tablespoons Swerve	1 teaspoon stevia glyceride
confectioners'-style sweetener or	⅛ teaspoon guar gum or xanthan
equivalent amount of liquid or	gum

1. Make the marinade: In a medium-sized shallow dish, stir together all the ingredients for the marinade until well combined. Place the salmon in the marinade. Cover and refrigerate for at least 2 hours or overnight. 2. Select Level 3. Select the "AIR FRY" function of Ninja Foodi Smart XL Pro Air Oven, set temperature to 400°F/200°C and time to 6 minutes. Select START/STOP to begin preheating. 3. Place

the marinated salmon in the air fryer, leaving space between them. Cook for 6 minutes, until cooked through and flakes easily with a fork. 4. While the salmon cooks, make the sauce, if using: Place all the sauce ingredients except the guar gum in a medium-sized bowl and stir until well combined. 5. Taste and adjust the sweetness to your liking. While whisking slowly, add the guar gum. Allow the sauce to thicken for 3 to 5 minutes. Drizzle the sauce over the salmon before serving. 6. Garnish the salmon with sliced green onions before serving.
Per Serving: Calories 354; Fat 7.9g; Sodium 704mg; Carbs 6g; Fiber 3.6g; Sugar 6g; Protein 18g

Delicious BLT Crab Cakes

Prep time: 10 minutes | Cook time: 19 minutes | Servings: 4

4 slices bacon

Crab Cakes:	
1 pound canned lump crabmeat,	½ teaspoon dried parsley
drained well	½ teaspoon dried dill weed
¼ cup plus 1 tablespoon	¼ teaspoon garlic powder
powdered Parmesan cheese	¼ teaspoon onion powder
3 tablespoons mayonnaise	⅛ teaspoon ground black pepper
1 large egg	1 cup pork dust
½ teaspoon dried chives	
For Serving:	
Leaves from 1 small head Boston	4 slices tomato
lettuce	¼ cup mayonnaise

1. Spray the air fryer basket with avocado oil. Select Level 3. Select the "AIR FRY" function of Ninja Foodi Smart XL Pro Air Oven, set temperature to 350°F/175°C and time to 9 minutes. Select START/STOP to begin preheating. 2. Place the bacon slices in the air fryer, leaving space between them, and cook for 7 to 9 minutes, until crispy. Remove the bacon and increase the heat to 400°F/200°C. Set the bacon aside. 3. Make the crab cakes: Place all the crab cake ingredients except the pork dust in a bowl and mix until well blended. Divide the mixture into 4 equal-sized crab cakes (they should each be about 1 inch thick). 4. Place the pork dust in a small bowl. Dredge the crab cakes in the pork dust to coat them well and use your hands to press the pork dust into the cakes. 5. Place them in the air fryer basket, leaving space between them, and cook for 10 minutes, or until crispy. 6. To serve, place 4 lettuce leaves on a serving platter and top each leaf with a slice of tomato, then a crab cake, then a dollop of mayo, and finally a slice of bacon.
Per Serving: Calories 354; Fat 7.9g; Sodium 704mg; Carbs 6g; Fiber 3.6g; Sugar 6g; Protein 18g

Cod over Creamy Leek Noodles

Prep time: 10 minutes | Cook time: 24 minutes | Servings: 4

1 small leek, sliced into long thin	1 teaspoon fine sea salt, divided
noodles	4 (4-ounce) cod fillets
½ cup heavy cream	½ teaspoon ground black pepper
2 cloves garlic, minced	
Coating:	
¼ cup grated Parmesan cheese	1 tablespoon chopped fresh
2 tablespoons mayonnaise	thyme, or ½ teaspoon dried thyme
2 tablespoons unsalted butter,	leaves, plus more for garnish
softened	

1. Select Level 3. Select the "AIR FRY" function of Ninja Foodi Smart XL Pro Air Oven, set temperature to 350°F/175°C and time to 10 minutes. Select START/STOP to begin preheating. 2. Place the leek noodles in a 6-inch casserole dish or a pan that will fit in your air fryer. 3. In a bowl, stir the cream, garlic, and ½ teaspoon of the salt. Pour the mixture over the leeks and cook in the air fryer for 10 minutes, or until the leeks are very tender. 4. Pat dry the fish and spice with the salt and the pepper. When the leeks are ready, open the air fryer and place the fish fillets on top of the leeks. Cook for 10 minutes, until the fish flakes easily with a fork. 5. While the fish cooks, make the coating: In a small bowl, combine the Parmesan, mayo, butter, and thyme. 6. When the fish is cooked; remove from fryer and increase the heat to 425°F/220°C. Spread the fillets with a ½-inch-thick to ¾-inch-thick layer of the coating. 7. Place the fish back in the air fryer and cook for 3 to 4 minutes, until the coating browns. 8. Garnish with fresh or dried thyme, if desired.
Per Serving: Calories 354; Fat 7.9g; Sodium 704mg; Carbs 6g; Fiber 3.6g; Sugar 6g; Protein 18g

Popcorn Shrimp

Prep time: 10 minutes | Cook time: 9 minutes | Servings: 4

4 large egg yolks
1 teaspoon prepared yellow mustard
1-pound small shrimp, peeled, deveined, and tails removed
For Serving/Garnish:
Prepared yellow mustard
Ranch Dressing

½ cup finely shredded Gouda or Parmesan cheese
½ cup pork dust
1 tablespoon Cajun seasoning

Tomato sauce
Sprig of fresh parsley

1. Spray the air fryer basket with avocado oil. Select Level 3. Select the "AIR FRY" function of Ninja Foodi Smart XL Pro Air Oven, set temperature to 400°F/200°C and time to 9 minutes. Select START/STOP to begin preheating. 2. Place the egg yolks in a bowl, add the mustard, and whisk until well combined. Add in the shrimp and toss to coat. 3. In a medium-sized bowl, mix together the cheese, pork dust, and Cajun seasoning until well combined. 4. One at a time, roll the coated shrimp in the pork dust mixture and use your hands to press it onto the shrimp. Spray the coated shrimp with avocado oil and place them in the air fryer basket, leaving space between them. 5. Cook in the air fryer for 9 minutes, or until cooked through and no longer translucent, flipping after 4 minutes. 6. Serve with your dipping sauces of choice and garnish with a sprig of fresh parsley.
Per Serving: Calories 354; Fat 7.9g; Sodium 704mg; Carbs 6g; Fiber 3.6g; Sugar 6g; Protein 18g

Garlicky Shrimp with Olives

Prep time: 5 minutes | Cook time: 12 minutes | Servings: 4

1-pound shrimp, peeled and deveined
4 garlic clove, minced
1 cup black olives, pitted and

chopped
3 tablespoons parsley
1 tablespoon olive oil

1. Select Level 3. Select the "AIR FRY" function of Ninja Foodi Smart XL Pro Air Oven, set temperature to 380°F/195°C and time to 12 minutes. Select START/STOP to begin preheating. 2. Combine all the ingredients in a Ninja sheet pan, toss, put the pan in the air fryer and cook for 12 minutes. 3. Divide between plates and serve.
Per Serving: Calories 354; Fat 7.9g; Sodium 704mg; Carbs 6g; Fiber 3.6g; Sugar 6g; Protein 18g

Herbed Parmesan Salmon

Prep time: 10 minutes | Cook time: 7 minutes | Servings: 2

10 oz. salmon fillet
1 teaspoon dried oregano
1 teaspoon sesame oil

2 oz. Parmesan, grated
¼ teaspoon chili flakes

1. Sprinkle the salmon fillet with dried oregano and chili flakes. Then brush it with sesame oil. 2. Select Level 3. Select the "AIR FRY" function of Ninja Foodi Smart XL Pro Air Oven, set temperature to 385°F/195°C and time to 5 minutes. Select START/STOP to begin preheating. 3. Place the salmon in the air fryer basket and cook it for 5 minutes. Then flip the fish on another side and top with Parmesan. Cook the fish for 2 minutes more.
Per Serving: Calories 354; Fat 7.9g; Sodium 704mg; Carbs 6g; Fiber 3.6g; Sugar 6g; Protein 18g

Crispy Fried Anchovies

Prep time: 20 minutes | Cook time: 6 minutes | Servings: 4

1-pound anchovies
¼ cup coconut flour
2 eggs, beaten
1 teaspoon salt

1 teaspoon ground black pepper
1 tablespoon lemon juice
1 tablespoon sesame oil

1. Trim and wash anchovies if needed and put them in the big bowl. Add salt and ground black pepper. Mix up the anchovies. 2. Then add eggs and lemon juice. Stir the fish until you get a homogenous mixture. After this coat every anchovies fish in the coconut flour. Brush the air fryer pan with sesame oil. Place the anchovies in the pan in one layer. 3. Select Level 3. Select the "AIR FRY" function of Ninja Foodi Smart XL Pro Air Oven, set temperature to 400°F/200°C and time to 6 minutes. Select START/STOP to begin preheating. 4. Put the pan with anchovies in the air fryer and cook them for 6 minutes or

until anchovies are golden brown.
Per Serving: Calories 354; Fat 7.9g; Sodium 704mg; Carbs 6g; Fiber 3.6g; Sugar 6g; Protein 18g

Trout with Crispy Asparagus

Prep time: 5 minutes | Cook time: 20 minutes | Servings: 4

4 trout fillets, boneless and skinless
1 tablespoon lemon juice
2 tablespoons olive oil

A pinch of salt and black pepper
1 bunch asparagus, trimmed
2 tablespoons ghee, melted
¼ cup mixed chives and tarragon

1. Select Level 3. Select the "AIR FRY" function of Ninja Foodi Smart XL Pro Air Oven, set temperature to 380°F/195°C and time to 6 minutes. Select START/STOP to begin preheating. 2. Mix the asparagus with half of the oil, salt and pepper, put it in your air fryer's basket, cook at 380/190°C °F for 6 minutes and divide between plates. 3. In a bowl, mix the trout with salt, pepper, lemon juice, the rest of the oil, chives and tarragon and toss. Put the fillets in your air fryer's basket and cook at 380 °F/190°C for 7 minutes on each side. 4. Divide the fish next to the asparagus, drizzle the melted ghee all over and serve.
Per Serving: Calories 354; Fat 7.9g; Sodium 704mg; Carbs 6g; Fiber 3.6g; Sugar 6g; Protein 18g

Refreshing Cilantro Salmon

Prep time: 5 minutes | Cook time: 12 minutes | Servings: 4

4 salmon fillets, boneless
Juice of ½ lemon
¼ cup chives, chopped

4 cilantro springs, chopped
3 tablespoons olive oil
Salt and black pepper to the taste

1. Select Level 3. Select the "AIR FRY" function of Ninja Foodi Smart XL Pro Air Oven, set temperature to 370°F/185°C and time to 12 minutes. Select START/STOP to begin preheating. 2. In a bowl, mix the salmon with all the other ingredients and toss. Put the fillets in your air fryer's basket and cook for 12 minutes, flipping the fish halfway. 3. Divide everything between plates and serve with a side salad.
Per Serving: Calories 354; Fat 7.9g; Sodium 704mg; Carbs 6g; Fiber 3.6g; Sugar 6g; Protein 18g

Mahi Mahi with Broccoli Cakes

Prep time: 15 minutes | Cook time: 11 minutes | Servings: 4

½ cup broccoli, shredded
1 tablespoon flax meal
1 egg, beaten
1 teaspoon ground coriander
1 oz. Monterey Jack cheese,

shredded
½ teaspoon salt
6 oz. Mahi Mahi, chopped
Cooking spray

1. In the mixing bowl mix up flax meal, egg, ground coriander, salt, broccoli, and chopped Mahi Mahi. Stir the ingredients gently with the help of the fork and add shredded Monterey Jack cheese. Stir the mixture until homogenous. Then make 4 cakes. 2. Install the wire rack on Level 3. Select the "BAKE" function of Ninja Foodi Smart XL Pro Air Oven, set temperature to 390°F/200°C and time to 11 minutes. Select START/STOP to begin preheating. 3. Place the Mahi Mahi cakes in the air fryer and spray them gently with cooking spray. Cook the fish cakes for 5 minutes and then flip on another side. 4. Cook the fish cakes for 6 minutes more.
Per Serving: Calories 354; Fat 7.9g; Sodium 704mg; Carbs 6g; Fiber 3.6g; Sugar 6g; Protein 18g

Balsamic Trout with Tomatoes &Pepper

Prep time: 5 minutes | Cook time: 16 minutes | Servings: 2

2 trout fillets, boneless
2 tomatoes, cubed
1 red bell pepper, chopped
2 garlic cloves, minced

1 tablespoon olive oil
1 tablespoon balsamic vinegar
A pinch of salt and black pepper
2 tablespoon almond flakes

1. Select Level 3. Select the "AIR FRY" function of Ninja Foodi Smart XL Pro Air Oven, set temperature to 370°F/185°C and time to 16 minutes. Select START/STOP to begin preheating. 2. Arrange the fish in a pan that fits your air fryer, add the rest of the ingredients and toss gently. 3. Cook for 16 minutes, divide between plates and serve.
Per Serving: Calories 354; Fat 7.9g; Sodium 704mg; Carbs 6g; Fiber 3.6g; Sugar 6g; Protein 18g

Squid Stuffed with Cauliflower

Prep time: 20 minutes | Cook time: 6 minutes | Servings: 4

4 squid tubes, trimmed
1 teaspoon ground paprika
½ teaspoon ground turmeric
½ teaspoon garlic, diced
½ cup cauliflower, shredded
1 egg, beaten
½ teaspoon salt
½ teaspoon ground ginger
Cooking spray

1. Clean the squid tubes if needed. After this, in the mixing bowl mix up ground paprika, turmeric, garlic, shredded cauliflower, salt, and ground ginger. Stir the mixture gently and add a beaten egg. Mix the mixture up. Then fill the squid tubes with shredded cauliflower mixture. Secure the edges of the squid tubes with toothpicks. 2. Install the wire rack on Level 3. Select the "BAKE" function of Ninja Foodi Smart XL Pro Air Oven, set temperature to 390°F/200°C and time to 6 minutes. Select START/STOP to begin preheating. 3. Place the stuffed squid tubes in the air fryer and spray with cooking spray. Cook the meal for 6 minutes.
Per Serving: Calories 354; Fat 7.9g; Sodium 704mg; Carbs 6g; Fiber 3.6g; Sugar 6g; Protein 18g

Nutty Trout

Prep time: 5 minutes | Cook time: 15 minutes | Servings: 2

2 trout fillets, boneless
2 tablespoons almonds, crushed
Zest of ½ lemon, grated
1 tablespoon olive oil
1 tablespoon ghee, melted
A pinch of salt and black pepper
1 tablespoon parsley, chopped

1. Select Level 3. Select the "AIR FRY" function of Ninja Foodi Smart XL Pro Air Oven, set temperature to 370°F/185°C and time to 5 minutes. Select START/STOP to begin preheating. 2. In a bowl, mix the trout with all the other ingredients except the parsley and toss. Put the fish in your air fryer's basket and cook for 15 minutes, flipping the fillets halfway. 3. Divide between serving plates, sprinkle the parsley on top and serve.
Per Serving: Calories 354; Fat 7.9g; Sodium 704mg; Carbs 6g; Fiber 3.6g; Sugar 6g; Protein 18g

Sea Bass and Olives

Prep time: 5 minutes | Cook time: 20 minutes | Servings: 2

2 sea bass, fillets
1 fennel bulb, sliced
Juice of 1 lemon
¼ cup black olives, pitted and
sliced
1 tablespoon olive oil
A pinch of salt and black pepper
¼ cup basil, chopped

1. Select Level 3. Select the "AIR FRY" function of Ninja Foodi Smart XL Pro Air Oven, set temperature to 380°F/195°C and time to 20 minutes. Select START/STOP to begin preheating. 2. In a pan that fits the air fryer, combine all the ingredients, introduce the pan in the Ninja Foodi air fryer and cook at 380°F/195°C for 20 minutes, shaking the fryer halfway. 3. Divide between plates and serve.
Per Serving: Calories 354; Fat 7.9g; Sodium 704mg; Carbs 6g; Fiber 3.6g; Sugar 6g; Protein 18g

Creole Crab Hush Puppies

Prep time: 15 minutes | Cook time: 6 minutes | Servings: 6

1 teaspoon Creole seasonings
4 tablespoons almond flour
¼ teaspoon baking powder
1 teaspoon apple cider vinegar
¼ teaspoon onion powder
1 teaspoon dried dill
1 teaspoon ghee
13 oz. crab meat, finely chopped
1 egg, beaten
Cooking spray

1. In the mixing bowl mix up crab meat, egg, dried dill, ghee, onion powder, apple cider vinegar, baking powder, and Creole seasonings. Then add almond flour and stir the mixture with the help of the fork until it is homogenous. Make the small balls (hushpuppies). 2. Select Level 3. Select the "AIR FRY" function of Ninja Foodi Smart XL Pro Air Oven, set temperature to 390°F/200°C and time to 6 minutes. Select START/STOP to begin preheating. 3. Put the hushpuppies in the air fryer basket and spray with cooking spray. Cook them for 3 minutes. 4. Then flip them on another side and cook for 3 minutes more or until the hushpuppies are golden brown.
Per Serving: Calories 354; Fat 7.9g; Sodium 704mg; Carbs 6g; Fiber 3.6g; Sugar 6g; Protein 18g

Sea Bass with Cauliflower Rice

Prep time: 5 minutes | Cook time: 25 minutes | Servings: 4

4 sea bass fillets, boneless
A pinch of salt and black pepper
1 tablespoon ghee, melted
1 garlic clove, minced
1 cup cauliflower rice
½ cup chicken stock
1 tablespoon parmesan, grated
1 tablespoon chervil, chopped
1 tablespoon parsley, chopped
1 tablespoon tarragon, chopped

1. Select Level 3. Select the "AIR FRY" function of Ninja Foodi Smart XL Pro Air Oven, set temperature to 380°F/195°C and time to 24 minutes. Select START/STOP to begin preheating. 2. In a pan that fits your air fryer, mix the cauliflower rice with the stock, parmesan, chervil, tarragon and parsley, toss, introduce the pan in the air fryer and cook for 12 minutes. 3. In a bowl, mix the fish with salt, pepper, garlic and melted ghee and toss gently. Put the fish over the cauliflower rice, cook for 12 minutes more, divide everything between plates and serve.
Per Serving: Calories 354; Fat 7.9g; Sodium 704mg; Carbs 6g; Fiber 3.6g; Sugar 6g; Protein 18g

Cheese and Lobster Lettuce Wraps

Prep time: 10 minutes | Cook time: 6 minutes | Servings: 4

4 lettuce leaves
½ teaspoon taco seasonings
4 lobster tails
1 teaspoon Splenda
½ teaspoon ground cumin
½ teaspoon chili flakes
1 tablespoon ricotta cheese
1 teaspoon avocado oil

1. Select Level 3. Select the "AIR FRY" function of Ninja Foodi Smart XL Pro Air Oven, set temperature to 380°F/195°C and time to 6 minutes. Select START/STOP to begin preheating. 2. Peel the lobster tails and sprinkle with ground cumin, taco seasonings, and chili flakes. 3. Arrange the lobster tails in the air fryer basket and sprinkle with avocado oil. Cook them for 6 minutes. 4. After this, remove the cooked lobster tails from the air fryer and chop them roughly. Transfer the lobster tails into the bowl. Add ricotta cheese and Splenda. Mix them up. 5. Place the lobster mixture on the lettuce leaves and fold them.
Per Serving: Calories 354; Fat 7.9g; Sodium 704mg; Carbs 6g; Fiber 3.6g; Sugar 6g; Protein 18g

Sea Bass with Tropical Sauce

Prep time: 5 minutes | Cook time: 20 minutes | Servings: 4

4 sea bass fillets, boneless
A pinch of salt and black pepper
2 spring onions, chopped
Juice of 1 lime
1 garlic clove, minced
2 tomatoes, cubed
2 cups coconut cream
½ cup okra
A handful coriander, chopped
2 red chilies, minced

1. Put the coconut cream in a pan that fits the air fryer, add garlic, spring onions, lime juice, tomatoes, okra, chilies and the coriander, toss, bring to a simmer and cook for 5-6 minutes. 2. Add the fish, toss gently. 3. Select Level 3. Select the "AIR FRY" function of Ninja Foodi Smart XL Pro Air Oven, set temperature to 380°F/195°C and time to 15 minutes. Select START/STOP to begin preheating. 4. Place the pan into the preheated air fryer and cook for 15 minutes. Divide between plates and serve.
Per Serving: Calories 354; Fat 7.9g; Sodium 704mg; Carbs 6g; Fiber 3.6g; Sugar 6g; Protein 18g

Shrimp with Scallions

Prep time: 3 minutes | Cook time: 10 minutes | Servings: 4

1-pound shrimp, peeled and deveined
2 tablespoons olive oil
1 tablespoon scallions, chopped
1 cup chicken stock

1. Select Level 3. Select the "AIR FRY" function of Ninja Foodi Smart XL Pro Air Oven, set temperature to 380°F/195°C and time to 10 minutes. Select START/STOP to begin preheating. 2. In a pan that fits your air fryer, mix the shrimp with the oil, scallions and the stock, introduce the pan in the fryer and cook for 10 minutes. 3. Divide into bowls and serve.
Per Serving: Calories 354; Fat 7.9g; Sodium 704mg; Carbs 6g; Fiber 3.6g; Sugar 6g; Protein 18g

Sausage and Shrimp Gumbo

Prep time: 10 minutes | Cook time: 12 minutes | Servings: 4

10 oz. shrimps, peeled
5 oz. smoked sausages, chopped
1 teaspoon olive oil
1 teaspoon ground black pepper
3 spring onions, diced

1 jalapeno pepper, chopped
½ cup chicken broth
1 teaspoon chili flakes
½ teaspoon dried cilantro
½ teaspoon salt

1. Select Level 3. Select the "AIR FRY" function of Ninja Foodi Smart XL Pro Air Oven, set temperature to 400°F/200°C and time to 4 minutes. Select START/STOP to begin preheating. 2. In the mixing bowl mix up smoked sausages, ground black pepper, and chili flakes. Put the smoked sausages in the air fryer and cook them for 4 minutes. 3. Meanwhile, in the mixing bowl mix up onion, jalapeno pepper, and salt. Remove the sausages from the air fryer. 4. Put the onion mixture in the air fryer sheet pan and sprinkle with olive oil. After this, Put the pan with onion in the air fryer and cook it for 2 minutes. 5. After this, add smoked sausages, dried cilantro, and shrimps. Add chicken broth. Stir the ingredients gently and cook the meal for 6 minutes.
Per Serving: Calories 354; Fat 7.9g; Sodium 704mg; Carbs 6g; Fiber 3.6g; Sugar 6g; Protein 18g

Clams with Coconut Lime Sauce

Prep time: 5 minutes | Cook time: 20 minutes | Servings: 4

15 small clams
1 tablespoon spring onions, chopped
Juice of 1 lime

10 ounces coconut cream
2 tablespoons cilantro, chopped
1 teaspoon olive oil

1. Heat up a pan that fits your air fryer with the oil over medium heat, add the spring onions and sauté for 2 minutes. Add lime juice, coconut cream and the cilantro, stir and cook for 2 minutes more. 2. Select Level 3. Select the "AIR FRY" function of Ninja Foodi Smart XL Pro Air Oven, set temperature to 390°F/200°C and time to 15 minutes. Select START/STOP to begin preheating. 3. Add the clams in the sauce, toss and introduce in the preheated air fryer and cook for 15 minutes. 4. Divide into bowls and serve hot.
Per Serving: Calories 354; Fat 7.9g; Sodium 704mg; Carbs 6g; Fiber 3.6g; Sugar 6g; Protein 18g

Fried Coconut Tilapia

Prep time: 10 minutes | Cook time: 12 minutes | Servings: 2

8 oz. tilapia fillet
1 teaspoon coconut cream
1 teaspoon coconut flour
½ teaspoon salt

¼ teaspoon smoked paprika
½ teaspoon dried oregano
½ teaspoon coconut oil, melted
¼ teaspoon ground cumin

1. Rub the tilapia fillet with ground cumin, dried oregano, smoked paprika, and salt. Then dip it in the coconut cream. Cut the tilapia fillet on 2 servings. After this, sprinkle every tilapia fillet with coconut flour gently. 2. Select Level 3. Select the "AIR FRY" function of Ninja Foodi Smart XL Pro Air Oven, set temperature to 385°F/195°C and time to 12 minutes. Select START/STOP to begin preheating. 3. Sprinkle the air fryer basket with coconut oil and put the tilapia fillets inside. Cook the fillets for 6 minutes from every side.
Per Serving: Calories 354; Fat 7.9g; Sodium 704mg; Carbs 6g; Fiber 3.6g; Sugar 6g; Protein 18g

Italian-Style Fennel Cod Fillets

Prep time: 5 minutes | Cook time: 15 minutes | Servings: 4

4 cod fillets, boneless
A pinch of salt and black pepper
1 tablespoon thyme, chopped
½ teaspoon black peppercorns
2 tablespoons olive oil

1 fennel, sliced
2 garlic cloves, minced
1 red bell pepper, chopped
2 teaspoons Italian seasoning

1. Select Level 3. Select the "AIR FRY" function of Ninja Foodi Smart XL Pro Air Oven, set temperature to 380°F/195°C and time to 15 minutes. Select START/STOP to begin preheating. 2. In a bowl, mix the fennel with bell pepper and the other ingredients except the fish fillets and toss. 3. Put this into a pan that fits the air fryer, add the fish on top, introduce the pan in your air fryer and cook for 15 minutes. 4. Divide between plates and serve.

Per Serving: Calories 354; Fat 7.9g; Sodium 704mg; Carbs 6g; Fiber 3.6g; Sugar 6g; Protein 18g

Fried Coconut Cod Strips

Prep time: 10 minutes | Cook time: 6 minutes | Servings: 4

10 oz. cod fillet
1 tablespoon coconut flour
1 tablespoon coconut flakes
1 egg, beaten

1 teaspoon ground turmeric
½ teaspoon salt
1 tablespoon heavy cream
1 teaspoon olive oil

1. Cut the cod fillets on the fries strips. After this, in the mixing bowl mix up coconut flour, coconut flakes, ground turmeric, and salt. In the other bowl mix up egg and heavy cream. After this, dip the fish fries in the egg mixture. Coat in the coconut flour mixture. Repeat the steps again. 2. Select Level 3. Select the "AIR FRY" function of Ninja Foodi Smart XL Pro Air Oven, set temperature to 400°F/200°C and time to 6 minutes. Select START/STOP to begin preheating. 3. Put the fish fries in the air fryer basket in one layer and sprinkle them with olive oil. Cook the meal for 3 minutes. 4. Then flip the fish fries on another side and cook for 3 minutes more.
Per Serving: Calories 354; Fat 7.9g; Sodium 704mg; Carbs 6g; Fiber 3.6g; Sugar 6g; Protein 18g

Chili Sea Bass

Prep time: 5 minutes | Cook time: 15 minutes | Servings: 4

4 sea bass fillets, boneless
4 garlic cloves, minced
Juice of 1 lime
1 cup veggie stock
A pinch of salt and black pepper
1 tablespoon black peppercorns,

crushed
1-inch ginger, grated
4 lemongrasses, chopped
4 small chilies, minced
1 bunch coriander, chopped

1. Select Level 3. Select the "AIR FRY" function of Ninja Foodi Smart XL Pro Air Oven, set temperature to 380°F/195°C and time to 15 minutes. Select START/STOP to begin preheating. 2. In a blender, mix all the ingredients instead of the fish and pulse well. Pour the mix in a pan that fits the air fryer, add the fish, toss, introduce in the fryer and cook for 15 minutes. 3. Divide between plates and serve.
Per Serving: Calories 354; Fat 7.9g; Sodium 704mg; Carbs 6g; Fiber 3.6g; Sugar 6g; Protein 18g

Buttery Haddock with Parsley

Prep time: 10 minutes | Cook time: 16 minutes | Servings: 2

7 oz. haddock fillet
2 tablespoons butter, melted
1 teaspoon minced garlic

½ teaspoon salt
1 teaspoon fresh parsley, chopped
½ teaspoon ground celery root

1. Cut the fish fillet on 2 servings. In the shallow bowl mix up butter and minced garlic. 2. Then add salt, celery root, and fresh parsley. After this, carefully brush the fish fillets with the butter mixture. Then wrap every fillet in the foil. 3. Select Level 3. Select the "AIR FRY" function of Ninja Foodi Smart XL Pro Air Oven, set temperature to 385°F/195°C and time to 16 minutes. Select START/STOP to begin preheating. 4. Put the wrapped haddock fillets in the air fryer and cook for 16 minutes.
Per Serving: Calories 354; Fat 7.9g; Sodium 704mg; Carbs 6g; Fiber 3.6g; Sugar 6g; Protein 18g

Italian Garlicky Shrimp

Prep time: 5 minutes | Cook time: 10 minutes | Servings: 4

2 pounds shrimp, peeled and deveined
A drizzle of olive oil
¼ cup chicken stock
1 tablespoon Italian seasoning

Salt and black pepper to the taste
1 teaspoon red pepper flakes, crushed
8 garlic cloves, crushed

1. Select Level 3. Select the "AIR FRY" function of Ninja Foodi Smart XL Pro Air Oven, set temperature to 390°F/200°C and time to 10 minutes. Select START/STOP to begin preheating. 2. Grease a pan that fits your air fryer with the oil, add the shrimp and the rest of the ingredients, toss, introduce the pan in the fryer and cook for 10 minutes. 3. Divide into bowls and serve.
Per Serving: Calories 354; Fat 7.9g; Sodium 704mg; Carbs 6g; Fiber 3.6g; Sugar 6g; Protein 18g

Tasty Salmon and Tarragon

Prep time: 15 minutes | Cook time: 15 minutes | Servings: 4

12 oz. salmon fillet
2 spring onions, chopped
1 tablespoon ghee, melted
1 teaspoon peppercorns
½ teaspoon salt
½ teaspoon ground black pepper
1 teaspoon tarragon
½ teaspoon dried cilantro

1. Cut the salmon fillet on 4 servings. Then make the parchment pockets and place the fish fillets in the parchment pockets. 2. Sprinkle the salmon with salt, ground black pepper, tarragon, and dried cilantro. After this, top the fish with spring onions, peppercorns, and ghee. 3. Select Level 3. Select the "AIR FRY" function of Ninja Foodi Smart XL Pro Air Oven, set temperature to 385°F/195°C and time to 15 minutes. Select START/STOP to begin preheating. 4. Arrange the salmon pockets in the air fryer in one layer and cook them for 15 minutes.
Per Serving: Calories 354; Fat 7.9g; Sodium 704mg; Carbs 6g; Fiber 3.6g; Sugar 6g; Protein 18g

Parsley Shrimp and Olives

Prep time: 5 minutes | Cook time: 12 minutes | Servings: 4

1-pound shrimp, peeled and deveined
4 garlic clove, minced
1 cup black olives, pitted and
chopped
3 tablespoons parsley
1 tablespoon olive oil

1. Select Level 3. Select the "AIR FRY" function of Ninja Foodi Smart XL Pro Air Oven, set temperature to 380°F/195°C and time to 12 minutes. Select START/STOP to begin preheating. 2. In a pan that fits the air fryer, combine all the ingredients, toss, put the pan in the Ninja Foodi air fryer and cook for 12 minutes. 3. Divide between plates and serve.
Per Serving: Calories 354; Fat 7.9g; Sodium 704mg; Carbs 6g; Fiber 3.6g; Sugar 6g; Protein 18g

Spicy Octopus

Prep time: 10 minutes | Cook time: 26 minutes | Servings: 4

11 oz. octopus
1 teaspoon chili flakes
1 chili pepper, chopped
1 tablespoon coconut oil, melted
½ teaspoon salt
1 cup of water
1 tablespoon lemon juice

1. Boil water in a saucepan. Chop the octopus and put it in the boiling water. Close and cook the seafood for 25 minutes. 2. Select Level 3. Select the "AIR FRY" function of Ninja Foodi Smart XL Pro Air Oven, set temperature to 390°F/200°C and time to 1 minute. Select START/STOP to begin preheating. 3. After this, remove the octopus from the water and sprinkle with chili flakes, chili pepper, coconut oil, salt, and lemon juice. 4. Transfer them in the air fryer and cook for 1 minute.
Per Serving: Calories 354; Fat 7.9g; Sodium 704mg; Carbs 6g; Fiber 3.6g; Sugar 6g; Protein 18g

Sea Bass and Tangy Balsamic Salsa

Prep time: 5 minutes | Cook time: 15 minutes | Servings: 4

4 sea bass fillets, boneless
1 tablespoon olive oil
3 tomatoes, roughly chopped
2 spring onions, chopped
¼ cup chicken stock
A pinch of salt and black pepper
3 garlic cloves, minced
1 tablespoon balsamic vinegar

1. Select Level 3. Select the "AIR FRY" function of Ninja Foodi Smart XL Pro Air Oven, set temperature to 380°F/195°C and time to 15 minutes. Select START/STOP to begin preheating. 2. In a blender, mix all the ingredients instead of the fish and pulse well. 3. Put the mix in a pan that fits the air fryer, add the fish, toss gently, introduce the pan in the fryer and cook for 15 minutes. 4. Divide between plates and serve.
Per Serving: Calories 354; Fat 7.9g; Sodium 704mg; Carbs 6g; Fiber 3.6g; Sugar 6g; Protein 18g

Chapter 6 Snack and Appetizer Recipes

Sweet Chicken Wings

Prep time: 10 minutes | Cook time: 20 minutes | Servings: 5

2 pounds chicken wings
¼ cup agave syrup
2 tablespoons soy sauce
2 tablespoons scallions, chopped
2 tablespoons olive oil

1 teaspoon ginger, peeled and grated
2 cloves garlic, minced
Black pepper and salt, to taste

1. Toss the chicken wings with the remaining recipe ingredients. 2. Cook on Air Fry mode and select level 3. Cook the chicken wings at 380°F/195°C for 18 minutes, turning them over halfway through the cooking time. 3. Serve.
Per Serving: Calories 284; Fat 16g; Sodium 252mg; Carbs 31.6g; Fiber 0.9g; Sugar 6.6g; Protein 3.7g

Yam Chips

Prep time: 10 minutes | Cook time: 15 minutes | Servings: 2

1 large-sized yam, peeled and cut into ¼-inch sticks
1 tablespoon olive oil

Kosher salt and red pepper, to taste

1. Select the "Air Fry" Mode, press level 3, and set its temperature to 360°F/180°C and set the time to 15 minutes. Press Start/Pause to initiate preheating. 2. Toss the yam with the remaining recipe ingredients and place them in the air fryer cooking basket. 3. Air fry the yam sticks for 15 minutes, tossing halfway through the cooking time and working in batches. Enjoy!
Per Serving: Calories 149; Fat 1.2g; Sodium 3mg; Carbs 37.6g; Fiber 5.8g; Sugar 29g; Protein 1.1g

Potato Chips

Prep time: 10 minutes | Cook time: 16 minutes | Servings: 3

2 large-sized potatoes, peeled and thinly sliced
2 tablespoons olive oil
1 teaspoon Sichuan peppercorns

1 teaspoon garlic powder
½ teaspoon Chinese five-spice powder
Salt, to taste

1. Select the "Air Fry" Mode, press level 3, and set its temperature to 360°F/180°C Press Start/Pause to initiate preheating. 2. Toss the potatoes with the remaining recipe ingredients and place them in the air fryer cooking basket. 3. Air fry the potato chips for 16 minutes, shaking the basket halfway through the cooking time and working in batches. 4. Enjoy!
Per Serving: Calories 127; Fat 14.2g; Sodium 672mg; Carbs 47.2g; Fiber 1.7g; Sugar 24.8g; Protein 4.4g

Butter Sriracha Chicken Wings

Prep time: 10 minutes | Cook time: 18minutes | Servings: 4

2 pounds chicken wings
1 tablespoon white vinegar
Black pepper and salt, to taste
1 teaspoon cayenne pepper
1 teaspoon garlic powder

½ teaspoon onion powder
4 tablespoons butter, room temperature
¼ cup sriracha sauce

1. Toss the chicken wings with the remaining recipe ingredients. 2. Cook on Air Fry mode and select level 3, cook the chicken wings at 380°F/195°C for 18 minutes, turning them over halfway through the cooking time. 3. Bon appétit!
Per Serving: Calories 192; Fat 9.3g; Sodium 133mg; Carbs 27.1g; Fiber 1.4g; Sugar 19g; Protein 3.2g

Eggplant Fries

Prep time: 10 minutes | Cook time: 15 minutes | Servings: 3

¾-pound eggplant
Black pepper and salt, to taste
½ teaspoon paprika

2 tablespoons olive oil
2 tablespoons balsamic vinegar

1. Toss the eggplant pieces with the remaining recipe ingredients until they are well coated on all sides. 2. Spread the eggplant in its air fryer basket. 3. Cook on Air Fry mode and select level 3, cook the eggplant at 400°F/200°C for about 15 minutes, shaking the basket halfway through the cooking time. 3. Bon appétit!

Per Serving: Calories 204; Fat 9g; Sodium 91mg; Carbs 27g; Fiber 2.4g; Sugar 15g; Protein 1.3g

Tomato Chips with Cheese

Prep time: 10 minutes | Cook time: 20 minutes | Servings: 3

1 large-sized beefsteak tomatoes
2 tablespoons olive oil
½ teaspoon paprika
Salt, to taste
1 teaspoon garlic powder

1 tablespoon fresh cilantro, chopped
4 tablespoons pecorino cheese, grated

1. Toss the tomato slices with the olive oil and spices until they are well coated on all sides. 2. Spread the tomato slices in the air fryer cooking basket. 3. Cook on Air Fry mode and select level 3, cook the tomato slices at 360°F/180°Cfor about 10 minutes. Turn the temperature to 330°F/165°C and top the tomato slices with the cheese; now, continue to cook for 5 minutes. Bon appétit!
Per Serving: Calories 157; Fat 1.3g; Sodium 27mg; Carbs 1.3g; Fiber 1g; Sugar 2.2g; Protein 8.2g

Spicy Nuts

Prep time: 10 minutes | Cook time: 6 minutes | Servings: 4

1 egg white lightly beaten
½ cup pecan halves
½ cup almonds
½ cup walnuts

Salt and cayenne pepper, to taste
1 teaspoon chili powder
½ teaspoon ground cinnamon
½ teaspoon ground allspice

1. Select the "Air Fry" Mode, press level 3. Set its temperature to 330°F/165°C. and set the time to 6 minutes. Press Start/Pause to initiate preheating. 2. Mix the nuts with the rest of the recipe ingredients and place them in the air fryer cooking basket. 3. Air fry the nuts for 6 minutes, shaking the basket halfway through the cooking time and working in batches. Enjoy!
Per Serving: Calories 258; Fat 12.4g; Sodium 79mg; Carbs 34.3g; Fiber 1g; Sugar 17g; Protein 3.2g

Golden Beet Chips

Prep time: 10 minutes | Cook time: 35 minutes | Servings: 2

½ pound golden beets, peeled and thinly sliced
Kosher salt and black pepper, to taste

1 teaspoon paprika
2 tablespoons olive oil
½ teaspoon garlic powder
1 teaspoon ground turmeric

1. Select the "Air Fry" Mode, press level 3, set its temperature to 330°F/165°C and set the time to 30 minutes. Press Start/Pause to initiate preheating. 2. Toss the beets with the remaining recipe ingredients and place them in the air fryer cooking basket. 3. Air fry your chips for 30 minutes, shaking the basket occasionally and working in batches. 4. Enjoy!
Per Serving: Calories 175; Fat 13.1g; Sodium 154mg; Carbs 14g; Fiber 0.8g; Sugar 8.9g; Protein 0.7g

Snack Granola Mix

Prep time: 10 minutes | Cook time: 30 minutes | Servings: 10

½ cup honey
3 tablespoons butter, melted
1 teaspoon salt
2 cups sesame sticks
2 cups pepitas [pumpkin seeds]

2 cups granola
1 cup cashews
2 cups crispy corn puff cereal
2 cup mini pretzel crisps

1. In a suitable bowl, mix the honey, butter, and salt. 2. In another bowl, mix the sesame sticks, pepitas, granola, cashews, corn puff cereal, and pretzel crisps. 3. Mix the contents of the two bowls. 4. Cook on Air Fry mode, pre-heat your air fryer to 370°F/185°C. Select Level "3" and set the time on your Ninja Foodi Smart XL Pro Air Fryer Oven to 10 minutes. Press Start/Pause to begin preheating. Continue to the next step when it is done preheating. 5. Put the prepared mixture in the fryer basket and air-fry for 10 - 12 minutes to toast the snack mixture, shaking the basket frequently. You will have to do this in two batches. 6. Place the snack mix on a cookie sheet and allow it to cool fully.
Per Serving: Calories 134; Fat 11 g; Sodium 14 mg; Carbs 8.7g; Fiber 4.2g; Sugar 4.5g; Protein 2.2 g

Cheese and Parsley Stuffed Mushrooms

Prep time: 10 minutes | Cook time: 10 minutes | Servings: 4

2 tablespoons olive oil
½ cup breadcrumbs
½ cup parmesan cheese, grated
1 teaspoon garlic, minced
1 tablespoon fresh parsley, chopped

1 tablespoon fresh chives, chopped
Black pepper and salt, to taste
1-pound button mushrooms, stems removed

1. In a mixing bowl, thoroughly mix the olive oil, breadcrumbs, parmesan cheese, garlic, parsley, chives, salt, and black pepper. 2. Divide the filling between your mushrooms. Spread the mushrooms in its air fryer basket. 3. Cook on Air Fry mode and select level 3, cook your mushrooms at 400°F/200°C for about 7 minutes, shaking the basket halfway through the cooking time. Bon appétit!
Per Serving: Calories 273; Fat 24 g; Sodium 1181 mg; Carbs 12.8g; Fiber 1g; Sugar 1.4g; Protein 20g

Feta Cheese Triangles

Prep time: 10 minutes | Cook time: 5 minutes | Servings: 5

1 egg yolk, beaten
4 ounces Feta cheese
2 tablespoons Flat-leafed parsley, finely chopped
1 scallion, finely chopped

2 sheets of frozen filo pastry, defrosted
2 tablespoons olive oil black pepper to taste

1. In a suitable bowl, mix the beaten egg yolk with the feta, parsley and scallion. Sprinkle on some pepper to taste. 2. Slice each sheet of filo dough into three strips. 3. Place a teaspoonful of the feta mixture on each strip of pastry. 4. Pinch the tip of the pastry and fold it up to enclose the filling and create a triangle. Continue folding the strip in zig-zags until the filling is wrapped in a triangle. Repeat with all of the strips of pastry. 5. Cook on Air Fry mode, pre-heat the air fryer to 390°F/200°C. Select Level "3" and set the time on your Ninja Foodi Smart XL Pro Air Fryer Oven to 10 minutes. Press Start/Pause to begin preheating. Continue to the next step when it is done preheating. 6. Coat the pastry with a light coating of oil and spread in the cooking basket. 7. Place the basket in its air fryer basket. Insert its air fryer basket into the level 3 of the oven and close the door. Cook for 3 minutes. 8. Lower the heat to 360°F/180°C and cook for a further 2 minutes until a golden color is achieved
Per Serving: Calories 164; Fat 16.9 g; Sodium 99 mg; Carbs 3.2g; Fiber 0.8g; Sugar 0.2g; Protein 2.3g

Naan Dippers

Prep time: 10 minutes | Cook time: 50 minutes | Servings: 10

4 naan bread, cut into 2-inch strips
3 tablespoons Butter, melted
12 ounces Light cream cheese, softened
1 cup plain yogurt
2 teaspoons curry powder
2 cups cooked chicken, shredded

4 scallions, minced
⅓ cup golden raisins
6 ounces Monterey jack cheese, grated [about 2 cups]
¼ cup fresh cilantro, chopped
Black pepper and salt
½ cup major grey's chutney

1. Select Air Fry mode, preheat air fryer to 400°F/200°C. Select Level "3" and set the time on your Ninja Foodi Smart XL Pro Air Fryer Oven to 5 minutes. Press Start/Pause to begin preheating. Continue to the next step when it is done preheating. 2. Slice up the naan in thirds lengthwise before cutting crosswise into 2-inch strips. In a suitable bowl, toss the strips with the melted butter. 3. Move the naan strips to air fryer basket. Air fry for 5 minutes, shaking the basket halfway through. You will have to do this in two batches. 4. Mix the softened cream cheese and yogurt with a hand mixer or in a food processor. Add in the curry powder and mix evenly. 5. Fold in the shredded chicken, scallions, golden raisins, Monterey jack cheese and chopped cilantro. 6. sprinkle with black pepper and salt as desired. 7. Pour the prepared mixture into a 1-quart baking dish and spread out evenly. Air-fry at 300°F/150°C for 25 minutes. 8. Put a dollop of major grey's chutney in the center of the dip and scatter the scallions on top. 9. Serve the naan dippers with the hot dip.
Per Serving: Calories 216; Fat 6.9 g; Sodium 31 mg; Carbs 38.5g; Fiber 5.6g; Sugar 6.7g; Protein 6.7g

Hot Dog Roll

Prep time: 10 minutes | Cook time: 10 minutes | Servings: 6

6 ounces crescent rolls, refrigerated

1 tablespoon mustard
10 ounces mini hot dogs

1. Separate the prepared dough into triangles. Cut them lengthwise into 3 small triangles. Spread each triangle with mustard. 2. Place a mini hot dog on the shortest side of each triangle and roll it up. 3. Place the rolls in the air fryer cooking basket. 4. Cook on Bake mode and select level 3, bake the rolls at 320°F/160°C for about 8 minutes, turning them over halfway through the cooking time. Bon appétit!
Per Serving: Calories 199; Fat 17.9g; Sodium 525mg; Carbs 1.1g; Fiber 0.3g; Sugar 0.6g; Protein 9.9g

Cheese Apple Pie Rolls

Prep time: 10 minutes | Cook time: 15 minutes | Servings: 4

6 ounces refrigerated crescent rolls
1 apple, peeled, cored, and grated

6 ounces cream cheese, crumbled
¼ cup brown sugar
1 teaspoon apple pie spice

1. Separate the prepared dough into rectangles. Mix the remaining recipe ingredients until well mixed. 2. Spread each rectangle with the cheese mixture; roll them up tightly. Place the rolls in the air fryer cooking basket. 3. Cook on Bake mode and select level 3, bake the rolls at 320°F/160°C for about 5 minutes. Turn them over and bake for a further 5 minutes. Bon appétit!
Per Serving: Calories 202; Fat 15.9g; Sodium 720 mg; Carbs 3.9g; Fiber 1.3g; Sugar 1.6g; Protein 12.4g

Kale Crisps

Prep time: 10 minutes | Cook time: 10 minutes | Servings: 4

5 cups kale leaves, torn into pieces, stems removed
1 tablespoon olive oil

1 teaspoon chili powder
Black pepper and salt, to taste
2 garlic cloves, minced

1. Select the "Air Fry" Mode, press level 3, set its temperature to 360°F/180°C and set the time to 8 minutes. Press Start/Pause to initiate preheating. 2. Toss the kale leaves with the remaining recipe ingredients and place them in the air fryer cooking basket. 3. Air fry the kale crisps for 8 minutes, shaking the basket occasionally and working in batches. 4. Enjoy!
Per Serving: Calories 315; Fat 28.6 g; Sodium 1020 mg; Carbs 3.1g; Fiber 0.6g; Sugar 1.7g; Protein 11.7g

Garlicky Kale Chips

Prep time: 10 minutes | Cook time: 10 minutes | Servings: 4

4 cups kale, torn into pieces
1 tablespoon sesame oil

1 teaspoon garlic powder
Black pepper and salt, to taste

1. Select the "Air Fry" Mode, press level 3, and set its temperature to 360°F/180°C Press Start/Pause to initiate preheating. 2. Toss the kale leaves with the remaining recipe ingredients and place them in the air fryer cooking basket. 3. Air fry your chips for 8 minutes, shaking the basket occasionally and working in batches. 4. Enjoy!
Per Serving: Calories 157; Fat 10.1 g; Sodium 423 mg; Carbs 1.6g; Fiber 0.5g; Sugar 0.4g; Protein 14.9g

Bacon-Wrapped Sausages

Prep time: 10 minutes | Cook time: 20 minutes | Servings: 4

1-pound mini sausages
2 tablespoons tamari sauce
2 tablespoons maple syrup

1 teaspoon chili powder
Black pepper, to taste
4 ounces bacon, thinly slices

1. Toss the mini sausages with the tamari sauce, maple syrup, chili powder, and black pepper. 2. Wrap the mini sausages with the bacon. 3. Place the sausages in a lightly oiled air fryer cooking basket. 4. Select the "Air Fry" Mode, press level 3, cook the sausages at 380°F/195°C for 15 minutes, tossing the basket halfway through the cooking time. 5. Serve warm and enjoy!
Per Serving: Calories 343; Fat 13.1 g; Sodium 1333 mg; Carbs 5.7g; Fiber 0.1g; Sugar 0.2g; Protein 43.6g

Herbed Beet Chips

Prep time: 10 minutes | Cook time: 35 minutes | Servings: 4

1 pound red and yellow beets, peeled and sliced	1 teaspoon dried rosemary
1 tablespoon olive oil	1 teaspoon dried parsley flakes
Black pepper and salt, to taste	1 teaspoon garlic
	2 tablespoons scallions, chopped

1. Select the "Air Fry" Mode, press level 3, set its temperature to 330°F/165°C and set the time to 30 minutes. Press Start/Pause to initiate preheating. 2. Toss the beets with the remaining recipe ingredients and place them in the air fryer cooking basket. 3. Air fry your chips for 30 minutes, shaking the basket occasionally and working in batches. 4. Enjoy!
Per Serving: Calories 96; Fat 5.8 g; Sodium 65 mg; Carbs 5.6g; Fiber 0.3g; Sugar 1.7g; Protein 36.4g

Sweet Onion Rings

Prep time: 10 minutes | Cook time: 10 minutes | Servings: 4

½ cup beer	Black pepper and salt, to taste
1 cup plain flour	2 eggs, whisked
1 teaspoon baking powder	1 cup tortilla chips, crushed
1 teaspoon cayenne pepper	2 sweet onions

1. Select the "Air Fry" Mode, press level 3, set its temperature to 380°F/195°C and set the time to 8 minutes. Press Start/Pause to initiate preheating. 2. In a shallow bowl, mix the beer, flour, baking powder, cayenne pepper, salt, and black pepper. 3. Whisk the egg in another shallow bowl. 4. Then place the crushed tortilla chips in a separate bowl. 5. Dip the onion rings in the flour mixture, then in the eggs, then in the tortilla chips. Place the onion rings in its air fryer basket. 6. Cook the onion rings for about 8 minutes until golden and cooked through. Bon appétit!
Per Serving: Calories 341; Fat 26.8 g; Sodium 525 mg; Carbs 9.8g; Fiber 0.4g; Sugar 1.1g; Protein 15.4g

Tortilla Chips

Prep time: 10 minutes | Cook time: 10 minutes | Servings: 4

4 corn tortillas, cut into wedges	1 teaspoon chili powder
1 tablespoon olive oil	1 teaspoon ground cumin
1 tablespoon Mexican oregano	Salt, to taste
2 tablespoons lime juice	

1. Toss the tortilla wedges with the remaining recipe ingredients. 2. Select the "Air Fry" Mode, press level 3, cook your tortilla chips at 360°F/180°C for about 5 minutes until crispy, working in batches. 3. Enjoy!
Per Serving: Calories 161; Fat 7.9 g; Sodium 595 mg; Carbs 10.8g; Fiber 1.7g; Sugar 0.5g; Protein 13.2g

Cajun Butter Snack

Prep time: 10 minutes | Cook time: 10 minutes | Servings: 5

2 tablespoons Cajun or creole seasoning	4 cups plain popcorn
½ cup butter, melted	1 teaspoon paprika
2 cups peanut	1 teaspoon garlic
2 cups mini wheat thin crackers	½ teaspoon thyme
2 cups mini pretzels	½ teaspoon oregano
2 teaspoons salt	1 teaspoon black pepper
1 teaspoon cayenne pepper	½ teaspoon onion powder

1. Select Air Fry mode, pre-heat the air fryer to 370°F/185°C. Select Level "3" and set the time on your Ninja Foodi Smart XL Pro Air Fryer Oven to 10 minutes. Press Start/Pause to begin preheating. Continue to the next step when it is done preheating. 2. In a bowl, mix the Cajun, melted butter and the remaining seasonings. 3. In a separate bowl, stir the peanuts, crackers, popcorn and pretzels. Coat the snacks with the butter mixture. 4. Place in the fryer and fry for 8 - 10 minutes, shaking the basket frequently during the cooking time. You will have to complete this step in two batches. 5. Put the snack mix on a cookie sheet and leave to cool. 6. The snacks can be kept in an airtight container for up to one week.
Per Serving: Calories 206; Fat 6.4 g; Sodium 911 mg; Carbs 28.9g; Fiber 3.6g; Sugar 20.4g; Protein 11g

Cheese and Bacon Stuffed Poblano Peppers

Prep time: 10 minutes | Cook time: 10 minutes | Servings: 4

8 poblano peppers, seeded and halved	4 ounces gruyere cheese
	4 ounces bacon, chopped

1. Stuff the poblano peppers with the cheese and bacon; transfer them to a lightly oiled air fryer basket. 2. Air fry the peppers on Air Fry mode on level 3 at 370°F/185°C or about 7 minutes until golden. Bon appétit!
Per Serving: Calories 220; Fat 13.5 g; Sodium 1395 mg; Carbs 6.9g; Fiber 1.7g; Sugar 3.8g; Protein 19.7g

Paprika Carrot Slices

Prep time: 10 minutes | Cook time: 20 minutes | Servings: 4

1 pound carrots, cut into slices	½ teaspoon dried oregano
2 tablespoons coconut oil	½ teaspoon dried parsley flakes
1 teaspoon paprika	Black pepper and salt, to taste
½ teaspoon garlic powder	

1. Toss the carrots with the remaining recipe ingredients; then, spread the carrots in the air fryer cooking basket. 2. Cook the carrots at Air Fry mode on level 3 at 380°F/195°C for 15 minutes, shaking the basket halfway through the cooking time. Bon appétit!
Per Serving: Calories 122; Fat 7.5 g; Sodium 465 mg; Carbs 9g; Fiber 3.8g; Sugar 2.8g; Protein 7.4g

Potato Wedges

Prep time: 10 minutes | Cook time: 40 minutes | Servings: 4

1 pound potatoes, cut into wedges	1 teaspoon paprika
2 tablespoons olive oil	1 teaspoon dried parsley flakes
Black pepper and salt, to taste	1 teaspoon Greek seasoning mix

1. Select the "Air Fry" Mode, press level 3, set its temperature to 400°F/200°C and set the time to 35 minutes. Press Start/Pause to initiate preheating. 2. Toss the potatoes with the remaining recipe ingredients and place them in the air fryer cooking basket. 3. Air fry the potato wedges for 35 minutes, shaking the basket halfway through the cooking time. 4. Enjoy!
Per Serving: Calories 179; Fat 7.5 g; Sodium 242 mg; Carbs 16g; Fiber 0.6g; Sugar 6.8g; Protein 10.6g

Air Fried Spare Ribs

Prep time: 10 minutes | Cook time: 40 minutes | Servings: 4

2 pounds spare ribs	¼ cup sesame oil
¼ cup soy sauce	2 garlic cloves, minced
¼ cup rice vinegar	

1. Toss all the recipe ingredients in a lightly greased air fryer cooking basket. 2. Cook the ribs on Air Fry mode on level 3 at 350°F/175°C for 35 minutes, turning them over halfway through the cooking time. Bon appétit!
Per Serving: Calories 445; Fat 27.5 g; Sodium 215 mg; Carbs 0.9g; Fiber 0.1g; Sugar 0.8g; Protein 46g

Parmesan Zucchini Fries

Prep time: 10 minutes | Cook time: 15 minutes | Servings: 4

1-pound zucchini, cut into sticks	2 tablespoons olive oil
½ cup parmesan cheese	1 teaspoon hot paprika
½ cup almond flour	Black pepper and salt, to taste
1 egg, whisked	

1. Select the "Air Fry" Mode, press level 3, set its temperature to 390°F/200°C and set the time to 10 minutes. Press Start/Pause to initiate preheating. 2. Toss the zucchini sticks with the remaining recipe ingredients and spread them in a single layer in the air fryer cooking basket. 3. Cook the zucchini sticks on Air Fry mode on level 3 for about 10 minutes at 390°F/200°C, shaking the basket halfway through the cooking time. Work in batches. Bon appétit!
Per Serving: Calories 451; Fat 8.4 g; Sodium 134 mg; Carbs 59.6g; Fiber 8.2g; Sugar 4.8g; Protein 32.9g

Cheese Cauliflower Bites

Prep time: 10 minutes | Cook time: 15 minutes | Servings: 4

1-pound cauliflower, grated
½ cup cheddar cheese, shredded
1-ounce butter, room temperature

Black pepper and salt, to taste
½ cup tortilla chips, crushed
2 eggs whisked

1. Thoroughly mix all the recipe ingredients in a mixing bowl. Shape the prepared mixture into bite-sized balls. 2. Cook on Air Fry mode and select level 3, cook the cauliflower balls at 350°F/175°C for about 13 minutes, turning them over halfway through the cooking time. Bon appétit!
Per Serving: Calories 241; Fat 16.8 g; Sodium 225 mg; Carbs 8g; Fiber 0.4g; Sugar 1.1g; Protein 15.4g

Pancetta-Wrapped Shrimp

Prep time: 10 minutes | Cook time: 10 minutes | Servings: 4

12 shrimp, peeled and deveined
3 slices pancetta, cut into strips

2 tablespoons maple syrup
1 tablespoon Dijon mustard

1. Wrap the shrimp in the pancetta strips and toss them with the maple syrup and mustard. 2. Place the shrimp in a lightly greased air fryer cooking basket. 3. Cook on Air Fry mode and select level 3, cook the shrimp at 400°F/200°C for 6 minutes, tossing the basket halfway through the cooking time. Bon appétit!
Per Serving: Calories 199; Fat 17.9g; Sodium 525mg; Carbs 1.1g; Fiber 0.3g; Sugar 0.6g; Protein 9.9g

Korean-Style Chicken Drumettes

Prep time: 10 minutes | Cook time: 20 minutes | Servings: 4

1-pound chicken drumettes
4 tablespoons soy sauce
¼ cup rice vinegar
4 tablespoons honey
2 tablespoons sesame oil

1 teaspoon gochutgaru, Korean chili powder
2 tablespoons scallions, chopped
2 garlic cloves, minced

1. Toss the chicken drumettes with the remaining recipe ingredients. 2. Cook the chicken drumettes on Air Fry mode on level 3 at 380°F/195°C for 18 minutes, turning them over halfway through the cooking time. Bon appétit!
Per Serving: Calories 208; Fat 10.5 g; Sodium 1755 mg; Carbs 26.9g; Fiber 4.1g; Sugar 2.5g; Protein 2.9g

Spicy Red Beet Chips

Prep time: 10 minutes | Cook time: 35 minutes | Servings: 4

1 pound red beets, peeled and cut into 1/8-inch slices
1 tablespoon olive oil

1 teaspoon cayenne pepper
Black pepper and salt, to taste

1. Select the "Air Fry" Mode, press level 3, set its temperature to 330°F/165°C and set the time to 30 minutes. Press Start/Pause to initiate preheating. 2. Toss the beets with the remaining recipe ingredients and place them in the air fryer cooking basket. 3. Air fry your chips for 30 minutes, shaking the basket occasionally and working in batches. 4. Enjoy!
Per Serving: Calories 281; Fat 15.5 g; Sodium 262 mg; Carbs 27.5g; Fiber 2.2g; Sugar 5g; Protein 8.5g

Ginger Chicken Wings

Prep time: 10 minutes | Cook time: 20 minutes | Servings: 4

2 pounds chicken wings
¼ cup honey
2 tablespoons fish sauce
2 garlic cloves, crushed

1 teaspoon ginger, peeled and grated
2 tablespoons butter, melted
Black pepper and salt, to taste

1. Toss the chicken wings with the remaining recipe ingredients. 2. Cook the chicken wings on Air Fry mode on level 3 at 380°F/195°C for 18 minutes, turning them over halfway through the cooking time. Bon appétit!
Per Serving: Calories 281; Fat 15.5 g; Sodium 262 mg; Carbs 27.5g; Fiber 2.2g; Sugar 5g; Protein 8.5g

Easy Corn Tortilla Chips

Prep time: 10 minutes | Cook time: 5 minutes | Servings: 2

8 corn tortillas
Salt to taste

1 tablespoon olive oil

1. Pre-heat your air fryer to 390°F/200°C. Cook on Air Fry mode and select Level "2" and set the time on your Ninja Foodi Smart XL Pro Air Fryer Oven to 3 minutes. Press Start/Pause to begin preheating. Continue to the next step when it is done preheating. 2. Slice the corn tortillas into triangles. Coat with a light brushing of olive oil. 3. Put the tortilla pieces in the wire basket and air fry for 3 minutes. You may need to do this in multiple batches. 4. Season with salt before serving.
Per Serving: Calories 149; Fat 12 g; Sodium 132 mg; Carbs 10.5g; Fiber 2.6g; Sugar 4.6g; Protein 1.5g

Sausage Onion Meatballs

Prep time: 10 minutes | Cook time: 15 minutes | Servings: 6

2 pounds Sausage meat
½ onion
½ teaspoon Garlic puree
1 teaspoon Sage

3 tablespoons bread crumbs
Pinch of salt
Black pepper

1. Mix all of the ingredients in a large bowl. 2. Take equal portions of the mixture, mold them into medium sized balls and put them in the air fryer. 3. Cook on "Air Fry" Mode, select level 3, and set its temperature to 355°F/180°C for 15 minutes. Serve.
Per Serving: Calories 170; Fat 13.1 g; Sodium 6 mg; Carbs 14.8 g; Fiber 2.5g; Sugar 9g; Protein 1.9g

Oats Poppers

Prep time: 10 minutes | Cook time: 8 minutes | Servings: 50 treats

½ cup unsweetened applesauce
1 cup peanut butter
2 cups oats

1 cup flour
1 teaspoon Baking powder

1. Mix the applesauce and peanut butter in a bowl to create a smooth consistency. 2. Pour in the oats, flour and baking powder. Continue mixing to form a soft dough. 3. Shape a half-teaspoon of dough into a ball and continue with the rest of the prepared dough. 4. Cook on Air Fry mode, pre-heat the air fryer to 350°F/175°C. Select Level "3" and set the time on your Ninja Foodi Smart XL Pro Air Fryer Oven to 8 minutes. Press Start/Pause to begin preheating. Continue to the next step when it is done preheating. 5. Grease the bottom of the basket with oil. 6. Place the poppers in the fryer and cook for 8 minutes, flipping the balls at the halfway point. You may need to cook the poppers in batches. 7. Let the poppers cool and serve immediately or keep in an airtight container for up to 2 weeks.
Per Serving: Calories 278; Fat 13 g; Sodium 15 mg; Carbs 38.5g; Fiber 4.2g; Sugar 2.4g; Protein 4.8g

Spicy Chicken Cheese Balls

Prep time: 10 minutes | Cook time: 16 minutes | Servings: 8

8 ounces cream cheese, softened
2 cups grated pepper jack cheese
1 Jalapeño pepper, diced
2 scallions, minced
1 teaspoon paprika
2 teaspoons salt, divided

3 cups shredded cooked chicken
¼ cup all-purpose flour
2 eggs, lightly beaten
1 cup panko breadcrumbs
olive oil, in a spray bottle
salsa

1. Beat the cream cheese and add the pepper jack cheese, Jalapeño pepper, scallions, paprika and salt. Fold in the shredded chicken and combine well. Roll this mixture into 1-inch balls. 2. Place the flour into a shallow dish. Place the eggs into another shallow dish. Finally, combine the panko breadcrumbs and salt in a third dish. 3. Coat the chicken cheese balls with flour first, then dip them into the eggs and finally roll them in the panko breadcrumbs to coat all sides. Refrigerate for at least 30 minutes. 4. Select Level 3. Select the "AIR FRY" function of Ninja Foodi Smart XL Pro Air Oven, set temperature to 400°F/200°C and time to 8 minutes. Select START/STOP to begin preheating. 5. Spray the chicken cheese balls with oil and air-fry in batches for 8 minutes. Shake the basket a few times throughout the cooking process to help the balls brown evenly. 6. Serve hot with salsa on the side.
Per Serving: Calories 310; Fat 20g; Sodium 614mg; Carbs 6g; Fiber 0g; Sugar 1g; Protein 25g

Spicy Cashew

Prep time: 10 minutes | Cook time: 20 minutes | Servings: 3

½ pound cashew nuts	1 teaspoon red chili powder
½ teaspoon garam masala powder	½ teaspoon black pepper
1 teaspoon coriander powder	2 teaspoons dry mango powder
1 teaspoon ghee	1 teaspoon salt

1. Put all the recipe ingredients in a suitable bowl and toss well. 2. Spread the cashew nuts in the basket of your air fryer. 3. Cook on "Air Fry" Mode, select level 3, and set its temperature to 250°F/120°C for 15 minutes until the nuts are brown and crispy. 4. let the nuts cool before serving or transferring to an airtight container to be stored for up to 2 weeks.
Per Serving: Calories 178; Fat 14.6 g; Sodium 67 mg; Carbs 12.4g; Fiber 4.8 g; Sugar 6.1g; Protein 2.9 g

Bacon Shrimp

Prep time: 10 minutes | Cook time: 7 minutes | Servings: 4

1 ¼ pound Tiger shrimp, peeled and deveined [16 pieces]	1-pound Bacon, thinly sliced, room temperature [16 slices]

1. Wrap each bacon slice around a piece of shrimp, from the head to the tail. Refrigerate for 20 minutes. 2. Cook on Air Fir mode, pre-heat the air fryer to 390°F/200°C. Select Level "3" and set the time on your Ninja Foodi Smart XL Pro Air Fryer Oven to 7 minutes. Press Start/Pause to begin preheating. Continue to the next step when it is done preheating. 3. Place the shrimp in the fryer's basket. Insert its air fryer basket into the level 3 of the oven and close the door. Cook for 5 – 7 minutes. 4. Allow to dry on a paper towel before serving.
Per Serving: Calories 187; Fat 10.9 g; Sodium 2512 mg; Carbs 12g; Fiber 1.7 g; Sugar 4.9g; Protein 13.7g

Avocado Egg Rolls

Prep time: 10 minutes | Cook time: 5 minutes | Servings: 5

10 egg roll wrappers	1 tomato, diced
3 avocados, peeled and pitted	Black pepper and salt, to taste

1. Select Air Fry mode, pre-heat your air fryer to 350°F/175°C. Select Level "3" and set the time on your Ninja Foodi Smart XL Pro Air Fryer Oven to 5 minutes. Press Start/Pause to begin preheating. Continue to the next step when it is done preheating. 2. Put the tomato and avocados in a bowl. Sprinkle on some black pepper and salt and mash with a fork until a smooth consistency is achieved. 3. Spoon equal amounts of the prepared mixture onto the wrappers. Roll the wrappers around the filling, enclosing them entirely. 4. Transfer the rolls to a lined baking dish and cook for 5 minutes.
Per Serving: Calories 169; Fat 7.1 g; Sodium 42 mg; Carbs 28.5g; Fiber 2.1g; Sugar 13.4g; Protein 1.2g

Fried Cheesy Ravioli with Marinara Sauce

Prep time: 7 minutes | Cook time: 14 minutes | Servings: 4 to 6

1-pound cheese ravioli, fresh or frozen	½ teaspoon dried oregano
	½ teaspoon salt
2 eggs, lightly beaten	grated Parmesan cheese
1 cup plain breadcrumbs	chopped fresh parsley
½ teaspoon paprika	1 to 2 cups marinara sauce

1. Boil the salted water. Boil the ravioli and then drain. Let the cooked ravioli cool to a temperature where you can comfortably handle them. 2. Place the eggs into one dish. Combine the breadcrumbs, paprika, dried oregano and salt in the other dish. 3. Select Level 3. Select the "AIR FRY" function of Ninja Foodi Smart XL Pro Air Oven, set temperature to 380°F/195°C and time to 5 minutes. Select START/STOP to begin preheating. 4. Working with one at a time, dip the cooked ravioli into the egg, coating all sides. Then press the ravioli into the breadcrumbs, making sure that all sides are covered. Transfer the ravioli to the air fryer basket, cooking in batches, one layer at a time. Air-fry F for 7 minutes. 5. While the ravioli is air-frying, bring the marinara sauce to a simmer on the stovetop. Transfer to a small bowl. 6. Sprinkle a little Parmesan cheese and chopped parsley on top of the fried ravioli and serve warm with the marinara sauce on the side for dipping.
Per Serving: Calories 60; Fat 1g; Sodium 154mg; Carbs 9g; Fiber 1g; Sugar 3g; Protein 3g

Saucy Meatballs

Prep time: 10 minutes | Cook time: 15 minutes | Servings: 4

1 small onion, chopped	thyme leaves
¾ pound ground beef	1 egg
1 tablespoon chopped fresh parsley	3 tablespoons bread crumbs
	Pepper and salt to taste
½ tablespoon chopped fresh	10 ounces tomato sauce

1. Put all the recipe ingredients in a bowl and mix well. 2. Use your hands to mold the prepared mixture into 10 - 12 balls. 3. Select Air Fry mode, pre-heat the air fryer to 390°F/200°C. Select Level "3" and set the time on your Ninja Foodi Smart XL Pro Air Fryer Oven to 8 minutes. Press Start/Pause to begin preheating. Continue to the next step when it is done preheating. 4. Put the meatballs in its air fryer basket and place the basket in the air fryer. Cook the meatballs for 8 minutes. 5. Put the meatballs in an oven dish, pour in the tomato sauce and set the dish in the basket of the air fryer. 6. Reduce the temperature to 330°F/165°C and warm the meatballs for 5 minutes.
Per Serving: Calories 343; Fat 13.1 g; Sodium 1333 mg; Carbs 5.7g; Fiber 0.1g; Sugar 0.2g; Protein 43.6g

Breaded Crab Croquettes

Prep time: 10 minutes | Cook time: 15 minutes | Servings: 6

For the Filling

1-pound lump crab meat	¼ teaspoon tarragon, chopped
2 egg whites, beaten	¼ teaspoon chives, chopped
1 tablespoon olive oil	½ teaspoon parsley, chopped
¼ cup red onion, chopped	½ teaspoon cayenne pepper
¼ red bell pepper, chopped	¼ cup mayonnaise
2 tablespoons celery, chopped	¼ cup sour cream

For the Breading

3 eggs, beaten	1 teaspoon olive oil
1 cup flour	½ teaspoon salt
1 cup friendly bread crumbs	

1. Sauté the olive oil, onions, peppers, and celery over a medium heat, allowing to sweat until the vegetables turn translucent. This should take about 4 – 5 minutes. 2. Take off the heat and allow to cool. 3. In a food processor, pulse the bread crumbs, olive oil and salt to form a fine crumb. 4. Place the eggs, panko mixture and flour in three separate bowls. 5. Mix the crabmeat, egg whites, mayonnaise, sour cream, spices and vegetables in a large bowl. 6. Select Air Fry mode, pre-heat the air fryer to 390°F/200°C. Select Level "3" and set the time on your Ninja Foodi Smart XL Pro Air Fryer Oven to 10 minutes. Press Start/Pause to begin preheating. Continue to the next step when it is done preheating. 7. Take equal amounts of the crab mixture and shape into golf balls. Coat the balls in the flour, before dipping them in the eggs and finally in the panko, making sure the bread crumbs stick well. 8. Put croquettes in the fryer basket in a single layer and well-spaced. 9. Cook the croquettes for 8 – 10 minutes until a golden color is achieved.
Per Serving: Calories 379; Fat 20.9 g; Sodium 1598 mg; Carbs 10g; Fiber 2.2g; Sugar 2.1g; Protein 37g

Ricotta Eggs Balls

Prep time: 10 minutes | Cook time: 25 minutes | Servings: 2 – 4

2 cups ricotta, grated	¼ teaspoon salt to taste
2 eggs, separated	¼ teaspoon pepper powder to taste
2 tablespoons chives, finely chopped	
	1 teaspoon orange zest, grated
2 tablespoons fresh basil, finely chopped	For coating
	¼ cup friendly bread crumbs
4 tablespoons flour	1 tablespoon vegetable oil

1. Cook on Air Fry mode, pre-heat your air fryer at 390°F/200°C. Select Level "3" and set the time on your Ninja Foodi Smart XL Pro Air Fryer Oven to 8 minutes. Press Start/Pause to begin preheating. Continue to the next step when it is done preheating. 2. In a suitable bowl, mix the yolks, flour, salt, pepper, chives and orange zest. Throw in the ricotta and incorporate with your hands. 3.Mold equal amounts of the prepared mixture into balls. 4. Mix the oil with the bread crumbs until a crumbly consistency is achieved. 5. Coat the prepared balls in the bread crumbs and transfer each one to the fryer's basket. 6. Put the basket in the fryer. Air fry for 8 minutes until a golden color is achieved. 7. Serve with a sauce of your choosing, such as ketchup.
Per Serving: Calories 363; Fat 17.1 g; Sodium1065 mg; Carbs 19.8g; Fiber 3.4g; Sugar 12.9g; Protein 33.7g

Air Fried Pumpkin Seeds

Prep time: 10 minutes | Cook time: 55 minutes | Servings: 1 ½ cups

1 ½ cups pumpkin seeds from a large whole pumpkin
Olive oil
1½ teaspoons salt
1 teaspoon Smoked paprika

1. Boil two quarts of well-salted water in a pot. Cook the pumpkin seeds in the boiling water for 10 minutes. 2. Dump the content of the pot into a sieve and dry the seeds on paper towels for at least 20 minutes. 3. Select Air Fry mode, pre-heat the air fryer to 350°F/175°C. Select Level "3" and set the time on your Ninja Foodi Smart XL Pro Air Fryer Oven to 35 minutes. Press Start/Pause to begin preheating. Continue to the next step when it is done preheating. 4. Cover the seeds with olive oil, salt and smoked paprika, before placing them in its air fryer basket. 5. Air fry for 35 minutes. Give the basket a good shake several times throughout the cooking process to ensure the pumpkin seeds are crispy and lightly browned. 6. Let the seeds cool before serving. Alternatively, you can keep them in an air-tight container or bag for snacking or for use as a yogurt topping.
Per Serving: Calories 183; Fat 0.4 g; Sodium 4347 mg; Carbs 5.6g; Fiber 0.6g; Sugar 8.4g; Protein 40.2g

Sweet and Salty Snack

Prep time: 10 minutes | Cook time: 20 minutes | Servings: 10

1 teaspoon salt
2 cups sesame sticks
½ cup honey
3 tablespoons butter, melted
1 cup pepitas
2 cups granola
1 cup cashews
2 cups crispy corn puff cereal
2 cups mini pretzel crisps
1 cup dried cherries

1. Combine the honey, butter and salt in a small bowl or measuring cup and stir until combined. 2. Mix the sesame sticks, pepitas, granola, cashews, corn puff cereal and pretzel crisps in a large bowl. Pour the honey mixture and toss to combine. 3. Select the "AIR FRY" function of Ninja Foodi Smart XL Pro Air Oven, set temperature to 370°F/185°C and time to 10 minutes. Select START/STOP to begin preheating. 4. Place half the mixture in the air fryer basket. Slide basket into rails of Level 3 and air-fry for 10 to 12 minutes, or until the snack mix is lightly toasted. 5. Toss the basket several times throughout the process so that the mixture cooks evenly and doesn't get too dark on top. 6. Transfer the snack mix to a cookie sheet and let it cool completely. Mix in the dried cherries and store the mix in an airtight container for up to a week or two.
Per Serving: Calories 270; Fat 12g; Sodium 633mg; Carbs 35g; Fiber 3g; Sugar 15g; Protein 6g

No-Corn Cheesy Hot Dogs

Prep time: 10 minutes | Cook time: 10 minutes | Servings: 4

1¾ cups shredded mozzarella cheese (about 7 ounces)
2 tablespoons unsalted butter
1 large egg
For Serving:
Prepared yellow mustard
No-sugar or reduced-sugar
¾ cup blanched almond flour
⅛ teaspoon fine sea salt
4 hot dogs

ketchup

1. Make the dough: Place the mozzarella cheese and butter in a large bowl and microwave for 2 minutes, until the cheese melted. Stir well. Add the egg and, using a hand mixer, combine well. Add the almond flour and salt and combine well with the mixer. 2. Lay a piece of parchment paper on the countertop, spray it with avocado oil, and place the dough on it. Knead for about 3 minutes. The dough should be thick yet pliable. 3. Spray the air fryer basket with avocado oil. Select Level 3. Select the "AIR FRY" function of Ninja Foodi Smart XL Pro Air Oven, set temperature to 390°F/200°C and time to 5 minutes. Select START/STOP to begin preheating. 4. Separate the dough into 4 equal portions. Pat each portion out with your hands to form a small oval, about 6 inches long and 2 inches wide. 5. Place one hot dog in each oval and form the dough around each hot dog using your hands. Place the dogs in the air fryer basket, leaving space between them, and cook for 8 minutes, or until golden brown, flipping halfway through. Drizzle with yellow mustard and serve with ketchup on the side, if desired. 6. Store leftovers in an airtight container in the refrigerator for up to 3 days.
Per Serving: Calories 354; Fat 7.9g; Sodium 704mg; Carbs 6g; Fiber 3.6g; Sugar 6g; Protein 18g

Garlic and Bread-Stuffed Mushrooms

Prep time: 10 minutes | Cook time: 10 minutes | Servings: 4

16 small button mushrooms
Stufffng
1 ½ slices bread
1 garlic clove, crushed
1 tablespoon flat-leafed parsley,
chopped
black pepper to taste
1½ tablespoons olive oil

1. Select Air Fry mode, pre-heat the air fryer to 390°F/200°C. Select Level "3" and set the time on your Ninja Foodi Smart XL Pro Air Fryer Oven to 10 minutes. Press Start/Pause to begin preheating. Continue to the next step when it is done preheating. 2. Blend the bread slices, garlic, parsley and pepper until a fine crumb is formed. 3. Mix in the olive oil. remove the mushroom stalks and spoon even amounts of the filling into the caps. Press the crumbs in well to make sure none fall out 4. Put the mushroom caps in the cooking basket and place it in the air fryer. 5. Cook the mushrooms for 7 – 8 minutes until they turn golden and crispy.
Per Serving: Calories 319; Fat 14.7 g; Sodium 92 mg; Carbs 30.3g; Fiber 4g; Sugar 12.3g; Protein 24g

Garlicky Eggplant Chips

Prep time: 10 minutes | Cook time: 45 minutes | Servings: 4

2 eggplants, peeled and sliced
Salt
½ cup tapioca starch
¼ cup canola oil
½ cup water
1 teaspoon garlic powder
½ teaspoon dried dill weed
½ teaspoon black pepper, to taste

1. Season the eggplant slices with salt and leave for half an hour. 2. Run them under cold water to rinse off any excess salt. 3. In a suitable bowl, coat the eggplant slices with all of the other ingredients. 4. Cook on "Air Fry" Mode, select level 3, and set its temperature to 390°F/200°C for 13 minutes. 5. Serve with the dipping sauce of your choice.
Per Serving: Calories 157; Fat 10.1 g; Sodium 423 mg; Carbs 1.6g; Fiber 0.5g; Sugar 0.4g; Protein 14.9g

Quinoa Meatballs

Prep time: 10 minutes | Cook time: 20 minutes | Servings: 6

½ pound ground pork
½ pound ground beef
1 cup quinoa, cooked
1 egg, beaten
2 scallions, finely chopped
½ teaspoon onion powder
1½ tablespoons Dijon mustard
¾ cup ketchup
1 teaspoon ancho chili powder
1 tablespoon sesame oil
2 tablespoons tamari sauce
¼ cup balsamic vinegar
2 tablespoons sugar

1. In a suitable bowl, stir all the recipe ingredients and mix well. 2. Use your hands to shape equal amounts of the prepared mixture into small meatballs. 3. Place the meatballs in its air fryer basket. Insert its air fryer basket into the level 3 of the oven and close the door. 4. Cook on "Air Fry" Mode, select level 3, and set its temperature to 370°F/185°C for 10 minutes. Give the basket a good shake and allow to cook for another 5 minutes.
Per Serving: Calories 380; Fat 7.7g; Sodium 403 mg; Carbs 7.6g; Fiber 0.1g; Sugar 5.4g; Protein 65.7g

Queso Fundido

Prep time: 10 minutes | Cook time: 25 minutes | Servings: 4

½ cup half and half
1 cup diced tomatoes
1 cup chopped onions
1 tablespoon minced garlic
2 diced jalapenos
2 teaspoons ground cumin
2 cups shredded mozzarella cheese
4 ounces' chorizo with the casings removed

1. Mix the cumin, jalapenos, garlic, onion, tomatoes and chorizo together. 2. Transfer the prepared mixture into the fryer basket. Cook on Air Fry mode. Insert its air fryer basket into the level 3 of the oven and close the door. air fry for 15 minutes at 400°F/200°C. 3. Add in the half and half, cheese and stir together. 4. Serve and enjoy as desired.
Per Serving: Calories 416; Fat 8.3 g; Sodium 208 mg; Carbs 22.9g; Fiber 0.5g; Sugar 19g; Protein 60.6g

Air Fried Blooming Onion

Prep time: 10 minutes | Cook time: 40 minutes | Servings: 4

4 medium/small onions
1 tablespoon olive oil

4 dollops of butter

1. Peel the onion. Cut off the top and bottom. 2. To make it bloom, cut as deeply as possible without slicing through it completely. 4 cuts (i.e. 8 segments) should do it. 3. Place the onions in a suitable bowl of salted water and allow to absorb for 4 hours to help eliminate the sharp taste and induce the blooming process. 4. Cook on Air Fry mode, pre-heat your air fryer to 355°F/180°C. Select Level "3" and set the time on your Ninja Foodi Smart XL Pro Air Fryer Oven to 30 minutes. Press Start/Pause to begin preheating. Continue to the next step when it is done preheating. 5. Transfer the onions to the air fryer. Pour over a light drizzle of olive oil and place a dollop of butter on top of each onion. 6. Cook for 30 minutes. Remove the outer layer before serving if it is too brown.
Per Serving: Calories 283; Fat 6.6g; Sodium 693mg; Carbs 8.5g; Fiber 1.4g; Sugar 3.4g; Protein 45.2g

Crunchy Cinnamon Nuts

Prep time: 10 minutes | Cook time: 40 minutes | Servings: 3 cups

1 egg white, beaten
¼ cup sugar
1 teaspoon Salt
½ teaspoon ground cinnamon
¼ teaspoon ground cloves

¼ teaspoon ground allspice
Pinch ground cayenne pepper
1 cup pecan halves
1 cup cashews
1 teaspoon vegetable oil

1. In a suitable bowl, mix the egg white with the sugar and spices. 2. Select Air Fry mode, pre-heat the air fryer to 300°F/150°C. Select Level "3" and set the time on your Ninja Foodi Smart XL Pro Air Fryer Oven to 25 minutes. Press Start/Pause to begin preheating. Continue to the next step when it is done preheating. 3. Coat the inside of the fryer's basket with vegetable oil. 4. Cover the nuts with the spiced egg white. Place half of them in the fryer. 5. Air fry for 25 minutes, giving the nuts a few good stirs throughout the cooking time, until they are crunchy and toasted. 6. Repeat with the other half of the nuts. 7. Serve immediately or store in an airtight container for up to two weeks.
Per Serving: Calories 297; Fat 18.4 g; Sodium 1151 mg; Carbs 11.6g; Fiber 0.6g; Sugar 10.9g; Protein 20.5g

Spicy Shrimp Bites

Prep time: 10 minutes | Cook time: 45 minutes | Servings: 10

1¼ pounds shrimp, peeled and deveined
1 teaspoon paprika
½ teaspoon black pepper
½ teaspoon red pepper flakes, crushed

1 tablespoon salt
1 teaspoon chili powder
1 tablespoon shallot powder
¼ teaspoon cumin powder
1¼ pounds thin bacon slices

1. Coat the shrimps with all of the seasonings. 2. Wrap a slice of bacon around each shrimp, and hold it in place with a toothpick. Refrigerate for half an hour. 3. Transfer to the air fryer and cook on Air Fry mode, select level 3, at 360°F/180°C for 7 - 8 minutes.
Per Serving: Calories 384; Fat 20.5g; Sodium 449 mg; Carbs 5.1g; Fiber 2.1g; Sugar 0.7g; Protein 45g

Tangy Olives Dip

Prep time: 5 minutes | Cook time: 5 minutes | Servings: 6

1 cup black olives, pitted and chopped
¼ cup capers
½ cup olive oil
3 tablespoons lemon juice

2 garlic cloves, minced
2 teaspoon apple cider vinegar
1 cup parsley leaves
1 cup basil leaves
A pinch of salt and black pepper

1. Select Level 3. Select the "AIR FRY" function of Ninja Foodi Smart XL Pro Air Oven, set temperature to 350°F/175°C and time to 5 minutes. Select START/STOP to begin preheating. 2. In a blender, blend all ingredients and transfer to a ramekin. Place the ramekin in your air fryer's basket and cook for 5 minutes. 3. Serve as a snack.
Per Serving: Calories 120; Fat 5g; Sodium 147mg; Carbs 3g; Fiber 2g; Sugar 1g; Protein 7g

Ranch Cashew Bowls

Prep time: 5 minutes | Cook time: 5 minutes | Servings: 4

4 oz. cashew
1 teaspoon ranch seasoning

1 teaspoon sesame oil

1. Select Level 3. Select the "AIR FRY" function of Ninja Foodi Smart XL Pro Air Oven, set temperature to 375°F/190°C and time to 5 minutes. Select START/STOP to begin preheating. 2. Mix up cashew with ranch seasoning and sesame oil and put in the air fryer. 3. Cook the cashew for 4 minutes. Then shake well and cook for 1 minute more.
Per Serving: Calories 6; Fat 117g; Sodium 213mg; Carbs 6.2g; Fiber 0.5g; Sugar 1g; Protein 2.9g

Broccoli Balls

Prep time: 10 minutes | Cook time: 20 minutes | Servings: 6

2 eggs, well whisked
2 cups Colby cheese, shredded
1 cup flour
Seasoned salt, to taste
¼ teaspoon Black pepper, or more

if preferred
1 head broccoli, chopped into florets
1 cup crushed saltines

1. Mix the eggs, cheese, flour, salt, pepper, and broccoli until a dough-like paste is formed. 2. Refrigerate for 1 hour. Divide the prepared mixture evenly and mold each portion into small balls. Coat the balls in the crushed saltines and spritz them all over with cooking spray. 3. Cook on "Air Fry" Mode, select level 3, and set its temperature to 360°F/180°C for 10 minutes. At this point, you should check how far along in the cooking process they are and allow to cook for a further 8-10 minutes as needed. 4. Serve with the dipping sauce of your choice.
Per Serving: Calories 322; Fat 14 g; Sodium 679 mg; Carbs 1.1g; Fiber 0.2g; Sugar 0.7g; Protein 45.5g

Cheese Jalapeno Poppers

Prep time: 10 minutes | Cook time: 7 minutes | Servings: 5

1 diced onion
1 minced garlic clove
4 ounces goat cheese
5 medium jalapenos

Salt, to taste
Powdered chili
Crushed red pepper
A handful of cilantro

1. Deseed the jalapenos then half each one of them. 2. Mix the onion, garlic, cilantro, red pepper, chili, salt and goat cheese. 3. Spoon the prepared cheese mixture into the halved jalapenos and spread in the fryer basket. 4. Cook on Air Fry mode. Insert the basket in the level 3 of the Ninja Foodi Smart XL Pro Oven. Air fry for 7 minutes at 350°F/175°C. 5. Serve and enjoy as desired.
Per Serving: Calories 327; Fat 14.2g; Sodium 672mg; Carbs 47.2g; Fiber 1.7g; Sugar 24.8g; Protein 4.4g

Lemony Ricotta with Capers

Prep time: 5 minutes | Cook time: 10 minutes | Servings: 4 to6

1½ cups ricotta cheese
zest of 1 lemon,
1 teaspoon chopped rosemary
pinch red pepper flakes
2 tablespoons capers, rinsed
2 tablespoons extra-virgin olive

oil
Salt and freshly ground black pepper
1 tablespoon grated Parmesan cheese

1. Select Level 3. Select the "AIR FRY" function of Ninja Foodi Smart XL Pro Air Oven, set temperature to 390°F/200°C and time to 10 minutes. Select START/STOP to begin preheating. 2. Combine the cheese with lemon zest, rosemary, red pepper flakes, capers, olive oil, salt and pepper and whisk together well. 3. Transfer the cheese mixture to a 7-inch pie dish and place the pie dish in the air fryer basket. Air-fry the ricotta for 8 to 10 minutes, or until the top is nicely browned in spots. 4. Remove the pie dish from the air fryer and immediately sprinkle the Parmesan cheese on top. 5. Drizzle with a bit of olive oil and add some freshly ground black pepper and lemon zest as garnish. 6. Serve warm with pita breads or crostini.
Per Serving: Calories 150; Fat 13g; Sodium 398mg; Carbs 2g; Fiber 0g; Sugar 0g; Protein 7g

Classic Cocktail Franks

Prep time: 10 minutes | Cook time: 45 minutes | Servings: 4

1x 12-ounces package cocktail franks

1x 8-ounces can crescent rolls

1. Drain the cocktail franks and dry with paper towels. 2. Unroll the crescent rolls and slice the prepared dough into rectangular strips, roughly 1" by 5". 3. Wrap the franks in the strips with the ends poking out. Leave in the freezer for 5 minutes. 4. Select Air Fry mode, pre-heat the air fryer to 330°F/165°C. Select Level "3" and set the time on your Ninja Foodi Smart XL Pro Air Fryer Oven to 10 minutes. Press Start/Pause to begin preheating. Continue to the next step when it is done preheating. 5. Take the franks out of the freezer and place them in the cooking basket. Cook for 6 – 8 minutes. 6. Reduce the heat to 390°F/200°C and cook for another 3 minutes until a golden-brown color is achieved.
Per Serving: Calories 210; Fat 5.4 g; Sodium 110 mg; Carbs 18.5g; Fiber 2.4g; Sugar 13.1g; Protein 23.5g

BBQ Meatballs

Prep time: 10 minutes | Cook time: 15 minutes | Servings: 5

¼ cup shredded cheddar cheese	1-pound ground beef
½ cup BBQ sauce	1 teaspoon steak seasoning
½ cup almond meal	1 teaspoon Worcestershire sauce
½ cup diced onions	2 minced garlic cloves
1 large egg	Salt & pepper, to taste

1. Using a suitable mixing bowl, then add in the Worcestershire sauce, cheddar cheese, egg, onions, almond meal, garlic, seasonings, ground beef and mix until molded into. 2. Scoop the prepared batter into bits and mold out 10 even meatballs then spread on a parchment paper. 3. Transfer the meatballs loaded parchment paper into the fryer basket. Cook on Air Fry mode. Insert its air fryer basket into the level 3 of the oven and close the door. air fry at 365°F/185°C for 8 minutes. 4. Flip the meatballs over then air fry for an extra 7 minutes. 5. Serve hot and enjoy drizzled with the sauce.
Per Serving: Calories 351; Fat 20.3 g; Sodium 298 mg; Carbs 40.9g; Fiber 0.5g; Sugar 35.5g; Protein3.6g

Sweet Potato Fries

Prep time: 10 minutes | Cook time: 20 minutes | Servings: 2 to 3

1 large sweet potato (about 1 pound)	¼ cup light mayonnaise
1 teaspoon vegetable or canola oil	1 tablespoon spicy brown mustard
salt	1 tablespoon sweet Thai chili sauce
Sweet & Spicy Dipping Sauce:	½ teaspoon sriracha sauce

1. Scrub the sweet potato well and cut it into ¼-inch French fries. (A mandolin slicer can really help with this.)2. Select Level 3. Select the "AIR FRY" function of Ninja Foodi Smart XL Pro Air Oven, set temperature to 250°F/125°C and time to 10 minutes. Select START/STOP to begin preheating. 3. Toss the sweet potato sticks with the oil and transfer them to the air fryer basket. Air-fry for 10 minutes, shaking the basket several times during the cooking process for even cooking. 4. Toss the fries with salt, increase the air fryer temperature to 400°F/200°C and air-fry for another 10 minutes, shaking the basket several times during the cooking process. 5. For dipping, mix all the ingredients in a bowl and stir until combined. 6. Serve the sweet potato fries warm with the dipping sauce on the side.
Per Serving: Calories 130; Fat 1g; Sodium 336mg; Carbs 28g; Fiber 4g; Sugar 9g; Protein 3g

Parmesan Eggplant Fries

Prep time: 5 minutes | Cook time: 18 minutes | Servings: 6

½ cup all-purpose flour	1 large eggplant
Salt and freshly ground black pepper	8 ounces mozzarella cheese
	Olive oil, in a spray bottle
2 eggs, beaten	Grated Parmesan cheese
1 cup seasoned breadcrumbs	1 (14-ounce) jar marinara sauce

1. Place the flour in a shallow dish and spice with salt and freshly ground black pepper. Put the eggs in the second shallow dish. Place the breadcrumbs in the third shallow dish. 2. Peel the eggplant and then slice it vertically into long ½-inch thick slices. Slice the mozzarella cheese into ½-inch thick slices and make a mozzarella sandwich, using the eggplant as the bread. Slice the eggplant-mozzarella sandwiches into rectangular strips about 1-inch by 3½-inches. 3. Coat the eggplant strips carefully, holding the sandwich together with your fingers. Dredge with flour first, then dip them into the eggs, and finally place them into the breadcrumbs. Pat the crumbs onto the eggplant strips and then coat them in the egg and breadcrumbs one more time, pressing gently with your hands so the crumbs stick evenly. 4. Select Level 3. Select the "AIR FRY" function of Ninja Foodi Smart XL Pro Air Oven, set temperature to 400°F/200°C and time to 9 minutes. Select START/STOP to begin preheating. 5. Spray the eggplant fries on all sides with olive oil, and transfer one layer at a time to the air-fryer basket. Air-fry in batches for 9 minutes, turning and rotating halfway through the cooking time. Spray the eggplant strips with additional oil when you turn them over. 6. While the fries are cooking, gently warm the marinara sauce on the stovetop in a small saucepan. 7. Serve eggplant fries fresh out of the air fryer with a little Parmesan cheese grated on top and the warmed marinara sauce on the side.
Per Serving: Calories 210; Fat 11g; Sodium 268mg; Carbs 16g; Fiber 4g; Sugar 7g; Protein 12g

Easy Ranch Roasted Chickpeas

Prep time: 4 minutes | Cook time: 10 minutes | Servings: 4

1 (15-ounce) can chickpeas, drained and rinsed	mix
	1 teaspoon salt
1 tablespoon olive oil	2 tablespoons freshly squeezed
3 tablespoons ranch seasoning	lemon juice

1. Grease the air fryer basket with olive oil. 2. Using paper towels, pat the chickpeas dry. 3. In a bowl, add the chickpeas, oil, seasoning mix, salt, and lemon juice. 4. Put the chickpeas in the air fryer basket and spread them out in a single layer. Install the wire rack on Level 3. Select the "AIR ROAST" function of Ninja Foodi Smart XL Pro Air Oven, set temperature to 350°F/175°C and time to 4 minutes. Select START/STOP to begin preheating. 5. Set the timer and roast for 4 minutes. Remove the drawer and shake vigorously to redistribute the chickpeas so they cook evenly. Reset the timer and roast for 6 minutes more. 6. When the time is up, release the air fryer basket from the drawer and pour the chickpeas into a bowl. Season with additional salt, if desired. Enjoy!
Per Serving: Calories 144; Fat 5g; Sodium 891mg; Carbs 19g; Fiber 5g; Sugar 3g; Protein 6g

Homemade Roasted Mixed Nuts

Prep time: 5 minutes | Cook time: 20 minutes | Servings: 6

2 cups mixed nuts (walnuts, pecans, and/or almonds)	1 teaspoon ground cinnamon
	2 tablespoons sugar
2 tablespoons egg white	1 teaspoon paprika

1. Install the wire rack on Level 3. Select the "AIR ROAST" function of Ninja Foodi Smart XL Pro Air Oven, set temperature to 300°F/150°C and time to 10 minutes. Select START/STOP to begin preheating. Spray the air fryer basket with olive oil. 2. In a mixing bowl, mix the nuts, egg white, cinnamon, sugar, and paprika, until the nuts are thoroughly coated. 3. Place the nuts in the greased air fryer basket; set the timer and roast for 10 minutes. 4. Pour the nuts into a bowl, and serve.
Per Serving: Calories 232; Fat 21g; Sodium 6mg; Carbs 10g; Fiber 3g; Sugar 5g; Protein 6g

Crispy Pickles Chips

Prep time: 10 minutes | Cook time: 10 minutes | Servings: 4

1 cup pickles, sliced	1 teaspoon dried cilantro
2 eggs, beaten	¼ cup Provolone cheese, grated
½ cup coconut flakes	

1. Mix up coconut flakes, dried cilantro, and Provolone cheese. Then dip the sliced pickles in the egg and coat in coconut flakes mixture. 2. Select Level 3. Select the "AIR FRY" function of Ninja Foodi Smart XL Pro Air Oven, set temperature to 400°F/200°C and time to 5 minutes. Select START/STOP to begin preheating. 3. Arrange the pickles in the air fryer in one layer and cook them for 5 minutes. 4. Then flip the pickles on another side and cook for another 5 minutes.
Per Serving: Calories 100; Fat 7.8g; Sodium 111mg; Carbs 2.8g; Fiber 1.4g; Sugar 1.2g; Protein 5.4g

Tomato and Basil Bruschetta

Prep time: 5 minutes | Cook time: 3 minutes | Servings: 6

4 tomatoes, diced
⅓ cup fresh basil, shredded
¼ cup shredded Parmesan cheese
1 tablespoon minced garlic
1 tablespoon balsamic vinegar
1 teaspoon olive oil
1 teaspoon salt
1 teaspoon freshly ground black pepper
1 loaf French bread

1. In a bowl, add the tomatoes and basil. 2. Mix in the Parmesan cheese, garlic, vinegar, olive oil, salt, and pepper. 3. Let the tomato mixture sit and marinate, while you prepare the bread. 4. Select Level 3. Select the "AIR FRY" function of Ninja Foodi Smart XL Pro Air Oven, set temperature to 250°F/125°C and time to 3 minutes. Select START/STOP to begin preheating. Grease the air fryer basket with olive oil. 5. Cut the bread into 1-inch-thick slices. 6. Place the slices in the greased air fryer basket in a single layer. 7. Spray the top of the bread with olive oil. 8. Set the temperature to 250°F/125°C. Set the timer and coo for 3 minutes. 9. Using tongs, remove the bread slices from the air fryer and place a spoonful of the bruschetta topping on each piece.
Per Serving: Calories 258; Fat 3g; Sodium 826mg; Carbs 47g; Fiber 3g; Sugar 4g; Protein 11g

Seasoned Sausage Rolls

Prep time: 5 minutes | Cook time: 5 minutes | Servings: 6

For the Seasoning:
2 tablespoons sesame seeds
1½ teaspoons poppy seeds
1½ teaspoons dried minced onion
1 teaspoon salt
1 teaspoon dried minced garlic
For the Sausages:
1 (8-ounce) package crescent roll dough
1 (12-ounce) package mini smoked sausages (cocktail franks)

1. To Make the Seasoning: In a bowl, combine the sesame seeds, poppy seeds, onion, salt, and garlic and set aside. 2.To Make the Sausages: Select Level 3. Select the "AIR FRY" function of Ninja Foodi Smart XL Pro Air Oven, set temperature to 330°F/165°C and time to 5 minutes. Select START/STOP to begin preheating. 3. Grease the air fryer basket with olive oil. Remove the crescent dough from the package and lay it out on a cutting board. 4. Separate the dough at the perforations. With sharp knife, cut each triangle of dough into fourths. 5. Drain the sausages and pat them dry with a paper towel. 6. Roll each sausage in a piece of dough. 7. Sprinkle seasoning on top of each roll. Place the seasoned sausage rolls into the greased air fryer basket in a single layer. 8. Air fry it for 5 minutes.
Per Serving: Calories 344; Fat 26g; Sodium 1145mg; Carbs 17g; Fiber 1g; Sugar 3g; Protein 10g

Mozzarella Sticks with Marinara Sauce

Prep time: 10 minutes | Cook time: 8 minutes | Servings: 6

1 (12-count) package mozzarella sticks
1 (8-ounce) package crescent roll dough
3 tablespoons unsalted butter, melted
¼ cup panko bread crumbs
Marinara sauce, for dipping

1. Grease the air fryer basket with olive oil. 2. Cut each cheese stick into thirds. 3. Unroll the crescent roll dough. With sharp knife, cut the dough into 36 even pieces. 4. Wrap each small cheese stick in a piece of dough. Make sure that the dough is wrapped tightly around the cheese. Close the dough by pinching them together at both ends, and pinch along the seam to ensure that the dough is completely sealed. 5. Using tongs, dip the wrapped cheese sticks in the melted butter, then dip the cheese sticks in the panko bread crumbs. 6. Place the cheese sticks in the greased air fryer basket in a single layer. (You may have to cook the cheese sticks in more than one batch.)7. Install the wire rack on Level 3. Select the "BAKE" function of Ninja Foodi Smart XL Pro Air Oven, set temperature to 370°F/185°C and time to 5 minutes. Select START/STOP to begin preheating. Set the timer and bake for 5 minutes. After 5 minutes, the tops should be golden brown. 8. Using tongs, flip the cheese sticks and bake for another 3 minutes, or until golden brown on all sides. 9. Plate, serve with the marinara sauce and enjoy!
Per Serving: Calories 348; Fat 23g; Sodium 811mg; Carbs 21g; Fiber 1g; Sugar 3g; Protein 17g

Air Fried Pita Chips

Prep time: 5 minutes | Cook time: 6 minutes | Servings: 4

2 pieces whole wheat pita bread
3 tablespoons olive oil
1 teaspoon freshly squeezed lemon juice
1 teaspoon salt
1 teaspoon dried basil
1 teaspoon garlic powder

1. Grease the air fryer basket with olive oil. 2. Use a pair of kitchen shears or a pizza cutter, cut the pita bread into small wedges. 3. Place the wedges in a small mixing bowl and add the olive oil, lemon juice, salt, dried basil, and garlic powder. 4. Mix well, coating each wedge. 5. Place the seasoned pita wedges in the greased air fryer basket in a single layer, being careful not to overcrowd them. (You may have to bake the pita chips in more than one batch.) 6. Install the wire rack on Level 3. Select the "BAKE" function of Ninja Foodi Smart XL Pro Air Oven, set temperature to 350°F/175°C and time to 6 minutes. Select START/STOP to begin preheating. 7. Set the timer and bake for 6 minutes. Every 2 minutes or so, remove the drawer and shake the pita chips so they redistribute in the basket for even cooking. 8. Serve with your choice of dip or alone as a tasty snack.
Per Serving: Calories 178; Fat 11g; Sodium 752mg; Carbs 18g; Fiber 3g; Sugar 1g; Protein 3g

Ham 'n' Cheese Pies

Prep time: 10 minutes | Cook time: 12 minutes | Servings: 1

Dough:
1¾ cups shredded mozzarella cheese (about 7 ounces)
2 tablespoons unsalted butter
Filling:
8 thin slices ham
4 slices provolone or cheddar cheese
1 large egg
¾ cup blanched almond flour
⅛ teaspoon fine sea salt
¼ cup mayonnaise
Prepared yellow mustard, for serving

1. Make the dough: Place the mozzarella cheese and butter in a large bowl and microwave for 2 minutes, until the cheese is entirely melted. Stir well. Add in the egg and combine well. Add the almond flour and salt and combine well with the mixer. 2. Lay a piece of parchment paper on the countertop, spray it with avocado oil, and place the dough on it. Knead for about 3 minutes. The dough should be thick yet pliable. 3. Spray the air fryer basket with avocado oil. Select Level 3. Select the "AIR FRY" function of Ninja Foodi Smart XL Pro Air Oven, set temperature to 350°F/175°C and time to 10 minutes. Select START/STOP to begin preheating. 4. Separate the dough into 4 equal portions. Pat each portion out with your hands to form a small circle, about 4 inches in diameter. 5. Place 2 slices of ham and one slice of cheese in the center of each dough circle and smear a tablespoon of mayo on top. Seal each pie closed by folding the dough circle in half and crimping the edges with your fingers. 6. Transfer the pies to the air fryer basket, leaving space between them. Cook for 10 minutes, or until golden brown. Drizzle with mustard before serving, if desired. 7. Store leftovers in an airtight container in the refrigerator for up to 3 days.
Per Serving: Calories 354; Fat 7.9g; Sodium 704mg; Carbs 6g; Fiber 3.6g; Sugar 6g; Protein 18g

Air Fryer Stuffed Button Mushrooms

Prep time: 5 minutes | Cook time: 10 minutes | Servings: 4

12 medium button mushrooms
½ cup bread crumbs
1 teaspoon salt
½ teaspoon freshly ground black pepper
5 to 6 tablespoons olive oil

1. Spray the air fryer basket with olive oil. 2. Separate the cap from the stem of each mushroom. Discard the stems. 3. In a mixing bowl, mix the bread crumbs, salt, pepper, and olive oil until you have a wet mixture. 4. Rub the mushrooms with olive oil on all sides. 5. Using a spoon, fill each mushroom with the bread crumb stuffing. 6. Place the mushrooms in the greased air fryer basket in a single layer. 7. Install the wire rack on Level 3. Select the "BAKE" function of Ninja Foodi Smart XL Pro Air Oven, set temperature to 360°F/180°C and time to 10 minutes. Select START/STOP to begin preheating. Set the timer and bake for 10 minutes. 8. Using tongs, remove the mushrooms from the air fryer, place them on a platter, and serve.
Per Serving: Calories 216; Fat 18g; Sodium 683mg; Carbs 12g; Fiber 1g; Sugar 2g; Protein 4g

Healthy Hot Dog Buns

Prep time: 10 minutes | Cook time: 25 minutes | Servings: 1

1½ cups blanched almond flour
¼ cup plus 1 tablespoon psyllium husk powder
2 teaspoons baking powder
1 teaspoon fine sea salt
2½ tablespoons apple cider vinegar
3 large egg whites
1 cup boiling water

1. Spray a 7-inch pie pan or a casserole dish that will fit inside your air fryer with avocado oil. Select Level 3. Select the "AIR FRY" function of Ninja Foodi Smart XL Pro Air Oven, set temperature to 325°F/160°C and time to 25 minutes. Select START/STOP to begin preheating. 2. In a medium-sized bowl, mix together the flour, psyllium husk powder, baking powder, and salt until well combined. Add the vinegar and egg whites and stir until a thick dough forms. Add the boiling water and mix until well combined. Let sit for 1 to 2 minutes, until the dough firms up. 3. Divide the dough into 8 equal-sized balls. Form each ball into a hot dog shape that's about 1-inch wide and 3½ inches long. Place the buns in the greased pie pan, spacing them about 1 inch apart. 4. Place the buns in the air fryer and cook for 15 minutes, then flip the buns over. Cook for another 5 to 10 minutes, until the buns are puffed up and cooked through and a toothpick inserts in the center of a bun comes out clean. 5. Store leftovers in an airtight container in the fridge for up to 5 days or in the freezer for up to a month.
Per Serving: Calories 354; Fat 7.9g; Sodium 704mg; Carbs 6g; Fiber 3.6g; Sugar 6g; Protein 18g

Crispy Ham 'n' Cheese Ravioli

Prep time: 15 minutes | Cook time: 10 minutes | Servings: 6

1 cup shredded cheddar cheese (about 4 ounces)
6 ounces cream cheese (¾ cup), softened
8 ounces thinly sliced ham (12 very large slices)
1 large egg
1 cup pork dust (see here)
Fresh parsley leaves, for garnish
Ranch Dressing (here), for serving

1. In a small bowl, stir together the cheddar cheese and cream cheese until well combined. 2. Assemble the ravioli: Lay one slice of ham on a sheet of parchment paper. Spoon about 2 heaping tablespoons of the filling into the center of the ham. Fold one end of the ham over the filling, making sure the ham completely covers the filling and meets the ham on the other side Fold the ends around the filling to make a square, making sure that the filling is covered well. 3. Using your fingers, press down around the filling to even the ravioli out into a square shape. Repeat with the rest of the ham and filling; you should have 12 raviolis. 4. Crack the egg into a shallow bowl and beat well with a fork. Place the pork dust in another shallow bowl. 5. Gently dip each ravioli into the egg, then dredge it in the pork dust. Use your hands to press the pork dust into the ravioli, coating it well. 6. Spray the ravioli with avocado oil and place it in the air fryer basket. Make sure to leave space between the ravioli. 7. Select Level 3. Select the "AIR FRY" function of Ninja Foodi Smart XL Pro Air Oven, set temperature to 400°F/200°C and time to 10 minutes. Select START/STOP to begin preheating. 8. Cook the ravioli in the air fryer for 10 minutes, or until crispy, flipping after 6 minutes. 9. Serve warm, garnished with fresh parsley and with ranch dressing for dipping if desired. 10. Store leftovers in an airtight container in the fridge for up to 4 days.
Per Serving: Calories 354; Fat 7.9g; Sodium 704mg; Carbs 6g; Fiber 3.6g; Sugar 6g; Protein 18g

Crispy Carrot Chips

Prep time: 5 minutes | Cook time: 6 to 8 minutes | Servings: 6

1 pound carrots, peeled and sliced ⅛ inch thick
2 tablespoons olive oil
1 teaspoon sea salt

1. In a bowl, combine the carrots, olive oil, and salt. Toss them together until the carrot slices are thoroughly coated with oil. 2. Place the carrot chips in the air fryer basket in a single layer. (You may have to bake the carrot chips in more than one batch.) 3. Install the wire rack on Level 3. Select the "BAKE" function of Ninja Foodi Smart XL Pro Air Oven, set temperature to 360°F/180°C and time to 3 minutes. Select START/STOP to begin preheating. Set the timer and bake for 3 minutes. 4. Remove the air fryer drawer and shake to redistribute the chips for even cooking. Reset the timer and bake for 3 minutes more. 5. Check the carrot chips for doneness. If you like them extra crispy, give the basket another shake and cook them for another 1 to 2 minutes. 6. When the chips are done, release the air fryer basket from the drawer, pour the chips into a bowl, and serve.
Per Serving: Calories 71; Fat 5g; Sodium 364mg; Carbs 7g; Fiber 2g; Sugar 4g; Protein 1g

Easy Potato Chips

Prep time: 5 minutes | Cook time: 15 to 20 minutes | Servings: 4

4 yellow potatoes
1 tablespoon olive oil
1 tablespoon salt (plus more for topping)

1. Using a mandoline or sharp knife, slice the potatoes into ⅛-inch-thick slices. 2. In a medium mixing bowl, toss the potato slices with the olive oil and salt until the potatoes are thoroughly coated with oil. 3. Place the potatoes in the air fryer basket in a single layer. (You may have to fry the potato chips in more than one batch.) 4. Select Level 3. Select the "AIR FRY" function of Ninja Foodi Smart XL Pro Air Oven, set temperature to 375°F/190°C and time to 15 minutes. Select START/STOP to begin preheating. Set the timer and fry for 15 minutes. 5. Shake the basket several times during cooking, so the chips crisp evenly and don't burn. 6. Check to see if they are fork-tender; if not, add another 5 to 10 minutes, checking frequently. They will crisp up after they are removed from the air fryer. 7. Season with additional salt, if desired.
Per Serving: Calories 177; Fat 4g; Sodium 1757mg; Carbs 34g; Fiber 5g; Sugar 3g; Protein 4g

Japanese BLT Sushi

Prep time: 15 minutes | Cook time: 8 minutes | Servings: 4

8 slices thin-cut bacon
¼ cup mayonnaise
1½ cups shredded lettuce
1 cup diced tomatoes

1. Select Level 3. Select the "AIR FRY" function of Ninja Foodi Smart XL Pro Air Oven, set temperature to 400°F/200°C and time to 8 minutes. Select START/STOP to begin preheating. 2. Remove the air fryer basket from the air fryer and place the bacon in it. Weave the bacon slices together in a square, 4 slices per side, threading each slice over and under the others. Make sure the grid is tight; if there are gaps, the mayo will leak through. 3. Return the air fryer basket to the air fryer and cook the bacon for 8 minutes, or until slightly crisp yet still flexible. 4. Place the bacon square on a cutting board crispy side down. Spread the mayo over the bacon. Place the shredded lettuce and tomatoes on the mayo. Roll the bacon square up tightly. Slice into 4 thick rolls and serve. 5. Best served fresh. Store leftovers in an airtight container in the fridge for up to 4 days.
Per Serving: Calories 354; Fat 7.9g; Sodium 704mg; Carbs 6g; Fiber 3.6g; Sugar 6g; Protein 18g

Crispy Parmesan Fried Dill Pickles

Prep time: 5 minutes | Cook time: 8 minutes | Servings: 4

1 (16-ounce) jar sliced dill pickles
⅔ cup panko bread crumbs
⅓ cup grated Parmesan cheese
¼ teaspoon dried dill
2 large eggs

1. Line a platter with a double thickness of paper towels. Spread the pickles out in a single layer on the paper towels. Let the pickles drain on the towels for 20 minutes. After 20 minutes have passed, pat the pickles again with a clean paper towel to get them as dry as possible before breading. 2. Select Level 3. Select the "AIR FRY" function of Ninja Foodi Smart XL Pro Air Oven, set temperature to 390°F/200°C and time to 4 minutes. Select START/STOP to begin preheating. Grease the air fryer basket with olive oil. 3. In a mixing bowl, combine the panko bread crumbs, Parmesan cheese, and dried dill. Mix well. 4. In a bowl, Whisk the eggs until frothy. 5. Dip each pickle into the egg mixture, then into the bread crumb mixture. Make sure the pickle is fully coated in breading. 6. Place the breaded pickle slices in the greased air fryer basket in a single layer. 7. Spray the pickles with a generous amount of olive oil. 8. Set the timer and fry for 4 minutes. 9. Open the air fryer drawer and use tongs to flip the pickles. Spray them again with olive oil. Reset the timer and fry for another 4 minutes. 10. Using tongs, remove the pickles from the drawer. Plate, serve, and enjoy!
Per Serving: Calories 153; Fat 6g; Sodium 1634mg; Carbs 16g; Fiber 2g; Sugar 3g; Protein 9g

Cheese and Bacon Stuffed Potato Skins

Prep time: 10 minutes | Cook time: 12 minutes | Servings: 4

4 medium russet potatoes, baked	4 slices cooked bacon, chopped
Olive oil	Finely chopped scallions, for
Salt	topping
Freshly ground black pepper	Sour cream, for topping
2 cups shredded Cheddar cheese	Finely chopped olives, for topping

1. Spray the air fryer basket with oil. 2. Cut each baked potato in half. 3. Using a large spoon, scoop out the center of each potato half, leaving about 1 inch of the potato flesh around the edges and the bottom. 4. Rub olive oil over the inside of each baked potato half and season with salt and pepper, then place the potato skins in the greased air fryer basket. 5. Select Level 3. Select the "AIR FRY" function of Ninja Foodi Smart XL Pro Air Oven, set temperature to 400°F/200°C and time to 10 minutes. Select START/STOP to begin preheating. Set the timer and fry for 10 minutes. 6. After 10 minutes, remove the potato skins and fill them with the shredded Cheddar cheese and bacon, then bake in the air fryer for another 2 minutes, just until the cheese is melted. 7. Garnish the potato skins with the scallions, sour cream, and olives.
Per Serving: Calories 487; Fat 31g; Sodium 986mg; Carbs 29g; Fiber 5g; Sugar 1g; Protein 24g

Spicy Potato Wedges

Prep time: 5 minutes | Cook time: 20 to 25 minutes | Servings: 4

4 russet potatoes	1 teaspoon paprika
2 teaspoons salt, divided	1 to 3 tablespoons olive oil,
1 teaspoon freshly ground black pepper	divided

1. Cut the potatoes into ½-inch-thick wedges. Try to make the wedges uniform in size, so they cook at an even rate. 2. In a mixing bowl, Spice the potato wedges with 1 teaspoon of salt, pepper, paprika, and 1 tablespoon of olive oil. Toss until potatoes are coated with oil. Add additional oil, if needed. 3. Place the potato wedges in the air fryer basket in a single layer. (You may have to roast them in batches.)4. Select Level 3. Select the "AIR FRY" function of Ninja Foodi Smart XL Pro Air Oven, set temperature to 400°F/200°C and time to 5 minutes. Select START/STOP to begin preheating. Set the timer and cook for 5 minutes. 5. After 5 minutes, remove the air fryer drawer and shake the potatoes to keep them from sticking. Reset the timer and roast the potatoes for another 5 minutes, then shake again. Repeat this process until the potatoes have cooked for a total of 20 minutes. 6. Check and see if the potatoes are cooked. If they are not fork-tender, roast for 5 minutes more. 7. Using tongs, remove the potato wedges from the air fryer basket and transfer them to a bowl. Toss with the remaining salt.
Per Serving: Calories 210; Fat 7g; Sodium 1176mg; Carbs 34g; Fiber 6g; Sugar 3g; Protein 4g

Scallions and Spinach Pie

Prep time: 15 minutes | Cook time: 15 minutes | Servings: 6

½ cup almond flour	1 tablespoon cream cheese
6 eggs	½ teaspoon baking powder
2 cup spinach, chopped	1 tablespoon butter, softened
1 oz. scallions, chopped	1 teaspoon ground black pepper
1 teaspoon sesame oil	

1. In the mixing bowl put almond flour, baking powder, and butter. Then crack 2 eggs and mix up the mixture gently. After this, knead the non-sticky dough. Transfer the dough in the air fryer sheet pan and flatten well to get the shape of the pie crust. Select Level 3. Select the "AIR FRY" function of Ninja Foodi Smart XL Pro Air Oven, set temperature to 365°F/185°C and time to 10 minutes. Select START/STOP to begin preheating. 2. Cook it for 10 minutes. Meanwhile, pour sesame oil in the skillet and heat it over the medium heat. 3. Cook scallions for 2 minutes. Then stir the vegetables and add chopped spinach and cream cheese. Cook the greens for 5 minutes over the medium heat. Then sprinkle it with ground black pepper. 4. Transfer the spinach mixture in the pie crust and flatten gently. Bake the pie for 5 minutes in the air fryer.
Per Serving: Calories 111; Fat 8.9g; Sodium 145mg; Carbs 2g; Fiber 0.7g; Sugar 0.9g; Protein 6.6g

Bacon-Wrapped Jalapeño Poppers

Prep time: 5 minutes | Cook time: 12 minutes | Servings: 12

12 jalapeño peppers	1 teaspoon salt
1 (8-ounce) cream cheese	½ teaspoon freshly ground black
1 cup shredded Cheddar cheese	pepper
1 teaspoon onion powder	12 slices bacon, cut in half

1. Spray the air fryer basket with olive oil. 2. Cut each pepper in half, then use a spoon to scrape out the veins and seeds. 3. In a bowl, mix the cream cheese, Cheddar cheese, onion powder, salt, and pepper. 4. Using a small spoon, fill each pepper half with the cheese mixture. 5. Wrap stuffed pepper with a slice of bacon. Place the bacon-wrapped peppers into the greased air fryer basket in a single layer. 6. Select Level 3. Select the "AIR FRY" function of Ninja Foodi Smart XL Pro Air Oven, set temperature to 320°F/160°C and time to 12 minutes. Select START/STOP to begin preheating. Set the timer and bake for 12 minutes. 7. Using tongs, remove the peppers from the air fryer, place them on a platter, and serve.
Per Serving: Calories 212; Fat 18g; Sodium 747mg; Carbs 2g; Fiber 0g; Sugar 1g; Protein 11g

Homemade Radish Chips

Prep time: 5 minutes | Cook time: 15 minutes | Servings: 4

16 ounces radishes, thinly sliced	2 tablespoons coconut oil, melted
A pinch of salt and black pepper	

1. Select Level 3. Select the "AIR FRY" function of Ninja Foodi Smart XL Pro Air Oven, set temperature to 400°F/200°C and time to 15 minutes. Select START/STOP to begin preheating. 2. In a bowl, mix the radish slices with salt, pepper and the oil, toss well, place them in your air fryer's basket and cook for 15 minutes, flipping them halfway. 3. Serve as a snack.
Per Serving: Calories 174; Fat 5g; Sodium 112mg; Carbs 3g; Fiber 1g; Sugar 1g; Protein 6g

Herbed Bacon Asparagus Wraps

Prep time: 5 minutes | Cook time: 15 minutes | Servings: 8

16 asparagus spears, trimmed	1 teaspoon thyme, chopped
16 bacon strips	1 teaspoon oregano, chopped
2 tablespoons olive oil	A pinch of salt and black pepper
1 tablespoon lemon juice	

1. Select Level 3. Select the "AIR FRY" function of Ninja Foodi Smart XL Pro Air Oven, set temperature to 390°F/200°C and time to 15 minutes. Select START/STOP to begin preheating. 2. In a bowl, mix the oil with lemon juice, the herbs, salt and pepper and whisk well. Brush the asparagus spears with this mix and wrap each in a bacon strip. 3. Arrange the asparagus wraps in your air fryer's basket and cook for 15 minutes. Serve as an appetizer.
Per Serving: Calories 173; Fat 4g; Sodium 322mg; Carbs 3g; Fiber 2g; Sugar 1g; Protein 6g

Healthy Cheesy Spinach Triangles

Prep time: 6 minutes | Cook time: 20 minutes | Servings: 6

3 cups mozzarella, shredded	6 ounces spinach, chopped
4 tablespoons coconut flour	¼ cup parmesan, grated
½ cup almond flour	4 ounces cream cheese, soft
2 eggs, whisked	2 tablespoons ghee, melted
A pinch of salt and black pepper	

1. Select Level 3. Select the "AIR FRY" function of Ninja Foodi Smart XL Pro Air Oven, set temperature to 360°F/180°C and time to 20 minutes. Select START/STOP to begin preheating. 2. In a bowl, mix the mozzarella with coconut and almond flour, eggs, salt and pepper, stir well until you obtain a dough and roll it well on a parchment paper. Cut into triangles and leave them aside for now. 3. In a bowl, mix the spinach with parmesan, cream cheese, salt and pepper and stir really well. Divide this into the center of each dough triangle, roll and seal the edges. 4. Brush the rolls with the ghee, place them in your air fryer's basket and cook for 20 minutes. 5. Serve as an appetizer.
Per Serving: Calories 210; Fat 8g; Sodium 100mg; Carbs 3g; Fiber 1g; Sugar 1g; Protein 8g

Refreshing Lime Tomato Salsa

Prep time: 5 minutes | Cook time: 8 minutes | Servings: 4

4 tomatoes, cubed
3 chili peppers, minced
2 spring onions, chopped
1 garlic clove, minced

2 tablespoons lime juice
2 teaspoons cilantro, chopped
2 teaspoons parsley, chopped
Cooking spray

1. Select Level 3. Select the "AIR FRY" function of Ninja Foodi Smart XL Pro Air Oven, set temperature to 360°F/180°C and time to 8 minutes. Select START/STOP to begin preheating. 2. Grease a pan that fits your air fryer with the cooking spray, and mix all the ingredients inside. 3. Introduce the pan in the Ninja Foodi air fryer and cook for 8 minutes. Divide into bowls and serve as an appetizer.
Per Serving: Calories 148; Fat 1g; Sodium 159mg; Carbs 3g; Fiber 2g; Sugar 1g; Protein 5g

Easy Fried Beetroot

Prep time: 5 minutes | Cook time: 30 minutes | Servings: 4

6 oz. beetroot, sliced   1 teaspoon salt

1. Sprinkle the beetroot slices with salt and mix up well. Select Level 3. Select the "AIR FRY" function of Ninja Foodi Smart XL Pro Air Oven, set temperature to 320°F/160°C and time to 30 minutes. Select START/STOP to begin preheating. 2. Put the beetroot slices in the air fryer basket. 3. Cook them for 30 minutes. Shake the beetroot chips every 5 minutes.
Per Serving: Calories 19; Fat 0.1g; Sodium 3mg; Carbs 64.2; Fiber 0.9g; Sugar 0.5g; Protein 0.7g

Cheesy Chives Salmon Dip

Prep time: 5 minutes | Cook time: 6 minutes | Servings: 4

8 ounces cream cheese, soft
2 tablespoons lemon juice
½ cup coconut cream
4 ounces smoked salmon,

skinless, boneless and minced
A pinch of salt and black pepper
1 tablespoon chives, chopped

1. Select Level 3. Select the "AIR FRY" function of Ninja Foodi Smart XL Pro Air Oven, set temperature to 360°F/180°C and time to 6 minutes. Select START/STOP to begin preheating. 2. In a bowl, mix all the ingredients and whisk them really well. Transfer the mix to a ramekin, place it in your air fryer's basket and cook for 6 minutes. 3. Serve as a party spread.
Per Serving: Calories 180; Fat 7g; Sodium 12mg; Carbs 5g; Fiber 1g; Sugar 1g; Protein 7g

Fried Jicama Wedges

Prep time: 10 minutes | Cook time: 3 minutes | Servings: 4

8 oz. Jicama, peeled
½ teaspoon ground turmeric

¼ teaspoon dried dill
1 tablespoon avocado oil

1. Cut the Jicama on the wedges and sprinkle them with turmeric and dried dill. Then sprinkle the vegetables with avocado oil. 2. Select Level 3. Select the "AIR FRY" function of Ninja Foodi Smart XL Pro Air Oven, set temperature to 400°F/200°C and time to 3 minutes. Select START/STOP to begin preheating. 3. Place the Jicama wedges in the air fryer basket in one layer and cook them for 3 minutes.
Per Serving: Calories 27; Fat 0.5g; Sodium 11mg; Carbs 5.4g; Fiber 3g; Sugar 2g; Protein 0.5g

Herbed Pork Skewers

Prep time: 10 minutes | Cook time: 20 minutes | Servings: 4

½ pound pork shoulder, cubed
¼ teaspoon sweet paprika
1 tablespoon coconut oil, melted
¼ teaspoon cumin, ground
¼ cup olive oil
¼ cup green bell peppers,

chopped
1½ tablespoons lemon juice
1 tablespoon cilantro, chopped
2 tablespoons parsley, chopped
2 garlic cloves, minced
A pinch of salt and black pepper

1. Select Level 3. Select the "AIR FRY" function of Ninja Foodi Smart XL Pro Air Oven, set temperature to 370°F/185°C and time to 20 minutes. Select START/STOP to begin preheating. 2. In a blender, blend the olive oil with bell peppers, lemon juice, cilantro, parsley,

garlic, salt and pepper and pulse well. 3. Thread the meat onto the skewers, sprinkle cumin and paprika all over and rub with the coconut oil. 4. In a bowl, mix the pork skewers with the herbed mix and rub well. 5. Place the skewers in your air fryer's basket, cook for 10 minutes on each side and serve as an appetizer.
Per Serving: Calories 249; Fat 16g; Sodium 211mg; Carbs 3g; Fiber 2g; Sugar 2g; Protein 17g

Spicy Kale Chips

Prep time: 5 minutes | Cook time: 5 minutes | Servings: 4

1 teaspoon nutritional yeast
1 teaspoon salt
2 cups kale, chopped

½ teaspoon chili flakes
1 teaspoon sesame oil

1. Mix up kale leaves with nutritional yeast, salt, chili flakes, and sesame oil. Shake the greens well. Select Level 3. Select the "AIR FRY" function of Ninja Foodi Smart XL Pro Air Oven, set temperature to 400°F/200°C and time to 5 minutes. Select START/STOP to begin preheating. 2. Put the kale leaves in the air fryer basket. Cook them for 3 minutes and then give a good shake. 3. Cook the kale leaves for 2 minutes more.
Per Serving: Calories 30; Fat 1.2g; Sodium 11mg; Carbs 3.9g; Fiber 0.7g; Sugar 0.4g; Protein 1.4g

Home-Fried Cheese Sticks

Prep time: 10 minutes | Cook time: 6 minutes | Servings: 4

8 oz. goat cheese
1 egg, beaten
1 tablespoon heavy cream

¼ cup coconut flour
¼ cup almond flour
1 teaspoon sesame oil

1. Slice the goat cheese on 4 slices. Then mix up beaten egg and heavy cream. In the separated bowl mix up coconut flour and almond flour. 2. Select Level 3. Select the "AIR FRY" function of Ninja Foodi Smart XL Pro Air Oven, set temperature to 400°F/200°C and time to 6 minutes. Select START/STOP to begin preheating. 3. Dip the cheese in the egg mix and then coat in the almond flour mixture. Repeat the last 2 steps two times. 4. Transfer the goat cheese slices in the air fryer basket and cook them for 3 minutes from each side or until the cheese slices are light brown.
Per Serving: Calories 340; Fat 25.4g; Sodium 110mg; Carbs 6.3g; Fiber 3.2g; Sugar 3g; Protein 20.6g

Pork Strips with Basil

Prep time: 10 minutes | Cook time: 25 minutes | Servings: 6

2 pounds pork belly, cut into strips
2 tablespoons olive oil

2 teaspoons fennel seeds
A pinch of salt and black pepper
A pinch of basil, dried

1. Select Level 3. Select the "AIR FRY" function of Ninja Foodi Smart XL Pro Air Oven, set temperature to 425°F/220°C and time to 25 minutes. Select START/STOP to begin preheating. 2. In a bowl, mix all the ingredients, toss and put the pork strips in your air fryer's basket and cook for 25 minutes. 3. Serve and enjoy.
Per Serving: Calories 251; Fat 14g; Sodium 122mg; Carbs 5g; Fiber 3g; Sugar 2g; Protein 18g

Cheesy Crab Dip

Prep time: 5 minutes | Cook time: 20 minutes | Servings: 4

8 ounces cream cheese, soft
1 tablespoon lemon juice
1 cup coconut cream
1 tablespoon lemon juice
1 bunch green onions, minced

1-pound artichoke hearts, drained and chopped
12 ounces jumbo crab meat
A pinch of salt and black pepper
1½ cups mozzarella, shredded

1. Select Level 3. Select the "AIR FRY" function of Ninja Foodi Smart XL Pro Air Oven, set temperature to 400°F/200°C and time to 15 minutes. Select START/STOP to begin preheating. 2. In a bowl, mix all ingredients instead of half of the cheese and whisk them really well. Transfer this to a pan that fits your air fryer, introduce in the Ninja Foodi air fryer and cook for 15 minutes. 3. Sprinkle the rest of the mozzarella on top and cook for 5 minutes more. Divide and serve as a party dip.
Per Serving: Calories 240; Fat 8g; Sodium 144mg; Carbs 4g; Fiber 2g; Sugar 2g; Protein 14g

Cheddar Tomato Platter

Prep time: 5 minutes | Cook time: 20 minutes | Servings: 6

6 tomatoes, halved
3 teaspoons sugar-free apricot jam
2 ounces watercress

2 teaspoons oregano, dried
1 tablespoon olive oil
A pinch of salt and black pepper
3 ounces cheddar cheese, grated

1. Select Level 3. Select the "AIR FRY" function of Ninja Foodi Smart XL Pro Air Oven, set temperature to 360°F/180°C and time to 20 minutes. Select START/STOP to begin preheating. 2. Spread the jam on each tomato half, sprinkle oregano, salt and pepper, and drizzle the oil all over them. Introduce them in the fryer's basket, sprinkle the cheese on top and cook for 20 minutes. 3. Arrange the tomatoes on a platter, top each half with some watercress and serve as an appetizer.
Per Serving: Calories 131; Fat 7g; Sodium 147mg; Carbs 4g; Fiber 2g; Sugar 2g; Protein 7g

Mixed Cheesy Veggie Bites

Prep time: 10 minutes | Cook time: 10 minutes | Servings: 6

1 cup zucchinis, cubed
1 cup eggplant, cubed
3 oz. Parmesan

1 tablespoon coconut cream
1 egg, beaten
½ tablespoon avocado oil

1. Select Level 3. Select the "AIR FRY" function of Ninja Foodi Smart XL Pro Air Oven, set temperature to 400°F/200°C and time to 10 minutes. Select START/STOP to begin preheating. 2. In the mixing bowl mix up beaten egg and coconut cream. Then dip the veggie cubes in the egg mixture and sprinkle with Parmesan. 3. Place the coated vegetables in the air fryer basket in one layer and cook for 10 minutes. 4. Serve as a snack.
Per Serving: Calories 75; Fat 4.6g; Sodium 33mg; Carbs 3.6g; Fiber 0.6g; Sugar 0.9g; Protein 5.9g

Parmesan Roasted Green Beans

Prep time: 5 minutes | Cook time: 12 minutes | Servings: 4

12 ounces green beans, trimmed
1 cup parmesan, grated
1 egg, whisked

A pinch of salt and black pepper
¼ teaspoon sweet paprika

1. Install the wire rack on Level 3. Select the "AIR ROAST" function of Ninja Foodi Smart XL Pro Air Oven, set temperature to 380°F/195°C and time to 12 minutes. Select START/STOP to begin preheating. 2. In a bowl, mix the parmesan with salt, pepper and the paprika and stir. Put the egg in a separate bowl, dredge the green beans in egg and then in the parmesan mix. 3. Arrange the green beans in your air fryer's basket and cook for 12 minutes. Serve as a snack.
Per Serving: Calories 112; Fat 6g; Sodium 85mg; Carbs 2g; Fiber 1g; Sugar 1g; Protein 9g

Spicy Calamari Rings

Prep time: 10 minutes | Cook time: 15 minutes | Servings: 2

1 pound calamari rings
1 teaspoon black pepper

½ teaspoon avocado oil
¼ teaspoon chili powder

1. Select Level 3. Select the "AIR FRY" function of Ninja Foodi Smart XL Pro Air Oven, set temperature to 400°F/200°C and time to 10 minutes. Select START/STOP to begin preheating. 2. In the air fryer, mix the calamari with black pepper and the other ingredients and toss. Cook the onion rings 10 minutes.
Per Serving: Calories 127; Fat 8.2g; Sodium 62mg; Carbs 5.7g; Fiber 1.3g; Sugar 1g; Protein 7.7g

Lemony Shrimp Bowls

Prep time: 5 minutes | Cook time: 10 minutes | Servings: 4

1-pound shrimp, peeled and deveined
3 garlic cloves, minced
¼ cup olive oil

Juice of ½ lemon
A pinch of salt and black pepper
¼ teaspoon cayenne pepper

1. Select Level 3. Select the "AIR FRY" function of Ninja Foodi Smart XL Pro Air Oven, set temperature to 370°F/185°C and time to 10 minutes. Select START/STOP to begin preheating. 2. In a pan that fits your air fryer, mix all the ingredients, toss, introduce in the fryer and cook for 10 minutes. Serve as a snack.
Per Serving: Calories 242; Fat 14g; Sodium 322mg; Carbs 3g; Fiber 2g; Sugar 3g; Protein 17g

Spicy Eggplant Nuggets

Prep time: 10 minutes | Cook time: 15 minutes | Servings: 4

1 eggplant, peeled
1 garlic clove, peeled
1 tablespoon sesame oil
¼ teaspoon ginger, grated
1 chili pepper, minced
½ tablespoon spring onions, chopped

½ teaspoon chili powder
¼ teaspoon ground coriander
¼ teaspoon turmeric
½ teaspoon fresh cilantro, chopped

1. Select Level 3. Select the "AIR FRY" function of Ninja Foodi Smart XL Pro Air Oven, set temperature to 400°F/200°C and time to 15 minutes. Select START/STOP to begin preheating. 2. Chop the eggplant into the cubes and put it in the air fryer. Add garlic and cook the vegetables for 15 minutes. Shake the vegetables every 5 minutes. 3. After this, transfer the soft eggplants and garlic in the bowl and mash them with the help of the fork. 4. Add sesame oil, ginger, minced chili pepper, onion, chili powder, ground coriander, and turmeric. Stir the mixture until homogenous and top with cilantro.
Per Serving: Calories 63; Fat 3.7g; Sodium 11mg; Carbs 7.5g; Fiber 4.3g; Sugar 3g; Protein 1.3g

Herbed Balsamic Mushroom

Prep time: 5 minutes | Cook time: 12 minutes | Servings: 4

2 tablespoons balsamic vinegar
2 tablespoons olive oil
½ teaspoon basil, dried
½ teaspoon tarragon, dried
½ teaspoon rosemary, dried

½ teaspoon thyme, dried
A pinch of salt and black pepper
12 ounces Portobello mushrooms, sliced

1. Select Level 3. Select the "AIR FRY" function of Ninja Foodi Smart XL Pro Air Oven, set temperature to 380°F/195°C and time to 12 minutes. Select START/STOP to begin preheating. 2. In a bowl, mix all the ingredients and toss well. Arrange the mushroom slices in your air fryer's basket and cook for 12 minutes. 3. Arrange the mushroom slices on a platter and serve.
Per Serving: Calories 147; Fat 8g; Sodium 333mg; Carbs 2g; Fiber 2g; Sugar 0g; Protein 3g

Cheesy Shrimp Dip

Prep time: 5 minutes | Cook time: 20 minutes | Servings: 4

1-pound shrimp, peeled, deveined and minced
2 tablespoons ghee, melted
¼ pound mushrooms, minced

½ cup mozzarella, shredded
4 garlic cloves, minced
1 tablespoon parsley, chopped
Salt and black pepper to the taste

1. Select Level 3. Select the "AIR FRY" function of Ninja Foodi Smart XL Pro Air Oven, set temperature to 360°F/180°C and time to 20 minutes. Select START/STOP to begin preheating. 2. In a bowl, mix all the ingredients, stir well, divide into small ramekins and place them in your air fryer's basket. 3. Cook for 20 minutes and serve as a party dip.
Per Serving: Calories 271; Fat 15g; Sodium 366mg; Carbs 4g; Fiber 3g; Sugar 1g; Protein 14g

Crispy Sage Radish Chips

Prep time: 10 minutes | Cook time: 35 minutes | Servings: 6

2 cups radish, sliced
½ teaspoon sage

2 teaspoons avocado oil
½ teaspoon salt

1. In the mixing bowl mix up radish, sage, avocado oil, and salt. Select Level 3. Select the "AIR FRY" function of Ninja Foodi Smart XL Pro Air Oven, set temperature to 320°F/160°C and time to 35 minutes. Select START/STOP to begin preheating. 2. Put the sliced radish in the air fryer basket and cook it for 35 minutes. 3. Shake the vegetables every 10 minutes.
Per Serving: Calories 8; Fat 0.3g; Sodium 5mg; Carbs 1.4g; Fiber 0.7g; Sugar 0.6g; Protein 0.3g

Herbed Eggplant Sticks

Prep time: 10 minutes | Cook time: 8 minutes | Servings: 3

6 oz. eggplant, trimmed
½ teaspoon dried oregano
½ teaspoon dried cilantro
½ teaspoon dried thyme
½ teaspoon ground cumin
½ teaspoon salt
1 tablespoon olive oil
¼ teaspoon garlic powder

1. Cut the eggplant into the fries and sprinkle with dried oregano, cilantro, thyme, cumin, salt, and garlic powder. Then sprinkle the eggplant fries with olive oil and shake well. 2. Select Level 3. Select the "AIR FRY" function of Ninja Foodi Smart XL Pro Air Oven, set temperature to 400°F/200°C and time to 8 minutes. Select START/STOP to begin preheating. 3. Place the eggplant in the air fryer and cook them for 4 minutes from each side.
Per Serving: Calories 58; Fat 4.9g; Sodium 112mg; Carbs 3.9g; Fiber 2.2g; Sugar 1.2g; Protein 0.7g

Cheesy Bacon Dip

Prep time: 5 minutes | Cook time: 20 minutes | Servings: 12

2 tablespoons ghee, melted
3 cups spring onions, chopped
A pinch of salt and black pepper
2 ounces cheddar cheese,
shredded
⅓ cup coconut cream
6 bacon slices, cooked and
crumbled

1. Select Level 3. Select the "AIR FRY" function of Ninja Foodi Smart XL Pro Air Oven, set temperature to 380°F/195°C and time to 13 minutes. Select START/STOP to begin preheating. 2. Heat up a pan that fits the fryer with the ghee over medium-high heat, add the onions, stir and sauté for 7 minutes. Add the remaining ingredients, instead of the bacon and stir well. 3. Sprinkle the bacon on top, introduce the pan in the Ninja Foodi air fryer and cook for 13 minutes. 4. Divide into bowls and serve as a party dip.

Tangy Tofu Cubes

Prep time: 10 minutes | Cook time: 7 minutes | Servings: 2

½ teaspoon ground coriander
1 tablespoon avocado oil
1 teaspoon lemon juice
½ teaspoon chili flakes
6 oz. tofu

1. In the shallow bowl, mix up ground coriander, avocado oil, lemon juice, and chili flakes. Chop the tofu into cubes and sprinkle with coriander mixture, shake the tofu. 2. Select Level 3. Select the

"AIR FRY" function of Ninja Foodi Smart XL Pro Air Oven, set temperature to 400°F/200°C and time to 7 minutes. Select START/STOP to begin preheating. 3. Put the tofu cubes in the air fryer basket, cook the tofu for 4 minutes. Then flip the tofu on another side and cook for 3 minutes more.
Per Serving: Calories 70; Fat 4.5g; Sodium 147mg; Carbs 1.9g; Fiber 1.1g; Sugar 0.3g; Protein 7.1g
Per Serving: Calories 220; Fat 12g; Sodium 74mg; Carbs 4g; Fiber 2g; Sugar 2g; Protein 15g

Healthy Tuna Bowls

Prep time: 5 minutes | Cook time: 10 minutes | Servings: 2

1-pound tuna, skinless, boneless
and cubed
3 scallion stalks, minced
1 chili pepper, minced
2 tablespoons olive oil
1 tablespoon coconut cream
1 tablespoon coconut aminos
2 tomatoes, cubed
1 teaspoon sesame seeds

1. Select Level 3. Select the "AIR FRY" function of Ninja Foodi Smart XL Pro Air Oven, set temperature to 360°F/180°C and time to 10 minutes. Select START/STOP to begin preheating. 2. In a pan that fits your air fryer, mix all the ingredients except the sesame seeds, toss, introduce in the fryer and cook for 10 minutes. 3. Serve as an appetizer with sesame seeds sprinkled on top.
Per Serving: Calories 231; Fat 18g; Sodium 147mg; Carbs 4g; Fiber 3g; Sugar 1g; Protein 18g

Crispy Avocado Wedges

Prep time: 5 minutes | Cook time: 8 minutes | Servings: 2

4 avocados, peeled, pitted and cut
into wedges
1 egg, whisked
1½ cups almond meal
A pinch of salt and black pepper
Cooking spray

1. Select Level 3. Select the "AIR FRY" function of Ninja Foodi Smart XL Pro Air Oven, set temperature to 400°F/200°C and time to 8 minutes. Select START/STOP to begin preheating. 2. Put the egg in a bowl, and the almond meal in another. Season avocado wedges with salt and pepper, coat them in egg and then in meal almond. 3. Arrange the avocado bites in your air fryer's basket, grease them with cooking spray and cook for 8 minutes. Serve as a snack right away.
Per Serving: Calories 200; Fat 12g; Sodium 325mg; Carbs 5g; Fiber 3g; Sugar 2g; Protein 16g

Chapter 7 Dessert Recipes

Sweet Chocolate Soufflés

Prep time: 10 minutes | Cook time: 14 minutes | Servings: 2

Butter and sugar for greasing the ramekins
3 ounces semi-sweet chocolate, chopped
3 tablespoons sugar
¼ cup unsalted butter
2 eggs, separate yolks and white
½ teaspoon vanilla extract
2 tablespoons all-purpose flour
Powdered sugar, for dusting
Heavy cream, for serving

1. Butter and sugar two 6-ounce ramekins. Melt the semi-sweet chocolate and butter in a bowl, in the microwave. 2. In a suitable bowl, beat the egg yolks. Stir in the sugar and the vanilla extract and beat well again. Drizzle in the melted chocolate and butter, mixing well. Add in the flour, combining until there are no lumps. 3. Cook on Air Fry mode. Pre-heat the Ninja Foodi Smart Xl Pro air fryer to 330°F/165°C. Select Level "3" and set the time on your Ninja Foodi Smart XL Pro Air Fryer Oven to 10 minutes. Press Start/Pause to begin preheating. 4. In another suitable bowl, beat the egg whites to soft peak stage. 5. Add the whipped egg whites into the chocolate mixture gently and in stages. 6. Transfer the prepared batter carefully to the buttered ramekins, leaving about ½-inch at the top. Place the ramekins into its air fryer basket and insert the basket in the level 3 of the Ninja Foodi Smart XL Pro Oven. Air-fry for 14 minutes. 7. Dust with sugar and serve with heavy cream
Per Serving: Calories 284; Fat 16g; Sodium 252mg; Carbs 31.6g; Fiber 0.9g; Sugar 6.6g; Protein 3.7g

Bananas Bread Pudding

Prep time: 10 minutes | Cook time: 50 minutes | Servings: 4

½ cup brown sugar
3 eggs
¾ cup half and half
1 teaspoon pure vanilla extract
6 cups cubed kings Hawaiian
bread (½-inch cubes), ½ pound
2 bananas, sliced
1 cup caramel sauce, plus more for serving

1. Mix the brown sugar, eggs, half and half and vanilla extract in a suitable bowl, whisking until the sugar has dissolved and the prepared mixture is smooth. Stir in the cubed bread and toss to coat all the cubes evenly. Let the bread sit for 10 minutes to absorb the liquid. 2. Mix the sliced bananas and caramel sauce in a separate bowl. 3. Fill the bottom of 4 (8-ounce) greased ramekins with half the bread cubes. Divide the caramel and bananas between the ramekins, spooning them on top of the bread cubes. Top with the remaining bread cubes and wrap each ramekin with aluminum foil, tenting the foil at the top to leave some room for the bread to puff up during the cooking process. 4. Cook on Air Fry mode, pre-heat the Ninja Foodi Smart Xl Pro air fryer to 350°F/175°C. Select Level "3" and set the time on your Ninja Foodi Smart XL Pro Air Fryer Oven to 25 minutes. Press Start/Pause to begin preheating. 5. Insert the basket in the level 3 of the Ninja Foodi Smart XL Pro Oven. Air-fry two bread puddings at a time for 25 minutes. Let the puddings cool a little and serve warm with additional caramel sauce drizzled on top. 6. Serve
Per Serving: Calories 386; Fat 10.3 g; Sodium 238 mg; Carbs 72.9g; Fiber 4.5g; Sugar 59g; Protein 2.6g

Apple Crumble

Prep time: 10 minutes | Cook time: 50 minutes | Servings: 6

4 apples, peeled and thinly sliced
2 tablespoons sugar
1 tablespoon flour
1 teaspoon ground cinnamon
Crumble Topping
¾ cup rolled oats
¼ cup sugar
⅓ cup flour
¼ teaspoon ground allspice
Healthy pinch ground nutmeg
10 caramel squares, cut into small pieces

¼ teaspoon ground cinnamon
6 tablespoons butter, melted

1. Mix the apples, sugar, flour, and spices in a suitable bowl and toss to coat. Add the caramel pieces and mix well. Pour the apple mixture into a 1-quart round baking dish that will fit in your air fryer basket (6-inch diameter). 2. To make the crumble topping, mix the rolled oats, sugar, flour and cinnamon in a suitable bowl. Add the melted butter and mix well. Top the apples with the crumble mixture. Cover this dish with foil and transfer the dish to its air fryer basket, lowering the dish into the basket using a sling made of aluminum foil. 3. Fold the ends of the aluminum foil over the top of the dish before returning the basket to the air fryer. 4. Cook on Air Fry mode. Pre-heat the

air fryer to 330°F/165°C. Select Level "3" and set the time on your Ninja Foodi Smart XL Pro Air Fryer Oven to 25 minutes. Press Start/Pause to begin preheating. Continue to the next step when it is done preheating. 5. Insert the basket in the level 3 of the Ninja Foodi Smart XL Pro Oven. Air-fry at 330°F/165°C for 25 minutes. Remove the aluminum foil and continue to air-fry for another 25 minutes. 6. Serve the crumble warm with whipped cream or vanilla ice cream, if desired.
Per Serving: Calories 426; Fat 36.3 g; Sodium 248 mg; Carbs 22.1g; Fiber 2g; Sugar 10.9g; Protein 6.6g

Exquisite Puff Pastry Apples

Prep time: 10 minutes | Cook time: 10 minutes | Servings: 4

3 Rome or gala apples, peeled
2 tablespoons sugar
1 teaspoon all-purpose flour
1 teaspoon ground cinnamon
⅛ teaspoon ground ginger
Pinch ground nutmeg
1 sheet puff pastry
1 tablespoon butter, cut into 4 pieces
1 egg, beaten
Vegetable oil
Vanilla ice cream
Caramel sauce

1. Remove the cores from the apples by cutting the four sides off the apple around the core. Slice the pieces of apple into thin half-moons, about ¼-inch thick. Mix the sugar, flour, cinnamon, ginger, and nutmeg in a suitable bowl. Add the apples to this bowl and gently toss until the apples are evenly coated with the spice mixture. Set aside. 2. Cut the puff pastry sheet into a 12- by 12-inch square. Then quarter the sheet into four 6-inch squares. 3. Save any remaining pastry for decorating the apples at the end. 4. Divide the spiced apples between the four puff pastry squares, stacking the apples in the center of each square and placing them flat on top of each other in a circle. Top the apples with a piece of the butter. 5. Brush the edges of the pastry with the egg wash. Bring the four corners of the pastry together, wrapping them around the apple slices and pinching them at the top in the style of a "beggars purse" appetizer. Fold the ends of the pastry corners down onto the apple making them look like leaves. Brush the entire apple with the egg wash. 6. Using the leftover dough, make leaves to decorate the apples. Cut out 8 leaf shapes, about 1½-inches long, "drawing" the leaf veins on the pastry leaves with a paring knife. Place 2 leaves on the top of each apple, tucking the ends of the leaves under the pastry in the center of the apples. Brush the top of the leaves with additional egg wash. Sprinkle the entire apple with some granulated sugar. 7. Spray or brush the inside of its air fryer basket with oil. Cook on Air Fry mode. Pre-heat the air fryer to 350°F/175°C. Select Level "3" and set the time on your Ninja Foodi Smart XL Pro Air Fryer Oven to 10 minutes. Press Start/Pause to begin preheating. Continue to the next step when it is done preheating. 8. Place the apples in the basket, insert the basket in the level 3 of the Ninja Foodi Smart XL Pro Oven. 9. Air-fry for 6 minutes. Carefully turn the apples over – it's easiest to remove one apple, then flip the others over and finally return the last apple to the air fryer. Air-fry for an additional 4 minutes. 10. Serve the puff pastry apples warm with vanilla ice cream and drizzle with some caramel sauce.
Per Serving: Calories 148; Fat 0.3 g; Sodium 3 mg; Carbs 38.9g; Fiber 0.5g; Sugar 33.9g; Protein 0.6g

Dark Chocolate Fudge

Prep time: 15 minutes | Cook time: 30 minutes | Servings:8

½ cup butter, melted
1 ounces dark chocolate, chopped, melted
2 tablespoons cocoa powder
3 tablespoons coconut flour
1 teaspoon vanilla extract
2 eggs, beaten
3 tablespoons Splenda
Cooking spray

1. In the bowl mix up melted butter and dark chocolate. Then add vanilla extract, eggs, and cocoa powder. Stir the prepared mixture until smooth and add Splenda, and coconut flour. Stir it again until smooth. 2. Then Select the Air Fry mode. Set the Ninja Foodi Smart XL Pro temperature to 325°F/160°C. Select Level "3" and set the time on your Ninja Foodi Smart XL Pro Air Fryer Oven to 30 minutes. Press Start/Pause to begin preheating. Continue to the next step when it is done preheating. 3. Line its air fryer basket with baking paper and spray it with cooking spray. 4. Pour the fudge mixture in its air fryer basket, flatten it gently with the help of the spatula. Insert its air fryer basket into the level 3 of the oven and close the door. Cook the fudge for 30 minutes. 5. Then cut it on the serving squares and cool the fudge completely.
Per Serving: Calories 416; Fat 8.3 g; Sodium 208 mg; Carbs 22.9g; Fiber 0.5g; Sugar 19g; Protein 6.6g

Currant Cookies

Prep time: 5 minutes | Cook time: 30 minutes | Servings: 6

2 cups almond flour
2 teaspoons baking soda
½ cup ghee, melted

½ cup swerve
1 teaspoon vanilla extract
½ cup currants

1. In a suitable bowl, mix all the recipe ingredients and whisk well. 2. Spread this on a suitable baking sheet lined with parchment paper, put the pan in its air fryer basket. Insert its air fryer basket into the level 3 of the oven and close the door. Cook on "Bake" mode, select level 3, and set its temperature to 350°F/175°C for 30 minutes. 3. Cool down, cut into rectangles and serve.
Per Serving: Calories 276; Fat 2.1 g; Sodium 18 mg; Carbs 65.9g; Fiber 4.5g; Sugar 59g; Protein 2.6g

Berry Pies

Prep time: 10 minutes | Cook time: 30 minutes | Servings: 4

¾ cup sugar
½ teaspoon ground cinnamon
1 tablespoon cornstarch
1 cup blueberries
1 cup blackberries
1 cup raspberries, divided

1 teaspoon water
1 package refrigerated pie dough (or your own homemade pie dough)
1 egg, beaten

1. Mix the sugar, cinnamon, and cornstarch in a suitable saucepan. Add the blueberries, blackberries, and ½ cup of the raspberries. Toss the berries gently to coat them evenly. 2. Add the teaspoon of water to the saucepan and turn the stovetop on to medium-high heat, stirring occasionally. 3. Once the berries break down, release their juice and start to simmer (about 5 minutes), simmer for another couple of minutes and then transfer the prepared mixture to a suitable bowl, stir in the remaining ½ cup of raspberries and let it cool. 4. Cut the pie dough into four 5-inch circles and four 6-inch circles. Spread the 6-inch circles on a flat surface. Divide the berry filling between all four circles. 5. Brush the perimeter of the prepared dough circles with a little water. Place the 5-inch circles on top of the filling and press the perimeter of the prepared dough circles to seal. 6. Roll the edges of the bottom circle up over the top circle to make a crust around the filling. Press a fork around the crust to make decorative indentations and to seal the crust shut. 7. Brush the pies with egg wash and topping with a little sugar. Poke a suitable hole in the center of each pie with a paring knife to vent the prepared dough. 8. Air-fry two pies at a time. Cook on Air Fry mode. Pre-heat the air fryer to 370°F/185°C. Select Level "3" and set the time on your Ninja Foodi Smart XL Pro Air Fryer Oven to 15 minutes. Press Start/Pause to begin preheating. 9. Continue to the next step when it is done preheating. 5. Brush or spray its air fryer basket with oil and place the pies into the basket. Insert the basket in the level 3 of the Ninja Foodi Smart XL Pro Oven. Air-fry for 9 minutes. 10. Turn the pies over and air-fry for another 6 minutes. Serve warm or at room temperature.
Per Serving: Calories 551; Fat 29.3 g; Sodium 74 mg; Carbs 73.9g; Fiber 3.5g; Sugar 55.9g; Protein 5g

Carrot Cake with Icing

Prep time: 10 minutes | Cook time: 55 minutes | Servings: 6

1¼ cups all-purpose flour
1 teaspoon baking powder
½ teaspoon baking soda
1 teaspoon ground cinnamon
¼ teaspoon ground nutmeg
¼ teaspoon salt
For the Icing:
8 ounces cream cheese, softened
8 tablespoons butter (4 ounces or 1 stick), softened at room

2 cups grated carrot (about 3 to 4 medium carrots or 2 large)
¾ cup granulated sugar
¼ cup brown sugar
2 eggs
¾ cup canola or vegetable oil

temperature
1 cup powdered sugar
1 teaspoon pure vanilla extract

1. Grease a 7-inch cake pan. Mix the flour, baking powder, baking soda, cinnamon, nutmeg and salt in a suitable bowl. Add the grated carrots and toss well. 2. In a separate bowl, beat the sugars and eggs until light and frothy. Drizzle in the oil, beating constantly. Fold the egg mixture into the dry ingredients until everything is just mixed and you no longer see any traces of flour. 3. Pour the prepared batter into the cake pan and wrap the pan completely in greased aluminum foil. 4. Lower the cake pan into its air fryer basket using a sling made of aluminum foil. Fold both the ends of the aluminum foil into the

air fryer, letting them rest on top of the cake. 5. Cook on Air Fry mode. Pre-heat the air fryer to 350°F/175°C. Select Level "3" and set the time on your Ninja Foodi Smart XL Pro Air Fryer Oven to 40 minutes. Press Start/Pause to begin preheating. 6. Continue to the next step when it is done preheating. Insert the basket in the level 3 of the Ninja Foodi Smart XL Pro Oven. Air-fry for 40 minutes. 7. While the cake is cooking, beat the cream cheese, butter, powdered sugar and vanilla extract using a hand mixer or food processor (or a lot of elbow grease!). 8. Remove the cake's pan from the air fryer and let the cake cool in the cake pan for 10 minutes or so. 9. Frost the cake with the cream cheese icing and serve.
Per Serving: Calories 276; Fat 2.1 g; Sodium 18 mg; Carbs 65.9g; Fiber 4.5g; Sugar 59g; Protein 2.6g

Boston Cream Donut

Prep time: 10 minutes | Cook time: 12 minutes | Servings: 12

1½ cups bread flour
1 teaspoon active dry yeast
1 tablespoon sugar
¼ teaspoon salt
½ cup warm milk
Custard Filling:
1 (4-ounce) box French vanilla instant pudding mix
Chocolate Glaze:
1 cup chocolate chips

½ teaspoon pure vanilla extract
2 egg yolks
2 tablespoons butter, melted
Vegetable oil

¾ cup whole milk
¼ cup heavy cream

⅓ cup heavy cream

1. In the bowl of a standing mixer, mix the flour, yeast, sugar, and salt. Add the butter, milk, vanilla, and egg yolks. Mix until a ball of the prepared dough begins to form. Place the prepared dough on a floured board and give it a 2-minute hand kneading. The prepared dough should be formed into a ball, placed in an appropriate oiled bowl, covered with a clean kitchen towel, and leave it to rise for one to eleven and a half hour. 2. When the prepared dough has risen, punch it down and roll it into a 24-inch log. Cut the prepared dough into 24 pieces and roll each piece into a ball. Place the prepared dough balls on a suitable baking sheet and let them rise for another 30 minutes. 3. Cook on Air Fry mode. Pre-heat the Ninja Foodi Smart Xl Pro air fryer to 400°F/200°C. Select Level "3" and set the time on your Ninja Foodi Smart XL Pro Air Fryer Oven to 4 minutes. Press Start/Pause to begin preheating. 4. Insert the basket in the level 3 of the Ninja Foodi Smart XL Pro Oven. Spray or brush the prepared dough balls lightly with vegetable oil and air-fry eight at a time for 4 minutes. 5. To make the filling, use an electric hand mixer to beat the French vanilla pudding, milk and ¼ cup of heavy cream for 2 minutes. 6. Put the chocolate chips in a medium-sized bowl to start the chocolate glaze. Over the chocolate chips, pour the heavy cream that has been heated on the stovetop to a boil. Stir the glaze and chips together until they are melted. 7. Place the custard stuffing in a pastry bag with a large tip and use it to fill the donut holes. Use a sharp knife to make a hole in the donut hole's side. 8. To accommodate the filling, wiggle the knife around. Squeeze the custard into the donut's center slowly by inserting the pastry bag tip into the hole. 9. Pour the chocolate glaze over the top half of the doughnut, allowing any extra icing drip back into the bowl.
Per Serving: Calories 116; Fat 4.3 g; Sodium 28 mg; Carbs 32.9g; Fiber 2.5g; Sugar 29g; Protein 1.6g

Cream Cheesecake

Prep time: 10 minutes | Cook time: 2 minutes | Servings: 2

½ cup erythritol
½ cup almond flour
½ teaspoon vanilla extract
2 tablespoons erythritol

4 tablespoons divided heavy cream
8 ounces cream cheese

1. Allow the cream cheese to soften then incorporate with the 2 tablespoons heavy cream, vanilla, and ½ cup erythritol until smooth and mixed. 2. Transfer the prepared mixture onto a suitable baking sheet lined with parchment paper then place in the freezer until firm. 3. Using a medium sized bowl, then add in the almond flour and tablespoons erythritol then mix together. 4. dip the cheesecake bites into the remaining heavy cream then run through the flour mixture. 5. Select Air Fry mode. Spread the bites into the fryer basket and insert the basket in the level 3 of the Ninja Foodi Smart XL Pro Oven. air fry at 300°F/150°C and set the time on your Ninja Foodi Smart XL Pro Air Fryer Oven to 2 minutes. 6. Serve and enjoy as desired.
Per Serving: Calories 391; Fat 24g; Sodium 142mg; Carbs 38.5g; Fiber 3.5g; Sugar 21g; Protein 6.6g

Cherry Turnovers

Prep time: 10 minutes | Cook time: 56 minutes | Servings: 8

2 sheets frozen puff pastry, thawed
1 (21-ounce) can premium cherry pie filling
2 teaspoons ground cinnamon
1 egg, beaten
1 cup sliced almonds
1 cup powdered sugar
2 tablespoons milk

1. Spread a sheet of puff pastry out into a square that is approximately 10-inches by 10-inches. Cut this large square into quarters. 2. Mix the cherry pie filling and cinnamon in a suitable bowl. Spoon ¼ cup of the cherry filling into the center of each puff pastry square. Brush the perimeter of the pastry square with the egg wash. 3. Fold one corner of the puff pastry over the cherry pie filling towards the opposite corner, forming a triangle. Seal the two edges of the pastry with the tip of a fork, making a design into the tines. 4. Brush the egg wash on the top of the turnovers and sprinkle sliced almonds over each one. Repeat these steps with the second sheet of puff pastry. You should have eight turnovers at the end. 5. Select Air Fry mode, pre-heat the air fryer to 370°F/185°C. Select Level "3" and set the time on your Ninja Foodi Smart XL Pro Air Fryer Oven to 14 minutes. Press Start/Pause to begin preheating. Continue to the next step when it is done preheating. 6. Insert the basket in the level 3 of the Ninja Foodi Smart XL Pro Oven. Air-fry two turnovers at a time for 14 minutes, carefully turning them over halfway through the cooking time. 7. While the turnovers are cooking, make the glaze by whisking the powdered sugar and milk in a suitable bowl until smooth. Let the glaze sit for a minute. 8. Let the cooked cherry turnovers sit for at least 10 minutes. Then drizzle the glaze over each turnover in a zigzag motion. 9. Serve warm or at room temperature.
Per Serving: Calories 506; Fat 48.3 g; Sodium 608 mg; Carbs 158.9g; Fiber 6.5g; Sugar 83.9g; Protein 12.6g

Orange Butter Cake

Prep time: 10 minutes | Cook time: 77 minutes | Servings: 6

Crust Layer:
½ cup flour
¼ cup sugar
½ teaspoon baking powder
⅛ teaspoon salt
2 ounces (½ stick) unsalted
European style butter, melted
1 egg
1 teaspoon orange extract
2 tablespoons orange zest

Gooey Butter Layer:
8 ounces cream cheese, softened
4 ounces (1 stick) unsalted European style butter, melted
2 eggs
2 teaspoons orange extract
2 tablespoons orange zest
4 cups powdered sugar

Garnish:
Powdered sugar
Orange slices

1. Grease a 7-inch cake pan and line the bottom with baking paper. Mix the flour, sugar, baking powder and salt in a suitable bowl. Add the melted butter, egg, orange extract and orange zest. 2. Mix well and press this mixture into the bottom of the greased cake pan. Lower the pan into the basket using an aluminum foil sling (fold a piece of aluminum foil into a strip about 2-inches wide by 24-inches long). Fold the ends of the foil over the top of the dish before returning the basket to the air fryer. Air-fry uncovered for 8 minutes. 3. To make the gooey butter layer, beat the cream cheese, melted butter, eggs, orange extract and orange zest in a suitable bowl using an electric hand mixer. 4. Add the powdered sugar in stages, beat until smooth with each addition. Pour this mixture on top of the baked crust in the cake pan. Wrap the pan with a piece of greased aluminum foil, tenting the top of the foil to leave a little room for the cake to rise. 5. Select Air Fry mode, pre-heat the air fryer to 350°F/175°C. Select Level "3" and set the time on your Ninja Foodi Smart XL Pro Air Fryer Oven to 60 minutes. Press Start/Pause to begin preheating. Continue to the next step when it is done preheating. 6. Place the pan in the oven and air-fry for 60 minutes. Remove the aluminum foil and insert the basket in the level 3 of the Ninja Foodi Smart XL Pro Oven. air-fry for an additional 17 minutes. 7. Let the cake cool inside the pan for at least 10 minutes. Then, run a butter knife around the cake and let the cake cool completely in the pan. 8. When cooled, run the butter knife around the edges of the cake again and invert it onto a plate and then back onto a serving platter. 9. Sprinkle the powdered sugar over the top of the cake and garnish with orange slices.
Per Serving: Calories 399; Fat 13 g; Sodium 626 mg; Carbs 52.9g; Fiber 8.8g; Sugar 3.9g; Protein 19.6g

Nutella Torte

Prep time: 10 minutes | Cook time: 55 minutes | Servings: 6

¼ cup unsalted butter, softened
½ cup sugar
2 eggs
1 teaspoon vanilla
1¼ cups Nutella (or other chocolate hazelnut spread), divided
¼ cup flour
1 teaspoon baking powder
¼ teaspoon salt
Dark chocolate fudge topping
Coarsely chopped toasted hazelnuts

1. Beat the butter and sugar with an electric hand mixer until light and fluffy. Add the eggs, vanilla, and ¾ cup of the Nutella and mix until mixed. Mix the flour, baking powder and salt together, and add these dry ingredients to the butter mixture, beating for 1 minute. 2. Grease a 7-inch cake pan with butter and then line the bottom of the pan with a circle of parchment paper. Grease the parchment paper circle as well. Pour the prepared batter into the prepared cake pan and wrap the pan completely with aluminum foil. Lower the pan into its air fryer basket with an aluminum sling. Fold the ends of the aluminum foil over the top of the dish before returning the basket to the air fryer. 3. Cook on Air Fry mode. Pre-heat the air fryer to 350°F/175°C. Select Level "3" and set the time on your Ninja Foodi Smart XL Pro Air Fryer Oven to 55 minutes. Press Start/Pause to begin preheating. Continue to the next step when it is done preheating. 4. Insert the basket in the level 3 of the Ninja Foodi Smart XL Pro Oven. Air-fry for 30 minutes. Remove the foil and air-fry for another 25 minutes. 5. Remove the cake from air fryer and let it cool for 10 minutes. Invert the cake onto a plate, remove the parchment paper and invert the cake back onto a serving platter. 6. While the cake is still warm, spread the remaining ½ cup of Nutella® over the top of the cake. Melt the dark chocolate fudge in the microwave for about 10 seconds so it melts enough to be pourable. 7. Drizzle the sauce on top of the cake in a zigzag motion. Turn the cake 90°F/45°C and drizzle more sauce in zigzags perpendicular to the first zigzags. 8. Garnish the edges of the torte with the toasted hazelnuts and serve.
Per Serving: Calories 116; Fat 2.3 g; Sodium 15 mg; Carbs 18.9g; Fiber 4.5g; Sugar 2.2g; Protein 6g

Banana S'mores

Prep time: 10 minutes | Cook time: 6 minutes | Servings: 4

4 bananas
3 tablespoons mini semi-sweet chocolate chips
3 tablespoons mini peanut butter
chips
3 tablespoons mini marshmallows
3 tablespoons graham cracker cereal

1. Cut into the unpeeled bananas lengthwise along the inside of the curve to make a pocket. 2. Fill each banana pocket with chocolate chips, peanut butter chips and marshmallows and poke the graham cracker cereal into the filling. 3. Cook on Air Fry mode, pre-heat the air fryer to 400°F/200°C. Select Level "3" and set the time on your Ninja Foodi Smart XL Pro Air Fryer Oven to 6 minutes. Press Start/Pause to begin preheating. Continue to the next step when it is done preheating. 4. Place the bananas in its air fryer basket, resting them on the side of the basket against each other so that they remain upright with the filling facing up. 5. Insert the basket in the level 3 of the Ninja Foodi Smart XL Pro Oven. Air-fry for 6 minutes, until the bananas are soft to the touch, the chocolate and marshmallows have melted and toasted. Serve.
Per Serving: Calories 416; Fat 8.3 g; Sodium 208 mg; Carbs 22.9g; Fiber 0.5g; Sugar 19g; Protein 60.6g

Coconut Bars

Prep time: 10 minutes | Cook time: 20 minutes | Servings: 12

1 cup coconut cream
¼ cup cashew butter, soft
¾ cup swerve
1 egg, whisked
Juice of 1 lemon
1 teaspoon lemon peel, grated
1 teaspoon baking powder

1. In a suitable bowl, mix all the recipe ingredients gradually and stir well. Spoon balls this on a suitable baking sheet lined with parchment paper and flatten them. 2. Put the sheet in the fryer and cook on "Bake" mode, select level 3, and set its temperature to 350°F 175°C for 20 minutes. 3. Cut into bars and serve cold.
Per Serving: Calories 368; Fat 32.8 g; Sodium 507 mg; Carbs 0.6g; Fiber 0.1g; Sugar 1.1g; Protein 8.5g

Chocolate Almond Cakes

Prep time: 10 minutes | Cook time: 13 minutes | Servings: 3

Butter and flour for the ramekins
4 ounces dark chocolate, chopped
½ cup unsalted butter
2 eggs
2 egg yolks
¼ cup sugar
½ teaspoon pure vanilla extract
1 tablespoon all-purpose flour

3 tablespoons ground almonds
8 to 12 semisweet chocolate discs
Cocoa powder or powdered sugar, for dusting
Toasted almonds, chopped
Butter and flour three (6-ounce) ramekins

1. Melt the dark chocolate and butter in a suitable by heating in the microwave. 2. In a suitable bowl, beat the eggs with egg yolks and sugar until smooth. 3. Add the vanilla extract. Whisk the chocolate mixture into the egg mixture. Stir in the flour and ground almonds. 4. Transfer the prepared batter carefully into the buttered ramekins, filling halfway. Place two or three chocolate discs in the center of the prepared batter and then fill the ramekins to ½-inch below the top with the remaining batter. 5. Cook on Air Fry mode. Pre-heat the air fryer to 330°F/165°C. Select Level "3" and set the time on your Ninja Foodi Smart XL Pro Air Fryer Oven to 13 minutes. Press Start/Pause to begin preheating. Continue to the next step when it is done preheating. 6. Place the ramekins into its air fryer basket, insert the basket in the level 3 of the Ninja Foodi Smart XL Pro Oven and air-fry at 330°F/165°C for 13 minutes. 7. Serve.
Per Serving: Calories 477; Fat 13.3 g; Sodium 128 mg; Carbs 89.5g; Fiber 6.5g; Sugar 59.2g; Protein 5.4g

Hazelnut Cookies

Prep time: 25 minutes | Cook time: 11 minutes | Servings: 6

1 tablespoon flaxseeds
¼ cup flax meal
½ cup coconut flour
½ teaspoon baking powder
1 ounces hazelnuts, chopped

1 teaspoon apple cider vinegar
3 tablespoons coconut cream
1 tablespoon butter, softened
3 teaspoons Splenda
Cooking spray

1. Put the flax meal in the bowl. Add flax seeds, coconut flour, baking powder, apple cider vinegar, and Splenda. Stir the prepared mixture gently with the help of the fork and add butter, coconut cream, hazelnuts, and knead the non-sticky dough. If the prepared dough is not sticky enough, then add more coconut cream. 2. Make the big ball from the prepared dough and put it in the freezer for 10-15 minutes. 3. After this, Select the Air Fry mode. Set the Ninja Foodi Smart XL Pro temperature to 365°F/185°C. Select Level "3" and set the time on your Ninja Foodi Smart XL Pro Air Fryer Oven to 10 minutes. Press Start/Pause to begin preheating. Continue to the next step when it is done preheating. 4. Make the small balls (cookies) from the flax meal dough and press them gently. Spray its air fryer basket with cooking spray from inside. Spread the cookies in its air fryer basket in one layer (cook 3-4 cookies per one time) and Insert its air fryer basket into the level 3 of the oven and close the door. cook them for 11 minutes. 5. Then transfer the cooked cookies on the plate and cool them completely. Repeat the same steps with remaining uncooked cookies. 6. Store the cookies in the glass jar with the closed lid.
Per Serving: Calories 426; Fat 36.3 g; Sodium 248 mg; Carbs 22.1g; Fiber 2g; Sugar 10.9g; Protein 6.6g

Coconut Currant Pudding

Prep time: 5 minutes | Cook time: 20 minutes | Servings: 6

1 cup red currants, blended
1 cup black currants, blended

3 tablespoons stevia
1 cup coconut cream

1. In a suitable bowl, mix all the recipe ingredients and stir well. Divide into ramekins, put them in the fryer and cook on "Bake" mode, select level 3, and set its temperature to 340°F /170°C for 20 minutes. 2. Serve the pudding cold.
Per Serving: Calories 551; Fat 29.3 g; Sodium 74 mg; Carbs 73.9g; Fiber 3.5g; Sugar 55.9g; Protein 5g

Clove Flaxseed Crackers

Prep time: 20 minutes | Cook time: 33 minutes | Servings: 8

1 cup almond flour
1 teaspoon xanthan gum
1 teaspoon flax meal

½ teaspoon salt
1 teaspoon baking powder
1 teaspoon lemon juice

½ teaspoon ground clove
2 tablespoons erythritol
1 egg, beaten

3 tablespoons coconut oil, softened

1. In the mixing bowl mix up almond flour, xanthan gum, flax meal, salt, baking powder, and ground clove. 2. Add erythritol, lemon juice, egg, and coconut oil. Stir the prepared mixture gently with the help of the fork. 3 Then knead the prepared mixture till you get a soft dough. Line the chopping board with parchment. 4. Put the prepared dough on the parchment and roll it up in a thin layer. Cut the thin dough into squares (crackers). 5. Select the Air Fry mode. Set the Ninja Foodi Smart XL Pro temperature to 360°F/180°C. Select Level "3" and set the time on your Ninja Foodi Smart XL Pro Air Fryer Oven to 11 minutes. Press Start/Pause to begin preheating. Continue to the next step when it is done preheating. 6. Line its air fryer basket with baking paper. Put the prepared crackers in its air fryer basket in one layer. Insert its air fryer basket into the level 3 of the oven and close the door. And cook them for 11 minutes until the crackers are dry and light brown. 7. Repeat the same steps with remaining uncooked crackers.
Per Serving: Calories 56; Fat 4.3 g; Sodium 21 mg; Carbs 2.9g; Fiber 0.3g; Sugar 3.9g; Protein 0.6g

Cranberries Cauliflower Pudding

Prep time: 5 minutes | Cook time: 20 minutes | Servings: 6

1 cup cauliflower rice
2 cups almond milk

½ cup cranberries
1 teaspoon vanilla extract

1. In a suitable pan that fits your air fryer, mix all the recipe ingredients, whisk a bit, put the pan in the fryer and cook on "Bake" mode, select level 3, and set its temperature to 360°F/180°C for 20 minutes. 2. Stir the pudding, divide into bowls and serve cold.
Per Serving: Calories 506; Fat 48.3 g; Sodium 608 mg; Carbs 158.9g; Fiber 6.5g; Sugar 83.9g; Protein 12.6g

Lime Merengues

Prep time: 15 minutes | Cook time: 65 minutes | Servings: 6

2 egg whites
1 teaspoon lime zest, grated

1 teaspoon lime juice
4 tablespoons erythritol

1. Whisk the egg whites until soft peaks. Then add erythritol and lime juice and whisk the egg whites until you get strong peaks. 2. After this, then add lime zest and carefully stir the egg white mixture. 3. Select the Air Fry mode. Set the Ninja Foodi Smart XL Pro temperature to 275°F/135°C. Select Level "3" and set the time on your Ninja Foodi Smart XL Pro Air Fryer Oven to 65 minutes. Press Start/Pause to begin preheating. Continue to the next step when it is done preheating. 4. Line its air fryer basket with baking paper. With the help of the spoon make the small merengues and put them in the air fryer in one layer. 5. Insert its air fryer basket into the level 3 of the oven and close the door. Cook the dessert for 65 minutes.
Per Serving: Calories 267; Fat 15.2 g; Sodium 479 mg; Carbs 13.9g; Fiber 0.1g; Sugar 12.9g; Protein 2.6g

Delicious Mini Strawberry Pies

Prep time: 7 minutes | Cook time: 8 minutes | Servings: 8

1 cup sugar
¼ teaspoon ground cloves
⅛ teaspoon cinnamon powder
1 teaspoon vanilla extract

1 (12-oz.) can biscuit dough
12 oz. strawberry pie filling
¼ cup butter, melted

1. Install the wire rack on Level 3. Select the "BAKE" function of Ninja Foodi Smart XL Pro Air Oven, set temperature to 340°F/170°C and time to 10 minutes. Select START/STOP to begin preheating. In a bowl, mix together the sugar, cloves, cinnamon, and vanilla. 2. With a rolling pin, roll each piece of the biscuit dough into a flat, round circle. 3. Spoon an equal amount of the strawberry pie filling onto the center of each biscuit. 4. Roll up the dough. Dip the biscuits into the melted butter and coat them with the sugar mixture. 5. Coat with a light brushing of non-stick cooking spray on all sides. 6. Transfer the cookies to the Air Fryer and bake them at 340°F/170°C for roughly 10 minutes, or until a golden-brown color is achieved. 7. Allow to cool for 5 minutes before serving.
Per Serving: Calories 23; Fat 1.3g; Sodium 40mg; Carbs 2g; Fiber 1g; Sugar 1g; Protein 1g

Banana & Vanilla Puffs

Prep time: 7 minutes | Cook time: 8 minutes | Servings: 8

1 package [8-oz.] crescent dinner rolls, refrigerated
1 cup milk
4 oz. instant vanilla pudding
4 oz. cream cheese, softened
2 bananas, peeled and sliced
1 egg, lightly beaten

1. Install the wire rack on Level 3. Select the "BAKE" function of Ninja Foodi Smart XL Pro Air Oven, set temperature to 355°F/180°C and time to 10 minutes. Select START/STOP to begin preheating. Roll out the crescent dinner rolls and slice each one into 8 squares. 2. Mix together the milk, pudding, and cream cheese using a whisk. 3. Scoop equal amounts of the mixture into the pastry squares. Add the banana slices on top. 4. Fold the squares around the filling, pressing down on the edges to seal them. 5. Apply a light brushing of the egg to each pastry puff before placing them in the Air Fryer. 6. Bake for 10 minutes.
Per Serving: Calories 104; Fat 2.5g; Sodium 29mg; Carbs 18g; Fiber 4g; Sugar 2g; Protein 3g

Cinnamon Cookies

Prep time: 15 minutes | Cook time: 24 minutes | Servings: 10

3 tablespoons cream cheese
3 tablespoons erythritol
1 teaspoon vanilla extract
½ teaspoon ground cinnamon
1 egg, beaten
1 cup almond flour
½ teaspoon baking powder
1 teaspoon butter, softened
½ teaspoon orange zest, grated

1.Put the cream cheese and erythritol in the bowl. Add vanilla extract, ground cinnamon, and almond flour. Stir the prepared mixture with the help of the spoon until homogenous. 2. Then add egg, almond flour, baking powder, and butter. Add orange zest and stir the mass until homogenous. Then knead it with the help of the fingertips. Roll up the prepared dough with the help of the rolling pin. Then make the cookies with the help of the cookies cutter. 3. Select the Bake mode. Set the Ninja Foodi Smart XL Pro temperature to 365°F/185°C. Select Level "3" and set the time on your Ninja Foodi Smart XL Pro Air Fryer Oven to 8 minutes. Press Start/Pause to begin preheating. Continue to the next step when it is done preheating. 4. Line its air fryer basket with baking paper. Put the cookies on the baking paper. Insert its air fryer basket into the level 3 of the oven and close the door. and cook them for 8 minutes. The time of cooking depends on the cooking size.
Per Serving: Calories 398; Fat 37.8 g; Sodium 1463 mg; Carbs 2.5g; Fiber 0.2g; Sugar 0.5g; Protein 3.6g

Almond Chocolate Cakes

Prep time: 10 minutes | Cook time: 20 minutes | Servings: 4

3 ounces dark chocolate, melted
¼ cup coconut oil, melted
2 tablespoons swerve
2 eggs, whisked
¼ teaspoon vanilla extract
1 tablespoon almond flour
Cooking spray

1. In bowl, mix all the recipe ingredients except the cooking spray and whisk really well. 2. Divide this into 4 ramekins greased with cooking spray, put them in the fryer. Insert its air fryer basket into the level 3 of the oven and close the door. 3. Cook on "Bake" mode, select level 3, and set its temperature to 360°F/180°C for 20 minutes. Serve warm.
Per Serving: Calories 398; Fat 27 g; Sodium 416mg; Carbs 34.9g; Fiber 6.5g; Sugar 6.9g; Protein 11.6g

Chia Protein Bites

Prep time: 15 minutes | Cook time: 8 minutes | Servings: 2

½ scoop of protein powder
1 egg, beaten
3 tablespoons almond flour
1 ounces hazelnuts, grinded
1 tablespoon flax meal
1 teaspoon Splenda
1 teaspoon butter, soften ed
1 teaspoon chia seeds, dried
¼ teaspoon ground clove

1. In the mixing bowl mix up protein powder, almond flour, grinded hazelnuts, flax meal, chia seeds, ground clove, and Splenda. 2. Then add egg and butter and stir it with the help of the spoon until you get a homogenous mixture. 3. Cut the prepared mixture into pieces and make 2 bites of any shape with the help of the fingertips. 4. Select the Air Fry mode. Set the Ninja Foodi Smart XL Pro temperature to 365°F/185°C. Select Level "3" and set the time on your Ninja Foodi Smart XL Pro Air Fryer Oven to 8 minutes. Press Start/Pause to begin preheating. Continue to the next step when it is done preheating. 5. Line its air fryer basket with baking paper and put the protein bites inside. Insert its air fryer basket into the level 3 of the oven and close the door. Cook them for 8 minutes.
Per Serving: Calories 539; Fat 17.5 g; Sodium 1875 mg; Carbs 79.2g; Fiber 4.5g; Sugar 26.9g; Protein 15.6g

Espresso Cookies

Prep time: 5 minutes | Cook time: 15 minutes | Servings: 12

8 tablespoons ghee, melted
1 cup almond flour
¼ cup brewed espresso
¼ cup swerve
½ tablespoon cinnamon powder
2 teaspoons baking powder
2 eggs, whisked

1. In a suitable bowl, mix all the recipe ingredients and whisk well. 2. Spread medium balls on a cookie sheet lined parchment paper, flatten them, put the cookie sheet in your air fryer. Insert its air fryer basket into the level 3 of the oven and close the door. 3. Cook on "Bake" mode, select level 3, and set its temperature to 350°F/175°C for 15 minutes. Serve the cookies cold.
Per Serving: Calories 324; Fat 17.8 g; Sodium 363 mg; Carbs 8.9g; Fiber 0.5g; Sugar 1.9g; Protein 36.6g

Almond Pie

Prep time: 20 minutes | Cook time: 35 minutes | Servings: 4

4 eggs, beaten
1 tablespoon poppy seeds
1 teaspoon ground turmeric
1 teaspoon vanilla extract
1 teaspoon baking powder
1 teaspoon lemon juice
1 cup almond flour
2 tablespoons heavy cream
¼ cup erythritol
1 teaspoon avocado oil

1. Put the eggs in the bowl. Add vanilla extract, baking powder, lemon juice, almond flour, heavy cream, and erythritol. 2. Then add avocado oil and poppy seeds. Add turmeric. With the help of a high-speed immersion blender, blend the pie batter until it is smooth. 3. Line the air fryer cake mold with baking paper. Pour the pie batter in the cake mold. Flatten the pie surface with the help of the spatula if needed. 4. Then Select the Air Fry mode. Set the Ninja Foodi Smart XL Pro temperature to 365°F/185°C. Select Level "3" and set the time on your Ninja Foodi Smart XL Pro Air Fryer Oven to 35 minutes. Press Start/Pause to begin preheating. Continue to the next step when it is done preheating. 5. Put the cake mold in its air fryer basket. Insert its air fryer basket into the level 3 of the oven and close the door. Cook the pie for 35 minutes. 6. When the pie is cooked, cool it completely and remove it from the cake mold. Cut the cooked pie into the servings.
Per Serving: Calories 382; Fat 32.5 g; Sodium 1363 mg; Carbs 3.2g; Fiber 0.2g; Sugar 1.9g; Protein 9.1g

Cinnamon Butter Pancakes

Prep time: 10 minutes | Cook time: 12 minutes | Servings: 2

1 teaspoon ground cinnamon
2 teaspoons butter, softened
1 teaspoon baking powder
½ teaspoon lemon juice
½ teaspoon vanilla extract
¼ cup heavy cream
4 tablespoons almond flour
2 teaspoons erythritol

1. Select the Air Fry mode. Set the Ninja Foodi Smart XL Pro temperature to 325°F/160°C. Select Level "3" and set the time on your Ninja Foodi Smart XL Pro Air Fryer Oven to 6 minutes. Press Start/Pause to begin preheating. Continue to the next step when it is done preheating. 2. Take 2 small cake mold and line them with baking paper. 3. After this, in the mixing bowl mix up ground cinnamon, butter, baking powder, lemon juice, vanilla extract, heavy cream, almond flour, and erythritol. Stir the prepared mixture until it is smooth. 4. Then pour the prepared mixture in the prepared cake molds. 5. Put the first cake mold in its air fryer basket. Insert its air fryer basket into the level 3 of the oven and close the door. Cook the pancake for 6 minutes. 6. Then check if the pancake is cooked (it should have light brown color) and remove it from the air fryer. 7. Repeat the same steps with the second pancake. It is recommended to serve the pancakes warm or hot.
Per Serving: Calories 404; Fat 20.3 g; Sodium 8 mg; Carbs 3.4g; Fiber 1g; Sugar 1.2g; Protein 3.4g

Cardamom Peanut Squares

Prep time: 15 minutes | Cook time: 20 minutes | Servings: 4

4 tablespoons peanut butter	½ cup coconut flour
1 tablespoon peanut, chopped	1 tablespoon erythritol
1 teaspoon vanilla extract	½ teaspoon ground cardamom

1. Put the peanut butter and peanut in the bowl. Add vanilla extract, coconut flour, and ground cardamom. Then add erythritol and stir the prepared mixture until homogenous. 2. Select the Air Fry mode. Set the Ninja Foodi Smart XL Pro temperature to 330°F/165°C. Select Level "3" and set the time on your Ninja Foodi Smart XL Pro Air Fryer Oven to 20 minutes. Press Start/Pause to begin preheating. Continue to the next step when it is done preheating. 3. Line its air fryer basket with baking paper and pour the peanut butter mixture over it. Flatten it gently. 4. Insert its air fryer basket into the level 3 of the oven and close the door. Cook for 20 minutes. 5. Then remove the cooked mixture from the air fryer and cool it completely. 6. Cut the dessert into the squares.
Per Serving: Calories 249; Fat 5.7 g; Sodium 574 mg; Carbs 23.9g; Fiber 0.9g; Sugar 1.9g; Protein 3.6g

Chocolate Coconut Brownies

Prep time: 7 minutes | Cook time: 15 minutes | Servings: 8

½ cup coconut oil	¼ teaspoon coconut extract
2 oz. dark chocolate	½ teaspoon vanilla extract
1 cup sugar	1 tablespoon honey
2½ tablespoons water	½ cup flour
4 whisked eggs	½ cup desiccated coconut
¼ teaspoon ground cinnamon	sugar, to dust
½ teaspoon ground anise star	

1. Install the wire rack on Level 3. Select the "BAKE" function of Ninja Foodi Smart XL Pro Air Oven, set temperature to 355°F/180°C and time to 15 minutes. Select START/STOP to begin preheating. Melt the chocolate and coconut oil in the microwave. 2. Combine the sugar, water, eggs, cinnamon, anise, coconut extract, vanilla, and honey in a large bowl. 3. Stir in the flour and desiccated coconut. Incorporate everything well. 4. Lightly grease a baking dish with butter. Transfer the mixture to the dish. 5. Place the dish in the Air Fryer and bake at 355°F/180°C for 15 minutes. 6. Remove from the fryer and allow to cool slightly. 7. Take care when taking it out of the baking dish. Slice it into squares. 8. Dust with sugar before serving.
Per Serving: Calories 80; Fat 6g; Sodium 444mg; Carbs 6g; Fiber 1g; Sugar 4g; Protein 1g

Sage Red Currants

Prep time: 5 minutes | Cook time: 30 minutes | Servings: 4

7 cups red currants	1 cup water
1 cup swerve	6 sage leaves

1. In a suitable pan that fits your air fryer, mix all the recipe ingredients, toss, put the pan in level 3 of the fryer and cook on "Air Fry" Mode, select level 3, and set its temperature to 330°F/165°C for 30 minutes. 2. Discard sage leaves, divide into cups and serve cold.
Per Serving: Calories 148; Fat 0.3 g; Sodium 3 mg; Carbs 38.9g; Fiber 0.5g; Sugar 33.9g; Protein 0.6g

Delicious Chocolate Cake

Prep time: 20 minutes | Cook time: 45 minutes | Servings: 8

½ cup sugar	1 egg
1¼ cups flour	¼ cup soda of your choice
1 teaspoon baking powder	¼ cup milk
⅓ cup cocoa powder	½ stick butter, melted
¼ teaspoon ground cloves	2 oz. bittersweet chocolate,
⅛ teaspoon freshly grated nutmeg	melted
Pinch of table salt	½ cup hot water

1. Install the wire rack on Level 3. Select the "BAKE" function of Ninja Foodi Smart XL Pro Air Oven, set temperature to 320°F/160°C and time to 35 minutes. Select START/STOP to begin preheating. 2. In a bowl, thoroughly combine the dry ingredients. In another bowl, mix together the egg, soda, milk, butter, and chocolate. 3. Combine the two mixtures. Add in the water and stir well. 4. Take a cake pan that can

fit inside your Air Fryer and transfer the mixture to the pan. 5. Place a sheet of foil on top and bake for 35 minutes. 6. Remove the foil and bake for further 10 minutes. 7. Frost the cake with buttercream if desired before serving.
Per Serving: Calories 42; Fat 2.8g; Sodium 126mg; Carbs 4g; Fiber 1g; Sugar 1g; Protein 1g

Sweet Butter Fritters

Prep time: 15 minutes | Cook time: 15 minutes | Servings: 16

For the Dough:

4 cups flour	temperature
1 teaspoon kosher salt	1 packet instant yeast
1 teaspoon sugar	1 ¼ cups lukewarm water
3 tablespoons butter, at room	

For the Cakes:

1 cup sugar	1 teaspoon cinnamon powder
Pinch of cardamom	1 stick butter, melted

1. Select Level 3. Select the "AIR FRY" function of Ninja Foodi Smart XL Pro Air Oven, set temperature to 360°F/180°C and time to 10 minutes. Select START/STOP to begin preheating. Place all ingredients in a bowl and combine well. 2. Add in the lukewarm water and mix until a soft, elastic dough forms. 3. Place the dough on a lightly floured surface and lay a greased sheet of aluminum foil on top of the dough. Refrigerate for 5 to 10 minutes. 4. Remove it from the refrigerator and divide it in two. Mold each half into a log and slice it into 20 pieces. 5. In a shallow bowl, combine the sugar, cardamom and cinnamon. 6. Coat the slices with a light brushing of melted butter and the sugar. 7. Spritz Air Fryer basket with cooking spray. 8. Transfer the slices to the fryer and air fry for roughly 10 minutes. Turn each slice once during the baking time. 9. Dust each slice with the sugar before serving.
Per Serving: Calories 134; Fat 2.8g; Sodium 64mg; Carbs 26g; Fiber 4g; Sugar 8g; Protein 3g

Pear & Apple Crisp with Walnuts

Prep time: 10 minutes | Cook time: 20 minutes | Servings: 6

½ lb. apples, cored and chopped	1 teaspoon ground cinnamon
½ lb. pears, cored and chopped	¼ teaspoon ground cloves
1 cup flour	1 teaspoon vanilla extract
1 cup sugar	¼ cup chopped walnuts
1 tablespoon butter	Whipped cream, to serve

1. Install the wire rack on Level 3. Select the "BAKE" function of Ninja Foodi Smart XL Pro Air Oven, set temperature to 340°F/170°C and time to 20 minutes. Select START/STOP to begin preheating. 2. Lightly grease a baking dish and place the apples and pears inside. Combine the rest of the ingredients, minus the walnuts and the whipped cream, until a coarse, crumbly texture is achieved. 3. Pour the mixture over the fruits and spread it evenly. Top with the chopped walnuts. 4. Bake for 20 minutes or until the top turns golden brown. 5. When cooked through, serve at room temperature with whipped cream.
Per Serving: Calories 134; Fat 2.8g; Sodium 64mg; Carbs 26g; Fiber 4g; Sugar 8g; Protein 3g

Sweet Breaded Bananas

Prep time: 10 minutes | Cook time: 10 minutes | Servings: 4

4 ripe bananas, peeled and halved	1 ½ tablespoon coconut oil
1 tablespoon meal	¼ cup flour
1 tablespoon cashew, crushed	1½ tablespoons sugar
1 egg, beaten	½ cup friendly bread crumbs

1. Select the "AIR FRY" function of Ninja Foodi Smart XL Pro Air Oven, set temperature to 350°F/175°C and time to 10 minutes. Select START/STOP to begin preheating. In a saucepan, heat the coconut oil, toast in the bread crumbs and cook, stirring continuously, for 4 minutes. 2. Transfer the bread crumbs to a bowl. 3. Add in the meal and crushed cashew. Mix well. 4. Coat each of the banana halves in the corn flour, before dipping it in the beaten egg and lastly coating it with the bread crumbs. 5. Put the coated banana halves in the Air Fryer basket. Season with the sugar. Slide basket into rails of Level 3. 6. Air fry for 10 minutes.
Per Serving: Calories 153; Fat 2.8g; Sodium 28mg; Carbs 26g; Fiber 1g; Sugar 1g; Protein 6g

Crunchy Shortbread Cookies

Prep time: 10 minutes | Cook time: 12 minutes | Servings: 10

1½ cups butter   ¾ cup sugar
1 cup flour   Cooking spray

1. Install the wire rack on Level 3. Select the "BAKE" function of Ninja Foodi Smart XL Pro Air Oven, set temperature to 350°F/175°C and time to 12 minutes. Select START/STOP to begin preheating. 2. In a bowl, combine the flour and sugar. 3. Cut each stick of butter into small chunks. Add the chunks into the flour and the sugar. 4. Blend the butter into the mixture to combine everything well. 5. Use your hands to knead the mixture, forming a smooth consistency. 6. Shape the mixture into 10 equal-sized finger shapes, marking them with the tines of a fork for decoration if desired. 7. Lightly spritz the Air Fryer basket with the cooking spray. Place the cookies inside, spacing them out well. 8. Bake the cookies for 12 minutes. Let cool slightly before serving. Alternatively, you can store the cookies in an airtight container for up to 3 days.
Per Serving: Calories 292; Fat 24.3g; Sodium 660mg; Carbs 5g; Fiber 0g; Sugar 3g; Protein 14g

Banana & Coconut Cake

Prep time: 15 minutes | Cook time: 60 minutes | Servings: 5

⅔ cup sugar, shaved   1 ripe banana, mashed
⅔ cup unsalted butter   ½ teaspoon vanilla extract
3 eggs   ⅛ teaspoon baking soda
1¼ cups flour   Sea salt to taste
Topping:
sugar to taste, shaved   Bananas to taste, sliced
Walnuts to taste, roughly chopped

1. Install the wire rack on Level 3. Select the "BAKE" function of Ninja Foodi Smart XL Pro Air Oven, set temperature to 360°F/180°C and time to 48 minutes. Select START/STOP to begin preheating. 2. Mix together the flour, baking soda, and a pinch of sea salt. 3. In a separate bowl, combine the butter, vanilla extract and sugar using an electric mixer or a blender, to achieve a fluffy consistency. 4. Beat in the eggs one at a time. 5. Throw in half of the flour mixture and stir thoroughly. Add in the mashed banana and continue to mix. Lastly, throw in the remaining half of the flour mixture and combine until a smooth batter is formed. 6. Transfer the batter to a baking tray and top with the banana slices. 7. Scatter the chopped walnuts on top before dusting with the sugar. 8. Place a sheet of foil over the tray and pierce several holes in it. 9. Put the covered tray in the Air Fryer. Cook for 48 minutes. 10. Decrease the temperature to 320°F/160°C, take off the foil, and allow to cook for an additional 10 minutes until golden brown.
Per Serving: Calories 193; Fat 8.9g; Sodium 93mg; Carbs 2g; Fiber 1g; Sugar 0g; Protein 25g

Healthy Banana Oatmeal Cookies

Prep time: 10 minutes | Cook time: 10 minutes | Servings: 6

2 cups quick oats   4 ripe bananas, mashed
¼ cup milk   ¼ cup coconut, shredded

1. Install the wire rack on Level 3. Select the "BAKE" function of Ninja Foodi Smart XL Pro Air Oven, set temperature to 350°F/175°C and time to 15 minutes. Select START/STOP to begin preheating. 2. Combine all of the ingredients in a bowl. 3. Scoop equal amounts of the cookie dough onto a baking sheet and put it in the Air Fryer. 4. Bake the cookies for 15 minutes.
Per Serving: Calories 1; Fat 0g; Sodium 114mg; Carbs 0g; Fiber 0g; Sugar 0g; Protein 0g

Roasted Cinnamon Pumpkin Seeds

Prep time: 15 minutes | Cook time: 20 minutes | Servings: 2

1 cup pumpkin raw seeds   1 cup water
1 tablespoon ground cinnamon   1 tablespoon olive oil
2 tablespoons sugar

1. In a frying pan, combine the pumpkin seeds, cinnamon and water. 2. Boil the mixture over a high heat for 2-3 minutes. 3. Pour out the water and place the seeds on a clean kitchen towel, allowing them to dry for 20-30 minutes. 4. In a bowl, mix together the sugar, dried seeds, a pinch of cinnamon and one tablespoon of olive oil. 5. Install the wire rack on Level 3. Select the "AIR ROAST" function of Ninja Foodi Smart XL Pro Air Oven, set temperature to 340°F/170°C and time to 15 minutes. Select START/STOP to begin preheating. 6. Place the seed mixture in the fryer basket and allow to cook for 15 minutes, shaking the basket periodically throughout.
Per Serving: Calories 101; Fat 5.4g; Sodium 106mg; Carbs 8g; Fiber 3g; Sugar 3g; Protein 7g

Lemon Tarts

Prep time: 15 minutes | Cook time: 15 minutes | Servings: 4

½ cup butter   1 large lemon, juiced and zested
½ lb. flour   2 tablespoons lemon curd
2 tablespoons sugar   Pinch of nutmeg

1. In a large bowl, combine the butter, flour and sugar until a crumbly consistency is achieved. 2. Add in the lemon zest and juice, followed by a pinch of nutmeg. Continue to combine. 3. Sprinkle the insides of a few small pastry tins with flour. Pour equal portions of the dough into each one and add sugar or lemon zest on top. 4. Select Level 3. Select the "AIR FRY" function of Ninja Foodi Smart XL Pro Air Oven, set temperature to 360°F/180°C and time to 15 minutes. Select START/STOP to begin preheating. 5. Place the lemon tarts inside the fryer and allow to cook for 15 minutes.
Per Serving: Calories 4; Fat 0.1g; Sodium 0mg; Carbs 1g; Fiber 1g; Sugar 0g; Protein 0g

Tasty Apple Turnovers

Prep time: 5 minutes | Cook time: 30 minutes | Servings: 4

3½ ounces (100g) dried apples   1 pound (455g) frozen puff pastry,
(about 2½ cups)   defrosted according to package
¼ cup (35g) golden raisins   instructions
1 tablespoon (13g) granulated   1 egg beaten with 1 tablespoon
sugar   (15ml) water
1 tablespoon (15ml) freshly   Turbinado or demerara sugar for
squeezed lemon juice   sprinkling
½ teaspoon cinnamon

1. Install the wire rack on Level 3. Select the "BAKE" function of Ninja Foodi Smart XL Pro Air Oven, set temperature to 325°F/160°C and time to 30 minutes. Select START/STOP to begin preheating. 2. Place the dried apples in a medium saucepan and cover with about 2 cups (480ml) of water. 3. Bring the mixture to a boil over medium-high heat, then reduce the heat to low, cover, and simmer until the apples have absorbed most of the liquid, about 20 minutes. 4. Remove the apples from the heat and allow to cool. Add the raisins, sugar, lemon juice, and cinnamon to the rehydrated apples and set aside. 5. On a well-floured board, roll the puff pastry out to a 12-inch (30 cm) square. Cut the square into 4 equal quarters. 6. Divide the filling equally among the 4 squares, mounding it in the middle of each square. Brush the edges of each square with water and fold the pastry diagonally over the apple mixture, creating a triangle. 7. Seal the edges by pressing them with the tines of a fork. Transfer the turnovers to a sheet pan lined with parchment paper. 8. Brush the top of 2 turnovers with egg wash and sprinkle with turbinado sugar. Make 2 small slits in the top of the turnovers for venting and bake for 25 to 30 minutes, until the top is browned and puffed and the pastry is cooked through. 9. Remove the cooked turnovers to a cooling rack and cook the remaining 2 turnovers in the same manner. Serve warm or at room temperature.
Per Serving: Calories 354; Fat 7.9g; Sodium 704mg; Carbs 6g; Fiber 3.6g; Sugar 6g; Protein 18g

Pineapple & Coconut Sticks

Prep time: 10 minutes | Cook time: 10 minutes | Servings: 4

½ fresh pineapple, cut into sticks   ¼ cup desiccated coconut

1. Select Level 3. Select the "AIR FTY" function of Ninja Foodi Smart XL Pro Air Oven, set temperature to 400°F/200°C and time to 10 minutes. Select START/STOP to begin preheating. 2. Coat the pineapple sticks in the desiccated coconut and put each one in the Air Fryer basket. Air fry for 10 minutes.
Per Serving: Calories 147; Fat 7.3g; Sodium 56mg; Carbs 20g; Fiber 5g; Sugar 11g; Protein 4g

Double Lemon Cake

Prep time: 15 minutes | Cook time: 35 minutes | Servings: 8

For the Cake:

9 oz. sugar
9 oz. butter
3 eggs
9 oz. flour

1 teaspoon vanilla extract
Zest of 1 lemon
1 teaspoon baking powder

For the Frosting:

Juice of 1 lemon
Zest of 1 lemon
1 teaspoon yellow food coloring

7 oz. sugar
4 egg whites

1. Install the wire rack on Level 3. Select the "BAKE" function of Ninja Foodi Smart XL Pro Air Oven, set temperature to 320°F/160°C and time to 15 minutes. Select START/STOP to begin preheating. 2. Use an electric mixer to combine all of the cake ingredients. 3. Grease the insides of two round cake pans. 4. Pour an equal amount of the batter into each pan. 5. Place one pan in the fryer and cook for 15 minutes, before repeating with the second pan. 6. Mix all of the frosting ingredients.7. Allow the cakes to cool. Spread the frosting and stack the other cake on top.
Per Serving: Calories 162; Fat 9.4g; Sodium 68mg; Carbs 21g; Fiber 4g; Sugar 16g; Protein 1g

Delicious Chocolate Lava Cake

Prep time: 10 minutes | Cook time: 12 minutes | Servings: 4

1 cup dark cocoa candy melts
1 stick butter
2 eggs
4 tablespoons sugar
1 tablespoon honey

4 tablespoons flour
Pinch of kosher salt
Pinch of ground cloves
¼ teaspoon grated nutmeg
¼ teaspoon cinnamon powder

1. Install the wire rack on Level 3. Select the "BAKE" function of Ninja Foodi Smart XL Pro Air Oven, set temperature to 350°F/175°C and time to 12 minutes. Select START/STOP to begin preheating. Spritz the insides of four custard cups with cooking spray. 2. Melt the cocoa candy melts and butter in the microwave for 30 seconds to 1 minute. 3. In a large bowl, combine the eggs, sugar and honey with a whisk until frothy. Pour in the melted chocolate mix. 4. Throw in the rest of the ingredients and combine well with an electric mixer or a manual whisk. 5. Transfer equal portions of the mixture into the prepared custard cups. 6. Place in the Air Fryer and air bake for 12 minutes. 7. Cool for 5 to 6 minutes. 8. Place each cup upside-down on a dessert plate and let the cake slide out. Serve with fruits and chocolate syrup if desired.
Per Serving: Calories 88; Fat 7.1g; Sodium 143mg; Carbs 4g; Fiber 3g; Sugar 1g; Protein 4g

Homemade Blueberry Pancakes

Prep time: 10 minutes | Cook time: 10 minutes | Servings: 4

½ teaspoon vanilla extract
2 tablespoons honey
½ cup blueberries
½ cup sugar
2 cups + 2 tablespoon flour

3 eggs, beaten
1 cup milk
1 teaspoon baking powder
Pinch of salt

1. Install the wire rack on Level 3. Select the "BAKE" function of Ninja Foodi Smart XL Pro Air Oven, set temperature to 390°F/200°C and time to 10 minutes. Select START/STOP to begin preheating. 2. In a bowl, mix together all of the dry ingredients. 3. Pour in the wet ingredients and combine with a whisk, ensuring the mixture becomes smooth. 4. Roll each blueberry in some flour to lightly coat it before folding it into the mixture. This is to ensure they do not change the color of the batter. 5. Coat the inside of a baking dish with a little oil or butter. 6. Spoon several equal amounts of the batter onto the baking dish, spreading them into pancake shapes and ensuring to space them out well. This may have to be completed in two batches. 7. Place the dish in the fryer and bake for about 10 minutes.
Per Serving: Calories 139; Fat 3.2g; Sodium 45mg; Carbs 26g; Fiber 4g; Sugar 8g; Protein 3g

Pumpkin Cake

Prep time: 15 minutes | Cook time: 35 minutes | Servings: 4

1 large egg

½ cup skimmed milk

7 oz. flour
2 tablespoons sugar
5 oz. pumpkin puree

Pinch of salt
Pinch of cinnamon (if desired)
Cooking spray

1. Stir together the pumpkin puree and sugar in a bowl. Crack in the egg and combine using a whisk until smooth. 2. Add in the flour and salt, stirring constantly. Pour in the milk, ensuring to combine everything well. 3. Spritz a baking tin with cooking spray. 4. Transfer the batter to the baking tin. 5. Install the wire rack on Level 3. Select the "BAKE" function of Ninja Foodi Smart XL Pro Air Oven, set temperature to 350°F/175°C and time to 15 minutes. Select START/STOP to begin preheating. 6. Put the tin in the Air Fryer basket and bake for 15 minutes.
Per Serving: Calories 409; Fat 18.9g; Sodium 214mg; Carbs 10g; Fiber 1g; Sugar 9g; Protein 48g

Chouquettes

Prep time: 15 minutes | Cook time: 45 minutes | Servings: 4 to 5

3 tablespoons (45g) unsalted butter
1 tablespoon (13g) granulated sugar
1 cup (240ml) water

1 cup (125g) all-purpose flour
3 eggs
1½ tablespoons (25ml) milk
Vegetable oil for brushing
½ cup (96g) pearl sugar

1. Combine the butter, granulated sugar, and water in a medium saucepan and melt the butter over low heat. Add in the flour to form a cohesive dough. Cook over medium-low heat for 2 minutes to get rid of the raw flour taste. 2. Remove from the heat and allow to cool to room temperature. Beat in 2 of the eggs, one at a time, making sure the first egg is fully incorporated before adding the second. 3. The dough will curdle, but keep beating vigorously until the dough becomes smooth. Once the eggs are fully incorporated, let the dough rest for 30 minutes. 4. Beat the remaining egg together with the milk in a small bowl. Lightly brush the basket of the air fryer with oil. 5. Using a small, spring-loaded cookie scoop or a tablespoon, scoop 6 to 8 circles of dough directly onto the basket of the air fryer. Brush top with the egg wash and sprinkle on pearl sugar. 6. Select Level 3. Select the "AIR FRY" function of Ninja Foodi Smart XL Pro Air Oven, set temperature to 360°F/180°C and time to 17 minutes. Select START/STOP to begin preheating. 7. Cook for 15 to 17 minutes until the outside of the chouquettes is golden brown and the inside fully cooked. 8. Serve immediately.
Per Serving: Calories 205; Fat 5.8g; Sodium 1481mg; Carbs 1g; Fiber 0g; Sugar 0g; Protein 35g

Strawberry Chocolate Cups

Prep time: 5 minutes | Cook time: 10 minutes | Servings: 8

16 strawberries, halved
2 tablespoons coconut oil

2 cups chocolate chips, melted

1. In a suitable pan that fits your air fryer, mix the strawberries with the oil and the melted chocolate chips, toss gently, put the pan in its air fryer basket. 2. Insert its air fryer basket into the level 3 of the oven and close the door. Cook on "Bake" mode, select level 3, and set its temperature to 340°F/170°C for 10 minutes. 3. Divide into cups and serve cold.
Per Serving: Calories 413; Fat 30.8 g; Sodium 1279 mg; Carbs 2.4g; Fiber 0.5g; Sugar 1.3g; Protein 1.6g

Sweet Cherry Pie

Prep time: 15 minutes | Cook time: 20 minutes | Servings: 8

1 tablespoon milk
2 ready-made pie crusts

21 oz. cherry pie filling
1 egg yolk

1. Select Level 3. Select the "AIR FRY" function of Ninja Foodi Smart XL Pro Air Oven, set temperature to 310°F/155°C and time to 15 minutes. Select START/STOP to begin preheating. 2.Coat the inside of a pie pan with a little oil or butter and lay one of the pie crusts inside. Use a fork to pierce a few holes in the pastry. 3. Spread the pie filling evenly over the crust. 4. Slice the other crust into strips and place them on top of the pie filling to make the pie look more homemade. 5. Place in the Air Fryer and cook for 15 minutes.
Per Serving: Calories 427; Fat 18.3g; Sodium 603mg; Carbs 44g; Fiber 6g; Sugar 3g; Protein 23g

Cinnamon Apple Pie

Prep time: 10 minutes | Cook time: 15 minutes | Servings: 7

2 large apples
½ cup flour
2 tablespoons unsalted butter

1 tablespoon sugar
½ teaspoon cinnamon

1. Select Level 3. Select the "AIR FRY" function of Ninja Foodi Smart XL Pro Air Oven, set temperature to 360°F/180°C and time to 15 minutes. Select START/STOP to begin preheating. 2. In a large bowl, combine the flour and butter. Pour in the sugar, continuing to mix. 3. Add in a 3 tablespoons water and combine everything to create a smooth dough. 4. Grease the insides of a few small pastry tins with butter. Divide the dough between each tin and lay each portion flat inside. 5. Peel, core and dice up the apples. Put the diced apples on top of the pastry and top with a sprinkling of sugar and cinnamon. 6. Place the pastry tins in your Air Fryer and cook for 15-17 minutes. Serve with ice cream if desired.
Per Serving: Calories 1646; Fat 146g; Sodium 498mg; Carbs 10g; Fiber 2g; Sugar 2g; Protein 77g

Peanut Butter Doughnut Holes

Prep time: 5 minutes | Cook time: 4 minutes | Servings: 12

1½ cups bread flour
1 teaspoon active dry yeast
1 tablespoon sugar
¼ teaspoon salt
½ cup warm milk
Doughnut Topping:
1 cup chocolate chips

½ teaspoon vanilla extract
2 egg yolks
2 tablespoons melted butter
24 miniature peanut butter cups
vegetable oil, in a spray bottle

2 tablespoons milk

1. Combine the flour with yeast, sugar and salt in a bowl. Add the milk along with vanilla, egg yolks and butter. Mix well until dough formed. knead the dough on floured surface by hand for about 2 minutes. Shape the dough and place it to an oiled bowl. Cover and let it rise in a warm place for 1 to 1½ hours, until doubled in size. 2. Punch the risen dough down and roll the flattered dough into a 24-inch log. Cut it into 24 pieces. a peanut butter into the center of each piece, Close the dough side with and roll in a ball shape. Place the balls on a sheet and let them rise in a warm place for 30 minutes. 3. Select Level 3. Select the "AIR FRY" function of Ninja Foodi Smart XL Pro Air Oven, set temperature to 400°F/200°C and time to 4 minutes. Select START/STOP to begin preheating. 4. Spray the dough balls lightly with oil. Air-fry eight at a time, at 400°F/200°C for 4 minutes, turning them over halfway through the cooking process. 5. Prepare the topping. in a bowl, Place the chocolate chips and milk. Microwave on high temp for 1 minute. Stir until melted and smooth. 6. Dip the half of the balls into the melted chocolate.
Per Serving: Calories 184; Fat 7.4g; Sodium 103mg; Carbs 7g; Fiber 1g; Sugar 1g; Protein 22g

Pakistani Gulab Jamun

Prep time: 10 minutes | Cook time: 10 minutes | Servings: 2 to 3

Fritters:
1 cup (128g) dried milk powder
¼ cup (31g) all-purpose flour
1 teaspoon powdered sugar
⅛ teaspoon baking soda
1 teaspoon ghee or vegetable oil
1 teaspoon freshly squeezed
Syrup:
1 cup (200g) granulated sugar
1 cup (240ml) water
3 or 4 cardamom pods, lightly

lemon juice
¼ cup (60ml) milk, slightly warmed
Vegetable oil for brushing
Sliced almonds for garnish

crushed
½ teaspoon rose water
½ teaspoon lemon juice

1. Whisk together the milk powder, flour, powdered sugar, and baking soda. Add the ghee and lemon juice and stir with a fork to combine. Gradually add the milk and stir with a fork just until the dough comes together. Let the dough rest and absorb the liquids for 10 to 15 minutes while you prepare the sugar syrup. 2. To make the syrup, combine the sugar, water, and cardamom pods in a small saucepan, bring the mixture to a boil over medium-high heat, stirring to dissolve the sugar. Lower the heat and manage to simmer for 5 minutes. The syrup should be thin and only slightly sticky. Add the rose water and lemon juice, cover, and keep warm over very low heat. 3. To make the fritters, divide the dough into 6 equal pieces. Gently roll each piece

into a smooth ball with your hands, then roll into a 3- to 4-inch (7.5 to 10 cm) cylinder. Select Level 3. Select the "AIR FRY" function of Ninja Foodi Smart XL Pro Air Oven, set temperature to 285°F/140°C and time to 5 minutes. Select START/STOP to begin preheating. 4. Brush the fritters on all sides with oil. Place the fritters in the basket of the air fryer and cook for 5 minutes until firm but still pale. Increase the heat to and cook until browned but not dark, 3 to 4 minutes. 5. Remove the fritters to a shallow bowl and poke them several times with a skewer to create holes. 6. Pour the warm syrup over the fritters and turn to coat. Allow the fritters to absorb the syrup for at least 15 minutes prior to serving. 7. Garnish with sliced almonds or chopped pistachios if desired.
Per Serving: Calories 295; Fat 21.2g; Sodium 94mg; Carbs 3g; Fiber 1g; Sugar 1g; Protein 23g

Crispy Apple Wedges

Prep time: 10 minutes | Cook time: 15 minutes | Servings: 4

4 large apples
2 tablespoons olive oil
½ cup dried apricots, chopped

1-2 tablespoons sugar
½ teaspoon ground cinnamon

1. Select Level 3. Select the "AIR FRY" function of Ninja Foodi Smart XL Pro Air Oven, set temperature to 350°F/175°C and time to 12 minutes. Select START/STOP to begin preheating. Peel the apples and slice them into eight wedges. Throw away the cores. 2. Coat the apple wedges with the oil. 3. Place each wedge in the Air Fryer and cook for 12 - 15 minutes. 4. Add in the apricots and allow to cook for a further 3 minutes. 5. Stir together the sugar and cinnamon. Sprinkle this mixture over the cooked apples before serving.
Per Serving: Calories 271; Fat 9.3g; Sodium 15mg; Carbs 43g; Fiber 6g; Sugar 2g; Protein 5g

Churros with Chocolate Sauce

Prep time: 10 minutes | Cook time: 30 minutes | Servings: 4

Chocolate Sauce:
4 ounces (115g) semisweet chocolate, finely chopped
½ cup (120ml) heavy cream
Churros:
3 tablespoons (45g) unsalted butter, divided
1 cup (240ml) water
½ cup (100g) granulated sugar plus 1 tablespoon (13g)

¼ cup (85g) light corn syrup
½ teaspoon cinnamon
¼ teaspoon cayenne pepper

Pinch kosher salt
1 cup (125g) all-purpose flour
2 eggs
Vegetable oil for spraying
2 teaspoons cinnamon

1. For chocolate sauce, place the chopped chocolate in a heat-proof bowl. Combine the cream with corn syrup in a saucepan and bring to a simmer. Pour the warm cream mixture over the chocolate and stir until the chocolate is melted. Add the cinnamon and cayenne pepper. Set aside. 2. To make the churros, combine 1 tablespoon (14g) of the butter, the water, 1 tablespoon (13g) of the sugar, and the salt in a medium saucepan. Melt the butter over low heat. Add the flour and stir vigorously to form a dough ball. 3. Continue to cook, stirring until the mixture looks dry and thick, 2 minutes. Remove from the heat and allow to cool to room temperature. 4. Once cool, beat in the eggs one at a time, making sure the first egg is fully incorporated before adding the second. Continue beating until the mixture is smooth. Let the dough rest for 30 minutes. 5. Place the churros batter into a piping bag outfitted with an extra-large tip, round or star-shaped. Spray the air fryer basket with oil. 6. Working in batches, pipe churros that are 5 to 6 inches (13 to 15 cm) long and ¾ to 1 inch (2 to 2.5 cm) in diameter directly onto the air fryer basket. Do not crowd the basket. 7. Cut the dough when you've reached the desired length. Spray the churros with oil. 8. Select Level 3. Select the "AIR FRY" function of Ninja Foodi Smart XL Pro Air Oven, set temperature to 360°F/180°C and time to 14 minutes. Select START/STOP to begin preheating. 9. Cook for 12 to 14 minutes until the outside is firm and brown and the inside is soft. While the churros are cooking, combine the remaining ½ cup (100g) sugar with the cinnamon on a plate and whisk to combine. Melt the butter and place in a small dish. 10. Remove the cooked churros from the air fryer and immediately brush with melted butter and dredge in the cinnamon sugar. 11. Repeat the process with the remaining churros. Serve hot with the chocolate sauce.
Per Serving: Calories 144; Fat 6.6g; Sodium 171mg; Carbs 2g; Fiber 0g; Sugar 1g; Protein 19g

Fried Bananas with Ice Cream

Prep time: 10 minutes | Cook time: 15 minutes | Servings: 2

2 large bananas
1 tablespoon butter
1 tablespoon sugar

2 tablespoons friendly bread crumbs
Vanilla ice cream for serving

1. Select Level 3. Select the "AIR FRY" function of Ninja Foodi Smart XL Pro Air Oven, set temperature to 350°F/175°C and time to 15 minutes. Select START/STOP to begin preheating. 2. Place the butter in the Air Fryer basket and allow it to melt for 1 minute. Combine the sugar and bread crumbs in a bowl. 3. Slice the bananas into 1-inch-round pieces. Drop them into the sugar mixture and coat them well. 4. Place the bananas in the Air Fryer and cook for 10-15 minutes. 5. Serve warm, with ice cream on the side if desired.
Per Serving: Calories 494; Fat 36g; Sodium 690mg; Carbs 17g; Fiber 11g; Sugar 2g; Protein 28g

Bamiyeh

Prep time: 10 minutes | Cook time: 35 minutes | Servings: 6

Doughnuts:
3 tablespoons (45g) unsalted butter
1 tablespoon (13g) granulated sugar
Syrup:
1 cup (200g) granulated sugar
¾ cup (180ml) water
1 teaspoon rose water

1 cup (240ml) water
1 cup (125g) all-purpose flour
2 eggs
Vegetable oil for spraying

Pinch saffron threads dissolved in ¼ cup (60ml) boiling water

1. Combine the butter, sugar, and water in a medium saucepan and melt the butter over low heat. Add in the flour to form a cohesive dough. Cook over medium-low heat for 2 minutes to get rid of the raw flour taste. 2. Remove from cooking and cool to room temperature. Beat the eggs in one at a time, making sure the first egg is fully incorporated before adding the second. 3. The dough will curdle but keep beating vigorously until the dough becomes smooth. Once the eggs are fully incorporated, let the dough rest for 30 minutes. 4. Prepare the rose water syrup. Add the sugar with water in a saucepan and bring to a boil, stirring to dissolve the sugar. Turn down the heat and simmer for 5 minutes until thickened. 5. Remove from the heat and add the rose water and 1 tablespoon (15ml) of the saffron water, reserving the remaining saffron water for another use, such as rice pilaf. Keep warm. 6. Once the dough has rested, place the dough in a piping bag outfitted with a large, star-shaped tip. 7. Lightly grease the air fryer basket. Pipe the dough directly onto the basket of the air fryer, forming doughnuts approximately 3 inches (7.5 cm) long and 1 inch (2.5 cm) wide. 8. Cut the dough when you have achieved the desired length. Work in batches so as not to overcrowd the basket. Spray lightly with oil. 9. Select Level 3. Select the "BAKE" function of Ninja Foodi Smart XL Pro Air Oven, set temperature to 360°F/180°C and time to 12 minutes. Select START/STOP to begin preheating. 10. Cook at 360°F/180°C shaking the basket once or twice, for 10 to 12 minutes until the outside of the doughnuts is golden brown and the inside is fully cooked. 11. Pour the warm syrup in a shallow bowl and place the first batch of doughnuts in the syrup. Soak for 5 minutes, then remove to a plate or platter. 12. Repeat the process with the remaining dough and syrup. Serve warm or at room temperature.
Per Serving: Calories 314; Fat 27.2g; Sodium 182mg; Carbs 0g; Fiber 0g; Sugar 0g; Protein 17g

Profiteroles

Prep time: 20 minutes | Cook time: 55 minutes | Servings: 4 to 5

Choux Puffs:
3 tablespoons (45g) unsalted butter
1 tablespoon (13g) granulated sugar
Chocolate Sauce:
4 ounces semisweet chocolate, finely chopped
2 tablespoons unsalted butter
1 cup (240ml) heavy cream

1 cup (235ml) water
1 cup (125g) all-purpose flour
2 eggs
Vegetable oil for brushing

¼ cup (85g) corn syrup
1 pint (285g) vanilla ice cream for serving

1. Combine the butter, sugar, and water in a medium saucepan and melt the butter over low heat. Add in the flour to form a cohesive

dough. 2. Cook over medium-low heat for 2 minutes to get rid of the raw flour taste. Remove from cooking and cool to room temperature. 3. Beat the eggs in one at a time, making sure the first egg is fully incorporated before adding the second. 4. The dough will curdle but keep beating vigorously until the dough becomes smooth. Once the eggs are fully incorporated, let the dough rest for 30 minutes. 5. Heat the chocolate and butter in a heat-proof bowl. Heat the cream and corn syrup in a small saucepan over medium heat until the cream is simmering. 6. Remove from the heat and pour the cream mixture over the chocolate in the bowl. Stir until sauce is smooth. Set aside. 7. Place it in a piping bag outfitted with a large, round tip. Lightly oil the basket of the air fryer. Working in 2 batches, pipe round puffs of dough approximately 2 inches (5 cm) wide and 1 inch (2.5 cm) tall directly onto the basket of the air fryer. 8. Cut the dough when you have achieved the desired size. With a damp finger, press down on the swirl at the top of each puff to round it. 9. Select Level 3. Select the "AIR FRY" function of Ninja Foodi Smart XL Pro Air Oven, set temperature to 360°F/180°C and time to 20 minutes. Select START/STOP to begin preheating. 10. Cook for 18 to 20 minutes until the outside of the puffs is golden brown and crisp and the inside is fully cooked and airy. 11. To serve, halve the choux puffs crosswise and place a scoop of ice cream inside each one. Replace the top of the puff and spoon chocolate sauce over the top. 12. Serve immediately.
Per Serving: Calories 143; Fat 7.5g; Sodium 5mg; Carbs 19g; Fiber 3g; Sugar 3g; Protein 3g

Mixed Berry Pastry

Prep time: 10 minutes | Cook time: 15 minutes | Servings: 3

3 pastry dough sheets
½ cup mixed berries, mashed
1 tablespoon honey

2 tablespoons cream cheese
3 tablespoons chopped walnuts
¼ teaspoon vanilla extract

1. Install the wire rack on Level 3. Select the "BAKE" function of Ninja Foodi Smart XL Pro Air Oven, set temperature to 375°F/190°C and time to 15 minutes. Select START/STOP to begin preheating. 2. Roll out the pastry sheets and spread the cream cheese over each one. 3. In a bowl, combine the berries, vanilla extract and honey. 4. Cover a baking sheet with parchment paper. 5. Spoon equal amounts of the berry mixture into the center of each sheet of pastry. Scatter the chopped walnuts on top. 6. Fold up the pastry around the filling and press down the edges with the back of a fork to seal them. 7. Transfer the baking sheet to the Air Fryer and cook for approximately 15 minutes.
Per Serving: Calories 716; Fat 62.6g; Sodium 302mg; Carbs 18g; Fiber 8g; Sugar 2g; Protein 34g

Traditional Apple Dumplings

Prep time: 15 minutes | Cook time: 25 minutes | Servings: 2

2 tablespoons sultanas
2 sheets puff pastry
2 tablespoons butter, melted

2 small apples, peeled and cored
1 tablespoon sugar

1. Install the wire rack on Level 3. Select the "BAKE" function of Ninja Foodi Smart XL Pro Air Oven, set temperature to 350°F/175°C and time to 25 minutes. Select START/STOP to begin preheating. 2. Peel the apples and remove the cores. 3. In a bowl, stir together the sugar and the sultanas. 4. Lay one apple on top of each pastry sheet and stuff the sugar and sultanas into the holes where the cores used to be. 5. Wrap the pastry around the apples, covering them completely. 6. Put them on a sheet of aluminum foil and coat each dumpling with a light brushing of melted butter. 7. Transfer to the Air Fryer and bake for 25 minutes until a golden brown color is achieved and the apples have softened inside.
Per Serving: Calories 387; Fat 26.3g; Sodium 602mg; Carbs 12g; Fiber 8g; Sugar 1g; Protein 26g

Nutty Peanut Butter Topping

¼ cup peanut butter
3 tablespoons milk

1 tablespoon powdered sugar

1. Add the milk and peanut butter into a bowl. Microwave for 30 seconds. Add in the powdered sugar and mix well until smooth. 2. Place the sauce in a bag and make a small hole. Drizzle over the chocolate layer on the doughnut holes.
Per Serving: Calories 170; Fat 9.5g; Sodium 158mg; Carbs 20g; Fiber 1g; Sugar 21g; Protein 5g

Coconut Crusted Bananas with Pineapple Sauce

Prep time: 10 minutes | Cook time: 10 minutes | Servings: 4

Pineapple Sauce:

1½ cups puréed fresh pineapple	1¼ cups shredded coconut
2 tablespoons sugar	⅓ cup crushed graham crackers
juice of 1 lemon	(crumbs)
¼ teaspoon ground cinnamon	Vegetable oil, in a spray bottle
3 firm bananas	Vanilla frozen yogurt or ice cream
¼ cup sweetened condensed milk	

1. Make the pineapple sauce by combining the pineapple, sugar, lemon juice and cinnamon in a saucepan. Simmer the mixture on the stovetop for 20 minutes, and then set it aside. 2. Slice the bananas diagonally into ½-inch thick slices and place them in a bowl. Pour the condensed milk into the bowl and toss the bananas gently to coat. Combine the coconut and graham cracker crumbs together in a shallow dish. 3. Remove the banana slices from the condensed milk and let any excess milk drip off. Dip the banana slices in the coconut and crumb mixture to coat both sides. Spray the coated slices with oil. 4. Select Level 3. Select the "AIR FRY" function of Ninja Foodi Smart XL Pro Air Oven, set temperature to 400°F/200°C and time to 5 minutes. Select START/STOP to begin preheating. 5. Grease the bottom of the air fryer basket with a little oil. Air-fry the bananas in batches for 5 minutes, turning them over halfway through the cooking time. Air-fry until the bananas are golden brown on both sides. 6. Serve warm over vanilla frozen yogurt with some of the pineapple sauce spooned over top.

Per Serving: Calories 290; Fat 4g; Sodium 100mg; Carbs 48g; Fiber 5g; Sugar 29g; Protein 3g

Lemony-Lavender Doughnuts

Prep time: 20 minutes | Cook time: 75 minutes | Servings: 3 to 4

½ cup (120ml) milk, warmed to between 100°F and 110°F (40°C to 45°C)	Zest and juice of 1 lemon
1 teaspoon yeast	4 tablespoons (55g) unsalted butter, melted
¼ cup (50g) granulated sugar, divided	1 egg
2 cups (250g) all-purpose flour	Vegetable oil for spraying
½ teaspoon kosher salt	1½ cups (150g) powdered sugar, sifted
	Dried lavender for culinary use

1. Combine the warm milk, yeast, and a pinch of the sugar in a small bowl and whisk to combine. Allow to sit until the yeast blooms and looks bubbly, about 5 to 10 minutes. Meanwhile, whisk together the remaining sugar, flour, and salt. Add the zest of the lemon to the dry ingredients. 2. When the yeast has bloomed, add the milk mixture to the dry ingredients and stir to combine. Add the melted butter and the egg and stir to form a thick dough. Turn out onto a well-floured board and knead until smooth, 1 to 2 minutes. Place the dough in an oiled bowl, cover, and allow to rise in the refrigerator overnight. 3. The following day, remove the dough from the refrigerator and allow it to come to room temperature. Turn out onto a well-floured board. Roll the dough out to ¼ inch (6 mm) thick. 4. Using a 3- or 4-inch (7.5 or 10 cm) circular cookie cutter, cut out as many doughnuts as possible. Use a 1-inch (2.5 cm) round cookie cutter to cut out holes from the center of each doughnut. 5. With the dough scraps, you can either cut out additional doughnut holes using the 1-inch (2.5 cm) cutter or, if desired, gather the scraps and roll them out again to cut out more doughnuts. 6. Transfer the doughnuts and doughnut holes to a lined baking sheet. Proof in a warm until puffy and, when pressed with a finger, the dough slowly springs back, 30 minutes to 1 hour. 7. While the dough is proofing, prepare the glaze. In a bowl, whisk the powdered sugar and the juice from the lemon. Set aside. 8. Select Level 3. Select the "AIR FRY" function of Ninja Foodi Smart XL Pro Air Oven, set temperature to 360°F/180°C and time to 6 minutes. Select START/STOP to begin preheating. 9. When the doughnuts have proofed, spray the basket of the air fryer with oil. Transfer no more than 3 or 4 of the doughnuts and 2 or 3 of the holes to the air fryer basket. 10. Spray the doughnuts lightly with oil. Cook for 5 to 6 minutes, flipping once halfway through, until browned and cooked through. Transfer the cooked doughnuts and holes to a cooling rack and repeat with the remaining doughnuts and holes. 11. Once the doughnuts are cool enough to handle, dip the tops into the glaze. Return the dipped doughnuts to the rack to allow the excess glaze to drip off. 12. Once the glaze has hardened, dip each doughnut again to create a nice opaque finish. While the second glaze is still wet, if desired, sprinkle a few buds of lavender on top of each doughnut.

Per Serving: Calories 543; Fat 38.1g; Sodium 134mg; Carbs 27g; Fiber 1g; Sugar 0g; Protein 23g

Charred Caramelized Peach Shortcakes

Prep time: 10 minutes | Cook time: 25 minutes | Servings: 4

Shortcakes:

1 cup (12g) self-rising flour	2 peaches, preferably freestone
½ cup (120ml) plus 1 tablespoon (15ml) heavy cream	1 tablespoon (14g) unsalted butter, melted
Vegetable oil for spraying	2 teaspoons brown sugar
Caramelized Peaches	1 teaspoon cinnamon

Whipped Cream:

1 cup (240ml) cold heavy cream	½ teaspoon vanilla extract
1 tablespoon (13g) granulated sugar	Zest of 1 lime

1. To make the shortcakes, place the flour in a medium bowl and whisk to remove any lumps. Make a hole in the flour like a well. While stirring with a fork, slowly pour in ½ cup (120ml) plus 1 tablespoon (15ml) of the heavy cream. Continue to stir until the dough has mostly come together. With your hands, gather the dough, incorporating any dry flour, and form into a ball. 2. Place the dough on floured board and pat into a rectangle that is ½ to ¾ inch (1.3 to 2 cm) thick. Fold in half. Turn and repeat. Pat the dough into a ¾-inch-thick (2 cm) square. Cut dough into 4 equally sized square biscuits. 3. Select Level 3. Select the "AIR FRY" function of Ninja Foodi Smart XL Pro Air Oven, set temperature to 325°F/160°C and time to 18 minutes. Select START/STOP to begin preheating. Spray the air fryer basket with oil to prevent sticking. Place the biscuits in the air fryer basket. Cook for 15 to 18 minutes until the tops are browned and the insides fully cooked. 4. To make the peaches, cut the peaches in half and remove the pit. Brush the peach with the butter and sprinkle ½ teaspoon of the brown sugar and ¼ teaspoon of the cinnamon on each peach half. Arrange the peaches in a single layer in the air fryer basket. Cook at 375°F/190°C for 8 to 10 minutes until the peaches are soft and the tops caramelized. 5. While the peaches are cooking, whip the cream. Pour the cold heavy cream, sugar, and vanilla (if using) into the bowl of a stand mixer or a metal mixing bowl. Beat with the whisk attachment for your stand mixer or a handheld electric mixer on high speed until stiff peaks form, about 1 minute. 6. To assemble the shortcakes, cut each biscuit in half horizontally. Place a peach on the bottom half of each biscuit and place the top half on top of the peach. 7. Top each shortcake with whipped cream and a sprinkle of lime zest. Serve immediately.

Per Serving: Calories 722; Fat 39g; Sodium 140mg; Carbs 7g; Fiber 2g; Sugar 4g; Protein 18g

Sugared Pizza Dough with Raspberry Cream Cheese Dip

Prep time: 12 minutes | Cook time: 16 minutes | Servings: 10 to 15

1-pound pizza dough	¾ to 1 cup sugar
½ cup butter, melted	

Raspberry Cream Cheese Dip:

4 ounces cream cheese, softened	1½ tablespoons milk
2 tablespoons powdered sugar	¼ cup raspberry preserves
½ teaspoon almond extract or almond paste	Fresh raspberries

1. Cut the ingredients in half or save half of the dough for another recipe. 2. When you're ready to make your sugared dough dippers, remove your pizza dough from the refrigerator at least 1 hour prior to baking and let it sit on the counter, covered gently with plastic wrap. 3. Roll the dough into two 15-inch logs. Cut each log into 20 slices and roll each slice so that it is 3- to 3½-inches long. Twist the dough halves 3 to 4 times. Place the it on a cookie sheet, grease with melted butter and sprinkle sugar over the dough twists. 4. Install the wire rack on Level 3. Select the "BAKE" function of Ninja Foodi Smart XL Pro Air Oven, set temperature to 390°F/200°C and time to 6 minutes. Select START/STOP to begin preheating. 5. Grease the air fryer basket with a little melted butter. Air-fry the dough twists in batches. Place 8 to 12 in the air fryer basket. 6. Air-fry for 6 minutes. Turn the dough strips over and brush the other side with butter. Air-fry for an additional 2 minutes. 7. While the dough twists are cooking, make the cream cheese and raspberry dip. Whip the cream cheese until fluffy. Add the powdered sugar, almond extract and milk, and beat until smooth. Fold in the raspberry preserves and transfer to a serving dish. 8. As the batches of dough twists are complete, place them into a shallow dish. Brush with more melted butter and generously coat with sugar, shaking the dish to cover both sides. 9. Serve the sugared dough dippers warm with the raspberry cream cheese dip on the side. Garnish with fresh raspberries.

Per Serving: Calories 250; Fat 11.5g; Sodium 178mg; Carbs 34g; Fiber 0g; Sugar 17g; Protein 4g

Chocolate Chunk Hazelnut Cookies

Prep time: 5 minutes | Cook time: 10 to 12 minutes | Servings: 12

1 cup butter, softened
1 cup brown sugar
½ cup granulated sugar
2 eggs, lightly beaten
1½ teaspoons vanilla extract
1½ cups all-purpose flour
½ cup rolled oats
1 teaspoon baking soda
½ teaspoon salt
2 cups chocolate chunks
½ cup toasted chopped hazelnuts

1. Cream the butter along with sugars until light and fluffy using a stand mixer or electric hand mixer. Add the eggs along with vanilla, and mix until well combined. 2. Combine the flour, rolled oats, baking soda and salt in a second bowl. Add the dry and wet ingredients in a bowl and mix with a wooden spoon or spatula. Stir in the chocolate chunks and hazelnuts until distributed throughout the dough. 3. Shape the cookies into small balls about the size of golf balls and place them on a baking sheet. Freeze the cookie balls for at least 30 minutes, or package them in as airtight a package as you can and keep them in your freezer. 4. When you're ready for a delicious snack or dessert. Install the wire rack on Level 3. Select the "BAKE" function of Ninja Foodi Smart XL Pro Air Oven, set temperature to 350°F/175°C and time to 12 minutes. Select START/STOP to begin preheating. Place the parchment down in the air fryer basket and place the frozen cookie ball or balls on top. 5. Air-fry the cookies for 10 to 12 minutes, or until they are done to your liking. Enjoy your freshly baked cookie.
Per Serving: Calories 210; Fat 12g; Sodium 311mg; Carbs 24g; Fiber 1g; Sugar 15g; Protein 3g

Strawberry Tart with Sweet and Sour Sauce

Prep time: 10 minutes | Cook time: 25 minutes | Servings: 2

1 pound (455g) strawberries, hulled and thinly sliced
1 tablespoon (15ml) balsamic vinegar
1 tablespoon (20g) honey
1 sprig basil
1 sheet frozen puff pastry, thawed according to package instructions
1 egg beaten

1. Place the strawberries in a 7-inch (18 cm) round pizza pan for the air fryer and mound them slightly in the center. 2. In a small bowl, whisk together the balsamic vinegar and honey. Drizzle the mixture over the strawberries. Slice the leaves from the sprig of basil into ribbons and sprinkle them over the strawberries. 3. Cut out an 8-inch (20 cm) square from the sheet of puff pastry. Drape the pastry over the strawberries in the pan. Poke holes in the puff pastry with the tines of a fork. 4. Brush the top of the pastry with the egg wash. Place the pan in the basket of the air fryer. 5. Install the wire rack on Level 3. Select the "BAKE" function of Ninja Foodi Smart XL Pro Air Oven, set temperature to 325°F/160°C and time to 25 minutes. Select START/STOP to begin preheating. 6. Bake for 25 to 30 minutes until the top of the pastry is golden brown and glossy and the underside of the pastry is cooked. 7. Remove the pan from the basket of the air fryer. If desired, cut the pastry in half and divide the dessert among 2 plates. 8. Alternatively, for less mess, two people can enjoy this tart right out of the pan.
Per Serving: Calories 300; Fat 24g; Sodium 117mg; Carbs 3g; Fiber 3g; Sugar 2g; Protein 18g

Tropical Pineapple Cake

Prep time: 15 minutes | Cook time: 35 minutes | Servings: 4

2 cups flour
¼ lb. butter
¼ cup sugar
½ lb. pineapple, chopped
½ cup pineapple juice
1 oz. dark chocolate, grated
1 large egg
2 tablespoons skimmed milk

1. Select Level 3. Select the "AIR FRY" function of Ninja Foodi Smart XL Pro Air Oven, set temperature to 370°F/185°C and time to 35 minutes. Select START/STOP to begin preheating. 2. Grease a cake tin with a little oil or butter. 3. In a bowl, combine the butter and flour to create a crumbly consistency. 4. Add in the sugar, diced pineapple, juice, and crushed dark chocolate and mix well. 5. In a separate bowl, combine the egg and milk. Add this mix to the flour and stir well until a soft dough forms. 6. Pour the batter into the cake tin and transfer to the Air Fryer. Cook for 35-40 minutes.
Per Serving: Calories 203; Fat 10.9g; Sodium 402mg; Carbs 2g; Fiber 0g; Sugar 1g; Protein 23g

Vanilla Donuts

Prep time: 10 minutes | Cook time: 15 minutes | Servings: 2 to 4

1 can (8 oz.) refrigerated croissant dough
Cooking spray
1 can (16 oz.) vanilla frosting

1. Select Level 3. Select the "BAKE" function of Ninja Foodi Smart XL Pro Air Oven, set temperature to 400°F/200°C and time to 5 minutes. Select START/STOP to begin preheating. Cut the croissant dough into 1-inch-round slices. Create a donut. 2. Put the donuts in the Air Fryer sheet pan, taking care not to overlap any, and spritz with cooking spray. 3. You may need to cook everything in multiple batches. 4. Bake for 2 minutes. Turn and cook for 3 minutes. 5. Place the rolls on a paper plate. 6. Microwave a half-cup of frosting for 30 seconds and pour a drizzling of the frosting over the donuts before serving.
Per Serving: Calories 463; Fat 15.5g; Sodium 553mg; Carbs 366g; Fiber 3g; Sugar 3g; Protein 41g

Charred Caramelized Pineapple with Mint and Lime

Prep time: 10 minutes | Cook time: 25 minutes | Servings: 4

1 pineapple
4 tablespoons (55g) unsalted butter, melted
2 tablespoons (30g) plus 2
teaspoons brown sugar
2 tablespoons (12g) fresh mint, cut into ribbons
1 lime

1. Cut off the top and bottom of the pineapple and stand it on a cut end. Slice off the outer skin, cutting deeply enough to remove the eyes of the pineapple. 2. Cut off any pointy edges to make the pineapple nice and round. Cut the peeled pineapple into 8 circles, approximately ½ to ¾ inch (1.3 to 2 cm) thick. 3. Remove the core of each slice using a small, circular cookie or biscuit cutter, or simply cut out the core using a paring knife. Place the pineapple rings on a plate. 4. Select Level 3. Select the "AIR FRY" function of Ninja Foodi Smart XL Pro Air Oven, set temperature to 400°F/200°C and time to 10 minutes. Select START/STOP to begin preheating. 5. Brush both sides of the pineapple rings with the melted butter. Working in 2 batches, arrange 4 slices in a single layer in the basket of the air fryer. 6. Sprinkle ½ teaspoon brown sugar on the top of each ring. Cook until the top side is browned and caramelized, about 10 minutes. 7. With tongs, carefully flip each ring and sprinkle brown sugar on the second side. Cook for 5 minutes until the second side is browned and caramelized. 8. Remove the cooked pineapple and repeat with the remaining pineapple rings. Arrange all the cooked pineapple rings on a serving plate or platter. 9. Sprinkle with mint and spritz with the juice of the lime. Serve warm.
Per Serving: Calories 153; Fat 39g; Sodium 108mg; Carbs 25g; Fiber 6g; Sugar 2g; Protein 37g

Delicious Chocolate Chip Pan Cookie Sundae

Prep time: 10 minutes | Cook time: 15 minutes | Servings: 4

1 stick (4 ounces, or 112g) unsalted butter, softened
3 tablespoons (39g) granulated sugar
3 tablespoons (28.5g) brown sugar
1 egg
1 teaspoon vanilla extract
½ cup (63g) all-purpose flour
¼ teaspoon baking soda
¼ teaspoon kosher salt
½ cup (88g) semisweet chocolate chips
Vegetable oil for spraying
Vanilla ice cream for serving
Hot fudge or caramel sauce for serving

1. In a medium bowl, using a handheld mixer, cream together the butter and sugar until light and fluffy. 2. Then add the egg and vanilla and mix until combined. In a bowl, whisk the flour, baking soda, and salt. Add the dry ingredients to the batter and mix until they are well combined. Add the chocolate chips and mix a final time. 3. Select Level 3. Select the "AIR FRY" function of Ninja Foodi Smart XL Pro Air Oven, set temperature to 325°F/160°C and time to 15 minutes. Select START/STOP to begin preheating. 4. Lightly grease a 7-inch (18 cm) pizza pan for the air fryer. Spread the batter evenly in the pan. 5. Place in the air fryer and cook for 12 to 15 minutes, until the top of the cookie is browned and the middle is gooey but cooked. 6. Remove the pan from the air fryer. Place 1 to 2 scoops of vanilla ice cream in the center of the cookie and top with hot fudge or caramel sauce, as you prefer. 7. Pass around spoons and eat the cookie sundae right out of the pan.
Per Serving: Calories 365; Fat 12.4gSodium 717mg; Carbs 29g; Fiber 3g; Sugar 10g; Protein 19g

Blueberry Tartlets

Prep time: 5 minutes | Cook time: 12 minutes | Servings: 4

8 ounces cream cheese, softened
¼ cup sugar
1 egg
½ teaspoon vanilla extract
Zest of 2 lemons, divided
9 mini graham cracker tartlet

shells
2 cups blueberries
½ teaspoon ground cinnamon
Juice of ½ lemon
¼ cup apricot preserves

1. Install the wire rack on Level 3. Select the "BAKE" function of Ninja Foodi Smart XL Pro Air Oven, set temperature to 330°F/165°C and time to 6 minutes. Select START/STOP to begin preheating. 2. Combine the cream cheese, sugar, egg, vanilla and the zest of one lemon in a medium bowl and blend until smooth by hand or with an electric hand mixer. Pour the cream cheese mixture into the tartlet shells. 3. Air-fry 3 tartlets at a time for 6 minutes, rotating them in halfway through the cooking time. 4. Combine the blueberries, cinnamon, zest of one lemon and juice of half a lemon in a bowl. Melt the apricot preserves in the microwave or over low heat in a saucepan. Pour the apricot preserves over the blueberries and gently toss to coat. 5. Allow the cheesecakes to cool completely and then top each one with some of the blueberry mixture. 6. Garnish the tartlets with a little sugared lemon peel and refrigerate until you are ready to serve.
Per Serving: Calories 12; Fat 12g; Sodium 147mg; Carbs 25g; Fiber 1g; Sugar 16g; Protein 3g

Nutty Pear Biscotti Crumble

Prep time: 20 minutes | Cook time: 65 minutes | Servings: 6

7-inch cake pan or ceramic dish
3 pears, peeled, cored and sliced
½ cup brown sugar
¼ teaspoon ground ginger
1 teaspoon ground cinnamon
⅛ teaspoon ground nutmeg

2 tablespoons cornstarch
1¼ cups (4 to 5) almond biscotti, coarsely crushed
¼ cup all-purpose flour
¼ cup sliced almonds
¼ cup butter, melted

1. Combine the pears, brown sugar, ginger, cinnamon, nutmeg and cornstarch in a bowl. Toss to combine and then pour the pear mixture into a greased 7-inch cake pan or ceramic dish. 2. Combine the crushed biscotti, flour, almonds and melted butter in a medium bowl. Toss with a fork until crumbles. Sprinkle the biscotti crumble over the pears and cover the pan with aluminum foil. 3. Select Level 3. Select the "AIR FRY" function of Ninja Foodi Smart XL Pro Air Oven, set temperature to 350°F/175°C and time to 60 minutes. Select START/STOP to begin preheating. 4. Air-fry for 60 minutes. Remove the aluminum foil and air-fry for an additional 5 minutes to brown the crumble layer. 5. Serve warm with cream.
Per Serving: Calories 330; Fat 15g; Sodium 155mg; Carbs 47g; Fiber 5g; Sugar 27g; Protein 5g

Tasty S'mores Pockets

Prep time: 10 minutes | Cook time: 10 minutes | Servings: 6

12 sheets phyllo dough, thawed
1½ cups butter, melted
¾ cup graham cracker crumbs

1 (7-ounce) milk chocolate bar
12 marshmallows, cut in half

1. Place one sheet of the phyllo on a large cutting board. Keep the rest of the phyllo sheets covered with a slightly damp, clean kitchen towel. Brush the phyllo sheet generously with some melted butter. 2. Place other phyllo sheet on top of the first and brush it with more butter. Repeat with one more phyllo sheet until you have a stack of 3 phyllo sheets with butter brushed between the layers. 3. Cover the phyllo sheets with one quarter of the graham cracker crumbs leaving a 1-inch border the rectangle. Cut the phyllo sheets lengthwise into 3 strips. 4. Take 2 of the strips and crisscross them to form a cross with the empty borders at the top and to the left. Place 2 of the chocolate rectangles in the center of the cross. 5. Place 4 of the marshmallow halves on top of the chocolate. Now fold the pocket together by folding the bottom phyllo strip up over the chocolate and marshmallows. 6. Then fold the right side over, then the top strip down and finally the left side over. Brush all the edges generously with melted butter to seal shut. Repeat with the next three sheets of phyllo, until all the sheets have been used. 7. You will be able to make 2 pockets with every second batch because you will have an extra graham cracker crumb strip from the previous set of sheets. 8. Select the "AIR FRY" function of Ninja Foodi Smart XL Pro Air Oven, set temperature to 350°F/175°C

and time to 5 minutes. Select START/STOP to begin preheating. 9. Transfer 3 pockets at a time to the air fryer basket. Slide basket into rails of Level 3. Air-fry at 350°F/175°C for 4 to 5 minutes, until the phyllo dough is light brown in color. 10. Flip the pockets over halfway through the cooking process. Repeat with the remaining 3 pockets. 11. Serve warm.
Per Serving: Calories 710; Fat 50g; Sodium 358mg; Carbs 61g; Fiber 1g; Sugar 30g; Protein 6g

Healthy Hasselback Apple Crisp

Prep time: 10 minutes | Cook time: 20 minutes | Servings: 4

2 large Gala apples, peeled, cored and cut in half
¼ cup butter, melted
Topping:
3 tablespoons butter, melted
2 tablespoons brown sugar
¼ cup chopped pecans
2 tablespoons rolled oats

½ teaspoon ground cinnamon
2 tablespoons sugar

1 tablespoon flour
Vanilla ice cream
Caramel sauce

1. Place the cut side down apples on a cutting board. Slicing from stem end to blossom end, make 8 to 10 slits down the apple halves but only slice three quarters of the way through the apple, not all the way through to the cutting board. 2. Select the "AIR FRY" function of Ninja Foodi Smart XL Pro Air Oven, set temperature to 330°F/165°C and time to 15 minutes. Select START/STOP to begin preheating. 3. Transfer the apples to the air fryer basket, flat side down. Slide basket into rails of Level 3. Combine ¼ cup of melted butter, cinnamon and sugar in a small bowl. Brush this butter mixture onto the apples and air-fry at 330°F/165°C for 15 minutes. Baste the apples several times with the butter mixture during the cooking process. 4. While the apples are air-frying, make the filling. Combine 3 tablespoons of melted butter with the brown sugar, pecans, rolled oats and flour in a bowl. Stir until resembles small crumbles. 5. When the timer is up, spoon the topping down the center of the apples. Air-fry at 330°F/165°C for an additional 5 minutes. 6. Serve with ice cream and caramel sauce.
Per Serving: Calories 330; Fat 24g; Sodium 158mg; Carbs 28g; Fiber 5g; Sugar 18g; Protein 2g

Delicious Honey Struffoli

Prep time: 10 minutes | Cook time: 20 minutes | Servings: 10

¼ cup butter, softened
⅔ cup sugar
5 eggs
2 teaspoons vanilla extract
Zest of 1 lemon
4 cups all-purpose flour
2 teaspoons baking soda

¼ teaspoon salt
16 ounces honey
1 teaspoon ground cinnamon
Zest of 1 orange
2 tablespoons water
Nonpareils candy sprinkles

1. Cream the butter along with sugar in a bowl until light and fluffy using a hand mixer. Add the eggs along with vanilla and lemon zest and mix. 2. In a separate bowl, combine the flour, baking soda and salt. Mix the dry ingredients to the wet ingredients and mix until you have a soft dough. Shape the dough and wrap it in plastic and let it rest for 30 minutes. 3. Divide the dough ball into four pieces. Roll each piece into a long rope. Cut each rope into about 25 (½-inch) pieces. Roll each piece into a tight ball. You should have 100 little balls when finished. 4. Select Level 3. Select the "AIR FRY" function of Ninja Foodi Smart XL Pro Air Oven, set temperature to 370°F/185°C and time to 4 minutes. Select START/STOP to begin preheating. 5. In batches of about 20, transfer the dough balls to the air fryer basket, leaving a small space in between them. Air-fry the dough balls at 370°F/185°C for 3 to 4 minutes, shaking the basket when one minute of cooking time remains. 6. After all the dough balls are air-fried, make the honey topping. Melt the honey in a small saucepan on the stovetop. Add the cinnamon, orange zest, and water. Simmer for one minute. 7. Place the air-fried dough balls in a large bowl and drizzle the honey mixture over top. Gently toss to coat all the dough balls evenly. 8. Transfer the coated struffoli to a platter and sprinkle the nonpareil candy sprinkles over top. You can dress the presentation up by piling the balls into the shape of a wreath or pile them high in a cone shape to resemble a Christmas tree. 9. Struffoli can be made ahead. Store covered tightly.
Per Serving: Calories 180; Fat 3g; Sodium 68mg; Carbs 35g; Fiber 1g; Sugar 20g; Protein 3g

Black and Blueberry Clafoutis

Prep time: 10 minutes | Cook time: 30 minutes | Servings: 4

6-inch pie pan
3 large eggs
½ cup sugar
1 teaspoon vanilla extract
2 tablespoons butter, melted 1 cup

milk
½ cup all-purpose flour
1 cup blackberries
1 cup blueberries
2 tablespoons confectioners' sugar

1. Install the wire rack on Level 3. Select the "BAKE" function of Ninja Foodi Smart XL Pro Air Oven, set temperature to 320°F/160°C and time to 15 minutes. Select START/STOP to begin preheating. 2. Combine the eggs along with sugar and whisk vigorously until smooth, lighter in color and well combined. Add the vanilla extract, butter and milk and whisk together well. Add in the flour and mix well until no streaks of white remain. 3. Scatter half the blueberries and blackberries in a greased (6-inch) pie pan or cake pan. Pour half of the batter (about 1¼ cups) on top of the berries and transfer the tart pan to the air fryer basket. 4. Air-fry for 12 to 15 minutes or until the clafoutis has puffed up and is still a little jiggly in the center. Remove the clafoutis from the air fryer, invert it onto a plate and let it cool while you bake the second batch. 5. Serve the clafoutis warm (not hot), dusted with confectioners' sugar on top.
Per Serving: Calories 340; Fat 11g; Sodium 149mg; Carbs 53g; Fiber 3g; Sugar 9g; Protein 9g

Strawberry Hand Tarts

Prep time: 10 minutes | Cook time: 18 minutes | Servings: 4

½ cup butter, softened
½ cup sugar
2 eggs
1 teaspoon vanilla extract
2 tablespoons lemon zest
2½ cups all-purpose flour

1 teaspoon baking powder
¼ teaspoon salt
1¼ cups strawberry jam, divided
1 egg white, beaten
1 cup powdered sugar
2 teaspoons milk

1. Combine the butter and sugar in a bowl and beat with an electric mixer until the mixture is light and fluffy. Add the eggs one at a time. Add the vanilla extract with lemon zest and mix well. 2. In a separate bowl, combine the flour, baking powder and salt. Add the dry and wet ingredients, mixing until dough forms. 3. Transfer the dough to a floured surface and knead by hand for 10 minutes. Cover and let rest for 30 minutes. 4. Divide the dough and roll each half out into a ¼-inch thick rectangle that measures 12-inches x 9-inches. Cut each rectangle of dough into nine 4-inch x 3-inch rectangles. You should have 18 rectangles. 5. Spread two teaspoons of strawberry jam in the center of nine of the rectangles, leaving a ¼-inch border around the edges. 6. Brush the egg white around the edges of each rectangle and top with the remaining nine rectangles of dough. Press the back of a fork around the edges to seal the tarts shut. 7. Brush the top of the tarts with the beaten egg white and pierce the dough three or four times down the center of the tart with a fork. 8. Select Level 3. Select the "AIR FRY" function of Ninja Foodi Smart XL Pro Air Oven, set temperature to 350°F/175°C and time to 9 minutes. Select START/STOP to begin preheating. 9. Air-fry the tarts in batches

at 350°F/175°C for 6 minutes. Flip the tarts over and air-fry for an additional 3 minutes. 10. While the tarts are air-frying, make the icing. Combine the powdered sugar, ¼ cup strawberry preserves and milk in a bowl, whisking until the icing is smooth. 11. Spread the icing, leaving an empty border around the edges. Decorate with sprinkles if desired.
Per Serving: Calories 420; Fat 12g; Sodium 179mg; Carbs 73g; Fiber 1g; Sugar 39g; Protein 6g

Baked Beignets

Prep time: 10 minutes | Cook time: 10 minutes | Servings: 12

¾ cup lukewarm water
¼ cup sugar
1 teaspoon active dry yeast
3½ to 4 cups all-purpose flour
½ teaspoon salt
2 tablespoons unsalted butter

1 egg, lightly beaten
½ cup evaporated milk
¼ cup melted butter
1 cup confectioners' sugar
Chocolate sauce or raspberry sauce, to dip

1. In a bowl, add a pinch of sugar, yeast and lukewarm water. Allow yeast to poof for 5 minutes. 2. In a bowl, Combine 3½ cups flour, salt, butter and sugar. Add the egg along with evaporated milk and yeast to the flour and mix with a wooden spoon until the dough form in a sticky ball. Transfer the dough to greased bowl, cover with kitchen towel and let it proof in a warm place until it has doubled in size. 3. Roll the dough to ½-inch thickness. Cut it into rectangular shaped pieces. 4. Install the wire rack on Level 3. Select the "BAKE" function of Ninja Foodi Smart XL Pro Air Oven, set temperature to 350°F/175°C and time to 5 minutes. Select START/STOP to begin preheating. 5. Brush the beignets on both sides with some of the melted butter and bake in batches for 5 minutes, turning them over halfway through if desired. 6. As soon as the beignets are finished, transfer them to a plate or baking sheet and dust with the confectioners' sugar. 7. Serve warm with a chocolate or raspberry sauce.
Per Serving: Calories 130; Fat 3.5g; Sodium 169mg; Carbs 22g; Fiber 1g; Sugar 7g; Protein 3g

Chocolaty Nutella Banana Sandwich

Prep time: 10 minutes | Cook time: 8 minutes | Servings: 2

4 slices white bread
¼ cup chocolate hazelnut spread

1 banana

1. Select the "AIR FRY" function of Ninja Foodi Smart XL Pro Air Oven, set temperature to 370°F/185°C and time to 8 minutes. Select START/STOP to begin preheating. 2. Butter one side of bread and place the slices buttered side down. Spread the chocolate spread on the other side of the bread. 3. Cut the banana lengthwise. Place the banana and top with the remaining slices of bread to make two sandwiches. Cut the sandwiches in half. Transfer the sandwiches to the air fryer basket. Slide basket into rails of Level 3. 4. Air-fry for 5 minutes. Flip the sandwiches over and air-fry for another 2 to 3 minutes, or until the top bread slices are nicely browned.
Per Serving: Calories 430; Fat 21g; Sodium 233mg; Carbs 57g; Fiber 4g; Sugar 31g; Protein 6g

Conclusion

The Ninja Foodi Smart Air Fryer Oven will help you cook everything that you want to serve at the table. Whether you are serving a large family gathering or cooking food for your homies, this kitchen miracle will help you cook all the portion sizes in just a few minutes. So, why buy all the different cooking appliances when you can replace them all with a single appliance which is simple to use and efficient in working? So, if you have made up your mind about the Ninja Foodi Smart Air Fryer Oven, then this cookbook can be your perfect cooking partner as it will give you all the smart cooking secrets that you need to use this machine up to its full potential.

Appendix 1 Measurement Conversion Chart

VOLUME EQUIVALENTS (LIQUID)

US STANDARD	US STANDARD (OUNCES)	METRIC (APPROXIMATE)
2 tablespoons	1 fl.oz	30 mL
¼ cup	2 fl.oz	60 mL
½ cup	4 fl.oz	120 mL
1 cup	8 fl.oz	240 mL
1½ cup	12 fl.oz	355 mL
2 cups or 1 pint	16 fl.oz	475 mL
4 cups or 1 quart	32 fl.oz	1 L
1 gallon	128 fl.oz	4 L

VOLUME EQUIVALENTS (DRY)

US STANDARD	METRIC (APPROXIMATE)
⅛ teaspoon	0.5 mL
¼ teaspoon	1 mL
½ teaspoon	2 mL
¾ teaspoon	4 mL
1 teaspoon	5 mL
1 tablespoon	15 mL
¼ cup	59 mL
½ cup	118 mL
¾ cup	177 mL
1 cup	235 mL
2 cups	475 mL
3 cups	700 mL
4 cups	1 L

TEMPERATURES EQUIVALENTS

FAHRENHEIT(F)	CELSIUS（C) (APPROXIMATE)
225 °F	107 °C
250 °F	120 °C
275 °F	135 °C
300 °F	150 °C
325 °F	160 °C
350 °F	180 °C
375 °F	190 °C
400 °F	205 °C
425 °F	220 °C
450 °F	235 °C
475 °F	245 °C
500 °F	260 °C

WEIGHT EQUIVALENTS

US STANDARD	METRIC (APPROXINATE)
1 ounce	28 g
2 ounces	57 g
5 ounces	142 g
10 ounces	284 g
15 ounces	425 g
16 ounces (1 pound)	455 g
1.5pounds	680 g
2pounds	907 g

Appendix 2 Air Fryer Cooking Chart

Vegetables	Temp (°F)	Time (min)
Asparagus	375	4 to 6
Baked Potatoes	400	35 to 45
Broccoli	400	8 to 10
Brussels Sprouts	350	15 to 18
Butternut Squash (cubed)	375	20 to 25
Carrots	375	15 to 25
Cauliflower	400	10 to 12
Corn on the Cob	390	6
Eggplant	400	15
Green Beans	375	16 to 20
Kale	250	12
Mushrooms	400	5
Peppers	375	8 to 10
Sweet Potatoes (whole)	380	30 to 35
Tomatoes (halved, sliced)	350	10
Zucchini (½-inch sticks)	400	12

Frozen Foods	Temp (°F)	Time (min)
Breaded Shrimp	400	9
Chicken Burger	360	11
Chicken Nudgets	400	10
Corn Dogs	400	7
Curly Fries (1 to 2 lbs.)	400	11 to 14
Fish Sticks (10 oz.)	400	10
French Fries	380	15 to 20
Hash Brown	360	15 to 18
Meatballs	380	6 to 8
Mozzarella Sticks	400	8
Onion Rings (8 oz.)	400	8
Pizza	390	5 to 10
Pot Pie	360	25
Pot Sticks (10 oz.)	400	8
Sausage Rolls	400	15
Spring Rolls	400	15 to 20

Meat and Seafood	Temp (°F)	Time (min)
Bacon	400	5 to 10
Beef Eye Round Roast (4 lbs.)	390	45 to 55
Bone to in Pork Chops	400	4 to 5 per side
Brats	400	8 to 10
Burgers	350	8 to 10
Chicken Breast	375	22 to 23
Chicken Tender	400	14 to 16
Chicken Thigh	400	25
Chicken Wings (2 lbs.)	400	10 to 12
Cod	370	8 to 10
Fillet Mignon (8 oz.)	400	14 to 18
Fish Fillet (0.5 lb., 1-inch)	400	10
Flank Steak(1.5 lbs.)	400	10 to 14
Lobster Tails (4 oz.)	380	5 to 7
Meatballs	400	7 to 10
Meat Loaf	325	35 to 45
Pork Chops	375	12 to 15
Salmon	400	5 to 7
Salmon Fillet (6 oz.)	380	12
Sausage Patties	400	8 to 10
Shrimp	375	8
Steak	400	7 to 14
Tilapia	400	8 to 12
Turkey Breast (3 lbs.)	360	40 to 50
Whole Chicken (6.5 lbs.)	360	75

Desserts	Temp (°F)	Time (min)
Apple Pie	320	30
Brownies	350	17
Churros	360	13
Cookies	350	5
Cupcakes	330	11
Doughnuts	360	5
Roasted Bananas	375	8
Peaches	350	5

Appendix 3 Recipes Index